"This volume offers a strong and diverse collection of chapters on the possibilities of AI in educational assessment. Its impressive breadth addresses many critical issues in this emerging field and highlights promising directions for leveraging AI to advance personalized, adaptive, and scalable assessment.

—**Jeff Douglas**, *University of Illinois*

"This is an exciting and timely book that summarizes contemporary perspectives on the use of AI in assessment. It is safe to say it is a 'revolution'—it remains to be seen if AI is an angel of salvation or a temptress and deluder. This book contributes in a meaningful way to discussions of the application of AI in educational assessment."

—**George Engelhard, Jr.**, *The University of Georgia*

"Speaking as a psychometrician, this is the book I've been waiting for! AI is clearly a critical part of the future of educational assessment. Many important issues are addressed in the book's chapters, including equity, validity and test security, making it a comprehensive resource for many audiences in the field."

—**Charles Lewis**, *Fordham University*

"Rarely is a book more perfectly timed for publication than this one. The winds of change stirred by developments in AI bring great opportunities to educational assessment but also potential risks. Readers of this volume will be better equipped to navigate the challenges posed by AI and make the most of its possibilities."

—**Mary J. Pitoniak**, *Pitoniak Educational Measurement LLC*

THE ROLE OF AI IN ASSESSMENT

The Role of AI in Assessment: Revolutionizing Education examines how artificial intelligence (AI) is transforming the evaluation of learning and addresses the urgent need for innovative assessment methodologies. It analyzes both the opportunities and the constraints of AI-driven assessment, responding to the growing demand for approaches that harness AI capabilities rigorously and responsibly.

Adopting an interdisciplinary perspective, this book introduces foundational AI concepts, including reinforcement learning, neural networks, deep learning, and large language models, and makes these complex topics accessible to educators, researchers, and policymakers. Chapters on ethics, equity, and personalized learning provide a systematic treatment of AI's implications for educational measurement and accountability.

With a practical and forward-looking orientation, this volume explores applications such as automatic item generation, automated essay scoring, game-based assessment, and test security. Case studies illustrate implementation strategies and provide guidance for integrating AI into contemporary assessment systems.

This resource is designed for educators, researchers, psychometricians, administrators, and policymakers seeking to design, evaluate, and govern AI-enabled assessment frameworks. It is also well suited for graduate courses in educational technology, assessment, data science in education, and AI ethics.

Dr. Xinhui Xiong is a chief psychometrician at Examroom AI and holds a PhD in Psychometrics from Fordham University, an MLA in Management from Harvard University, and a Master's degree in Computer Science. Her work centers on scalable, defensible assessment design, including validation, equating, fairness analysis, and test security. She has published in leading journals and presented extensively at national and international conferences on measurement.

Dr. Mark D. Shermis was the principal investigator and academic adviser for the Automated Student Assessment Prize (ASAP). He is currently a consultant for Performance Assessment Analytics, LLC. Dr. Shermis has also held faculty and administrative positions at multiple universities. He is a frequently cited expert on machine scoring and co-editor (with Dr. Joshua Wilson) and author of *The Routledge International Handbook of Automated Essay Evaluation.*

Dr. Jiawei Xiong is a research scientist at Curriculum Associates. He earned his PhD in Educational Psychology (Quantitative Methodology) from the University of Georgia. He has co-edited multiple volumes, published widely, and contributed to numerous national and state assessment and learning programs. He is the recipient of the Brenda H. Loyd Outstanding Dissertation Award from the National Council on Measurement in Education.

THE ROLE OF AI IN ASSESSMENT

Revolutionizing Education

Edited by
Xinhui Xiong, Mark D. Shermis,
and Jiawei Xiong

Routledge
Taylor & Francis Group
LONDON AND NEW YORK

Designed cover image: Getty Images @Photoraidz

First published 2027
by Routledge
4 Park Square, Milton Park, Abingdon, Oxon OX14 4RN

and by Routledge
605 Third Avenue, New York, NY 10158

Routledge is an imprint of the Taylor & Francis Group, an informa business

British Library Cataloguing-in-Publication Data
A catalogue record for this book is available from the British Library

ISBN: 9781041029335 (hbk)
ISBN: 9781041028031 (pbk)
ISBN: 9781003621522 (ebk)

DOI: 10.4324/9781003621522

Typeset in Times New Roman
by codeMantra

CONTENTS

ACKNOWLEDGMENTS

We extend our sincere gratitude to the following individuals for their careful and constructive reviews of the chapters included in this volume:

Soyeon Ahn, University of Miami
Erin Banjanovic, Curriculum Associates
Maggie Beiting-Parrish, Federation of American Scientists
Derek Briggs, University of Colorado Boulder
Okan Bulut, University of Alberta
Amy Burkhardt, Cambium Assessment, Inc.
Jeffrey Douglas, University of Illinois at Urbana-Champaign
Susan Embretson, Georgia Institute of Technology
Tahereh Firoozi, University of Alberta
Brian F. French, Washington State University
Amy Hendrickson, College Board
Jietai Hou, Hong Kong University
Justin Kern, University of Illinois at Urbana-Champaign
Richard M. Luecht, University of North Carolina Greensboro
Tim Moses, Buros Center for Testing
Christopher Ormerod, College Board
Corey Palermo, Measurement, Inc.
Mark Reckase, Michigan State University
Jon S. Twing, HumPRO
Jordan Wheeler, University of Nebraska-Lincoln
James Wollack, University of Wisconsin-Madison
Susu Zhang, University of Illinois at Urbana-Champaign

Their insightful feedback, critical engagement, and collegial support substantially strengthened the conceptual coherence, methodological rigor, and overall quality of this collection. We deeply appreciate the time and expertise they generously contributed to this project.

NOTES ON THE CONTRIBUTORS

Dr. Sergio Araneda is a research scientist at Caveon, working remotely from many places, including Chile. He holds a PhD in Educational Measurement and Psychometrics from the University of Massachusetts Amherst. His research focuses on validity theory, test security, generative AI in assessment, and the conceptualization of tests as socio-technical artifacts. He is the author of *An Experiential Approach to Test Design and Validation* (2023) and has organized international conference sessions on AI and test security (NCME, COTS, ITC, AIMEcon). He currently investigates the validation and security implications of LLM-generated item pools and AI-driven assessment technologies.

Dr. Burcu Arslan is a research scientist at the ETS Research Institute with a PhD in artificial intelligence (AI). Her interdisciplinary work combines AI, cognitive science, and statistical modeling to advance educational assessment through personalization, process data modeling, and interactive tasks measuring complex skills. She has published in journals, including *Child Development*, *European Journal of Psychological Assessment*, and *Educational Measurement: Issues and Practice* and held editorial roles with *PLoS One* and the *Journal of Memory and Cognition*. She currently leads a project on a learner-driven, AI-enabled context personalization and co-leads a project on assessing empathy with a conversation-based assessment.

Dr. Randy E. Bennett is a principal at Assessment Innovation Matters, with an EdD in Education of Students with Disabilities. He conducts research and consults internationally on assessment innovations that emphasize equity and positive impact, including personalizing assessment through generative AI and non-AI means, responsibly incorporating AI into assessment, validity and fairness, socioculturally responsive assessment, and formative assessment. He is an elected member of the National Academy of Education, a fellow of the American Educational Research Association, and recipient of the AERA E. F. Lindquist Award, the AERA Cognition and Assessment SIG Outstanding Contribution to Research Award, and the NCME Bradley Hanson Award.

Dr. Ummugul Bezirhan is Assistant Research Director for Advanced Psychometrics and Machine Learning Applications at the TIMSS & PIRLS International Study Center. She holds a PhD in Measurement, Evaluation, and Applied Statistics from Columbia University. Her research focuses on latent variable modeling, item response theory, and the integration of AI in international large-scale assessments, including automated scoring, item generation, and classification. Her dissertation was recognized with the Dissertation Award from the Psychometric Society. She currently leads research initiatives modernizing psychometric practices and contributes to the operational scaling of TIMSS, PIRLS, and special studies.

Dr. Amy Burkhardt is lead scientist and manager of the Applied Language Modeling and Evaluation group within the Machine Learning team at Cambium Assessment, Inc. She holds a PhD in Research and Evaluation Methodology from the University of Colorado Boulder, United States. Her research focuses on automated writing evaluation, applied language modeling, and the responsible design and evaluation of AI-based feedback systems.

Dr. Ikkyu Choi is a Research Director at ETS Research Institute, where he leads efforts to ensure AI is used responsibly in educational assessment. His work focuses on developing AI-driven solutions that are valid, reliable, and fair to help advance innovation without compromising integrity. He holds a PhD in Applied Linguistics from the University of California, Los Angeles, and his research combines statistical modeling, machine learning, and natural language processing to develop new capabilities in educational measurement.

Dr. Allan S. Cohen (PhD, 1972, University of Iowa) is a Professor Emeritus in the Department of Educational Psychology at the University of Georgia. He is a former O.C. and E.P. Aderhold Professor of Research Methodology, Director, Georgia Center for Assessment, and Director, Institute for Interdisciplinary Research in Education and Human Development. He studies methodological issues in educational measurement, primarily in test design and development, and new methods for understanding examinees' test-taking behaviors, especially in the context of latent variable models. He received the 2012 Career Contributions to Educational Measurement Award from the National Council on Measurement in Education.

Dr. Kadriye Ercikan is Senior Vice President of Global Research at ETS and a Professor Emerita at the University of British Columbia. Her research focuses on validity and fairness issues in assessment, including validity and fairness issues in innovative digital assessments using response process data, AI applications, personalization, and adaptivity. Dr. Ercikan is the President and a fellow of the International Academy of Education, President of the International Test Commission, and the Vice President of the National Council on Measurement in Education.

Dr. Deniz Eseryel is the Founder of Aurora Learning Solutions and a former Associate Professor in the Learning, Design & Technology program at North Carolina State University, where she also served as senior research fellow in the Chancellor's Faculty Excellence Program on Digital Transformation of Education. She earned her PhD in Instructional Design, Development & Evaluation from Syracuse University. Her work centers on digital simulations, game-based learning, and stealth assessment to develop and measure complex problem-solving skills. She has co-edited multiple volumes, published widely, and received the Outstanding International Research Collaboration Award from AERA. She currently leads an AI-based stealth assessment research initiative.

Dr. Tahereh Firoozi is an Assistant Clinical Professor in the School of Dentistry at the University of Alberta, Edmonton, Alberta, Canada. She recently completed a two-year Alberta Innovates Postdoctoral Fellowship in the Faculty of Medicine and Dentistry. She received her first PhD in Applied Linguistics from Shahid Chamran University in Iran. She completed her second PhD in Measurement, Evaluation, and Data Science at the University of Alberta. Her research is focused on the application of large language models (LLMs) in Education and Health Sciences.

Dr. Peter W. Foltz is a Research Professor at the Institute of Cognitive Science at the University of Colorado, Boulder. His research focuses on AI-based approaches for educational assessments, large-scale data analytics, and supporting learning of higher-order cognitive skills. He has worked in academic and industry settings with a history of leading innovative research and development teams resulting in the transition from ideas to proofs of concept to revenue-generating products. He was a founder and chief scientist at Knowledge Analysis Technologies, which was acquired by Pearson Education and then served as Vice President for Research at Pearson before returning to academia.

Dr. Mark Gierl is Professor of Educational Psychology and a member of the Measurement, Evaluation, and Data Science program at the University of Alberta in Edmonton, Alberta, Canada. He received his PhD in Educational Measurement and Quantitative Methods from the University of Illinois at Urbana-Champaign. His current research program is focused on automatic item generation and automated essay scoring. He is the co-author of the 2021 book *Advanced Method in Automatic Item Generation* with Dr. Hollis Lai and Vasily Tanygin. Professor Gierl holds the Tier I Canada Research Chair in Educational Measurement.

Dr. Hong Jiao is a Professor in the Department of Human Development and Quantitative Psychology at the University of Maryland, College Park, USA. She holds a PhD in Measurement and Statistics from Florida State University. Her research focuses on psychometrics in large-scale assessments, multilevel testlet models, Bayesian estimation for Item Response Theory (IRT) models, and applications of AI on cheating detection, automated scoring, item difficulty modeling, item content alignment, and large language model evaluation. Her works on multilevel testlet model and process data have been recognized with two awards from the National Council on Measurement in Education. She currently is working on the applications of machine learning, encoder-only language models, and large language models to improve the methods and practices for educational assessment.

Dr. Matthew S. Johnson is Managing Director of Foundational and Innovation Research within the ETS Research Institute. He holds a PhD in Statistics from Carnegie Mellon University and leads research on psychometrics, educational measurement, and the responsible use of AI in assessment. His work spans item response theory, Bayesian methods, large-scale assessment, and human-centered AI. He has published extensively in leading journals, has contributed to national and international large-scale assessment programs, and currently focuses on advancing valid, fair, and interpretable AI-enabled assessment systems.

Dr. Alexander Kwako is a lead scientist at Cambium Assessment. He holds a PhD in Education from the University of California, Los Angeles. His research focuses on exploring novel methodologies in education and educational assessment, with emphases on natural language processing and student agency.

Dr. Hongyun Liu is a Professor at Beijing Normal University, China. She earned her PhD in Psychometrics from Beijing Normal University. Her research focuses on large-scale educational assessment, process data analysis, and advanced statistical modeling. She has published over 200 papers in leading journals such as *Psychological Methods*, *Psychometrika*, and *Behavior Research Methods*. She is currently leading a research project on the application of AI for the prediction and control of item difficulty in educational testing.

Chandramani Lnu is an LLM AI Research Engineer at Upfeat Canada. He holds an MS in Machine Learning. His research focuses on LLMs, multimodal reasoning, and reinforcement learning–based alignment methods. His work includes synthetic data generation, automated assessment systems, and optimization of foundation models using advanced policy optimization techniques. He is currently exploring representation learning and world modeling approaches for next-generation AI systems.

Dr. Fang Luo is a Professor and Vice Dean in the Faculty of Psychology at Beijing Normal University, China. She holds a PhD in Psychometrics from Beijing Normal

University. Her research expertise covers psychological statistics and assessment, test theory, and technology. She has presided over multiple projects funded by the National Natural Science Foundation of China and published in *Nature Human Behaviour*. She currently leads research on human–computer interactive test development and process data mining in educational assessment.

Dr. Sue Lottridge is the Head of Scoring and Insights at Pearson School Assessment, USA. She holds a PhD in Assessment and Measurement from the James Madison University, USA. Her research focuses on automated scoring and processing of student responses. She has recently been appointed chair of the ITC Guidelines on Generative AI Use in Assessment. She currently leads all of human and automated scoring and Pearson School Assessment.

Dr. Constanza Mardones-Segovia is a Research Data Analyst II at the University of California, San Diego, and holds a PhD in Quantitative Methodology from the University of Georgia. Her research advances latent variable modeling using psychometric methods, natural language processing, and machine learning to analyze text-based and process data. She has published on model selection and estimation in topic modeling and diagnostic classification models. Her work emphasizes fairness, validity, and reproducible analytic pipelines, including open-source R packages and interactive Shiny applications for complex behavioral and clinical data. She has received University of Georgia (UGA) Outstanding Scholarship and Outstanding MA Awards in Quantitative Methodology.

Dr. Andrew McEachin is a Senior Research Director at the ETS Research Institute. He holds a PhD in Education Policy and an MA in Economics from the University of Southern California. His research focuses on educational inequality, school choice, math education policy, and discipline disparities. He is currently interested in investigating how policymakers can make more informed decisions about the fair and ethical implementation of AI technologies in K–12 school systems.

Dr. Kai North is a senior data scientist at Cambium Assessment, Inc. Kai earned his PhD in Information Technology at George Mason University, Virginia. He specializes in machine learning and natural language processing applied to educational and assessment technologies and has multiple top-tier publications at venues such as ACL, COLING, and ACM Computing Surveys.

Dr. Christopher Ormerod is the Executive Director of Natural Language Measurement at the College Board, USA. He holds a PhD in Mathematics from the University of Sydney, Australia. His research is highly interdisciplinary, spanning mathematics, systems biology, data science, and education. He currently focuses on applying AI to educational assessment, particularly on fine-tuning open-source LLMs for automated scoring and educational feedback.

Dr. Mark D. Shermis was the principal investigator and academic adviser for the Automated Student Assessment Prize (ASAP). He is currently a consultant for Performance Assessment Analytics, LLC. Dr. Shermis has also held faculty and administrative positions at the University of Houston, Clear Lake, University of Akron, University of Florida, Florida International, IUPUI, and the University of Texas. He is a frequently cited expert on machine scoring and co-editor (with Dr. Joshua Wilson) and author of *The Routledge International Handbook of Automated Essay Evaluation.*

Dr. Sandip Sinharay is the Linda Cook Chair in the Science of Measurement, ETS Research Institute. He has a PhD in Statistics. His primary research interests include understandardized assessments, item response theory, assessment of model fit, fairness, reporting of subscores, and statistical methods for detecting test fraud. He received the Career Contributions Award from the National Council on Measurement in Education in 2026. He is currently working on a project regarding the development of advanced psychometric methods for personalized assessments.

Dr. Stephen G. Sireci is a Distinguished University Professor and the Executive Director of the Center for Educational Assessment Education at University of Massachusetts Amherst. He has published widely on topics such as test fairness and validation, cross-lingual assessment, standard setting, and computerized adaptive testing. He is co-architect of the Massachusetts Adult Proficiency Tests, a fellow of Division 5 of the American Psychological Association, a fellow of AERA, and an elected member of the National Academy of Education.

Dr. Jesse R. Sparks is a Research Director at the ETS Research Institute with a PhD in Learning Sciences and a certificate in Cognitive Science. Her research leverages theory and research in the cognitive and learning sciences toward the design of educational assessments, including personalized, socioculturally responsive, and scenario-based assessments, especially for digital and AI literacy. She has published in *Educational Measurement: Issues and Practice*, *Practical Assessment Research and Evaluation*, and *Applied Measurement in Education* and is co-editor of the forthcoming *International Handbook of Research in Digital Literacies* (Routledge). She currently leads research on new paradigms for personalized assessment and AI literacy assessment.

Dr. Javier Suárez-Álvarez is an Associate Professor in the Research, Educational Measurement, and Psychometrics (REMP) program at the University of Massachusetts Amherst, USA. His current research focuses on integrating validity and fairness in technology-enhanced assessment systems. He serves on the Council of the International Test Commission and the Benchmarking Working Group at the National Center on Education and the Economy. He is an Associate Editor of *Psychological Assessment* and *Psicothema.* He has contributed to major international assessments, including OECD PISA and UNICEF MICS and holds a PhD in Psychometrics from the University of Oviedo, Spain.

Dr. Kimberly Swygert is Director, Test Development Innovations, at National Board of Medical Examiners (NBME). She earned her PhD in Quantitative Psychology from UNC-Chapel Hill in 1998. Since then, she has presented and published in research areas such as medical licensure assessment, performance-based assessments, test security innovations, and the responsible use of generative AI in test development. She currently leads the innovative item development, test construction, multimedia, and application development teams at NBME. She is a member of ATP's Board of Directors, and in 2018 was made a fellow of the College of Physicians of Philadelphia for her contribution to medical education research.

Cheng Tang is a PhD candidate in Educational Psychology (Quantitative Methodology Program) at the University of Georgia. He has an MS in Computer Science from the University of Georgia and both an ME and BE in Civil Engineering from Chongqing University. Cheng Tang's research integrates psychometric theories with AI, focusing on automated scoring, adaptive testing, and process data analytics using machine learning and LLMs. He has publications in the *Journal of Educational Measurement*, *Education Sciences*, and *Data* and serves as a co-developer of the TopicTestlet R package on CRAN. He currently serves as a Graduate Research Assistant and is an active reviewer for AERA, NCME, and ISLS.

Dr. Matthias von Davier is the Monan Professor in Education at Boston College and the Executive Director of the TIMSS & PIRLS International Study Center. He received his PhD in Psychology, with a specialization in psychometrics, from the University of Kiel, Germany. His scholarship has substantially advanced item response theory, diagnostic classification models, mixture modeling, process data analytics, and the integration of AI in large-scale assessment. He has played a leading role in shaping the methodological and scaling frameworks of international studies including TIMSS, PIRLS, PISA, and PIAAC. He has authored more than 200 scholarly publications and multiple books, is a fellow of the American Educational Research Association and a member of the National Academy of Education, and has served as the editor of *Psychometrika* and the *British Journal of Mathematical and Statistical Psychology*.

Dr. Shiyu Wang is an Associate Professor and a Program Coordinator of the Quantitative Methodology Program in the Department of Educational Psychology at the University of Georgia, where she also directs the NewGen Psychometrics and Data Science Analytics Lab. She holds a PhD in Statistics from the University of Illinois at Urbana-Champaign. Her research focuses on computerized adaptive testing, cognitive diagnostic models, and next-generation psychometric and data science methods. Her work has received multiple honors, including Early Career

Award from Psychometric Society (2026), Jason Millman Promising Measurement Scholar Award from NCME (2020), and the Early Career Researcher Award from IACAT (2019).

Dr. Jiawei Xiong is a research scientist at Curriculum Associates. He earned his PhD in Educational Psychology (Quantitative Methodology) from the University of Georgia. His research focuses on quantitative methods, measurement, and personalized learning. He has co-edited multiple volumes, published widely, and contributed to numerous national and state assessment and learning programs. Currently, he leads research on personalized instruction serving over 17 million K–8 students and more than 1 million educators across the USA.

Dr. Xinhui Xiong is a psychometrician and researcher specializing in longitudinal measurement, computer adaptive testing, automated test assembly, and AI-enhanced scoring and learning systems. She is Chief Psychometrician at ExamRoom AI and holds a PhD in Psychometrics from Fordham University. Her work focuses on scalable, defensible assessment design, including validation, equating, fairness analysis, and test security. She has published in leading journals and has presented extensively at national and international conference on measurement. She currently leads research on AI-integrated assessment systems for large-scale workforce and educational measurement.

Yaxuan Yang is a PhD student in the Quantitative Methodology Program at the University of Georgia. She received her MS in Learning Analytics from Teachers College, Columbia University, and her BA from the University of North Carolina at Chapel Hill. Her research focuses on integrating LLMs and natural language processing with psychometric and statistical methods in educational measurement. Her work has appeared in journals and conference proceedings in educational measurement and AI. She currently serves as a Graduate Research Assistant and contributes to interdisciplinary research in educational measurement.

Dr. Yongmei Zhang is a Research Professor at Beijing Academy of Educational Sciences, China. She received her PhD in Psychometrics from Beijing Normal University. Her research focuses on quantitative methodology for K–12 large-scale assessment, with particular interests in test design, linking and equating, and performance assessment. She is the sole author of *The Development of Large-Scale Assessment: Theory, Methodology and Application* and *Theory and Practice of Performance Assessment*. She currently leads research on computer-based assessment of higher-order thinking and LLM-enabled automated scoring for K–12 assessment programs.

FOREWORD

Richard J. Patz

Education is being reshaped by artificial intelligence (AI) at a pace and scale that few could have anticipated even a short time ago. Institutions are responding in markedly different ways. Some are embracing AI as an integral learning tool, encouraging students to use it in solving problems, drafting text, and exploring ideas. Others, perceiving threats to individual dignity, social cohesion, or the purposes of schooling itself, are retreating from digital technologies altogether, reaffirming more traditional approaches to teaching, learning, and assessment. These divergent responses are not merely differences in policy or pedagogy; they reflect deeper uncertainties about the aims of education, what counts as evidence of learning, and how responsibility should be exercised in the face of powerful and rapidly evolving tools.

Educational measurement sits squarely within this turbulence. Indeed, it may be affected at least as profoundly as other domains of educational practice. Measurement has long been tasked with providing stable, interpretable inferences about inherently complex learners, using tools and procedures that are deliberately simplified, transparent, and governable. That asymmetry, complex objects of measurement and comparatively simple, well-understood instruments, has been foundational to validity, interpretability, and trust. AI unsettles this arrangement. In introducing AI systems into assessment, we are not merely refining familiar tools; we are incorporating agents whose internal operations are opaque even to their designers, and whose behavior must therefore be observed, documented, and studied rather than fully specified in advance.

There is historical precedent for this moment, though not a perfect analogue. Automated essay scoring, for example, dates back to the work of Ellis Page in the 1960s and evolved steadily through successive generations of natural language processing, text mining, and statistical learning methods. Along the way, educational measurement intersected productively with computer science and related disciplines, while also encountering persistent resistance. How, critics asked, could a machine replace human judgment about the quality of student writing? Contrived examples, such as nonsensical essays receiving high scores, were often offered as evidence of fundamental flaws. Yet the practical advantages of automation, including cost efficiency, scalability, consistency, and eventually the promise of timely feedback, proved too compelling to ignore. Similar dynamics accompanied the adoption of computer-based testing and computer adaptive testing. In each case, skepticism was warranted, but wholesale rejection ultimately gave way to careful integration as the field developed appropriate standards, validation practices, and safeguards.

What distinguishes the present moment is not that these tensions exist, but the speed and scale at which they are unfolding. Generative AI systems are advancing rapidly, diffusing widely, and being taken up in educational contexts faster than traditional research cycles can comfortably accommodate. The challenge before us is therefore unprecedented in degree, if not in kind. It cannot be met by enthusiasm alone, nor by rigid adherence to past paradigms. It requires a combination of ethical principles, professional standards, empirical research, and open-mindedness, an approach that is both disciplined and adaptive.

Educational measurement is, in important respects, well positioned to provide ballast in these turbulent seas. The field brings to bear a long-standing commitment to validity as an organizing concept; a robust set of professional standards (currently under revision) that articulate shared responsibilities; a vibrant and collaborative community of scholars and practitioners spanning universities, research organizations, and commercial settings; and well-established mechanisms for peer review and collective deliberation. Volumes such as this one are part of that infrastructure. They create space for careful thinking, for methodological and ethical reflection, and for the exchange of ideas across disciplinary and professional boundaries.

At the same time, the challenges posed by AI demand a reexamination of some of our assumptions. In measurement, we have typically treated the tools we use, models, algorithms, and scoring rules, as fully articulated and resting on inputs observed without error, even as we acknowledge the complexity and variability of the learners we study. When human raters are introduced into the process, their fallibility becomes an object of systematic attention, managed through training, monitoring, and empirical evaluation. AI systems occupy an ambiguous position. From the perspective of the measurer, they are in some ways more like learners or raters than like traditional tools: they generate outputs through processes that are not fully transparent, that may change over time, and that must be evaluated on the basis of their performance rather than their internal logic alone. One response to this development is to insist that only fully explainable operations may be permitted in the creation of tests and the production of test scores. Another is to treat AI systems more as we do human contributors to assessment, by setting benchmarks for correctness, consistency, fairness, and bias and by subjecting their outputs to ongoing validation and scrutiny. Given the pace of change, the latter approach may offer a more practical path toward scholarship and practice that remain relevant without abandoning core commitments.

This volume enters the fray with ambition and breadth. Its scope is wide, encompassing technical, theoretical, methodological, ethical, and practical considerations. It addresses the full range of activities that undergird modern assessment practice and the educational contexts in which learning occurs, from item development and scoring to interpretation, validity argumentation, instructional impact, and large-scale implementation. The authors are actively engaged in this work, bringing perspectives informed by research, development, and use. The result is not a single argument or a unified position, but a collection of carefully reasoned and empirically grounded examinations of the current state of the field.

Readers are unlikely to approach this book linearly, nor should they. Most will come seeking insight on particular questions or challenges, and they will find chapters that speak directly to those concerns. Taken together, this volume offers something more: a springboard for further innovation and a set of guideposts that keep measurable learning improvements front and center. While the specific AI tools discussed here will undoubtedly evolve, the forms of reasoning on display, the ways in which evidence is weighed, limitations are acknowledged, and implications are traced, will endure somewhat longer. In that sense, this book models a kind of scholarship that is theoretically grounded, practically engaged, and candid about its own provisionality.

There are two failure modes that loom large in the current environment, and they stand in tension with one another. The first is the uncritical embrace of flashy technologies whose apparent benefits obscure deeper costs: impairments to meaningful learning, exacerbation of existing inequalities, diversion of scarce resources, or broader social and environmental consequences. The second is a defensive retreat into established paradigms and evidentiary standards so rigid that they paralyze inquiry and foreclose timely, responsible experimentation. Navigating between these extremes requires judgment. Readers of this volume, particularly those responsible for consequential decisions, will be better equipped to exercise that judgment with care.

The title of this book speaks of revolution, and there is no denying that AI has the potential to transform education in profound ways. Yet transformation without direction is as likely to impair as to enable meaningful progress. Educational measurement must retain its fundamental character, grounded in validity, interpretability, and responsibility, if it is to guide that transformation toward a future defined by expanded opportunity and improved outcomes for all learners. The chapters that follow do not offer simple answers, nor do they promise permanence in a rapidly changing landscape. What they offer instead is a call to disciplined imagination: an invitation to think seriously, act responsibly, and contribute thoughtfully to a field, and an educational system, very much in the making.

1

INTRODUCTION TO ARTIFICIAL INTELLIGENCE IN EDUCATIONAL ASSESSMENT

Xinhui Xiong

1.1 Introduction to Artificial Intelligence

1.1.1 Definition and Scope

1.1.1.1 AI Overview for Beginners

Artificial Intelligence (AI) is a branch of computer science focused on developing algorithms that can perform tasks such as understanding natural language, learning from experience, predicting outcomes, rating written work, recognizing speech. Tasks like those usually require human intelligence to execute. John McCarthy, often referred to as the father of AI, defines AI as "the science and engineering of making intelligent machines, especially intelligent computer programs." AI has found applications across numerous industries, including education, due to its ability to handle repetitive tasks, provide continuous availability, and eliminate concerns related to physical risks. AI is an expansive field that spans various disciplines like computer science, data analytics, linguistics, and psychology. The core of AI lies in its capacity for cognitive simulation and adaptability, enabling machines to carry out simple or complex tasks with varying levels of autonomy (Russell & Norvig, 2021).

Based on its capabilities, AI can be categorized into three broad types: narrow AI (weak AI), general AI (strong AI), and super AI.

Narrow AI is developed to perform specific tasks or a limited range of tasks. Examples of these tasks include virtual assistants like Siri or Alexa, recommendation algorithms used by streaming platforms, and conventional automated grading systems. Although narrow AI excels within its assigned domain, it cannot function beyond its programmed boundaries. Advanced applications, such as large language

DOI: 10.4324/9781003621522-1

models (LLMs) employed in automated grading, demonstrate increased sophistication in their specialized areas but remain constrained within the limits of narrow AI (Brown et al., 2020).

General AI is a hypothetical form of AI that can understand, learn, and apply knowledge across various tasks, similar to human cognitive abilities. As of now, it remains a concept without real-world implementation (Goodfellow et al., 2018).

Super AI is currently purely theoretical. If realized, it would surpass human beings in learning, reasoning, and other cognitive abilities.

Among the three types of AI, only narrow AI has been developed and applied in real-world scenarios. Unlike general AI, which would have the capacity to perform any intellectual task that humans can, or super AI, which would exceed human intelligence, narrow AI is specialized, excelling in specific tasks but lacking the ability to generalize across different domains.

1.1.1.2 Essential Characteristics and Objectives

AI has transitioned from basic rule-based systems of the past to advanced, adaptive technologies. Several defining attributes characterize modern AI systems. In the field of educational assessment, notable features include natural language processing (NLP), adaptability, predictive capabilities, reasoning, and autonomy (Goodfellow et al., 2018; Russell & Norvig, 2021; Silver et al., 2017; Devlin et al., 2019).

A fundamental feature of AI is its capacity to learn from data. The ability to iterate is often made possible through machine learning (ML), a subset of AI where algorithms are trained on extensive datasets to identify patterns and make predictions or decisions without explicit programming for each task. For example, AI learns from analyzing actual essay data and corresponding human ratings in automated essay scoring while applying pre-programmed rating criteria. Beyond ML, AI can also learn through reinforcement learning, which involves learning from interactions with an environment, and symbolic reasoning, which relies on predefined rules.

NLP enables AI to understand, interpret, and analyze human language. NLP is essential for various applications, such as chatbots, providing customer support, language translation services bridging communication across languages, and automated content generation tools efficiently producing written material. For instance, in an automated item generation system, an NLP-powered item generator can analyze existing test questions, understand their structure and content, and generate new questions that match style and difficulty.

AI systems can adjust their operations based on new data or changing conditions, improving their performance over time and managing unforeseen situations more effectively. For instance, adaptive tests adjust the difficulty of subsequent questions based on a student's previous answer. If the student answers a question correctly, the system presents a more challenging question. Conversely, if the student answers incorrectly, the system provides a question of less difficulty.

A fundamental capability of AI systems is its ability to leverage data analysis to forecast future outcomes by assessing current and historical data. With sophisticated algorithms and ML techniques, these systems can uncover patterns, trends, and correlations that may not be immediately apparent. For example, an AI system can analyze a student's homework, test results, and class participation in an educational context. The AI can accurately predict the student's future assessment performance by evaluating these data points. Furthermore, it can offer personalized recommendations, such as suggesting targeted practice exercises, designing custom revision schedules, or providing additional resources to address specific areas of improvement. This predictive ability allows educators to implement timely and individualized interventions, thereby enhancing each student's learning experience and improving their potential for academic success.

AI systems analyze data and make decisions through logical inference, mimicking human reasoning. For instance, in education, an AI system used for personalized learning can evaluate a student's performance data, such as test results and homework submissions, to determine their strengths and weaknesses. Based on this analysis, the AI generates customized learning materials and strategies to address the student's specific needs, similar to how a teacher would tailor instruction based on a student's progress and challenges.

Many AI systems operate with a degree of autonomy, meaning that they can perform tasks independently once properly trained or programmed. This characteristic is crucial for various applications. For example, AI can autonomously assess student progress in personalized learning platforms, adapt learning materials to individual needs, and provide feedback without constant human oversight. The unsupervised nature of the work allows educators to focus on more complex instructional tasks, while the AI handles routine assessments and personalized content delivery.

While features like pattern recognition and image recognition are important, they do not fully reflect the broader, more flexible, and adaptive nature of AI.

The overarching objectives of AI research and application span many goals. These include enhancing human capabilities by boosting productivity, streamlining routine and tedious tasks to increase operational efficiency, solving complex real-world problems that exceed the limitations of traditional computational methods, and driving innovation across multiple fields. Ultimately, AI strives to develop systems that can adapt, learn, and evolve, empowering individuals and organizations (He et al., 2016; Hu et al., 2018; Silver et al., 2018; LeCun et al., 2015).

AI is crafted to augment human abilities by simplifying complex tasks and boosting efficiency. Through advanced algorithms and ML, AI revolutionizes our approach to various challenges. For example, AI-powered diagnostic tools enable educators to identify students' weaknesses with enhanced accuracy and speed, allowing for more tailored interventions that effectively address individual needs. Consequently, educators can concentrate on strategic aspects of teaching, leading to improved outcomes and greater productivity.

By automating routine and repetitive tasks, AI can significantly boost organizational efficiency. This automation encompasses various activities, such as administrative processes, data cleaning, and interactions between humans and software. Consequently, AI liberates employees from monotonous and laborious duties, freeing them to dedicate their efforts to concentrate on more creative, strategic, and high-value tasks. This transition not only streamlines workflows but also promotes strategic thinking.

AI has substantial potential for addressing complex challenges that often exceed human capabilities. By utilizing advanced algorithms and significant computational power, AI systems can sift through massive amounts of data to uncover patterns and insights that traditional methods might overlook. AI's game-changing role in education is apparent in its capacity to personalize learning experiences according to each student's unique needs and preferences. Additionally, it improves teaching strategies by offering real-time feedback and identifying appropriate instructional methods.

AI is a potent driver of innovation, propelling advancements across various sectors and spawning groundbreaking products, services, and technologies. Its transformative impact is evident in personalized education and assessment, redefining traditional paradigms and creating new opportunities. AI enhances evaluation methods by making them more personalized, adaptive, and efficient. This adaptability leads to more accurate and comprehensive assessments, providing educators with deeper insights into student progress and allowing for tailored support to meet individual needs. As AI technology evolves, its role in educational assessment is poised to grow, offering further opportunities to elevate academic success and cultivate a more welcoming learning atmosphere.

1.1.2 Brief History

1.1.2.1 The Significant Benchmarks in AI Development Relevant to Assessments

AI has evolved through several key stages. Each phase has significantly shaped its development, moving from the early days of symbolic AI to the advancements seen in ML, deep learning, and LLMs. Additionally, notable figures and recent innovations have further contributed to its progress.

The origins of AI can be traced back to the mid-20th century, when symbolic AI, which concentrated on rule-based systems and logical reasoning, was introduced. The Dartmouth Conference of 1956, organized by John McCarthy and his colleagues, is widely regarded as the formal birth of AI (McCarthy et al., 2006). This foundational work established the basis for initial assessment tools using rule-based logic to evaluate student performance. For instance, in the early 1960s, systems like the "General Problem Solver" developed by Allen Newell and Herbert A. Simon were among the first to apply rule-based logic to problem-solving, which paved the way for future educational assessments leveraging similar methodologies.

In the 1980s and 1990s, the direction of AI research pivoted toward ML, where systems learn from data rather than relying solely on rule-based methods. This shift led to the development of advanced algorithms such as decision trees and neural networks, which significantly improved the analysis of educational data and the automation of assessments, including tasks like grading multiple-choice questions (Mitchell, 1997). For instance, in a classroom setting, an ML-based system employing neural networks can analyze patterns in student responses to identify common misconceptions and deliver targeted feedback, thus streamlining the grading process.

Recent advancements in AI include the development of deep learning technologies, which utilize neural networks with multiple layers that can learn representations of data with increasing levels of abstraction. This capability has enabled more accurate classification in complex datasets. In educational settings, deep learning has been used to improve the accuracy of automated essay scoring (Shermis & Wilson, 2024) and enhance adaptive learning systems by analyzing and interpreting student data to tailor educational experiences.

LLMs, such as Generative Pre-trained Transformer (GPT)-3 and GPT-4, represent another significant advancement in AI. These models excel at processing and generating human-like text, transforming how to analyze and respond to student inputs. By leveraging LLMs, educators can provide more sophisticated tools for analyzing complex student responses and delivering personalized feedback. These models have been integrated into adaptive learning systems and automated essay scoring, offering a more nuanced and responsive approach to educational assessment (Brown et al., 2020; Gan et al., 2023).

1.1.2.2 Memorable Figures and Events in AI's Evolution

In addition to foundational figures such as Alan Turing and Marvin Minsky, who laid the groundwork for AI, contemporary researchers, including Yann LeCun, Geoffrey Hinton, and Yoshua Bengio, have driven recent advancements. Their groundbreaking work on neural networks and deep learning has catalyzed significant progress in AI. The research of LeCun, Hinton, and Bengio has led to developing sophisticated algorithms that underpin modern AI systems, which are increasingly being leveraged in educational assessment (LeCun et al., 2015).

The emergence of advanced LLMs and their integration into educational technologies mark critical milestones in the evolution of AI. These models, as explored in Collins et al.'s 2022 research, represent a leap forward in the ability of AI systems to understand and generate human-like text, thereby enhancing their application in educational contexts. The deployment of these technologies has opened new avenues for improving educational assessment, offering innovative solutions that were previously unattainable.

1.2 Key Concepts in AI Relevant to Educational Assessment and Current Applications

1.2.1 Machine Learning

1.2.1.1 Rationale and Categories

Unlike traditional programming, where explicit instructions are provided for each task, ML[1] algorithms improve performance by recognizing insights from large datasets. Based on the approaches used in training models and their objectives, three broad types of ML are commonly employed: supervised learning, unsupervised learning, and reinforcement learning.

In supervised learning[2], the primary goal is to predict new, unseen data outcomes by leveraging patterns learned from the labeled training set. Common algorithms used in supervised learning include decision trees and support vector machines (SVMs). For example, in educational assessment, supervised learning can be applied to classify students into different performance levels based on examples of correct classifications used during training. Additional examples are available in Alachiotis et al. (2022).

Conversely, unsupervised learning[3] focuses on uncovering hidden patterns within the data. Standard techniques include clustering and dimensionality reduction. Clustering methods, such as k-means and hierarchical clustering, group data points based on similarity, revealing natural groupings within the dataset that can help identify patterns, make predictions, or inform decision-making. Techniques for reducing dimensionality, such as principal component analysis and t-distributed stochastic neighbor embedding, simplify data by reducing the number of variables while preserving essential relationships. As an illustration, unsupervised learning can segment students based on performance data or identify trends in learning behaviors (Crivei et al., 2020).

Reinforcement learning[4], on the other hand, aims to develop strategies that maximize cumulative rewards over time by learning from errors. Reinforcement learning is especially pertinent for developing adaptive learning systems that adjust instructional strategies based on student responses and progress (Li et al., 2023).

Each ML type has unique applications and is suited to different problems, reflecting the versatility and potential of ML technologies in various fields.

1.2.1.2 Key Algorithms and Models

Several vital algorithms and models are pivotal in ML applications for educational assessment. These algorithms are the backbone of sophisticated systems that analyze, predict, and improve educational outcomes. Each model has unique strengths and applications, making understanding their roles and functionalities essential.

Decision trees are tree-like models used for classification and regression tasks. They operate by recursively splitting the dataset into subsets based on feature values, resulting in a tree-like structure where each node represents a decision criterion. Decision trees' transparency and interpretability make them particularly useful for tasks that require clear and understandable outcomes, such as diagnosing student performance and identifying factors influencing educational outcomes. For example, they can be employed to predict student performance and pinpoint factors contributing to academic success or failure (Chen & Lin, 2023).

Neural networks are computational models inspired by the human brain, featuring layers of interlinked nodes that flexibly process and learn from data. Their capability to model complex, non-linear relationships allows them to uncover intricate patterns within data. Cutting-edge deep learning frameworks, such as convolutional neural networks (CNNs) and recurrent neural networks (RNNs), enable neural networks to perform sophisticated tasks like personalized learning recommendations and predictive analytics. These models push the boundaries of educational assessment, demonstrating their effectiveness in complex applications such as essay scoring and NLP (Huang et al., 2017).

SVMs find broad application in classification and regression tasks because they can determine the ideal hyperplane to maximize the gap between groups. In classification problems, particularly binary classification, SVMs are highly effective in distinguishing between two groups by identifying the boundary that best separates them. For instance, they can predict outcomes such as the probability of a student succeeding or not based on features like test scores or engagement metrics (Naicker et al., 2020). By using kernel functions to map input data into higher dimensional spaces, SVMs are well suited for capturing complex, non-linear relationships. Additionally, their ability to perform well with smaller datasets while minimizing overfitting further underscores their versatility.

Each algorithm offers a unique set of capabilities for educational assessment, enhancing the precision, scalability, and adaptability of ML applications. By leveraging these diverse approaches, educators and researchers can develop more innovative, personalized, and effective assessments that support a broad spectrum of learning and assessment needs and settings.

1.2.2 Natural Language Processing

1.2.2.1 Work Mechanics and Components

NLP[5] enables computers to interact with humans through natural language in a meaningful and efficient way. The process starts with data collection, where large volumes of textual data are sourced from websites, social media platforms, documents, and other repositories. Next, data preprocessing is carried out, which is a critical phase involving the cleaning and standardization of the text to ensure accuracy and consistency for subsequent analysis. Techniques such as stop-word removal, tokenization (breaking text into words or phrases), lemmatization (converting words to their base form), and stemming (reducing words to their root form) are applied to ensure consistency and uniformity across the dataset (Harme, 2024).

After preprocessing, the text is converted into numerical representations suitable for ML models. Common techniques include bag-of-words, which represents text based on word frequencies, and N-grams, which capture sequences of words. More advanced methods, such as Word2Vec and GloVe embeddings, transform the text into vectors that capture both syntactic features (word order and structure) and semantic features (meaning and context).

At this stage, ML algorithms or deep learning models are utilized to analyze the data and perform various NLP tasks, including text classification, emotion classification, entity tagging, and linguistic translation. Depending on the complexity of the task and the data, algorithms like Naïve Bayes, SVMs, or advanced neural networks and transformers may be applied.

Upon completion of training, the model is assessed with metrics such as accuracy, precision, and recall to gauge its effectiveness. Based on these results, it may be fine-tuned and optimized. Once the desired outcomes are achieved, the NLP model is deployed for real-world use. Continuous monitoring and iterative improvements ensure the model stays effective as it processes new data (Geeksforgeeks, 2024).

The intricate mechanics of NLP showcase a complex interplay of various components that work together to achieve a comprehensive understanding of language. Central to NLP is syntax analysis, which examines the structure of words by breaking them down into their constituent parts to understand how they combine. This foundational layer lays the groundwork for syntactic analysis, where the grammatical relationships among words are carefully evaluated, ensuring that sentences conform to the language rules.

As we dive deeper into understanding, semantic analysis emerges, focusing on the meanings of words and phrases in various contexts. This aspect is vital, as it transforms simple text strings into meaningful concepts. Complementing this step is discourse analysis, which examines how sentences relate to one another and how meaning is constructed across longer stretches of text, allowing the system to maintain coherence and flow in communication.

Finally, pragmatic analysis elevates understanding by extracting insights from the text. This process involves interpreting the intended meaning behind the words while considering factors such as the speaker's intent, social context, and cultural nuances. Each of these components, while distinct, collaborates to enhance the performance of NLP systems, transforming raw data into meaningful information and facilitating seamless interactions between humans and machines. This collective effort highlights the sophistication of NLP technology, demonstrating its potential to comprehend and process human language with accuracy and depth (Datacamp, 2024; Harme, 2024).

1.2.2.2 Applications

NLP has transformed industries like healthcare, law, and education. Its integration into chatbots has become essential for providing 24/7 customer service, allowing businesses to address various inquiries in real time. This capability not only enhances user experience but also improves operational efficiency. NLP is especially beneficial for beginners using online learning or assessment tools, simplifying interactions and making these platforms more accessible.

In the field of educational assessment, NLP is driving significant innovation. For example, speech recognition, powered by NLP, has made it possible to incorporate more oral responses into assessments, previously limited due to the enormous human labor required to listen to and score such responses. With NLP, assessments can incorporate diverse question formats, such as spoken answers, offering a more comprehensive evaluation of student abilities.

NLP techniques can enhance personalized learning by offering immediate, AI-driven feedback on students' writing. This capability allows teachers to provide more targeted guidance while enabling students to engage in self-directed learning. NLP's capacity to analyze text and offer tailored suggestions fosters an individualized learning experience that caters to the individual requirements and growth of every student, ultimately improving educational outcomes.

1.2.3 Neural Networks and Deep Learning

1.2.3.1 Structure and Function of Neural Networks

The core of a neural network[6] consists of neurons, the fundamental units that connect through multiple layers. The input layer receives data, and the output layer generates the final result. Between these are hidden layers, where the network performs calculations and transformations, enabling it to recognize complex patterns and relationships within the data.

A basic neural network structure connects layers sequentially, passing information from the input layer through the hidden layers to the output layer. To fine-tune the learning process, weights and biases are introduced. Weights control the strength of the signal passed between neurons by scaling the input values. Biases, on the other hand, allow the network to adjust the activation function, thereby providing flexibility. By adding a constant term to the weighted sum of inputs, biases enable the network to make more accurate predictions, even when specific inputs are zero. This adjustment allows the model to fit the data better and helps prevent underfitting. The initial input data moves through the network forward to generate an output (forward propagation).

In advanced neural networks, backpropagation adjusts weights and biases by calculating the error between the predicted and actual outputs. Gradient descent, an optimization technique, helps reduce this error by computing the gradient (or slope) of the error function in relation to the model's parameters. It then updates the parameters in the direction that lowers the error, taking small steps toward minimizing it. Over time, this iterative process fine-tunes the model, improving its accuracy in making predictions (Jons, 2021; IBM, 2024).

Neural networks demonstrate exceptional performance across various applications, particularly when it comes to making predictions and identifying patterns within large datasets. For example, in educational contexts, they can predict a student's end-of-year performance by analyzing trends from interim assessments, homework submissions, and participation records. In addition, neural networks are highly effective at recognizing patterns that might go unnoticed. This capability can be applied to detect irregular or suspicious behaviors during exams, such as potential instances of cheating. By analyzing deviations in response patterns or identifying anomalies in time spent on specific questions, neural networks offer a sophisticated layer of analysis that supports the integrity of the assessment process. Beyond these, neural networks can assist in curriculum development by analyzing historical performance data to recommend personalized learning pathways for students, ensuring that instructional content is designed to suit their distinct needs and learning styles.

1.2.3.2 Advances in Deep Learning and Their Applications

Neural networks are the foundation of deep learning[7], a specialized area of AI that employs multi-layered neural networks to capture and model complex patterns in large datasets. Recent developments in this field underscore the evolution of neural network architectures, particularly deep neural networks (DNNs). DNNs enable the training of models with an impressive number of parameters, significantly improving the accuracy and efficiency of tasks like image recognition and NLP. In automated scoring systems, DNNs can evaluate essays by analyzing complexity, coherence, and grammar. This capability allows for more nuanced assessments that closely resemble human grading standards.

CNNs mark another advancement in deep learning, designed specifically for processing visual data. They excel in object detection and image classification by leveraging spatial hierarchies. In education, CNNs can be utilized in tools that analyze students' handwriting in scanned documents or images, enabling automated grading of written assessments and identifying areas where students may struggle with their writing skills.

RNNs, along with their advanced variants like long short-term memory (LSTM) networks, are specifically designed to handle sequential data. This capability makes them highly effective for tasks such as time-series predictions, speech recognition, and language modeling. In educational contexts, LSTMs can be incorporated into intelligent tutoring systems, allowing these systems to adapt to the unique needs of individual learners by analyzing their interactions over time.

These diverse neural network architectures illustrate the growing sophistication of deep learning models, enabling them to tackle a broader range of complex, real-world challenges, especially in education. As these technologies progress, they set the stage for innovations in automated scoring, personalized learning platforms, and other systems. This expanding versatility highlights the transformative potential of deep learning in educational settings, ultimately resulting in enhanced outcomes for both students and educators.

1.2.4 Large Language Models

1.2.4.1 Framework Snapshot

Built on sophisticated deep learning architectures, particularly transformers, LLMs[8] excel in processing and predicting text (Vaswani et al., 2017). Trained on extensive and diverse datasets covering a broad range of languages and topics, LLMs capture and comprehend the nuances of human language. This extensive training enables them to perform exceptionally well in various language-related tasks, including prompt engineering. Their ability to produce contextually relevant and coherent text has made them indispensable in content creation and automated writing applications.

Here are some key examples of LLMs:

GPT-4, developed by OpenAI, is the latest advancement in the GPT series. It demonstrates exceptional abilities in generating coherent text and understanding complex prompts, showcasing remarkable proficiency in content creation and executing advanced NLP applications.

Claude, developed by Anthropic, is named after Claude Shannon, the "father of information theory." It emphasizes helpful, ethical, and collaborative interactions. With a focus on safety and responsible AI practices, Claude offers refined text generation capabilities similar to GPT-4.

Turing-NLG, developed by Microsoft, is a sophisticated language model optimized for various language-related tasks. Engineered to generate high-quality text, it adapts seamlessly to various linguistic contexts and user needs. Its versatility positions Turing-NLG as a potent tool in NLP (Open AI, 2023).

Bidirectional Encoder Representations from Transformers (BERT) is a transformer-based model developed by Google that excels at understanding the context of words with the surrounding text. Unlike GPT models, which focus on generating text, BERT is designed primarily for text comprehension and interpretation. It performs exceptionally well in question answering, sentiment analysis, and sentence classification tasks. Gray Boxes 1 and 2 articulate how BERT's structure functions and how BERT predicts the following words (Devlin et al., 2019).

GRAY BOX 1

BERT architecture

1 Input embeddings
   - Converts tokens into high-dimensional vectors.

2 Multi-head attention
   - Attention mechanism for capturing word dependencies and context.

3 Feedforward layers
   - Process the embeddings and enhance feature extraction using DNNs.

4 Output layer
   - Produces contextualized word representations for downstream applications.

GRAY BOX 2

How BERT predicts next words

Masked language modeling (MLM): During training, BERT replaces some words in a sentence with a special [MASK] token. The model then predicts the original words based on the surrounding context. For example, in the sentence "The national results are in line with [MASK]," BERT might mask out the word "polls," resulting in "The national results are in line with [MASK]." The model's task is to predict the masked word based on the surrounding context.

Contextual understanding: BERT's bidirectional attention mechanism allows it to consider the context from both directions (left and right of the [MASK] token). This bidirectional approach helps BERT accurately predict the missing words based on the full sentence context. In the example, BERT uses the context from "The national results are in line with" to predict that the masked word is "polls."

Fine-tuning for specific tasks: BERT is pre-trained using MLM and then fine-tuned on specific tasks with labeled data. For instance, after learning from examples like "The national results are in line with [MASK]" and predicting "polls," BERT can be fine-tuned for tasks such as sentiment analysis or named entity recognition, applying its contextual understanding to these applications.

1.2.4.2 Capabilities and Utilizations in Education

LLMs mark a significant advancement in AI and NLP. These models leverage neural networks to process extensive text datasets, learning intricate relationships among words, phrases, syntax, and tone. Through training on large-scale corpora, they develop the capacity to understand and generate human language with notable accuracy. As they are exposed to more data, their ability to grasp the context and produce coherent responses continuously improves, enhancing their proficiency in comprehending and replicating natural language (IBM, 2024).

LLMs are highly versatile, with applications across various domains. They can generate human-like text for tasks such as translation, question answering, text summarization, and sentiment analysis. Their strength lies in recognizing linguistic nuances, enabling them to handle both surface-level understanding and deeper semantic interpretation.

In the educational domain, LLMs hold immense potential. They can generate sample writings for students, serving as models of well-structured text and appropriate vocabulary for various contexts. Beyond this, LLMs can enhance personalized learning by providing automated feedback, adaptive tutoring, and customized learning materials, ultimately improving both teaching and learning experiences.

1.3 The Transformative Potential of AI in Educational Assessment

1.3.1 Tailored Teaching and Assessment

Advances in technology are reshaping the future of educational assessment (Xiong, 2024), with AI-driven solutions leading this transformation. These systems can potentially revolutionize both teaching and assessment by enabling personalized teaching experiences tailored to individual student needs. This capability is especially important in today's diverse classrooms, where students have different learning styles, abilities, and cultural backgrounds. AI empowers educators to adopt more adaptive and inclusive approaches, ensuring every student receives the support they need to succeed.

By analyzing data in real time, AI-powered assessments can pinpoint student strengths and areas for improvement, enabling educators to offer timely, targeted support. This approach enhances student engagement and promotes deeper learning and retention. Additionally, AI can address biases commonly found in traditional assessments, fostering more equitable educational practices. By personalizing assessments to each learner's unique path, AI-driven technologies help improve learning outcomes and create environments where all students can thrive (Zawacki-Richter et al., 2019).

In this evolving landscape, educators are better equipped to make informed decisions, shaping a future where education becomes increasingly dynamic, responsive, and inclusive.

1.3.2 Enhanced Assessment Accuracy and Efficiency

AI-powered assessment holds transformative potential to significantly enhance both the accuracy and efficiency of the evaluation process. Leveraging advanced algorithms and ML models, AI can analyze vast amounts of data in real time, producing accurate insights into student performance, learning patterns, and cognitive engagement. This technological capability minimizes the risk of human error, ensuring that evaluations are more objective and consistent. Additionally, AI accelerates grading and feedback cycles, enabling educators to provide timely, data-driven, and personalized feedback. This capability supports individualized learning, promotes deeper student engagement, and fosters ongoing growth by more effectively addressing each learner's unique needs. As a result, educators can shift their focus from administrative tasks to instructional strategies that enhance student success (Ruya & Bedizel, 2023).

In addition, AI systems are designed to be adaptive, enabling them to personalize assessments to the unique needs of individual learners. This adaptability allows for more customized evaluations that go beyond a snapshot of a student's current abilities. By continuously monitoring and analyzing a learner's progress over time, these systems provide a richer and more nuanced understanding of their strengths, areas for improvement, and learning patterns. AI-driven assessments don't just stop at grading; they can uncover trends in student learning behaviors, predict future performance, and even suggest targeted interventions. These tailored interventions are essential for identifying and supporting students at risk of falling behind, ensuring that no one slips through the cracks. Ultimately, AI systems have the potential to foster more equitable educational outcomes by offering personalized pathways to success for every learner.

1.3.3 Strengthened Support for Students and Educators

AI-powered assessment has the potential to revolutionize the educational landscape by improving support for both students and educators. By offering personalized feedback, pinpointing learning gaps, and customizing instruction to address individual needs, AI can foster a more responsive and effective educational experience.

AI-driven assessments offer students personalized learning pathways that adjust in real time to their individual strengths and weaknesses. This tailored approach enhances engagement with the material and encourages a sense of ownership in their learning journey, ultimately resulting in better academic outcomes. Additionally, AI provides immediate feedback, allowing students to quickly grasp their progress and identify areas for improvement, surpassing the pace of traditional assessment methods (Balaraman, 2024).

Educators can also gain significantly from AI's capabilities. By automating routine administrative tasks like grading and monitoring student progress, AI liberates valuable time for educators to concentrate on instruction and mentoring. Furthermore, AI can analyze extensive datasets to reveal trends and insights that may not be readily visible. These actionable insights can guide instructional strategies, enabling educators to enhance their teaching methods and provide enhanced support to their students.

In this way, AI-powered assessment enhances individual learning experiences while fostering a more efficient and effective learning environment. By connecting students' needs with educators' capabilities, AI promotes a more inclusive and adaptive educational ecosystem, empowering all learners to thrive.

1.4 Challenges and Considerations

1.4.1 Ethical and Fairness Issues

Ethical and fairness concerns encompass bias, data security, and privacy. Fairness issues arise when algorithms and AI systems inadvertently favor certain groups, potentially perpetuating existing inequalities or creating new forms of discrimination. Bias can be introduced through various means, such as biased training data or flawed assumptions in model design, leading to skewed outcomes that affect marginalized populations disproportionately.

Data security and privacy are also components of ethical discussions surrounding AI. As these technologies often rely on large volumes of personal data, ensuring this information from unauthorized access and breaches is crucial. Moreover, individuals should have clear visibility into how their data is collected, used, and stored. Tackling these ethical and fairness issues is fundamental for establishing confidence in AI systems and guaranteeing they function in a manner that honors the rights and dignity of all users.

1.4.1.1 Fairness and Bias Concerns

Fairness and bias in AI-powered learning and assessment are critical issues that require thoughtful attention as they can impact the outcomes and effectiveness of these systems. Bias can arise from various sources, including data, algorithms, and human involvement, each contributing differently to how AI models behave and make decisions (Ferrara, 2023).

Data bias is one of the challenges in AI that is often overlooked, leading to unreliable output, commonly described as "garbage in garbage out." Since AI systems rely on data to learn and make predictions, biases present in the training data can be carried into the system. For example, if historical data reflects societal biases related to gender, race, or socioeconomic status, the AI system may not only mirror these biases but could also amplify them. In educational settings, this can lead to unfair assessments, where certain groups of students are systematically disadvantaged due to biased data.

Algorithmic bias is another critical concern that stems from the design of AI algorithms. Even if the data is relatively unbiased, the algorithm may still process information in ways that disproportionately favor or disadvantage certain groups. This bias can happen when certain features or variables in the algorithm's decision-making process better represent one group than another, leading to skewed outcomes. In educational assessments, this could result in unfair scoring, with some students being rated higher or lower based on factors unrelated to their actual performance. In high-stakes tests, such as licensure exams, this could even lead to individuals losing their credentials.

Human decision bias also plays a crucial role. The individuals who develop, implement, and manage AI systems can inadvertently introduce their own biases, consciously or unconsciously. This bias can occur at various stages of AI development, such as labeling data, selecting models, or interpreting outcomes. These human decisions shape the system's performance, and if biases are present, they will be reflected in the AI's assessments. For example, a developer might unintentionally select features that favor specific student populations, reinforcing existing inequities.

Addressing fairness and bias in AI requires ongoing attention to these sources of bias throughout the entire AI lifecycle, from data collection and algorithm development to human oversight and interpretation.

Bias in AI-powered assessments has profound consequences, leading to unfair results and reinforcing existing educational inequities. When AI systems exhibit bias, assessment results can disproportionately disadvantage certain student groups. For example, an AI system designed to evaluate student essays may consistently score lower for students from particular backgrounds, even when their work is similar to others. Bias creates skewed academic evaluations, where some students are unfairly penalized, not due to the quality of their work, but because of the biases embedded in the system (MIT Horizon, 2024; Abrams, 2024).

Beyond individual assessment outcomes, these biases have broader implications. If left unaddressed, they can reinforce existing inequities in education, making it more challenging for marginalized groups to succeed. When AI systems consistently disadvantage certain students, they contribute to systemic barriers that already exist, widening the gap between privileged and underrepresented groups. This cycle of bias, once embedded in AI, becomes self-reinforcing, hindering efforts to promote educational equity and inclusiveness across diverse student populations.

Transparency, reproducibility, and bias awareness are essential strategies for mitigating the risks associated with AI systems, especially in sensitive domains such as assessment and decision-making (MIT Horizon, 2024; Ferrara, 2023). Transparency requires that AI systems disclose their decision-making process, offering clear and comprehensible explanations for the outcomes they produce. This approach entails clarifying the logic behind scores, assessments, or recommendations, fostering user trust and establishing a foundation for accountability.

Reproducibility is vital for AI systems, highlighting the necessity for consistent results under the same conditions. When an AI system demonstrates reproducibility, it boosts trust in its reliability and fairness, enhancing its credibility and allowing for effective testing and validation.

Equally important is bias awareness, which calls for developers to diligently detect and resolve biases in AI systems. This approach involves utilizing diverse and representative training data, as well as conducting regular audits to detect and mitigate any emerging biases over time. By being aware of bias and striving to counteract it, developers can help ensure that AI systems make fair and equitable decisions, avoiding unintended discrimination or harm.

1.4.1.2 Privacy and Data Security Concerns

Privacy and data security are paramount in AI systems, primarily because of the enormous volumes of data they handle and the associated risks. From the initial stages of data collection to the training of AI models and ultimately the use of these models by end users, privacy concerns permeate every step of the process (Gomstyn & Jonker, 2024; Gulen, 2023; Megas, 2024).

Data collection, which frequently contains sensitive personal information, poses considerable challenges, especially regarding obtaining consent and ensuring ethical data use. Organizations must navigate the complexities of acquiring extensive datasets while upholding ethical standards.

As the volume of data processed by AI systems escalates, the threat of data breaches becomes greater. Unauthorized entry into personal information can bring about serious consequences, including identity theft and fraud targeting students, highlighting the critical priority of data security for developers and organizations. Additionally, the capacity of AI to analyze and cross-reference information from various sources raises another issue: the risk of re-identifying individuals from datasets that were meant to be anonymized.

AI systems also improve surveillance capabilities, potentially infringing on individual privacy rights. Furthermore, biases embedded within AI algorithms may lead to discriminatory outcomes, unfairly impacting individuals based on traits such as race or gender.

During the training phase of AI models, there is a risk of data leakage, where sensitive information could be unintentionally exposed, thereby complicating data security issues. As AI technology continues to evolve, so do the regulatory frameworks that govern its application. Organizations must navigate the ongoing challenge of ensuring adherence to privacy laws and regulations, which constantly adapt to new developments in the field.

To effectively tackle these complex issues, organizations must implement robust data governance frameworks, embrace transparent AI practices, and engage in continuous monitoring to safeguard individual privacy and ensure data security.

1.4.2 Implementation Challenges

Implementation challenges encompass several vital factors. Data quality is essential, as inaccuracies lead to poor decisions and ineffective systems. Additionally, robust infrastructure and technology are essential to support new systems, including adequate hardware, software, and network capabilities.

Another major challenge is the shortage of skilled professionals. This gap often leads to delays in implementing and maintaining these systems, highlighting the urgent need for targeted training and recruitment strategies. Finally, high upfront costs and uncertainty surrounding return on investment (ROI) can hinder efforts to justify expenditures to stakeholders. By tackling these issues, organizations can improve their prospects for successful implementation and fully leverage the benefits of their initiatives (Pappas, 2023; RapidCanvas, 2024).

1.4.2.1 Technical Requirements and Infrastructure

Building and maintaining AI systems requires a robust infrastructure that seamlessly integrates various hardware and software components. Central to these systems is extensive data storage, as AI relies on vast amounts of data to operate optimally. To accommodate this, scalable storage solutions, such as cloud storage and distributed databases, are essential. Once the data is stored, it must be processed efficiently. Tools like Apache Hadoop and Apache Spark are instrumental in handling large datasets, enabling information to be processed and analyzed effectively (Flinders & Smalley, 2024; RedHat, 2023).

Training AI models requires substantial computational resources, making specialized hardware essential. Specialized processors such as GPUs[9] and TPUs[10] are critical in managing the intensive computations involved in this process. Once the appropriate computing resources are in place, developers utilize ML frameworks to construct and train AI models. Frameworks such as TensorFlow and PyTorch offer the necessary tools and libraries that facilitate and streamline the model-building process.

ML operations platforms are essential for ensuring the smooth operation of ML models throughout their lifecycle. Tools such as MLflow and Kubeflow facilitate the management of all stages, from development to deployment and monitoring, providing a comprehensive framework for overseeing AI projects.

Networking is fundamental in this infrastructure. Fast and reliable networks are essential for transferring large datasets and model parameters among various components of the AI system. Cloud platforms, including Amazon Web Services (AWS), Google Cloud, and Azure, offer scalable networking solutions tailored for AI workloads, ensuring efficient data flow and connectivity.

Lastly, development and deployment tools are indispensable for creating and implementing AI models. Integrated development environments such as Jupyter Notebooks and PyCharm are commonly used for model development. Meanwhile, deployment tools like Docker and Kubernetes facilitate the scalable and efficient launch of these models. Together, these components create a robust AI infrastructure that supports the seamless development, deployment, and maintenance of advanced AI systems.

1.4.2.2 Training and Support

Training and support help address the challenges that often arise when implementing AI systems. One practical approach is to organize regular workshops and seminars. These sessions keep the team updated on the latest AI trends, tools, and technologies while fostering a culture of continuous learning and innovation. They also provide a collaborative environment where team members can exchange ideas, discuss challenges, and develop new skills relevant to their roles.

In addition to workshops, teams are encouraged to take online courses and pursue certifications in AI and ML to deepen their understanding and expertise. This structured, self-paced learning provides flexibility and allows employees to develop specialized knowledge, making them more effective in their roles. Certifications can also bolster their professional credentials, boosting both confidence and value within the organization.

Mentorship programs are another powerful strategy for overcoming implementation challenges. By pairing less experienced team members with AI experts, organizations can promote hands-on learning and personalized guidance. This one-on-one approach allows mentees to ask targeted questions, receive practical advice, and apply their knowledge directly to real-world projects. At the same time, mentors have the opportunity to refine their skills through teaching, fostering a culture of shared growth and development across the team.

Moreover, continuous technical support is crucial for the smooth and efficient operation of AI systems. Establishing a solid support infrastructure enables the team to troubleshoot technical issues quickly and optimize the performance of AI applications. Whether resolving system bugs, fine-tuning algorithms, or improving integration with existing systems, reliable technical support minimizes disruptions and keeps AI initiatives moving forward.

By implementing these strategies, ongoing education through workshops and courses, mentorship for skill development, and dedicated technical support, organizations can not only overcome the challenges of AI implementation but also create a foundation for long-term success and innovation in AI adoption.

1.5 Conclusion

AI has rapidly transformed various fields, including education and assessment, surpassing the capabilities of traditional technologies. In education, AI has revolutionized traditional methods, enhancing both teaching and learning by enabling personalized instruction tailored to individual learning styles and paces. As a result, education has become more accessible and practical. In the realm of assessment, innovations such as automatic item generation and prompt engineering have streamlined the creation of test items. At the same time, automated scoring and immediate feedback have improved the efficiency, objectivity, and timeliness of assessments. These advancements have increased assessment accuracy and freed educators to focus on personalized instruction, thereby improving the learning experience.

Despite these significant improvements, AI's transformative potential in education has not yet been fully realized. There is still immense opportunity to introduce more innovative assessment methods that address diverse learning needs and improve educational outcomes. For example, adaptive assessments that adjust in real time on student responses and AI-driven predictive analytics, offering more profound insights into student performance, are areas ripe for growth.

However, this potential also brings a set of ethical and practical challenges. Fairness and bias in AI algorithms are critical, particularly when considering the diverse student populations that educational systems serve. Concerns around the transparency of AI-driven decisions are valid, especially when these systems could unintentionally reinforce existing inequalities. The issues of privacy and data security are paramount, as AI often relies on vast amounts of sensitive student data. Without proper safeguards, students and educators are at risk of facing unnecessary risks.

The implementation of AI in education faces several logistical challenges. The maintenance of high-quality data is crucial for optimal AI performance; however, many educational institutions face challenges in upholding this standard. Building the necessary infrastructure to support AI technologies can be expensive and time-consuming, requiring robust systems capable of handling the complexities of AI algorithms. Moreover, the limited expertise in AI within educational institutions poses a significant barrier, with many educators and administrators uncertain about how to effectively integrate these technologies into their existing frameworks. Furthermore, determining the ROI for AI in education remains challenging, given that the benefits are often neither immediate nor easily quantifiable.

While these challenges are substantial, they are not insurmountable. With proper training, support, and a commitment to fostering continuous learning, organizations can successfully navigate the complexities of AI integration. Empowering educators with the expertise to effectively employ AI tools is vital. Furthermore, as AI technologies evolve, organizations must continuously develop and refine policies and guidelines that address ethical concerns, ensure data privacy, and mitigate risks related to fairness and bias. By doing so, education can better unlock the potential of AI, paving the way for more personalized, equitable, and innovative approaches to both teaching and assessment.

Notes

1 ML is a subset of AI that involves the development of algorithms capable of learning from and making predictions or decisions based on data.
2 Supervised learning relies on labeled data, where each training example is associated with a known output. The model learns to map inputs to these known outputs, enabling it to make predictions or classifications.
3 Unlike supervised learning, unsupervised learning deals with unlabeled data to explore and analyze without predefined categories or outcomes.
4 Reinforcement learning is grounded in the principle of learning through interaction. It involves training an agent to make decisions by rewarding desirable outcomes and penalizing undesirable ones.
5 NLP refers to a set of programs that utilize ML technologies to facilitate interactions between computers and human beings using natural language.
6 Neural networks are designed to process information in a way that resembles how the human brain functions.
7 Deep learning employs neural networks with multiple layers to extract complex patterns from data.
8 LLMs are advanced AI systems that understand, generate, and manipulate natural language text.
9 Graphics processing units.
10 Tensor processing units.

References

Abrams, Z. (2024). Addressing equity and ethics in artificial intelligence. *American Psychological Association*, *55*(3), 24. https://www.apa.org/monitor/2024/04/addressing-equity-ethics-artificial-intelligence

Alachiotis, N., Kotsiantis, S., Sakkopiulos, E., & Verykios, V. (2022). Supervised machine learning for student performance prediction. *Intelligent Decision Technology*, *16*(1), 93–106. https://doi.org/ content.iospress.com/articles/intelligent-decision-technologies/idt210251

Balaraman, K. (2024). Empowering personalized learning paths: The transformative role of AI. *Integra*. https://integranxt.com/blog/empowering-personalized-learning-paths-the-transformative-role-of-ai/

Brown, T., Mann, B., Ryder, N., Subbiah, M., Kaplan, J., Dhariwal, P., … & Amodei, D. (2020). Language models are few-shot learners. *Proceedings of the 33rd Conference on Neural Information Processing Systems (NeurIPS 2020)*. https://arxiv.org/abs/2005.14165

Chen, S., & Lin, X. (2023). Application of Decision Tree algorithm in educational data mining. *Curriculum and Teaching Methodology*, *6*(8), 120–127. https://doi.org/10.23977/curtm.2023.060818

Collins, K. M., Wong, C., Feng, J., Wei, M., & Tenenbaum, J. B. (2022). Structured, flexible, and robust: Benchmarking and improving large language models towards more human-like behavior in out-of-distribution reasoning tasks. *ArXiv*. https://doi.org/10.48550/arXiv.2205.05718

Crivei, L. M., Czibula, G., Ciubotariu G., & Dindelegan, M. (2020). Unsupervised learning based mining of academic data sets for students' performance analysis. *2020 IEEE 14th International Symposium on Applied Computational Intelligence and Informatics (SACI)*, Timisoara, Romania, 11–16. https://doi.org/10.1109/SACI49304.2020.9118835

Datacamp (2024). What is natural language processing? A comprehensive guide for beginners. *Datacamp*. https://www.datacamp.com/blog/what-is-natural-language-processing

Devlin, J., Chang, M. W., Lee, K., & Toutanova, K. (2019). BERT: Pre-training of deep bidirectional transformers for language understanding. *Proceedings of the 2019 Conference of the North American Chapter of the Association for Computational Linguistics (NAACL-HLT 2019)*, Minneapolis, MN, 4171–4186. https://aclanthology.org/N19-1423.pdf

Ferrara, E. (2023). Fairness and bias in artificial intelligence: A brief survey of sources, impacts, and mitigation strategies. *Sci*, *6*(1), 3–17. https://doi.org/10.3390/sci6010003

Flinders, M., & Smalley, I. (2024). What is AI infrastructure. *IBM*. https://www.ibm.com/topics/ai-infrastructure

Gan, W., Qi, Z., & Wu, J., & Lin J. (2023). Large language models in education: Vision and opportunities. *2023 IEEE International Conference on Big Data*, Sorrento, Italy, 4776–4785. https://doi.org/10.1109/BigData59044.2023.10386291

Geeksforgeeks (2024). Natural language processing – Overview. *Geeksforgeeks*. https://www.geeksforgeeks.org/natural-language-processing-overview/

Gomstyn, A., & Jonker, A. (2024). Exploring privacy issues in the age of AI. *IBM*. https://www.ibm.com/think/topics/ai-privacy

Goodfellow, I., Bengio, Y., & Courville, A. (2018). Deep learning. *Genet Program Evolvable Mach*, *19*, 305–307. https://doi.org/10.1007/s10710-017-9314-z

Gulen, K. (2023). AI and ethics: Balancing progress and protection. *DATA CONOMY*. https://dataconomy.com/2023/01/16/artificial-intelligence-security-issues/

Harme, K. M. (2024). Components and implementations of natural language processing. *Hackerearth*. https://www.hackerearth.com/blog/developers/natural-language-processing-components-and-implementations/

He, K., Zhang, X., Ren, S., & Sun, J. (2016). Deep residual learning for image recognition. *Proceedings of the IEEE Conference on Computer Vision and Pattern Recognition (CVPR)*, Las Vegas, 770–778. https://doi.org/10.1109/CVPR.2016.90

Hu, J., Shen, L., & Sun, G. (2018). Squeeze-and-excitation networks. *2018 IEEE/CVF Conference on Computer Vision and Pattern Recognition*, Salt Lake City, UT, 7132–7141. https://doi.org/10.1109/CVPR.2018.00745

Huang, G., Liu, Z., Van Der Maaten, L., & Weinberger, K. Q. (2017). Densely connected convolutional networks. *2017 IEEE Conference on Computer Vision and Pattern Recognition (CVPR)*, Honolulu, HI, 2261–2269. https://doi.org/10.1109/CVPR.2017.243

IBM (2024). What is a neural network? *IBM.* https://www.ibm.com/topics/neural-networks
Jons, R. (2021) Neural networks: Structure, types, and possibilities. *IEEE Computer Society.* https://www.computer.org/publications/tech-news/neural-network-structures
LeCun, Y., Bengio, Y., & Hinton, G. (2015). Deep learning. *Nature, 521*, 436–444. https://doi.org/10.1038/nature14539
Li, X., Xu, H., Zhang, J., & Chang, H. (2023). Deep reinforcement learning for adaptive learning systems. *Journal of Educational and Behavioral Statistics, 48*(2), 220–243. https://doi.org/10.3102/10769986221129847
McCarthy, J., Minsky, M. L., Rochester, N., & Shannon, C. E. (2006). A proposal for the Dartmouth summer research project on artificial intelligence, August 31, 1955. *AI Magazine, 27*(4), 12–16. https://doi.org/10.1609/aimag.v27i4.1904
Megas, K. (2024). Managing cybersecurity and privacy risks in the age of artificial intelligence: Launching a new program at NIST. *NIST.* https://www.nist.gov/blogs/cybersecurity-insights/managing-cybersecurity-and-privacy-risks-age-artificial-intelligence
MIT Horizon (2024). Ethics and AI-powered learning and assessment. *MIT Open Learning.* https://openlearning.mit.edu/news/ethics-and-ai-powered-learning-and-assessment
Mitchell, T. M. (1997). *Machine Learning.* McGraw-Hill.
Naicker, N., Adeliyi, T., & Wing J. (2020). Linear support vector machines for prediction of student performance in school-based education. *Mathematical Problems in Engineering, 2020*, Article ID 4761468. https://doi.org/10.1155/2020/4761468
Open AI (2023). GPT-4 technical report. *ArXiv.* https://doi.org/10.48550/arXiv.2303.08774
Pappas, C. (2023). 6 AI implementation challenges and how to overcome them. *eLearning Industry.* https://elearningindustry.com/ai-implementation-challenges-and-how-to-overcome-them
RapidCanvas (2024). Overcoming AI implementation challenges: strategies for success. *AI & ML TECH TREND.* https://www.rapidcanvas.ai/blogs/overcoming-ai-implementation-challenges-strategies-for-success
RedHat (2023). AI infrastructure explained. *RedHat.* https://www.redhat.com/en/topics/ai/ai-infrastructure-explained
Russell, S., & Norvig, P. (2021). *Artificial Intelligence: A Modern Approach* (4th ed.). Pearson.
Ruya, N., & Bedizel, T. (2023). Evolving landscape of artificial intelligence (AI) and assessment in education: A bibliometric analysis. *International Journal of Assessment Tools in Education, 10*, special issue, 208–223.
Shermis, M. D., & Wilson, J. (2024). *The Routledge International Handbook of Automated Essay Evaluation.* Routledge.
Silver, D., Hubert, T., Schrittwieser, J., Antonoglou, I., Lai, M., Guez, A., … & Hassabis, D. (2017). Mastering chess and shogi by self-play with a general reinforcement learning algorithm. *Nature, 550*(7676), 354–359. https://doi.org/10.48550/arXiv.1712.01815
Silver, D., Hubert, T., Schrittwieser, J., Antonoglou, I., Lai, M., Guez, A., … & Hassabis, D. (2018). A general reinforcement learning algorithm that masters chess, shogi, and Go through self-play. *Science, 362*(6419), 1140–1144. https://doi.org/10.1126/science.aar6404
Xiong, X. (2024). Transforming educational assessment: innovative methods and future pathways. *Journal of China Examinations, 2024*(10), 81–93.
Vaswani, A., Shazeer, N., Parmar, N., Uszkoreit, J., Jones, L., Gomez, A. N., Kaiser, Ł., & Polosukhin, I. (2017). Attention is all you need. *NIPS'17: Proceedings of the 31st International Conference on Neural Information Processing Systems*, Long Beach, CA, 6000–6010. https://dl.acm.org/doi/10.5555/3295222.3295349
Zawacki-Richter, O., Marín, V. I., Bond, M., & Gouverneur, F. (2019). Systematic review of research on artificial intelligence applications in higher education where educators are not involved in the loop. *International Journal of Educational Technology in Higher Education, 16*(39), 1–27. https://doi.org/10.1186/s41239-019-0171-0

2

ETHICAL CONSIDERATIONS AND CHALLENGES IN AI-BASED EDUCATIONAL ASSESSMENT

Matthew S. Johnson, Ikkyu Choi, and Andrew McEachin

2.1 Introduction

2.1.1 The Rise of AI in Educational Assessment

The rapid expansion of artificial intelligence (AI) technologies within educational contexts is reshaping the landscape of assessment at an unprecedented pace. AI systems, according to a High-Level Expert Group of the European Commission, are "systems that display intelligent behaviour by analysing their environment and taking actions – with some degree of autonomy – to achieve specific goals" (High-Level Expert Group on AI, 2019; Sheikh et al., 2023, p. 19). In educational assessment, AI encompasses a sweeping range of applications: from automated scoring and adaptive testing to intelligent tutoring systems and the personalized generation of assessment content (Bulut et al., 2024; Burstein et al., 2024; Burstein, 2025; Johnson, 2025).

These innovations improve efficiency, enable real-time feedback, and provide scalability and flexibility in measuring learner skills and knowledge. For instance, generative AI now supports the creation of novel and adaptive test items (Choi & Zu, 2022; Song et al., 2025; Tan et al., 2025; Zawacki-Richter et al., 2019; Zu et al., 2023), while advanced algorithms enable multimodal data analysis incorporating audio, video, and text to assess complex constructs such as communication or collaboration (Hao et al., 2024; Jiang et al., 2025). At the same time, AI-powered analytics can deliver insights to educators, learners, and policymakers, catalyzing data-informed instruction and supporting educational mobility (UNESCO, 2023; U.S. Department of Education, Office of Educational Technology, 2023).

As these systems become deeply embedded in assessment infrastructure, it is crucial to recognize that an AI assessment solution is not just a single model but a

DOI: 10.4324/9781003621522-2

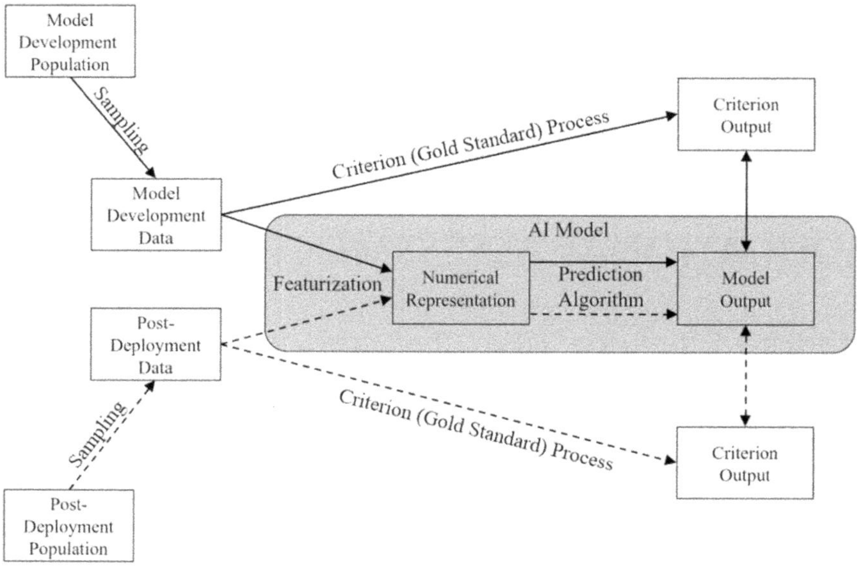

FIGURE 2.1 Schematic representation of a typical AI-based assessment system, spanning both the model development and post-deployment phases across data, population, numerical representation, and gold-standard evaluation criteria. Each stage, from sampling and featurization to model output and criterion processes, can introduce error or bias into the assessment process.

complex, multi-component process. Figure 2.1 illustrates a typical architecture of an AI-based assessment system.

The figure highlights how development begins with the sampling of representative populations and data, followed by the transformation of this data into numerical features suitable for modeling and prediction. Crucially, each prediction generated by the AI-based system is interpreted in reference to "criterion" or gold-standard processes, such as human rater scores or expert benchmarks, that anchor system validity. Once deployed, the system continues processing new data from diverse populations, requiring ongoing evaluation of predictions against updated criteria to monitor both accuracy and fairness.

This system-level perspective is critical: ethical vulnerabilities, including bias, reliability threats, and unfairness, may originate not only in the modeling algorithms themselves but also from upstream influences (such as data sampling and feature selection) or downstream criteria and interpretive practices. Accordingly, high-stakes, AI-generated inferences can influence access to educational opportunities, career advancement, and lifelong learning trajectories. Therefore, it is imperative that the deployment of AI in educational assessment proceeds in a manner that is not only technically robust but also ethically responsible and socially just (Johnson, 2025; UNESCO, 2022).

2.1.2 Why Ethical Considerations Matter

Ethical challenges permeate every stage of the AI assessment lifecycle, from data collection and model development to system deployment and monitoring. Algorithmic bias, lack of transparency, opacity in decision-making, and the risks of misuse can undermine the foundational goals of educational measurement: supporting learning, ensuring equity, and safeguarding individual rights.

Biases in AI systems may emerge from unrepresentative data, flawed modeling assumptions, or interactions with complex sociotechnical contexts (Baker & Hawn, 2022; Barocas et al., 2023). Such biases can perpetuate or even amplify historical disadvantages, inadvertently disadvantaging entire demographic groups or individuals with distinct learning needs. This raises critical questions about fairness, not merely as a statistical property but as a lived reality for learners navigating educational systems shaped by AI.

Moreover, the opacity of many state-of-the-art AI-based systems, the so-called black box problem, undermines the explainability and interpretability necessary for meaningful human oversight. Stakeholders, including learners and educators, may be unable to contest, understand, or trust system outputs absent clear explanations and robust accountability mechanisms (Khosravi et al., 2022; Phillips et al., 2021). Data privacy and security remain omnipresent concerns, particularly as assessment systems collect and process increasingly granular and sensitive learner data (CISA, 2023b).

International and national bodies, including UNESCO, OECD, NIST, the U.S. Department of Education, and professional measurement organizations such as American Educational Research Association, American Psychological Association, and National Council on Measurement in Education, have articulated convergent sets of principles for the ethical governance of AI in education (NIST, 2023; OECD, 2019; UNESCO, 2022; U.S. Department of Education, Office of Educational Technology, 2023). These principles emphasize fairness and bias mitigation, transparency, explainability, human oversight, personal autonomy, accountability, privacy and security, and ongoing monitoring for continuous improvement (Johnson, 2025).

Striking a balance between the innovative disruptive potential of AI and the ethical responsibilities inherent in educational measurement is thus a central challenge for researchers, developers, and practitioners alike.

2.1.3 Aims and Organization of This Chapter

This chapter critically examines the ethical challenges and responsibilities associated with integrating AI in educational assessment. Drawing on international standards and current research, our goal is to provide practitioners, researchers, and policymakers with clear frameworks and practical strategies for responsible AI use.

We begin by clarifying foundational concepts, including ethics, fairness, and compliance, and introducing philosophical approaches that inform ethical decision-making in assessment. The core of this chapter explores major ethical issues:

- Algorithmic bias and its impact on fairness, with discussion of mechanisms and mitigation strategies.
- Transparency and explainability as necessary conditions for stakeholder trust and accountability.
- Human oversight and the risks of automation bias, emphasizing the importance of professional judgment and institutional safeguards.
- Privacy and security concerns, focusing on protecting sensitive learner data.

To illustrate these themes, we present a detailed case study of an AI-based grading platform, analyzing its strengths and limitations from an ethical standpoint. We conclude with actionable recommendations for continuous monitoring, stakeholder engagement, and policy development, underscoring that ethical innovation must balance technical progress with a commitment to equity and the public good.

2.2 Framing the Ethical Landscape

The term *ethical* broadly refers to applying moral principles and standards, distinguishing right from wrong, and acting in ways that align with accepted codes of conduct and values. In professional practice, ethics provides a compass for decision-making, guiding individuals and organizations to act with integrity, fairness, and respect for all stakeholders. AI-enhanced assessment systems prompt renewed attention to these ethical principles.

2.2.1 Distinguishing Ethics, Fairness, and Compliance

In discussions about AI-enabled educational assessment, the terms *ethics*, *fairness*, and *compliance* are sometimes treated as interchangeable. However, while these concepts are closely related, they have distinct meanings and implications for the research, development, and deployment of assessment systems.

Ethics encompasses broad principles about what is right, just, and beneficial for individuals and society. Ethical considerations demand reflection on moral values, the possible consequences of decisions, and the obligations to various stakeholders, including learners, educators, families, and the broader community. In educational assessment, ethics involves not only technical accuracy but also the moral imperative to respect and empower learners, foster equity, and promote positive educational and social outcomes (AERA et al., 2014).

Fairness is a central, but narrower, component of ethics. In the context of educational measurement, fairness refers specifically to ensuring that assessments do not produce or reinforce unjust advantages or disadvantages for any group or individual. This encompasses

- Avoiding bias based on race, gender, socioeconomic status, disability, language, or other attributes;
- Providing equitable access and opportunity;
- Treating similar cases similarly and different cases appropriately differently;
- Carefully considering how assessment systems might differentially affect diverse populations (Barocas et al., 2023; Johnson et al., 2022; Johnson & McCaffrey, 2023; Suk & Han, 2024).

Fairness is often operationalized with measurable criteria in testing and machine learning, for example, by evaluating differential outcomes, disparate impact, or differential item functioning. Nevertheless, technical metrics alone cannot substitute for continuous ethical reflection, as definitions and expectations of fairness can vary across societies and contexts (Castelnovo et al., 2022).

Compliance, by contrast, refers to adherence to established laws, regulations, and institutional policies. These may include data privacy statutes (such as FERPA or GDPR), anti-discrimination laws, professional testing standards, or specific organizational procedures for test security and integrity. While compliance provides important guardrails and clear minimum standards for practice, it does not guarantee ethical or fair outcomes by itself. There can be situations where compliant systems still produce results or impacts that are ethically questionable or unfair in practice (Castelnovo et al., 2022; High-Level Expert Group on AI, 2019; Johnson, 2025; NIST, 2023).

While the distinctions between ethics, fairness, and compliance provide a practical foundation for responsible AI use in educational assessment, understanding how to navigate complex ethical dilemmas often requires deeper reflection. Here, philosophical traditions offer invaluable resources. By examining different schools of ethical thought, we can better appreciate the values, priorities, and trade-offs that shape our judgments, especially when technical metrics or regulatory standards fall short of resolving complex cases. In the context of AI-driven assessment, these philosophical perspectives not only inform how we define and pursue fairness or justice but also help us recognize our broader obligations to learners and society. The following section introduces key philosophical approaches that can enrich ethical decision-making in this evolving landscape.

2.2.2 Philosophical Approaches to Ethics

Diverse philosophical traditions have shaped ethical reasoning, each offering a different perspective on what it means to act morally or make ethical decisions. Understanding these theories can help clarify how we approach ethical questions in educational assessment, particularly when new dilemmas arise from the use of AI and algorithmic tools.

Consequentialism (utilitarianism): This tradition evaluates the morality of decisions by their outcomes, asking whether an AI system improves educational results for the most significant number of learners (Mill, 1861; Sinnott-Armstrong, 2023). While a consequentialist might support an algorithm if it boosts overall achievement, this approach risks overlooking harms to minorities or marginalized groups, highlighting the need for careful consideration of who benefits and who may be disadvantaged (Barocas et al., 2023).

Deontology (duty-based ethics): Deontological ethics focuses on principles and rights that we should not violate, regardless of the consequences (Alexander & Moore, 2024; Kant, 1785/2011). In educational measurement, this means upholding duties such as non-discrimination and informed consent. For example, a scoring model that systematically disadvantages a particular group is unethical from a deontological perspective, even if it improves average performance (AERA et al., 2014; Floridi & Taddeo, 2016).

Virtue ethics: Rather than focusing solely on rules or outcomes, virtue ethics emphasizes the character and intentions of practitioners (Aristotle, 1999; Hursthouse & Pettigrove, 2023). For those developing and deploying AI assessment systems, this means cultivating qualities such as honesty, humility, and a willingness to accept and address feedback, especially when confronted with system limitations or ethical uncertainty (Mittelstadt et al., 2016; Wiltshire, 2015).

Care ethics: This perspective centers on contexts, relationships, and a commitment to respond to vulnerability (Gilligan, 1982; Noddings, 1984; Partsei et al., 2025). Applied to AI-based assessment, care ethics urges us to consider the real-world impacts on individuals, especially those least able to advocate for themselves, such as non-native speakers or students with disabilities.

Principle-based, pluralistic approaches: Most contemporary regulatory frameworks, such as those from UNESCO, OECD, and NIST, draw from multiple traditions, emphasizing core values like fairness, transparency, accountability, privacy, and autonomy (NIST, 2023; OECD, 2019; UNESCO, 2022). These pluralistic approaches guide ethical decision-making in complex contexts, helping practitioners balance competing priorities such as accuracy versus explainability, or efficiency versus equity.

2.2.3 Overview of Key Ethical Issues

In practice, these philosophical perspectives equip us to confront the ethical challenges posed by AI in educational assessment, moving beyond technical compliance to ensure our decisions reflect both sound measurement and a genuine commitment to justice for all learners.

A review of contemporary research, international guidelines, and professional standards reveals a set of recurring ethical concerns that are especially salient for

AI-based assessment systems (Barocas et al., 2023; Bulut et al., 2024; Burstein et al., 2024; Burstein, 2025; Johnson, 2025; UNESCO, 2022, 2023):

- **Bias and fairness**: AI-based assessment systems can replicate and even intensify historical patterns of inequality if they draw on data or assumptions that reflect existing social biases. Ensuring that assessment systems are fair, i.e., providing equitable access and opportunity to all learners, requires ongoing vigilance, robust bias detection and mitigation strategies, and a readiness to continually evaluate what constitutes "fair" in diverse and evolving contexts (Baker & Hawn, 2022; Johnson, 2025).
- **Transparency and explainability**: The complexity and opacity of many AI systems make it difficult for stakeholders to understand how AI-based assessment systems make decisions or challenge outcomes they perceive as unjust. Explainable AI is necessary not only for earned trust and stakeholder acceptance but also for upholding ethical responsibilities of accountability (Binns, 2018) and participatory decision-making (Khosravi et al., 2022; Phillips et al., 2021).
- **Human oversight**: As assessment systems become more automated, there is heightened risk of "automation bias," where decision-makers and users defer too readily to algorithmic outputs. Maintaining human agency and professional judgment is critical for effective oversight, error correction, and alignment with core educational values (U.S. Department of Education, Office of Educational Technology, 2023).
- **Privacy and security**: With AI-enhanced assessment comes the collection and analysis of large quantities of sensitive educational data. Safeguarding the privacy, dignity, and security of learners is both a regulatory requirement and an ethical imperative, one that calls for strict data governance, transparency in data use, and vigilance against new threats (CISA, 2023a, 2023b, 2023c; NIST, 2023).

These issues are overlapping and often interdependent in practice. For example, efforts to make models more explainable can impact predictive performance, and data minimization for privacy can create tension with the need for robust fairness analyses (Buijsman, 2023; Corbett-Davies et al., 2017, 2023; Veale & Binns, 2017). Navigating such trade-offs requires reflective practice, broad consultation, and a continual return to the principal goal of serving learners and the public good.

The following sections of this chapter will examine each of these domains in depth, analyzing the mechanisms by which ethical risks emerge in AI-driven assessment, presenting practical mitigation strategies, and highlighting real-world lessons from recent advances and challenges in the field.

2.3 Algorithmic Bias in Educational Assessment

With the ongoing integration of AI and machine learning in educational assessment, stakeholders must pay meticulous attention to the presence and effects of algorithmic bias. As in traditional assessment, fairness remains central to the validity and utility of AI-driven scores, probably even more so given the scale and opacity with which machine learning models operate. Without careful design and monitoring, automated assessment systems risk perpetuating or even exacerbating the very inequities they promise to redress.

2.3.1 How Bias Arises in AI-Driven Assessment

AI and machine learning models inherit and sometimes amplify biases present in their design, data, and deployment. In automated scoring, for instance, both the NLP and traditional statistical algorithms that underpin AI-based assessment systems have been documented to generate disparate and sometimes detrimental impacts for specific demographic groups (Johnson et al., 2022; Johnson & McCaffrey, 2023; Mehrabi et al., 2021; Suk & Han, 2024). This can occur across a range of applications, from simple automated short-answer scoring to multimodal analysis of complex open-ended tasks.

Suresh and Guttag's "Seven Sources of Harm in Machine Learning" (Suresh & Guttag, 2021a; Suresh & Guttag, 2021b) provides a helpful framework for understanding the emergence of bias in AI systems by offering a comprehensive lens for practitioners to systematically identify, anticipate, and address risks. Extending and contextualizing this for the assessment domain, we see the following:

- **Historical bias**: When training data reflect past patterns of discrimination, be it due to prior policies, curriculum design, or societal trends, AI-based assessment systems can enshrine these patterns into present-day predictions. For example, automated scoring systems trained on responses from predominantly affluent or majority-culture students may struggle with the linguistic styles, topics, or experiences common among underrepresented or lower socioeconomic status groups. As the composition of test-takers changes over time, reliance on historical data may yield scores that systematically misrepresent the abilities of contemporary or historically marginalized learners.
- **Representation bias**: This emerges when the development data for AI-based assessment systems underrepresents specific populations. For example, if training data lack sufficient examples from English language learners, rural students, or students from minoritized racial backgrounds, the resulting algorithms risk producing less accurate or reliable scores for these groups, potentially widening educational disparities.
- **Measurement bias**: Flaws in how assessment features are conceptualized or operationalized can generate biased outputs. This may arise due to omitted variables (features important for adequate scoring are left out), use of proxies (using imperfect measures in place of what raters actually score), or reliance on confounded variables (e.g., features correlated with both group membership and score but irrelevant to the rubric). Each can introduce systematic error

differentially across groups. For example, if an automated essay scoring system focuses exclusively on surface grammar without accounting for content relevance, and if relevant content knowledge varies systematically by background, group disparities may emerge.

- **Aggregation bias**: When models are fit to data pooled from diverse subpopulations, but underlying relationships differ between those groups, bias emerges. For example, if students from urban and rural contexts or from different cultural backgrounds employ distinct rhetorical norms in writing or speech, a single model may fail to accurately score all subgroups. Large-scale AI scoring deployments that cover multiple states, regions, or countries frequently reveal this problem.
- **Learning/Algorithmic bias**: Technical aspects of model construction, including the choice of loss function, regularization, or training paradigm, can inadvertently shape outcomes for specific groups. For instance, if a model is tuned to minimize overall mean squared error in a dataset where one group dominates numerically, the model will optimize error for that group at the expense of underrepresented minorities.
- **Evaluation bias**: The process by which AI-based assessment systems are tested and validated may itself introduce bias if evaluative benchmarks or performance metrics ignore subgroups of interest. If fairness analyses only consider aggregate population performance or a limited set of demographic indicators, meaningful disparities in smaller or less visible populations may go undetected.
- **Deployment bias**: Even fair and robust models may generate harm if used in ways that depart from the intended context, such as presenting continuous model scores as categorical decisions, or post-processing scores without considering group-level performance or validity. Furthermore, if automated scores are used to make high-stakes decisions (e.g., course placement or graduation) with insufficient human review, small group-level biases can yield significant real-world consequences.

Understanding and addressing these sources of bias is critical for anyone developing or deploying AI in assessment, particularly in contexts characterized by diversity and persistent inequity.

2.3.2 Mitigation Strategies

Mitigating algorithmic bias in educational assessment requires an ongoing, multi-layered approach. Rather than relying on one-time fixes, responsible AI development integrates fairness and bias reduction throughout data collection, system design, evaluation, and deployment. Johnson (2025) discusses two major areas when considering bias mitigation strategies for AI-based assessment systems: data representativeness and bias analysis.

2.3.2.1 Data Representativeness

Ensuring that the data used to train and evaluate AI assessment systems is representative of the populations served is a foundational strategy (Clemmensen & Kjærsgaard, 2023). This means explicitly defining the population of interest and seeking data that reflects its diversity in terms of demographic characteristics, educational backgrounds, and contextual factors. For example, it is important to include examples from groups such as English language learners, rural students, and students from minoritized backgrounds. Without such representation, AI-based assessment systems may perform poorly or unfairly for underrepresented groups, exacerbating existing disparities.

Developers should also be mindful of how contextual variables, such as disability status or access to learning resources, may influence assessment outcomes. As student populations and educational practices evolve, data must be regularly updated to reflect these changes and to maintain the relevance and fairness of AI-driven assessments.

There are many interpretations of what it means for data to be representative (Clemmensen & Kjærsgaard, 2023; Kruskal & Mosteller, 1979a, 1979b, 1979c, 1980), so it is important to be mindful about how data selected for training and evaluating AI-based assessment systems can affect their performance and outputs (Johnson, 2025).

2.3.2.2 Bias Analysis and Evaluation

Thorough bias analysis is essential at all stages of AI system development. This begins with engaging stakeholders, including learners, educators, administrators, and community representatives, to define what fairness and bias mean in a particular educational context. The literature offers multiple definitions of fairness. Barocas et al. (2023) boil down the many definitions of fairness into three different conceptions defined in terms of different independence assumptions among three variables: the output of the AI system, the target variable, or gold-standard output that the system is trying to produce, and the sensitive attribute being considered (e.g., race, urbanicity, sex). The three types of fairness are:

- Independence: the sensitive attribute is statistically independent of the prediction;
- Separation: the prediction or AI output is conditionally independent of the sensitive attribute, given the target variable;
- Sufficiency: the prediction is sufficient for describing the relationship between the sensitive attribute and the target variable; that is, the target variable is conditionally independent of the sensitive attribute, given the prediction.

Differential item functioning (Holland & Thayer, 1988; Holland & Wainer, 1993), differential algorithmic functioning (Suk & Han, 2024), and the automated scoring fairness metrics of Johnson et al. (2022) and Johnson and McCaffrey (2023) are all aligned with the separation definition of fairness.

Developers and deployers of AI-based assessment systems should evaluate them using a mix of approaches, including both group and individual fairness perspectives. For example, group fairness focuses on equitable outcomes across demographic groups, while individual fairness considers whether similar individuals receive similar treatment (Dwork et al., 2011). Counterfactual fairness provides yet another lens, asking whether decisions would remain unchanged if sensitive attributes were altered, holding all else constant (Kusner et al., 2017).

Importantly, evaluation reports should not only provide aggregated results; instead, they should present results disaggregated by relevant subgroups to ensure that disparities are recognized and addressed (Johnson & Zhang, 2024). Continuous stakeholder involvement helps ensure that fairness remains aligned with community values and educational goals.

2.3.2.3 Remediation and Ongoing Monitoring

Addressing bias in AI-driven educational assessment requires a combination of technical interventions, ethical reflection, and ongoing vigilance. At the modeling stage, several algorithmic strategies can help reduce bias and promote fairness. Fairness-aware algorithms, for example, introduce constraints or penalties during training to ensure that fairness objectives are balanced alongside predictive accuracy (Dwork et al., 2011). Recent work by Johnson and McCaffrey (2023) proposes penalizing or constraining automated scoring models that produce non-zero bias estimates, providing a concrete means to limit group-based disparities in scores. Additionally, cost-sensitive learning and constrained optimization methods can be employed to prioritize accuracy or minimize errors for historically marginalized groups, further reducing potential disparities in outcomes (Elkan, 2001). Regular audits and validation with diverse, real-world datasets are essential for detecting new or emerging sources of bias as assessment systems evolve.

When evaluations identify bias, remediation may involve rebalancing datasets, refining feature selection, or revising model objectives to address disparities. Developers should be transparent about the trade-offs involved in these interventions, as efforts to enhance fairness for one group may sometimes reduce overall predictive accuracy or create unintended effects for others (Buijsman, 2023; Corbett-Davies et al., 2017, 2023). Open documentation of bias analyses and mitigation efforts, along with regular monitoring, supports accountability and continuous improvement.

Technical measures alone cannot guarantee fairness. Legal and ethical frameworks, such as anti-discrimination statutes, the Joint Standards, and guidance from organizations like UNESCO, must also inform bias mitigation strategies. While regulatory compliance is necessary, it is equally important to consider the broader ethical implications of system outputs, especially as societal values and expectations evolve (NIST, 2023; Schwartz et al., 2022).

Ultimately, bias mitigation in educational AI is an ongoing process that requires thoughtful integration of data practices, stakeholder collaboration, technical innovation, and ethical consideration. By embedding these principles throughout the entire system lifecycle, developers and educators can better ensure that AI assessment technologies foster equitable opportunities and outcomes for all learners.

2.3.3 Limitations and Ongoing Challenges

Despite significant advances, persistent limitations challenge our ability to entirely eliminate bias in AI-based assessment systems. Some bias may be structural, rooted in broader societal patterns that data-driven techniques cannot easily redress. Trade-offs may arise between maximizing predictive accuracy and minimizing error for the most vulnerable groups, or between model interpretability and technical performance. Moreover, real-world assessment settings are dynamic; both student populations and language practices shift over time, requiring ongoing vigilance and flexibility in AI governance. Finally, no technical solution can substitute for meaningful human judgment: supporting educators and institutions in recognizing, interrogating, and acting on algorithmic bias remains a central, enduring task.

Algorithmic bias is one of the most critical and persistent ethical challenges in the use of AI for educational measurement and assessment. Although assessment developers have long recognized bias as a threat to fairness and validity in conventional testing, the adoption of complex AI and machine learning systems introduces new sources, forms, and consequences of bias, often operating at a greater scale and with less transparency than traditional assessment tools.

2.4 Transparency, Explainability, and Trust

Transparency occupies a foundational place in the responsible deployment of AI within educational assessment. In psychometrics, transparency has long been recognized as essential for building trust in tests, supporting valid score interpretations, and ensuring that stakeholders can make well-informed decisions based on assessment outcomes (AERA et al., 2014). With the integration of AI, however, the conceptual demands of transparency have become still more complex and pressing.

Unlike traditional assessments, AI-powered systems operate through multilayered algorithms, often using large datasets, sophisticated feature extraction, and, in some cases, "black box" models such as deep neural networks. These systems can generate inferences that appear inscrutable even to expert practitioners (Kay et al., 2023). As such, a commitment to transparency requires that organizations do more than offer basic technical disclosure. They must provide stakeholders with clear, meaningful, and timely information about how the system makes decisions, how developers build and validate models, how they collect and use data, and what assumptions and limitations shape the system's outputs (U.S. Department of Education, Office of Educational Technology, 2023). It is not enough for algorithms merely to be accurate; they must also be understandable, accessible, and open to scrutiny by the broad community of educational stakeholders, including learners, educators, administrators, policymakers, and even the wider public (Doshi-Velez & Kim, 2017; Mitchell et al., 2019).

2.4.1 The Role of Transparency in AI Assessment Systems

At its core, *transparency* in AI assessment refers to the clear and open disclosure of how systems are constructed, deployed, and maintained, and how the pipeline from data collection to algorithmic decision-making unfolds (High-Level Expert Group on AI, 2019; NIST, 2023). In practice, this involves much more than releasing pseudocode or summaries of model performance metrics. It requires:

- Clear documentation of dataset provenance, selection criteria, and potential biases present in the data.
- Openness about the kinds of features and variables incorporated into model design, and the rationale for their inclusion or exclusion.
- Disclosure of model assumptions, optimization criteria, and details of post-processing steps, such as rescaling or rounding of automated scores.
- Articulation of the intended use-cases, known limitations, and the steps taken to protect privacy and security (Mitchell et al., 2019).

Transparency lays the groundwork for trust. It creates the conditions necessary for external auditing, enables stakeholders to interpret system outputs, and signals institutional commitment to ethical conduct. Particularly in high-stakes educational settings, where AI-driven scores can affect course placement, graduation, or access to opportunities, transparency serves as a safeguard against "black box" risk, where AI systems make critical decisions in ways inaccessible even to those most affected.

In practical terms, transparency serves several critical roles:

Fostering informed stakeholder engagement: Transparency empowers all educational actors, including students, families, educators, administrators, and policymakers, to critically appraise the functioning and implications of AI-based assessments. For instance, when a high-stakes admission is an AI-based assessment system, explicit documentation about the system's structure, performance, and sources of potential bias enables overseers and affected individuals to ask pertinent questions: are models responsive to changes in the applicant population? Do technical limitations create disproportionate burdens for students from less-resourced schools? Is the training data representative of diverse learning trajectories?

Supporting fairness, accountability, and due process: Only when stakeholders understand the criteria by which AI-based assessment systems evaluate student work or potential can they meaningfully challenge, appeal, or seek redress for adverse or erroneous decisions. This is particularly important in contexts where AI-derived scores significantly influence educational advancement, scholarship opportunities, or access to gifted programs.

For example, a school district implementing AI-driven essay scoring must not only communicate average scoring reliability but also explain to educators and students how specific response features (e.g., grammar, coherence, topic relevance) are weighted, and whether the algorithms in use systematically disadvantaged particular groups (e.g., non-native speakers, students from underrepresented backgrounds).

Enabling technical scrutiny and continuous improvement: Technical transparency is necessary for psychometricians, data scientists, and independent researchers to audit, validate, and improve AI assessment systems. This includes publishing model architectures, training regimens, evaluation criteria, and error distributions across demographic groups or item types. Transparent systems allow for the systematic identification of performance gaps, support bias mitigation efforts, and promote an open culture of measurement science.

It is important to acknowledge, however, that complete transparency sometimes collides with other legitimate priorities. For example, regulations to prevent gaming of the test may limit complete disclosure of algorithmic details. Similarly, protecting proprietary information or the privacy of training data may require carefully balanced disclosures. Striking the right balance is, as always, context-dependent and informed by ongoing dialogue between technical and non-technical stakeholders (High-Level Expert Group on AI, 2019; NIST, 2023).

A notable example of this tension arose in the context of automated essay scoring systems, particularly with Educational Testing Service's (ETS) e-rater (Burstein et al., 2013). As e-rater became widely used for scoring high-stakes assessments, concerns grew about the potential for test-takers to exploit weaknesses in the system's scoring algorithms. The BABEL generator, a program developed by Les Perelman to produce essays that were essentially meaningless but structured in a way that could deceive automated scoring engines into assigning high scores (Perelman, 2020), vividly illustrated this issue. The existence of BABEL highlighted the risks of making algorithmic details too transparent: public knowledge about system vulnerabilities enabled adversarial attacks, undermining the validity of test results.

In response, ETS researchers developed methods to detect BABEL-generated text and other forms of adversarial input (Cahill et al., 2018). Their work demonstrated the ongoing need for protective measures in system design, while also reinforcing the importance of adaptive transparency. Full algorithmic disclosure may not always be possible or desirable; instead, organizations must strike a careful balance between openness and security, ensuring that transparency serves both the public interest and the integrity of assessment systems.

2.4.2 Explainability

Explainability refers to the degree to which the internal mechanics and outputs of an AI system can be made intelligible to human stakeholders. In assessment, this means more than interpreting feature weights or opening the "algorithmic black box." Explainability compels us to ask: can learners, teachers, and administrators understand the reasons why an AI assigned a particular score, recommendation, or classification?

Phillips et al. (2021) identify four foundational principles of explainable AI systems:

1. **Explanation**: The system should produce explanations or rationales for its predictions or decisions.
2. **Meaningful**: Explanations must be understandable and context-appropriate for their intended audience. For example, what is meaningful for a psychometrician may be impenetrable to a student, and vice versa.
3. **Explanation accuracy**: The explanation should reflect, with fidelity, the actual data, features, and steps that led to the output, rather than a simplified or "marketing" narrative.
4. **Knowledge limits**: The system should identify cases for which the system was not designed to function, or in situations where the outputs may be problematic (e.g., low reliability, bias issues).

The pursuit of explainability in AI for educational measurement confronts several enduring challenges:

- **Complexity of underlying models**: State-of-the-art systems, such as deep neural networks, ensemble methods, or large language models, are often less inherently interpretable than simpler statistical models, making it difficult to provide clear rationales for individual predictions.
- **Trade-offs with system performance**: There is a well-documented tension (Johnson, 2025) between model transparency or interpretability and overall predictive accuracy. Simpler, more transparent models may sacrifice nuance and subtlety, whereas more complex models may deliver higher accuracy but defy straightforward explanation. Educational institutions must weigh when greater simplicity is warranted, especially when trust or high-stakes fairness is of significant concern.
- **Audience diversity**: Different users require different kinds of explanations. A system that is explainable to psychometricians may not be easily understood by learners or parents. Thus, explainability must be tailored, with layered or audience-specific resources, ranging from technical documentation to simplified guides, to interactive visualizations demonstrating system logic.

Despite these challenges, explainability remains a central vehicle for advancing fairness, trust, and responsible adoption of AI in educational assessment. Importantly, explainability is both a technical and an organizational property, and it is advanced not just through algorithmic choices but also through policy, documentation, and professional development.

2.4.3 Impact on Trust and Stakeholder Acceptance

Empirical research demonstrates that stakeholder trust in AI-driven assessments is inextricably linked to transparency and explainability (Khosravi et al., 2022). When users do not understand how or why scores are determined, acceptance drops, contestation rises, and calls for human intervention or appeals increase. Conversely, well-communicated explanations, such as instructors' guides, interface tooltips, or walkthroughs, can significantly increase perceived fairness and facilitate ongoing learning and improvement.

A concrete example arises in automated essay scoring platforms. Systems that display the linguistic features or structural elements influencing a score and can relate them to scoring rubrics known to users are more likely to be trusted and adopted by both students and teachers. Conversely, proprietary "black box" algorithms, where even the test provider cannot reason through a specific score assignment, face resistance and skepticism, particularly when scores deviate from human expectations or appear to penalize minoritized populations.

Similarly, in large-scale deployments of adaptive learning technologies, institutions that clearly describe how they make recommendations by providing accessible documentation, backed by user testing and feedback cycles, see greater willingness among educators and learners to integrate these technologies into everyday practice.

2.4.4 Challenges and Tensions

Despite its virtues, operationalizing transparency in AI-based assessments presents significant technical and practical challenges. Highly complex models may resist intuitive explanation; proprietary constraints or intellectual property considerations may limit disclosure; and, as noted earlier, model sophistication often comes at the expense of clarity, making it harder to explain the system's inner workings to lay stakeholders.

Moreover, if transparency is poorly implemented, it may degenerate into a ceremonial practice, overwhelming stakeholders with jargon-laden technical minutiae or selectively omitting uncomfortable sources of model error or bias. Thus, transparency must be grounded in effective communication, tailored to the needs of diverse audiences, and always attentive to the underlying ethical imperative: to make the workings and consequences of AI assessment visible, comprehensible, and contestable.

In summary, transparency is not a panacea, but it is an indispensable foundation for ethical AI in educational assessment. It illuminates the "how" and "why" behind automated judgments, supports accountability, and undergirds the ongoing collaborative enterprise of measurement science in the service of educational equity and improvement.

2.5 Human Oversight and Responsible Use

While advances in AI-powered assessment promise transformative benefits for education, these systems are not, and should not be, autonomous arbiters of student potential or achievement. The responsible integration of AI into educational measurement requires a steadfast commitment to meaningful human oversight at every stage of the assessment lifecycle. Human judgment, contextual awareness, and ethical discernment remain irreplaceable, especially in high-stakes or sensitive decision-making scenarios.

Human oversight encompasses a broad spectrum of activities, from the design and validation of AI-based assessment systems to the ongoing monitoring of their outputs and impacts in real-world contexts. Educators, assessment professionals, and policymakers must retain ultimate authority over consequential decisions, ensuring that AI serves as a tool for informed judgment rather than as an unquestionable source of truth. This "human-in-the-loop" approach not only supports the detection and correction of errors or biases that may elude automated systems but also upholds foundational principles of fairness, due process, and accountability in education (Binns, 2018; U.S. Department of Education, Office of Educational Technology, 2023).

Moreover, responsible use of AI in assessment is not merely a technical or procedural matter; it is an ongoing ethical and professional obligation. This involves cultivating a culture of critical reflection, continuous improvement, and stakeholder engagement, where developers and deployers openly communicate about the affordances and limitations of AI, and what the mechanisms for appeal, redress, and transparency are. By centering human oversight and ethical stewardship, educational institutions can ensure that the adoption of AI assessment technologies advances, rather than undermines, their core mission of supporting learning, equity, and student well-being.

2.5.1 The Role of Human Judgment with AI

Even as AI systems in educational assessment grow in sophistication, the irreplaceable value of human judgment persists. Human experts bring interpretive nuance, contextual understanding, and ethical discernment that AI, regardless of its advances, cannot fully replicate (Baker, 2016). While AI can rapidly process vast datasets, identify subtle statistical patterns, and provide consistent scoring at scale, it cannot weigh factors such as cultural context, individual learning histories, or non-standard student responses that may warrant special consideration.

Human judgment plays a critical role in several phases of the assessment process. During the design stage, educators and psychometricians define learning objectives, select relevant features, and set boundaries for appropriate model use, decisions that require pedagogical expertise and value-based reasoning (Hao, 2025). In operational settings, human oversight is essential for monitoring anomalous outputs, adjudicating borderline cases, and reviewing instances where AI-generated scores conflict with teacher assessments or student self-reports (Ninaus & Sailer, 2022). For example, when an automated essay scorer flags an essay as off-topic or assigns an unexpectedly low score, a human reviewer can consider contextual factors, such as language proficiency, prompt interpretation, or evidence of creative expression, that the algorithm may fully capture (Bulut et al., 2024).

Furthermore, human judgment is vital for maintaining fairness and equity. Automated systems, if left unchecked, risk perpetuating or amplifying existing biases in educational data. By providing opportunities for appeal, audit, and intervention, human reviewers can identify and address unjust outcomes, ensuring that AI serves as an aid to, rather than a substitute for, professional expertise and ethical responsibility (Binns, 2018). Ultimately, the most trustworthy and effective assessment systems are those that combine the efficiency and analytical power of AI with the discernment, empathy, and critical insight of human educators and decision-makers.

As AI becomes integral to educational assessment, ensuring that robust human oversight remains paramount. AI promises improvements in efficiency, scalability, and sometimes objectivity, but research and policy guidance affirm that human judgment is indispensable for ensuring the ethical, fair, and valid use of assessment technology (Johnson, 2025; UNESCO, 2023; U.S. Department of Education, Office of Educational Technology, 2023).

2.5.2 Risks of Automation Bias and Over-Reliance

The rapid integration of AI into educational assessment brings significant risks related to automation bias and over-reliance on algorithmic decision-making. Automation bias refers to the tendency for users to uncritically accept, or favor, recommendations made by automated systems, even in the presence of conflicting evidence or common sense (SKITKA et al., 1999). In educational contexts, this bias can lead teachers, administrators, and policymakers to defer to AI-generated scores or classifications without adequately questioning their validity, accuracy, or fairness.

Such over-reliance can have profound consequences, including the perpetuation of existing biases, the marginalization of non-standard learners, and a diminished role for human judgment in interpreting complex or context-dependent student responses (Binns, 2018). Automated systems, while powerful, are only as fair and effective as the data and assumptions they use; unchecked trust in their outputs can erode critical safeguards, such as appeal mechanisms and individualized review, that are essential for upholding equity and accountability in education (UNESCO, 2022). Ethical use of AI requires ongoing vigilance against automation bias, ensuring that human educators remain actively engaged in oversight, critical reflection, and the final decision-making process.

2.5.3 Ensuring Meaningful Human Involvement

To truly harness the benefits of AI in educational assessment while guarding against its risks, intentional and systemic approaches to human oversight are essential. Robust involvement of educators, administrators, and other stakeholders should be embedded throughout every phase of AI system design, implementation, and use. This begins with comprehensive professional development: schools and districts must invest in ongoing, hands-on learning that builds AI literacy, clarifies the capabilities and limitations of assessment technologies, and empowers staff to interpret critically and, when necessary, challenge algorithmic outputs (UNESCO, 2023; U.S. Department of Education, Office of Educational Technology, 2023). Scenario-based training can help educators reconcile AI-generated recommendations with the complex realities of their classrooms, developing the judgment needed to recognize when intervention is warranted.

Beyond training, effective oversight protocols are crucial. Policies should require that substantial academic, placement, or disciplinary decisions are reviewed by qualified educators, ensuring that no AI output is treated as the final say in the absence of human judgment (AERA et al., 2014; High-Level Expert Group on AI, 2019). Transparent redress mechanisms must be in place so that students, families, or educators can contest or appeal AI-generated outcomes. Structured review panels should be empowered to intervene when necessary, providing essential safeguards against potential errors or injustices (High-Level Expert Group on Artificial Intelligence (AI HLEG), 2020; UNESCO, 2023). These processes not only protect individual learners but also uphold the integrity and accountability of the educational system.

Moreover, meaningful human involvement depends on distributed and collaborative accountability. Oversight of AI decisions should be a shared responsibility, leveraging the diverse expertise of teachers, administrators, technical experts, and, where appropriate, students and families themselves (Johnson, 2025). Institutions should conduct regular audits of AI-generated decisions to identify systematic patterns of error or bias and actively solicit stakeholder feedback to guide ongoing improvements (AERA et al., 2014). This participatory approach builds trust in technology and ensures that assessment processes remain fair, transparent, and responsive to the evolving needs of all learners.

Ethical and effective use of AI in educational assessment depends not on replacing, but on augmenting, professional expertise. AI-based assessment systems should provide valuable evidence for human deliberation, not acting as arbiters, but as partners. With robust professional development, strong institutional policies, and vigilant oversight, education can realize the promise of AI while steadfastly preserving fairness, autonomy, and trust at the heart of assessment practice. By creating structures that support ongoing reflection, transparent communication, and stakeholder engagement, educational systems can ensure that AI technologies advance rather than undermine their core mission of supporting learning, equity, and student well-being.

2.6 Privacy and Security Considerations

As AI systems become foundational in educational measurement, they increasingly rely on collecting, storing, and analyzing vast amounts of sensitive learner data. This includes not only test scores and written responses but also potentially rich behavioral, biometric, or multimedia data (e.g., facial video, voice recordings). While these data streams enable greater personalization and powerful analytics, they simultaneously magnify privacy and security risks, risks that go well beyond technical failures, touching on profound ethical and social questions (Johnson, 2025; UNESCO, 2022; U.S. Department of Education, Office of Educational Technology, 2023).

The unique context of educational assessment heightens the stakes. Learners, who are often minors, and their families may not always have the knowledge, power, or resources to provide informed consent, contest inappropriate data collection, or recognize subtle threats. A breach, misuse, or unintended sharing of assessment data can lead to identity theft, reputational damage, discrimination, or even psychological harm. Further, large-scale educational data are increasingly targeted by malicious actors (e.g., ransomware), and regulatory environments (FERPA, GDPR) impose legal obligations (AERA et al., 2014; CISA, 2023c).

2.6.1 Ethical Implications Beyond the Technical

Deployers of AI-based assessment systems must understand privacy and security not merely as compliance checkboxes or engineering challenges but as ethical imperatives fundamental to trust and justice in educational settings (Johnson, 2025; UNESCO, 2023). The protection of learner data relates directly to principles of autonomy, dignity, and fairness.

- **Autonomy**: Students should retain meaningful control over what data is collected about them and how the systems use, share, and retain these data. In practice, this means strong policies for informed consent, age-appropriate privacy notices, and options to opt out where feasible (UNESCO, 2022).
- **Dignity and non-discrimination**: Mishandling of sensitive data may expose students to unfair treatment. For example, assessment records leaked or shared without consent could lead to bias in placement, college admissions, or employment.

- **Power and equity**: Marginalized groups may be more vulnerable to privacy harms, lacking the ability to challenge inappropriate data collection or usage, and suffering disproportionately from breaches. Responsible stewardship thus entails additional vigilance and proactive support for these learners (UNESCO, 2023).

2.6.2 Supporting Responsible Stewardship

Responsible data stewardship is an ongoing process that requires technical rigor, institutional investment, and a culture of transparency and vigilance. The following list provides recommended practices for the ethical handling of data.

- **Secure by design**: Following guidance from cybersecurity agencies, systems should be architected from the ground up to prevent unauthorized access, minimize stored sensitive data, and ensure isolation of security-critical components (CISA, 2023b, 2023c). Encryption, access controls, and regular vulnerability assessments are baseline requirements.
- **Minimization and purpose limitation**: Collect only data that are strictly necessary for assessment or learning purposes, and limit retention to what is required to fulfill those purposes. Unnecessary accumulation of data not only increases breach risk but may violate ethical and legal standards (UNESCO, 2022; U.S. Department of Education, Office of Educational Technology, 2023).
- **Transparency and consent**: Provide learners and guardians with plain-language explanations of what is being collected, how it will be used, and with whom it will be shared. Consent should be informed, voluntary, and revisable; policies should comply with legal norms while aspiring to genuinely honor individual autonomy (Johnson, 2025; UNESCO, 2023).
- **Continuous monitoring and incident response**: Educational organizations should develop, rehearse, and regularly update their protocols for detecting, reporting, and responding to breaches or inappropriate data usage. Incident response is not simply a technical matter; communication with affected learners and families is critical (CISA, 2023a).
- **Regular privacy audits**: Conduct periodic privacy impact assessments and third-party security reviews, especially when AI systems are significantly updated or new data modalities are introduced (AERA et al., 2014).

2.7 Case Study: Ethical Analysis of an AI-Based Grading Platform

2.7.1 Ethical Evaluation Protocol for AI-Based Assessment Systems

The adoption of AI-based grading platforms in educational settings is expanding rapidly, but their use raises significant ethical, technical, and practical questions.

TABLE 2.1 Protocol for Evaluating the Ethical Application of AI

Evaluation Step	*Key Questions*
Documentation, transparency, and explainability	Is technical and procedural documentation available? Are system logic, data flows, and model details clearly described? Do teachers and students receive clear explanations for scores?
Validity and reliability	Is there published evidence that AI-generated grades are accurate and consistent compared to qualified human raters?
Fairness and bias	Have subgroup analyses or bias audits been conducted and reported? Are there mechanisms for mitigating discovered bias?
User oversight	Can teachers override AI outputs? Are appeals processes present?
Privacy and security	Are privacy safeguards robust and transparent? Is compliance with regulations such as FERPA clearly demonstrated?
Limitations and accountability	Are the limitations of the system clearly stated? Is there public acknowledgment of potential errors, independent auditing, and clear assignment of responsibility for mistakes or harms? Are there mechanisms for third-party review and ongoing accountability?

Before implementation or procurement, it is essential to systematically assess such platforms using a protocol that covers key ethical and operational dimensions. The following table provides a structured protocol with guiding questions (Table 2.1).

2.7.2 Application of the Protocol: Commercial AI Grading Platform

To explore current offerings in automated essay scoring, we conducted a Google search using the phrase "AI Grading for Teachers." We selected the first non-sponsored (non-promoted) result, which led us to the landing page for an AI-powered grading platform designed for educators.

The landing page immediately positions the platform as a solution for reducing teacher workload and improving the quality and speed of feedback on student writing. The main headline emphasizes substantial time savings ("grade essays in 80% less time"), while the supporting text highlights that the tool is already in use at over a thousand schools.

The page presents the system as an "AI Essay Grader" that allows teachers to provide individualized, standards-aligned feedback more efficiently, with features, including

- Integration with common learning management systems (Google Classroom, Canvas, Schoology)

- Support for state test rubrics and custom grading criteria
- Data-driven insights for lesson planning and identifying learning gaps
- Emphasis on "equity in grading" and minimizing human bias through rubric-based, objective scoring
- Differentiated feedback tailored to each student's needs

The platform further appeals to prospective users through a series of teacher testimonials, praising the tool for its ability to deliver detailed, timely feedback, reduce grading subjectivity, and save time. Multiple teachers cite transformative effects on their workload and classroom practices.

The page also provides practical information about how the system operates: teachers import assignments, define grading criteria or rubrics, receive AI-generated grades and feedback, and retain the ability to review and adjust both before sharing with students. The platform asserts that educators maintain complete control over final grades.

In the frequently asked questions section, the platform addresses topics such as compatibility with various state standards, privacy, and data security (including FERPA and NIST compliance, data encryption, and minimal data collection), and the use of anonymized data with third-party AI providers. The company asserts that they (and third parties) do not use student data to train models and that final grading responsibility remains with the teacher.

Overall, the landing page markets the grading platform as a time-saving, objective, and teacher-friendly AI assistant that supports best practices in education, while also gesturing toward issues of privacy, reliability, and fairness, albeit with few technical details provided on these fronts.

2.7.2.1 Evaluation

Examining the multiple dimensions of ethical AI adoption, we note the following:

Documentation, explainability, and transparency: The platform explains basic data flows but does not provide details on its underlying models, training data, or scoring logic. It is unclear how AI scores are generated or what explanations, if any, are provided to justify individual grades. Technical documentation and explainability are limited.

Validity and reliability: No independent or peer-reviewed evidence is provided to compare the accuracy or consistency of AI-generated grades against expert human judgment. The platform's claims are supported by user testimonials rather than empirical studies or published evaluations of reliability or error rates.

Fairness and bias: Marketing language emphasizes "equity in grading" and minimizing human subjectivity, but there is no evidence of subgroup analysis or fairness/bias audits (e.g., performance comparison by race/ethnicity, gender, English proficiency). No differential algorithmic functioning studies or mitigation strategies are described.

Human oversight: Teachers import student assignments, define grading rubrics, review AI-generated grades and feedback, and retain the ability to adjust or override these decisions before sharing with students. The platform asserts that "teachers maintain full control over final grades." There is also no standardized mechanism for students to appeal or query scores.

Privacy and security: It follows standard data protection measures and claims compliance with FERPA and NIST but relies on teachers and schools to manage consent; the system also transmits some data to third-party AI providers.

Limitations and accountability: The platform acknowledges that AI-generated grades and feedback may contain errors and advises teachers to review outputs. However, it lacks rigorous evaluation, public reporting, or independent audits of its reliability, fairness, and privacy practices. Membership in industry organizations signals intent, but without concrete evidence or transparent accountability mechanisms, stakeholders must rely on company assurances.

The results of our evaluation and recommendations for next steps are provided in Table 2.2.

The ethical deployment of AI grading platforms demands more than broad commitments and industry affiliation. It requires concrete, transparent documentation of system logic, reliability, fairness evaluation, and privacy safeguards. While the platform under review has made strides in disclosing its basic data flows and limitations, unresolved questions remain regarding the explainability of its outputs, the robustness of its fairness and reliability measures, and the adequacy of its privacy protections. Until system developers and deployers substantively address these concerns with open evidence and independent validation, caution is warranted in relying on such systems for consequential educational decisions.

TABLE 2.2 Protocol Results

Evaluation Area	*Platform Status*	*Key Recommendations*
Documentation, explainability, and transparency	High-level only; lacks technical detail, rationales for scores, and audit results	Publicly release model documentation, audit reports; provide score rationales
Validity and reliability	No empirical validation reported	Commission/report studies with human rater comparisons
Fairness and bias	No public subgroup or bias analyses	Conduct and publish regular bias/fairness audits
Human oversight	Teachers can review; no clear appeals process	Formalize appeals process
Privacy and security	Claims basic compliance; details lacking	Disclose detailed policies; enable third-party audits
Limitations and accountability	Basic disclaimer about possible error; no public audits or redress mechanisms	Routinely report limitations; enable independent review and establish redress pathways

2.8 Conclusion

2.8.1 Key Points

Integrating AI into educational assessment marks both a profound opportunity and an enduring challenge. As we have seen throughout this chapter, AI-driven systems have the capacity to enrich educational measurement by improving efficiency, broadening access, and facilitating forms of analysis previously unimaginable. However, these gains are contingent on a vigilant and sustained commitment to core ethical values: fairness, transparency, explainability, accountability, privacy, and responsible stewardship.

Algorithmic bias, whether inherited from historical data, embedded in design, or emergent in deployment, poses persistent risks, especially for learners from underrepresented or minoritized backgrounds. Transparency and explainability remain critical for building and sustaining trust among stakeholders, but advancements in technical performance must not come at the expense of comprehension or contestability. Human oversight is indispensable: we must not position educators and administrators as passive consumers of algorithmic output, but as active partners, questioning, interpreting, and, where necessary, redressing AI-mediated decisions.

We must therefore understand ethical innovation in this space as a multidimensional project: one that weaves together technological vigilance, policy formation, institutional training, ongoing empirical research, and continuous dialogue with those most affected by assessment outcomes.

2.8.2 Practical Recommendations

Drawing on the analysis in this chapter and consolidated guidance from international frameworks (AERA et al., 2014; NIST, 2023; UNESCO, 2023; U.S. Department of Education, Office of Educational Technology, 2023) and measurement organizations (Bulut et al., 2024; Burstein et al., 2024; Burstein, 2025; Johnson, 2025), we offer the following recommendations for practice:

- **Commit to continuous monitoring and improvement:** AI assessment systems must be subject to regular audit for fairness and accuracy across all subgroups and recalibrated as new risks or shifts in learner populations emerge.
- **Prioritize transparency and meaningful explanation:** Design outputs and interfaces to ensure not only technical disclosure but also actionable, audience-appropriate explanations for educators, learners, and families.
- **Institutionalize human oversight:** Develop clear protocols for human review of high-stakes or ambiguous cases, and equip all staff charged with oversight with AI literacy and critical interpretation skills.
- **Engage stakeholders in design and evaluation:** Foster inclusive processes that elevate the voices of diverse learners, practitioners, and communities, from problem formulation to deployment and post-launch monitoring.

- **Center data privacy and security:** Treat the ethical and legal imperatives of privacy as non-negotiable, adopting secure-by-design principles and ensuring individuals retain agency over their own educational data.
- **Establish redress mechanisms:** Provide clear, accessible pathways for appeals and corrections, with third-party review where appropriate, so that developers can swiftly address errors and biases.

2.8.3 Future Directions

Despite significant progress, many open questions remain about the ethical integration of AI in educational assessment. Future work should focus on developing robust metrics and methods for fairness and transparency, understanding long-term impacts on equity, and improving collaboration between AI systems and human judgment. Scaling effective professional development and translating ethical guidelines into policy and everyday practice are also crucial.

Ultimately, the promise of AI in assessment depends not only on technical innovation but also on our collective commitment to ethical responsibility, ongoing reflection, and inclusive engagement with all stakeholders. By centering ethics as an evolving, participatory practice, educational assessment can advance both measurement science and educational justice.

References

Alexander, L., & Moore, M. (2024). Deontological ethics. In E. N. Zalta & U. Nodelman (Eds.), *The Stanford encyclopedia of philosophy* (Winter 2024). Metaphysics Research Lab, Stanford University. https://plato.stanford.edu/archives/win2024/entries/ethics-deontological/.

American Educational Research Association (AERA), American Psychological Association (APA), & National Council on Measurement in Education (NCME). (2014). *Standards for educational and psychological testing*. American Educational Research Association. https://www.testingstandards.net/open-access-files.html

Aristotle. (1999). *Nicomachean ethics* (T. Irwin, Trans.; 2nd ed.). Hackett Publishing Company.

Baker, R. S. (2016). Stupid tutoring systems, intelligent humans. *International Journal of Artificial Intelligence in Education*, *26*(2), 600–614. https://doi.org/10.1007/s40593-016-0105-0

Baker, R. S., & Hawn, A. (2022). Algorithmic bias in education. *International Journal of Artificial Intelligence in Education, 32,* 1052–1092.

Barocas, S., Hardt, M., & Narayanan, A. (2023). *Fairness and machine learning: Limitations and opportunities*. The MIT Press. https://fairmlbook.org

Binns, R. (2018). Algorithmic accountability and public reason. *Philosophy & Technology*, *31*(4), 543–556.

Buijsman, S. (2023). Navigating fairness measures and trade-offs. *AI and Ethics*, *4,* 1323–1334. https://doi.org/10.1007/s43681-023-00318-0

Bulut, O., Beiting-Parrish, M., Casabianca, J. M., Slater, S. C., Jiao, H., Song, D., Ormerod, C., Fabiyi, D. G., Ivan, R., Walsh, C., Rios, O., Wilson, J., Yildirim-Erbasli, S. N., Wongvorachan, T., Liu, J. X., Tan, B., & Morilova, P. (2024). The rise of artificial intelligence in educational measurement: Opportunities and ethical challenges. *Chinese/*

English Journal of Educational Measurement and Evaluation, *5*(3), 1–32. https://doi.org/10.59863/MIQL7785

Burstein, J. (2025). *Duolingo research report, 2025* (DRR-25-05). https://duolingo-papers.s3.us-east-1.amazonaws.com/other/Duolingo+English+Test+Responsible+AI.pdf

Burstein, J., LaFlair, G. T., Yancey, K., Davier, A. A. v., & Dotan, R. (2024). *Responsible AI for test equity and quality: The duolingo English test as a case study*. arXiv preprint arXiv:2409.07476. https://arxiv.org/abs/2409.07476

Burstein, J., Tetreault, J., & Madnani, N. (2013). The E-rater automated essay scoring system. In M. D. Shermis & J. Burstein (Eds.), *Handbook of automated essay evaluation: Current applications and new directions* (pp. 55–67). Routledge.

Cahill, A., Chodorow, M., & Flor, M. (2018). Developing an e-rater advisory to detect babel-generated essays. *Journal of Writing Analytics*, *2*, 203–224.

Castelnovo, A., Crupi, R., Greco, G., Regoli, D., Penco, I. G., & Cosentini, A. C. (2022). A clarification of the nuances in the fairness metrics landscape. *Scientific Reports*. *12*(2409). https://doi.org/10.1038/s41598-022-07939-1

Choi, I., & Zu, J. (2022). The impact of using synthetically generated listening stimuli on test-taker performance: A case study with multiple-choice, single-selection items. *ETS Research Report Series*, *2022*(1), 1–14. https://doi.org/10.1002/ets2.12347

CISA. (2023a). *K-12 education technology secure by design pledge*. CISA. https://www.cisa.gov/securebydesign/k-12-education-technology-pledge

CISA. (2023b). *Secure by design*. CISA. https://www.cisa.gov/securebydesign

CISA. (2023c). *Shifting the balance of cybersecurity risk: Principles and approaches for secure by design software*. CISA. https://www.cisa.gov/sites/default/files/2023-10/SecureByDesign_1025_508c.pdf

Clemmensen, L. H., & Kjærsgaard, R. D. (2023). *Data representativity for machine learning and AI systems*. arXiv preprint arXiv:2203.04706. https://arxiv.org/abs/2203.04706

Corbett-Davies, S., Gaebler, J. D., Nilforoshan, H., Shroff, R., & Goel, S. (2023). The measure and mismeasure of fairness. *Journal of Machine Learning Research*, *24*(1), 14730–14846.

Corbett-Davies, S., Pierson, E., Feller, A., Goel, S., & Huq, A. (2017). Algorithmic decision making and the cost of fairness. *Proceedings of the 23rd ACM SIGKDD International Conference on Knowledge Discovery and Data Mining*, 797–806. https://doi.org/10.1145/3097983.3098095

Doshi-Velez, F., & Kim, B. (2017). Towards a rigorous science of interpretable machine learning. *arXiv: Machine Learning*. arXiv:1702.08608. https://arxiv.org/abs/1702.0860

Dwork, C., Hardt, M., Pitassi, T., Reingold, O., & Zemel, R. (2011). *Fairness through awareness*. https://arxiv.org/abs/1104.3913

Elkan, C. (2001). The foundations of cost-sensitive learning. *Proceedings of the Seventeenth International Conference on Artificial Intelligence: 4–10 August 2001; Seattle*, 1.

Floridi, L., & Taddeo, M. (2016). What is data ethics? *Philosophical Transactions of the Royal Society A: Mathematical, Physical and Engineering Sciences*, *374*(2083), 20160360. https://doi.org/10.1098/rsta.2016.0360

Gilligan, C. (1982). *In a different voice: Psychological theory and women's development*. Harvard University Press.

Hao, J. (2025). *AI for educational assessment: Opportunities and challenges through the lens of evidence-centered design and measurement values*. EdArXiv. https://doi.org/10.35542/osf.io/dacxj_v2

Hao, J., Davier, A. A. v., Yaneva, V., Lottridge, S., Davier, M. v., & Harris, D. J. (2024). Transforming assessment: The impacts and implications of large language models and generative AI. *Educational Measurement: Issues and Practice*, *43*, 16–29. https://doi.org/10.1111/emip.12602

High-Level Expert Group on AI. (2019). *Ethics guidelines for trustworthy artificial intelligence*. European Commission. https://digital-strategy.ec.europa.eu/en/library/ethics-guidelines-trustworthy-ai

High-Level Expert Group on Artificial Intelligence (AI HLEG). (2020). *Assessment list for trustworthy artificial intelligence (ALTAI)*. European Commission. https://digital-strategy.ec.europa.eu/en/library/assessment-list-trustworthy-artificial-intelligence-altai-self-assessment

Holland, P. W., & Thayer, D. T. (1988). Differential item performance and the Mantel-Haenszel procedure. In H. Wainer & H. Braun (Eds.), *Test validity* (pp. 129–145). Lawrence Erlbaum Associates.

Holland, P. W., & Wainer, H. (1993). *Differential item functioning*. Lawrence Erlbaum Associates.

Hursthouse, R., & Pettigrove, G. (2023). Virtue ethics. In E. N. Zalta & U. Nodelman (Eds.), *The Stanford encyclopedia of philosophy* (Fall 2023). Metaphysics Research Lab, Stanford University. https://plato.stanford.edu/archives/fall2023/entries/ethics-virtue/

Jiang, Y., Hao, J., Cui, W., Kerzabi, E., & Kyllonen, P. (2025). Uncovering transferable collaboration patterns across tasks using large language models. In A. I. Cristea, E. Walker, Y. Lu, O. C. Santos, & S. Isotani (Eds.), *Artificial intelligence in education. AIED 2025. Lecture notes in computer science* (Vol. 15878, pp. 320–335). Springer. https://doi.org/10.1007/978-3-031-98417-4_23

Johnson, M. S. (2025). Responsible AI for measurement and learning: Principles and practices. *ETS Research Report Series*, RR-25-03. https://rr.ets.org/index.php/etsrr/article/view/9

Johnson, M. S., Liu, X., & McCaffrey, D. F. (2022). Psychometric methods to evaluate measurement and algorithmic bias in automated scoring. *Journal of Educational Measurement*, *59*(3), 338–361. https://doi.org/https://doi.org/10.1111/jedm.12335

Johnson, M. S., & McCaffrey, D. F. (2023). Evaluating fairness of automated scoring in educational measurement. In V. Yaneva & M. von Davier (Eds.), *Advancing natural language processing in educational assessment* (pp. 142–164). Routledge.

Johnson, M. S., & Zhang, M. (2024). Examining the responsible use of zero-shot AI approaches to scoring essays. *Scientific Reports*, *14*, 30064. https://doi.org/10.1038/s41598-024-79208-2

Kant, I. (1785/2011). *Groundwork of the metaphysics of morals* (J. Timmermann, Ed.; M. Gregor, Trans.). Cambridge University Press.

Kay, J., Kummerfeld, B., Conati, C., Porayska-Pomsta, K., & Holstein, K. (2023). Chapter 6: Scrutable AIED. In B. du Boulay, A. Mitrovic, & K. Yacef (Eds.), *Handbook of artificial intelligence in education* (pp. 101–125). Edward Elgar Publishing. https://doi.org/10.4337/9781800375413.00015

Khosravi, H., Shum, S. B., Chen, G., Conati, C., Tsai, Y.-S., Kay, J., Knight, S., Martinez-Maldonado, R., Sadiq, S., & Gašević, D. (2022). Explainable artificial intelligence in education. *Computers and Education: Artificial Intelligence*, *3*, 100074. https://doi.org/https://doi.org/10.1016/j.caeai.2022.100074

Kruskal, W., & Mosteller, F. (1979a). Representative sampling, i: Non-scientific literature. *International Statistical Review / Revue Internationale de Statistique*, *47*(1), 13–24. https://www.jstor.org/stable/1403202

Kruskal, W., & Mosteller, F. (1979b). Representative sampling, II: Scientific literature, excluding statistics. *International Statistical Review / Revue Internationale de Statistique*, *47*(2), 111–127. https://www.jstor.org/stable/1402564

Kruskal, W., & Mosteller, F. (1979c). Representative sampling, III: The current statistical literature. *International Statistical Review / Revue Internationale de Statistique*, *47*(3), 245–265. https://www.jstor.org/stable/1402647

Kruskal, W., & Mosteller, F. (1980). Representative sampling, IV: The history of the concept in statistics, 1895–1939. *International Statistical Review / Revue Internationale de Statistique*, *48*(2), 169–195. https://www.jstor.org/stable/1403151

Kusner, M. J., Loftus, J., Russell, C., & Silva, R. (2017). Counterfactual fairness. In I. Guyon, U. V. Luxburg, S. Bengio, H. Wallach, R. Fergus, S. Vishwanathan, & R. Garnett (Eds.), *Proceedings of the 31st International Conference on Neural Information Processing Systems,* 4069–4079. Curran Associates, Inc. https://proceedings.neurips.cc/paper_files/paper/2017/file/a486cd07e4ac3d270571622f4f316ec5-Paper.pdf

Mehrabi, N., Morstatter, F., Saxena, N., Lerman, K., & Galstyan, A. (2021). A survey on bias and fairness in machine learning. *ACM Computing Surveys*, *54*(6), 1–35. https://doi.org/10.1145/3457607

Mill, J. S. (1861). *Utilitarianism*. Parker, Son, and Bourn.

Mitchell, M., Wu, S., Zaldivar, A., Barnes, P., Vasserman, L., Hutchinson, B., Spitzer, E., Raji, I. D., & Gebru, T. (2019). Model cards for model reporting. *Proceedings of the Conference on Fairness, Accountability, and Transparency*, 220–229. https://doi.org/10.1145/3287560.3287596

Mittelstadt, B. D., Allo, P., Taddeo, M., Wachter, S., & Floridi, L. (2016). The ethics of algorithms: Mapping the debate. *Big Data & Society*, *3*(2), 2053951716679679. https://doi.org/10.1177/2053951716679679

Ninaus, M., & Sailer, M. (2022). Closing the loop – The human role in artificial intelligence for education. *Frontiers in Psychology*, *13*. https://doi.org/10.3389/fpsyg.2022.956798

NIST. (2023). *Artificial intelligence risk management framework (AI RMF 1.0)*. National Institute of Standards; Technology. https://doi.org/10.6028/NIST.AI.100-1

Noddings, N. (1984). *Caring: A feminine approach to ethics and moral education*. University of California Press.

OECD. (2019). *Scoping the OECD AI principles: Deliberations of the expert group on artificial intelligence at the OECD (AIGO)*. OECD. https://doi.org/10.1787/d62f618a-en

Partsei, K., Berezova, L., Pryimak, V., Bilozerska, S., & Kravchenko-Dzondza, O. (2025). Ethics of educational innovations in the context of constant change and social instability. *InternationalJournalonCulture,History,andReligion*, *7*(SI1),564–584.https://doi.org/10.63931/ijchr.v7iSI1.152

Perelman, L. (2020). The BABEL generator and e-rater: 21st century writing constructs and automated essay scoring (AES). *Journal of Writing Assessment*, *13*(1), 1–9.

Phillips, P. J., Phillips, P. J., Hahn, C. A., Fontana, P. C., Yates, A. N., Greene, K., Broniatowski, D. A., & Przybocki, M. A. (2021). *Four principles of explainable artificial intelligence* (NISTIR 8312). US Department of Commerce, National Institute of Standards; Technology. https://doi.org/10.6028/NIST.IR.8312

Schwartz, R., Vassilev, A., Greene, K. K., Perine, L., Burt, A., & Hall, P. (2022). *Towards a standard for identifying and managing bias in artificial intelligence*. National Institute of Standards; Technology (NIST). https://doi.org/10.6028/NIST.SP.1270

Sheikh, H., Prins, C., & Schrijvers, E. (2023). *Mission AI: The new system technology*. Springer Cham. https://doi.org/10.1007/978-3-031-21448-6

Sinnott-Armstrong, W. (2023). Consequentialism. In E. N. Zalta & U. Nodelman (Eds.), *The Stanford encyclopedia of philosophy* (Winter 2023). Metaphysics Research Lab, Stanford University. https://plato.stanford.edu/archives/win2023/entries/consequentialism/.

Skitka, L. J., Mosier, K. L., & Burdick, M. (1999). Does automation bias decision-making? *International Journal of Human-Computer Studies*, *51*(5), 991–1006. https://doi.org/https://doi.org/10.1006/ijhc.1999.0252

Song, Y., Du, J., & Zheng, Q. (2025). Automatic item generation for educational assessments: A systematic literature review. *Interactive Learning Environments*, *33*(9), 5386–5405. https://doi.org/10.1080/10494820.2025.2482588

Suk, Y., & Han, K. T. (2024). A psychometric framework for evaluating fairness in algorithmic decision making: Differential algorithmic functioning. *Journal of Educational and Behavioral Statistics*, *49*(2), 151–172. https://doi.org/10.3102/10769986231171711

Suresh, H., & Guttag, J. (2021a). Understanding potential sources of harm throughout the machine learning life cycle. *MIT case studies in social and ethical responsibilities of computing, Summer 2021*. https://doi.org/10.21428/2c646de5.c16a07bb

Suresh, H., & Guttag, J. V. (2021b). *A framework for understanding sources of harm throughout the machine learning life cycle*. https://arxiv.org/abs/1901.10002

Tan, B., Armoush, N., Mazzullo, E., & Bulut, O. (2025). A review of automatic item generation techniques leveraging large language models. *International Journal of Assessment Tools in Education*, *12*(2), 317–340. https://doi.org/10.21449/ijate.1602294

UNESCO. (2022). *Recommendations on the ethics of artificial intelligence*. UNESCO. https://unesdoc.unesco.org/ark:/48223/pf0000381137

UNESCO. (2023). *Guidance for generative AI in education and research*. UNESCO. https://unesdoc.unesco.org/ark:/48223/pf0000386693

U.S. Department of Education, Office of Educational Technology. (2023). *Artificial intelligence and future of teaching and learning: Insights and recommendations*. U.S. Department of Education. https://www.ed.gov/sites/ed/files/documents/ai-report/ai-report.pdf

Veale, M., & Binns, R. (2017). Fairer machine learning in the real world: Mitigating discrimination without collecting sensitive data. *Big Data & Society*, *4*(2), 2053951717743530. https://doi.org/10.1177/2053951717743530

Wiltshire, T. J. (2015). A prospective framework for the design of ideal artificial moral agents: Insights from the science of heroism in humans. *Minds & Machines*, *25*(1), 57–71. https://doi.org/10.1007/s11023-015-9361-2

Zawacki-Richter, O., Marín, V. I., Bond, M., & Gouverneur, F. (2019). Systematic review of research on artificial intelligence applications in higher education – Where are the educators? *International Journal of Educational Technology in Higher Education*, *16*(1), 39. https://doi.org/10.1186/s41239-019-0171-0

Zu, J., Choi, I., & Hao, J. (2023). Automated distractor generation for fill-in-the-blank items using a prompt-based learning approach. *Psychological Test and Assessment Modeling*, *65*(1), 55–75. https://www.proquest.com/scholarly-journals/automated-distractor-generation-fill-blank-items/docview/2799814401/se-2

3

THE EVOLUTION OF ASSESSMENT WITH AI TECHNOLOGIES

Mark D. Shermis

3.1 Introduction

This chapter explores the transformative role of artificial intelligence (AI) in educational measurement, a field that has undergone significant changes over the past century. Educational assessments have long been used to evaluate students' knowledge and abilities, but traditional models are increasingly seen as inadequate in addressing the demands of the 21st-century education landscape. Integrating AI into educational measurement is a technological advancement and a fundamental shift in how educators, policymakers, and researchers think about and implement assessments.

This chapter provides a comprehensive overview of AI-driven innovations in educational measurement, examining both the historical context and contemporary significance of assessment practices. It will highlight how AI is reshaping traditional approaches to testing and outline the potential for new, more dynamic assessment models. These models promise to improve education accuracy, efficiency, and equity, addressing long-standing challenges associated with standardized testing and traditional assessment frameworks.

The scope of this chapter includes an exploration of critical themes central to understanding the impact of AI on educational assessments. First, it will address the limitations of traditional assessments, such as issues related to fairness, accessibility, and the narrow focus on academic knowledge. Second, this chapter will explore educational institutions' modern challenges, such as the need for assessments that can measure complex, non-cognitive skills and provide personalized learning experiences. Finally, it will delve into the innovative solutions made possible by AI, such as adaptive testing, real-time feedback systems, and machine learning algorithms to analyze large datasets.

DOI: 10.4324/9781003621522-3

3.2 Overview of the Historical and Contemporary Significance of Educational Assessments

Educational assessments have a long and complex history, with roots in the oral and written examinations of ancient and medieval societies. In the 20th century, standardized tests became a cornerstone of educational systems worldwide, driven by a need for objective measures of academic achievement (Koretz, 2008). These tests, such as the SAT and ACT in the United States, have been used to make high-stakes decisions about students' academic and professional futures. However, standardized testing has been criticized for its inability to capture the full range of student abilities and for perpetuating inequities based on socioeconomic status, race, and cultural background (Au, 2022).

In response to these limitations, educational researchers and policymakers have called for more comprehensive assessment models. The advent of AI technologies has opened new possibilities for educational measurement, allowing for assessments that are more efficient, personalized, and responsive to individual learning needs. AI-driven assessments can analyze vast amounts of data to provide previously unattainable insights, potentially revolutionizing educational practices (Luckin & Holmes, 2016).

This chapter will examine how AI is used to address the challenges of traditional assessments and create more meaningful learning experiences. It will discuss the implications of these innovations for students, educators, and policymakers, emphasizing the need for thoughtful integration of AI technologies into educational systems.

3.3 Brief Summary of Key Themes

The key themes of this chapter revolve around the contrast between traditional assessments and the opportunities presented by AI. Traditional assessments, such as standardized tests, are often criticized for being one-size-fits-all and failing to measure higher-order thinking skills or non-cognitive abilities, such as creativity and emotional intelligence (Heissel et al., 2017). These assessments also tend to reinforce inequities, as students from marginalized backgrounds may not have access to the same resources and opportunities for test preparation as their more advantaged peers (Reardon, 2011).

Modern educational challenges require innovative solutions, such as needing assessments that can adapt to diverse learning styles and provide real-time feedback. AI has the potential to meet these needs through adaptive testing, which adjusts the difficulty of questions based on a student's performance, and through data-driven insights that inform personalized instruction. Furthermore, AI can develop assessments that measure complex competencies, such as problem-solving and collaboration, essential for success in the 21st-century workforce (Pellegrino & Hilton, 2012).

3.4 Definitions and Concepts

A clear understanding of key terms and concepts is essential for navigating the discussions in this chapter. Educational assessment systematically evaluates student learning through tests, assignments, or other measures to gauge knowledge and skills. Traditional assessments include standardized tests and summative evaluations administered at the end of an instructional period. These assessments have been widely used but are increasingly viewed as limited in scope and effectiveness.

Innovative assessment methods, in contrast, encompass a range of practices that aim to provide a more comprehensive understanding of student learning. These methods include formative assessments, which monitor student progress and guide instruction, and performance-based assessments (PBAs), which require students to demonstrate their skills through real-world tasks (Black & Wiliam, 1998a). AI-based assessments represent a subset of innovative methods that leverage technology to enhance assessment practices. They include tools such as computerized adaptive testing (CAT) and automated essay scoring, which use machine learning algorithms to analyze student responses and provide feedback.

This chapter's critical analysis framework will explore the benefits and limitations of AI-driven assessments. It will consider ethical and practical concerns, such as data privacy, algorithmic bias, and the need for transparency in AI systems. Additionally, this chapter will discuss the role of AI in promoting educational equity, examining the opportunities and challenges associated with implementing these technologies on a large scale.

3.5 The Historical Development of Educational Assessments

3.5.1 *Early Forms of Assessments*

The roots of educational assessments can be traced back thousands of years, with diverse forms and functions emerging across different civilizations. Early assessments were typically informal and centered around practical skills demonstration and oral questioning. In ancient Egypt, for instance, scribal schools used oral recitations to evaluate students' mastery of hieroglyphic writing (Tyack & Hansot, 1982). Students were required to memorize and reproduce complex texts, and their proficiency was judged by more experienced scribes, reflecting a highly subjective but contextually effective form of evaluation.

In ancient Greece, education was heavily influenced by the Socratic method, which emphasized oral dialogues to stimulate critical thinking. These discussions served as both instruction and assessment, as students' responses to probing questions revealed their understanding of philosophical and mathematical concepts (Klein, 1990). Similarly, in medieval Europe, learning assessment was closely tied to the apprentice system, where practical demonstration of skills, rather than academic knowledge, was the primary focus (Meyer, 2021). This approach was not limited to crafts and trades but extended to professions such as medicine and law, where mastery was judged through oral examinations known as *disputations* (Rothblatt, 1976).

In medieval Europe, the apprenticeship model dominated. Evaluations were performance-based, mainly focusing on mastering practical skills within crafts and trades (Meyer, 2021). An apprentice's progress was evaluated based on their ability to replicate the skills of a master, culminating in a final piece known as a "masterpiece," which was used to determine if the apprentice was qualified to become a master craftsman (Thorndike, 1910).

The evolution from oral to written assessments represented a fundamental shift in educational practice. The Chinese imperial examination system began as early as 605 AD during the Sui Dynasty and is one of the earliest examples of large-scale written examinations (Fukuyama, 2014). Designed to select candidates for civil service positions, these exams tested knowledge of Confucian classics and became a model for standardized testing. In the 19th century, European and American educators began adopting similar methods, spreading written examinations in schools and universities (Tyack & Hansot, 1982).

The emergence of written examinations can be traced back to 19th-century Europe and America. Inspired by the Chinese imperial examination system, European and American educational systems began adopting written assessments to standardize qualifications and create objective criteria for academic advancement. By the late 1800s, written examinations had become common in secondary and higher education (Terman, 1916). This shift marked a significant departure from the personalized, oral evaluations of the past, laying the groundwork for more formalized and structured assessment systems (Brookhart & McMillan, 2020).

This period also saw the formalization of assessments through developing grading systems and using essay questions to gauge analytical abilities. By the late 1800s, universities in the United States, such as Harvard and Yale, used written exams as the primary criterion for admission, marking the transition to a more structured and standardized approach to evaluation (Lemann, 2000). These changes set the stage for the rise of modern standardized testing in the 20th century, which would transform educational assessment practices worldwide.

3.5.2 Rise of Standardized Testing in the 20th Century

The rise of standardized testing in the 20th century can be traced back to the burgeoning field of educational psychology and the quest to develop objective measures of intelligence and academic aptitude. Alfred Binet and Théodore Simon's work in the early 1900s laid the foundation for modern intelligence testing. Their goal was to create a tool that could identify students needing special educational support, leading to the development of the Binet-Simon scale in 1905 (Binet & Simon, 1916). Lewis Terman, an American psychologist, adapted this scale to create the Stanford-Binet Intelligence Scale in 1916, introducing the concept of the intelligence quotient (Terman, 1916).

The widespread adoption of IQ testing in the United States during the early 20th century coincided with a growing belief in the power of science and measurement to improve education and society. The use of intelligence tests to classify and track students became a dominant theme, influencing educational policy and practices (Thorndike, 1910). Another prominent figure, Robert Yerkes, developed the Army Alpha and Beta tests during World War I, which were used to evaluate the cognitive abilities of military recruits (Yerkes, 1921). These tests demonstrated the potential of standardized assessments to efficiently evaluate large groups, further cementing their role in educational and societal decision-making.

In the post-war period, standardized testing expanded beyond intelligence testing to include academic aptitude and achievement measures. The development of the SAT by the College Entrance Examination Board in 1926 was a pivotal moment in the history of educational assessments. The SAT aimed to provide a standard metric for comparing students from diverse educational backgrounds, thereby democratizing access to higher education (Croft & Beard, 2021). The ACT, introduced in 1959, sought to offer an alternative by focusing more on academic achievement than innate aptitude (Atkinson, 2001).

The rise of standardized testing was subject to controversy. Critics argued that these tests reinforced social inequalities by privileging specific knowledge and cognitive skills over others (Good, 1973). Despite these critiques, standardized tests gained widespread acceptance due to their perceived objectivity, reliability, and efficiency. By the mid-20th century, standardized testing had become a central feature of American education, influencing everything from student tracking and curriculum design to college admissions and educational policy.

3.5.3 Key Milestones in Assessment History

The mid- to late 20th century saw significant developments in educational assessments, driven by changes in educational policy, advances in psychometrics, and growing public scrutiny of educational outcomes. One of the most consequential developments was the rise of high-stakes testing, which linked test results to educational funding, accountability measures, and policy decisions.

The No Child Left Behind Act (NCLB), signed into law by President George W. Bush in 2002, exemplifies this trend (Ravitch, 2010). NCLB mandated annual testing in reading and mathematics for students in grades 3–8 and once in high school, with the results used to evaluate school performance. Schools failing to meet adequate yearly progress faced sanctions, including losing funding and potential restructuring. This policy marked a shift toward using standardized assessments to measure student learning and as a tool for enforcing accountability and driving educational reform.

The NCLB era highlighted both the strengths and limitations of high-stakes testing. While proponents argued that the policy brought much-needed attention to achievement gaps and educational inequities, critics contended that it led to teaching to the test, narrowed curricula, and increased stress for students and educators

(Shepard, 2000). These debates continue to shape discussions about the role of standardized testing in education.

Simultaneously, international assessments such as the Programme for International Student Assessment (PISA) and the Trends in International Mathematics and Science Study (TIMSS) gained prominence. PISA, first conducted by the Organisation for Economic Cooperation and Development (OECD) in 2000, assesses 15-year-olds' ability to apply knowledge in real-world contexts (OECD, 2010). TIMSS, administered by the International Association for the Evaluation of Educational Achievement, evaluates mathematics and science knowledge among 4th and 8th graders (Mullis et al., 2012).

These international assessments have influenced educational policy by providing benchmarks for comparing the performance of educational systems across countries. Nations that perform poorly on PISA or TIMSS often face pressure to reform their educational systems, leading to changes in curriculum standards, teacher training, and assessment practices (OECD, 2010). The global spread of standardized testing has also raised questions about cultural biases, the validity of cross-national comparisons, and the impact of these assessments on educational equity.

3.5.4 *Contemporary Developments and Challenges*

The 21st century has brought new challenges and opportunities for educational assessments. Advances in technology have transformed assessment practices, enabling the development of computer-based and adaptive testing. These innovations allow for more precise measurement of student abilities, real-time feedback, and the ability to assess complex cognitive skills (Bennett, 2011). Computer-based assessments, such as those used in PISA since 2015, offer new ways to evaluate students' problem-solving and collaborative skills, which are increasingly valued in the modern workforce.

Despite these advances, the role of standardized testing in education remains contentious. Critics argue that standardized tests often fail to capture the full range of students' abilities, exceptionally creative and non-cognitive skills (Broadfoot, 1996). The rise of the "opt-out" movement in the United States, where parents refuse to allow their children to participate in standardized tests, reflects growing dissatisfaction with the current state of educational assessments (Wiliam, 2011).

In response, educators and policymakers are exploring alternative approaches to assessment. Formative assessments, which provide ongoing feedback to support learning rather than measure it, are gaining traction to create a more balanced and supportive assessment system (Harlen, 2007). Similarly, PBAs, which require students to demonstrate their understanding through projects, presentations, and real-world tasks, are being integrated into some educational systems (Resnick & Resnick, 1992).

The future of educational assessments will likely involve a combination of traditional and innovative approaches, balancing the need for standardization with the recognition that education is a complex and multifaceted process. As educational systems continue to evolve, the challenge will be to develop assessments that are fair, valid, and aligned with the broader goals of education in a rapidly changing world.

3.6 Limitations of Conventional Assessments

Conventional assessments, often typified by standardized tests, have been the cornerstone of educational evaluation for decades. However, their limitations are increasingly evident in today's complex educational landscape. These limitations can be grouped into three primary categories: concerns around accuracy and validity, issues of equity and accessibility, and questions of relevance in the 21st-century educational context. This chapter thoroughly explores these limitations, drawing on various scholarly sources highlighting the need for more effective and inclusive assessment practices (Shermis & Di Vesta, 2011).

3.6.1 Accuracy and Validity Concerns

Conventional assessments frequently fail to reflect student abilities accurately. The focus on standardized test scores as a measure of student learning, teacher effectiveness, and school performance has been widely critiqued. According to Darling-Hammond et al. (2013), standardized tests often measure a narrow band of student knowledge, ignoring the breadth of skills necessary for real-world success. This misalignment calls into question these assessments' validity as educational evaluation tools.

3.6.1.1 Mismatch between Assessment Outcomes and Real-World Competencies

The primary purpose of educational assessment should be to measure how students have acquired relevant competencies beyond the classroom. However, as Linn (2000) argues, the dominant assessment paradigms prioritize knowledge recall and basic procedural skills over critical thinking and creativity. This narrow focus can result in "teaching to the test," where instructional time is redirected toward test preparation rather than deeper learning (Au, 2007). This shift undermines the development of transferable skills, such as collaboration, innovation, and problem-solving, which are increasingly recognized as crucial for success in the 21st century (Care et al., 2017).

Further complicating the picture, studies have shown that standardized test results often correlate more strongly with students' socioeconomic backgrounds than their actual academic abilities (Rothstein, 2004). This relationship suggests that what is being measured may be more indicative of external factors, such as access to resources and support, than of the competencies students have developed.

3.6.1.2 *Issues of Test Design and Psychometric Flaws*

The design and psychometric properties of conventional assessments also present significant challenges. Traditional tests are grounded in classical test theory, prioritizing reliability and standardization. However, Messick (1994) highlights that this approach can lead to construct underrepresentation and construct-irrelevant variance, where important aspects of the competency are omitted or unintended factors influence test scores. For example, students' familiarity with the test format or language used in the items can unfairly affect their performance, leading to scores not truly reflective of their abilities (Sireci et al., 2003).

Another concern is the presence of item bias, where test questions may be more favorable to certain demographic groups. For instance, Abedi (2004) found that English language learners (ELLs) often score lower on standardized tests, not because of a lack of content knowledge but due to linguistic barriers embedded within test items. These flaws compromise the fairness and validity of assessments, making them inadequate tools for evaluating diverse student populations.

Moreover, high-stakes testing environments contribute to a phenomenon known as "test anxiety," which can disproportionately affect students' performance, particularly among those from marginalized backgrounds or with learning disabilities (Segool et al., 2013). Such anxiety can distort results, leading to an inaccurate representation of students' true abilities and exacerbating existing educational inequities.

3.6.2 *Equity and Accessibility Challenges*

Equity and accessibility are critical considerations in educational assessment. Conventional assessments often fail to account for students' diverse backgrounds and needs, leading to disparities in performance that reflect broader social inequalities. According to Buchmann et al. (2010), socioeconomic factors, such as access to test preparation resources, play a pivotal role in shaping performance outcomes, perpetuating a cycle of inequality.

3.6.2.1 *Socioeconomic Disparities in Test Preparation and Access*

Students from affluent families have access to many resources, including private tutoring, test preparation courses, and extracurricular activities that bolster academic performance (Buchmann et al., 2010). In contrast, students from low-income backgrounds often lack these supports, contributing to a performance gap that reflects economic disparities more than academic potential (Rothstein, 2004). This issue is compounded by the "Matthew Effect," where students who start with advantages accumulate more educational gains over time, while those without these advantages fall further behind (Stanovich, 2009).

Moreover, the increasing commercialization of test preparation services has exacerbated these disparities. Studies have shown that participation in intensive test prep programs can significantly boost scores, providing a competitive edge to those who can afford them (Buchmann et al., 2010). This dynamic raises ethical concerns about the fairness of using standardized tests for high-stakes decisions, such as college admissions and scholarship allocations.

3.6.2.2 Bias against Non-Traditional Learners (e.g., Neurodivergent Students, ELLs)

Conventional assessments often need to be more aligned with the needs of non-traditional learners, including neurodivergent students and ELLs. These groups frequently encounter tests that do not accommodate their unique learning profiles. For instance, neurodivergent students, such as those with ADHD or dyslexia, may struggle with standardized testing formats that emphasize speed and precision, leading to underestimation of their abilities (Hehir et al., 2016).

For ELLs, linguistic complexity in test items can obscure content understanding, resulting in scores that reflect language proficiency rather than content knowledge (Abedi, 2004). Such biases highlight the need for more inclusive assessment designs that accommodate diverse learners and accurately reflect their knowledge and skills.

3.6.3 Relevance in a 21st-Century Educational Context

The relevance of conventional assessments is increasingly questioned in light of the evolving educational landscape. As society shifts toward a knowledge-based economy, critical thinking, digital literacy, and collaborative problem-solving are gaining prominence (Binkley et al., 2012). However, most standardized tests are rooted in 20th-century educational models prioritizing static knowledge over these dynamic competencies.

3.6.3.1 Outdated Assessment Frameworks That Ignore Digital Literacy and Critical Thinking

Current assessment frameworks must pay more attention to digital literacy, creativity, and other 21st-century skills critical for success in a rapidly changing world (Griffin et al., 2012). For instance, while digital tools are ubiquitous in modern workplaces, many assessments still rely on paper-and-pencil formats that do not measure students' ability to navigate and analyze information using digital resources (Care et al., 2017). This disconnect has led to calls for new assessment models that capture the full spectrum of skills students need to thrive in the digital age.

3.6.3.2 Overemphasis on Rote Memorization and Decontextualized Knowledge

Conventional assessments also emphasize rote memorization and decontextualized knowledge, which are increasingly viewed as inadequate measures of student learning (Pellegrino & Hilton, 2012). As Hattie (2008) points out, assessments focusing solely on content recall fail to capture students' ability to apply knowledge meaningfully. This focus on low-level cognitive skills contributes to a lack of engagement and motivation among students, diminishing the educational value of these assessments.

In sum, conventional assessments' limitations are evident in their inability to measure student competencies accurately, their inequitable impact on diverse populations, and their lack of relevance in modern education. Addressing these limitations requires a shift toward more holistic and inclusive assessment models prioritizing validity, equity, and relevance. As educational systems evolve, there is a pressing need to develop new approaches that better align with the complexities of teaching and learning in the 21st century.

3.7 Contemporary Approaches to Educational Assessment

3.7.1 Formative and Diagnostic Assessments

Formative and diagnostic assessments have widely become essential tools in modern educational practices. Unlike traditional summative assessments that evaluate student learning at the end of an instructional period, formative assessments are administered throughout the learning process to provide feedback that can be used to improve both teaching and learning (Black & Wiliam, 1998a). On the other hand, diagnostic assessments are used at the beginning of a learning unit or academic year to identify students' existing knowledge, skills, and misconceptions (Brookhart, 2013). Together, these approaches create a dynamic feedback system that enables teachers to tailor instruction to meet individual student needs.

3.7.1.1 Use of Ongoing Assessments to Inform Instruction

Ongoing formative assessment is integral to effective instruction. Techniques such as quizzes, concept maps, exit tickets, and reflective journals allow teachers to gauge students' understanding in real time and adjust their teaching strategies accordingly (Heritage, 2021). For example, concept maps help teachers visualize students' understanding of a topic and identify gaps in knowledge. This information can then guide subsequent lessons to address these areas of weakness.

The continuous feedback provided by formative assessments encourages a growth mindset in students by emphasizing learning as a process. Instead of focusing solely on grades, students are motivated to improve through constructive feedback, fostering self-regulation and metacognitive skills (Nicol & Macfarlane-Dick, 2006). Diagnostic assessments play a crucial role in identifying specific learning needs. For instance, in a K–12 setting, diagnostic tests can identify areas where a student may need additional support, such as foundational math skills or reading comprehension, enabling targeted intervention (Chappuis & Stiggins, 2016).

3.7.1.2 Case Studies of Successful Implementation in K–12 and Higher Education

Numerous case studies highlight the successful implementation of formative and diagnostic assessments in K–12 and higher education. In a study by Black and Wiliam (1998a), a group of middle school teachers incorporated formative assessments into their math and science instruction, significantly improving student achievement. Another example is higher education, where the University of Edinburgh adopted formative assessments in its engineering courses. Professors used weekly quizzes and peer-assessment activities, leading to a notable increase in student engagement and understanding of core concepts (Carless, 2007).

Similarly, the "Formative Assessment for Teachers" initiative in New York City Public Schools trained teachers to integrate diagnostic assessments into daily instruction. The program showed that students in classrooms with regular formative assessments performed better in standardized tests, reflecting the potential of these assessments to drive meaningful learning (Fisher & Frey, 2021).

3.7.2 Performance-Based Assessments

PBAs represent a shift from traditional testing toward evaluating students' abilities to apply knowledge in real-world scenarios. PBAs require students to engage in tasks demonstrating their knowledge and skills, such as projects, presentations, and portfolios (Gulikers et al., 2004). These assessments encourage higher-order thinking and creativity, as students are often required to analyze, synthesize, and evaluate information rather than recall facts.

3.7.2.1 Project-Based Learning and Portfolio Assessments

Project-based learning (PBL) has become a popular instructional strategy that aligns well with PBAs. In PBL, students work on complex, real-world projects over an extended period, culminating in a final product or presentation (Kokotsaki et al., 2016). This method develops content knowledge and builds essential skills like collaboration, problem-solving, and time management. Teachers assess students based on their project engagement, the quality of the final product, and the reflection process.

Portfolio assessments offer a comprehensive view of a student's progress over time. In this approach, students collect and curate a selection of their work, reflecting on their growth and learning journey (Paulson et al., 1991). Portfolios provide a richer, more holistic picture of a student's capabilities, capturing strengths and improvement areas. They are particularly effective in subjects requiring creative expression, such as art, writing, and design, and are used extensively in K–12 and higher education settings (Gardner, 2008).

3.7.2.2 Rubric Design and Evaluation Criteria

A critical component of effective PBAs is the use of well-designed rubrics. Rubrics serve as a guide for teachers and students by providing clear criteria for each level of performance (Andrade, 2005). Rubrics should be specific, fair, and aligned with learning objectives, helping to standardize grading and reduce subjectivity. For instance, a rubric for a science project may include criteria such as "demonstrates understanding of scientific principles," "application of research," and "creativity in presentation."

Developing a rubric involves identifying the essential skills and knowledge areas the assessment aims to measure. A well-constructed rubric helps students understand the expectations and allows them to self-assess their work. Rubrics also facilitate meaningful feedback, as teachers can provide specific comments on each criterion, guiding students toward improvement (Brookhart, 2013).

3.7.3 Digital and Adaptive Assessments

Digital technology has revolutionized educational assessment by enabling personalized and adaptive testing. Computer-based assessments offer flexibility, interactivity, and the ability to collect data on student performance to inform teaching and learning in real time. One of the most innovative forms of digital assessment is CAT, which adjusts the difficulty of questions based on the student's responses (Weiss, 2004).

3.7.3.1 Use of Technology for Personalized and Adaptive Testing

Adaptive testing provides a more individualized assessment experience by adjusting question difficulty in response to each answer. Adaptive testing allows for more precise measurements of a student's ability, particularly in subjects where skill levels vary widely, such as mathematics and language arts (Kingsbury & Houser, 1993). For instance, if a student answers a question correctly, the next question may be more challenging, whereas an incorrect answer may lead to an easier question. This adaptability provides a more accurate picture of a student's skill level and reduces test anxiety.

Digital assessments are increasingly used in standardized testing, as seen in programs like the GRE and GMAT, where CAT models provide efficient testing experiences while maintaining accuracy. In K–12 education, tools like the i-Ready diagnostic assessment adapt to each student's responses, providing educators with detailed insights into student strengths and weaknesses (Frey & Schmitt, 2007). These insights enable targeted interventions and differentiated instruction, supporting a more personalized learning experience.

3.7.3.2 The Potential of AI-Driven Assessments for Real-Time Feedback

AI has the potential to further transform educational assessments by providing real-time, data-driven feedback. AI-driven platforms, such as adaptive learning systems, continuously analyze student performance and offer personalized guidance based on individual needs (Luckin & Holmes, 2016). For example, an AI-based assessment tool might detect patterns in a student's errors, offering specific exercises to target those weaknesses.

AI also enables automated scoring for complex tasks, such as essays and open-ended questions, which traditionally require significant time and effort from educators. Natural Language Processing technologies can assess writing quality, coherence, and grammar, providing immediate feedback to students and freeing teachers to focus on other instructional activities (Shermis & Burstein, 2013). AI-based assessments are particularly promising in remote learning contexts, where real-time feedback can help bridge the gap between teacher and student.

3.8 Innovative Assessment Models for 21st-Century Education

3.8.1 Competency-Based Education

Competency-Based Education (CBE) represents a paradigm shift in assessment, focusing on student mastery of specific skills and knowledge rather than time spent in class. Traditional education models emphasize "seat-time," where students progress based on how long they have attended a course rather than actual learning or mastery. In contrast, CBE allows students to advance at their own pace, ensuring that each individual demonstrates competency before moving on to the next topic or skill (Le et al., 2014).

3.8.1.1 Shifting Focus from Seat-Time to Mastery of Skills

CBE challenges the traditional assessment framework by prioritizing skill mastery over rote memorization. In CBE systems, students are assessed on their ability to apply knowledge to real-world problems. This approach aligns with Bloom's Taxonomy, which emphasizes higher-order thinking skills such as analysis, synthesis, and evaluation (Guskey, 2005). By focusing on mastery, CBE prepares students for practical applications of knowledge, equipping them with skills directly relevant to their careers and lives.

For instance, rather than assessing a math student solely through exams, CBE might require students to demonstrate their mathematical skills in solving complex, real-life problems. Similarly, a language student might show proficiency by composing a comprehensive report or engaging in a structured debate (Sturgis, 2015). These PBAs require students to demonstrate their understanding through projects and practical tasks rather than traditional tests.

3.8.1.2 Examples from Innovative School Systems and Universities

CBE is gaining traction in K–12 and higher education systems across the United States and globally. For example, Western Governors University (WGU) operates exclusively on a competency-based model, allowing students to progress at their own pace and achieve mastery in targeted areas (Johnstone & Soares, 2014). WGU assesses students based on completing assessments and projects, which measure their ability to apply knowledge in practical scenarios rather than through seat-time requirements.

In K–12 education, the New Hampshire Department of Education has implemented CBE across several school districts. Students' progress through personalized learning pathways is structured around competencies rather than grade levels (Patrick & Sturgis, 2015). This model ensures that students acquire essential skills before advancing, creating a more customized and relevant educational experience.

3.8.2 *Holistic and Culturally Responsive Assessments*

As educational systems become more diverse, there is a growing need for assessments that recognize and respect students' cultural backgrounds. Holistic and culturally responsive assessments provide a more comprehensive understanding of students by considering the cultural context in which they live and learn (Gay, 2018). These models go beyond traditional assessments by valuing qualitative data, such as personal experiences and social interactions, often revealing insights into students' learning that quantitative assessments might overlook.

3.8.2.1 *Incorporating Students' Cultural Backgrounds into Assessment*

Culturally responsive assessments acknowledge that students' cultural identities shape their learning experiences. Educators can more accurately evaluate students' understanding and skills by incorporating cultural context into the assessment process. For example, a culturally responsive approach to history might involve assessing a student's ability to interpret historical events from multiple cultural perspectives or asking students to draw connections between historical content and cultural backgrounds (Ladson-Billings, 2022).

This approach also includes language assessments that consider multilingual students' linguistic diversity a strength rather than a barrier. Rather than penalizing students for using vernacular expressions or code-switching, culturally responsive assessments evaluate students' language proficiency across various contexts, recognizing the richness of bilingual or multilingual skills (Paris & Alim, 2017).

3.8.2.2 *Qualitative Methods: Interviews, Ethnographic Observations*

Holistic assessments often rely on qualitative methods, such as interviews and ethnographic observations, to capture the nuances of students' cultural backgrounds. These methods allow educators to gather deeper insights into students' thought processes, motivations, and cultural values (Banks & Banks, 2019). For instance, interviews can reveal how students relate to specific content areas, providing valuable context for understanding their academic performance.

Ethnographic observations, which involve in-depth, contextualized study of students' behavior and interactions, are instrumental in assessing collaborative and social skills. These observations help educators understand how students interact with peers from diverse backgrounds and how they apply their cultural knowledge in social situations (Villegas & Lucas, 2002).

3.8.3 Social-Emotional and Non-Cognitive Skills Measurement

Success depends on academic knowledge and social-emotional and non-cognitive skills in today's complex world. Collaboration, emotional intelligence, and creativity are increasingly recognized as essential for personal and professional growth (Duckworth & Yeager, 2015). Consequently, educational assessments are evolving to include measures of these non-academic skills, ensuring a more comprehensive approach to student development.

3.8.3.1 Assessing Collaboration, Emotional Intelligence, and Creativity

Assessing social-emotional skills involves evaluating students' ability to understand and manage their emotions, empathize with others, and maintain positive relationships. Emotional intelligence assessments, for instance, might evaluate how well students identify their emotions, respond to stress, and demonstrate empathy (Goleman, 1996). Similarly, assessments of collaboration skills examine students' ability to work effectively in groups, manage conflict, and contribute constructively to shared goals (Johnson & Johnson, 2013).

Creativity, another key non-cognitive skill, is often assessed through tasks that require innovative thinking, problem-solving, and artistic expression. For example, a creativity assessment might ask students to design a product prototype or develop a unique solution to a real-world issue. Rubrics for these tasks focus on originality, flexibility, and the ability to think "outside the box" (Sternberg & Lubart, 1999).

3.9 Tools and Frameworks for Non-Academic Skill Evaluation

Various frameworks and tools have been developed to assess non-cognitive skills effectively. The Collaborative for Academic, Social, and Emotional Learning (CASEL) provides a comprehensive framework for social-emotional learning (SEL), identifying five core competencies: self-awareness, self-management, social awareness, relationship skills, and responsible decision-making (CASEL, 2013). Schools and educators can use this framework to design assessments that evaluate students' growth in each area.

Tools like the Devereux Student Strengths Assessment (DESSA) provide structured methods for assessing social-emotional competencies in K–12 students. The DESSA includes teacher-rated scales that measure self-regulation, resilience, and cooperation, enabling educators to monitor students' social-emotional development over time (LeBuffe et al., 2018). Similarly, the Big Five Inventory measures non-cognitive traits such as openness, conscientiousness, and agreeableness, offering valuable insights into students' personalities and behavioral tendencies (John & Srivastava, 1999).

3.10 Implications for Educational Policy and Practice

3.10.1 Policy Recommendations

The shift toward innovative assessment models in education has significant implications for educational policy and accountability systems. As the emphasis moves from traditional standardized testing to more holistic, competency-based, and formative assessments, policymakers must rethink the structures and measures used to evaluate educational outcomes. This shift requires a critical examination of existing accountability frameworks to ensure they support, rather than hinder, the adoption of innovative practices.

3.10.1.1 Rethinking Accountability Systems in Light of Innovative Assessments

Current accountability systems in many educational contexts heavily rely on standardized tests, which primarily measure academic achievement in a narrow set of skills, such as math and reading. These systems often overlook broader learning goals, such as critical thinking, collaboration, and creativity (Darling-Hammond, 2015). To foster a more comprehensive approach to education, policymakers should develop accountability systems that incorporate multiple measures of student learning, including PBAs and SEL metrics.

For example, some states in the United States, like New Hampshire, have begun to pilot innovative accountability models through initiatives such as the Performance Assessment of Competency Education (Marion & Shepard, 2010). These systems include locally developed performance assessments alongside standardized tests, providing a more balanced picture of student learning. Policymakers should consider expanding such initiatives and providing resources for scaling successful models across districts and states.

Moreover, accountability systems should emphasize continuous improvement rather than punitive measures. By prioritizing formative assessment data and school-wide reflection on practices, schools can focus on meaningful improvements rather than "teaching to the test" (Chappuis & Stiggins, 2016). This requires policies incentivizing schools to experiment with and adopt innovative assessment methods and mechanisms for sharing best practices across educational networks.

3.10.1.2 Need for Policy Support for Assessment Innovation

Schools and districts need robust policy support to implement innovative assessment models successfully. Policy support includes funding for research and development of new assessment tools, grants for pilot programs, and investments in the technological infrastructure required for digital and adaptive assessments (Darling-Hammond & Adamson, 2014). Policymakers should also consider establishing partnerships with educational technology companies and research institutions to develop valid and reliable assessments.

Legislative frameworks must be flexible enough to accommodate new assessment forms while ensuring student learning remains the top priority. For instance, policies could provide waivers or exemptions from certain standardized testing requirements for schools implementing innovative assessment systems and demonstrating success through alternative measures (Linn, 2000). Additionally, there should be clear guidelines and support for ensuring equity in assessment so that all students, regardless of background, can access fair and culturally responsive evaluations.

3.10.2 Professional Development for Educators

The successful implementation of innovative assessment models depends highly on educators' skills and knowledge. Teachers must be equipped not only to administer these new assessments but also to interpret the data they generate and use it to inform instruction. This requires a fundamental shift in teacher training and professional development.

3.10.2.1 Preparing Teachers to Implement and Interpret New Forms of Assessment

Educators need comprehensive professional development programs that focus on both the theory and practice of innovative assessments. For example, training sessions should cover the principles of formative and performance-based assessments, the design of effective rubrics, and strategies for providing constructive feedback to students (Heritage, 2021). Teachers should also learn to use assessment data to make informed instructional decisions, differentiate learning experiences, and support student growth.

Professional development should be ongoing and embedded within teachers' daily practice. This can be achieved through professional learning communities (PLCs) where teachers collaborate, share experiences, and learn from one another (DuFour, 2004). PLCs provide a supportive environment for educators to experiment with new assessment methods, reflect on their effectiveness, and make necessary adjustments. Additionally, schools should offer coaching and mentoring programs that pair teachers with assessment experts who can provide personalized guidance and support.

3.10.2.2 Training Needs for a Paradigm Shift

The move toward innovative assessments requires a paradigm shift in how teachers view student learning and their role as facilitators of that learning. Traditional assessments often reinforce a teacher-centered model of instruction, while formative and performance-based assessments encourage a student-centered approach emphasizing active learning and self-assessment (Black & Wiliam, 1998b). To navigate this shift, teachers must be trained to foster a classroom culture that values inquiry, collaboration, and reflection.

Teacher education programs must also address changing assessment practices' emotional and practical challenges. For instance, teachers may feel overwhelmed by the perceived complexity of PBAs or need clarification about how to evaluate student work fairly. Training should provide teachers with practical tools, examples, and opportunities for hands-on practice to build their confidence and competence (Wiliam, 2011).

Furthermore, professional development should emphasize cultural competence and the ability to create inclusive assessments representative of diverse student backgrounds. Teachers should learn to recognize and address cultural biases in assessment design and ensure that their evaluations are equitable and respectful of students' unique experiences (Gay, 2018). By investing in comprehensive and culturally responsive training programs, educational systems can better support teachers and improve student outcomes.

References

Abedi, J. (2004). The no child left behind act and English language learners: Assessment and accountability issues. *Educational Researcher*, *33*(1), 4–14. https://doi.org/10.3102/0013189X033001004

Andrade, H. G. (2005). Teaching with rubrics: The good, the bad, and the ugly. *College Teaching*, *53*(1), 27–31. https://doi.org/10.3200/CTCH.53.1.27-31

Atkinson, R. (2001). *Standardized Tests and Access to American Universities*. https://escholarship.org/uc/item/6182126z

Au, W. (2007). High-stakes testing and curricular control: A qualitative meta-synthesis. *Educational Researcher*, *36*(5), 258–267. https://doi.org/10.3102/0013189X07306523

Au, W. (2022). *Unequal by Design: High-stakes Testing and the Standardization of Inequality*. Routledge. https://doi.org/10.4324/9781003005179

Banks, J. A., & Banks, C. A. M. (Eds.). (2019). *Multicultural Education: Issues and Perspectives* (10 ed.). John Wiley & Sons.

Bennett, R. E. (2011). *Automated Scoring of Constructed-Response Literacy and Mathematics Items*. A. P. Advisors.

Binet, A., & Simon, T. (1916). *The Development of Intelligence in Children: The Binet-Simon Scale*. Williams & Wilkins.

Binkley, M., Erstad, O., Herman, J. L., Riaizen, S., Ripley, M., Miller-Ricci, M., & Rumble, M. (2012). Defining twenty-first-century skills. In P. Griffin, B. McGraw, & E. Care (Eds.), *Assessment and Teaching of 21st Century Skills* (pp. 17–66). Springer. https://doi.org/10.1007/978-94-007-2324-5_2

Black, P., & Wiliam, D. (1998a). Assessment and classroom learning. *Assessment in Education: Principles, Policy & Practice*, *5*(1), 7–74. https://doi.org/10.1080/0969595980050102

Black, P., & Wiliam, D. (1998b). Inside the black box: Raising standards through classroom assessment. *Phi Delta Kappan*, *80*(2), 139–148.

Broadfoot, P. (1996). Performance assessment in perspective. In A. Craft (Ed.), *Primary Education: Assessing and Planning Learning* (pp. 35–65). Routledge.

Brookhart, S. M. (2013). *How to Create and Use Rubrics for Formative Assessment and Grading*. ASCD.
Brookhart, S. M., & McMillan, J. H. (2020). *Classroom Assessment and Educational Measurement*. Routledge. https://doi.org/10.4324/9780429507533
Buchmann, C., Condron, D. J., & Roscigno, V. J. (2010). Shadow education, American style: Test preparation, the SAT and college enrollment. *Social Forces*, *89*(2), 435–461. https://doi.org/10.1353/sof.2010.0105
Care, E., Kim, H., Anderson, K., & Gustafsson-Wright, E. (2017). *Skills for a Changing World: National Perspectives and the Global Movement* (ED583031). Center for Universal Education at the Brookings Institution, Issue.
Carless, D. (2007). Learning-oriented assessment: conceptual bases and practical implications. *Innovations in Education and Teaching International*, *44*(1), 57–66. https://doi.org/10.1080/14703290601081332
CASEL. (2013). *Effective Social and Emotional Learning Programs (Preschool and Elementary School Edition)*. Collaborative for Academic, Social, and Emotional Learning.
Chappuis, J., & Stiggins, R. (2016). *An Introduction to Student-involved Assessment FOR Learning* (7 ed.). Pearson.
Croft, M., & Beard, J. J. (2021). Development and evolution of the SAT and ACT. In B. Clauser (Ed.), *The History of Educational Measurement* (pp. 22–41). Routledge. https://doi.org/10.4324/9780367815318
Darling-Hammond, L. (2015). *The Flat World and Education: How America's Commitment to Equity Will Determine Our Future*. Teachers College Press.
Darling-Hammond, L., & Adamson, F. (2014). *Beyond the Bubble Test: How Performance Assessments Support 21st Century Learning*. John Wiley & Sons.
Darling-Hammond, L., Herman, J., Pellegrino, J., Abedi, J., Aber, J. L., Baker, E., & Steele, C. (2013). *Criteria for High-Quality Assessment*. Stanford Center for Opportunity Policy in Education (Stanford University), Center for Research on Student Standards and Testing (University of California at Los Angeles), Learning Sciences Research Institute (University of Illinois at Chicago).
Duckworth, A. L., & Yeager, D. S. (2015). Measurement matters: Assessing personal qualities other than cognitive ability for educational purposes. *Educational Researcher*, *44*(4), 237–251. https://doi.org/10.3102/0013189X15584327
DuFour, R. (2004). What is a "professional learning community"? *Educational Leadership*, *61*(8), 6–11.
Fisher, D., & Frey, N. (2021). *Better Learning through Structured Teaching: A Framework for the Gradual Release of Responsibility* (3 ed.). ASCD.
Frey, B. B., & Schmitt, V. L. (2007). Coming to terms with classroom assessment. *Journal of Advanced Academics*, *18*(3), 402–423. https://doi.org/10.4219/jaa-2007-495
Fukuyama, F. (2014). *Political Order and Political Decay: From the Industrial Revolution to the Globalization of Democracy*. Farrar, Straus and Giroux.
Gardner, H. E. (2008). *Multiple Intelligences: New Horizons in Theory and Practice* (2 ed.). Basic Books.
Gay, G. (2018). *Culturally Responsive Teaching: Theory, Research, and Practice*. Teachers College Press.
Goleman, D. (1996). Emotional intelligence. Why it can matter more than IQ. *Learning*, *24*(6), 49–50.
Good, C. V. (1973). *Dictionary of Education*. McGraw-Hill Book Company.
Griffin, P., McGraw, B., & Care, E. (Eds.). (2012). *Assessment and Teaching of 21st Century Skills*. Springer. https://doi.org/10.1007/978-94-007-2324-5

Gulikers, J. T., Bastiaens, T. J., & Kirschner, P. A. (2004). A five-dimensional framework for authentic assessment. *Educational Technology Research and Development*, *52*(3), 67–86. https://doi.org/10.1007/BF02504676

Guskey, T. R. (2005, April 11–15). *Formative Classroom Assessment and Benjamin S. Bloom: Theory, Research, and Implications*. American Educational Research Association.

Harlen, W. (2007). Criteria for evaluating systems for student assessment. *Studies in Educational Evaluation*, *33*(1), 15–28. https://doi.org/10.1016/j.stueduc.2007.01.003

Hattie, J. (2008). *Visible Learning: A Synthesis of over 800 Meta-analyses Relating to Achievement*. Routledge. https://doi.org/10.4324/9780203887332

Hehir, T., Grindal, T., Freeman, B., Lamoreau, R., Borquaye, Y., & Burke, S. (2016). *A Summary of the Evidence on Inclusive Education* (ED596134). Instituto Alana & Abt Associates.

Heissel, J. A., Levy, D. J., & Adam, E. K. (2017). Stress, sleep, and performance on standardized tests: Understudied pathways to the achievement gap. *AERA Open*, *3*(3), 2332858417713488. https://doi.org/10.1177/2332858417713488

Heritage, M. (2021). *Formative Assessment: Making It Happen in the Classroom*. Corwin Press.

John, O. P., & Srivastava, S. (1999). The Big-Five trait taxonomy: History, measurement, and theoretical perspectives. In L. A. Pervin & O. P. John (Eds.), *Handbook of Personality: Theory and Research* (pp. 102–138). The Guilford Press.

Johnson, D. W., & Johnson, R. T. (2013). Cooperative, competitive, and individualistic learning environments. In J. Hattie & E. M. Anderman (Eds.), *International Guide to Student Achievement* (pp. 372–374). Routledge.

Johnstone, S. M., & Soares, L. (2014). Principles for developing competency-based education programs. *Change: The Magazine of Higher Learning*, *46*(2), 12–19. https://doi.org/10.1080/00091383.2014.896705

Kingsbury, G. G., & Houser, R. L. (1993). Assessing the utility of item response models: Computerized adaptive testing. *Educational Measurement: Issues and Practice*, *12*(1), 21–27. https://doi.org/10.1111/j.1745-3992.1993.tb00520.x

Klein, J. T. (1990). *Interdisciplinarity: History, Theory, and Practice*. Wayne State University Press. https://doi.org/10.1093/acrefore/9780190201098.013.988

Kokotsaki, D., Menzies, V., & Wiggins, A. (2016). Project-based learning: A review of the literature. *Improving Schools*, *19*(3), 267–277. https://doi.org/10.1177/1365480216659733

Koretz, D. M. (2008). *Measuring Up*. Harvard University Press. https://doi.org/10.4159/9780674039728

Ladson-Billings, G. (2022). *The Dreamkeepers: Successful Teachers of African American Children* (3 ed.). Jossey-Bass.

Le, C., Wolfe, R. E., & Steinberg, A. (2014). *The Past and the Promise: Today's Competency Education Movement. Students at the Center: Competency Education Research Series*. Boston, MA: Jobs for the Future (ED561253).

LeBuffe, P. A., Shapiro, V. B., & Robitaille, J. L. (2018). The Devereux Student Strengths Assessment (DESSA) comprehensive system: Screening, assessing, planning, and monitoring. *Journal of Applied Developmental Psychology*, *55*, 62–70. https://doi.org/10.1016/j.appdev.2017.05.002

Lemann, N. (2000). *The Big Test: The Secret History of the American Meritocracy*. Farrar, Straus and Giroux.

Linn, R. L. (2000). Assessments and accountability. *Educational Researcher*, *29*(2), 4–16. https://doi.org/10.3102/0013189X029002004

Luckin, R., & Holmes, W. (2016). *Intelligence Unleashed: An Argument for AI in Education*. https://discovery.ucl.ac.uk/id/eprint/1475756/

Marion, S., & Shepard, L. (2010). *Let's Not Forget about Opportunity to Learn: Curricular Supports for Innovative Assessments*. https://www.nciea.org/wp-content/uploads/2021/11/Marion_Shepard_Curricular_units_042610.pdf

Messick, S. (1994). The interplay of evidence and consequences in the validation of performance assessments. *Educational Researcher*, *23*(2), 13–23. https://doi.org/10.3102/0013189X023002013

Meyer, J. W. (2021). Institutional theory and world society (2009). In R. Jepperson & J. W. Meyer (Eds.), *Institutional Theory: The Cultural Construction of Organizations, States, and Identities* (pp. 243–280). Cambridge University Press. https://doi.org/10.1017/9781139939744

Mullis, I. V. S., Martin, M. O., Foy, P., & Arora, A. (2012). *TIMSS 2011 International Results in Mathematics*. https://timssandpirls.bc.edu/timss2011/downloads/T11_IR_Mathematics_FullBook.pdf

Nicol, D. J., & Macfarlane-Dick, D. (2006). Formative assessment and self-regulated learning: A model and seven principles of good feedback practice. *Studies in Higher Education*, *31*(2), 199–218. https://doi.org/10.1080/03075070600572090

OECD. (2010). *PISA 2009 Results: What Students Know and Can Do: Student Performance in Reading, Mathematics and Science* (6612985526). OECD. https://doi.org/10.1787/9789264091450-en

Paris, D., & Alim, H. S. (Eds.). (2017). *Culturally Sustaining Pedagogies: Teaching and Learning for Justice in a Changing World*. Teachers College Press.

Patrick, S., & Sturgis, C. (2015). *Maximizing Competency Education and Blended Learning: Insights from Experts. Competency Works Issue Brief*. International Association for K-12 Online Learning.

Paulson, F. L., Paulson, P. R., & Meyer, C. A. (1991). What makes a portfolio a portfolio? *Educational Leadership*, *48*(5), 60–63.

Pellegrino, J. W., & Hilton, M. L. (Eds.). (2012). *Education for Life and Work: Developing Transferable Knowledge and Skills in the 21st Century*. The National Academies Press. https://www.fsba.org/wp-content/uploads/2014/04/Education-for-life-and-work.pdf

Ravitch, D. (2010). *The Death and Life of the Great American School System: How Testing and Choice Are Undermining Education*. Basic Books.

Reardon, S. F. (2011). The widening academic achievement gap between the rich and the poor: New evidence and possible explanations. In G. J. Duncan & R. J. Murnane (Eds.), *Whither Opportunity?: Rising Inequality, Schools, and Children's Life Chances* (pp. 91–116). Russell Sage Foundation.

Resnick, L. B., & Resnick, D. P. (1992). Assessing the thinking curriculum: New tools for educational reform. In B. R. Gifford & M. C. O'Connor (Eds.), *Changing Assessments: Alternative Views of Aptitude, Achievement, and Instruction* (Vol. 30, pp. 37–75). Springer.

Rothblatt, S. (1976). *Tradition and Change in English Liberal Education: An Essay in History and Culture*. Faber and Faber.

Rothstein, R. (2004). *Class and Schools: Using Social, Economic, and Educational Reform to Close the Black-White Achievement Gap*. https://coilink.org/20.500.12592/dg3d6c

Segool, N. K., Carlson, J. S., Goforth, A. N., Von Der Embse, N., & Barterian, J. A. (2013). Heightened test anxiety among children: Elementary school students' anxious responses to high-stakes testing. *Psychology in the Schools*, *50*(5), 489–499. https://onlinelibrary.wiley.com/doi/10.1002/pits.21689

Shepard, L. A. (2000). The role of assessment in a learning culture. *Educational Researcher, 29*(7), 4–14. https://doi.org/10.3102/0013189X029007004

Shermis, M. D., & Burstein, J. (Eds.). (2013). *Handbook of Automated Essay Evaluation: Current Applications and New Directions*. Routledge. https://doi.org/10.4324/9780203122761.

Shermis, M. D., & Di Vesta, F. (2011). *Classroom Assessment in Action*. Rowman & Littlefield.

Sireci, S. G., Li, S., & Scarpati, S. (2003). *The Effects of Test Accommodations on Test Performance: A Review of the Literature*. Amherst, MA: University of Massachusetts, Center for Educational Assessment, Research Report 485.

Stanovich, K. E. (2009). Matthew effects in reading: Some consequences of individual differences in the acquisition of literacy. *Journal of Education, 189*(1–2), 23–55. https://doi.org/10.1177/0022057409189001-204

Sternberg, R. J., & Lubart, T. I. (1999). The concept of creativity: Prospects and paradigms. In R. J. Sternberg (Ed.), *Handbook of Creativity* (pp. 3–15). Cambridge University Press.

Sturgis, C. (2015). *Implementing Competency Education in K-12 Systems: Insights from Local Leaders. CompetencyWorks Issue Brief* (ED 557750). International Association for K-12 Online Learning.

Terman, L. M. (1916). *The Measurement of Intelligence: An Explanation of and a Complete Guide for the Use of the Stanford Revision and Extension of the Binet-Simon Intelligence Scale*. Houghton Mifflin.

Thorndike, E. L. (1910). *Educational Psychology*. Teachers College Press.

Tyack, D. T., & Hansot, E. (1982). *Managers of Virtue: Public School Leadership in America, 1820–1980*. Basic Books. https://doi.org/10.2307/3323663

Villegas, A. M., & Lucas, T. (2002). Preparing culturally responsive teachers: Rethinking the curriculum. *Journal of Teacher Education, 53*(1), 20–32. https://doi.org/10.1177/0022487102053001003

Weiss, D. J. (2004). Computerized adaptive testing for effective and efficient measurement in counseling and education. *Measurement and Evaluation in Counseling and Development, 37*(2), 70–84. https://doi.org/10.1080/07481756.2004.11909751

Wiliam, D. (2011). *Embedded Formative Assessment*. Solution Tree Press.

Yerkes, R. M. (Ed.). (1921). *Psychological Examining in the United States Army* (Vol. 15). US Government Printing Office.

4

A CALL FOR TRANSPARENCY IN THE DEVELOPMENT AND VALIDATION OF AI-BASED WRITING EVALUATION SYSTEMS

Sue Lottridge and Amy Burkhardt

Algorithms have long been able to assign scores to essays by mimicking how humans do so, following scoring rubrics. Through such algorithms, an automatic score may immediately inform a student where their writing falls on a rubric. Yet, this alone does not help students to understand *why* they landed at that level or *what* they need to do to move to the next one. Such actionable guidance is often essential for feedback to be effective (e.g., Hattie & Timperley, 2007). While such detailed feedback is critical for supporting students' growth as writers, it is also time-intensive to create. Teachers often have limited availability for one-on-one conferencing with their students or time to provide detailed feedback on each student's essay and version. One solution that can support both educators and students in this feedback process is the use of automated writing evaluation (AWE) tools. Recent advances in artificial intelligence, or AI, enable these tools to move beyond rubric-based scoring to deliver more nuanced feedback on the quality and features of student writing. As these AI capabilities expand, the creation of AWE tools and subsequent adoption by students and teachers in classrooms is likely to accelerate.

Writing is multifaceted, and AI feedback may prioritize one writing area over another. For example, feedback may attend to grammar and conventions, or more substantive aspects, such as coherence, reasoning, or organizational structure. Regardless of a tool's specific focus, all AWE solutions – at their core – aim to support students in their development as writers. A substantial risk of these tools, however, is that the opposite is achieved: namely, that these tools inadvertently hinder writing development if not designed or used appropriately. Early evidence of AI tool use more broadly gives reason for caution. A recent systematic review found that students' over-reliance on AI systems may erode skills that are foundational to strong written communication – critical thinking, decision making, and analytic reasoning (Zahi et al., 2024). We also know that motivation is a key element of

DOI: 10.4324/9781003621522-4

learning, and the lack of human involvement in the feedback process may reduce levels of engagement with tools (Ahmad et al., 2023; Chu et al., 2025; Shi et al., 2025; Holt, 2024). Relatedly, AWE tools can inadvertently reduce critical interactions between students and teachers, or between students (e.g., Pershan, 2025). We must be mindful of these risks and account for their likelihood when designing, implementing, and evaluating AWE tools.

The purpose of evaluating AWE tools is not to merely ensure they avoid harm but to determine whether they genuinely support students' growth as writers. Doing so requires scrutiny of the evidence surrounding the design, development, implementation, and validation of these tools. A key question becomes: which elements of the development and evaluation process must be present for an AWE tool to enable rigorous external review?

To address this question, it may help to envision five areas for what a fully mature writing tool would entail: (1) a clearly defined purpose with corresponding use cases; (2) evidence that substantiates those uses; (3) transparency in how the AI model is trained and functions within the tool; (4) transparent reporting of model performance on well-defined datasets; and (5) explicitly designed safeguards to protect student privacy and safety. Underlying these areas is the construct of writing itself – that is, how students themselves evolve as writers over time, and what they need to improve their writing skill.

It may be unrealistic to expect any current AWE tool to achieve full maturity, given the recency of AI feedback tooling and products. Additionally, we expect tools to vary in maturity across the five areas, given developers' priorities and the specific problems they may be designed to solve. That said, even at various levels of maturity, current tools may still offer meaningful support to students, particularly in schools where little or no feedback is provided. As the education community grapples with the responsible integration of AI into classrooms (e.g., Oregon Department of Education, 2025), transparency about the maturity of an AWE tool is an essential guardrail to ensure AI writing tools are evaluated not only on their stated claims but also on the evidence that underpins those claims. Such transparency can aid local, state, and federal agencies as they review and approve teaching tools; it can also support teachers as they make individual classroom decisions about which tools to use and how to use them.

To support this, we propose a framework for evaluating the maturity of AWE tools along these five dimensions. While maturity alone is not a guarantee of quality, it is suggestive of quality. Mature tools, having undergone multiple development cycles, documentation iterations, and multiple efficacy studies, can be examined and held accountable in ways early stage tools cannot. Just as a Phase I clinical drug is not "bad" but simply too new to know whether it is effective or safe, an AWE tool in its early stages cannot be fully judged. Likewise, a Phase III drug may still fail, but it provides evidence to support further evaluation. In the same way, maturity in AWE tools identifies the level of transparency and evidence available for scrutiny. In the case of education, a maturity matrix can leverage the tiers of evidence, such as those outlined in ESSA (IES, 2025).

We therefore introduce a "maturity matrix" that outlines criteria at different stages of development. In our view, a maturity matrix offers a structured way to align expectations around quality and efficacy, thereby encouraging developers and researchers to disclose more information as tools evolve and enabling educators and policymakers to make evidence-informed decisions around which tools to use for which purpose and for/by whom (Ho, 2022). The maturity matrix considers this most directly by examining the theory-of-action claims as well as the evidence collected that supports those claims, along with examinations of AI technology, validation, and considerations of student safety, security, and privacy. We begin by presenting key AWE tools and situating them within this conversation. Then, we introduce the maturity matrix, discuss each focus area, and place each tool at the maturity levels outlined in the rubric to illustrate and clarify the criteria.

Our vision of transparency closely maps to NIST's *AI Risk Management Framework* (2023), which outlines elements of application context, data and input, AI model and validation, application context, as well as considerations for individuals, communities, and the planet (see p. 11). While the NIST framework is general to all AI applications, our focus is on AWE tool design and use within the classroom. Our vision also aligns with the U.S. DOE OET *Designing for Education with Artificial Intelligence* (2024) document which argues that designing for education requires the provision of evidence for the tool rationale and impact while also ensuring safety and security (p. 10). Both federal documents outline the need for transparency as a key way to build trust when using AI-enhanced or enabled tools in education.

4.1 Automatic Writing Evaluation Tools

As noted above, AWE tools are designed with different approaches to support specific aspects of writing. Four examples, currently used in classrooms, illustrate the range of purposes and AI technologies. Khanmigo *Writing Coach*, Khan Academy's AI tutor that engages students in dialogue about their drafts using generative AI, was released in 2024 (Robertson, 2025). *MI Write*, a widely used AWE tool available for more than ten years, generates overall writing scores using automated scoring using Project Essay Grade and the Six Trait Rubric (Wilson, Myers, & Potter, 2022; Education Northwest, n.d.). *eRevise+RF* provides revision-oriented feedback, focusing on students' use of evidence and reasoning in argumentative writing, and has been studied in multiple classrooms across two states (Liu et al., 2025). *Write-On with Cambi!* (hereafter, *Cambi*) guides students through drafting and revision, emphasizing key compositional elements, was released in 2024 and has been used primarily in one state by over 2,000 teachers and 40,000 students (Lottridge, Ormerod, & Burkhardt, 2025). These tools were chosen because of their long-standing use across states (e.g., *MI Write*), because of their innovative use of AI (*eRevise+RF*, *Cambi*), and/or because of the large volume of use in one feedback area (math) using generative AI with a new adaptation to the domain of writing (*Writing Coach*).

Our focus is to explicate the maturity matrix using these tools, as each tool offers elements that reflect the matrix's key focus areas and levels. We intend to illustrate how the matrix can be interpreted using these tools as exemplars rather than provide a definitive judgment on the tools themselves. This choice is driven by a desire to mitigate a conflict of interest: the authors of this chapter contributed to the development of *Cambi*. Research published in journals and conferences, as well as blog posts, was used to obtain information from each AWE tool when the maturity matrix was applied.

4.2 The AWE Maturity Matrix

In this framework, we describe what evaluators – educators, policymakers, researchers – should reasonably expect to see at different levels of a tool's development maturity. As presented in Table 4.1, the maturity matrix has five focus areas: *Theory of Action*, *Outcome Evaluation*, *AI Technology*, *Model Validation*, and *Safety, Security & Privacy*. Each area has four maturity levels: *Early*, *Developing*, *Established*, and *Mature*. We expect that the maturity levels can be applied individually to each area; for example, a tool may have a strong theory of action but little evidence to support the claims. Alternatively, a tool may have an exhaustive description of the AI technology and model validation process but lack a theory of action. This is in part because the development of AWE tools may be driven and designed by different groups, such as learning scientists, AI engineers, or assessment experts. In this way, we expect tools to have patterns of maturity levels across the five areas; these patterns indicate the strengths and weaknesses of the evidence supporting them. We do expect that the tools with the most substantial evidence supporting their use will have *Established* or *Mature* levels across all five areas.

Next, we describe each of the five focus areas of the maturity matrix and briefly outline example maturity levels for each. We also provide examples from the four AWE tools to illustrate the levels.

4.2.1 Theory of Action

The first framework element is a theory of action, a critical component in defining the purpose and design of the AWE system. A theory of action is "an explicit theory of how an intervention, such as project, a program, a strategy, an initiative, or a policy, contributes to a chain of intermediate results and finally to the intended or observed outcomes" (Funnell & Rogers, 2011). The National Council on Measurement in Education (NCME) 2018 position statement requires explicit delineation of "program's constituent parts; its intended (short- and long-term) outcomes; the causal mechanisms posited as responsible for the intended change; and the ideal implementation of the program that is believed to be most likely to lead to those outcomes." Logic models further explicate the theory of action by delineating the

TABLE 4.1 AWE Maturity Matrix

Maturity Level	*Theory of Action*	*Outcome Evaluation*	*AI Technology*	*Model Validation*	*Safety, Security, and Privacy*
Early	No theory of action described.	No supporting evidence provided.	No description of AI technology.	No model validation results.	No evidence of safety, security, or privacy measures.
Developing	Tool's purpose is stated but lacks a clear explanation of how goals will be achieved. Introduces the tool's central construct.	Correlational studies or small-scale qualitative research exist that focus on short-term goals, usability, or perceptions.	Minimal description of AI technology, modeling approach, training data, and feedback.	Limited evidence of model performance and description of data to support that evaluation.	Basic mention of student data security and privacy. Minimal description of how potential harmful effects are managed.
Established	Purpose is stated with limited articulation of how the tool achieves its goals. This may include a logic model of inputs, activities, outputs, and outcomes.	Some multi-methods evidence (e.g., quasi-experimental, qualitative, process data) with sufficient sample sizes across schools or districts, focused on evaluating short-term goals.	Modeling approach described but lacks key details such as rationale for model choice, training data, or explanation of feedback mechanisms.	Evidence of model's ability to predict scores or feedback accurately, with limited alignment of predictions to the construct definition outlined in the theory of action.	Some information on privacy protections, model housing, and data use agreements. Some description of how potential harmful effects are managed.

(*Continued*)

TABLE 4.1 (Continued)

Maturity Level	*Theory of Action*	*Outcome Evaluation*	*AI Technology*	*Model Validation*	*Safety, Security, and Privacy*
Mature	Clear articulation of tool's purpose, including short- and long-term goals, supported by a logic model. Describes how the building blocks of the theory of change are connected.	Evidence across multiple methods, including qualitative research, process data, and experimental or quasi-experimental designs, to evaluate both short- and long-term outcomes. Sample size and representation support results interpretation.	Transparent rationale and description of modeling approach, data, and design features that support feedback.	Evidence of model's ability to predict scores or feedback accurately, aligned to construct definition in the theory of action. Evidence of accuracy across a broad range of students, classes, and regions.	Comprehensive data privacy and security protocols: models stored in secure environments, encrypted data, contractual data use agreements, and mitigation of adversarial risks.

inputs, activities, and outputs linked to the desired outcomes (Lemire, Porowski, & Mumma, 2023; d'Brot, 2019).

A theory of action details how specific activities and outputs lead to specific outcomes, and how contextual factors influence these. In the case of an AWE tool, contextual factors may include a teacher's support and engagement with students using the tool in the classroom. In essence, the theory of action is the claim of what the tool is intended to accomplish and how it does that. Note that the theory of action parallels the OET guidance on designing tools for education and providing evidence and rationale for impact (U.S. DOE OET, 2024, p. 10); the OET guidance itself recommends the use of theories of action in the design, development, and validation of educational tools using AI.

Key elements of the theory of action include both the construct definition and the assessment feedback provided to the student and/or teachers. The construct definition refers to the elements of writing evaluated in the AWE tool. It situates the use of these elements in writing literature or writing assessment (e.g., standards, rubrics, expert range-finding decisions, and learning science). The construct definition for a tool may be broad (e.g., covering all aspects of writing defined in a standard or rubric) or narrow (e.g., focusing only on certain conventions elements or argumentation elements). Regardless of choice, the construct assessed in the tool should be well-defined and grounded in research. Assessment feedback refers to the mechanisms that translate the evaluated elements into formats that are accessible and usable for students and teachers. For students, this may be reflected in how they interact with AWE feedback via a user interface. For teachers, this can be reflected in how they use feedback in instruction and their evaluation of student writing. For both, assessment feedback also includes any supplemental information that helps users understand the tool (e.g., user guides). These guides inform the user that they are interacting with an "AI model" and focus on describing the intended use of the AWE system, how to use the AWE system tools, and, at least in the context of k12 assessment, how the tools align with state standards and rubrics. In essence, assessment feedback is a key mechanism that enacts the theory of action; it is the programmatic implementation of the assumptions underlying how the AWE information can be interpreted and used by teachers and students.

To explore what a theory of action for an AWE tool may look like in practice, we have developed one for a fictional writing tool. This fictional tool's purpose is to help students improve their transition strategies. Table 4.2 presents a logic model of the inputs, activities, outputs, and the short- and long-term outcomes expected from this tool's use. Note that the construct of "transitions" is an underlying element to the logic model; namely, the tool must be able to identify transitions in student essays accurately and to provide an evaluation of the quality of a transition (e.g., weak/strong). In this sense, the logic model consists of two levels of claims: (1) the construct can be assessed accurately, and (2) the use of the tool results in the expected short- and long-term outcomes.

TABLE 4.2 Fictitious AWE Tool Logic Model to Demonstrate a Mature Theory of Action

Inputs	*Activities*	*Outputs*	*Short-Term Outcomes*	*Long-Term Outcomes*
- Student drafts an essay and presses the "get feedback" button within the AWE software	- The tool highlights weak/missing transitions and prompts the student to make revisions - The student makes changes to existing transitional text - The student adds new transitional text	- Final essay submitted to system	- Increased use of varied transition words and phrases - More cohesive paragraph connections - Higher rubric score on organization dimension - Improved confidence in connecting ideas	- Students transfer transition skills to non-tool writing tasks - Student essays demonstrate stronger logical flow - Improve overall essay score beyond coherence

The theory of action then connects these inputs, activities, and outputs to theorize the causal mechanisms that lead to the outcomes. In this example, the theory of action can build upon the logic model with the following explication:

> Transitional statements and text are a critical aspect of sophisticated writing. They signal relationships between ideas, guiding the reader from one sentence or paragraph to the next. Without them, even strong individual points can feel disjointed or abrupt. Effective transitions do more than add flow; they clarify logical connections (cause, contrast, sequence, emphasis), help readers anticipate what comes next, and reinforce the overall coherence of an argument or narrative. When a student submits a draft essay, AWE technology detects transitional statements. This, in turn, allows the tool to highlight and prompt the student to focus on areas with weak or missing transitions. This prompting leads to the student engaging in metacognition to review, evaluate, and edit their text. In the context of this AWE, teachers provide support by answering questions and clarifying concepts, which helps students deepen their use of transitional strategies. The cycle of revisions produces a final essay, which leads to:
>
> - Increased use of varied transition types,
> - Stronger connections between paragraphs,
> - Higher rubric scores in domains such as organization, and
> - Improved student confidence in connecting ideas.
>
> Over time, these short-term gains transfer through generalization and self-regulation: students begin to monitor for weak or missing transitions on their own, across different writing tasks.

As noted above, this theory of action begins by identifying – and, to some extent, defining – the construct of transitional statements. It is essential to clarify *which* aspects of writing the tool focuses on; this becomes critical for detailing specific short- and long-term outcomes. A theory of action for a less developed tool may not explicitly define the construct, may omit a logic model altogether, or, if one is present, may fail to connect inputs, activities, and outputs to the mechanisms that generate outcomes.

Table 4.3 presents the theories of action for the four AWE tools, illustrating the range of maturity levels outlined in the matrix. Tools with low specificity in explicating the inputs, activities, and outputs received a level of *Developing*. Tools that offered more specificity around these elements without the detail of the fictional example received a level of *Established*, and tools with extensive levels of specificity in the detail of feedback, as well as the systems contributing to that feedback and outcomes, received a level of *Mature.*

TABLE 4.3 Maturity Levels of the AWE Tools for the Theory-of-Action Focus

AWE Tool	*Description*	*Maturity Level*
Writing Coach	By providing students with access to Writing Coach, students engage with the writing process, resulting in improved immediate essay output and improved essay output on future essays. The student engages with the entire process of essay development in four steps: (1) understanding the assignment; (2) outlining; (3) drafting; and (4) feedback and revision. Students receive AI-generated feedback on five writing elements: introduction, evidence, structure, style and tone, and conclusion (Di Cerbo, personal communication; Robertson, 2025).	Developing
MI Write	By easing the burden of providing feedback, MI Write allows teachers to assign more writing and focus their feedback efforts. In turn, MI Write affords students the increased writing practice opportunities they need to improve writing quality. Moreover, MI Write's automated writing quality scores provide timely and reliable assessment data – which can be used to examine changes in performance over time – and automated feedback helps students improve their knowledge of writing quality criteria (MI Write, n.d.-a). MI Write provides a number of features theorized to improve writing skill, including multiple opportunities for writing practice, graphical organizers to increase planning behaviors, score reporting across times to support self-monitoring of progress by students, peer review that can prompt further revisions, and interactive skill-building lessons (Wilson et al., 2021b).	Established

(*Continued*)

TABLE 4.3 (Continued)

AWE Tool	*Description*	*Maturity Level*
eRevise + RF	The eRevise+RF theory of action is grounded in sociocultural theories of formative assessment, emphasizing the “situated and social nature of learning.” The authors argue that AWE tools should consider disciplinary norms for text-based argumentation, the values and goals of teachers and students, the mediation of the AWE tool by teachers, and the outcomes of student use, including student revisions that improve the essay. To this end, the AWE tool must accurately capture meaningful features of evidence use. Teachers must perceive the tool as aligned with their pedagogical aims, and students must find the tool interpretable and beneficial. Teachers are likely to vary in their support for students in interpreting eRevise+RF feedback, although substantive dialogue between teachers and students supports effective essay revisions and skills. Combined, these result in improved essays that use evidence in ways aligned with the feedback provided, and students can describe how their learning aligns with the feedback (Summarized from Correnti et al., 2022).	Mature
Cambi	Students who are guided through a structured review of their essays with immediate, well-aligned, annotated feedback will produce essays of higher overall quality. This guidance can minimize or eliminate the need for repetitive teacher review and enable more substantive (and likely more interesting and engaging) conversations between teachers and students about their writing. This feedback will be most helpful for lower proficiency students because it can scaffold the feedback that teachers often do not have time to provide. As students meaningfully engage with Cambi over time, they will develop a practice of reviewing their writing and an understanding of the basic elements of an essay; this, in turn, will help them become better writers overall. A key part of this claim is that the support provided by Cambi does not encourage the student to over-rely on AI and that teachers will remain actively involved in offering writing feedback and instruction (Lottridge, Ormerod, & Burkhardt, 2025).	Established

4.2.2 Outcome Evaluation

Theories of action make claims about intended outcomes and the causal mechanisms underlying the claims. Outcome evaluation examines the degree to which these claims are supported by evidence. As noted by NCME (2018), "… a theory of action must be regularly evaluated with empirical evidence that examines whether it is operating as intended." Below, we describe four areas to consider in evaluating AWE systems: perceptions, implementation, immediate/short-term effects on student writing, and long-term/distal effects on student writing skill. Mature tools will have evidence across all areas, building toward the assessment of long-term impacts; less mature tools will have evidence on short-term effects or limited evidence on implementation or perceptions. In all cases, the number, representation, and type of study participants are important considerations in study design and interpretation of results. Most AWE use by teachers is likely to be voluntary, and mitigating the effects of non-random convenience samples will be necessary; this requires either matched comparison groups or another method to approximate a counterfactual, thereby limiting the extent to which one can generalize the findings. Still, the collection of evidence across studies should provide support for or against the theory-of-action claims.

Sociocultural theories of formative assessment suggest that learning outcomes include metacognition and self-regulation, and that learning occurs within the dynamic social context of a classroom with teachers and students, as well as within the larger contexts of school, district, and state requirements and policies (e.g., Correnti et al., 2022). Using this lens, student and teacher perceptions are critically important aspects of a mature theory of action, as they can be an outcome of the theory of action (e.g., students report more confidence in writing) or a mediating factor in achieving an outcome (e.g., students find the tool helpful and engaging and use it as a result). Understanding how teachers perceive the tool in relation to their theory of teaching, enacted curriculum, state standards, feelings about AI, and classroom practice is clearly an important lens for understanding outcomes. Relatedly, understanding how students perceive the tool in relation to their perceptions of their writing skills, interest in technology and AI, and the tool's usefulness for their writing is also important. Mature outcome evaluation studies will consider both teacher and student perceptions in their study design, either to better interpret the outcome results or as outcomes themselves. Such feedback can be obtained through surveys and interviews focused on the theory of action's key claims.

Implementation refers to whether and how students and teachers are using the AWE tool. The degree of implementation can be examined in multiple ways, including usability labs, cognitive labs, analysis of writing process/log data, and classroom observations. Usability and cognitive labs involve observing one or more students as they interact with the AWE tool. In usability studies, the focus is typically on whether students understand how to use the tool and its various features. The nature and type of feedback provided by AI-based tools may complicate this analysis, especially when responses are dynamic and varied. The outcomes of the usability studies will be formative; namely, they will drive UI/UX changes, assessment feedback changes, or result in the development of additional supporting resources. Cognitive labs focus primarily on how students engage with the tool to edit their essays. These labs may ask students to "think aloud" as they interact with the tool, to illustrate how they interpret the feedback and what they do with their essay in response. The setup, coding, and analysis of the cognitive labs are again likely to be complicated by the nature and type of feedback provided by the system, as well as by variations in student essays and students' editing skills. These labs offer insight into what students report thinking and doing in response to feedback, and how they consider revising their essays. These then can form the basis for writing process/log data evaluations. Process data examine the stored information collected on how the students use the tool – that is, what screens they access, when they edit their essay (and the relationship between feedback and editing behavior), how they edit their essay, how long they take for each of these pieces on each step of the writing process, and how they interact with their teachers or one another. Most critically, the process data need to align the feedback mechanism with the edits themselves and are likely to provide a rich source of interactions and edits to evaluate, particularly when analyzed alongside cognitive lab data. Analyzing the process data, then, not only contextualizes how students use the tool but also offers an opportunity to test the causal mechanisms posited in the theory of action.

Short-term effects focus on the impact of AWE tool use for students and teachers during essay review and revision, assessing whether and how student essays improve following interaction with the system, and which students experience benefits. These immediate impacts can be examined by comparing rubric-based scores (teacher-, automated-, or professional-scored) for students of similar ability who interact with and do not interact with the AWE tool. This analysis can illustrate which students benefit and whether those benefits are consistent across student groups or classrooms. In addition to rubric scores, the analysis can include changes in essays as expected by the theory of action (e.g., the addition of transitional phrasing when prompted to do so, or the lack of change when not encouraged to make them). These conclusions rely on a research design that involves either randomized controlled trials or a quasi-experimental design, with a focus on representativeness of both teachers and students for making and generalizing inferences.

Long-term effects examine the impact of AWE tool use on students' overall writing ability over time, with the theory of action guiding the specific areas of ability assessed. Time can vary from classroom use over a few weeks to repeated use over the course of an academic year. These studies necessarily use an independent writing assessment administered without feedback. This external measure could include a writing prompt in a later classroom session, the evolution of writing scores over time, and/or the student's performance on a state-level writing assessment (summative or otherwise). Finally, these studies should collect data on students' and teachers' perceptions and practices to inform the interpretation of the results.

Table 4.4 presents the maturity levels for the four AWE tools. All four levels are exhibited across the AWE tools, reflecting the body of evidence collected for each tool across the areas of perceptions, implementation, short-term, and long-term effects. Note that the descriptions do not focus on the actual outcomes but rather the purpose and methods of research in examining the theory-of-action claims. The key distinction across the AWE tools is the amount of evidence in the four areas when evaluating outcomes. *MI Write* has the most exhaustive analysis of the evidence, followed by *eRevise+RF.* The *Cambi* tool has a limited set of studies to support its use, focusing on perceptions and short-term effects. *Writing Coach* has not yet published evidence to support its theory-of-action claims.

4.2.3 AI Technology

AI technology enables AWE tools by underpinning the ability to provide immediate feedback. AI technology can range from classical feature-based approaches to transformer-based large language models (LLMs) fine-tuned for prediction (e.g., BERT) to prompting with generative AI models such as ChatGPT. Regardless of the AI technology chosen, a rationale for all elements of engine design, the AI training or prompting method, and data use is critical to the maturity of an AWE tool. While it is evident that AI technology should align with the theory of action, purpose, and methods, there are likely many candidate approaches to choosing an AI technology. *Mature* tools will consider all factors. *Early* tools will have little or no explanation of each factor. *Developing* tools will have minimal explanation, and *Established* tools will have some, but an incomplete level of reason for the choices. Below, we outline the key elements of AI technology: architecture, training, and data.

Engine architecture is a critical factor in AI technology. By architecture, we refer to the design of the engine that produces the output, as well as the nature of the input and output. Early versions of AWE systems used expert-designed features focused on identifying spelling or grammar errors, detecting word patterns associated with high-quality essays, and assessing sentence-formation characteristics (e.g., Cahill & Evanini, 2020). These features were then used in a parametric statistical model (e.g., multivariate regression) or a nonparametric model (e.g., gradient-boosted regression trees or support vector machines) to predict a score or other value. More recent methods either leverage large language model embeddings as "implicit features" (Lottridge et al., 2024; Lottridge et al., 2023) for prediction or leverage generative AI via prompting to support the student (DiCerbo et al., 2025). Importantly, these methods may use closed-source LLMs (e.g., OpenAI) via an application programming interface (API) or open-source LLMs (e.g., Llama 3, deBERTa) available for download and fine-tuning via software hubs such as HuggingFace (HuggingFace, n.d.). An important distinction between the closed-source and open-source/custom approaches is that the engine architecture underlying

TABLE 4.4 Maturity Levels of the AWE Tools for the Outcome Evaluation Focus

AWE Tool	*Description*	*Maturity Level*
Writing Coach	No supporting evidence has been published for *Writing Coach*. While there is outcome evidence to support the *Khanmigo* math tool (Khan Academy Blog, 2025), it is not yet clear how those studies apply to the *Writing Coach*.	Early
MI Write	*MI Write* has an extensive body of outcome evaluation research, including that of teacher and student perceptions, implementation in the classroom, short-term effects, and long-term effects. Below, we provide a subset of key studies that illustrate the outcome evaluation analyses on *MI Write*. Palermo and Thompson (2018) examined three methods for incorporating *MI Write* into the classroom: one using ad hoc approaches to writing instruction with *MI Write*, another using a Self-Regulated Strategy Development (SRSD) approach with *MI Write*, and a baseline with no *MI Write*. This study also tracked *MI Write* use. This quasi-experimental, mixed-methods study interviewed and surveyed teachers and students and collected evidence of implementation fidelity through log files to examine the system's use. The pre-test essay scores, treatment fidelity, and treatment type were used as inputs to a multi-level model, with the dependent variables being the final essay score, the final essay length, and the number of compositional elements in the final essay. Data were collected in one state, across five districts, with 19 teachers and approximately 800 middle school students. Palermo and Wilson (2020) extended these analyses to focus on student essay changes (measured by overall score, length, and use of compositional elements) in classrooms that used *MI* Write with the two strategies and on how student and teacher perceptions varied across the two strategies. Data were also analyzed by race/ethnicity. Wilson et al. (2021a) used focus groups to examine teachers' attitudes and experiences with *MI Write*; this study focused on how 90 mid-Atlantic teachers perceived AWE's influence on their own and their students' writing and how they thought AWE might transform teaching and learning. Wilson, Myers, and Potter (2022) extended this analysis to using a multi-level analysis of student data to examine changes in essay performance over the course of an academic year. Wilson et al. (2021b) examined the short- and long-term impacts of *MI Write* use in elementary grades (3–5), focusing on implementation and motivational factors. The sample consisted of 1935 students and 135 teachers	Mature

	from 14 elementary schools. Teacher and student attitudes toward *MI Write* were assessed via surveys. Student performance on the state assessment essay and the post-test essay score in *MI Write* was used as the dependent variables. Predictor variables were the number of essays written by students using *MI Write*, the number of essay drafts, the average gain score between first and final drafts, and total time in minutes in *MI Write*. Covariates were the pre-test MI Write essay score, the average first draft MI Write score, student writing self-efficacy score, as well as demographics (gender, race, special education status, English Language Learner status, and percent of students receiving free or reduced lunch in the school). Teacher and student perceptions of *MI Write* were examined, and its use was assessed via log files. Hierarchical linear modeling was used to predict the two dependent variables using the predictors and covariates. Wilson et al. (2023) used a randomized controlled trial (at the classroom level) to examine the impact of *MI Write* usage on summative essay scores and found no effect over the course of a year; however, they examined scores by level of usage and found an impact for those schools that used *MI Write* appropriately and often. The hierarchical model included treatment group, a pre-test score, special education status, and a priority population control. They examined treatment fidelity, writing self-efficacy, and enjoyment of writing. The sample comprised 2,547 middle school students (grades 7 and 8) from 14 schools across three districts. The authors also examined performance by district. Wilson et al. (2024) extended this evaluation by focusing on factors that influence students' perceptions of *MI Write*.	
eRevise + RF	*eRevise+RF* has a solid body of outcome evaluation research, including that of teacher and student perceptions, implementation in the classroom, and short-term effects. Research is primarily focused on two states and using two prompts. Teachers and students completed surveys about their experience and use of the tool. All 16 teacher participants underwent semi-structured interviews about students' experience with the tool, whether feedback was aligned to the teacher's goals, how the tool might impact their writing instruction, and how often teachers might use the tool. Student surveys focused on whether students understood the feedback, what to do with the feedback, and how much of the advice they used when revising their essays. Teachers also were asked to keep an implementation log of questions asked by students during tool use and how they interacted with students during tool use; these data were compared to the scores of students to determine how teacher interactions impacted performance using a hierarchical linear model (Correnti et al., 2022).	Established

(*Continued*)

TABLE 4.4 (Continued)

AWE Tool	*Description*	*Maturity Level*
	An evaluation of short-term quality improvement was based upon the amount and type of evidence provided, reasons about the evidence use, and the integration of evidence/reasons across drafts written across three sessions (Liu et al., 2025; Correnti et al., 2022; Zhang et al., 2019). Researchers also examined the degree of improvement across drafts by type of feedback provided and quality of initial draft to explore how the feedback was associated with student edits (Liu et al., 2025; Correnti et al., 2022).	
Cambi	*Cambi* has a small set of studies focused on teacher perceptions, the immediate impact of using *Cambi* on essay scores in a randomized controlled trial, and the analysis of essay evolution over a single writing session. Semi-structured teacher interviews were used to gauge how well a convenience sample of 20 teachers across two states felt the tool aligned with their instruction before its use, and to understand their views after using it in their classrooms. Interview data were used to improve the tool and to determine how well the tool aligned with their teaching. A small study with *Cambi* was conducted on a convenience sample of 11 teacher-led classrooms across two states, in which students were randomly assigned to either access to *Cambi* feedback or not to have access but receive static *Cambi*-like guidance. The dependent variable was the rubric score, as provided by an automated scoring engine. Results were compared across the two groups using mean scores and score distributions. This study also examined the kinds of changes students made (appending text and in-essay edits of two types: surface-level and substantive) during the writing session across the two groups (Lottridge, Ormerod, & Burkhardt, 2025; Sairam, Burkhardt, & Lottridge, 2025).	Developing

predictions in closed-source models is not made public and is managed by an external vendor (e.g., OpenAI, Amazon, or Anthropic). In this latter case, only the code surrounding the LLM can be made explicit (e.g., the API call and the prompt); however, the LLM itself cannot be described.

Mature AWE tools demonstrate a clear rationale for using the closed/open/custom approaches. For AWE tools that use open or custom approaches, the rationale for the model choice itself should be described; typically, this choice is made based upon prior performance on related task, data, and method used to pretrain the model in the case of LLMs, the number of model parameters and transformer architecture, and any limitations around essay features (e.g., length of the context window). The complexity of writing will likely require the use of multiple engines supporting the AWE system (e.g., Lottridge, Ormerod, & Burkhardt, 2025; Liu et al., 2025), and each should be described. Finally, *Mature* tools should describe the nature of the model outputs, such as labels associated with essay sentences (e.g., labeling a sentence as evidence or reasons), labels for phrases (e.g., identifying a grammar error in a sentence), and scores assigned to the entire essay, typically associated with a rubric description.

The approach to training the engine is also a key element in understanding the AI technology. *Mature* systems will describe this process in detail, outlining all components. In some cases, there may be no fine-tuning, but rather simply LLM prompting. In other cases, there may be minimal fine-tuning, such as providing the LLM with examples as part of the prompt (e.g., few-shot learning; Brown et al., 2020) or combining with information retrieval techniques to dynamically prompt the LLM (Gao et al., 2024). In other cases, fine-tuning or training may directly update model weights to improve the prediction task rather than simply prompting the model to produce outputs. This approach is typically used with open-source LLMs and custom architectures to optimize predictive task performance and has been quite successful at delivering results that mimic human output (IES, 2022; Lottridge et al., 2025). *Mature* AWE tools provide extensive detail around the hyperparameters/features used to fine-tune or train the models. In the case of open-source LLMs, this can include a number of epochs, batch size, learning rate, loss function, and stopping criterion.

Finally, *Mature* AWE tools describe the data used to fine-tune or prompt the model, including a rationale for the data selection and the data management approach. For example, data should represent the intended population for which the feedback will be used, demonstrate adequate quality of human labeling and scoring, and have sample sizes sufficient for AI model training and validation. In our view, generating high-quality, labeled, and representative data should be a key focus of AWE systems and is often among the most significant expenses in building them. It is also this area that requires substantive expertise in human labeling and scoring to obtain information that represents the intended construct. Because AI models are rapidly evolving, the same validation data can be used to examine model evolution and investigate performance improvements or to obtain additional types of feedback. Finally, metrics and criteria for evaluating human labeling (and AI labeling) are also essential in the fine-tuning process, as they define what success looks like for the model and drive the choice of engine architecture and hyperparameters used in training. Synthetically generated data, such as that produced by generative AI and used in training, should be specified, as should any AI-based methods used to monitor engine outputs (e.g., AI as judge, DiCerbo et al., 2025; Weatherholtz et al., 2025).

Table 4.5 presents the AI technology maturity levels and descriptions for the four AWE tools. *Writing Coach* receives an *Early* rating due to the lack of research on the AI technology in the tool; however, we do provide information on the *Khanmigo* math tutor AI technology, under the assumption that these tools will inform its use in *Writing Coach.* Both *eRevise+RF* and *Cambi* received *Mature* ratings because the body of work describing the AI development was comprehensive, covering the data used to train the models, the rationale and analysis of model choice, and the alignment of the model outputs with feedback. The *MI Write* tool received an *Established* level only because the data used to train the models was not defined in the literature, and the modeling was described only at a high level. That said, the overall modeling process was explained, as well as the link between the modeling and the feedback.

4.2.4 Model Validation

The evaluation of AI model performance is typically conducted relative to human performance using well-defined metrics and criteria (James et al., 2017; Williamson, Xi, & Breyer, 2012) and aligned with the construct definition outlined in the theory of action. The purpose of the model validation is to understand the degree to which the AI output approximates human performance in ways that generalize to a broader population. This analysis typically builds on the same data used to train the AI engine, or on data gathered after the engine is deployed for use in the AWE tool. To ensure that models are not biased, analyses should examine not just overall performance but also for key student subgroups (e.g., race/ethnicity, gender, primary language, disability, socio-economic status), classrooms, or regions. The outcomes of the evaluation can inform decisions about whether, what, and how AI-generated outputs are used in assessment feedback.

In cases where predictions are categorical or continuous, the validation approach is reasonably straightforward. Here, the strategy focuses on agreement metrics and criteria such as accuracy, correlation, kappa values, F1 scores, and standardized mean difference, using human agreement as the benchmark. In cases where predictions are qualitative and/or iterative as in the use of chatbots or AI-generated text feedback, the validation process is less well-defined and an emerging area of research. For these approaches, the validation process needs to consider the dynamic interplay of the student and AI system within the feedback session, while correctly classifying

TABLE 4.5 Maturity Levels of the AWE Tools for the AI Technology Focus

AWE Tool	*Description*	*Maturity Level*
Writing Coach	No description of the AI technology, but presumably *Writing Coach* will leverage the closed-source GPT-4 with prompting (Ofgang, 2024). Research on math tutoring suggests either use of open-source or closed-source models as AI judges the evaluate correctness of the student response (Miller & DiCerbo, 2024) and the AI tool generates text based on the student response and the extent to which that text is appropriate (i.e., correctly interpreting the student response, providing adequate questioning of the response or guiding the student to the correct response) (Weatherholtz et al., 2025; Dicerbo et al., 2025; Burleigh et al., 2025b). Khan Academy released a dataset for modeling the correctness of students' math responses (Miller & DiCerbo, 2024). Finally, researchers have examined ways to use synthetic data to reduce deployment times for new math items (Burleigh et al., 2025a). We expect these methodologies to be adapted for *Writing Coach.*	Early
MI Write	Scoring is produced by Project Essay Grade (PEG) using a custom, classical feature-based model based on the Six Trait model (ideas, organization, style, sentence fluency, word choice, and conventions), with each trait rubric having five levels. Models are trained for each trait, three genres (narrative, informative, argumentative), and for five grade bands (3–4, 5–6, 7–8, 9–10, 11–12). Models were trained so that scores were vertically aligned across grade bands within a genre (i.e., the same essay would receive a lower score from a grade 3–4 model than from a grade 5–6 model). The model is adapted for essay revisions by examining changes in key variables for each trait and how those changes affect the gradient; the AI score is intended to represent the improvement in the score based on those changes. Students can receive up to five feedback statements for each trait, presumably tied to the automated score, and receive some level of in-line grammatical feedback (Wilson et al., 2021b). A description of the data used to train the engine were not available in the literature.	Established
eRevise + RF	Custom feature-based models are used to provide feedback on the Number of Pieces of Evidence (NPE), which provides the number of topics in an essay, and the specificity (SPC), which provides the number of details of evidence. Manually derived lists are provided for the NPE and SPC engines; the words are encoded using open-source embeddings. A sliding window is applied to the essay to obtain the NPE and SPC counts. NPE and SPC are intended to represent the breadth and depth of the evidence used in an essay. Currently, only two prompts are evaluated in the system.	Mature

(*Continued*)

TABLE 4.5 (Continued)

AWE Tool	*Description*	*Maturity Level*
	Students have two opportunities to revise their essays. In the first draft, the NPE and SPC measures are provided to the student as feedback. After the second draft is submitted, the system uses custom, feature-based models to assess the nature of the revision based on the NPE and SPC scores. The system compares two drafts and identifies revised sentences or new sentences. An open-source LLM classifier, fine-tuned on college essays, is used to classify revisions as surface-level or content revisions. A separate closed-source classifier (via GPT-4) is then used to predict whether the identified revision is evidence or reasoning and to identify the context space of the argument itself. Finally, an open-source, fine-tuned classifier is used to determine whether the revision is successful or unsuccessful. The classification of evidence/reasoning and success/non-success yields four revision labels: successful evidence, unsuccessful evidence, successful reasoning, and unsuccessful reasoning. These labels are then mapped to feedback provided to students using a combination of the NPE and SPC scores and the revision scores: feedback to provide more evidence, feedback to provide more details, or feedback to offer more explanation of the connection between the evidence and the argument. Students can then use this feedback in their third revision. Details summarizing the AI technology can be found in Liu et al. (2025). The research underpinning the development of the elements of the system appears across multiple papers: development of a revision rubric (Afrin et al., 2020), revision success modeling (Liu et al., 2023; Li et al., 2024), NPE and SPC development and word-list creation (Zhang et al., 2019; Zhang & Litman, 2020a; Zhang & Litman, 2020b), and revision patterns (Li et al., 2025).	
Cambi	Fine-tuned open-source transformer models are used for all AI feedback. Models were trained to identify compositional elements and conventions elements. Compositional element models were trained across two grade bands (3–5 and 6–8) and two genres (argumentative and informative). Training data consisted of responses from one state's summative assessment program across multiple years. Models were trained on sentences labeled by humans using standard scoring procedures.	Mature

Different models were trained on conventions elements. One transformer model was fine-tuned, using human-labeled student sentences from the same state, to identify whether sentences were run-ons, fragments, or normal. Another transformer model was fine-tuned on a publicly available dataset (C4–200m; Stahlberg & Kumar, 2021) to take as input sentences and output corrected sentences. The outputs of this model were entered into a rule-based grammar tool (ERRANT; Bryant et al., 2017) that identified the type and nature of correction in the output sentence. These two models then provided a sentence-based conventions analysis that identified the kind of conventions error in a sentence.

All AI outputs for a response were then mapped to feedback codes that aligned with common state-level rubrics. Custom-written student-facing feedback was provided and linked to highlighted segments in the response.

Details summarizing the AI technology can be found in Burkhardt et al. (2025), Lottridge et al. (2025), Lottridge et al. (2024), and Ormerod et al. (2023).

student responses across the range of student answer types, providing accurate but not leading answers, and managing conceptual shifts by students in a conversation (Miller & DiCerbo, 2024). The use of chatbots requires a strong theory of action that outlines the space of all reasonable inputs and outputs across interactions, and the use of well-defined rubrics and methods to evaluate the accuracy and appropriateness of those inputs and outputs (DiCerbo et al., 2025; Weatherholtz et al., 2025). This area of work is nascent, given the recency of AI chatbots and their incorporation into AWE tools.

We expect AWE tools that have a *Mature* model validation consider all areas described above with extensive evidence to support claims that the AI models perform well. *Established* AWE tools will consider key metrics but may lack analysis by demographic groups. *Developing* AWE tools may use a subset of the key metrics. *Early* AWE tools have no metrics on model performance. The maturity levels of the AWE tools for model validation appear in Table 4.6. *Writing Coach* has been assigned a rating of *Early* because its results have not yet been published on its performance. The remaining three AWE tools received ratings of *Established* either because results are not available for the specific models used in the AWE tool (e.g., *MI Write*) but are provided more generally for the underlying engine, or because the results do not examine performance by student groups (e.g., *eRevise+RF and Cambi*).

TABLE 4.6 Maturity Levels of the AWE Tools for the Model Validation Focus

AWE Tool	*Description*	*Maturity Level*
Writing Coach	Model evaluation results are not available for *Writing Coach.* We expect that results will build upon those produced for math, including the accuracy of scoring student work (Miller & DiCerbo, 2024) and the nature and quality of automated feedback (Weatherholtz et al., 2025; DiCerbo et al., 2025; Burleigh et al., 2025b). For each, human labels and operational responses serve as ground truth, with evaluations examining exact agreement, Krippendorf's alpha, Matthew's correlation coefficient, Fleiss' kappa, precision, and recall.	Early
MI Write	While there appears to be no published evidence on the models used in *MI Write*, the authors argue that the models leverage PEG. The quality of PEG scoring, as measured by quadratic weighted kappa, exact agreement, and standardized mean difference across a variety of grades, genres, and rubrics, has been reported in multiple papers (e.g., Shermis, 2014; Shermis & Hamner, 2013; Bunch, Vaughn, & Miel, 2016).	Established

(*Continued*)

TABLE 4.6 (Continued)

AWE Tool	*Description*	*Maturity Level*
eRevise + RF	The accuracy of *eRevise+RF* NPE, SPC, and revision metrics was compared to human evaluations; the exact agreements, intra-class correlations, and quadratic weighted kappa were used to examine agreement using operational responses and scores. The NPE and SPC scores were also analyzed for sensitivity to change in student revisions by examining improvements in the scores relative to the degree and type of changes. This work was conducted via multiple studies as AI models were evaluated for use. Studies were conducted in two states, with two prompts, and involved a relatively small number of teachers and students. Research outlining results spans across multiple papers, including Liu et al. (2025), Li et al. (2024, 2025), Liu et al. (2023), Zhang et al. (2019), Zhang and Litman (2020a), and Zhang and Litman (2020b).	Established
Cambi	Human-labeled data from one state were used to evaluate models of compositional elements. Annotation rubrics were designed and used during the human labeling process, and 15% of essays received a second human label. AI engine performance was evaluated against human labels using kappa and exact agreement. Cross-genre and grade models were also assessed to examine the robustness of model performance across grade spans and genres. See Lottridge et al. (2025), Lottridge et al. (2024), and Burkhardt et al. (2025) for more details. The sentence-formation model was evaluated in two phases: first, using a held-out set of human-labeled sentences, again using kappa and exact agreement; second, using open-source datasets and examining the percentage of false and true positives (Lottridge et al., 2025; Young et al., 2025). The final conventions model was also evaluated in two phases: first, using publicly available test sets and the Generalized Language Evaluation Understanding (GLEU) metric; second, using open-source datasets and examining the false and true positives (Lottridge et al., 2025; Young et al., 2025).	Established

4.2.5 Data Safety and Security

Mature AWE tools must secure the safety, privacy, and security of students and their data. These dimensions are emphasized in OET AI guidelines, the *Standards* (AERA, APA & NCME, 2014), NIST guidelines, federal legislation (e.g., Family Educational Rights and Privacy Act [FERPA], the Protection of Pupil Rights Amendment [PPRA], and Children's Online Privacy Protection Act [COPPA]), and state guidelines (e.g., WDPI, 2024) and laws (e.g., The Connecticut Data Privacy Act). Indeed, the *Standards* themselves outline the need to protect student data as part of good measurement practice around test takers' rights and responsibilities (see Standards 8.5 and 8.6). These issues are particularly notable in the age of LLMs and AI. The use of closed-source models and the evolving legal landscape surrounding them raise serious concerns. Vendors may vary in their treatment of the privacy and security of user data, and care needs to be taken to ensure that systems do not use student or other data to train models and that such data are not leaked in downstream uses. As noted earlier, the use of AI – if not properly validated – can have impacts on student safety. Chatbot systems can be "jail broken" to act in rogue, potentially harmful ways; they can also confidently steer a student in the wrong direction, do work for the student thereby creating an over-reliance that results in worse learning outcomes, or simply be wrong (US DOE EOT, 2024, p. 35). Evaluation of such adverse impacts is again a reflection of a strong theory of action that "anticipates ways that an improper implementation of the program may lead to unintended negative consequences" (NCME, 2018).

AI tools should "not under defined conditions, lead to a state in which human life, health, property, or the environment is endangered" (NIST, 2023, p. 14). Notably, harm can occur to people, to organizations, and to ecosystems. The OET guidelines outline examples of potential harm to students, including feedback that is biased against particular students or simply wrong, and a tendency for people to defer to AI and thereby offload thinking to the AI system (see pp. 34 and 35). Thus, the framework for AWE evaluation should consider these potential harms in its measurement and efficacy evaluations. The safety of organizations, such as schools, can also be impacted by AWE tools if they rely too heavily on system outputs without teacher input and oversight, if they attempt to replace teachers with such tools, or if they seek to reduce the collaborative nature of classroom instruction. The safety of ecosystems, such as education systems and communities, can be compromised if the extensive use of AWE tools negatively affects overall student learning. *Mature* AWE tools should consider and evaluate the potential negative impacts of their use on students, teachers, classrooms, and schools.

The NIST framework defines privacy as the "norms and practices that help to safeguard human autonomy, identity, and dignity" (p. 17). In the case of AWE tools, this means ensuring that student and teacher data remain private throughout interactions with the tool. Data in this case means any identifying information, student responses, and feedback. For systems that use closed-source AI, this means ensuring that the data submitted to, and received from, the tool also maintains that privacy. Examples of this assurance are three-fold: that any data sent to the consumer-facing version are not used in training a more general model that has other uses; any data sent to the consumer-facing version cannot be generated by the more general model available to others outside the AWE tool; and the outputs generated by the tool adhere to the same data privacy rules.

Table 4.7 presents the maturity level ratings for the four AWE tools. *MI Write* and *Cambi* were assigned a *Mature* level based on their organizational policies regarding data and software handling, the use of AI that produces limited predictions of scores or feedback, and system design or research that supports the safe

TABLE 4.7 Maturity Levels of the AWE Tools for the Safety, Security, and Privacy Focus

AWE Tool	*Description*	*Maturity Level*
Writing Coach	Khan Academy provides information on managing personally identifiable information using encryption techniques (Khan Academy Blog, 2022). The Khan Academy website also discusses safety features such as detecting inappropriate, harmful, or unsafe content, limiting interactions with the AI tool, providing in-product messaging about the limitations of AI, and allowing parents and teachers to view all chat history (Khan Academy Help Center, n.d.). The Khan Academy also provides a detailed privacy policy on its website (Khan Academy, 2024). While the accuracy of the *Writing Coach* feedback is not known, we expect similar research to be applied to that tool.	Established
MI Write	*MI Write* provides a detailed privacy policy around data privacy, security, and handling (MI Write, n.d-a; MI Write, n.d.-b) as well as defined terms of service (MI Write, n.d.-c). The limited use of AI tools to automate scoring, tied to scores and text feedback, as well as the highlighting of some grammatical errors, suggests minimal negative impacts on students beyond potentially providing incorrect scores or feedback. The suite of outcome evaluation studies on *MI Write* that examine student and teacher perceptions, implementation, and short- and long-term effects suggests that *MI Write* poses few or no safety risks.	Mature

(*Continued*)

TABLE 4.7 (Continued)

AWE Tool	*Description*	*Maturity Level*
eRevise + RF	*eRevise+RF* does not provide web-based information on how the software manages data privacy. That said, most research appears to be reviewed by an Institutional Review Board, suggesting adherence to ethical data use and the protection of human subjects. The limited use of AI tools to automate scoring tied to scores and text feedback, as well as the highlighting of some grammatical errors, suggests limited negative impacts to students beyond potentially providing incorrect scores or feedback. The suite of outcome evaluation studies examining student and teacher perceptions, implementation, and short- and long-term effects suggests that *eRevise+RF* poses few or no safety risks.	Established
Cambi	*Cambi* is ISO 27001/27018 certified (Cambium Assessment, n.d.), ensuring that all *Cambi* data is stored securely and that privacy is fully protected. All student demographic and response data are strictly de-identified before use in training AI engines. *Cambi* uses open-source large language models hosted on Cambium Assessment Inc. (CAI) infrastructure, mitigating the risks of using 3rd-party APIs that may use this data for other purposes. *Cambi* uses a structured interface designed for a specific purpose to ensure the feedback is appropriate. To ensure feedback is always consistent, the feedback mechanism and language are scripted rather than provided by generative AI. The student-facing feedback is positively phrased and uses easy-to-understand language that places the onus on the student to make edits. *Cambi* also hedges the feedback so the student does not assume that the engine is correct. This approach supports students in the editing process without providing the "right" answer or doing the work for them. Students can choose to disregard guidance if they choose. Feedback is also available via speech, using automated text-to-speech technology.	Mature

use of AI. *Writing Coach* was assigned a level of *Established* based on Khan Academy's privacy policy statements and the research underpinning Khanmigo's math chatbot. *eRevise+RF* was assigned a level of *Established* based on their use of Institutional Research Board review, use of AI that produces limited predictions of scores or feedback, and the underlying research.

4.2.6 Summary and Conclusion

We introduced the AWE maturity matrix to provide a structured framework for educators and policymakers to make evidence-informed decisions about which tools to use for which purposes, while also encouraging AWE tool developers to consider key areas that can shape the design, development, implementation, and research of these tools. We described each AWE tool for each of the five focus areas and proposed a level for each tool and focus area. The purpose of this evaluation was to illustrate the application of the rubric using the publicly available information on the AWE tools. Table 4.8 summarizes our proposed ratings for each AWE tool across the five focus areas. Note that AWE tools varied in their rating levels across the four focus areas. Long-standing tools (e.g., *MI Write*, *erevise+RF*) tended to have more mature ratings (e.g., *Established* or *Mature*). AWE tools released more recently vary in their levels based on the maturity of their development and evaluation process. *Cambi*, for instance, underwent substantial validation before release and so had reasonably mature levels for some focus areas but has a small set of research to support the outcome evaluation. *Writing Coach* was recently released, with no published articles on its design and development; however, it includes a theory of action and is built on the technical foundations of the Khan Academy.

A widely used metaphor that has gained traction beyond education and assessment is the "AI Nutrition Label." This label serves as an accessible heuristic – an invitation to disclose what is "inside" an AI tool, including data origins, model architecture, known limitations, and potential biases, presented in a standardized way (e.g., Pundhir, 2025; Motorola Solutions, 2025; Twilio, n.d.; Open Ethics Initiative, n.d.). Although organizations interpret and implement this concept differently, the underlying purpose remains consistent: to promote self-disclosure so that consumers can better understand what is beneficial or harmful.

In the context of educational assessment, however, AI tools are inherently more complex. They not only make inferences about unobservable latent traits but also provide feedback intended to support students' development of those traits. As a result, the evidence needed to evaluate the use of such tools does not fit neatly within a single, uniform label or document. Even so, the spirit of the AI Nutrition Label – the commitment to transparency, clarity, and informed evaluation – remains highly relevant. Rather than proposing a label, we offer a matrix that helps tool

TABLE 4.8 AWE Maturity Matrix Levels for the Four AWE Tools

Maturity Level	*Theory of Action*	*Outcome Evaluation*	*AI Technology*	*Model Validation*	*Safety, Security, and Privacy*
Writing Coach	Developing	Early	Early	Early	Established
MI Write	Established	Mature	Established	Established	Mature
eRevise+RF	Mature	Established	Mature	Established	Established
Cambi	Established	Developing	Mature	Established	Mature

developers identify what information is important to disclose and guides evaluators in determining what is reasonable to expect as they assess the benefits of a tool for students and educators.

References

Afrin, T., Wang, E., Litman, D., Matsumura, C., & Correnti, C. (2020). Annotation and classification of evidence and reasoning revisions in argumentative writing. In *Proceedings of the Fifteenth Workshop on Innovative Use of NLP for Building Educational Applications*, Seattle, WA, pp. 75–84.

Ahmad, K., Iqhal, W., El-Hassain, A., Qadir, J., Benhaddou, D., Ayyash, M., & Al-Fuqaaha, A. (2023). Data-driven artificial intelligence in education: A comprehensive review. *IEEE Transactions in Learning Technologies, 17*, 12–31.

American Educational Research Association, American Psychological Association, & National Council on Measurement in Education (AERA/APA/NCME). (2014). *Standards for Educational and Psychological Testing*. Washington, DC: American Educational Research Association, American Psychological Association, & National Council on Measurement in Education (AERA/APA/NCME).

Brown, T., Mann, B., Ryder, N., Subbiah, M., Kaplan, J., Dhariwal, P., Neelakantan, A, Shyam, P., Sastry, G., Askell, A., Agarwal, S., Herbert-Voss, A., Krueger, G., Henighan, T., Child, R., Ramesh, A., Ziegler, D., Wu, J., Winter, C., Hesse, C. Chen, M., Sigler, E., Litwin, M., Gray, S., Chess, B., Clark, J, Berner, C., McCandlish, S., Radford, A., Sutskever, I. & Amodei, D. (2020). *Language Models Are Few-Shot Learners.* arXiv. https://doi.org/10.48550/arXiv.2005.14165.

Bryant, C., Felice, M., & Briscoe, T. (2017). Automatic annotation and evaluation of error types for grammatical error correction. In *Proceedings of the 55th Annual Meeting of the Association for Computational Linguistics*, Vancouver, Canada, pp. 793–805. https://aclanthology.org/P17-1074.pdf.

Bunch, M., Vaughn, D., & Miel, S. (2016). Automated scoring in assessment systems. In Y. Rosen, S. Ferrar, & M. Mosharraf (Eds.), *Technology Tools for Real-World Skill Development* (pp. 611–626). Hershey, PA: IGI Global.

Burkhardt, A., Woolf, S., Ormerod, C., Kehat, G., & Lottridge, S. (2025, April). *Extending Human and AI Annotations Beyond Argumentative Writing: A Model Transfer Inquiry.* Paper presented at the Annual Meeting of the National Council on Measurement in Education, Denver, CO.

Burleigh, T., Chen, J., & DiCerbo, K. (2025a, October). Pre-pilot optimization of conversation-based assessment items using synthetic response data. In *Proceedings of the Artificial Intelligence in Measurement and Education Conference*, Pittsburgh, PA, pp. 61–68.https://aclanthology.org/2025.aimecon-sessions.7.pdf.

Burleigh, T., Han, J., & DiCerbo, K. (2025b, October). Beyond the hint: Using self-critique to constrain LLM feedback in conversation-based assessment. In *Proceedings of the Artificial Intelligence in Measurement and Education Conference*, Pittsburgh, PA, pp. 71–85. https://aclanthology.org/2025.aimecon-sessions.9.pdf.

Cahill, A., & Evanini, K. (2020). Natural language processing for writing and speaking. In D. Yan, A. Rupp, & P. W. Foltz (Eds.), *Handbook of Automated Scoring: Theory into Practice* (pp. 69–92). Boca Raton, FL: CRC Press.

Cambium Assessment. (n.d.). Did you know? https://www.cambiumassessment.com/did-you-know.html.

Chu, Z., Liu, C., Zahn, J., Wang, Z., Hao, X., Zhang, S., & Chen, X. (2025). Effect of collaboration in digital game-based learning: The rules of flow experience and intrinsic motivation. *Journal of Computer Assisted Learning, 41*(4), e70065.

Correnti, R., Matsumara, L.C., Wang, E.L., Litman, D., & Zhang, H. (2022). Building a validity argument for an automated writing evaluation system (eRevise) as a formative assessment. *Computers and Education Open, 3*, 100084 https://doi.org/10.1016/j.caeo.2022.100084.

D'Brot, J. (2019, November). *Theories of Action Aren't Enough: An Argument for Logic Models.* https://www.nciea.org/blog/theories-of-action-arent-enough-an-argument-for-logic-models/.

DiCerbo, K., Burleigh, T., & Deters, L. (2025, April). *Comparing LLMs in Conversational Interactions*. Paper presented at the annual conference of the National Council on Measurement in Education, Denver, CO.

Education Northwest. (n.d.). *6+1 Trait Rubrics.* https://educationnorthwest.org/resources/61-trait-rubrics.

Funnell, S., & Rogers, P. (2011). *Purposeful Program Theory: Effective Use of Theories of Change and Logic Models*, 1st edition. San Francisco, CA: Jossy-Bass.

Gao, Y., Xiong, Y., Gao, X, Jia, K., Pan, J., Bi, Y., Dai, Y., Sun, J., Wang, M., &Wang, H. (2024). *Retrieval-augmented Generation for Large Language Models: A Survey.* arXiv. https://arxiv.org/abs/2312.10997.

Hattie, J., & Timperley, H. (2007). The power of feedback. *Review of Educational Research, 77*(1), 81–112.

Ho, A. (2022). Specifying the three Ws in educational measurement: Who uses which scores for what purpose? *Journal of Educational Measurement, 59*(4), 418–422. https://onlinelibrary.wiley.com/doi/10.1111/jedm.12355

Holt, L. (2024, April). The 5 percent problem: Online mathematics programs may benefit most the kids who need it the least. *Education Next, 24*(4), 26–30. https://www.educationnext.org/5-percent-problem-online-mathematics-programs-may-benefit-most-kids-who-need-it-least/.

HuggingFace. (n.d.). *The AI Community for Building the Future*. https://huggingface.co/.

Institute of Education Sciences. (2022, January). *Four Teams Win Top Prize in Automated Scoring Challenge for the Nation's Report Card.* https://github.com/NAEP-AS-Challenge/reading-prediction/blob/main/automated_scoring_press_release.pdf.

Institute of Education Sciences. (2025). *ESSA Tiers of Evidence: What You Need to Know.* https://ies.ed.gov/ies/2025/01/essa-tiers-evidence.

James, G., Witten, D., Hastie, T., & Tibshirani, R. (2017). *An Introduction to Statistical Learning with Applications in R.* New York: Springer.

Khan Academy. (2024, November 1). *Khan Academy Privacy Policy.* https://www.khanacademy.org/about/privacy-policy.

Khan Academy Blog. (2022, January 26). *We Count on You! Protecting Privacy, Enabling Analytics*. https://blog.khanacademy.org/we-count-on-you-balancing-privacy-and-analytics/.

Khan Academy Blog. (2025, August 1). *Khan Academy Improves State Test Scores: Results from New 3-Year Efficacy Study.* https://blog.khanacademy.org/khan-academy-improves-state-test-scores-results-from-new-3-year-efficacy-study/.

Khan Academy Help Center. (n.d.). *What Safety Features Does Khanmigo Have?* https://support.khanacademy.org/hc/en-us/articles/14394814244365-What-safety-features-does-Khanmigo-have.

Lemire, S., Porowski, A., & Mumma, K. (2023). *How We Model Matters: Visualizing Program Theories*. Rockville, MD: Abt Associates.

Li, T., Hong, M., Matsumura, L., Wang, E., Litman, D., & Correnti, R. (2025, October). Chain-of-thought prompting for automated evaluation of revision patterns in young student writing. In *Proceedings of the Artificial Intelligence in Measurement in Education Conference*, Pittsburgh, PA, 49–65.

Li, T., Liu, Z., Matsumura, L., Wang, E., Litman, D., & Correnti, R. (2024). Using large language models to assess young students' writing revisions. In *Proceedings of the 19th Workshop on Innovative Use of NLP for Building Educational Applications,* Mexico City, Mexico, pp. 365–380.

Liu, Z., Litman, D., Wang, E., Li, T., Gobat, M., Matsumura, L., & Correnti, R. (2025, April). eRevise+RF: A writing evaluation system for assessing student essay revisions and providing formative feedback. In *Proceedings of the 2025 Conference of the Nations of the Americas Chapter of the Association for Computational Linguistics: Human Language Technologies (System Demonstrations)*, Albuquerque, NM, pp. 173–190. https://arxiv.org/abs/2501.00715.

Liu, Z., Litman, D., Wang, E., Matsumura, L., & Correnti, R. (2023). Predicting the quality of revisions in argumentative writing. In *Proceedings of the Eighteenth Workshop on Innovative Use of NLP for Building Educational Applications,* Toronto, CA, pp. 275–287.

Lottridge, S., Ormerod, C., & Burkhardt (2025, April). *Development and Validation of an AWE System "Write on with Cambi!".* Paper presented at the annual conference of the National Council on Measurement in Education, Denver, CO. https://files.portal.cambiumast.com/corporate-site/documents/CAI-Development-and-Validation-of-Write-on-With-Cambi.pdf.

Lottridge, S., Ormerod, C., & Jafari, A. (2023). Psychometric considerations in using deep learning models for automated scoring. In V. Yaneva & M. von Davier (Eds.), *Natural Language Processing Applications in Assessment*, NCME Educational Measurement and Assessment Book Series (pp. 15–30). New York, NY: Routledge.

Lottridge, S., Ormerod, C., & Patel, M. (2024). Redesigning automated scoring engines to include deep learning models. In M. Shermis & J. Wilson (Eds.), *The Routledge International Handbook of Automated Essay Evaluation* (pp. 487–503). New York: Taylor and Francis.

Miller, P., & DiCerbo, K. (2024). LLM based math tutoring: Challenges and dataset. *Khan Academy GitHub.* https://github.com/Khan/tutoring-accuracy-dataset.

MI Write. (n.d.-a). *What Is MI Write?* https://www.miwrite.com/research.

MI Write. (n.d.-b). *Privacy Policy.* https://www.miwrite.com/privacy-policy.

MI Write. (n.d.-c). *Terms of Service.* https://www.miwrite.com/terms-of-service.

Motorola Solutions. (2025, July 24). *Motorola Solutions Introduces 'AI nutrition labels,' A First for Public Safety & Enterprise Security Products.* https://www.motorolasolutions.com/newsroom/press-releases/motorola-solutions-introduces-ai-nutrition-labels.html.

National Council on Measurement in Education. (2018). *Position Statement on Theories of Action for Testing Programs.* https://higherlogicdownload.s3.amazonaws.com/NCME/c53581e4-9882-4137-987b-4475f6cb502a/UploadedImages/Documents/NCME_Position_Paper_on_Theories_of_Action_-_Final_July__2018.pdf.

National Institute of Standards and Technology. (2023). *Artificial Intelligence Risk Management Framework (AI RMF 1.0).* https://nvlpubs.nist.gov/nistpubs/ai/NIST.AI.100-1.pdf.

Ofgang, E. (2024, April 17). What is Khanmigo? The GPT-4 learning tool explained by Sal Khan. *Tech & Learning.* https://www.techlearning.com/news/what-is-khanmigo-the-gpt-4-learning-tool-explained-by-sal-khan.

Open Ethics Initiative. (n.d.). *Open Ethics Label: AI Nutrition Labels.* https://openethics.ai/label/.

Oregon Department of Education. (2025, March). *Generative Artificial Intelligence (AI) in K-12 Classrooms.* https://www.oregon.gov/ode/educator-resources/teachingcontent/Documents/Generative%20Artificial%20Intelligence%20(AI)%20in%20K-12%20Classrooms%20v2.pdf.

Ormerod, C., Burkhardt, A., Young, M., & Lottridge, S. (2023). *Argumentation Element Annotation Modeling Using XLNet.* arXiv:2311.06239.

Palermo, C., & Thompson, M.M. (2018). Teacher implementation of self-regulated strategy development with an automated writing evaluation system: Effects on the argumentative writing performance of middle school students. *Contemporary Educational Psychology, 54*, 255–270.

Palermo, C., & Wilson, J. (2020). Implementing automated writing evaluation in different instructional contexts: A mixed-methods study. *Journal of Writing Research, 12*(1), 63–108. https://doi.org/10.17239/jowr-2020.12.01.04.

Pershan, M. (2025, August 10). *Practice Software Is Struggling: Why Whole-Group Teaching Is Easier Than Individual Practice.* https://pershmail.substack.com/p/practice-software-is-struggling?utm_campaign=post&utm_medium=web&triedRedirect=true.

Pundhir, A. (2025, December 9). The AI nutrition label: The case for AI transparency in 2026. *Forbes.* https://www.forbes.com/councils/forbestechcouncil/2025/12/09/the-ai-nutrition-label-the-case-for-ai-transparency-in-2026/.

Robertson, S. (2025, March 20). Meet Khanmigo Writing Coach: Helping learners become better writers. *Khan Academy Blog.* https://blog.khanacademy.org/meet-khanmigo-writing-coach-helping-learners-become-better-writers/.

Sairam, K., Burkhardt, A., & Lottridge, S. (2025, October). The impact of an NLP-based writing tool on student writing. In *Proceedings of the Artificial Intelligence in Measurement and Education Conference*, Pittsburgh, PA, pp. 115–123. https://aclanthology.org/2025.aimecon-sessions.14.pdf.

Shermis, M. D. (2014). State-of-the-art automated essay scoring: Competition, results, and future directions from a United States demonstration. *Assessing Writing, 20*, 53–76. https://doi.org/10.1016/j.asw.2013.04.001.

Shermis, M. D., & Hamner, B. (2013). Contrasting state-of-the-art automated scoring of essays. In M. Shermis & J Berstein (Eds.), *Handbook of Automated Essay Evaluation: Current Applications and New Directions* (pp. 313–346). New York, NY: Routledge.

Shi, H., Zhang, N., Caskurlu, S., & Na, H. (2025). Applications of machine learning for at-risk student prediction of online education: A 10-year systemic review of literature. *Journal of Computer Assisted Learning, 41*(4), e70058.

Stahlberg, F., & Kumar, S. (2021). Synthetic data generation for grammatical error correction with tagged corruption models. In *Proceedings of the 16th Workshop on Innovative Use of NLP for Building Educational Applications*, Online (pp. 37–47). Retrieved from https://www.aclweb.org/ anthology/2021.bea-1.4.

Twilio. (n.d.). *AI Nutrition Facts.* https://nutrition-facts.ai/.

U.S. Department of Education, Office of Educational Technology. (2024). *Designing for Education with Artificial Intelligence: An Essential Guide for Developers.* Washington, DC: U.S. Department of Education, Office of Educational Technology. https://files.eric.ed.gov/fulltext/ED661949.pdf

Weatherholtz, K., Millwood Hill, K., DiCerbo, K., Wells, W., Grimaldi, P., Miller-Vedam, M., Hogg, C., & Yamkovenko, B. (2025, October). Cognitive engagement in genAI tutor conversations: At-scale measurement and impact on learning. In *Proceedings of the Artificial Intelligence in Measurement and Education Conference*, Pittsburgh, PA, pp. 40–48. https://aclanthology.org/2025.aimecon-wip.6.pdf.

Williamson, D., Xi, X., & Breyer, J. (2012). A framework for the evaluation and use of automated scoring. *Educational Measurement: Issues and Practice, 31*(1), 2–13.
Wilson, J., Ahrendt, C., Fudge, E., Raiche, A., Beard, G, & MacArther, C. (2021a). Elementary teachers' perceptions of automated feedback and automated scoring: Transforming teaching and learning of writing using automated writing evaluation. *Computers & Education, 168*, 104208.
Wilson, J., Huang, Y., Palermo, C., Beard, G., & MacArthur, C. (2021b). Automated feedback and automated scoring in the elementary grades: Usage, attitudes, and associates with writing outcomes in a districtwide implementation of MI Write. *International Journal of Artificial Intelligence in Education, 31*, 234–276.
Wilson, J., Myers, M.C., & Potter, A. (2022). Investigating the promise of automated writing evaluation for supporting formative writing assessment at scale. *Assessment in Education: Principles, Policy & Practice, 29*(2), 183–199.
Wilson, J., Palermo, C., Myers, M., Cordero, T.C., Eacker, H., Coles, J., & Potter, A. (2023). *Impact of MI Write Automated Evaluation of Middle-Grade Writing Outcomes.* Paper presented at the Annual Meeting of the National Council of Measurement in Education, Chicago, IL.
Wilson, J., Zhang, F., Palermo, C., Cordero, T.C., Myers, M., Eacker, H., Pottery, A., & Coles, J. (2024). Predictors of middle school students' perceptions of automated writing evaluation. *Computers & Education, 211*, 104985.
Wisconsin Department of Public Instruction. (2024, December). *AI Guidance for Enhancing K-12 and Library Education.* https://dpi.wi.gov/sites/default/files/imce/imt/doc/AI_Guidance_for_Enhancing_K-12_and_Library_Education.pdf.
Young, M., Burkhardt, A., Wilson, Q., & Lottridge, S. (2025, April). *A Framework for Evaluating Automated Conventions Feedback.* Paper presented at the Annual Meeting of the National Council of Measurement in Education, Denver, CO.
Zahi, C., Wibowo, S., & Lily, D. (2024). The effects of over-reliance on AI dialogue systems on student's cognitive abilities: A systematic review. *Smart Learning Environments, 11*(28). https://doi.org/10.1186/s40561-024-00316-7
Zhang, H., & Litman, D. (2020a). Automated topical component extractions using neural network attention scores from source-based essay scoring. In *Proceedings of the 58th Annual Meeting of the Association for Computational Linguistics*, Online, 8569–8584.
Zhang, H., & Litman, D. (2020b). Essay quality signals as weak supervision for source-based essay scoring. In *Proceedings of the 16th Workshop on Innovative Use of NLP for Building Educational Applications*, Online, pp. 85–96.
Zhang, H., Magooda, A., Litman, D., Correnti, R., Wang, E., Matsumura, L., Howe, E., & Quintana, R. (2019, February). eRevise: Using natural language processing to provide formative feedback on text evidence usage in student writing. In *Proceedings of the 31st AAAI Conference on Innovative Applications in Artificial Intelligence*, Honolulu, HI, vol. 33, pp. 9619–9625.

5

PERSONALIZATION IN ASSESSMENT TO OPTIMIZE ENGAGEMENT AND PERFORMANCE

Burcu Arslan, Randy E. Bennett, Sandip Sinharay, Jesse R. Sparks, and Kadriye Ercikan

5.1 Why Personalize?

In educational measurement, standardization generally has two meanings. One meaning relates to creating norms for referencing scores, as in a "test standardization sample." A second meaning is the one of interest here, which is that of giving examinees equal treatment. In its strict form, this type of standardization gives each examinee essentially the same test content in the same format under the same conditions, with their responses judged using the same rules. This meaning of standardization was brought to the emerging field of educational measurement in the early 20th century from the physical sciences via the also-new field of experimental psychology[1]. In an experimental context, the idea is simple: manipulate one variable while holding all other factors constant to identify the effect of the manipulated variable on some outcome. In testing, standardization is intended to isolate the measured variable by holding all other conditions constant. What standardization cannot do, of course, is hold *examinee* characteristics constant. The practice works very effectively when examinee populations are relatively homogeneous; that is, when construct-irrelevant characteristics that might be correlated with the measured variable do not in fact vary much (e.g., all examinees are of a similar social class). In the ideal case, when all examinees are exactly the same on every related characteristic except for the one being measured, the only factor significantly influencing the test score will be the target variable.

Ironically, among the first to remark on the need for relative homogeneity was Carl Brigham. In his book, *A Study of American Intelligence* (1923), he compared the performance of different racial/ethnic groups on the Army Alpha and Beta intelligence tests. Being recruited for service during World War I, the tested population was highly heterogeneous on multiple dimensions. Using unquestionably

DOI: 10.4324/9781003621522-5

racist language, Brigham, a eugenicist, interpreted the observed racial/ethnic group differences as signaling the impending progressive decline of the national population's intelligence. Seven years later, he published an article in *Psychological Review* (Brigham, 1930) that ended with a one-sentence retraction. Leading up to the retraction, he wrote,

> For purposes of comparing individuals or groups, it is apparent that tests in the vernacular must be used only with individuals having equal opportunities to acquire the vernacular of the test. This requirement precludes the use of such tests in making comparative studies of individuals brought up in homes in which the vernacular of the test is not used, or in which two vernaculars are used.
>
> *(p. 165)*

The consequential uses of standardized tests that followed World War I were largely restricted to college and university admissions, where the examinee populations tended to be highly homogeneous, especially for selective institutions where White, male, upper-class applicants constituted the overwhelming majority. Over time, the populations in which consequential tests were used became more diverse. Just before World War II, Harvard adopted the SAT for use in the evaluation of scholarship applicants as a means of attracting a more economically diverse entering class (Conant, 2017; Fuess, 1950). After World War II, the GI Bill funded post-secondary education for a broader social class of applicants, soldiers exiting the service (US Congress, 1944). In both the Harvard and GI Bill cases, however, the examinee populations remained principally male and White.

The U.S. population itself was relatively homogeneous racially/ethnically and linguistically until only recently. In 1980, the population was 20% non-White, 6.2% foreign-born, and 11% speaking a language other than English at home (Dietrich & Hernandez, 2022, Table 1; Frey, 2020; Gibson & Lennon, 1999, Table 1; Hobbs & Stoops, 2002). By 2020, only four decades later, each of those figures had doubled, with 42% non-White, 13.7% foreign-born, and 19% speaking a language other than English at home (Jensen et al., 2021; US Census Bureau, 2024, n.d.). The public-school population, as of 2022, was both majority non-White and eligible for free or reduced-price lunch (National Center for Education Statistics [NCES], 2023, Tables 203.70 and 204.10), an indicator of economic class. This condition has been referred to by Vertovec (2023) as "superdiversity," meaning levels not having been seen before. In addition to heterogeneity of cultural and linguistic backgrounds, examinees come from diverse societal and cultural contexts as well as educational experiences. These contexts shape how individuals learn, how they approach solving problems, and what levels of motivation and engagement they bring to taking assessments (Ercikan & Solano-Flores, in press 2025).

Dramatically increased heterogeneity of populations as well as sociocultural and educational contexts, in the U.S. and elsewhere, suggests the need for assessment approaches that account for differences in language, ways of knowing, cultural identity, interests, prior knowledge, and other sociocultural factors that we have in the past presumed to be approximately equal or otherwise irrelevant in a standardized testing context. In fact, departures from standardization in response to population heterogeneity have been emerging piecemeal for some time (Bennett, 2024). Such departures include adaptive testing to better account for differences in competency level, accommodations for individuals with exceptionalities, language versions for English learners, offering of problem choice to cater to variation of interests and prior knowledge, and at-home testing for those who find a non-center context more conducive. All these departures intend to provide better and fairer measurement by giving individuals opportunities to show what they know and can do in ways suited to them. Additionally, through various justifications and sometimes through statistical linking, the resulting scores may be considered comparable to those from the standardized administration.

5.2 Forms and Types of Personalization

5.2.1 Forms of Personalization

All the above-cited departures are, in essence, micro-personalizations. Micro-personalizations are, as the name implies, quite limited in nature. Typical adaptive testing, for instance, personalizes on only one variable, the competency being measured, choosing the next item (or set) based on a dynamically updated competency estimate. Personalized assessment in fuller realization is far more complex, and similar to personalized learning, it can be achieved in several ways (see Plass & Pawar, 2020, for a taxonomy of adaptivity in learning).

The most straightforward form of personalization is to design the assessment so that individuals can adjust aspects of it to their particular interests, prior knowledge, cultural identity, and other relevant characteristics. This form of human-driven personalization, or adaptability, involves learners actively making choices about the assessment content and experience, which can promote agency, intrinsic motivation, and engagement (Bernacki et al., 2021; Plass & Pawar, 2020; Walkington & Bernacki, 2020). For example, examinees may choose the difficulty of the items (e.g., self-adaptive testing; Wise et al., 1992, 2002) or response formats (Wilschut et al., 2024). Notably, human-driven personalization aligns with self-determination theory, which emphasizes agency as a basic human need and central factor for intrinsic motivation (Ryan & Deci, 2000, 2024). Agency is a multi-faceted construct beyond offering choice and is considered critical for self-regulated learning (Brod, 2026; Brod et al., 2023). Although offering choice in assessments can boost examinee intrinsic motivation and engagement, effectively implementing choice requires careful consideration. Research has shown that too many options can actually decrease engagement (Iyengar & Lepper, 2000), prompting some scholars to suggest limiting the number of choices to between two and four options (O'Neill & Padden, 2022; Patall et al., 2010). One key challenge in applying choice within large-scale assessments is the psychometric complexity of ensuring equivalence across different task options (Wainer & Thissen, 1994), an issue we return to in the "Validation and Related Issues for Personalized Assessments" section. The Advanced Placement (AP) Program's research assessment is an example of human-driven personalization (College Board, 2023). This through-course performance task includes an academic paper on a topic of the student's choice, a presentation, and an oral defense, all of which contribute to their score. The personalization is in the choice afforded the examinee as to topic, method, and other aspects of the project's substance and conduct, all of which allow the examinee to bring their characteristics to the examination in whatever ways they feel might best show their capability. One complexity attendant to this approach is in scoring, as each examinee produces a unique performance.

Another form of personalization includes a machine-driven approach. Rather than the examinee making adjustments to suit the assessment to themselves, the machine uses information it has about the examinee to design an assessment uniquely for them. That is, from a vector of values describing the examinee's characteristics, an assessment is created to be "optimal" for them, the precise meaning of optimality being one of the complexities. This approach utilizes computational cognitive models or (generative) artificial intelligence (AI) methods (Bulut et al., 2025; Corbett et al., 2000; Falmagne et al., 1990; Shin & Bulut, 2022) to personalize the assessment in real time, ideally based on a (scrutable or integrated) learner model (Bellarhmouch et al., 2023; Sparks et al., 2024; Zapata-Rivera, 2020; Zapata-Rivera & Arslan, 2021; Zapata-Rivera et al., 2020) that provides a transparent, cohesive understanding of a learner's progress, strengths, and needs across multiple dimensions and which can support more personalized, timely, and effective interventions while also maintaining trust in the system. Despite the advantages of machine-driven personalization, fully automated systems risk misalignment with learner needs, especially for neurodivergent populations, whose behaviors may deviate from normative models (Arslan et al., 2025b). Learner models may also fail to capture nuanced cognitive, affective, or contextual states, leading to ineffective adaptations (Arslan et al., 2025b). To mitigate these risks related to uncertainty in the machine-driven adaptations, a human-in-the-loop approach is essential. Realizing this type of personalized assessment, especially in the high-stakes assessment context, is hugely challenging, so it is reasonable that no operational examples yet exist at scale. However, with the prodigious advances in AI that have occurred over the past several years, examples may soon be coming.

A final approach for personalization is to combine the two methods in a hybrid fashion. Instead of a unidimensional view of giving control to humans versus machines, human-centered AI frameworks, such as the two-dimensional model proposed by Shneiderman (2022), emphasize the importance of balancing high levels of machine-driven automation with strong human control to ensure transparency, safety, and user satisfaction. In the context of educational assessment, recommender systems exemplify this balance by using AI algorithms to suggest one or more options, while still allowing learners to override or select from the provided recommendations (Arslan et al., 2025b). Generative AI (genAI) can further support a hybrid model of personalization due to its on-the-fly generative capabilities, in which learners provide input to the genAI model and the genAI model personalizes the content in real time (e.g., Arslan, 2024; Arslan et al., 2025a). Additionally, genAI-enabled chatbots could assist learners by answering usability questions or providing language support (Arslan et al., 2024). However, assessment designers should proceed cautiously when implementing on-the-fly personalization using genAI, especially in the high-stakes assessment context. It is critical to ensure that the core principles of educational assessment (i.e., validity, reliability, and fairness) are upheld and that genAI tools are used responsibly and ethically (Arslan et al., 2024; see also Johnson, 2025, for principles and practices for responsible AI for measurement and learning).

5.2.2 On What Student Characteristics Should We Personalize?

Beyond different approaches to personalization, it is also important to consider the student-level characteristics, or individual differences, on which assessments should be personalized. The targeted factors can contribute to a *student profile* that includes information about students' characteristics (e.g., knowledge, interests, linguistic and cultural backgrounds) as well as contextual factors such as their prior opportunities to learn (Lehman et al., 2024b; Sparks et al., 2024). These student profiles can be used to adapt the assessment in ways that offer a more personalized experience tuned to the characteristics that students bring with them to the assessment. For our purposes, we focus on the following student characteristics to drive personalization, given their critical relevance to learning and assessment: prior performance, prior knowledge, cognitive effort and interests, language background, and cultural backgrounds.

Prior performance. Traditionally, approaches to adaptivity have primarily considered students' prior performance as the basis on which to personalize. In the context of personalized learning, adaptive learning technologies typically adjust the level or type of content to align with students' current level of competency, based on their performance to date on related tasks, to help students develop toward skill mastery (Peng et al., 2019; Shemshack et al., 2021). In educational assessment, personalization based on student performance is best exemplified by computerized adaptive testing (CAT; Lord, 1980; van der Linden & Glas, 2000). In a typical CAT, an examinee's competency level estimated from performance on prior items is used to determine what item(s) to present next, usually in terms of the appropriate level of difficulty (i.e., neither too easy nor too difficult) given the current estimate of the examinee's ability (Wainer et al., 2000). Such approaches are commonly implemented in operational standardized testing programs. However, reliance on cognitive factors like prior performance alone may be insufficient as a means for deeper personalization in educational assessment that reflects a more holistic conception of students' experiences (du Boulay, 2018; Sparks et al., 2024; Zapata-Rivera, 2017).

Prior knowledge. Personalized assessments should be grounded in an understanding of each student's prior knowledge. Domain-specific knowledge can have both facilitative (e.g., chunking, strategy use, evaluation) and inhibitive (e.g., misconceptions, biases) effects on learning and performance (see Simonsmeier et al., 2022). Students enter educational environments with diverse experiences, knowledge, and skill levels, which influence how they process information during the assessment (Arslan & Tenison, 2025). When students are presented with a novel assessment task, to provide a response, they need to retrieve prior knowledge from their long-term memory and use it with their previously learned procedural skills and strategies (Anderson, 2007; Taatgen, 2013). Therefore, personalized assessment environments should make the adaptations by considering both declarative (factual) knowledge and procedural skills to guide content selection, feedback, and scheduling. Developers should consider both the quantity of knowledge (high vs. low) and the quality (domain-specific vs. general, accurate vs. inaccurate) of knowledge in determining how to personalize assessment tasks (McCarthy et al., 2018, 2023; O'Reilly et al., 2019; Sparks et al., 2026; Wang et al., 2021).

Cognitive effort and interests. Student motivation and engagement are critical to better assess what students know and can do (Nakkula & Toshalis, 2025). When students do not give full cognitive effort when responding to an assessment task, the validity of the interpretation of assessment scores can be threatened (Finn, 2015; Lehman et al., 2024a; Wise & DeMars, 2005). In low-stakes assessment contexts, examinees may not always be cognitively engaged with assessment tasks due to the lack of direct consequences for them. In these contexts, optimizing engagement becomes necessary in order to support a valid interpretation of assessment results (Wise & DeMars, 2005). A way of optimizing engagement is personalizing the assessment task context based on student interests. For example, students could input their out-of-school interests, and genAI could dynamically tailor mathematics word problem contexts in real time (Arslan, 2024). Another way of optimizing engagement is detecting disengaged or not (fully) effortful responses and introducing warnings or nudges to students during the assessment (e.g., Arslan & Finn, 2023; Wise et al., 2006) or selecting the assessment questions or content considering student engagement (e.g., Bulut et al., 2025).

Language background. Personalization in terms of students' language background is a commonly implemented operational practice, especially in the context of large-scale international assessments such as the Programme for International Student Assessment (PISA), Program for the International Assessment of Adult Competencies, Trends in International Mathematics and Science Study, and Progress in International Reading Literacy Study. Administering test forms in different languages as appropriate for the sample populations enables cross-national comparisons in terms of the targeted knowledge, skills, and abilities. In these cases, assessment design is tightly controlled to ensure that items remain comparable, locally relevant, and comprehensible throughout the process of translating the test into the different languages. Rigorous statistical analyses are also performed after administration to facilitate comparability across groups (OECD, 2024).

Cultural background. Recent decades have seen a resurgence of interest in personalizing educational assessments to students' cultural backgrounds and identities, toward culturally (or socioculturally) relevant, responsive, and sustaining assessment approaches (Bennett, 2023, 2024; Bennett et al., 2025; Evans & Taylor, 2025; Hood, 1998; Lee, 1998). Collectively, these approaches aim to "design assessment for the social, cultural, and other relevant characteristics of diverse students and the contexts in which they live" (Bennett, 2023, p. 86), with the intent to make assessments that are aligned with the knowledge, experiences, interests, and values of students from diverse backgrounds who otherwise may not be well served or see themselves represented in traditional assessments that reflect dominant majority cultures (Bennett, 2023; Randall, 2021; Randall et al., 2021; Walker et al., 2023). Thus, designing assessments to be socioculturally responsive necessitates intentional consideration of a wide range of student characteristics, including prior knowledge, interests, languages, and identities, incorporating assessment content and contexts that celebrate these cultural characteristics as assets (O'Dwyer et al., 2023) and responding in ways that meaningfully reflect their intersections (Lehman et al., 2024b; Sparks et al., 2024).

5.2.3 Implementing Personalization in Item, Task, and Test Designs

Once developers have determined the characteristics and behaviors on which to personalize, they must make design decisions regarding how to implement personalization in response to those qualities. Here, we briefly discuss several relevant frameworks and approaches to support the design of personalization in assessment.

Caring assessment. Implementing personalization in assessment requires designing and deploying adaptations to assessment content and contexts to meet individual students' needs and in response to their characteristics and behaviors. This personalization can occur at the item level, through adjustments to content, difficulty, or order, or at the assessment level, through supports such as language accommodations, nudges, or feedback. The framework for caring assessment (Zapata-Rivera, 2017; see also Lehman et al., 2024b; Sparks et al., 2024) specifies that personalized adaptations, supports, and feedback can be implemented at three time points: before, during, and after students take the assessment. Adaptations *before the assessment* can leverage information embedded in student profiles or integrated learner models to deliver different assessment or task versions to examinees based on known characteristics of the student. Assigning different language versions of an assessment based on students' home language or language of instruction reflects this type of adaptation. As another example, students with limited prior knowledge of a topic may be routed to an alternate assessment form with a more familiar topic, or to a version with supplemental background material that can enable them to engage with the target topic (Sparks et al., 2026). Personalized supports can be dynamically implemented *during the assessment* by tracking students' actions and interactions within the task (e.g., item responses, behavioral engagement) and responding by providing just-in-time interventions (e.g., nudges, messaging) in response to the detected states (Arslan & Finn, 2023; Wise et al., 2006). Personalized feedback can be provided *after the assessment* by tailoring score reports by contextualizing students' performance in terms of their characteristics (e.g., prior knowledge, interest, language proficiency) and demonstrated behaviors (e.g., engagement, technical issues) to support deeper interpretations and more precise next steps for instruction or assessment (Zapata-Rivera et al., 2025).

Universal design of assessment. More generally, personalized assessments should be designed to maximize fairness for *all* examinees. The Standards for Educational and Psychological Testing (AERA, APA, & NCME, 2014) emphasizes the application of *universal design* principles to promote fairness by maximizing the accessibility of assessments across diverse individuals and subgroups, while minimizing the introduction of construct-irrelevant variance that may differentially affect particular subgroups (Ketterlin-Geller, 2005). Universal Design for Learning guidelines recommend offering multiple means of engagement (e.g., offering personalized choices that align with learner identities and motivations), multiple means of representation (e.g., presenting information in multiple modalities as appropriate for the construct of interest), and multiple means of action and expression (e.g., flexibility in response modes by which students can demonstrate their knowledge, skills, and other attributes, including affordances for students with perceptual and motor disabilities; CAST, 2024).

Recently, Laitusis and Karvonen (2025) expanded prior work into an overarching framework of Universal Design of Assessment Systems (UDAS) that goes beyond the design and administration of large-scale assessments to consider how universal design can be applied to different kinds of assessments (e.g., classroom and formative assessments) and can consider the needs of all relevant stakeholders (e.g., teachers, parents, and score users outside of the student by item interactions). UDAS emphasizes that assessments should (1) meet psychological needs, including autonomy, competence, and relatedness; (2) design for flexibility and learner variability, including inclusiveness in construct definition, flexibility in representations, and flexibility in action and expression; and (3) safeguard for fair, responsible, and equitable use, including proactively evaluating validity, promoting intended interpretations and discouraging inappropriate uses, promoting assessment literacy, and building in consequences for misuse of scores. Application of UDAS and related principles can help to ensure that personalized assessments flexibly and responsibly meet the needs of all students.

Evidence-based dynamic personalization for learning and assessment tools (ED-PLAT). Forms of personalization (i.e., human-driven, machine-driven, or hybrid) require evidence-based decisions. Currently, there is insufficient evidence regarding when, at what level, and on which features control should be given to examinees and/or machines. To this end, Arslan et al. (2025b) recently introduced a framework, ED-PLAT, comprising three steps. The first step involves identifying the necessary features of the learning and assessment environment (e.g., item context, response method) and reviewing existing theories and literature to identify the effects of selected features on learners' motivation, affect, cognition, and perception/motor characteristics so that the intended effects are explicit. The second step involves collecting empirical evidence (e.g., controlled experiments, A/B tests, user feedback) on whether learner agency or system automation best improves the defined outcomes for the targeted population, including neurodiverse learners who are most at risk from misaligned learner models used for machine-driven personalization. Finally, the third step involves assigning control at the feature level to the learner, machine, or both and dynamically updating the control assignment based on empirical evidence, while keeping teachers as active monitors who can intervene when data are sparse or context shifts.

5.3 Evidence Supporting Efficacy of Personalization

While there are many possible rationales for and theoretical conceptions to guide the implementation of personalization in assessment contexts, empirical evidence demonstrating that such personalization achieves its goal of optimizing performance and engagement is still in an emergent stage. Evidence for the efficacy of *personalized learning* approaches has been summarized in various systematic reviews and meta-analyses (e.g., Alrawashdeh et al., 2024; Bernacki et al., 2021; Lin et al., 2024; Major et al., 2021; Zheng et al., 2022).

For example, a meta-analysis of 34 publications, covering 34 effect sizes, examined the effects of technology-facilitated personalized learning (vs. control groups that did not use technology-facilitated personalized learning) and reported a medium-to-large effect (Hedges' $g = 0.67$) on learning achievements and a small-sized effect (Hedges' $g = 0.26$) on learning perceptions (e.g., attitudes, motivation) with variation in effect sizes based on moderators such as number of learning methods used and the type of personalized learning software used (i.e., personalized prompts showed the largest effect size, followed by personalized guidance, personalized diagnosis, and personalized learning suggestions; Zheng et al., 2022).

In the domain of reading literacy, a meta-analysis of 27 publications, covering 27 effect sizes, examined the effects of personalized and adaptive learning technology (as compared to non-personalized learning software or traditional, non-technology-based learning materials) for K–12 students and observed an overall small but positive effect size (Hedges' $g = 0.29$) on reading skill proficiency, with variation in effect sizes based on study features (i.e., teachers' role, intervention dosage, and use of blended instruction) and student characteristics (e.g., grade level, socioeconomic status; Alrawashdeh et al., 2024).

Going beyond performance-based outcomes, Lin et al.'s (2024) a meta-analysis on interest-based personalization, covering 26 interest effect sizes, eight cognitive load effect sizes, 46 retention effect sizes, and six transfer effect sizes from 34 publications, reported that when compared to non-personalization control conditions, personalization showed a medium-to-large effect on interest (overall Hedges' $g = 0.55$; in math Hedges' $g = 0.64$), a medium-to-large effect on cognitive load (Hedges' $g = 0.54$), a medium effect on learning retention (Hedges' $g = 0.48$), and a medium effect on learning transfer (Hedges' $g = 0.36$). Lin et al. (2024) reported significant heterogeneity of interest effect sizes based on diagnostic approach (significant effects for survey-based vs. technology-based approaches to personalization), grain size (significant effects for personalization to individuals vs. group-level personalization), and content domain (significant effects obtained for math vs. other domains), and significant heterogeneity of retention effect sizes based on continent (studies conducted in Asia and North America showed significant effects, but studies conducted in Europe and Africa did not) and methodology (quasi-experiments showed larger effect sizes than experiments, but both effects were statistically significant). Generally, then, evidence favors implementation of personalized learning, conditional on what types of personalization are implemented, how they are implemented, and with whom.

With respect to evidence supporting *personalized assessment*, as noted previously, there are as yet very few existing operational examples of personalized assessment being implemented at scale to determine the impacts of personalization on students' assessment performance, although no doubt more examples will emerge and evidence will soon be available as advances in AI enable more instances of personalization at scale. However, several notable recent examples indicate the promise of aligning assessment features to students' characteristics (Sinharay et al., 2025a; Sparks et al., 2026; Wang et al., 2025) in ways that are consistent with a caring assessment approach.

Wang et al. (2025) examined the impact of socioculturally relevant assessment in the context of scenario-based assessments (SBAs) of reading comprehension skills in a digital environment. The authors examined the reading comprehension performance of approximately 7,000 high school students responding to one of three SBA forms covering different topics, including ecosystems and invasive species, European immigration to the U.S., and the Harlem Renaissance cultural movement of the early 20th century. Because the Harlem Renaissance has historical and cultural significance for African Americans, it was predicted that this topic should be more familiar, and the assessment more engaging and supportive of performance, for Black students as compared to the other topics. Indeed, results indicated that Black students had significantly lower topic knowledge of ecosystems and immigration compared to non-Black students, but comparable knowledge of the Harlem Renaissance topic, based on topical background knowledge measures administered prior to the assessment. Differences in topical knowledge coincided with differences in test-taking engagement; Black and non-Black students demonstrated similar levels of engagement (based on time-on-task) on the Harlem Renaissance topic, while Black students showed lower levels of engagement on the other two topics. Finally, score differences between Black and non-Black student groups were smaller on the Harlem Renaissance form (both groups demonstrated comparable performance, controlling for prior achievement based on state standardized test scores for English Language Arts), while Black students showed lower scores than non-Black students on the other two forms. All SBA forms demonstrated comparable reliability and psychometric quality, indicating that culturally relevant test forms can be administered to target student groups in ways that maximize engagement, minimize group-level score differences, and maintain technical quality.

Sparks et al. (2026) further examined relationships between examinees' prior knowledge and their engagement and performance on a reading comprehension SBA. Using data from approximately 1,300 middle school students, the authors administered measures of topical background knowledge, as well as novel measures of self-reported funds of knowledge and experiences, to examine relationships among different facets of prior knowledge and students' performance on an SBA on the topic of organic farming. After controlling for student demographics (i.e., race/ethnicity, gender, grade level, free/reduced lunch eligibility, special education status, and English learner status), topical vocabulary measures explained an additional 27% of variance in SBA scores. Incorporating self-reported knowledge and experience measures into the model explained a small, but statistically significant, additional amount of variance (2%) over and above demographics and topic knowledge. Adding test-taking engagement (based on time-on-task) explained a further 18% of variance in SBA scores. The authors concluded that by administering self-report measures of knowledge and experience in addition to topical vocabulary knowledge measures commonly used in SBA contexts, more nuanced personalized test versions or dynamic supports could be implemented within the SBA to enhance the degree to which students can effectively access the test materials.

Sinharay et al. (2025b) examined the impact of presenting test items adapted to contain vocabulary, contexts, and scenarios relevant to Hispanic cultures (i.e., Mexican, Dominican, and Puerto Rican) prevalent in the U.S. Adaptations were made of NAEP Grade 8 mathematics items and were administered in adapted and original versions to approximately 950 students from different states. Analyses indicated that adapted test items resulted in a 25% reduction in the average score difference between Hispanic and White students and, as would be expected, no notable reduction in the gap between White and African American students. Although only modest effects were obtained for the contextualized items, the adaptations were themselves minimal and largely reflected surface-level, as opposed to deeper, customizations (for the importance of depth, see Walkington & Bernacki, 2014). The authors suggested potential future directions in terms of expanding the degree of adaptation, exploring adaptations for other subgroups of examinees (e.g., African American students), examining effects of similar adaptations in other domains (e.g., literacy), and exploring additional sources of evidence (e.g., richer process data from students' interactions within the assessment). Thus, the findings of Sinharay et al. (2025b) indicate that even surface-level adaptations have the potential to impact students' assessment experiences in ways that enhance fairness.

5.4 Validation and Related Issues for Personalized Assessments

While personalization in assessment may lead to several benefits, there is a lack of theory and empirical research on its measurement characteristics, including validation (e.g., Buzick et al., 2023). There are several key issues to consider in creating scores from assessments that may vary in content and format across individuals, but for which valid, fair, and comparable interpretations are desired. Key to validity and fairness is the degree to which personalized assessments produce construct comparability and score comparability. In the sections below, we first discuss data versus construct comparability and comparability of scores and then turn to validation and fairness.

5.4.1 Data versus Construct Comparability

Associated with the extremes of strict standardization and full personalization, Mislevy et al. (2025, p. 202) introduced the notions of data comparability and construct comparability, both of which are maximized in tandem under conditions of strict standardization and high population homogeneity, where scores can be rendered exchangeable across test forms. Under conditions of high population diversity, however, maximizing data comparability through standardization inevitably compromises construct comparability. Requiring all examinees to show what they know and can do within narrow presentation and response constraints, for example, prevents examinees who are unable to work within those constraints from being able to demonstrate competency (e.g., on a test of verbal reasoning presented in written form, decoding challenges may irrelevantly interfere). In contrast, under the same high diversity conditions, departures from standardization afforded by full personalization should work to enhance construct comparability because each examinee is ideally measured in a suitable way. However, data comparability is consequently reduced, as everyone is assessed uniquely.

Construct comparability is a claim that needs to be backed with a validity argument (e.g., Sinharay et al., 2025a). That argument should ideally be founded in theory, logic, and data. The theoretical and logical elements can include descriptions of how a high-level construct definition, scoring rubric, and scoring processes work together to allow for unique performances or artifacts to be mapped onto the same common scale. Empirical evidence could include the results of factor analysis, cognitive task analysis, logfile analysis, or other methodologies to demonstrate that scores have approximately similar meanings.

5.4.2 Comparability of Scores on Personalized Assessments

According to the *Standards for Educational and Psychological Testing*, "comparable scores" refer to scores that can be considered interchangeable (e.g., AERA, APA & NCME, 2014, p. 128). In standardized tests, the psychometric procedure of equating allows treating scores as interchangeable (e.g., Dorans, 2012). Several experts, including Dorans and Middleton (2012) and Thissen (2016, p. 203), noted that when a test is adapted for various population groups to account for differences in language, culture, etc., the various versions of the test are essentially "disparate tests." Personalized assessments involve adaptation based on various individual characteristics to different extents, so the different versions of these assessments constitute disparate tests. Thissen (2016) also noted that it is extremely difficult to produce equated scores for disparate tests because of the lack of common items and common examinees, which preclude equating for these tests. Mislevy (2018, p. 242), Sireci (2020), and Winter (2010) also implied the possibility of reduced comparability for personalized assessments. Additionally, it is problematic to collect data that would allow one to equate scores or to examine the extent to which scores on personalized assessments are interchangeable. However, operational practice from other disparate assessments, including translated assessments (e.g., PISA) and assessments involving accommodations, can be brought to bear in the context of personalized assessments to develop several strategies that may allow claiming at least some degree of score comparability.

First, if one is assessing a competency that may be expressed in a wide variety of ways, one can specify an assessment structure that allows for such broad expressions, establish scoring criteria to accommodate that breadth, and then train raters extensively to develop shared standards in how to render reasonably comparable scores on student responses to tasks that may look very different. These scores may then be considered as comparable judgments of achievement across students, conditional on context and the materials, processes, and ideas that they chose to pursue. The scoring for the AP Art and Design Portfolio assessments, which are personalized assessments, follows this procedure.

Second, the use of a theory-based framework for item development may allow one to make relatively strong comparability claims for personalized assessments. Such a framework would describe abstract features of situations, behaviors, or cognition that can instantiate a construct as it manifests in different contexts. One such theory-based framework is learning progressions (Alonzo & Gotwals, 2012), which are research-based hypotheses about how students' capabilities in a domain develop over time. Applications of evidence-centered design (Mislevy et al., 2003a, 2003b) that draw on well-established theory in defining the student, task, and evidence models underlying the assessment design may also be useful in establishing comparable items.

Third, Mislevy et al. (2025) noted that careful test development and assembly may help with making claims about the comparability of scores on personalized assessments. One can start from a collection of items with certain characteristics or a schematic procedure for creating such items (Gierl & Haladyna, 2012). In the first approach, subsets of items are assigned to different test forms, either randomly or balanced with respect to various factors like item content and examinee characteristics. In the "schematic procedure" approach, items are created according to specifications as to item type, content, cognitive demands, etc., so that each new test form is constructed to a similar mix of items. Both approaches would enhance comparability claims across and within test forms.

Fourth, it is possible to depend on the judgment of a group of experts to decide whether various versions of the same item provide comparable evidence on the construct of interest and, consequently, whether the various forms of a personalized assessment can be considered parallel. In some cases, expert judgment is readily accepted. The equivalence of a mathematics test in Braille to the same test in print is not seriously debated. Tests that are translations from a base form are generally accepted as being comparable if the translations are done carefully. An example is the PISA that administers translations of the same items in a multitude of country-by-language versions (e.g., Joo et al., 2020) and hence leads to disparate tests. Comparability claims for scores from these translated versions of tests rely on human expert evaluations, as well as psychometric linking studies.[2]

5.4.3 Validation for Personalized Assessments

Personalized assessments can be considered extensions of CATs, which adjust the assessment to each examinee based on a single cognitive characteristic (i.e., the construct being assessed). Validation for personalized assessments, compared to traditional CATs, is much more complex, primarily because of the consideration of additional examinee characteristics and personalization variables. Sinharay et al. (2025a) proposed a framework for validation for personalized assessments. The framework is based on the threats-to-validity approach of Crooks et al. (1996) that treats an assessment as divided into the following eight linked stages:

1. *Administration* of assessment tasks to the student.
2. *Scoring* of the student's performances on the tasks.
3. *Aggregation* of the scores on individual tasks to produce one or more combined scores (total score or subscale scores).
4. *Generalization* from the particular tasks included in a combined score to the whole domain of similar tasks (the assessed domain).
5. *Extrapolation* from the assessed domain to a larger target domain containing all tasks relevant to the proposed interpretation.
6. *Evaluation* of the student's performance, forming judgments.
7. *Decision* on actions to be taken in light of the judgments.
8. *Impact* on the student and other participants arising from the assessment processes, interpretations, and decisions.

Validation is performed through careful scrutiny of each stage. Examination of each link, with the goal of finding potential weaknesses in the chain of inference, provides a systematic approach to validation. The validators should begin by considering the administration link and then move through the above list, evaluating the threats to validity associated with each link. The final step in validation should be the identification of the weakest links in the chain. The weakest links will be the appropriate places to focus particular effort when trying to improve the assessment.

Sinharay et al. (2025a) examined the threats associated with each of the above links for a personalized assessment and discussed whether the severity of the threat is ameliorated or exacerbated in comparison to a (hypothetical) standardized assessment that attempts to measure similar knowledge, skills, and abilities for a similar population. They also examined the threats to validity for two personalized assessments, including the AP 3D Art and Design Portfolio examination and an experimental culturally relevant assessment contextualized for Indigenous students. Sinharay et al. (2025a) concluded that several threats to validity seem to be ameliorated for personalized assessments. These threats include those of:

- low motivation and task or response not communicated (under the "Administration" link);
- poor grasp of assessment information and its limitations, inadequately supported construct interpretation, and biased interpretation or explanation ("Evaluation" link);
- poor pedagogical decisions ("Decision" link); and
- positive consequences are not achieved, and a serious negative impact occurs ("Impact" link).

However, Sinharay et al. (2025a) noted that a major threat to the validity of personalized assessments is associated with the "Scoring" link because of questions regarding the comparability of scores. They also noted that the scores may be comparable for some inferences (e.g., abstract-level construct interpretations) and some score uses, but not for others. The extent of this threat to validity depends on the use of the test scores and the conception of comparability one adopts. For a licensure or certification examination, the extent may be severe if interchangeability is required for a particular use. However, if the use can accommodate variations in conditions that preclude interchangeability but that are thought to enhance validity (e.g., using one's own car for a driving test), the threat may be considerably less severe. Lower severity may also occur in uses in which the consequences of wrong decisions are both low and easily reversible, as in personalized assessment intended for adjusting classroom instruction. Alternatively, if one is able to use any of the four strategies discussed in the previous section to claim comparability, then the threat to validity associated with the "Scoring" link is considerably ameliorated.

It is possible to adopt other validation approaches, including Messick's unified framework (e.g., Messick, 1989) or the framework of Embretson (2007), where validity is conceptualized as a universal and interactive system. However, the issue of score comparability is likely to loom large for any other approach. For example, the framework of Embretson (2007) involves 11 categories of evidence about test meaning and significance and includes the categories "psychometric properties" and "scoring models." Consequently, a potential lack of comparability would make the validity evidence weak in these two categories.

5.5 Fairness of Interpretations of Scores from Personalized Assessments

Kane (2006) emphasizes two key aspects of fairness: (1) consistency of score meaning and (2) equitable treatment of groups. Consistency of score meaning involves ensuring that the same conclusions and inferences can be drawn from test results for various groups. This aspect of fairness has been the primary focus of fairness research. This aspect means assessments provide similar opportunities for engagement with assessments, equivalence of constructs measured, and comparable scores for individuals from different backgrounds. For highly heterogeneous populations, focusing on fairness for groups presents significant challenges. The typical demographic groups that fairness research generally considers, such as those based on gender, race/ethnicity, or native language, are usually highly heterogeneous. In fact, personalization challenges the notion that a key measurement principle, such as fairness, should focus on group-level evidence of consistency of score meaning at all. Specifically, personalization grounded in sociocultural perspectives contests the assumption of within-group homogeneity in statistical analyses for detecting differential item functioning (DIF), typically used for evaluating fairness in assessments. Previous research shows that increased heterogeneity in focal-group samples decreases the detection of biased items (Ercikan et al., 2014; Oliveri et al., 2014). This research suggests that violating the homogeneity assumption has significant implications for the usual fairness and bias analyses. The limitations of DIF methodologies for highly heterogeneous populations highlight the fact that our current concepts of fairness defined at the group level are not applicable to individuals. Personalized assessments open the door for rethinking fairness at the individual level.

Equal treatment of groups refers to the uniformity of testing conditions across examinees. Traditionally, equal treatment has been addressed through standardization. This concept assumes that while certain aspects of an assessment may benefit some students, other aspects will benefit others, thereby balancing out advantages and disadvantages on average (Mislevy et al., 2013). However, as previously discussed, standardization does not always create equivalent testing conditions for individuals from diverse sociocultural backgrounds. Consequently, it may not consistently provide comparable evidence of students' knowledge, skills, and abilities. Individuals with varying experiences in testing, such as familiarity with test formats and technology-rich environments, and those from cultures and contexts unaccustomed to performing cognitive tasks within limited time frames or who relate differently to assessment tasks, may engage with tests in distinct ways that produce less valid scores.

Building on the concept of "marginal fairness" introduced by Hansen et al. (2005) for test accessibility, Mislevy et al. (2013) proposed the "conditional sense of fairness," which means considering, for inference purposes, specific information at the individual level rather than averaging over its variations. This consideration means that aspects of an assessment are intentionally varied so that individual students can access, interact with, and respond to tasks with minimal difficulty, ensuring that the primary challenges are central to the intended construct (Mislevy, 2018, p. 220). This approach diverges from standardization and emphasizes systematic variations across individuals in assessment and assessment conditions to provide equivalent evidence of the target construct. Examples of such deviations include testing students with disabilities using accommodations (Kopriva et al., 2016; Mislevy et al., 2013; Thurlow & Kopriva, 2015), adapting tests to different languages (Ercikan & Por, 2020; Solano-Flores et al., 2009), and personalized assessments discussed earlier in this chapter.

In personalized assessments, notions of fairness, consistency of score meaning, and equitable treatment are related to the degree to which personalization achieves its goals for individuals: optimizing performance and engagement, and accurate measurement of individuals' competencies (Arslan et al., 2024; Bennett, 2024). Hence, a key aspect of fairness in personalized assessments is the degree to which personalization goals are met. In fairness evaluation, empirical evidence is required to ascertain whether personalization:

- Better aligns with learners' interests, characteristics, and backgrounds; and
- Improves engagement, performance, and measurement precision, ideally for all individuals.

5.6 Final Note

Effective personalization requires a thoughtful, evidence-based approach that considers both machine-driven adaptivity and human-driven adaptability. That approach should holistically treat learners by leveraging their prior performance, knowledge and skills, effort, interest, language background, and cultural identity to guide personalization of assessment contexts, tasks, and items. While AI can scale and optimize personalization, learner agency remains essential to ensure the assessment experience remains inclusive, engaging, and aligned with each learner's needs and potential. Leveraging frameworks such as caring assessment, UDAS, and ED-PLAT can help assessment developers guide when, where, and how they implement personalization.

One of the significant challenges in personalized assessment is ensuring the validity, fairness, and comparability of the resulting assessment claims, challenges that become more complex as the assessment consequences increase. These challenges include addressing the compatibility of measurement across different tasks and across individuals from different backgrounds. Additionally, there is a need for empirical evidence to support personalization for different contexts and purposes, to establish how and when to personalize based on which characteristics and behaviors, and to identify which learner qualities should *not* be considered (e.g., the persistent but discredited notion of learning styles; see Laitusis & Karvonen, 2025; Pashler et al., 2008). Most of all, research should focus on the validation, comparability, and fairness of this form of personalized assessments, as well as on the impact of different types of personalization on learner engagement, performance, and measurement precision.

Notes

1 The practice, of course, goes back much farther, found in the ancient Chinese Imperial Civil Service Examinations, which date to the Sui Dynasty, almost 1,500 years ago.
2 It should be noted that comparability is a more crucial requirement for high-stakes uses of scores as in licensing or admissions decisions. In high-stakes situations where it is difficult to apply the above strategies, one option, as recommended by Dorans et al. (1997) in the context of concordance tables, is to treat as comparable only scores for individuals with very similar characteristics. For low-stakes uses, like classroom instruction or comparing group means for monitoring trends, comparability is not a crucial issue.

References

Alonzo, A. C., & Gotwals, A. W. (Eds.). (2012). *Learning Progressions in Science: Current Challenges and Future Directions.* Rotterdam: Sense Publishers. https://www.worldcat.org/title/learningprogressions-in-science-current-challenges-and-future-directions/oclc/858351407

Alrawashdeh, G. S., Fyffe, S., Azevedo, R. F. L., & Castillo, N. M. (2024). Exploring the impact of personalized and adaptive learning technologies on reading literacy: A global meta-analysis. *Educational Research Review, 42.* https://doi.org/10.1016/j.edurev.2023.100587

American Educational Research Association [AERA], American Psychological Association [APA], & National Council for Measurement in Education [NCME]. (2014). *Standards for Educational and Psychological Testing.* Washington, DC: American Educational Research Association.

Anderson, J. R. (2007). *How Can the Human Mind Occur in the Physical Universe?* New York: Oxford University Press. https://doi.org/10.1093/acprof:oso/9780195324259.001.0001

Arslan, B. (2024). Personalized, adaptive, and inclusive digital assessment and learning environments [conference presentation]. E-ADAPT conference, Potsdam, Germany. Available at: https://osf.io/82p5f/?view_only=cba3f410bc1e462fb086e3361ffed0bc (Accessed August 4, 2025).

Arslan, B., & Finn, B. (2023). The effects of personalized nudges on cognitively disengaged student behavior in low-stakes assessments. *Journal of Intelligence, 11*(11), 204. https://doi.org/10.3390/jintelligence11110204

Arslan, B., Lehman, B., Tenison, C., Sparks, J. R., López, A. A., Gu, L., & Zapata-Rivera, D. (2024). Opportunities and challenges of using generative AI to personalize educational assessment. *Frontiers in Artificial Intelligence*, *7*, 1460651. https://doi.org/10.3389/frai.2024.1460651

Arslan, B., & Tenison, C. (2025). Adapting to prior and developing knowledge. In M. L. Bernacki, C. Walkington, A. Emery, & L. Zhang (Eds.), *Handbook of Personalized Learning* (pp. 95–111). Routledge.

Arslan, B., Tenison, C., & Gooch, R. (2025a, April). *On-the-fly context personalization with generative AI in mathematics assessments: Co-designing with teachers.* Presentation at the annual meeting of the American Educational Research Association, Denver, CO.

Arslan, B., Wilschut, T., van Rijn, H., & van der Velde, M. (2025b). Evidence-based dynamic personalization for learning and assessment tools (ED-PLAT): Machine- and learner-driven adaptation to support all learners. In *International Conference on Artificial Intelligence in Education* (pp. 477–491). Cham: Springer Nature Switzerland.

Bellarhmouch, Y., Jeghal, A., Tairi, H., & Benjelloun, N. (2023). A proposed architectural learner model for a personalized learning environment. *Education and Information Technologies*, *28*(4), 4243–4263. https://doi.org/10.1007/s10639-022-11392-y

Bennett, R. E. (2023). Toward a theory of socioculturally responsive assessment. *Educational Assessment*, *28*(2), 83–104. https://doi.org/10.1080/10627197.2023.2202312

Bennett, R. E. (2024). Personalizing assessment: Dream or nightmare? *Educational Measurement: Issues and Practice*, 43(4), 119–125. https://doi.org/10.1111/emip.12652

Bennett, R. E., Darling-Hammond, L., & Badrinarayan, A. (2025). *Socioculturally Responsive Assessment: Implications for Theory, Measurement, and Systems-level Policy*. New York: Routledge.

Bernacki, M. L., Greene, M. J., & Lobczowski, N. G. (2021). A systematic review of research on personalized learning: Personalized by whom, to what, how, and for what purpose(s)? *Educational Psychology Review*, *33*(4), 1675–1715. https://doi.org/10.1007/s10648-021-09615-8

Brigham, C. C. (1930). Intelligence tests of immigrant groups. *Psychological Review*, *37*(2), 158–165. https://doi.org/10.1037/h0072570

Brod, G. (2026). Agency does not equal choice-conceptualizing agency for learning in the age of AI. *Learning and Individual Differences*, *125*, 102841. https://doi.org/10.1016/j.lindif.2025.102841

Brod, G., Kucirkova, N., Shepherd, J., Jolles, D., & Molenaar, I. (2023). Agency in educational technology: Interdisciplinary perspectives and implications for learning design. *Educational Psychology Review*, *35*(1), 25. https://doi.org/10.1007/s10648-023-09749-x

Bulut, O., Liu, J. X., & Demir, H. (2025). Deep reinforcement learning for engagement-aware question selection in adaptive assessment systems. In *International Conference on Artificial Intelligence in Education* (pp. 27–34). Cham: Springer Nature Switzerland.

Buzick, H. M., Casabianca, J. M., & Gholson, M. L. (2023). Personalizing large-scale assessment in practice. *Educational Measurement: Issues and Practice*, *42*(2), 5–11. https://doi.org/10.1111/emip.12551

CAST (2024). Universal design for learning guidelines version 3.0. Wakefield, MA. https://udlguidelines.cast.org/

College Board. (2023). *AP Research: Course and Exam Description.* https://apcentral.collegeboard.org/courses/ap-research

Conant, J. (2017). *Man of the Hour: James B. Conant–Warrior Scientist*. New York: Simon and Schuster.

Corbett, A., McLaughlin, M., & Scarpinatto, K. C. (2000). Modeling student knowledge: Cognitive tutors in high school and college. *User Modeling and User-Adapted Interaction*, *10*(2/3), 81–108. https://doi.org/10.1023/A:1026505626690

Crooks, T. J., Kane, M. T., & Cohen, A. S. (1996). Threats to the valid use of assessments, assessment in education: Principles. *Policy & Practice*, *3*(3), 265–286. https://doi.org/10.1080/0969594960030302

Dietrich, S., & Hernandez, E. (2022). Language use in the United States: 2019 (American Community Survey Reports). U.S. Census Bureau. https://www.census.gov/library/publications/2022/acs/acs-50.html

Dorans, N. J. (2012). The contestant perspective on taking tests: Emanations from the statue within. *Educational Measurement: Issues and Practice*, *31*(4), 20–37. https://doi.org/10.1111/j.1745-3992.2012.00250.x

Dorans, N. J., Lyu, C. F., Pommerich, M., & Houston, W. M. (1997). Concordance between ACT assessment and recentered SAT I sum scores. *College and University*, *73*, 24–34.

Dorans, N. J., & Middleton, K. (2012). Addressing the extreme assumptions of presumed linkings. *Journal of Educational Measurement*, *49*, 1–18. https://doi.org/10.1111/j.1745-3984.2011.00157.x

Du Boulay, B. (2018). Intelligent tutoring systems that adapt to learner motivation. In S. D. Craig (Ed.), *Tutoring and Intelligent Tutoring Systems* (pp. 103–128). New York: Nova Science Publishers, Inc.

Embretson, S. E. (2007). Construct validity: A universal validity system or just another test evaluation procedure? *Educational Researcher*, *36*(8), 449–455. https://doi.org/10.3102/0013189X07311600

Ercikan, K., Roth, W. M., Simon, M., Sandilands, D., & Lyons-Thomas, J. (2014). Inconsistencies in DIF detection for sub-groups in heterogeneous language groups. *Applied Measurement in Education*, *27*(4), 273–285. https://doi.org/10.1080/08957347.2014.944306

Ercikan, K., & Solano-Flores, G. (2025). Sociocultural context on assessment. In L. Cook & M. Pitoniak (Eds.), *Educational Measurement* (5th ed.). (pp. 115–191). New York: Oxford University Press.

Ercikan, K., & Por, H. H. (2020). Comparability in multilingual and multicultural assessment contexts. In A. Berman, E. Haertel, & J. Pellegrino (Eds.), *Comparability of large-scale educational assessments: Issues and recommendations* (pp. 205–226). National Academy of Education.

Evans, C. M., & Taylor, C. S. (2025). *Culturally Responsive Assessment in Classrooms and Large-Scale Contexts: Theory, Research, and Practice.* New York: Routledge.

Falmagne, J.-C., Koppen, M., Villano, M., Doignon, J.-P., & Johannesen, L. (1990). Introduction to knowledge spaces: How to build, test, and search them. *Psychological Review*, *97*(2), 201–224. https://doi.org/10.1037/0033-295X.97.2.201

Finn, B. (2015). Measuring motivation in low-stakes assessments. *ETS Research Report Series*, *2015*, 1–17. https://doi.org/10.1002/ets2.12067

Frey, W. H. (2020). *The nation is diversifying even faster than predicted, according to new Census data.* Brookings. https://www.brookings.edu/articles/new-census-data-shows-the-nation-is-diversifying-even-faster-than-predicted/

Fuess, C. M. (1950). *The College Board: Its First Fifty Years.* New York: Columbia University Press.

Gibson, C. J., & Lennon, E. (1999). *Historical Census Statistics on the Foreign-born Population of the United States: 1850–1990.* https://www.census.gov/library/working-papers/1999/demo/POP-twps0029.html

Gierl, M. J., & Haladyna, T. M. (Eds.). (2012). *Automatic Item Generation: Theory and Practice.* Routledge.

Hansen, E. G., Mislevy, R. J., Steinberg, L. S., Lee, M. J., & Forer, D. C. (2005). Accessibility of tests within a validity framework. *System: An International Journal of Educational Technology and Applied Linguistics*, *33*, 107–133. doi:10.1016/j.system.2004.11.002

Hobbs, F., & Stoops, N. (2002). *Demographic Trends in the 20th Century: Census 2000 Special Reports* (CENSR-4). U.S. Census Bureau. https://eric.ed.gov/?id=ED477270

Hood, S. (1998). Culturally responsive performance-based assessment: Conceptual and psychometric considerations. *Journal of Negro Education*, *67*(3), 187–196. https://doi.org/10.2307/2668188

Iyengar, S. S., & Lepper, M. R. (2000). When choice is demotivating: Can one desire too much of a good thing? *Journal of Personality and Social Psychology*, *79*(6), 995.

Jensen, E., Jones, N., Rabe, M., Pratt, B., Medina, L., Orozco, K., & Spell, L. (2021, August 12). *2020 U.S. Population More Racially and Ethnically Diverse Than Measured in 2010*. US Census Bureau. https://www.census.gov/library/stories/2021/08/2020-united-states-population-more-racially-ethnically-diverse-than-2010.html

Johnson, M. S. (2025). Responsible AI for Measurement and Learning: Principles and Practices. *Research Report. RR-25-03. ETS Research Report Series*. Princeton, NJ: Educational Testing Service

Joo, S.-H., Khorramdel, L., Yamamoto, K., Shin, H. J., & Robin, F. (2020). Evaluating item fit statistic thresholds in PISA: Analysis of cross-country comparability of cognitive items. *Educational Measurement: Issues and Practice*, *40*(2), 37–48. https://doi.org/10.1111/emip.12404

Kane M. T. (2006). Content-related validity evidence in test development. In: S. M. Downing, & T. M. Haladyna (Eds.), *Handbook of Test Development*. Mahwah, NJ: Lawrence Erlbaum Associates.

Ketterlin-Geller, L. R. (2005). Knowing what all students know: Procedures for developing universal design for assessment. *Journal of Technology, Learning, and Assessment*, *4*(2). https://ejournals.bc.edu/index.php/jtla/article/view/1649

Kopriva, R. J., Thurlow, M. L., Perie, M., Lazarus, S. S., & Clark, A. (2016). Test takers and the validity of score interpretations. *Educational Psychologist, 51*(1), 108–128.

Laitusis, C. C., & Karvonen, M. (2025). A case for reimagining universal design of assessment systems. *Educational Measurement: Issues and Practice, 44*(3), 5–14. https://doi.org/10.1111/emip.12674

Lee, C. D. (1998). Culturally responsive pedagogy and performance-based assessment. *Journal of Negro Education*, *67*(3), 268–279. https://doi.org/10.2307/2668195

Lehman, B., Sparks, J. R., & Steinberg, J. (2024a). *Detecting Test-taking Engagement in Changing Test Contexts*. ETS Research Report Series. Princeton, NJ: Educational Testing Service. https://doi.org/10.1002/ets2.12384

Lehman, B., Sparks, J. R., Zapata-Rivera, D., Steinberg, J., & Forsyth, C. (2024b). A culturally enhanced framework of caring assessments for diverse learners. *Practical Assessment, Research, & Evaluation*, *29*(1), 9. https://doi.org/10.7275/pare.2102

Lin, L., Lin, X., Zhang, X., & Ginns, P. (2024). The personalized learning by interest effect on interest, cognitive load, retention, and transfer: A meta-analysis. *Educational Psychology Review*, *36*(3), 88. https://doi.org/10.1007/s10648-024-09933-7

Lord, F. M. (1980). *Applications of Item Response Theory to Practical Testing Problems.* Hillsdale, NJ: Lawrence Erlbaum Associates.

Major, L., Francis, G. A., & Tsapali, M. (2021). The effectiveness of technology - supported personalised learning in low - and middle - income countries: A

meta - analysis. *British Journal of Educational Technology*, *52*(5), 1935–1964. https://doi.org/10.1111/bjet.13116
McCarthy, K. S., Guerrero, T. A., Kent, K. M., Allen, L. K., McNamara, D. S., Chao, S.-F., Steinberg, J., O'Reilly, T., & Sabatini, J. (2018). Comprehension in a scenario-based assessment: Domain and topic-specific knowledge. *Discourse Processes*, *55*(5–6), 510–524. https://doi.org/10.1080/0163853X.2018.1460159
McCarthy, K. S., Steinberg, J., Dreier, K., O'Reilly, T., Sabatini, J., Butterfuss, R., & McNamara, D. S. (2023). The effects of prior knowledge in a scenario-based comprehension assessment: A multidimensional approach. *Learning and Individual Differences*, *103*, 102283. https://doi.org/10.1016/j.lindif.2023.102283
Messick, S. (1989). Validity. In R. L. Linn (Ed.), *Educational Measurement* (3rd ed., pp. 13–103). New York: American Council on Education/Macmillan.
Mislevy, R. J., Almond, R. G., & Lukas, J. F. (2003a). *A Brief Introduction to Evidence-centered Design*. ETS Research Report (RR-03–16). Princeton, NJ: ETS. https://doi.org/10.1002/j.2333-8504.2003.tb01908.x
Mislevy, R. J., Oliveri, M. E., Slomp, D., Crop Eared Wolf, A., & Elliot, N. (2025). An evidentiary-reasoning lens for socioculturally responsive assessment. In R. E. Bennett, L. Darling-Hammond, & A. Badrinarayan (Eds.), *Socioculturally Responsive Assessment: Implications for Theory, Measurement, and Systems-level Policy* (pp. 199–242). New York: Routledge.
Mislevy, R. J. (2018). *Sociocognitive Foundations of Educational Measurement*. New York: Routledge.
Mislevy, R. J., Haertel, G., Cheng, B. H., Ructtinger, L., DeBarger, A., Murray, E., ... & Vendlinski, T. (2013). A "conditional" sense of fairness in assessment. *Educational Research and Evaluation*, 19(2–3), 121–140.
Mislevy, R. J., Steinberg, L. S., & Almond, R. G. (2003b). Focus article: On the structure of educational assessments. *Measurement: Interdisciplinary Research and Perspectives*, *1*(1), 3–62. https://doi.org/10.1207/S15366359MEA0101_02
Nakkula, M., & Toshalis, E. (2025). Student engagement, motivation, and assessment. In C. M. Evans, & C. S. Taylor (Eds.), *Culturally Responsive Assessment in Classrooms and Large-Scale Contexts* (pp. 34–51). New York: Routledge. https://doi.org/10.4324/9781003392217-4
National Center for Education Statistics (NCES). (2023). *Digest of Education Statistics: 2023 Tables and Figures*. US Department of Education. https://nces.ed.gov/programs/digest/2023menu_tables.asp
O'Dwyer, E., Sparks, J. R., & Nabors Oláh, L. (2023). Enacting a process for developing culturally relevant classroom assessments. *Applied Measurement in Education*, *36*(3), 286–303. https://doi.org/10.1080/08957347.2023.2214652
O'Neill, G., & Padden, L. (2022). Diversifying assessment methods: Barriers, benefits and enablers. *Innovations in Education and Teaching International*, *59*(4), 398–409. https://doi.org/10.1080/14703297.2021.1880462
O'Reilly, T., Wang, Z., & Sabatini, J. (2019). How much knowledge is too little? When a lack of knowledge becomes a barrier to comprehension. *Psychological Science*, *30*(9), 1344–1351. https://doi.org/10.1177/0956797619862276
OECD. (2024). *PISA 2022 Technical Report*. Paris: OECD Publishing. https://doi.org/10.1787/01820d6d-en
Oliveri, M. E., Ercikan, K., & Zumbo, B. D. (2014). Effects of population heterogeneity on accuracy of DIF detection. *Applied Measurement in Education*, *27*(4), 286–300. https://doi.org/10.1080/08957347.2014.944305

Pashler, H., McDaniel, M., Rohrer, D., & Bjork, R. (2008). Learning styles: Concepts and evidence. *Psychological Science in the Public Interest*, *9*(3), 105–119. https://doi.org/10.1111/j.1539-6053.2009.01038.x

Patall, E. A., Cooper, H., & Wynn, S. R. (2010). The effectiveness and relative importance of choice in the classroom. *Journal of Educational Psychology*, *102*(4), 896.

Peng, H., Ma, S., Spector, J. M. (2019). Personalized adaptive learning: An emerging pedagogical approach enabled by a smart learning environment. In M. Chang, E. Popescu, Kinshuk, N. Chen, M. Jemni, R. Huang, J. M. Spector, D. G. Sampson (Eds.), *Foundations and Trends in Smart Learning. Lecture Notes in Educational Technology* (pp. 171–176). Singapore: Springer. https://doi.org/10.1007/978-981-13-6908-7_24

Plass, J. L., & Pawar, S. (2020). Toward a taxonomy of adaptivity for learning. *Journal of Research on Technology in Education*, *52*(3), 275–300. https://doi.org/10.1080/15391523.2020.1719943

Randall, J. (2021). "Color-neutral" is not a thing: Redefining construct definition and representation through a justice-oriented critical antiracist lens. *Educational Measurement: Issues and Practice*, *40*(4), 82–90. https://doi.org/10.1111/emip.12429

Randall, J., Poe, M., & Slomp, D. (2021). Ain't oughta be in the dictionary: Getting to justice by dismantling anti-black literacy assessment practices. *Journal of Adolescent and Adult Literacy*, *64*(5), 594–599. https://doi.org/10.1002/jaal.1142

Ryan, R. M., & Deci, E. L. (2000). Self-determination theory and the facilitation of intrinsic motivation, social development, and well-being. *American Psychologist*, *55*(1), 68–78.

Ryan, R. M., & Deci, E. L. (2024). Self-determination theory. In F. Maggino (Ed.), *Encyclopedia of Quality of Life and Well-Being Research* (pp. 6229–6235). Cham: Springer.

Shemshack, A., Kinshuk, & Spector, J. M. (2021). A comprehensive analysis of personalized learning components. *Journal of Computers in Education*, *8*, 485–503. https://doi.org/10.1007/s40692-021-00188-7

Shin, J., & Bulut, O. (2022). Building an intelligent recommendation system for personalized test scheduling in computerized assessments: A reinforcement learning approach. *Behavior Research Methods*, *54*(1), 216–232. https://doi.org/10.3758/s13428-021-01602-9

Shneiderman, B. (2022). *Human-Centered AI.* Oxford: Oxford University Press.

Simonsmeier, B. A., Flaig, M., Deiglmayr, A., Schalk, L., & Schneider, M. (2022). Domain-specific prior knowledge and learning: A meta-analysis. *Educational Psychologist*, *57*(1), 31–54. https://doi.org/10.1080/00461520.2021.1939700

Sinharay, S., Bennett, R. E., Kane, M., & Sparks, J. R. (2025a). Validation for personalized assessments: A threats-to-validity approach. *Journal of Educational Measurement*, *62*(2), 282–310. https://doi.org/10.1111/jedm.12434

Sinharay, S., Johnson, M. S., Bennett, R. E., Lopez, R., Guzman-Orth, D., Sparks, J. R., & Pillarisetti, S. (2025b). Culturally responsive assessments in the context of the National Assessment of Educational Progress: An initial look. *Educational Measurement: Issues and Practice, 44*(4), 33–51.

Sireci, S. G. (2020). Standardization and UNDERSTANDardization in educational assessment. *Educational Measurement: Issues and Practice*, *39*(3), 100–105. https://doi.org/10.1111/emip.12377

Solano-Flores, G., Backhoff, E., & Contreras-Niño, L. Á. (2009). Theory of test translation error. *International Journal of Testing*, *9*(2), 78–91.

Sparks, J. R., Lehman, B., & Zapata-Rivera, D. (2024). Caring assessments: Challenges and opportunities. *Frontiers in Education - Assessment, Testing, and Applied Measurement*, *9,* 1216481. https://doi.org/10.3389/feduc.2024.1216481

Sparks, J. R., Ober, T., & Lehman, B. (2026). Leveraging measures of students' prior knowledge and lived experiences toward more personalized culturally responsive assessment. *Practical Assessment, Research, and Evaluation, 30*(2).

Taatgen, N. A. (2013). The nature and transfer of cognitive skills. *Psychological Review, 120*(3), 439. https://doi.org/10.1037/a0033138

Thissen, D. (2016). Commentary on the assessment of the fairness of comparisons under divergent measurement conditions. In N. J. Dorans & L. Cook (Eds.), *Fairness in Educational Assessment and Measurement* (pp. 219–230). New York: Routledge. https://doi.org/10.4324/9781315774527-13

Thurlow, M. L., & Kopriva, R. J. (2015). Advancing accessibility and accommodations in content assessments for students with disabilities and English learners. *Review of Research in Education*, 39(1), 331–369.

US Census Bureau. (2024, April 9). *New Report on the Nation's Foreign-born Population* (Press Release Number CB24-TPS.34). https://www.census.gov/newsroom/press-releases/2024/foreign-born-population.html

US Census Bureau. (n.d.). *Language Spoken at Home*. https://www.census.gov/acs/www/about/why-we-ask-each-question/language/

US Congress. (1944). *An Act to Provide Federal Government Aid for the Readjustment in Civilian Life of Returning World War II Veterans, June 22, 1944*. Enrolled Acts and Resolutions of Congress, 1789–1996, General Records of the United States Government, Record Group 11. National Archives.

van der Linden, W. J., & Glas, C. A. W. (2000). *Computerized Adaptive Testing: Theory and Practice*. Dordrecht: Springer. https://doi.org/10.1007/0-306-47531-6

Vertovec, S. (2023). *Superdiversity: Migration and Social Complexity*. Routledge: Oxon, UK.

Wainer, H., Dorans, N. J., Eignor, D., Flaugher, R., Green, B. F., Mislevy, R. J., Steinberg, L., & Thissen, D. (2000). *Computerized Adaptive Testing: A Primer* (2nd ed.). Mahwah, NJ: Lawrence Erlbaum Associates.

Wainer, H., & Thissen, D. (1994). On examinee choice in educational testing. *ETS Research Report Series, 1994*(2), 159–195. https://doi.org/10.1002/j.2333-8504.1994.tb01604.x

Walker, M. E., Olivera-Aguilar, M., Lehman, B., Laitusis, C., Guzman-Orth, D., & Gholson, M. (2023). *Culturally Responsive Assessment: Provisional Principles* (ETS Research Report No. RR-23-11). Princeton, NJ: ETS. https://doi.org/10.1002/ets2.12374

Walkington, C., & Bernacki, M. L. (2014). Motivating students by "personalizing" learning around individual interests: A consideration of theory, design, and implementation issues. In S. Karabenick & T. Urdan (Eds.), *Advances in Motivation and Achievement* (vol. 18, pp. 139–176). Emerald Group Publishing Limited. 10.1108/S0749-742320140000018004

Walkington, C., & Bernacki, M. (2020). Appraising research on personalized learning: Definitions, theoretical alignment, advancements, and future directions. *Journal of Research on Technology in Education, 52*(3), 235–252. https://doi.org/10.1080/15391523.2020.1747757

Wang, Z., O'Reilly, T., Sabatini, J., McCarthy, K. S., & McNamara, D. S. (2021). A tale of two tests: The role of topic and general academic knowledge in traditional versus contemporary scenario-based reading. *Learning and Instruction, 73*, 1001462. https://doi.org/10.1016/j.learninstruc.2021.101462

Wang, Z., Sparks, J. R., Walker, M., O'Reilly, T., & Bruce, K. (2025). Group differences across scenario-based reading assessments: Examining the effects of culturally relevant test content. In R. Bennett, L. Darling-Hammond, & A. Badrinarayan (Eds.), *Socioculturally Responsive Assessment: Implications for Theory, Measurement, and Systems-Level Policy* (pp. 369–398). New York: Routledge.

Winter, P. C. (2010). Comparability and test variations. In P. C. Winter (Ed.), *Evaluating the Comparability of Scores from Test Variations,*(pp. 1–11). Washington, DC: Council of Chief State School Officers.

Wise, S. L., & DeMars. C. E. (2005). Low examinee effort in low-stakes assessment: Problems and potential solutions. *Educational Assessment, 10*, 1–17. https://doi.org/10.1207/s15326977ea1001_1

Wise, S. L., Plake, B. S., Johnson, P. L., & Roos, L. L. (1992). A comparison of self - adapted and computerized adaptive tests. *Journal of Educational Measurement, 29*(4), 329–339.

Wise, S. L., Ponsoda, V., & Olea, J. (2002). Self-adapted testing: An overview. *International Journal of Continuing Engineering Education and Life Long Learning, 12*(1–4), 107–122. https://doi.org/10.1504/IJCEELL.2002.000422

Wise, S. L., Bhola, D. S., & Yang, S.-T. (2006). Taking the time to improve the validity of low-stakes tests: The effort-monitoring CBT. *Educational Measurement: Issues and Practice, 25*, 21–30. https://doi.org/10.1111/j.1745-3992.2006.00054.x

Wilschut, T., Sense, F., & van Rijn, H. (2024). Speaking to remember: Model-based adaptive vocabulary learning using automatic speech recognition. *Computer Speech & Language, 84*, 101578. https://doi.org/10.1016/j.csl.2023.101578

Zapata-Rivera, D. (2017). Toward caring assessment systems. In M. Tkalcic, D. Thakker, P. Germanakos, K. Yacef, C. Paris, & O. Santos (Eds.), *Adjunct Publication of the 25th Conference on User Modeling, Adaptation and Personalization (UMAP '17)* (pp. 97–100). New York: ACM.

Zapata-Rivera, D. (2020). Open student modeling research and its connections to educational assessment. *International Journal of Artificial Intelligence in Education, 31*, 380–396. https://doi.org/10.1007/s40593-020-00206-2

Zapata-Rivera, D., & Arslan, B. (2021). Enhancing personalization by integrating top-down and bottom-up approaches to learner modeling. In R. A. Sottilare and J. Schwarz (Eds.), *Proceedings of HCII 2021* (pp. 234–246). Switzerland: Springer Nature.

Zapata-Rivera, D., Lehman, B., Lopez, A. A., Gooch, R. M., & Long, R. (2025, April). *Designing and evaluating AI-enhanced interactive reports with teachers.* Paper presented at the annual meeting of the American Educational Research Association, Denver, CO.

Zapata-Rivera, D., Lehman, B., & Sparks, J. R. (2020). Learner modeling in the context of caring assessments. In R. A. Sottilare & J. Schwarz (Eds.), *Adaptive Instructional Systems: Second International Conference (AIS) 2020* (pp. 422–431). Cham: Springer. https://doi.org/10.1007/978-3-030-50788-6_31

Zheng, L., Long, M., Zhong, L., & Gyasi, J. F. (2022). The effectiveness of technology-facilitated personalized learning on learning achievements and learning perceptions: A meta-analysis. *Education and Information Technologies*, 27(8), 11807–11830. https://doi.org/10.1007/s10639-022-11092-7

6

MODERN NLP PIPELINE IN EDUCATIONAL MEASUREMENT

From Text Analysis to Scoring and Reasoning

Constanza Mardones-Segovia, Yaxuan Yang, Cheng Tang, Jiawei Xiong, Shiyu Wang, and Allan S. Cohen

Rapid technological advances have expanded assessment data to include constructed-response (CR) items, in which examinees present their responses as a written text with one or more paragraphs or as spoken responses of varying lengths (e.g., Burstein, McCaffrey, Holtzman, & Klebanov, 2023; Yaneva et al., 2023). These items offer multiple benefits, such as assessing students' higher-order thinking, semantic organization, and identifying misconceptions (e.g., Kuechler & Simkin, 2010). Most research efforts in CR items have focused on developing techniques to automatically score these items, minimizing reliance on manual rating, reducing the time required for scoring, and enhancing score consistency (Liu et al., 2014; Lottridge, Ormerod, & Jafari, 2023).

However, unlike scores to multiple-choice items, written and speech responses do not follow a fixed format. Language is a complex system with grammar rules, semantic structures, and writing conventions (Palmer, 2010), where the meaning of words often shifts with context. As a result, the complex relationships among words have not been easily captured by categorical or numerical values (Ellis, 2008).

Natural language processing (NLP) has addressed these complexities through a pipeline-based approach that transforms unstructured text, hereafter denoted as a document (e.g., an examinee's response to CR items), into a structured numerical representation to improve the interpretability and reliability of downstream data analyses (Hickman, Thapa, Tay, Cao, & Srinivasan, 2022). Early approaches to text analysis emerged in the 1960s with the development of bag-of-words representation and document-term matrices (DTMs), which quantify the frequency with which words appear within each document. These representations laid the foundation for what later became a standardized NLP pipeline emphasizing text cleaning (e.g., eliminating punctuations and words that, although frequent, do not add interpretative meaning), lemmatization (e.g., transforming different tenses of

DOI: 10.4324/9781003621522-6

the word *begin* to its infinitive form), tokenization (i.e., separating a document into tokens such as words), and feature extraction (i.e., mapping documents and words into a DTM).

This sequence of steps, hereafter referred to as the traditional NLP pipeline, has been extensively used in educational research, including early automated scoring systems (AESs) applications through latent semantic analysis (Deerwester, Dumais, Furnas, Landauer, & Harshman, 1990) and exploring students' reasoning when answering CR items (e.g., Cardozo-Gaibisso, Kim, Buxton, & Cohen, 2019) using latent Dirichlet allocation (LDA; Blei, Ng, & Jordan, 2003). More recent research has integrated NLP techniques to support writing analysis and feedback, as well as AESs (Tang, Xiong, & Engelhard, 2025; Xiong & Li, 2023). While representing documents as a DTM provides a structured representation of examinees' answers, this traditional approach assumes that words are independent features, ignoring their order and contextual relationships. This limitation can be counterproductive when analyzing complex, context-dependent responses, as traditional feature-extraction methods may fall short (Jing & Xu, 2019).

Recent advances in artificial intelligence have addressed challenges encountered with traditional NLP pipelines by using deep learning language models, commonly referred to as large language models (LLMs; Arisoy, Sainath, Kingsbury, & Ramabhadran, 2012). These models are termed *deep* because they use multiple neural network layers that work together to understand language patterns, including semantics and syntax, rather than relying on manually engineered features. LLMs are trained on massive external datasets (e.g., books, articles, and web pages), which enables them to learn word meanings from context. By modeling context, modern NLP produces continuous numerical representations of words and documents, commonly referred to as *embeddings,* that automatically capture semantic meaning and relationships, including cases in which the same word can take on different meanings depending on its linguistic context (Hadi et al., 2024). As a result, these models require less text preprocessing than a traditional NLP pipeline (Jurafsky & Martin, 2026).

This paradigm, hereafter referred to as the modern NLP pipeline, represents a shift from count-based representations toward context-aware representations of language. One of the most versatile LLMs is the bidirectional encoder representations from transformers (BERT; Devlin, Chang, & Lee, 2019). BERT is a flexible model that serves two distinct roles in text analysis. First, BERT can be used as a feature extractor, transforming written responses into embeddings that can serve as inputs to downstream models, such as topic modeling or regression-based analyses. In this role, BERT serves as a modular component that provides context-aware document representations, while relying on separate statistical or machine learning models for exploration or inference. Second, BERT can be used as an end-to-end framework, where the embeddings are fine-tuned to directly predict or classify outcomes from raw examinees' responses, for example, for automated scoring tasks. In this case, feature extraction and prediction are jointly learned within a single model, rather than as separate steps (Lottridge et al., 2023).

For researchers and practitioners in educational measurement, this shift can feel unfamiliar. Rather than relying solely on observable item scores and explicit parametric assumptions, modern NLP models learn complex patterns automatically. They may function as "black boxes," raising important questions about interpretability, validation, and alignment within measurement theory. An additional challenge is that, because models such as BERT can be used for different purposes, the NLP pipeline is not uniform across tasks; instead, it must be adapted to a specific research goal.

This chapter provides a comprehensive review of a modern NLP pipeline for educational measurement tasks involving students' written responses to CR items using BERT. This chapter is primarily intended for readers in educational measurement with limited prior exposure to NLP. We keep notation light, define technical terms on first use, and connect modeling choices to familiar concerns in educational measurement. It covers key steps of the pipeline, illustrating how unstructured text can be transformed into meaningful representations for data analysis and interpretation. To clarify BERT's dual role and the resulting differences in the pipeline, we present two educational applications.

First, for an automated scoring task, BERT is used as an end-to-end framework in which embeddings and score predictions are jointly learned. Second, for exploratory analyses that aim to discover examinees' reasoning and thinking patterns, BERT is used as a feature extractor to generate embeddings that serve as inputs to topic modeling, resulting in an integrating approach commonly referred to as BERTopic (Grootendorst, 2022).

6.1 The General BERT-Based NLP Pipeline

This section outlines the key steps of the BERT-based NLP pipeline, including (1) text preprocessing, (2) feature extraction, and (3) modeling and evaluation. While these steps are common across tasks, their implementation varies based on the objective of the educational measurement task.

6.1.1 Text Preprocessing

Because raw examinees' written responses are often noisy, unstructured, and inconsistent, the NLP pipeline typically begins by transforming written responses into a structured sequence of linguistically meaningful numerical units to reduce variability in language while preserving information that is relevant for interpreting and/or scoring the responses (Hickman et al., 2022). In a BERT-based pipeline, however, while lemmatizing and removing stopwords is often unnecessary when using language models, spell correction can still improve model performance, particularly when the misspellings are severe enough to distort the models' interpretation (Lottridge et al., 2023). Because it relies on pretrained models, tokenization is not part of text preprocessing; instead, it is handled internally during feature extraction.

6.1.2 Feature Extraction

Following text preprocessing, feature-extraction methods transform textual data into numerical representations suitable for downstream data analyses. Early embedding methods, such as Word2Vec, rely on a simple neural network language model that learns fixed representations for each word rather than updating their meanings based on context.

For instance, the word *bank* would receive identical representations whether referring to a financial institution or the edge of a river. This representation, however, becomes problematic in educational assessment as examinees may use words creatively, and subtle differences in meaning can be critical for accurate scoring.

BERT addresses this limitation by using a transformer architecture that incorporates positional encoding to retain word order and employs multi-head self-attention layers to dynamically adjust word representations based on context (Jiao & Zhang, 2021), thereby overcoming the limitations of early word embeddings (Jurafsky & Martin, 2026). BERT implements this approach using a multi-layer bidirectional transformer encoder (Devlin et al., 2019). In this architecture, word representations are refined across successive layers, incorporating information from both preceding and following words in the response. Within each layer, BERT first identifies which other words in the response are most relevant for interpreting a given word using self-attention. Then, it combines this contextual information through a feed-forward neural network to update the word's representation. For example, the word *bank* is influenced more strongly by *loan* in a financial context and by *river* in a geographical context. Repeating this process across layers enables BERT to construct rich, context-sensitive representations of examinees' responses.

Depending on the educational measurement task, BERT models vary in architectural complexity (e.g., number of layers, attention heads, and parameters) and in the types of embeddings they produce (Wolf et al., 2020). Common general-purpose models include *bert-base-uncased*, *bert-base-cased*, and the lighter *DistilBERT-base-uncased* (Sanh, Debut, Chaumond, & Wolf, 2019). Domain-specific models, such as BioBERT and ClinicalBERT, have shown improved performance in scientific and biomedical contexts (e.g., Yaneva et al., 2023). However, no consensus evidence has yet appeared on the optimal model for educational measurement, leading researchers to evaluate multiple architectures for task-specific performance. Moreover, depending on the specific educational task, BERT can be used to extract word-level embeddings, which capture the semantic information of words, or document-level embeddings, which summarize the overall meaning of examinees' written responses.

6.1.3 Modeling and Evaluation

BERT can be incorporated into educational measurement analyses in two distinct ways, depending on the study's aim. First, when the purpose is predicting scores for a new sample of examinees, as in the automated scoring task, responses previously scored by experts are split into training and evaluation sets, and BERT is fine-tuned directly on the prediction task. In other words, embeddings and scoring parameters are learned jointly to optimize accuracy in predicting scores for unseen examinees' responses. Second, when the purpose is to uncover underlying latent structures reflected through examinees' written responses, we employ topic modeling approaches. In this case, learned document-level embeddings are used to extract patterns related to reasoning, thinking processes, or other latent constructs that emerge from the response data. Because this approach relies on embeddings rather than DTMs, the resulting topic model is called BERTopic (Grootendorst, 2022). Each of them will be further explained in the Sections 6.2 and 6.3, respectively.

After applying a machine learning technique and obtaining results, an evaluation mechanism is needed to assess the model's performance quality, tailored to the specific educational measurement task (Mardones-Segovia, Wang, & Cohen, 2025). For example, when the purpose is to predict examinees' scores, researchers typically assess agreement between BERT-based predicted scores and reference scores assigned by human raters (Doewes, Kurdhi, & Saxena, 2023). In contrast, when the aim is to explore or summarize examinees' written answers into clusters or topics, the evaluation process focuses on assessing the semantic coherence of words within each topic and the dissimilarity of words across topics (Grootendorst, 2022).

6.2 BERT-Based NLP Pipeline for Automated Scoring

This section outlines how a BERT-based pipeline can be adapted for automated scoring. An overview of such a pipeline is shown in Figure 6.1, and each component is described in detail in the subsections that follow. Finally, it concludes with an empirical example that illustrates how the pipeline is implemented in practice.

A BERT-based pipeline for automated scoring typically consists of four main stages: (1) text preprocessing; (2) partitioning the preprocessed data into training, validation, and test sets; (3) feature extraction; and (4) model fine-tuning and evaluation on held-out data.

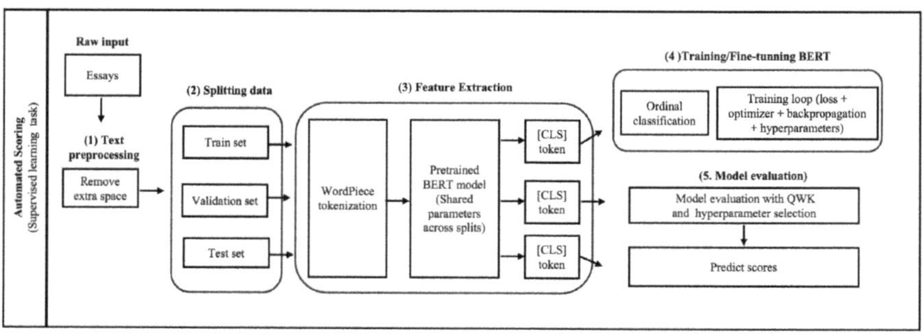

FIGURE 6.1 NLP pipeline for automated scoring using BERT.

6.2.1 *Text Preprocessing*

Following Section 6.1, the first stage of the NLP pipeline is to transform raw examinees' essays into a structured format that the model can process. In general, the only preprocessing task in this setup involves whitespace normalization, including stripping leading and trailing spaces, and fixing spacing errors.

6.2.2 *Data Partitioning*

With preprocessed text, the data are partitioned into three subsets: (1) training, (2) validation, and (3) testing, supporting reliable model development and evaluation (Goodfellow, Bengio, Courville, & Bengio, 2016). The training set is used to fine-tune BERT's parameters by learning patterns from embedded text. The validation set is used to monitor performance across iterations and select hyperparameter configurations that help prevent overfitting. Once the final model configuration is selected, performance is evaluated on the test set, which is kept completely unseen during fine-tuning and model selection and is used only to provide an unbiased evaluation of how well the trained model generalizes to unseen data. In summary, the training set is used to learn model parameters, the validation set is used to select the optimal model configuration, and the test set is used solely to evaluate final agreement between model predictions and human raters. This partitioning is usually done randomly, or with stratification for class balance, to ensure that each subset is representative of the overall dataset (Shin & Oh, 2021).

6.2.3 *Feature Extraction*

Feature extraction in this application focuses on transforming examinees' written responses into numerical representations for score prediction. This process is model-dependent and begins with selecting a pretrained BERT architecture, which determines how written responses are converted into model-compatible units and defines the granularity of the learned representations.

Once a pretrained model is selected, examinees' responses are passed to the model's corresponding tokenizer using the WordPiece (Wu et al., 2016) tokenization technique. WordPiece segments words into subwords based on their frequency and assigns each subword a unique identifier from a pretrained vocabulary. As a result, common words such as *those* and *kids* remain intact. In contrast, less frequent words such as *bioluminescence* are decomposed into subword pieces (e.g., *bio*, *##lum*, *##ine*, *##scence*), where the prefix ## indicates that the word is attached to the previous one. This approach allows the model to reuse previously learned representations to interpret unfamiliar or rare words rather than treating them as unknown.

During the tokenization process, BERT also inserts special tokens to support automated scoring task. [*CLS*] is a token added at the beginning of each document, acting as an aggregate representation for the entire sequence. [*SEP*] is a token that reflects the boundary between two sentences (Devlin et al., 2019). To improve processing efficiency, BERT processes text in batches, i.e., it handles multiple responses in parallel. Since not all answers are the same length, BERT adds [*PAD*] tokens, which carry no meaning, to the shortest documents. For an illustrative example of this process, refer to Example 6.1.

After tokenization, examinees' responses are passed through an embedding layer that generates a numerical representation for each token (i.e., each word or subword, including the [*CLS*] token), along with positional embeddings that encode word order (Adoma, Henry, Chen, & Andre, 2020). Across successive layers, tokens interact via self-attention mechanisms, allowing their representations to be updated based on surrounding context (Jurafsky & Martin, 2026).

In particular, the [*CLS*] token aggregates contextual information from all other tokens and is commonly used as a fixed-length representation of the entire document. In automated essay scoring, this final [*CLS*] embedding typically acts as the input feature for prediction models. At this stage, the [*CLS*] embeddings are general-purpose representations learned during BERT's pre-training process. These embeddings are then fine-tuned during model training to capture patterns specific to the automated scoring task. Illustrative examples of this process are provided in Examples 6.2 and 6.3.

Example 6.1: WordPiece Tokenization and Padding in BERT

Special Tokens

- [*CLS*] is placed at the beginning of an examinee's answer (for classification tasks).
- [*SEP*] marks the end of an examinee's answer or separates multiple sentences within the examinee's answer.
- [*PAD*] added to shorter sequence so that all inputs in a batch have the same length.

Example. Suppose a researcher processes four examinees' written answers simultaneously (batch size = 4). Three of the answers contain 13 tokens, but the fourth has only 11. To ensure consistent input length, BERT adds two padding tokens to the shorter sequence.

- **Sequence before padding**: [*CLS*] those kids like eating ice ##cream every single day [*SEP*].
- **Sequence after padding**: [*CLS*] those kids like eating ice ##cream every single day [*SEP*] [*PAD*] [*PAD*].

BERT also creates an ***attention mask*** (or input mask) indicating which tokens are real (1) and which are padding (0). For this example, the attention mask for the fourth examinee would be: ***[1, 1, 1, 1, 1, 1, 1, 1, 1, 1, 1, 0, 0]***.

Example 6.2: Word Embeddings in BERT

1 **Tokenization**:

$[CLS]$ *those kids like eating ice ## cream* $[SEP][PAD][PAD]$

2 **Embedding**: Each token is converted into a high-dimensional vector of length 768 (in *BERT_base*) or 1,024 (in *BERT_large*).

$ice \rightarrow [0.31,-0.12,0.45,...,0.27]$ $\quad \#\#cream \rightarrow [0.12,-0.34,0.56,...,-0.09]$

3 **Contextualization through self-attention**: At every transformer layer, each token's vector is updated based on its relationship to all other tokens in the sentence, such that the vector dimension represents a latent feature capturing semantic, syntactic, and contextual information.

$Layer1: \quad \#\#cream = [0.2,-0.3,0.5,...,0.1]$

$Layer6: \quad \#\#cream = [0.5,-0.1,0.7,...,0.4]$

$Layer12: \quad \#\#cream = [0.8,0.3,0.1,...,0.6]$

4 **Output**: After the final layer, the 768-dimensional vector should encode the token's meaning in its specific context. For instance, the final representation of "##cream" should differ across sentences:

$ice\#\#cream \neq whipped\#\#cream$

The special [*CLS*] token, shown at the beginning of the sequence, serves as an aggregate representation of the entire response and is typically used as input for automated scoring tasks.

Example 6.3: Self-Attention + Feedforward Network

This example uses the same sentence as Example 6.2 but zooms in on what happens inside a single transformer encoder layer.

1 **Input to Layer *l***: Suppose the previous layer outputs contextual vectors for each token:

$ice \rightarrow [0.31,-0.12,0.45,...,0.27]$ $\quad \#\#cream \rightarrow [0.12,-0.34,0.56,...,-0.09]$

$kids \rightarrow [0.08,0.41,-0.10,...,0.05]$ $\quad eating \rightarrow [-0.02,0.22,0.18,...,0.11]$

2 **Self-attention**: Within this layer, *##cream* forms attention weights over all tokens. (Weights shown below are illustrative and simplified for exposition purposes.)

$\alpha_{[CLS]} = 0.05,\ \alpha_{kids} = 0.10,\ \alpha_{like} = 0.07,\ \alpha_{eating} = 0.09,\ \alpha_{ice} = 0.30,\ \alpha_{\#\#cream} = 0.35$

The attention output is a weighted sum of value vectors:

$$att_{\#\#\,cream} = \sum_j \alpha_j x_j$$

For example, the first two dimensions are:

$$att_{\#\#\,cream}[1] = 0.05x_{[CLS]}[1] + \cdots + 0.30x_{ice}[1] + 0.35x_{\#\#\,cream}[1] \approx 0.20,$$
$$att_{\#\#\,cream}[2] = 0.05x_{[CLS]}[2] + \cdots + 0.30x_{ice}[2] + 0.35x_{\#\#\,cream}[2] \approx -0.30.$$

Thus, the updated vector after self-attention is:

$$att_{\#\#\,cream} \rightarrow [0.20, -0.30, 0.50, \ldots, 0.10]$$

3 **Feedforward neural network**: Next, a position-wise Feedforward neural network (FFN) with weight, bias, and activation function is applied to each token independently:

$$FFN(h) = W_2\sigma(W_1h + b_1) + b_2$$

Applied to the attention output for *##cream*, this yields:

$$ffn_{\#\#\,cream} = FFN\left(att_{\#\#\,cream}\right) \rightarrow [0.26, -0.18, 0.63, \ldots, 0.15]$$

4 **Output of Layer *l***: With residual connection and layer normalization, the layer produces the next representation:

$$x^{(l)}_{\#\#\,cream} \rightarrow [0.24, -0.25, 0.58, \ldots, 0.12]$$

Interpretation: Self-attention updates *##cream* by mixing information from related tokens, and the FFN nonlinearly re-encodes that mixed context. Repeating this two-step update across layers produces the evolving vectors shown in Example 6.3.

6.2.4 *Modeling and Evaluation*

Following feature extraction, the automated scoring task is performed using an end-to-end deep learning architecture. The architecture consists of two primary components: (1) the encoder and (2) the prediction head. The encoder corresponds to the pretrained BERT model described in the previous subsection and processes tokenized responses through multiple layers of bidirectional transformer layers. Through self-attention, the initial word embeddings, which were learned initially from large general-purpose corpora, are dynamically contextualized. The final output of this encoder is the high-dimensional vector associated with the [*CLS*] token, which serves as a fixed, aggregated semantic representation of the entire response. This representation is then passed to the prediction head, implemented as a feed-forward neural network that projects the high-dimensional embedding to a single scalar value representing the predicted essay score.

6.2.4.1 Fine-Tuning

The training process employed in this stage is hereafter referred to as *fine-tuning*. In general, training typically implies learning task-specific parameters with randomly initialized weights. However, fine-tuning begins with a model that already possesses a deep understanding of language structure from pre-training. During this stage, the model is adapted to the specific characteristics of the automated scoring task and dataset by updating its parameters using labeled essay scores from the training set.

6.2.4.1.1 Learning Procedure

The fine-tuning process is executed through an iterative learning loop, in which BERT gradually learns how to assign scores that align with human judgments. During each iteration, the model performs three steps: (1) a forward pass, (2) loss calculation, and (3) backpropagation and optimization. First, during the forward pass, the model processes a batch of essays and computes predicted scores. Second, a loss function is calculated by comparing these predicted scores to the scores assigned by human raters. This comparison is typically conducted using mean squared error (MSE) as it provides a differentiable measure of predicted error. Finally, an optimizer uses this error signal to adjust the model's parameters, which include the weights of the prediction head, the internal attention mechanisms of the transformer layers, and the original word embeddings.

Thereby, allowing the word embeddings to be updated, the model can shift the semantic representations of words to better align with the specific scoring rubrics. This optimization minimizes the loss over time, gradually refining the model's ability to map linguistic patterns to holistic quality scores.

6.2.4.2 Hyperparameter Configuration

While the BERT model provides a robust foundation, its successful application for an automated scoring task depends heavily on the choice of hyperparameters.

These are user-defined settings that control how the model learns during fine-tuning. Unlike internal parameters, which are learned from the data, hyperparameters must be specified before fine-tuning begins. In general, six hyperparameters are critical for the model's performance. Each of them is described in the following:

1. *Batch size*: The number of examinees' essays that are processed before the model's parameters are updated. Smaller batch sizes result in more frequent weight updates, helping achieve convergence faster. Larger sizes, on the other hand, result in less frequent updates, leading to a slower convergence rate (Devlin et al., 2019).
2. *Epoch*: The number of times the model has seen the complete training dataset. In other words, once the model has processed all the batches, one epoch is completed. Training the model for a few epochs may lead to underfitting. Conversely, training for too many epochs may lead to overfitting, where the model memorizes specific patterns in the training data, including noise, rather than learning general objective patterns.
3. *Learning rate*: Determines the magnitude of parameter adjustments during training. A low rate can lead to excessively slow convergence, whereas a high rate can cause the training to become unstable.
4. *Dropout rate*: A regularization technique that randomly sets the outputs of a fraction of neurons to zero during each training step to prevent overfitting.
5. *Optimizer*: Algorithm responsible for updating the model's parameters to minimize the loss function. Common options are Adam Kingma and Ba (2014) and its successor, AdamW Loshchilov and Hutter (2017). While both are adaptive learning rate algorithms, AdamW improves upon Adam by implementing a more effective weight decay mechanism, offering higher generalization.
6. *Activation function*: Function that enables the model to learn complex nonlinear patterns. This function is applied to each layer's output, transforming the values before they are passed to the next layer. Some of the most widely used activation functions are the hyperbolic tangent (Tanh) and Rectified Linear Unit (ReLU) (e.g., Hendrycks & Gimpel, 2016; LeCun, Bottou, Bengio, & Haffner, 2002; Maas et al., 2013; Nair & Hinton, 2010).

The interaction among these hyperparameters is complex, as changes in one hyperparameter configuration often affect the behavior of others. For example, a change in batch size typically requires a corresponding adjustment in the learning rate. Therefore, rather than relying on default settings, empirical studies often employ a grid search to identify the configuration that yields the highest reliability for a specific essay prompt.

6.2.4.3 Evaluation

Once the model parameters are optimized, it is essential to validate the system's performance using a metric that reflects meaningful agreement with human raters.

It is essential to distinguish this evaluation phase from the training phase described in Section 6.2.4.1. During training, the model minimizes a loss function denoted as mean squared error (MSE), which provides a smooth, mathematical gradient necessary for adjusting weights. However, MSE values can be difficult to interpret intuitively and do not account for the ordinal nature of essay scoring. Therefore, for evaluation, we employ a distinct metric, quadratic weighted kappa (QWK). QWK is an agreement metric that penalizes significant scoring discrepancies more heavily than minor ones, unlike simple accuracy measures that treat all errors as equivalent (Doewes et al., 2023).

QWK is defined in Equation (6.1), where k is the number of possible rating categories (e.g., for a score range of 0–3, $k = 4$), and i and j are the specific ratings from the human rater and the model, respectively. O is a confusion matrix, and its element O_{ij} contains the number of items that received a score of i from the human rater and a score of j from the model. w is a matrix defining the penalty for disagreement. In QWK, the weights are the squared differences between the ratings: $w_{ij} = (i - j)^2$. E is a matrix representing the agreement expected by chance. It is the outer product of the two raters' score distributions:

$$k = 1 - \frac{\sum_{i=1}^{k}\sum_{j=1}^{k} w_{ij}O_{ij}}{\sum_{i=1}^{k}\sum_{j=1}^{k} w_{ij}E_{ij}} \tag{6.1}$$

QWK ranges from −1 to 1. A higher QWK indicates stronger agreement between predictions and true scores. A perfect score of 1 indicates that the model fully agrees with human raters. Conversely, a value of 0 shows poor agreement, and the prediction is no better than chance. Negative scores, while rare in practice, indicate that the model agrees with the human raters less than what would be expected by chance.

6.2.5 *Educational Study 1: Automated Essay Scoring*

The following sections present the details of an empirical case study demonstrating how to apply the BERT-based pipeline to an automated scoring task.

6.2.5.1 Data

This study uses the Automated Student Assessment Prize dataset,[1] which includes eight unique essay items, each with a corresponding set of student responses (Hamner, Morgan, Lynnvandev, & Ark, 2012). For demonstration purposes, we focused on Item 1 as the running example. Table 6.1 summarizes the basic characteristics of Item 1.

The essays vary in length and quality, reflecting a diverse range of student writing abilities. The target variable for the scoring engine is the holistic score, which ranges from 2 to 12. The dataset was partitioned into three distinct subsets: 1,426 essays in the training set, 357 in the validation set, and 589 in the test set.

6.2.5.2 Study Design

Consistent with the modern NLP pipeline described in previous sections, we applied a minimal preprocessing strategy to the raw essays. The application was limited to whitespace normalization to remove formatting issues. We then utilized WordPiece tokenization to obtain the initial word embedding, ensuring that the semantic representation of the essays was preserved.

A constrained grid search was conducted in Python (version 3.11.4) over three hyperparameters: (1) learning rate, (2) batch size, and (3) dropout rate. This design aimed to provide data-driven evidence of the effectiveness of modeling strategies for the automated scoring task by isolating the effects of these hyperparameters while holding all other components constant. Each hyperparameter was manipulated at three levels.

Learning rate was varied across 1×10^{-5}, 2×10^{-5}, and 3×10^{-5}. These values were chosen because they sit at the lower end of the standard fine-tuning range, minimizing the risk of "forgetting" pretrained knowledge. *Batch sizes were* set to 8, 16, and 32, allowing us to evaluate the trade-off between noisy, frequent updates from small batches and stable, smoothed gradients from larger batches. Finally, the *dropout rate* was varied across 0.10, 0.20, and 0.30, with higher values providing stronger regularization to prevent overfitting. The adjustments yielded 27 distinct hyperparameter configurations.

To isolate their impact, the base model architecture, optimizer, and activation function were held constant across all experimental conditions. Specifically, we used *DistilBERT-base-uncased* as the pretrained transformer architecture, selected for its computational efficiency and high feature-extraction performance in such settings. DistilBERT is a six-layer compressed model pretrained on BooksCorpus (Zhu et al., 2015) and English Wikipedia. For optimization, we chose the AdamW with a weight decay of 0.01, which is a modern variant of Adam with improved generalization (Loshchilov & Hutter, 2017). We also implemented a three-layer regression head with hidden dimensions [512, 256, 128] and ReLU activation (Nair & Hinton, 2010). The pooling strategy was set to the [*CLS*] token.

Each configuration was fine-tuned for up to 50 epochs. Typical recommendations of two to four epochs for BERT models are based on extensive, stable classification benchmarks. However, AES is a prompt-specific regression task with a comparatively smaller sample size and potentially noisier supervision. Therefore, allowing more potential epochs is expected to help ensure that promising configurations are not terminated prematurely due to short-term metric fluctuations. However, to ensure we captured the optimal model and prevent overfitting, we employed

TABLE 6.1 ASAP Dataset Summary (Set 1)

Item	*Prompt Background*	*Training*	*Validation*	*Test*	*Score Range*
1	Write an essay stating your opinion on the effects computers have on people.	1,426	357	589	(2, 12)

an early stopping mechanism with a patience of ten epochs. The consequence of the settings means that if the QWK on the validation set did not improve for ten consecutive epochs, fine-tuning was halted. During fine-tuning, all internal parameters, including word embeddings, were updated at each epoch. The final model for each configuration was selected based on the highest validation QWK, and it was then evaluated on the held-out test set to report the final results.

6.2.5.3 Results

The results of the hyperparameter grid search are summarized in Table 6.2, highlighting that BERT's performance is sensitive to the interaction between hyperparameters. Across the 27 configurations, validation QWK ranged from 0.78 to 0.86, and test QWK ranged from 0.61 to 0.85. Hyperparameters showed well-defined effects.

Configurations using the highest learning rate (3×10^{-5}) combined with high dropout (0.30) demonstrated marked instability; for instance, Config 24 yielded the lowest validation performance in the high-learning-rate bracket with a QWK of 0.78. The reconfiguration suggests that when the model weights are updated too aggressively while simultaneously losing too much information via dropout, the fine-tuning process struggles to converge on a generalized solution. In contrast, the most stable performance was observed with the lowest learning rate (1×10^{-5}). Across all batch sizes and dropout rates in this tier (Configs ID 1–9), the model consistently achieved validation QWKs between 0.8388 and 0.8574. The results indicate that a conservative optimization strategy effectively mitigates the risk of catastrophic forgetting, preserving the pretrained linguistic features necessary for scoring.

Model selection was based on the validation QWK, because the validation split was reserved for hyperparameter tuning and the test split was held out for final evaluation. The winning configuration was Config 16, which utilized a learning rate of 2×10^{-5}, a batch size of 32, and a dropout rate of 0.10. This model achieved the highest peak performance during training with a validation QWK of 0.86. When applied to the held-out test set, it yielded a QWK of 0.74, which suggests

TABLE 6.2 Grid Search Results

Config ID	*Learning Rate*	*Batch Size*	*Dropout*	*Validation QWK*	*Test QWK*
1	1×10^{-5}	8	0.1	0.85	0.82
2	1×10^{-5}	8	0.2	0.84	0.80
3	1×10^{-5}	8	0.3	0.85	0.72
4	1×10^{-5}	16	0.1	0.86	0.79
5	1×10^{-5}	16	0.2	0.84	0.80
6	1×10^{-5}	16	0.3	0.84	0.74
7	1×10^{-5}	32	0.1	0.85	0.83
8	1×10^{-5}	32	0.2	0.86	0.85
9	1×10^{-5}	32	0.3	0.85	0.81
10	2×10^{-5}	8	0.1	0.84	0.82
11	2×10^{-5}	8	0.2	0.85	0.69
12	2×10^{-5}	8	0.3	0.85	0.80
13	2×10^{-5}	16	0.1	0.85	0.81
14	2×10^{-5}	16	0.2	0.83	0.74
15	2×10^{-5}	16	0.3	0.81	0.65
16	2×10^{-5}	32	0.1	0.86	0.74
17	2×10^{-5}	32	0.2	0.85	0.81
18	2×10^{-5}	32	0.3	0.84	0.80
19	3×10^{-5}	8	0.1	0.84	0.84
20	3×10^{-5}	8	0.2	0.83	0.82
21	3×10^{-5}	8	0.3	0.84	0.79
22	3×10^{-5}	16	0.1	0.84	0.69
23	3×10^{-5}	16	0.2	0.84	0.81
24	3×10^{-5}	16	0.3	0.78	0.69
25	3×10^{-5}	32	0.1	0.85	0.74
26	3×10^{-5}	32	0.2	0.85	0.79
27	3×10^{-5}	32	0.3	0.84	0.61

some overfitting to the validation sample. Notably, the configuration with the highest test QWK used a slightly different setting (learning rate 1×10^{-5}, batch size 32, dropout 0.20) and achieved a validation QWK (0.86).

This pattern highlights that performance is driven by the interaction of hyperparameters rather than any single setting in isolation, and that the configuration that maximizes validation performance is not guaranteed to be the top performer on the test set. Although the process follows a rigorous selection protocol, the validation set is used repeatedly during model selection across many candidate configurations. As a result, the maximum validation QWK among a grid of configurations can be an optimistic estimate of true generalization, because it is selected from noisy validation measurements, an effect known as the winner's curse. To reduce sensitivity to validation noise, some advanced approaches can be applied to choose hyperparameters from a set of strong candidates rather than a single best point estimate. Specifically, we recommend creating a set of candidate's configurations within a small margin of the best validation QWK. From this set, select the configuration that has the highest average validation QWK across repeated samples, such as repeated train/validation splits or *K*-fold cross-validation.

6.3 BERT-Based NLP Pipeline for Reasoning and Thinking

This section outlines how a BERT-based NLP pipeline can be adapted to explore examinees' reasoning and thinking beyond assigning a score to their responses to CR items. Figure 6.2 provides a visual summary of the NLP pipeline using BERTopic (Grootendorst, 2022). The following subsections describe each step of the pipeline, which concludes with an empirical example illustrating its implementation for this educational measurement task.

A BERT-based pipeline for exploring reasoning and thinking is implemented using the topic modeling framework BERTopic (Grootendorst, 2022). In contrast to BERT-based automated scoring, which fine-tunes models to predict scores, BERTopic adopts a modular, unsupervised (i.e., exploratory) approach to uncover latent topics from examinees' responses. Thereby, rather than prioritizing prediction accuracy, BERTopic focuses on identifying and interpreting common themes, hereafter referred to as topics, that reflect how examinees articulate their reasoning. Because it focuses on document-level features, responses are represented using dense semantic embeddings, which are then clustered into topics and defined using the most predominant words per topic. The pipeline consists of three main steps: (1) text preprocessing; (2) feature extraction through document embeddings; and (3) modeling and evaluation, including dimensionality reduction, clustering, topic representation, and model evaluation.

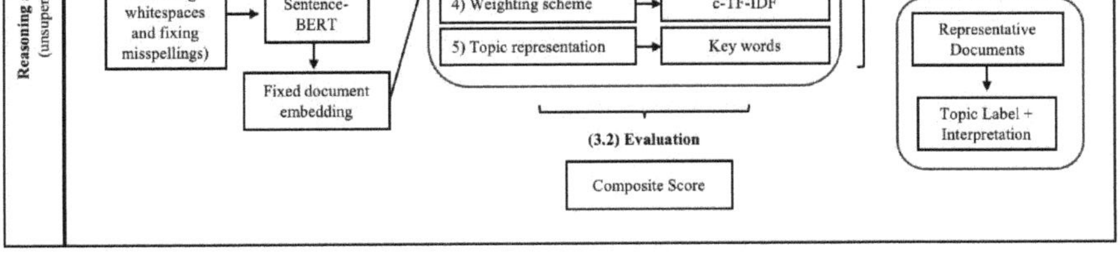

FIGURE 6.2 NLP pipeline for exploring examinees' reasoning and thinking using BERTopic.

6.3.1 Text Preprocessing

In datasets composed of brief, content-specific texts, such as short CR item responses, minimal preprocessing is often preferred to preserve the linguistic diversity and subtle variations in student expression (Grootendorst, 2022). Consistent with the preprocessing strategy used in the automated scoring task, text preprocessing is limited to whitespace normalization, such as stripping leading and trailing spaces and correcting spacing errors.

6.3.2 Feature Extraction

To explore examinees' reasoning and thinking, BERTopic uses document-level embeddings that generate a single vector representation per examinee response, enabling responses to be clustered based on their semantic similarity (Grootendorst, 2022). These embeddings are typically obtained using sentence-BERT, also referred to as the sentence-transformer framework (Reimers & Gurevych, 2019). Unlike predictive educational tasks such as AES, sentence-BERT employs an additional pooling layer, typically referred to as mean pooling, that aggregates contextualized word embeddings into a single document-level representation, known as document embeddings.

Sentence-BERT models are pretrained and fine-tuned on external semantic similarity tasks to map semantically similar sentences closer together within the embedding space. The original sentence-BERT was fine-tuned on external datasets such as (1) the Stanford Natural Language Inference corpus, a collection of 570,000 English sentence pairs labeled into entailment, contradiction, and semantic independence (Bowman, Angeli, Potts, & Manning, 2015); and (2) the semantic textual similarity corpus, which contains sentence pairs annotated with human scores. Nowadays, many pretrained models are available, often fine-tuned on broader corpora and optimized for various tasks, including clustering and semantic search (Reimers & Gurevych, 2019). Note this fine-tuning occurs before BERTopic and does not form part of the topic modeling process; document embeddings are therefore used as fixed representations.

6.3.3 Modeling and Evaluation

Once the examinees' answers have been converted into document embeddings, BERTopic initiates its modeling phase, which involves dimension reduction, clustering, tokenizer, weighting scheme, and topic representation. Because the structure and quality of the extracted topics depend on modeling choices and their corresponding hyperparameter settings, evaluation is conducted alongside modeling to ensure interpretable and distinct topics.

6.3.3.1 Modeling

1 *Dimension reduction*: Since cluster models struggle to handle high-dimensional data (Haviana et al., 2024), document embeddings need to be

reduced to yield more coherent topics (George & Sumathy, 2023). By default, BERTopic uses uniform manifold approximation and projection (UMAP), a nonlinear technique designed to preserve both local and global data structure (Haviana et al., 2024). UMAP calculates pairwise distances in the original embedding space and projects the data into a lower-dimensional space while maintaining these relationships through stochastic optimization (Asyaky & Mandala, 2021). Three hyperparameters need to be user-defined to begin dimensionality reduction with UMAP: (1) *distance metric*, specified in Python as *metric*, which determines the distance function used to compute similarities in a high-dimensional space, typically conducted using cosine similarity; (2) *number of neighbors*, specified as *n_neighbors*, which define how many sample points will be used when conducting the manifold approximation; and (3) *number of components*, specified as *n_components*, which indicates the expected dimensionality of the embedding after dimensionality reduction.

2 *Clustering*: After reducing the dimensionality of the embeddings, BERTopic utilizes clustering algorithms to group semantically related responses into coherent topics. This process is typically conducted via hierarchical density-based spatial clustering of applications with noise (HDBSCAN) or K-means, with HDBSCAN being the default algorithm in BERTopic. HDBSCAN is a non-parametric method that identifies clusters of varying shapes and densities while treating sparse data points as noise (Bu, Shu, Kang, Hu, & Zhao, 2023). It estimates the local density of data points in the reduced embedding space and automatically determines the number of clusters based on the underlying data structure. A notable advantage of HDBSCAN, particularly compared to probabilistic models such as LDA, is its ability to identify outlier documents. In Python, documents labeled as −1 indicate those noise examinees' answers that do not belong to any coherent topic cluster. Some of the hyperparameters that can be hyper-tuned are *minimal cluster size*, specified in Python as *min_cluster_size*, which controls the minimal number of examinees' responses to form a cluster, and the *minimal sample*, specified as *min_samples*, which controls how many outliers are allowed. In contrast, K-means partitions the data into a pre-specified number of clusters by minimizing within-cluster variance. Although less flexible than HDBSCAN, it allows for more direct control over topic granularity.

3 *Tokenizer*: Unlike AES, tokenization in BERTopic is not part of feature extraction and does not affect document embeddings or clustering results. Instead, tokenization is applied after clustering and serves exclusively to support topic representation. Specifically, BERTopic applies a traditional unigram-based tokenization procedure to extract keywords from documents within each topic. By default, it applies the tokenizer built into *CountVectorizer*, which separates words based on whitespace and punctuation (Rachel, Bhuvaneswari, &

Kumudha, 2024). Although this procedure resembles tokenization used in traditional topic models such as LDA, it is employed solely for identifying interpretable keywords and does not contribute to learning the topic structure.

4 *Weighting scheme*: The tokens obtained in the previous step are used with a class-based term frequency–inverse document frequency (c-TF–IDF) weighting scheme to determine the importance of words within each topic (Grootendorst, 2022). Unlike traditional TF–IDF, which calculates term importance at the document level, c-TF–IDF aggregates term frequencies across all documents assigned to a cluster and compares them to their frequency in the entire corpus. This approach emphasizes terms characteristic of a particular topic while downweighting common terms shared across topics. Refer to Mardones-Segovia et al. (2025) for more details on a traditional TF–IDF approach.
5 *Topic representation*: Topic representations in BERTopic are constructed by extracting the top-ranked words with the highest c-TF–IDF scores within each topic (Rachel et al., 2024). These keywords serve as concise summaries of the underlying thinking and reasoning process present in each topic.

After clustering and topic representation, BERTopic generates *topic assignments*, which indicate the topic label that each examinee's response receives based on its cluster membership. When the model is fit with *calculate_probabilities = True*, it also generates *topic proportions*, indicating the probability distribution of topics for each document.

These proportions enable a soft-clustering interpretation of topic membership, similar to LDA, allowing identification of documents most strongly associated with each topic. Such documents can then be used to guide LLMs' labeling and interpretation of topics (e.g., GPT, Gemini). However, these LLM-based interpretations must be carefully reviewed by domain experts to ensure their validity and accuracy.

6.3.3.2 Evaluation

Topic models can be evaluated using two complementary criteria: (1) topic coherence and (2) topic dissimilarity. Topic coherence measures the average semantic similarity among the top keywords within each topic, thereby reflecting the degree to which topics are internally consistent and semantically meaningful. In contrast, topic dissimilarity was computed as the average pairwise distance between all topic embeddings, where distance was defined as 1 − cosine similarity. This measure serves as a proxy for topic separability, ensuring that topics reflect semantically different aspects of examinees' reasoning rather than redundant or overlapping content (Grootendorst, 2022).

Dissimilarity values range from 0 to 1, with higher values indicating better separated topics and lower values indicating greater overlap. Embedding-based coherence ranges from −1 to 1, where higher values reflect stronger semantic relatedness among a topic's top words. To balance coherence and dissimilarity, we developed a *composite score*. Because these metrics operate on different scales, standardization is required before combining them into a unified quality index:

$$composite\ score = 0.5z\_dissimilarity + 0.5z\_coherence. \qquad (6.2)$$

Because the *z*-scores are standardized across all hyperparameter configurations evaluated in the grid search, the *composite score* is intended for *within-study* model selection rather than cross-study comparison. The distribution of scores, and therefore the meaning of a high value, is specific to the search space used in this study. Higher scores indicate configurations that achieve more coherent topics (internal consistency) and greater topic separability (non-redundancy), whereas lower scores reflect either reduced coherence, greater overlap among topics, or both.

In practice, hyperparameter configurations with the highest composite score represent the most interpretable and distinct topic solution. However, to ensure that the extracted topics are semantically coherent and aligned with the dataset's educational content, human raters should also conduct a qualitative review of the top-ranked keywords and representative examinee responses within each topic structure (Mardones-Segovia et al., 2025).

6.3.4 Educational Study 2: Reasoning and Thinking Analysis Using BERTopic

The following section showcases how BERTopic can be used to analyze examinees' reasoning in a science context and conduct a grid search to identify the hyperparameter configurations that yield the most coherent and diverse topic structure.

6.3.4.1 Data

The dataset included responses from 870 fifth-grade students who completed a test comprising 23 multiple-choice items and three CR items (items 23–25). This case study focuses on Item 25, which includes three CR sub-items about electricity use in everyday life. These responses were short and domain-specific, reflecting elementary-level scientific reasoning and conceptual understanding. This dataset was previously analyzed using traditional NLP methods, and LDA analysis indicated that a four-topic model yielded the most interpretable structure. The resulting topic structure extracted different aspects of students' reasoning regarding electricity, including (1) *Properties of current versus static electricity*, (2) *Connecting natural phenomena and human-made electricity*, (3) *Electricity distribution systems*, and (4) *Everyday uses of electricity* (Mardones-Segovia et al., 2025).

6.3.4.2 Study Design

We conducted a grid search in Python 3.11.4 using a full-factorial experimental design, systematically varying text preprocessing strategies, BERTopic hyperparameter configurations, and topic modeling strategies (i.e., free- versus fixed-topic structures). The following paragraphs describe the selected levels for each factor and provide a rationale for each decision.

In datasets composed of content-specific texts, such as the science responses examined here, minimal preprocessing is often preferred (Grootendorst, 2022). However, there is currently limited empirical evidence on how preprocessing choices affect BERTopic in educational contexts. Drawing on this rationale, we examined four preprocessing strategies applied cumulatively: (1) minimal preprocessing, involving lowercase conversion and whitespace normalization; (2) fixing misspellings, which builds on the first strategy by correcting spelling errors; (3) stopword removal, which incorporates the previous steps and eliminates common stopwords; and (4) lemmatization, which includes all prior steps and standardizes words to their base or dictionary form. For feature extraction, we used the default pretrained language model called *all-MiniLM-L6-v2*.

The model was selected based on two key considerations: It adapts well to domain-specific datasets of limited size (Yin & Zhang, 2024) and supports strong topic coherence in unsupervised settings (Sontheimer, Fahlbusch, Chou, & Kuo, 2025). To reduce the dimensionality of the high-dimensional sentence embeddings, we applied UMAP, varying two key hyperparameters: the number of neighbors (*n_neighbors* = 10 or 15) and the number of output components (*n_components* = 5 or 10).

Two strategies were used to determine the topic structure: (1) a free-topic structure using HDBSCAN, which allowed the number of topics to emerge naturally, and (2) a fixed-topic structure, where similar topics were merged post hoc to enforce a predefined number of topics. In this setting, the *candidate_n_topics* parameter was varied from 3 to 10 to examine how topic granularity influences interpretability and redundancy in the resulting topic structures (Yuan & Yang, 2019). For both strategies, two *min_samples* parameters were varied (5 or 10), with lower values detecting finer-grained clusters, at the expense of increasing noise. In contrast, higher values result in fewer but more robust clusters. Finally, to construct interpretable topic representations, we employed c-TF–IDF to prioritize words that are frequent within a topic but less frequent across other topics, thereby improving topic distinctiveness.

6.3.4.3 Evaluation and Interpretation

For each hyperparameter configuration, we computed topic dissimilarity and topic coherence, and then ranked these models using the *composite score* defined in Equation (6.2). Although qualitative analyses are essential for thoroughly assessing topic interpretability, the aim of this empirical study was methodological and illustrative. Therefore, we do not provide manual topic interpretation and instead focus on the quantitative evaluation derived from the grid search.

6.3.4.4 Results

Figures 6.3a and 6.3b present the results of the grid search of the two modeling strategies: (1) fixed topic and (2) free topic, respectively.

Under the fixed-topic strategy, composite scores varied across UMAP configurations. Overall, higher scores were observed with *n_components* = 5 compared to *n_components* = 10. For *n_components* = 5, composite scores tended to increase as the number of candidate topics rose from two to four or five. Beyond this point, however, improvements in composite scores plateaued, suggesting diminishing returns from adding additional topics. The highest-scoring configuration within this strategy (composite score = 1.27) was obtained using minimal preprocessing with a three-topic structure (before removing the outlier topic), *n_neighbors* = 10, *n_components* = 5, and *min_samples* =10. Minimal preprocessing also achieved a final score of 1.27 under a different configuration, also with a three-topic structure (before removing the outlier topic), but with *n_neighbors* = 15, *n_components* = 5, and *min_samples* = 5, indicating robustness to changes in neighborhood size and clustering density when the text preprocessing strategy was held constant. For *n_components* = 10, minimal preprocessing did not yield the highest composite score; instead, values remained relatively steady around zero across candidate topic models ranging from three to 10. Under this configuration, the highest composite scores across UMAP neighborhood sizes were achieved when misspellings were corrected or stopwords removed, particularly with *min_samples* = 5. Lemmatization, on the other hand, consistently resulted in the lowest composite scores.

Under the free-topic strategy (Figure 6.3b), the model automatically determined the number of topics based on the underlying clustering structure. The best performing model across all configurations (composite score = 1.56) was obtained with minimal preprocessing, a three-topic model (after removing the outlier topic), *n_neighbors* = 15, *n_components* = 5, and *min_samples* = 5. Minimal preprocessing also achieved the same composite score (1.56) under a different configuration, also with a three-topic structure (after removing the outlier topic), but with *n_neighbors* = 15, *n_components* = 5, and *min_samples* = 10. These results suggest that BERTopic's performance remained stable across different HDBSCAN settings when the UMAP embedding was fixed. In contrast

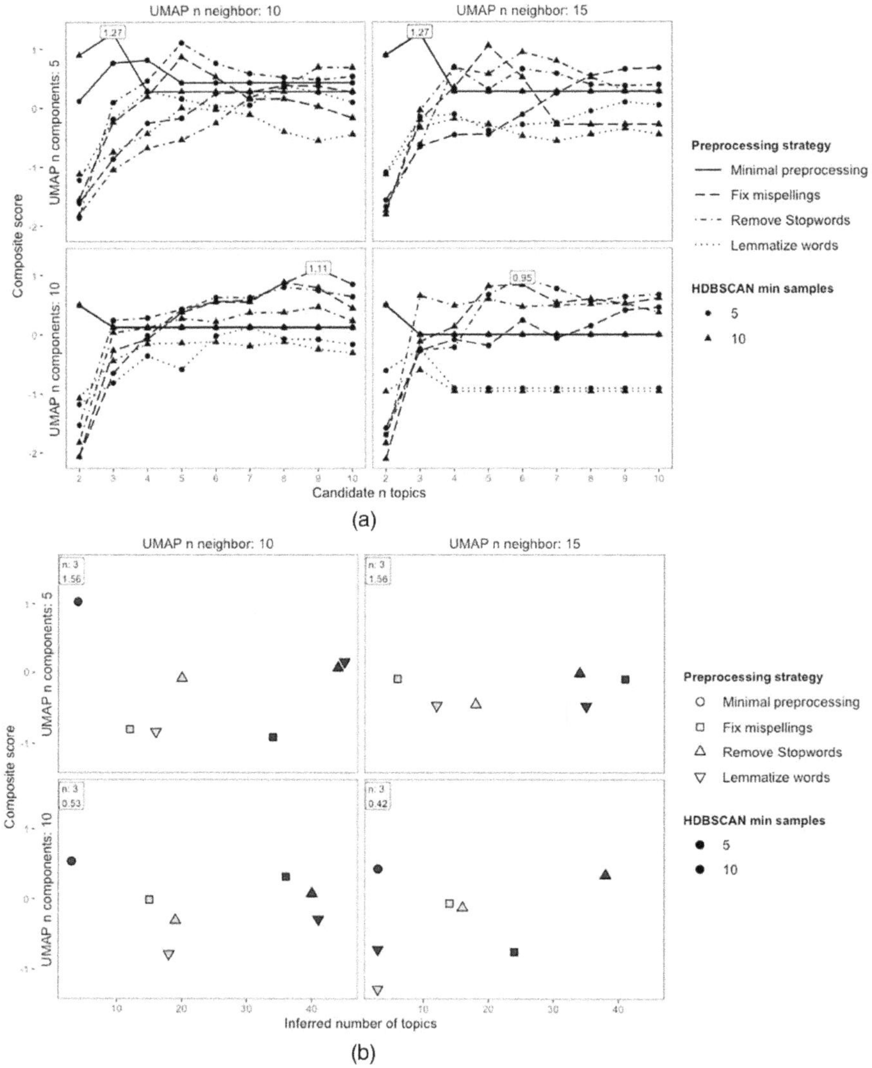

FIGURE 6.3 Comparison of fixed and free modeling strategies in topic modeling.

Note. In the fixed-topic strategy, a candidate number of topics may retain an outlier topic. Final score = $0.5z_{dissimilarity} + 0.5z_{coherence}$. For the highlighted configurations, the raw metric values were approximately fixed topic: coherence = 0.35, dissimilarity = 0.36; free-topic: coherence = 0.34, dissimilarity = 0.35.

to the fixed-topic strategy, minimal preprocessing consistently yielded the highest-scoring configurations, whereas fixing misspellings or stopword removal did not appear among the top configurations.

TABLE 6.3 Glossary of NLP Terms Used in This Chapter

Term	*Definition*
NLP pipeline	End-to-end workflow for text analysis: preprocessing, feature extraction (embeddings), modeling, and evaluation.
Token	The minimal text unit processed by a model (e.g., word, subword, or special symbol).
Tokenization	The procedure that splits text into tokens; can be word-, character-, or subword-based.
Subword tokenization	Strategy that decomposes rare words into frequent subunits to balance vocabulary size and coverage.
WordPiece	A data-driven subword algorithm used by BERT to build a compact vocabulary of tokens and sub-tokens.
Document-term matrix (DTM)	Matrix with documents as rows and terms as columns; entries are counts or weights (e.g., TF–IDF).
n-gram	Contiguous sequence of *n* tokens (e.g., bigram, trigram) used as simple context features.
Embedding	A dense, real-valued vector representation of linguistic units (tokens, sentences, documents).
Word embedding (static)	Context-independent vector for a word (e.g., Word2Vec); same vector across all contexts.
Contextualized embedding	Vector whose values depend on the surrounding context (e.g., BERT token or sentence embeddings).
Sentence embedding	A single vector summarizing a sentence or short text (e.g., from sentence-BERT).
Transformer	Neural architecture built from stacked self-attention and position-wise feedforward sublayers.
Positional encoding	Numeric encoding was added to token vectors so that a transformer can exploit word order.
Self-attention	Mechanism that computes context-dependent representations by weighting token-to-token relations via queries, keys, and values.
Multi-head attention	Parallel self-attention "heads" that capture complementary relational patterns.
Feedforward neural network (FFN)	Position-wise nonlinear mapping (typically implemented as two affine layers with an activation) is applied to each token independently within a transformer layer.
Residual connection	Skip connection that adds a layer's input to its output to stabilize optimization and preserve information.
Layer normalization	Normalization applied to hidden features within a layer to improve training stability.
Encoder (transformer)	Stack of attention+FFN blocks that maps an input sequence to contextualized representations (used by BERT).
Decoder (transformer)	Stack with masked self-attention (and optional cross-attention) used for generation.
BERT	Bidirectional encoder representations from transformers; an encoder-only model used for feature extraction or fine-tuning.

(*Continued*)

TABLE 6.3 (Continued)

Term	*Definition*
[*CLS*], [*SEP*], [*PAD*]	Special tokens for sequence-level representation, segment separation, and padding, respectively.
Attention mask	Binary vector that marks real tokens (1) versus padding (0) to restrict attention to valid inputs.
Embedding dimension pre-training	The length of the vector representation (e.g., 768 for *BERT_base*). Large-scale self-supervised training (e.g., masked language modeling) that learns general linguistic representations.
Fine-tuning or training	Task-specific supervised adaptation of a pretrained model's parameters on labeled data.
Loss function	Objective minimized during training (e.g., mean squared error for regression, cross-entropy for classification).
Optimizer	Algorithm that updates parameters using gradients (e.g., Adam, AdamW).
Learning rate	Step size controls the magnitude of parameter updates during optimization.
Batch size	Number of examples processed before a parameter update.
Epoch	One complete pass through the training set.
Dropout	Regularization that randomly sets activations to zero during training to reduce overfitting.
Activation function	Nonlinear mapping within neural networks (e.g., ReLU, GELU, Tanh).
Hyperparameter	User-specified setting controlling model architecture or training (e.g., learning rate, batch size).
Grid/random search	Systematic (grid) or stochastic (random) procedures to explore hyperparameter configurations.
Quadratic weighted kappa (QWK)	An agreement index for ordinal scores that penalizes larger disagreements more heavily.
LSA	Latent semantic analysis; matrix-factorization method applied to DTMs for semantic structure.
LDA	Latent Dirichlet Allocation; probabilistic topic model over DTMs producing distributions over topics and words.
BERTopic	A topic modeling framework using sentence embeddings, dimensionality reduction, clustering, and c-TF–IDF for topic representation.
UMAP	Uniform manifold approximation and projection; nonlinear dimensionality reduction preserving local/global structure.
HDBSCAN	Density-based clustering that discovers variable-density clusters and labels sparse points as noise.
c-TF–IDF	Class-based TF–IDF that aggregates documents in a cluster to highlight topic-specific tokens.
Topic coherence	Measure of semantic relatedness among a topic's top words (higher indicates more interpretable topics).
Topic dissimilarity	Separation among topic representations (e.g., 1 − cosine similarity), indicating non-redundancy.

(*Continued*)

TABLE 6.3 (Continued)

Term	*Definition*
Attention head	One of the parallel attention mechanisms within multi-head attention.
Classification head	Task-specific layer(s) placed on top of embeddings (e.g., using the [*CLS*] vector) for prediction.
Early stopping	Training halt criterion triggered when validation performance no longer improves, to prevent overfitting.

6.4 Conclusion and Discussion

This chapter provides a comprehensive review of a BERT-based NLP pipeline for evaluating examinees' written responses to CR items. It outlines the general workflow in the Section 6.2 and illustrates how each pipeline component can be adapted through two educational measurement tasks. The key technical terms used throughout this chapter are summarized in Table 6.3.

The first measurement task focused on AES and illustrated how a pretrained BERT model can be adapted for automated scoring through different hyperparameter configurations. With minimal preprocessing and a stratified data split, we conducted a constrained grid search over learning rate, batch size, and dropout while holding the model architecture and other training components constant.

The grid search results showed that DistilBERT's scoring performance was primarily shaped by interactions among hyperparameters rather than by any single setting in isolation. Across the 27 configurations, validation QWK ranged from 0.78 to 0.86, and test QWK ranged from 0.61 to 0.85, with an unstable behavior emerging when a high learning rate was paired with high dropout, suggesting difficulty in converging to a generalized solution under overly aggressive updates and heavy regularization. Modest differences across individual parameter values were still observable. For example, the lowest learning rate tier consistently produced strong validation performance across batch sizes and dropout settings, indicating that single-parameter effects exist but are best interpreted in context. Importantly, the configuration that maximized validation QWK did not yield the highest test performance.

In contrast, the strongest test QWK was achieved by a nearby but different setting, underscoring that validation-optimal choices may reflect overfitting or noise when many candidates are compared. Overall, the tuning results provide a practical basis for selecting a strong configuration for this task. Moreover, it also suggests that when computational budget permits, confirming the choice across a small set of top-performing settings with cross-validation can further strengthen confidence in generalization.

The second measurement task illustrated the use of BERTopic to explore reasoning and thinking in examinees' answers to CR items. A grid search was conducted to identify the hyperparameter combination that yielded the most coherent topic representations and the most remarkable dissimilarity between topics. The consistent improvement in final scores, achieved with minimal preprocessing across search strategies, highlights the advantage of retaining richer linguistic information when using BERTopic. These results show practical benefits compared to traditional NLP pipeline guidelines, where aggressive text preprocessing, which is often iterative, time-consuming, and dependent on expert judgment, is often pointed out as a critical aspect to achieve interpretable results.

When comparing BERTopic's performance across search strategies, the results showed that post hoc topic fixing did not outperform the final scores obtained with a free-topic structure. These results thereby highlight that using an automatic approach to identify the best topic structure can lead to a more coherent and diverse topic representation, particularly when minimal preprocessing is applied. This pattern is consistent with previous evidence reported in computer science contexts (e.g., Grootendorst, 2022). Similar to the automated scoring task results, BERTopic's performance appears to vary with hyperparameter settings, suggesting that optimal configurations may be corpus-dependent. Future applications of BERTopic in educational contexts may therefore require testing different hyperparameter sets to identify the topic structure that best summarizes examinees' thinking and reasoning.

Compared to traditional LDA applied to this dataset by Mardones-Segovia et al. (2025), BERTopic identified fewer topics, likely due to the combined influence of embedding-based clustering and the composite final score, which explicitly balanced topic coherence and dissimilarity. Note, however, that because the present study focused on illustration and methodological evaluation, the interpretability of the highest performing topic structures was not assessed. Future work should therefore directly compare LDA and BERTopic results with respect to topic interpretability and coherence.

In summary, both studies demonstrated how to use BERT-based NLP techniques for educational measurement tasks and the importance of selecting an appropriate set of hyperparameters within such an architecture. However, this chapter also acknowledges its limitations. Both studies relied on quantitative approaches to evaluate the performance of BERT-based models, potentially overlooking other factors that affect the validity of their interpretations. Likewise, although the empirical results show important patterns, future studies should investigate the performance of BERT-based models across multiple hyperparameter configurations, sample sizes, text lengths, and score ranges to guide researchers and practitioners aligned with educational measurement standards.

Note

1 https://www.kaggle.com/c/asap-aes/data.

References

Adoma, A. F., Henry, N.-M., Chen, W., & Andre, N. R. (2020, December). Recognizing emotions from texts using a bert-based approach. In *2020 17th international computer conference on wavelet active media technology and information processing (ICCWAMTIP), Chengdu, China* (pp. 62–66).

Arisoy, E., Sainath, T. N., Kingsbury, B., & Ramabhadran, B. (2012, June). Deep neural network language models. In *Proceedings of the NAACL-HLT 2012 workshop: Will we ever really replace the n-gram model? on the future of language modeling for HLT* (pp. 20–28).

Asyaky, M. S., & Mandala, R. (2021, September). Improving the performance of HDBSCAN on short text clustering by using word embedding and UMAP. In *2021 8th international conference on advanced informatics: Concepts, theory and applications (ICAICTA)* (pp. 1–6).

Blei, D. M., Ng, A. Y., & Jordan, M. I. (2003). Latent Dirichlet allocation. *Journal of Machine Learning Research, 3*, 993–1022.

Bowman, S. R., Angeli, G., Potts, C., & Manning, C. D. (2015, September). A large annotated corpus for learning natural language inference. In *Proceedings of the 2015 conference on empirical methods in natural language processing* (pp. 632–642).

Bu, W., Shu, H., Kang, F., Hu, Q., & Zhao, Y. (2023). Software subclassification based on bertopic-bert-bilstm model. *Electronics, 12*(18), 3798.

Burstein, J., McCaffrey, D. F., Holtzman, S., & Klebanov, B. B. (2023). Making sense of college students' writing achievement and retention with automated writing evaluation. In V. Yaneva & M. Von Davier (Eds.), *Advancing Natural Language Processing in Educational Assessment* (p. 217). Routledge.

Cardozo-Gaibisso, L., Kim, S., Buxton, C., & Cohen, A. (2019). Thinking beyond the score: Multidimensional analysis of student performance to inform the next generation of science assessments. *Journal of Research in Science Teaching, 1*(57), 856–878.

Deerwester, S., Dumais, S. T., Furnas, G. W., Landauer, T. K., & Harshman, R. (1990). Indexing by latent semantic analysis. *Journal of the American Society for Information Science, 41*(6), 391–407.

Devlin, J., Chang, M.-W., Lee, K., & Toutanova, K. (2019, June). Bert: Pre-training of deep bidirectional transformers for language understanding. In *Proceedings of the 2019 conference of the North American chapter of the association for computational linguistics: human language technologies, volume 1 (long and short papers)* (pp. 4171–4186).

Doewes, A., Kurdhi, N., & Saxena, A. (2023, July). Evaluating quadratic weighted kappa as the standard performance metric for automated essay scoring. In *16th international conference on educational data mining, EDM 2023* (pp. 103–113).

Ellis, N. C. (2008). The dynamics of second language emergence: Cycles of language use, language change, and language acquisition. *The Modern Language Journal, 92*(2), 232–249.

George, L., & Sumathy, P. (2023). An integrated clustering and bert framework for improved topic modeling. *International Journal of Information Technology, 15*(4), 2187–2195.

Goodfellow, I., Bengio, Y., Courville, A., & Bengio, Y. (2016). *Deep learning* (Vol. 1) (No. 2). MIT Press Cambridge.

Grootendorst, M. (2022). Bertopic: Neural topic modeling with a class-based tf-idf procedure. *arXiv preprint arXiv:2203.05794.*

Hadi, M. U., Qureshi, R., Shah, A., Irfan, M., Zafar, A., Shaikh, M. B., … & Mirjalili, S. (2023). Large language models: A comprehensive survey of its applications, challenges, limitations, and future prospects. *Authorea Preprints*, *1*(3), 1–26.

Hamner, B., Morgan, J., Lynnvandev, M., & Ark, T. (2012). The hewlett foundation: Automated essay scoring. Kaggle. [Google Scholar].

Haviana, S. F. C., Mulyono, S., Salim, C. A., Adli, M. F., Febriansah, M. T., Sulaiman, N. S., & Yaqob, A. (2024, September). Leveraging transformer-based topic modeling using BERTopic for publication venue recommendation. In *2024 11th international conference on electrical engineering, computer science and informatics (EECSI)* (pp. 556–562).

Hendrycks, D., & Gimpel, K. (2016). Gaussian error linear units (gelus). *arXiv preprint arXiv:1606.08415.*

Hickman, L., Thapa, S., Tay, L., Cao, M., & Srinivasan, P. (2022). Text preprocessing for text mining in organizational research: Review and recommendations. *Organizational Research Methods*, *25*(1), 114–146.

Jiao, Q., & Zhang, S. (2021, March). A brief survey of word embedding and its recent development. In *2021 IEEE 5th advanced information technology, electronic and automation control conference (IAEAC)* (Vol. 5, pp. 1697–1701).

Jing, K., & Xu, J. (2019). A survey on neural network language models. *arXiv preprint arXiv:1906.03591.*

Jurafsky, D., & Martin, J. H. (2026). *Speech and language processing: An introduction to natural language processing, computational linguistics, and speech recognition* (3rd edition). Internet: https://web.stanford.edu/~jurafsky/slp3/ed3book_jan26.pdf [Accessed: April 19, 2026].

Kingma, D. P., & Ba, J. (2014). Adam: A method for stochastic optimization. *arXiv preprint arXiv:1412.6980.*

Kuechler, W. L., & Simkin, M. G. (2010). Why is performance on multiple-choice tests and constructed-response tests not more closely related? Theory and an empirical test. *Decision Sciences Journal of Innovative Education*, *8*(1), 55–73.

LeCun, Y., Bottou, L., Bengio, Y., & Haffner, P. (2002). Gradient-based learning applied to document recognition. *Proceedings of the IEEE*, *86*(11), 2278–2324.

Liu, O. L., Brew, C., Blackmore, J., Gerard, L., Madhok, J., & Linn, M. C. (2014). Automated scoring of constructed-response science items: Prospects and obstacles. *Educational Measurement: Issues and Practice*, *33*(2), 19–28.

Loshchilov, I., & Hutter, F. (2017). Decoupled weight decay regularization. *arXiv preprint arXiv:1711.05101.*

Lottridge, S., Ormerod, C., & Jafari, A. (2023). Psychometric considerations when using deep learning for automated scoring. In V. Yaneva & M. Von Davier (Eds.), *Advancing Natural Language Processing in Educational Assessment* (pp. 15–30). Routledge.

Maas, A. L., Hannun, A. Y., & Ng, A. Y. (2013). Rectifier nonlinearities improve neural network acoustic models. In *Proceeding of the 30th International Conference in Machine Learning* (Vol. 30, No.1, p. 3).

Mardones-Segovia, C., Wang, S., & Cohen, A. S. (2025). Natural language processing pipeline for assessment data: An r-based tutorial. *Chinese/English Journal of Educational Measurement and Evaluation*, *6*(2), 3.

Nair, V., & Hinton, G. E. (2010). Rectified linear units improve restricted boltzmann machines. In *Proceedings of the 27th international conference on machine learning (ICML-10)* (pp. 807–814).

Palmer, D. D. (2010). Text preprocessing. In R. Dale, H. Moisl, & H. Somers (Eds.), *Handbook of natural language processing* (pp. 11–35). New York: Marcel Dekker, Inc.

Rachel, J, J. L., Bhuvaneswari, A., & Kumudha, M. (2024, April). Topic modeling based clustering of disaster tweets using BERTopic. In *2024 MIT art, design and technology school of computing international conference (MITADTSoCiCon)* (pp. 1–6).

Reimers, N., & Gurevych, I. (2019). Sentence-bert: Sentence embeddings using siamese bert-networks. *arXiv preprint arXiv:1908.10084.*

Sanh, V., Debut, L., Chaumond, J., & Wolf, T. (2019). Distilbert, a distilled version of bert: Smaller, faster, cheaper and lighter. *arXiv preprint arXiv:1910.01108.*

Shin, H., & Oh, S. (2021). Feature-weighted sampling for proper evaluation of classification models. *Applied Sciences, 11*(5), 2039.

Sontheimer, M., Fahlbusch, J., Chou, S.-Y., & Kuo, Y.-L. (2025). Content analysis of e-participation platforms in Taiwan with topic modeling: How to train and evaluate neural topic models? *Applied Sciences, 15*(5), 2263.

Tang, C., Xiong, J., & Engelhard, G. (2025). Identification of writing strategies in educational assessments with an unsupervised learning measurement framework. *Education Sciences, 15*(7), 912.

Wolf, T., Debut, L., Sanh, V., Chaumond, J., Delangue, C., Moi, A., … & Rush, A. M. (2020, October). Transformers: State-of-the-art natural language processing. In *Proceedings of the 2020 conference on empirical methods in natural language processing: System demonstrations* (pp. 38–45).

Wu, Y., Schuster, M., Chen, Z., Le, Q. V., Norouzi, M., Macherey, W., … & Dean, J. (2016). Google's neural machine translation system: Bridging the gap between human and machine translation. *arXiv preprint arXiv:1609.08144.*

Xiong, J., & Li, F. (2023). Bilevel topic model-based multitask learning for constructed-responses multidimensional automated scoring and interpretation. *Educational Measurement: Issues and Practice, 42*(2), 42–61.

Yaneva, V., Baldwin, P., Ha, L., A., & Runyon, C. (2023). Extracting linguistic signal from item text and its application to modeling item characteristics. In V. Yaneva & M. Von Davier (Eds.), *Advancing natural language processing in educational assessment* (pp. 167–182). Routledge.

Yin, C., & Zhang, Z. (2024, October). A study of sentence similarity based on the all-minilm-l6-v2 model with "same semantics, different structure" after fine tuning. In *2024 2nd international conference on image, algorithms and artificial intelligence (ICIAAI 2024)* (pp. 677–684). Atlantis Press.

Yuan, C., & Yang, H. (2019). Research on k-value selection method of k-means clustering algorithm. *J, 2*(2), 226–235.

Zhu, Y., Kiros, R., Zemel, R., Salakhutdinov, R., Urtasun, R., Torralba, A., & Fidler, S. (2015). Aligning books and movies: Towards story-like visual explanations by watching movies and reading books. In *Proceedings of the IEEE international conference on computer vision* (pp. 19–27).

7

RAPID ITEM GENERATION AND THE REVOLUTIONARY IMPACT OF GENERATIVE AI

Kimberly Swygert, Tahereh Firoozi, and Mark Gierl

7.1 Introduction to Traditional Item Development

The item serves as the fundamental unit of analysis in educational and psychological testing, where each item provides a building block required to create the final test form (Lane, Raymond, & Haladyna, 2016). Test score reliability and validity evidence for test score uses are directly linked to the performance of items, and the concept of "high-quality" assessments is based on the psychometric characteristics of items (Kane, 1992, 2013; American Educational Research Association, the American Psychological Association, and the National Council on Measurement in Education, 2014). Therefore, it comes as no surprise that item development is often characterized as the most important activity in the testing process (Haladyna & Rodriguez, 2013; Rodriguez & Haladyna, 2013).

The traditional approach to creating test items, defined here as single best option multiple-choice questions, or MCQs, relies on subject matter experts (SMEs) writing each item individually. Item writing is iterative: SMEs apply judgment and expertise to draft items, which are then edited, reviewed, and revised until they meet quality standards. SMEs play a critical role by identifying, organizing, and evaluating content. Each item reflects an SME's unique conceptualization of knowledge and skills; this introduces subjectivity into the item development process and renders each item unique. This individuality makes item writing an "art" grounded in SME knowledge and insight that carries the risk of introducing subjective bias into MCQs (Schmeiser & Welch, 2006).

Due to this subjectivity, guidelines and review processes are used to increase standardization of the item output. Item-writing guidelines are used to ensure fairness and equity (Haladyna, Downing, & Rodriguez, 2002). These guidelines summarize best practices, common errors, and expectations. Haladyna and Downing

DOI: 10.4324/9781003621522-7

(1989) introduced one of the first comprehensive MCQ guidelines, a 46-rule taxonomy based on authoritative references and expert input, with the goal to consolidate standards for producing clear, fair, and valid items. In 2002, Haladyna, Downing, and Rodriguez refined this taxonomy into a concise 31-rule guideline using empirical evidence and expert consensus. These oft-cited guidelines have been extremely influential for item writing in the fields of social sciences, medicine, and psychology. Iterative refinement via item review is used to evaluate whether the item has met the important outcomes described in the guidelines. Reviews are usually conducted by committees of SMEs who were not involved in the initial item-writing activities. This review yields detailed feedback on different standards of item quality that, in turn, can be used to revise and improve the original item.

7.2 Limitations of Traditional Item Writing

The traditional item-writing approach has two limitations. First, it is time-consuming and costly because each item is treated as a unique unit requiring individual writing, editing, and review (Drasgow, Luecht, & Bennett, 2006). Numerous quality components such as curriculum alignment, difficulty, clarity, and format must be assessed for every item, often by SMEs whose time is costly. Rudner (2010) estimated that the cost of developing one operational item for a large-scale test using the traditional item-writing approach ranged from $1,500 to $2,500 USD (p. 157). As Drasgow et al. (2006) noted:

> The demand for large numbers of items is challenging to satisfy because the traditional approach to test development uses the item as the fundamental unit of currency. That is, each item is individually hand-crafted — written, reviewed, revised, edited, entered into a computer, and calibrated — as if no other like it had ever been created before.
>
> *(p. 473)*

Second, the traditional approach to item writing is expensive and possibly infeasible to scale. When 500 items are needed, 500 items must be individually written and reviewed. Large-scale production does not shorten or simplify the process for each; despite overall increase in output, the process remains labor-intensive due to the human effort required for drafting, reviewing, and revising items.

7.3 From Traditional Item Development to Automatic Item Generation

Automatic item generation (AIG) is an alternative approach to item writing that can address the need to produce large numbers of new test items in an efficient and economical manner (AIG; Gierl & Haladyna, 2013; Gierl, Lai, & Tanygin, 2021; Irvine & Kyllonen, 2002). AIG as a way to leverage technology was described by Bormuth (1970) more than 50 years ago; it has recently gained renewed interest because testing organizations require large numbers of high-quality, content-specific test items. One factor in this increased demand is the popularization of multiple test forms (Roid & Haladyna, 1982) to address item exposure and test security concerns. The longstanding use of a single form meant the content could easily become exposed because all examinees viewed the same set of items; this led to the concept of developing parallel test forms, containing different items measuring the same content and construct, that can be administered concurrently. Because parallel forms are used interchangeably, items on each form must be equivalent in their content and statistical specifications, meaning that a larger volume of generated items and a process to ensure comparable content and statistical characteristics are required.

7.4 Early Developments in Automatic Item Generation

The demand for more items initially led to a predecessor of AIG as we currently know it, *systematic item writing*. Guttman (1959) proposed facet theory, which organizes related knowledge into components called "facets." This approach enabled item creation through knowledge substitution, reducing subjectivity by constraining item structure. Building on this logic, Bormuth (1970) introduced a rule-based method using prose transformations and algorithmic expressions. While innovative, Bormuth's approach was limited to text-based items and relied on transformational grammar, which was unfamiliar to most test developers (Haladyna, 1994).

The first widely adopted systematic framework was *item shell* development (Roid & Haladyna, 1982). A shell contains an outline of the item's structure; this structure is then replicated to produce new items by manually substituting content into the shell to produce similar items. Unlike Bormuth's method, shells were concrete, generalizable to text and numeric content, and practical for SMEs (Haladyna, 1994). This approach, sometimes called *templating* or *cloning*, ensured comparable statistical properties by controlling substitution content (Glas, 2006).

7.5 Item Modeling: The First Modern Approach to Automatic Item Generation

With the introduction of *item modeling* (LaDuca, Staples Templeton, & Holzman, 1986; Bejar et al., 2003), an inductive approach for generating items that uses structures of knowledge, the unit of analysis changed from the individual item to groups or sets of items. An item model differs from an item shell by having a modular structure composed of elements. An item model must contain at least one element, where an element is a component in the item that contains variable content and rules determining how that content can vary. An element can take on many different forms, as a part of a sentence, a whole sentence, a key term, or a numerical value.

When an item model with elements is manipulated, two types of items can be created: *variants* or *isomorphs*. Unlike clones or templated items, variants are expected to be psychometrically different from one another (e.g., different difficulty values). Since generated items differ only by their varied elements defined within the item model, elements that affect the psychometric properties are known as *radicals* (Bejar, 2002). However, it is possible to constrain item models to generate isomorphs that are expected to be psychometrically comparable to one another (e.g., similar difficulty values); in these models, the elements that affect the psychometric properties are known as *incidentals* (Bejar, 2002). In short, models with radical elements can be used to generate variant items across a range of difficulty levels, whereas models with incidental elements can be used to generate isomorph items within a specific range of difficulty levels.

The orchestration of incidental and radical elements in AIG requires a theoretical framework, referred to as *strong and weak theory* (Bejar, 2002; Drasgow, Luecht, & Bennett, 2006). Strong theory represents a deterministic approach where items are generated precisely to measure specific skills and knowledge at predictable difficulty levels. Cognitive models anchored to a theoretical framework prescribe how knowledge and skills are organized within a content area, guiding item model development to generate isomorphs where the psychometric properties can be estimated for each manipulated component (Drasgow et al., 2006). When successful, this approach strengthens the inferential link between item performance and score interpretation because cognitive model features predict test performance (Bejar, 2012).

In the absence of well-defined cognitive models, item-writing guidelines (e.g., Haladyna & Downing, 1989; Haladyna, Downing, & Rodriguez, 2002) form the basis of weak theory where SMEs develop radicals based on judgment and experience, identifying features expected to affect difficulty without theoretical defensibility. While less precise than strong theory, weak theory offers a practical solution when cognitive models or knowledge structures are unavailable.

7.6 Limitations of Item Modeling

Item modeling faced notable limitations, and few organizations were quick to adopt it for creating live test items. It was most successful in predictable content areas like mathematics (Gierl, Lai, Hogan, & Matovinovic, 2015) but showed less success in areas within language arts. Methods such as transformational grammar (Bormuth, 1970) and item design rules (Hornke, 2002) were proposed for verbal analogies and reading comprehension yet produced only small, non-isomorphic item sets. Text-rich domains posed challenges because language arts items often rely on fixed facts, limiting systematic variation.

Another limiting factor was the absence of guidance for implementing item modeling. Research often emphasized psychometric properties while neglecting content-related issues (Janssen, Schepers, & Peres, 2004; Sinharay, Johnson, &

Williamson, 2003); focused on content without addressing technology (Pugh et al., 2016); or explored technology without considering the psychometrics (Karamanis, Ha, & Mitkov, 2006; Reiter & Dale, 1997). A comprehensive framework to orchestrate tasks from conceptualizing content to generating operational items was missing.

Evaluating item quality posed another challenge. Traditional item writing relies on established guidelines, but no comparable standards existed for item models capable of producing hundreds of items. While strong theory, AIG, was ideal for capturing content expertise, examples were limited to specialized areas such as spatial reasoning (Bejar, 1990; Janssen, 2010), mental rotation (Arendasy, Sommer, & Gittler, 2010), and word fluency (Arendasy, Sommer, & Mayr, 2012). Demonstrations in broader domains like mathematics or medicine were rare due to the lack of well-defined cognitive models for implementing strong theory (Leighton & Gierl, 2011). Ultimately, item modeling provided a systematic process that often yielded overly similar items and lacked a unifying framework for guiding development from start to finish.

7.7 Cognitive Modeling: The Second Modern Approach to Automatic Item Generation

Gierl and Lai (2013, 2016) introduced a three-step workflow for generating test items that combined human expertise with computer-based assembly (for a diagrammatic representation, *see* Gierl, Lai, & Tanygin, 2021, Figure 1.1). This AIG approach using *cognitive modeling* presents a structured representation of how examinees think and solve problems, thus ensuring item generation is grounded in domain-specific reasoning.

In Step 1, SMEs identify the content using a cognitive model as the framework that organizes the knowledge, skills, and abilities required to solve problems in a specific domain (Gierl, Lai, & Turner, 2012). In Step 2, SMEs create an item model, which serves as the template for assessment tasks (LaDuca, Staples, Templeton, & Holzman, 1986). Item models define manipulable components such as stems, options, and auxiliary materials like graphs or tables. For typical selected-response MCQs, stems, correct options, and distractors are manipulable to allow systematic variation of item components based on the cognitive model. In Step 3, items are generated using computer-based systems to manage the complex combinatorial tasks that are needed. Programs such as IGOR (Gierl, Zhou, & Alves, 2008) implement logical-constraint programming to combine cognitive model content with item model structures. The system iterates through all possible combinations of elements, applying SME-defined constraints to ensure meaningful outcomes, thus enabling the generation of hundreds or thousands of items.

Cognitive models themselves follow an abstraction-decomposition approach (Hoffman & Lintern, 2006) and consist of three components: *problem and scenario*, *sources of information*, and *features*. Problems define the assessment focus; scenarios provide specific content; sources of information organize cues relevant to problem-solving; and features specify manipulable elements and constraints. Constraints act as logical rules to ensure valid item assembly. SMEs construct these models by defining relationships between scenarios and features to guide systematic item generation.

By outlining domain knowledge in cognitive models and embedding it into item models, this approach ensures transparency and replicability. Unlike earlier AIG methods focused on psychometrics or technology alone, cognitive modeling emphasizes SME involvement throughout the process. SMEs define both the content and structure before technology is applied, reinforcing their essential role in producing high-quality items. This integration of human expertise and automation represents a practical, scalable method for generating items grounded in theory and content validity.

7.8 Benefits and Limitations of Cognitive Modeling

Cognitive-model-based AIG offers significant benefits for producing large numbers of diverse, high-quality items. This approach is easy for SMEs to learn (Falcao et al., 2022; Pugh et al., 2016) and replicable (Gierl et al., 2021, pp. 8–9) and includes a validation framework for evaluating item quality (Falcao et al., 2022; Gierl & Lai, 2016; Gierl et al., 2021, Chapter 7). As Falcao et al. (2022) concluded:

> AIG is a next gen assessment method that combines human expertise with computer algorithms. Through this review, we collected data that allows us to conclude that AIG is a feasible and valid item development method capable of generating quality items.

AIG with cognitive modeling also addresses the traditional item-writing limitations of scalability and cost. Item models act as templates that can be reused and adapted across content areas, reducing the need to create each item individually. AIG has been used to generate hundreds of items in domains such as science (Gierl et al., 2016), mathematics (Gierl & Lai, 2016; Gierl et al., 2015), medicine (Gierl & Lai, 2013; Gierl et al., 2018), pharmacy (Leslie & Gierl, 2023), and dentistry (Lai et al., 2016). Analyses show that AIG items measure performance across a wide ability range and provide strong discrimination using both classical test theory and item response theory indices (Lai et al., 2016). Item statistics for correct options are comparable to those of traditionally developed items (Gierl et al., 2016). AIG with cognitive modeling also supports post-processing for item banking via appropriate content coding or metadata that can be set at the model or item level (Gierl et al., 2021). Metadata enables test bank management, test form assembly, and tracking after administration, all of which may become even more challenging when working with large volumes of generated items (Gierl et al., 2022).

Cognitive modeling does introduce some limitations. First, no explicit definition or description exists for characterizing item similarity. Item similarity therefore remains an important concern to be defined by the test developer and addressed via model refinement or review and editing post-production. Additionally, generated items come without pre-established statistics, meaning the pretesting bottleneck is still in place. Strong theory AIG aimed to predict item characteristics without pretesting but was limited to narrow domains such as analogical reasoning, mental rotation, and word fluency. Weak theory AIG, guided by SME judgment rather than formal models, remains a practical alternative when theoretical frameworks are unavailable (Leighton & Gierl, 2011) but requires pretesting to confirm psychometric properties.

7.9 The Next Generation of Item Development

The traditional item development process as described here underscores that SMEs control the majority of the process via meticulous effort in a way that supports high item quality and strong validity arguments but is inherently time-consuming, costly, and difficult to scale. To address these limitations, the psychometric field gradually moved toward more automated approaches, culminating in the 2010s in template-based AIG using cognitive modeling. This approach introduced new challenges such as the need for more precise measures of item uniqueness, increased pressure on the pretesting bottleneck, and a limited applicability of strong theory AIG.

As assessment practices evolve, the next stage beyond traditional item writing and AIG will almost certainly involve the integration of *artificial intelligence* (AI) capabilities. AI is advancing at an extraordinary pace and, in just a few years, has demonstrated remarkable potential to address longstanding challenges in item generation. In the remainder of this chapter, we examine how emerging AI capabilities might allow us to mitigate the known limitations of automating item development, while also presenting the potential risks specific to AI.

7.10 Emerging AI Capabilities in Assessment

AI is defined here as an umbrella term for technologies enabling computers to perform tasks typically requiring human cognition, judgment, and decision-making. *Machine learning* (ML), a subset of AI, uses statistical techniques to classify and predict based on large datasets, retaining variables for predictive power rather than theoretical explanation. *Deep learning,* a subset of ML, employs neural networks and massive datasets to allow machines to train and predict independently. *Natural language processing* (NLP) bridges human and computer language, enabling interpretation, analysis, and generation of text or speech (ATP, 2025a).

It is within the NLP arena that the potential for AI to support high-quality assessments first emerged with a focus on text interpretation, categorization, and analysis. In the early 1990s, NLP-supported matching to predetermined scoring rubrics enabled automated scoring of text-heavy assessment responses such as essays. Systems like ETS's eRater (Burstein, 2003; Attali & Burstein, 2004) automated the process of essay scoring with high accuracy while effectively reducing reliance on human raters. By the late 2010s, NLP research in assessment expanded beyond analysis of existing text into generation of new text via the use of extensive researcher-assembled corpora of structured training data. Duolingo combined public language resources and labeled datasets to create content for the Duolingo English Test (Settles, LaFlair, & Hagiwara, 2020; Burstein et al., 2021).

This approach required significant, specialized human expertise along with substantial technical investments and resources. The advent of *large language models* (LLMs) integrating NLP and deep learning made generation feasible with fewer in-house resources (a useful high-level LLM summary is provided by Wang et al., 2024). NLP provided the linguistic framework, such as syntax, semantics, and context, while the deep learning component enabled LLMs to learn complex relationships and representations across words, sentences, and documents. Models such as BERT (Devlin et al., 2019) introduced encoder-only architectures for text inputting and classification, while decoder-only models such as GPT that process text left-to-right enabled predictive text generation.

The potential for LLMs to support whole item creation became evident as models improved in areas such as contextual understanding. von Davier's publication in *Psychometrika* (2018) was one of the first publications in the field of assessment that explored the potential of language models supported by deep learning, via the use of a public database of personality inventory items. The study concluded that generation of entire items was possible but noted limitations of the usefulness of such a small training set. However, the substantial technical and resource needs for this kind of exploration limited the early uses of NLP to more feasible analyses of existing items. NLP was evaluated as a potential solution for critical large-scale item bank review and coding tasks such as item matching for test security efforts, where external plagiarism software could not feasibly be used (Swygert, Micir, & Adler, 2019). A specific open-source LLM with scientific text, SciBERT, was used with clustering algorithms to identify hidden patterns in the item pool that could potentially indicate stereotypical or biased language in existing items (Padhee, Swygert, & Micir, 2021).

Despite this early promise, the use of NLP to transform content creation via generation of complete, accurate, and high-quality items at scale remained largely a research exercise into the late 2010s. Psychometricians in general were not yet well-versed in NLP. Access to the type and amount of data needed to refine the output from LLMs was limited within organizations. In addition, the reliance on SMEs necessitated item generation processes that were explainable and intuitive, and NLP methodology was neither transparent nor easily explainable to those outside the field. Unknown to most in the assessment field at that time, one particular LLM-based application was waiting in the wings that would address the accessibility and transparency elements so well that it would have a transformative impact not just on the educational technology sphere but on the entire world.

7.11 The Impact of ChatGPT

Although our framing may oversimplify a complex evolution, we suggest that it is still useful for understanding the impact of AI on item development to divide the educational technology landscape into "pre-ChatGPT" and "post-ChatGPT" eras, with December 2022, marked by OpenAI's release of ChatGPT, serving as the pivotal point (OpenAI, 2022). Prior to ChatGPT, access to LLMs was largely restricted to individuals with advanced technical and mathematical expertise, limiting their practical application. The introduction of ChatGPT, with its intuitive and conversational interface, fundamentally changed this dynamic. Almost overnight, the general public eagerly began exploring this powerful tool capable of generating coherent, contextually relevant text on virtually any topic. This breakthrough also sparked widespread recognition of the transformative potential these systems hold for item development.

Within the education world, the first and most prominent topic for research was, "How well can ChatGPT *answer* a specific set of test items?" In the medical licensure field, to use one example, multiple studies benchmarked ChatGPT's performance on licensing exams like the United States Medical Licensing Examination (USMLE). A publication from NBME on this topic evaluated ChatGPT's performance against a comprehensive set of retired USMLE® items for all three-step exams (Yaneva et al., 2024a). The authors concluded that the application performed well below expectations for a typical USMLE examinee and below an estimated passing score for two of the three exams. Investigations into ChatGPT's capacity to answer multistate bar exam practice items revealed a similar trend: the application performed well above chance but was not yet at an estimated passing level for the exams (Bommarito & Katz, 2022). Many studies evaluating ChatGPT's performance across a variety of admissions and licensure exams quickly emerged; most had limited relevance due to reliance on public practice items that were overly simplistic (e.g., text-based only) and not equivalent to items used on the actual exams.

Notwithstanding these limitations, the conclusions from initial ChatGPT studies (where the specific version of GPT used varied based on the timing of the data analysis) were promising, and with each updated version of GPT that was released, the performance against existing test items improved. However, researchers quickly zeroed in on potential limitations as well. A summary of ChatGPT's performance across a variety of test items in the first three months of its release (Leiter et al., 2024) noted that it often produced answers that sounded plausible but were entirely incorrect, a phenomenon known as a "hallucination." The application's reliance on existing statistical patterns in language meant that deeper reasoning or domain-specific logic was not applied, leading to inconsistent performance across domains. The lack of transparent reasoning or justifications for the generated answers limited ChatGPT's use as a formative learning tool, as did the training data bias toward the English language. Because many of the items against which ChatGPT performance was compared were sourced from public practice material, they could have been included in the training data, making the items easier for ChatGPT to answer. Researchers often noted that just because ChatGPT could answer MCQs, that did not necessarily impact the validity statements for MCQ-based assessments. There was still a need for humans to demonstrate knowledge of the test material, and there was still a defensible argument for using MCQs to assess that knowledge.

7.12 Using AI to Generate MCQs

Despite these emerging limitations, researchers quickly moved on to the next logical question about the potential of ChatGPT: "Can ChatGPT be used to reliably *generate* accurate, high-quality test items?" For this question, the assessment field has seen an astounding volume of research published since 2022, not least because of the variety of LLM-based applications with engaging user interfaces that have since emerged. Already the testing industry is publishing entire editions on the promise of generative AI [e.g., *Journal of Educational Measurement*, volume 59(3) for an example], along with high-level guidelines to address the logistics and business decisions needed to integrate generative AI into a variety of test development (ATP, 2025b). Thus, a chronological developmental narrative as used in this chapter up until now is unlikely to be helpful.

Instead, we shift focus to present-day insights and recommendations for the use of generative AI models from a perspective intended to be applicable across LLMs. Our recommendations are grouped into critical areas for test developers, psychometricians, subject matters experts, and others tasked with making decisions about the best uses of such models: selecting an LLM, generating effective prompts, using automated coding and rationale generation, and reviewing AI-generated items. These recommendations are intended to be applicable regardless of whether organizations are building their own solutions or contracting with a vendor.

7.13 Selecting the LLM

The initial step in leveraging LLMs for MCQ generation is to compare and select the most appropriate model for an organization's specific testing needs. This begins with defining clear requirements, such as the need for domain-specific knowledge, review of documentation on the high factual accuracy or low hallucination rates of the LLM, and the demonstrated ability to follow structured prompts. Once these criteria are established, test developers should evaluate leading models (e.g., GPT-5, Claude, Gemini) by running small-scale pilot tests that simulate item development tasks. These pilots help assess each model's strengths and limitations.

Beyond accuracy and efficiency, fairness and bias must be central considerations in model selection. Public LLMs are trained on massive datasets that often include uncontrolled internet sources, which can embed societal biases related to race, gender, socioeconomic status, and other protected characteristics (Gallegos et al., 2024; Kumar et al., 2025). Studies have shown that different models exhibit varying levels of bias, with some demonstrating systematic preferences in educational contexts (Baldwin, 2025; Shetty et al., 2024). Therefore, organizations should review available documentation on bias mitigation strategies for the LLM in question and examine independent audits or benchmarks that measure fairness (Simpson et al., 2025).

After gathering performance and fairness data, the selection process should focus on identifying the model that best balances quality, efficiency, scalability, and equity. This includes evaluating aspects such as how well the model handles nuanced educational prompts without introducing stereotypes, its ability to generate plausible distractors without cultural bias, and its responsiveness to iterative refinement. Organizations should also consider whether the model supports transparency features, such as explainability tools or audit trails, which can be critical for maintaining trust in high-stakes testing environments (Miguelañez, 2025).

Finally, the chosen LLM must align with organizational constraints, particularly the data security and responsible AI principles. Test developers should document the desired level of security for generated content, including how the model handles input data, whether prompts and outputs are stored or logged, and whether any part of the generation process involves human review by the vendor. For high-stakes assessments, organizations should prioritize a structure where the LLM will operate in a secure, enterprise-grade environment ensuring data isolation and non-retention of user inputs or outputs. If contracting with a vendor, organizations should require clear documentation on data handling policies, including whether content is used for model training or quality assurance and whether the vendor will have access to generated material.

7.13.1 Creating Effective Prompts for Item Generation

Effective prompt engineering is essential in guiding LLMs to produce high-quality MCQs, but communication with an LLM is not the same as training or evaluating a human item writer, and finding the correct level of complexity for a prompt is more challenging than it may first appear. Because of this, developers must spend some time becoming familiar with the best practices of prompt modeling and should plan for prompt development to be an iterative and lengthy process. Effective prompt engineering is not a one-time task but an ongoing process that evolves with feedback from reviewers and performance data. Best practices for prompt engineering in MCQ generation evolve over time, but some recommendations have emerged in the following areas (see Artsi et al., 2024; Kiyak et al., 2024 for more details).

- Clarity and specificity – Clearly state the task, constraints, and desired output format.
- Contextual anchoring. Provide relevant background reference material already owned and used by your organization to guide responses. For MCQ generation, this can include the exam blueprints, organization-specific item writing or style guides, and accepted curricula.

- Role assignment. Assign the model a role (e.g., "You are a board-certified practitioner in this content area") to frame its perspective.
- Examples and few-shot learning. Include high-performing example items to set expectations for tone, complexity, and structure. Low-performing examples can be included as well, although it is usually more effective to prompt LLMs on what to do rather than what *not* to do.
- Iterative refinement. Use multi-step prompting or feedback loops to improve accuracy and consistency.
- Bias and fairness controls. Explicitly instruct the model to avoid stereotypes or biased language.

Early adoption examples of AI item generation can be found within some fields that had pre-existing public, relevant knowledge bases online and an emphasis on recall items that made prompt-writing relatively straightforward, such as law (see Deroy, Ghosh, & Ghosh, 2025, for examples). More extensive prompting is required for MCQs that are not based solely on factual recall, especially for those that require the test-taker to synthesize the information in the item and where the knowledge sources may be numerous, reliant on field-specific terminology, and/or inaccessible to the general public. Two literature reviews of MCQ generation in the medical field document a wide variety of possible prompts (Artsi et al., 2024; Kiyak et al., 2024), with the latter providing 19 prompts sampled from publications. A review of these examples suggest that a complex prompt might reference any of the following: a specific exam's item style; desired tone or difficulty level; designated public or provided reference sources; test-taker educational level; detailed learning objectives; identity of item writer; complex clinical scenarios and diagnoses; and specific item stem and option formats.

Existing structures that guide item development need not be set aside, as these can be incorporated into item generation prompts. Programs that use an evidence-centered design approach can repurpose elements of the claims about what test-takers should know and be able to do into item generation prompts (Kaldaras, Akaeze, & Reckase, 2024). Prompts can also be designed to account for cognitive model structures by embedding components such as problems/scenarios, sources of information, and features into the instructions (Kiyak et al., 2024, 2025). This approach ensures that generated items align with the intended knowledge structure and difficulty level, reinforcing validity and reducing variation in item content.

Iterative testing and refinement of prompts are crucial steps. Even streamlined few-shot approaches can significantly improve output quality (Brown et al., 2020). Isley et al. (2025) documented a three-step iterative process: initial prompt with course material and sample items, LLM-based labeling of generated items as "good" or "bad," and a final prompt incorporating these labels to produce improved items. Their findings showed slightly lower item difficulty but higher discrimination, with acceptable reliability across diverse student ability levels.

7.14 Automated Coding and Rationale Generation

The utility of LLMs for MCQ generation extends beyond item creation. Items require metadata, such as content area, item format, and cognitive level, to ensure alignment with test blueprints. Traditionally, this coding process has been manual and expert-driven and thus associated with unavoidable bottlenecks. NLP has proven effective for coding existing items (Zhou & Ostrow, 2022; Butterfuss & Doran, 2025); the logical next step is integrating automated coding into prompts during or after item generation. LLMs can analyze linguistic and conceptual features to predict metadata such as cognitive level, content domain, and skill classification. Using reference material in prompts improves accuracy, and diversity in coding perspectives (e.g., textbook vs. collaborative experts) can be incorporated (Moore et al., 2024). When paired with ML classifiers trained on historical item data, LLMs refine predictions over time, increasing consistency across large item pools.

Items used in practice assessments usually include rationales for correct and incorrect options. Effective rationales reference textual evidence, explain why the correct answer is supported, and clarify why distractors are incorrect. Rationales also support quality control by ensuring alignment with intended competencies and plausibility of distractors. However, writing rationales has traditionally been an inefficient process, especially when SMEs create them separately from item writing. LLMs offer a scalable solution for rationale generation. In intelligent tutoring systems, frameworks such as Hang et al. (2024) combine GPT-4 with retrieval-augmented generation of instructor- and student-written rationales along with iterative prompt engineering. Human raters gave perfect scores for grammatical fluidity and relevance, though diversity and complexity were rated lower. Even the most streamlined approach where text generation was requested in the absence of concrete examples (aka, a zero-shot approach) yielded promising results. Ch'en et al. (2025) used GPT-4 with a basic prompt on ten clinical vignette MCQs: "Answer the following single best answer MCQ and tell me why each answer is right or wrong?" Course directors judged 93.8% of rationales appropriate and 77.5% accurate, with most accuracy achieved on the first attempt.

7.15 Reviewing Generated MCQs

SMEs can introduce biases and flaws in test items; these are typically addressed through training and item-writing guides that provide explicit rules and standardized templates (NBME, 2020). AI-generated MCQs, while efficient, do not eliminate these risks and may introduce new challenges that are harder to identify and remediate.

Public LLMs are trained on massive, uncontrolled datasets, making it reasonable to assume that biases from the training data may appear in generated items. Items may seem valid yet contain inaccuracies, from subtle flaws to outright hallucinations (Sommer & Arendasy, 2025). A systematic review in medical education noted issues such as multiple correct answers, overly simplistic items, and biased language (Artsi et al., 2024). Prompt quality affects item complexity and accuracy, underscoring the need for quality controls throughout the process, not just at final review. Prompts should specify style, format, and content scope, and iterative prompting can include checks for accuracy and alignment with educational levels.

AI faces similar challenges as human authors in creating plausible MCQ distractors, which are critical for item difficulty and discrimination. Historically, distractor generation has been one of the most difficult aspects of item writing (Gierl et al., 2017), and early distractor attempts with local LLMs were discouraging, with 50% of distractors deemed implausible. However, as GPT-based models have evolved, so has their utility for improved distractor generation (Bitew et al., 2023). For history items, ChatGPT achieved high-quality distractor rates near 60% even in zero-shot scenarios, though performance was weaker for language items due to difficulty in generating grammatically incorrect responses (Bitew et al., 2023). Potential solutions to improve distractor quality include using correct-answer-only items as prompts and comparing generated distractors to actual distractors for quality assurance (Baldwin et al., 2022).

7.16 Using AI to Address Limitations of Bulk Item Generation

Traditional item-writing methods have limitations around scalability and cost. Solutions such as AIG can produce items that are very similar to one another or introduce an even more severe pretesting bottleneck. An AI solution for item writing can speed up the process even more, at lower cost, but both AIG and AI might generate many items that are highly similar or unusable in the absence of additional pretest space. Luckily, the NLP methodology that underpins LLMs can itself be used to tackle these two limitations. Here, we present information for the test developer who would like to explore the use of NLP and LLMs for quantifying textual similarities in generated items or easing the burden on pretesting with NLP-supported predictions of item difficulty.

7.16.1 Quantifying Item Textual Similarity

Best practices for accurate item coding and test development include a systematic review by SMEs to ensure that any pair of items with a high degree of textual similarity should be coded as enemies and not used on the same form (Lane, Raymond & Haladyna, 2016; NBME, 2020; Gierl, Lai, & Tanygin, 2021). Item enemy pairs can be identified and tagged in advance of form construction or flagged after construction via form review. This review process is laborious even for traditional item writing and verges on impossible when large quantities of items are generated.

Research into the suitability of NLP methods for automated item similarity/item enemy identification emerged just prior to the release of transformer-based models and is highly promising (Peng, 2020; Gierl, Lai & Tanygin, 2021; Mao & Zhang,

2021). An NLP clustering methodology, used on an AIG-generated item bank, is effective in grouping more closely together the items with the most textual overlap to allow for faster human review of potential enemy items (Cole et al., 2020). Other studies have outlined how lexical NLP techniques that combined cosine similarity indices with ML models can efficiently quantify item text overlap, prioritize edge cases for human review, and efficiently finalize or change flags to more accurately reflect enemy status (Micir, Swygert, & D'Angelo, 2022; Becker & Kao, 2022; Meng & Li, 2024; Stevenor, McBride, & Anyanwu, 2025).

The results in the literature are encouraging, and test developers should be encouraged to explore the utility of lexical and semantic models for automating at least some part of the item enemy identification process. It should be noted that these studies also name several challenges. First, the existing human-applied enemy codes in the item bank will almost certainly contain some amount of error, meaning manual effort may be required to provide accurate training data and support prediction models. Second, enemy pairs represent very small segments of item banks, meaning even small increases in sensitivity with new models can result in an increase in false positive codes. Finally, these NLP methodologies can only quantify and rank-order the amount of similarity among all possible item pairs. For the automated enemy coding process to truly save time and effort, human experts should review the outcomes and select the threshold for lexical or semantic similarity above which all items can be automatically classified as enemies, thus greatly reducing the expert workload to only the borderline pairs or those outliers that should be enemies despite relatively little similarity.

7.16.2 Predicting Item Difficulty

Efforts to use NLP to predict item difficulty, response time, and other factors with linguistic signals are of relatively recent origin and have resulted in less promising results than with item enemy identification. Early efforts to predict item difficulty for medical licensing MCQs were not encouraging (Baldwin et al., 2022; Yaneva, Baldwin, & Runyon, 2023). Another study compared direct estimation of difficulty via the LLM vs a feature-based two-step strategy on K-5 reading and math assessments (Razavi & Powers, 2025). This strategy of using the LLM to first extract cognitive and linguistic features and then using ML to predict item difficulty from those, rather than directly from the item itself, produced more accurate predictions, though not consistently so for all grade levels.

This topic remains a high priority within the NLP in assessment field. A major effort known as the *First Shared Task on Automated Prediction of Difficulty and Response Time for Multiple-Choice Items* that solicited solutions for item difficulty and response time predictions has released its first report (Yaneva et al., 2024b). For this initiative, a dataset was first compiled of item text, mean response times, and Rasch model difficulty values from 667 items recently retired from the USMLE® series. This dataset was provided to 17 teams across the world, where teams could submit up to three solutions each, with results judged by the greatest reduction in root mean square error (RMSE) as compared to the RMSE for a baseline dummy regression. The various models all reduced the baseline RMSE by a small amount, although with surprisingly little variation among the models.

While the potential of AI to support multiple aspects of item generation is undeniable, these advancements also introduce critical responsibilities that are unique to AI use. In the next section, we discuss topics related to legal requirements and responsible use expectations. Test developers should be prepared to address these considerations proactively to safeguard the integrity of assessments and maintain stakeholder trust in the testing process and the scores that result from it.

7.17 Legal and Responsible Use Considerations

One huge advantage of traditional item or model generation is that it is transparent and easily explainable to stakeholders. The item writer can be directly questioned about potential biases, and organizations can be transparent about training methods and reference materials. While the creation, handling, and storage of personally identifiable information/PII on test-takers may be impacted by legislation such as the General Data Protection Regulation (Regulation (EU) 2016/679) and other data privacy protections, the process of traditional item writing is unlikely to ever require compliance with additional legislation at any jurisdiction level. Finally, the ownership of the resulting items is never in doubt, and full copyright protection is possible given the clear human authorship.

The use of AI to generate MCQs, on the other hand, introduces potential challenges for every one of these elements; this use is accompanied by much higher stakeholder awareness of the existence, use, and implications of AI. Figure 7.1

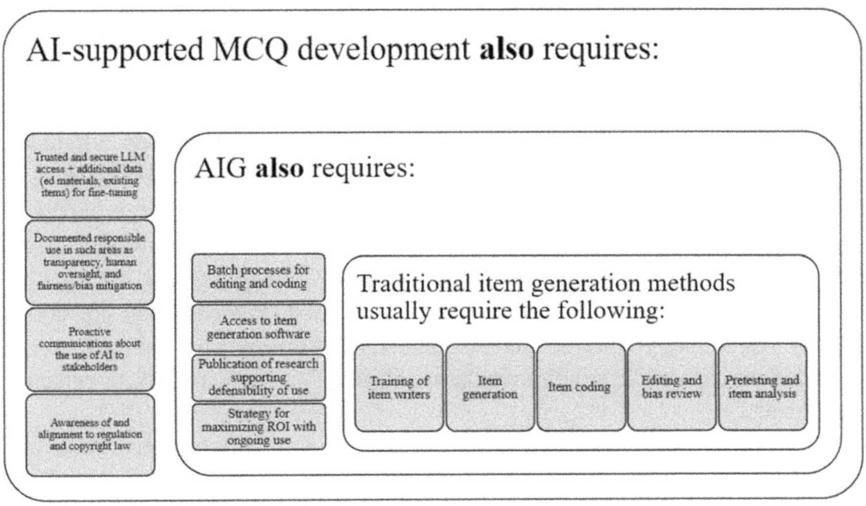

FIGURE 7.1 A diagram of the nested requirements for three item development methods.

represents the nested requirements across item-writing method, where each level includes all the elements in the level nested in it. Thus, training SMEs is required for any item development method; using AIG means also including processes for editing and coding large amounts of items at once; using AI requires responsible use policies and awareness of AI-related regulations in addition to that.

The selection and use of LLMs have been covered earlier in this chapter. Here, we turn to common stakeholder concerns about responsible AI use (fairness/bias, transparency, and human oversight), guidelines for proactive communications, and discussion of two pressing legal issues with AI-assisted MCQ generation.

7.17.1 Responsible AI Use and Stakeholder Communications

Bias in assessment items, whether cultural, linguistic, or socioeconomic, can distort measurement by introducing construct-irrelevant variance, thereby compromising fairness and the validity argument for the use of the test scores (Kaldaras, Akaeze, & Reckase, 2024). The standard of ensuring fairness and mitigating bias in any AI use, including AI generation of MCQs, emerges as one of the most common responsible AI use principles across all organizations (Hagendorff, 2019). Thus, organizations using AI for MCQ generation should be prepared to provide substantial documentation to support fairness arguments, including details about the training data sources, model architecture, and any preprocessing steps as well as the rationales for prompt design and item refinement. This documentation should record details of the fairness and bias reviews that already exist for traditional item writing and acceptance and how these have been updated for AI use, including the demographic representativeness of human reviewers of AI-generated items and additional criteria used to evaluate AI-generated items for bias. These records can be key in the defensibility argument for the validity of the exam scores.

In addition to documentation, organizations should establish formal processes for investigating potential bias in AI-generated items to avoid the perception or reality of a negative impact on test validity. Best practices include conducting quantitative analyses such as differential item functioning to detect subgroup differences that human reviewers may overlook (Belzak et al., 2023). Automated bias detection methods, such as embedding association tests, can complement human review by providing scalable and reproducible evaluations of bias in large item pools (Peng et al., 2025). These investigations should be iterative and integrated into the test development cycle, ensuring that identified biases are addressed before operational use. By combining robust documentation with systematic bias analysis, testing organizations can uphold validity standards and maintain public trust in AI-enhanced assessments.

Transparency in AI-assisted MCQ development requires clear communication with stakeholders, including test-takers. Organizations should be prepared to state publicly why a specific AI method was chosen, how it is used, and its expected value. Any supporting research may necessitate early release of pilot data. Strategies for allowing test-takers to opt out of AI-related research or assessments may be required, depending on legislation. One major challenge is the "black-box" nature of LLMs, where speed and accuracy often come at the cost of explainability. To address this, organizations might begin with simpler, more interpretable AI uses, such as NLP-based similarity methods, before adopting complex encoder models with ML elements, even if simpler methods are less accurate (ATP, 2025b). Documented human oversight (*aka* "humans in the loop") is emphasized in public ethical guidelines (ATP, 2025b) and other examples cited in this chapter, yet universal standards for the extent and timing of human involvement do not yet exist. Testing organizations should create their own guidelines informed by stakeholder input, risk analyses, known item-writing error points, and updated training materials (for an example process, see Burstein et al. (2024)).

Testing organizations must also communicate in advance changes to exam programs to maintain transparency and trust. While minor shifts in item-writing methodology are usually not advertised to test-takers and other score users, the use of AI, even in formative assessments, should be proactively disclosed. Public sentiment toward AI can be negative, with concerns about output quality, automation bias, and reduced human involvement in high-stakes decisions. Effective communication should address the rationale for using LLMs, supporting data, human oversight, and safeguards for accuracy and fairness. Outreach should extend beyond white papers to include webinars, press releases, website updates, and revised test-taker materials. A key challenge is balancing transparency with test security: details such as prompts, fine-tuning data, or generation processes may need to remain confidential to prevent replication of exam content.

7.17.2 High-Risk Uses of AI

Emerging legislation on AI use is typically organized by risk, with the greatest concern for technologies that pose significant harm and are either prohibited or require substantial oversight. Definitions of high risk vary across jurisdictions, but most legislation, including the EU AI Act (Regulation (EU) 2024/1689 (Artificial Intelligence Act)) and the Colorado AI Act (Colorado General Assembly, 2024), classify AI applications that can impact educational opportunities, vocational training, and employment as high risk. As of 2025, there is no published industry consensus on when AI-generated items would trigger such rules. It is generally assumed that formative assessments will be considered low- or no-risk but testing organizations should anticipate that AI-generated MCQs for high-stakes exams could be classified as high risk, thus requiring compliance documentation and auditing of data sources.

7.17.3 Copyright Considerations

The US Copyright Office stated in 2023 that copyright protection would apply "only [to] material that is the product of human creativity" (US Copyright Office, 2023). Recent rulings reaffirm what wholesale generation of items with minimal human review may prevent copyright claims, partly due to concerns that LLM output may not be transformative enough for fair use. Because users cannot verify all training sources, there is also a risk of inadvertently reproducing copyrighted material. However, there is also the potential that where AI is used to assist rather than wholly create, the portion of MCQs that are documented as created by humans might be copyrightable. Thus, one recommendation is to design AI systems and workflows where LLMs serve only as initial drafting tools; the subsequent human review and revision should be significant, documented, and, if possible, quantified. If the potential for copyrighting still seems low, organizations can consider adopting alternative protections such as the Defend Trade Secrets Act (DTSA, 2016). Under DTSA, AI-generated MCQs can qualify as trade secrets if they provide economic value from being confidential and if reasonable steps are taken to maintain secrecy.

7.18 Conclusion

The history of item development offers critical lessons. Traditional item writing provides authenticity but is often slow and costly. Item modeling improved efficiency and cognitive modeling strengthened theoretical alignment, but issues of item similarity and pretesting bottlenecks were amplified. Each stage solved some problems while creating new challenges, underscoring that no method is without trade-offs. AI continues this pattern, offering speed, adaptability, and creativity, while introducing risks related to bias, lack of transparency, and legal challenges. The task for psychometricians is to determine how to integrate AI responsibly to safeguard validity and fairness while leveraging its potential.

Legal, ethical, and responsible use considerations are especially urgent. Copyright law protects only human-created material, leaving ownership of AI-generated content uncertain, while trade secret protections demand strict confidentiality and economic justification. Questions abound: can organizations realistically protect large volumes of AI-generated items as trade secrets? How should human involvement be documented to maintain copyright eligibility? And what happens when models unintentionally reproduce elements of their training data? At the same time, LLMs trained on massive datasets may embed cultural or demographic biases, potentially disadvantaging certain groups of learners. Technical bias detection methods are emerging, but they cannot replace the nuance and judgment of human experts. SMEs remain indispensable but their repurposed efforts must be well-designed and carefully managed.

Transparency and collaboration are cornerstones of responsible AI integration. Stakeholders must work together to ensure openness about how items are created, what constructs they measure, and how fairness is maintained. Transparency is complicated by AI's "black-box" nature and the need to protect intellectual property, requiring organizations to balance disclosure with security while developing agile strategies that allow innovation without compromising validity. The integration of AI is not an endpoint but an opening, as a call for dialogue and shared responsibility. Decisions made today about efficiency, cost, and fairness will shape the future of assessment, and whether AI use strengthens or undermines validity evidence will depend on how thoughtfully organizations address the issues noted in this chapter.

References

AERA, APA, and NCME (2014). *Standards for Educational and Psychological Testing.* Washington, DC: AERA.

Arendasy, M., Sommer, M., & Gittler, G. (2010). Combining automatic item generation and experimental designs to investigate the contribution of cognitive components to the gender difference in mental rotation. *Intelligence, 38*, 506–512.

Arendasy, M., Sommer, M., & Mayr, F. (2012). Using automatic item generation to simultaneously construct German and English versions of a word fluency test. *Journal of Cross-Cultural Psychology, 43*, 464–479.

ATP. (2025a). *AI in Assessment Glossary*. Accessed at https://www.testpublishers.org/assets/ATP%20AI%20Glossary%20April%202025.pdf.

ATP. (2025b). *Considerations for the Use of Generative AI in Test Development.* Accessed at https://www.testpublishers.org/assets/Considerations%20for%20the%20Use%20of%20GenAI%20in%20Test%20Development%20May%202025%201.pdf.

Artsi, Y., Sorin, V., Konen, E., Glicksberg, B. S., Nadkarni, G., & Klang, E. (2024). Large language models for generating medical examinations: Systematic review. *BMC Medical Education, 24*, 354.

Attali, Y., & Burstein, J. (2004). Automated essay scoring with e-rater® v. 2.0. *ETS Research Report Series, 2004*(2), i–21.

Baldwin, P. (2025, October). Audit-style framework for evaluating bias in large language models. *Frontiers in Education, 10*, 1592037.

Baldwin, P., Mee, J., Yaneva, V., Paniagua, M., D'Angelo, J., Swygert, K., & Clauser, B. E. (2022). A natural-language-processing-based procedure for generating distractors for multiple-choice items. *Evaluation & the Health Professions, 45*(4), 327–340.

Becker, K. A., & Kao, S. C. (2022). Identifying enemy item pairs using natural language processing. *Journal of Applied Testing Technology*, *23*(Special Issue 1), 41–52.

Bejar, I. (1990). A generative analysis of a three-dimensional spatial task. *Applied Psychological Measurement, 14*, 237–245.

Bejar, I. (2002). Generative testing: From conception to implementation. In S. H. Irvine & P. C. Kyllonen (Eds.), *Item Generation for Test Development* (pp. 199–217). Hillsdale, NJ: Erlbaum.

Bejar, I. I. (2010). Recent Development and Prospects in Item Generation. In S. E. Embretson (Ed.), *Measuring Psychological Constructs: Advances in Model-Based Approaches* (pp. 201–226). Washington, DC: American Psychological Association.

Bejar, I. (2012). Item generation: Implications for a validity argument. In M. Gierl & T. Haladyna (Eds.), *Automatic Item Generation: Theory and Practice.* New York: Routledge.

Bejar, I., Lawless, R., Morley, M., Wagner, M., Bennett, & Revuelta, J. (2003). A feasibility study of on-the-fly item generation in adaptive testing. *Journal of Technology, Learning, and Assessment, 2*(3).

Belzak, W.C.M., Naismith, B., & Burstein, J. (2023). Ensuring fairness of human- and AI-generated test items. In N. Wang, G. Rebolledo-Mendez, V. Dimitrova, N. Matsuda, & O. C. Santos (Eds.), *Artificial Intelligence in Education. Posters and Late Breaking Results, Workshops and Tutorials, Industry and Innovation Tracks, Practitioners, Doctoral Consortium and Blue Sky.* AIED 2023. Communications in Computer and Information Science, *1831*, 701–707.

Bitew, S.K., Deleu, J., Develder, C., & Demeester, T. (2023). Distractor generation for multiple-choice questions with predictive prompting and large language models. In: R. Meo & F. Silvestri (Eds.), *Machine Learning and Principles and Practice of*

Knowledge Discovery in Databases. ECML PKDD 2023. Communications in Computer and Information Science, *2134*, 48–63.

Bommarito II, M., & Katz, D. M. (2022). GPT takes the bar exam. *arXiv preprint arXiv:2212.14402*.

Bormuth, J. (1970). *On a Theory of Achievement Test Items*. Chicago, IL: University of Chicago Press.

Brown, T. B., Mann, B., Ryder, N., Subbiah, M., Kaplan, J., Dhariwal, P., Neelakantan, A., Shyam, P., Sastry, G., Askell, A., Agarwal, S., Herbert-Voss, A., Krueger, G., Henighan, T., Child, R., Ramesh, A., Ziegler, D. M., Wu, J., Winter, C., Hesse, C., Chen, M., Sigler, E., Litwin, M., Gray, S., Chess, B., Clark, J., Berner, C., McCandlish, S., Radford, A., Sutskever, I., & Amodei, D. (2020). Language models are few-shot learners. *Advances in Neural Information Processing Systems, 33*, 1877–1901.

Burstein, J. (2003). The e-rater scoring engine: Automated essay scoring with natural language processing. In M. D. Shermis & J. Burstein (Eds.), *Automated Essay Scoring: A Cross-Disciplinary Perspective* (pp. 113–121). Mahwah, NJ: Lawrence Erlbaum Associates Publishers.

Burstein, J., LaFlair, G. T., Kunnan, A. J., & von Davier, A. A. (2021). A theoretical assessment ecosystem for a digital-first assessment: The Duolingo English Test. *Duolingo Research Report DRR-25-0*.

Burstein, J., LaFlair, G. T., Yancey, K., von Davier, A. A., & Dotan, R. (2024). Responsible AI for test equity and quality: The Duolingo English test as a case study. *arXiv preprint. arXiv:2409.07476*.

Butterfuss, R., & Doran, H. (2025). An application of text embeddings to support alignment of educational content standards. *Educational Measurement: Issues and Practice, 44*(1), 73–83.

Ch'en, P. Y., Day, W., Pekson, R. C., Barrientos, J., Burton, W. B., Ludwig, A. B., Jariwala, S. P., & Cassese, T. (2025). GPT-4 generated answer rationales to multiple choice assessment items in undergraduate medical education. *BMC Medical Education, 25*(1), 333.

Cole, B. S., Lima-Walton, E., Brunnert, K., Vesey, W. B., & Raha, K. (2020). Taming the firehose: Unsupervised machine learning for syntactic partitioning of large volumes of automatically generated items to assist automated test assembly. *Journal of Applied Testing Technology, 21*(1), 1–11.

Colorado General Assembly. (2024, May 17). Senate Bill 24–205: Consumer Protections for Artificial Intelligence. Colorado State Legislature. Accessed at: https://legiscan.com/CO/text/SB205/id/2996839.

Deroy, A., Ghosh, K. & Ghosh, S. (2025). Investigating legal question generation using large language models. *Artificial Intelligence and Law.* https://doi.org/10.1007/s10506-025-09452-y.

Devlin, J., Chang, M. W., Lee, K., & Toutanova, K. (2019, June). Bert: Pre-training of deep bidirectional transformers for language understanding. In *Proceedings of the 2019 Conference of the North American Chapter of the Association for Computational Linguistics: Human Language Technologies*, Volume 1 (long and short papers), 4171–4186.

Drasgow, F., Luecht, R. M., & Bennett, R. (2006). Technology and testing. In R. L. Brennan (Ed.), *Educational Measurement* (4th ed., pp. 471–516). Washington, DC: American Council on Education.

Falcao, F., Costa, P., & Pego, J. M. (2022). Feasibility assurance: A review of automatic item generation in medical assessment. *Advances in Health Sciences Education, 27*(2), 405–425.

Gallegos, I. O., Rossi, R. A., Barrow, J., Tanjim, M. M., Kim, S., Dernoncourt, F., Yu, T., Zhang, R., & Ahmed, N. K. (2024). Bias and fairness in large language models: A survey. *Computational Linguistics,* 50(3), 1097–1179.

Gierl, M. J., Bulut, O., Guo, Q., & Zhang, X. (2017). Developing, analyzing, and using distractors for multiple-choice tests in education: A comprehensive review. *Review of Educational Research, 87*(6), 1082–1116.
Gierl, M. J., & Haladyna, T. (2013). *Automatic Item Generation: Theory and Practice*. New York: Routledge.
Gierl, M. J., & Lai, H. (2013). Evaluating the quality of medical multiple-choice items created with automated generation processes. *Medical Education, 47*, 726–733.
Gierl, M. J., & Lai, H. (2016). A process for reviewing and evaluating generated test items. *Educational Measurement: Issues and Practice, 35*, 6–20.
Gierl, M. J., Lai, H., Hogan, J., & Matovinovic, D. (2015). A method for generating test items that are aligned to the Common Core State Standards. *Journal of Applied Testing Technology, 16*, 1–18.
Gierl, M. J., Lai, H., Pugh, D., Touchie, C., Boulais, A.-P., & De Champlain, A. (2016). Evaluating the psychometric characteristics of generated multiple-choice test items. *Applied Measurement in Education, 29*, 196–210.
Gierl, M. J., Lai, J., & Tanygin, V. (2021). *Advanced Methods in Automatic Item Generation*. New York: Routledge.
Gierl, M. J., Lai, H., & Turner, S. (2012). Using automatic item generation to create multiple-choice items for assessments in medical education. *Medical Education, 46*, 757–765.
Gierl, M. J., Lai, H., & Zhang, X. (2018). Automatic item generation. In M. Khosrow-Pour (Ed.), *Encyclopedia of Information Science and Technology* (4th ed., pp. 2369–2379). Hershey, PA: IGI Global.
Gierl, M. J., Shin, J., Firoozi, T., & Lai, H. (2022). Using content coding and automatic item generation to improve test security. *Frontiers in Education, 07*, 853578.
Gierl, M. J., Zhou, J., & Alves, C. (2008). Developing a taxonomy of item model types to promote assessment engineering. *Journal of Technology, Learning, and Assessment, 7*(2). Accessed at https://ejournals.bc.edu/index.php/jtla/article/view/1629/1664.
Glas, C. (2006). Alternative approaches to updating item parameter estimates in tests with item cloning. *LSAC Research Report Series* 03-01, 1–7.
Guttman, L. (1959). Introduction to facet design and analysis. *Acta Psychologica, 15*, 130–138.
Hagendorff, T. (2019). The ethics of AI ethics–an evaluation of guidelines. *arXiv preprint arXiv:1903.03425*.
Haladyna, T. (1994). *Developing and Validation Multiple-Choice Test Items*. Hillsdale, NJ: LEA.
Haladyna, T. M., & Downing, S. M. (1989). Validity of a taxonomy of multiple-choice item-writing rules. *Applied Measurement in Education, 2*(1), 51–78.
Haladyna, T. M., Downing, S. M., & Rodriguez, M. C. (2002). A review of multiple-choice item-writing guidelines for classroom assessment. *Applied Measurement in Education, 15*(3), 309–334.
Haladyna, T. M., & Rodriguez, M. C. (2013). *Developing and Validating Test Items*. New York and London: Routledge.
Hang, C. N., Tan, C., & Yu, P. D. (2024). MCQGen: A large language model-driven MCQ generator for personalized learning. *IEEE Access, 12*, 102261–102273.
Hoffman, R., & Lintern, G. (2006). Eliciting and representing the knowledge of experts. In K. Ericsson, N. Charness, P. Feltovich, & R. Hoffman (Eds.), *Cambridge Handbook of Expertise and Expert Performance* (pp. 203–222). New York: Cambridge University Press.
Hornke, L. (2002). Item generation models for higher cognitive functions. In S. Irvine & P. Kyllonen (Eds.), *Item Generation for Test Development* (pp. 159–178). Hillsdale, NJ: Erlbaum.

Irvine, S., & Kyllonen, P. (2002). *Item Generation for Test Development.* Hillsdale, NJ: Erlbaum.

Isley, C., Gilbert, J., Kassos, E., Kocher, M., Nie, A., Brunskill, E., ... & Goel, S. (2025). Assessing the quality of AI-generated exams: A large-scale field study. *arXiv preprint arXiv:2508.08314.*

Janssen, R. (2010). Modeling the effect of item designs within the Rasch model. In S. E. Embretson (Ed.), *Measuring Psychological Constructs: Advances in Model-Based Approaches* (pp. 227–245). Washington, DC: American Psychological Association.

Janssen, R., Schepers, J., & Peres, D. (2004). Models with item and group predictors. In P. DeBoeck & M. Wilson (Eds.), *Explanatory Item Response Models: A Generalized Linear and Non-linear Approach* (pp. 189–212). New York: Springer.

Kaldaras, L., Akaeze, H. O., & Reckase, M. D. (2024, August). Developing valid assessments in the era of generative artificial intelligence. *Frontiers in Education, 9,* 1399377.

Kane, M. T. (1992). An argument-based approach to validity. *Psychological Bulletin, 112*(3), 527.

Kane, M. T. (2013). Validating the interpretation and uses of test scores. *Journal of Educational Measurement, 50*(1), 1–73.

Karamanis, N., Ha, L., & Mitkov, R. (2006). Generating multiple-choice test items from medical text: A pilot study. In *Proceedings of the Fourth International Natural Language Generation Conference (INLG '06)* (pp. 111–113). Association for Computational Linguistics.

Kiyak, Y. S., & Kononowicz, A. A. (2025). Using a hybrid of AI and template-based method in automatic item generation to create multiple-choice questions in medical education: Hybrid AIG. *JMIR Formative Research, 9,* e65726.

Kiyak, Y. S., Kononowicz, A. A., & Górski, S. (2024). Multilingual template-based automatic item generation for medical education supported by generative artificial intelligence models ChatGPT and Claude. *Bio-Algorithms and Med-Systems, 20*(1), 81–89.

Kumar, C. V., Urlana, A., Kanumolu, G., Garlapati, B. M., & Mishra, P. (2025). No LLM is free from bias: A comprehensive study of bias evaluation in large language models. *arXiv preprint arXiv:2503.11985.*

LaDuca, A., Staples, W. I., Templeton, B., & Holzman, G. B. (1986). Item modeling procedures for constructing content-equivalent multiple-choice items. *Medical Education, 20,* 53–56.

Lai, H., Gierl, M. J., Byrne, B. E., Spielman, A., & Waldschmidt, D. (2016). Three modeling applications to promote automatic item generation for examinations in dentistry. *Journal of Dental Education, 80,* 339–347.

Lane, S., Raymond, M., & Haladyna, R. (2016). Test development process. In S. Lane, M. Raymond, & T. Haladyna (Eds.), *Handbook of Test Development* (2nd ed., pp. 3–18). New York: Routledge.

Leighton, J. P., & Gierl, M. J. (2011). *The Learning Sciences in Educational Assessment: The Role of Cognitive Models.* Cambridge: Cambridge University Press.

Leiter, C., Zhang, R., Chen, Y., Belouadi, J., Larionov, D., Fresen, V., & Eger, S. (2024). ChatGPT: A meta-analysis after 2.5 months. *Machine Learning with Applications, 16,* 100541.

Leslie, T., & Gierl, M. J. (2023). Using automatic item generation to create multiple-choice items for pharmacy assessment. *Journal of Pharmaceutical Education, 87*(10), 100081.

Mao, X., & Zhang, Q. (2021). An exploration of an integrated approach for enemy item identification. *International Journal of Intelligent Technologies & Applied Statistics, 14*(2), 123–134.

Meng, H., & Li, J. (2024, May). Automatic enemy identification—Are we there yet? *Artificial Intelligence and Applications, 2*(4), 295–306.

Micir, I., Swygert, K., & D'Angelo, J. (2022). Leveraging machine learning technology to improve accuracy and efficiency of identification of enemy item pairs. *Journal of Applied Testing Technology, 23*(Special Issue 1), 30–40.

Miguelañez, C. (2025, April 22). How to build auditing frameworks for LLM transparency. *Latitude Blog.* Accessed at https://latitude-blog.ghost.io/blog/how-to-build-auditing-frameworks-for-llm-transparency/.

Moore, S., Schmucker, R., Mitchell, T., & Stamper, J. (2024, July). Automated generation and tagging of knowledge components from multiple-choice items. In *Proceedings of the Eleventh ACM Conference on Learning@Scale* (pp. 122–133).

National Board of Medical Examiners. (2020). *Constructing Written Test Questions for the Basic and Clinical Sciences* (6th ed.). Philadelphia, PA: NBME.

OpenAI. (2022, November 30). ChatGPT [Large language model]. Accessed at https://openai.com/blog/chatgpt/.

Padhee, S., Swygert, K., & Micir, I. (2021, December). Exploring language patterns in a medical licensure exam item bank. In *2021 IEEE International Conference on Bioinformatics and Biomedicine (BIBM)* (pp. 503–508). IEEE.

Peng, F. (2020). *Automatic Enemy Item Detection using Natural Language Processing* (Doctoral dissertation, University of Illinois at Chicago).

Peng, J., Shen, W., Rao, J., Lin, J. (2025). Automated bias assessment in AI-generated educational content using CEAT framework. In A. I. Cristea, E. Walker, Y. Lu, O. C. Santos, & S. Isotani (Eds.), *Artificial Intelligence in Education. Posters and Late Breaking Results, Workshops and Tutorials, Industry and Innovation Tracks, Practitioners, Doctoral Consortium, Blue Sky, and WideAIED.* AIED 2025. Communications in Computer and Information Science, *2591*, 352–358.

Pugh, D., De Champlain, A., Gierl, M. J., Lai, H, & Touchie, C. (2016). Using cognitive models to develop quality multiple-choice items. *Medical Teacher, 38*, 838–843.

Regulation (EU) 2024/1689 of the European Parliament and of the Council of 13 June 2024 laying down harmonised rules on artificial intelligence (Artificial Intelligence Act). *Official Journal of the European Union*, L 2024/1689. Accessed at https://eur-lex.europa.eu/eli/reg/2024/1689/oj/eng.

Reiter, E. & Dale, R. (1997). Building applied natural Language generation systems. *Natural Language Engineering, 3*, 57–87.

Razavi, P., & Powers, S. J. (2025). Estimating item difficulty using large language models and tree-based machine learning algorithms. *arXiv preprint arXiv:2504.08804.*

Rodriguez, M. C., & Haladyna, T. M. (2013). Objective testing of educational achievement. In K. F. Geisinger, B. A. Bracken, J. F. Carlson, J.-I. C. Hansen, N. R. Kuncel, S. P. Reise, & M. C. Rodriguez (Eds.), *APA Handbook of Testing and Assessment in Psychology, Vol. 1. Test Theory and Testing and Assessment in Industrial and Organizational Psychology* (pp. 305–314). APA.

Roid, G., & Haladyna, T. (1982). *A Technology for Test-Item Writing.* Maryland Heights, MO: Academic Press.

Rudner, L. (2010). Implementing the graduate management admission test computerized adaptive test. In W. van der Linden & C. Glas (Eds.), *Elements of Adaptive Testing* (pp. 151–165). New York: Springer.

Schmeiser, C. B., & Welch, C. J. (2006). Test development. In R. L. Brennan (Ed.), *Educational Measurement* (4th ed., pp. 307–353). Westport, CT: NCME, ACE.

Settles, B., LaFlair, G. T., & Hagiwara, M. (2020). Machine learning-driven language assessment. *Transactions of the Association for Computational Linguistics, 8*, 247–263.

Shetty, P., Rao, V. S., & Muralikrishna, S. N. (2024, December). Assessing bias in large language models: A comparative study of ChatGPT, Gemini, and Claude. In *2024 International Conference on Modeling, Simulation & Intelligent Computing (MoSICom)* (pp. 133–137).

Simpson, S., Nukpezah, J., Brooks, K., & Pandya, R. (2025). Parity benchmark for measuring bias in LLMs. *AI and Ethics, 5*(3), 3087–3101.

Sinharay, S., Johnson, M. S., & Williamson, D. M. (2003). Calibrating item families and summarizing the results using family expected response functions. *Journal of Educational and Behavioral Statistics, 28*, 295–313.

Sommer, M., & Arendasy, M. (2025) Automatic- and transformer-based automatic item generation: A critical review. *Journal of Intelligence, 13*(8), 102.

Stevenor, B. A., McBride, N. L. L., & Anyanwu, C. (2025). Comparing lexical and semantic techniques for identifying enemy items via natural language processing. *Journal of Applied Testing Technology, 26*(1), 14–20.

Swygert, K. A., Micir, I., & Adler, L. (2019, October). Lessons learned: Leveraging technology to efficiently evaluate potentially-compromised test items on tests containing foundational and clinical science content. Paper presented at the Conference on Test Security annual conference, Miami, FL.

U. S. Congress. (2016). Defend Trade Secrets Act of 2016, Pub. L. No. 114–153, 130 Stat. 376. Accessed at https://www.congress.gov/114/plaws/publ153/PLAW-114publ153.pdf.

U.S. Copyright Office. (2023, March 16). *Copyright Registration Guidance: Works Containing Material Generated by Artificial Intelligence* (88 FR 16190–16194; FR Doc. 202305321). Federal Register. Accessed at https://www.federalregister.gov/documents/2023/03/16/2023-05321/copyright-registration-guidance-works-containing-material-generated-by-artificial-intelligence.

von Davier, M. (2018). Automated item generation with recurrent neural networks. *Psychometrika, 83*(4), 847–857.

Wang, Y., Tian, J., Yazar, Y., Ones, D. S., & Landers, R. N. (2024). Using natural language processing and machine learning to replace human content coders. *Psychological Methods, 29*(6), 1148–1163.

Yaneva, V., Baldwin, P., Jurich, D. P., Swygert, K., & Clauser, B. E. (2024a). Examining ChatGPT performance on USMLE sample items and implications for assessment. *Academic Medicine, 99*(2), 192–197.

Yaneva, V., Baldwin, P., & Runyon, C. (2023). Extracting linguistic signal from item text and its application to modeling item characteristics. In *Advancing Natural Language Processing in Educational Assessment* (pp. 167–182). Routledge.

Yaneva, V., North, K., Baldwin, P., Ha, L. A., Rezayi, S., Zhou, Y., … & Clauser, B. (2024b, June). Findings from the first shared task on automated prediction of difficulty and response time for multiple-choice items. In E. Kochmar, M. Bexte, J. Burstein, A. Horbach, R. Laarmann-Quante, A. Tack, V. Yaneva, & Z. Yuan (Eds.), *Proceedings of the 19th Workshop on Innovative Use of NLP for Building Educational Applications (BEA 2024)* (pp. 470–482).

Zhou, Z., & Ostrow, K. S. (2022). Transformer-based automated content-standards alignment: A pilot study. In G. Meiselwitz, A. Moallem, P. Zaphiris, A. Ioannou, R. A. Sottilare, J. Schwarz, & X. Fang (Eds.), *HCI International 2022-Late Breaking Papers. Interaction in New Media, Learning and Games - 24th International Conference on Human-Computer Interaction, HCII 2022, Virtual Event, June 26–July 1, 2022, Proceedings* (Vol. 13517, pp. 525–542).

8

MEASURING LEARNING THROUGH PLAY

AI-Enabled Game-Based Assessment

Xinhui Xiong and Deniz Eseryel

8.1 Measurement Matters in Educational Games

Game-based learning (GBL) has evolved well beyond its early role as a motivational supplement to traditional instruction. Contemporary educational games increasingly function as complex learning environments that engage learners in sustained problem-solving, strategic decision-making, collaboration, and reflection. Through these interactions, games elicit rich cognitive, behavioral, and affective processes that unfold dynamically over time (Gee, 2007; Eseryel et al., 2011; Clark et al., 2016). As learners play, they generate continuous streams of data, choices made, strategies attempted, errors revised, patterns of persistence, and responses to feedback that hold considerable potential as evidence of learning. Without principled measurement frameworks, however, these data remain largely descriptive, offering limited insight into what learners know, how they reason, or what they are capable of doing. Measurement is therefore central to transforming gameplay activity into meaningful and defensible evidence of learning (Ifenthaler, Eseryel, & Ge, 2012).

Educational measurement provides systematic approaches for interpreting learner behavior through explicit construct definition, structured inference processes, and validity theory (Pellegrino, Chudowsky, & Glaser, 2001). In the context of educational games, measurement clarifies what forms of learning are intended, how those forms of learning are expected to manifest through gameplay, and under what assumptions observed behaviors can support claims about learner knowledge, skills, or dispositions. Constructs such as problem-solving ability, critical thinking, or collaboration cannot be inferred directly from gameplay traces (Eseryel, Ifenthaler, & Ge, 2013). Rather, they must be explicitly articulated and theoretically grounded, with clear links established between latent constructs and

DOI: 10.4324/9781003621522-8

observable in-game actions. Validity arguments then connect these observations to intended interpretations, ensuring that inferences drawn from gameplay data are justified by theory and evidence rather than intuition or surface-level correlations (Eseryel et al., 2014).

A critical distinction in this domain lies between using games as instructional tools and using gameplay data as assessment evidence (Eseryel, Ifenthaler, & Ge, 2011). Many educational games are designed primarily to promote learning through engagement, exploration, and practice. An emerging body of research, however, emphasizes games as embedded or "stealth" assessment environments, in which assessment is an integral feature of the game system itself rather than an external testing layer (Shute & Ventura, 2013). In this paradigm, learners are evaluated through their natural interactions with the game world, often without explicit awareness that assessment is occurring. This approach has the potential to reduce test anxiety, increase ecological validity, and capture learning processes as they unfold in authentic contexts. Measurement, in this sense, is what enables gameplay data to function as assessment data, supporting formative feedback, adaptive learning pathways, and summative interpretations of performance (Ifenthaler, Eseryel, & Ge, 2012).

Importantly, careful measurement design allows educational games to serve as valid assessment environments without undermining engagement, authenticity, or learner agency. Poorly aligned metrics, opaque scoring rules, or intrusive testing mechanisms risk disrupting immersion and distorting learner behavior, thereby compromising both engagement and validity. By contrast, well-designed measurement systems leverage the affordances of games, their interactivity, adaptivity, and contextual richness, to capture learning in situ. Aligning game mechanics, learning objectives, and measurement models is therefore essential for preserving the motivational strengths of games while producing reliable, interpretable, and actionable evidence of learning (Eseryel & Law, 2012).

In sum, measurement matters in educational games because it bridges the gap between engagement and evidence. It enables educational games to move beyond being compelling learning experiences toward becoming credible environments for understanding, supporting, and evaluating learning in complex, dynamic contexts.

8.1.1 Research Problem and Contribution

Despite the rapid growth and adoption of GBL environments, substantial challenges remain in how assessment embedded within games is conceptualized, validated, and interpreted. Much of the existing GBL literature emphasizes engagement, motivation, or learning outcomes, while giving comparatively limited attention to assessment as a rigorous inferential enterprise (Eseryel, Guo, & Law, 2012). Core issues of construct definition, validity, inference, and fairness are often under-specified or treated implicitly, with gameplay data assumed to be self-evident indicators of learning rather than evidence requiring principled interpretation (Mislevy et al., 2012; Shaffer et al., 2005). As a result, many game-based assessments (GBAs) yield findings that are difficult to justify, compare, or generalize across learners, contexts, and populations.

A central research problem, therefore, is the lack of coherent frameworks that integrate learning theory, game design, and educational measurement (Ifenthaler, Eseryel, & Ge, 2012). Advances in learning analytics have enabled the collection and analysis of fine-grained process data from games, but these analytic approaches are not always grounded in explicit construct models or articulated validity arguments (Siemens & Baker, 2012). Evidence-centered design (ECD) has been widely cited as a promising framework for GBA, yet its implementation is often partial. In many cases, ECD is applied primarily at the level of task design, while warrants, assumptions, and alternative explanations underlying inference remain underdeveloped (Mislevy et al., 2003).

Concerns related to fairness and bias further complicate the use of games as assessment environments. Differences in prior gaming experience, familiarity with digital interfaces, cultural interpretations of game mechanics, and algorithmic decision-making processes may introduce construct-irrelevant variance and systematic disadvantage for particular groups (Dorans & Cook, 2016). When such factors are not explicitly modeled or evaluated, artificial intelligence (AI)-driven inferences risk amplifying inequities rather than mitigating them.

This chapter addresses these challenges by synthesizing educational measurement theory, ECD, and AI-driven learning analytics to articulate principled approaches for designing, validating, and interpreting assessment embedded in educational games. Rather than treating games primarily as novel data sources, this chapter frames GBA as a measurement problem that requires explicit construct modeling, defensible inference chains, and systematic validity evaluation. It examines how observable in-game behaviors can function as evidence for assessment claims, the assumptions under which those inferences are warranted, and the implications for fairness, transparency, and interpretability.

The contribution of this work is both conceptual and methodological. Conceptually, it reframes educational games as measurement systems embedded within dynamic learning environments. Methodologically, it provides guidance for researchers and designers seeking to move beyond descriptive analytics toward theory-driven, transparent, and equitable measurement practices. In doing so, this chapter aims to support the development of GBAs that are not only engaging and innovative but also valid, interpretable, and credible for educational decision-making.

8.2 Conceptual Foundations

8.2.1 Design Frameworks for Game-Based Assessment

A central framework for the design of GBA, particularly in AI-enabled and interactive environments, is ECD. ECD provides a principled approach to assessment by explicitly structuring the inferential chain that connects observable behaviors to claims about learner knowledge, skills, or dispositions (Mislevy, Steinberg, & Almond, 2003; Mislevy, Almond, Lukas, & Steinberg, 2002). Rather than treating assessment as a scoring procedure applied after task completion, ECD conceptualizes assessment as an evidentiary argument composed of three interrelated elements: (a) claims specifying what learners know or can do, (b) evidence required to support those claims, and (c) tasks designed to elicit that evidence.

In game-based environments, these elements can be systematically aligned with game mechanics, telemetry features, and AI-driven analytic models. Claims correspond to targeted competencies or latent learner states, such as strategic reasoning, systems thinking, or collaborative problem-solving. Evidence is instantiated in fine-grained gameplay traces, including action sequences, strategy shifts, error patterns, persistence trajectories, or responses to feedback. Tasks are realized through game challenges, scenarios, and affordances that structure opportunities for learners to demonstrate these behaviors. Within this framework, AI models, such as probabilistic graphical models, sequence models, or machine learning classifiers, operate as inference engines that transform high-volume gameplay data into estimates of learner proficiency or state.

The strength of ECD lies in its explicit articulation of inference assumptions and validity warrants. By requiring designers to specify constructs, evidentiary relationships, and task demands a priori, ECD supports defensible interpretation of AI-generated inferences and provides a coherent basis for validation. This feature is especially critical in data-rich, adaptive game environments, where the complexity of interaction can otherwise obscure the relationship between observed behavior and intended constructs. ECD does not prescribe specific analytic techniques; rather, it constrains their use by embedding them within an explicit measurement argument.

Other perspectives on assessment and learning offer complementary insights but provide less direct guidance for algorithmic inference. Assessment-as-learning emphasizes learner reflection and formative use of assessment information (Earl, 2013), while learning progressions focus on developmental trajectories of competence over time (National Research Council, 2007). Both perspectives are valuable for instructional design and interpretation, particularly in formative contexts. However, neither provides a fully articulated framework for specifying how complex behavioral data should be translated into defensible claims through computational models. ECD's focus on claims, evidence, and tasks makes it particularly well suited for integrating game design, educational measurement, and AI-based analytics within embedded assessment systems.

8.2.2 *Forms of Assessment in Game-Based Learning*

Assessment in GBL environments can take multiple forms, differing in their degree of integration with gameplay and their analytic sophistication. One common approach involves assessments administered outside the game, such as pretests and posttests. These measures provide summative or comparative information about learning outcomes and are often psychometrically well understood. However, they remain largely disconnected from in-game activity and do not capitalize on the richness of gameplay data. As a result, they offer limited insight into learning processes or strategy use during play.

A second form relies on in-game metrics, such as scores, levels, badges, completion times, or achievement indicators. These measures are tightly coupled with gameplay and are often easy to compute and communicate. However, they are frequently weakly specified in terms of underlying constructs and are rarely accompanied by explicit validity arguments (Shute, 2011). In many cases, such indicators conflate performance, engagement, and progression mechanics, making it difficult to interpret what they actually represent in terms of learning.

A third and increasingly influential form is AI-supported stealth assessment, in which assessment is embedded directly into gameplay and operates continuously as learners interact with the game. Rather than interrupting play with explicit testing events, stealth assessment leverages naturally occurring player behaviors, choices, strategies, errors, and persistence, as evidence of learning (Shute & Ventura, 2013). This typology reflects a progression from assessment around games, to assessment in games, to assessment through games, with corresponding increases in ecological validity, diagnostic resolution, and alignment between learning processes and measurement.

Crucially, the movement toward embedded and stealth assessment does not eliminate the need for measurement rigor. Instead, it heightens the importance of explicit construct modeling and principled inference. When assessment is inseparable from gameplay, the interpretive burden shifts from discrete test items to continuous streams of interaction data, making frameworks such as ECD essential for maintaining clarity about what is being measured and why.

8.2.3 Stealth Assessment and AI-Based Inference

Stealth assessment refers to unobtrusive, formative, and continuous assessment that is seamlessly integrated into gameplay (Shute & Ventura, 2013). In this approach, assessment is not experienced by learners as a separate evaluative activity. Instead, learners demonstrate their competencies through natural interaction with the game environment, and these interactions are captured as telemetry data. AI-based inference models analyze these data in real time to update estimates of learner knowledge, skills, or dispositions.

Stealth assessment systems are typically grounded in ECD principles. Claims specify the competencies of interest; evidence models identify features of gameplay that are informative about those competencies; and task models define the conditions under which such evidence can be elicited. AI-driven inference enables dynamic updating of learner models, allowing assessment and instruction to co-evolve during play. This integration supports adaptive feedback, personalized scaffolding, and responsive task sequencing, all without disrupting immersion.

From a measurement perspective, stealth assessment represents a shift from static performance snapshots to dynamic representations of learning processes. Rather than asking whether a learner can produce a correct response at a single point in time, stealth assessment examines how learners approach problems, revise strategies, and respond to challenge over extended interaction sequences. This process-oriented focus not only aligns well with contemporary theories of learning and competence but also introduces new challenges for inference, validity, and fairness. Because inferences are based on patterns accumulated over time, explicit modeling of temporal dependency and learning trajectories becomes essential.

Moreover, the unobtrusive nature of stealth assessment places additional responsibility on designers and researchers to ensure transparency and interpretability. Learners may not be aware of how their actions are being interpreted, making it critical that inference models are theoretically grounded and that validity arguments clearly justify the proposed interpretations and uses of assessment information.

8.2.4 Learning Theory Foundations and Measurable Interaction

The design and interpretation of GBAs are further informed by learning theories that emphasize interaction, participation, and motivation. Constructivist and situative perspectives conceptualize learning as an active process of meaning-making situated within authentic contexts and social practices (Gee, 2007; Greeno, 1998). From this standpoint, games are not merely delivery systems for content but participatory environments in which learners engage in problem-solving, experimentation, and collaboration. Knowledge is constructed through interaction with tools, representations, and other players, rather than transmitted through isolated tasks.

Self-determination theory complements these perspectives by identifying autonomy, competence, and relatedness as key drivers of engagement and learning (Ryan & Deci, 2000). Game-based environments are particularly well positioned to support these psychological needs through player choice, adaptive challenge, and responsive feedback. When augmented with AI-driven adaptation, games can dynamically adjust task difficulty and feedback to sustain optimal challenge, thereby influencing both motivation and observable learning behaviors (Shute, 2011).

These learning theories also provide a basis for measurability. Cognitive strategies, motivational states, and self-regulatory behaviors are expected to manifest as detectable gameplay signals, such as exploration patterns, persistence trajectories, help-seeking behaviors, collaboration dynamics, or responses to feedback. By explicitly mapping theoretical constructs to observable interaction data, designers can ensure that AI models ground their inferences in theory rather than relying solely on data-driven correlations. This linkage strengthens interpretability, supports validity arguments, and enhances the explanatory power of AI-supported GBA systems.

At the same time, learning theory highlights the risk of construct-irrelevant variance. Behaviors observed in games may reflect factors such as prior gaming experience, familiarity with interfaces, or personal play styles rather than the targeted construct. Recognizing this distinction reinforces the need for careful construct specification, task design, and validity evaluation, issues that become even more salient in AI-driven, adaptive environments.

8.3 Psychometrics for AI-Based Games

AI-based games used for assessment represent a substantive departure from conventional testing formats in educational and psychological measurement. These systems integrate AI, adaptive algorithms, and continuous data capture to support real-time inference about learner competencies. Although the technological affordances of such systems differ markedly from those of traditional assessments, foundational psychometric principles remain essential for ensuring that AI-driven inferences are meaningful, defensible, and fair. The central challenge is therefore not whether psychometrics applies to AI-based games, but how established principles must be extended to accommodate dynamic, sequential, and adaptive assessment environments.

8.3.1 Core Measurement Principles

Validity, reliability, fairness, and generalizability remain foundational considerations, even when inferences are generated through AI-driven models rather than fixed scoring rules (Pellegrino, Chudowsky, & Glaser, 2001). Validity concerns whether interpretations derived from AI-mediated gameplay data are appropriate for their intended uses, while reliability refers to the stability and consistency of those inferences across time, contexts, and algorithmic states. In AI-based games, reliability can no longer be conceptualized solely in terms of internal consistency; instead, it must encompass temporal stability, robustness across adaptive pathways, and sensitivity to changes in model parameters and training data.

AI-based assessment systems must also explicitly account for learning trajectories and temporal dependency. Gameplay in adaptive environments is typically designed to promote learning, experimentation, and strategy refinement over time. As a result, observations are inherently dependent, and performance at any given moment reflects both current proficiency and prior interactions with the system. Embretson's (1998) work on dynamic testing and learning-oriented measurement provides a theoretical foundation for modeling such trajectories, emphasizing the need to distinguish meaningful growth from measurement error and to treat change as a substantive outcome rather than a nuisance variable.

Generalizability and fairness are particularly salient in AI-based games, given the heterogeneity of player backgrounds, interaction styles, and prior experience with digital technologies. AI models trained on gameplay data may inadvertently encode systematic biases related to interface familiarity, gaming conventions, or culturally patterned approaches to exploration and risk-taking. Generalizability theory offers a useful framework for decomposing multiple sources of variance, such as player-by-time, player-by-context, and player-by-algorithm interactions, and for evaluating whether inferences remain stable across populations and conditions.

Comparability across AI-adaptive game states presents additional psychometric challenges. AI-driven systems often tailor difficulty, content, or feedback in response to player behavior, resulting in non-equivalent experiences across individuals. Ensuring comparability under such conditions requires extensions of traditional linking and equating approaches. While foundational work on equating provides a conceptual basis (Kolen & Brennan, 2014), AI-based games demand new methods capable of accommodating continuous adaptation, branching pathways, and evolving task pools.

8.3.2 Inference Models for Gameplay Data

Classical test theory and item response theory continue to play important roles in AI-based games, particularly as baseline models or as components within hybrid systems. However, their core assumptions, independent observations, discrete items, and static parameters, are often violated in environments characterized by continuous interaction, sequential decision-making, and adaptive task selection. Consequently, AI-based games increasingly rely on more flexible inference models capable of handling complex, temporally structured data.

Bayesian networks and cognitive diagnostic models (CDMs) have proven especially valuable in this context. Bayesian networks support the integration of multiple sources of evidence and allow for explicit modeling of uncertainty, enabling real-time updating of proficiency estimates as new data are observed (DiCerbo & Behrens, 2012). CDMs facilitate fine-grained diagnostic inference by modeling mastery profiles across multiple skills or attributes, aligning well with the instructional and feedback-oriented goals of AI-based games.

In parallel, machine learning algorithms are increasingly used to detect patterns in large-scale gameplay data, including action sequences, timing information, and strategy use. These approaches can substantially improve predictive accuracy and scalability. However, from a psychometric perspective, they raise important concerns regarding interpretability, construct representation, and generalizability. Machine learning models must therefore be embedded within explicit measurement frameworks that link algorithmic outputs to theoretically grounded constructs, rather than treated as standalone predictors optimized solely for performance.

8.3.3 Validity Threats in AI-Based Games

AI-based games introduce distinctive threats to validity, particularly through construct-irrelevant variance associated with the game and interface itself. Factors such as prior gaming experience, interface proficiency, exploratory behavior, and risk tolerance may systematically influence gameplay patterns independently of the targeted construct (Clark, Tanner-Smith, & Killingsworth, 2016). When AI models learn from such patterns without appropriate controls, they risk conflating engagement, familiarity, or stylistic preferences with competence.

Adaptive and learning algorithms further complicate validity by obscuring the relationship between observed behavior and underlying constructs. Changes in task difficulty, feedback, or system behavior may alter player strategies in ways that are difficult to disentangle from true changes in proficiency. Consistent with principles articulated in the Standards for Educational and Psychological Testing (AERA, NCME and APA, 2014), such adaptations raise important concerns regarding construct representation, fairness, and the validity of score interpretations. Without careful design and analysis, AI-driven adaptation can introduce feedback loops that reinforce initial differences among learners and threaten fairness across groups.

Argument-based validity theory provides a coherent framework for addressing these challenges. From this perspective, validity depends on the degree to which evidence and theory support the proposed interpretations and uses of AI-generated scores and classifications (Kane, 2013). In AI-based games, this requires explicit justification of how gameplay data are selected, encoded, modeled, and transformed into inferences, as well as transparency regarding the assumptions embedded in AI algorithms and adaptive mechanisms.

8.3.4 Validity Arguments for AI-Driven Use

Robust validity arguments for AI-based games must draw on multiple sources of evidence, including internal structure, response processes, relations to external variables, and consequences of use (Kane, 2006; Pellegrino et al., 2001). Evidence based on internal structure examines whether relationships among AI-derived indicators align with theoretical expectations about the construct. Response process evidence investigates whether the cognitive and behavioral processes elicited by the game and inferred by AI models correspond to the intended competencies.

Relations to external variables provide convergent and discriminant evidence by examining associations between AI-based game inferences and external criteria, such as standardized assessments, instructional outcomes, or expert judgments. Finally, evidence concerning consequences addresses the impact of AI-driven GBA use, including benefits for learning and instruction as well as potential unintended effects, particularly in high-stakes or automated decision-making contexts.

In sum, psychometric principles remain central to AI-based games, but they must be thoughtfully extended to accommodate adaptive algorithms, temporal dependency, and complex inference models. Grounding AI-driven GBA in rigorous measurement theory and comprehensive validity arguments is essential for ensuring that innovation does not come at the expense of interpretability or fairness.

8.4 AI Analytics and Multimodal Evidence

8.4.1 *Game Telemetry as Analytic Substrate*

Digital educational games function as instrumented systems that generate dense, fine-grained telemetry, including time-stamped logs, sequences of player actions, decision paths, resource usage, and interaction traces (Baker & Inventado, 2014). Such data enable continuous, process-oriented observation of learning behaviors, providing insights into planning, strategy use, and problem-solving dynamics that are inaccessible through traditional outcome measures. AI methods are particularly well suited to modeling this high-frequency, sequential data; however, their analytic value depends on principled alignment with learning constructs to ensure that inferences are meaningful rather than merely descriptive.

8.4.2 *Multimodal Data for Enriching Learning Evidence*

Beyond interaction logs, multimodal learning analytics offer opportunities to enrich evidence about learning processes by integrating behavioral, physiological, affective, and social signals. Data sources such as eye gaze, speech, posture, facial expression, and biometric measures can be combined with game telemetry to triangulate inferences about cognitive load, engagement, self-regulation, and collaboration (Ifenthaler & Yau, 2020). When carefully designed, multimodal evidence can strengthen validity by capturing aspects of learning that are only indirectly observable through gameplay actions alone.

At the same time, multimodal data introduce additional challenges related to synchronization, noise, privacy, and construct definition. Without explicit theoretical grounding and rigorous preprocessing, multimodal correlations risk being spurious or uninterpretable. Consequently, the inclusion of multimodal data should be guided by clear measurement purposes and integrated within explicit evidence models.

8.4.3 *Embedding AI Analytics within Evidence-Centered Design*

To translate AI-derived analytics into defensible assessment evidence, analytic methods must be embedded within the framework of ECD. ECD provides a conceptual and inferential structure that constrains model development by requiring explicit specification of competency claims, evidence rules, and task characteristics (Mislevy et al., 2003). Embedding analytics within this framework promotes interpretability, transparency, and auditability, mitigating concerns about opaque or "black-box" AI while enabling scalable, analytics-driven assessment.

8.4.4 *Challenges of Analytics-Based Assessment*

Despite their promise, AI-driven analytics-based assessments face persistent challenges. Algorithmic opacity, limited explainability, overfitting to specific game contexts, and construct drift over time complicate interpretation and validation

(Siemens, 2013). Central to these concerns is the translation problem: AI-generated predictions must be theoretically justified and empirically validated to function as assessment evidence, rather than being treated as evidence in themselves (Williamson, Bejar, & Mislevy, 2006). Increasing data volume alone does not improve measurement quality; without disciplined construct definition and evidence modeling, analytics remain descriptive rather than inferential (Wise & Shaffer, 2015).

8.5 AI-Informed Game Design

AI-informed game design extends measurement-driven educational game design by explicitly integrating computational inference models into alignment, evidence, and validation processes. In such systems, AI does not merely personalize experiences but functions as a core component of assessment, interpreting gameplay data to generate inferences about learner competencies. Effective AI-informed design therefore requires principled coordination among learning objectives, evidence models, engagement strategies, and validation workflows.

8.5.1 Outcome Alignment

Learning outcomes must be explicitly aligned with the features and signals used by AI models for inference. Competencies should be operationalized as patterns of observable gameplay behavior that can be reliably detected, represented, and interpreted by probabilistic or machine learning models. This alignment ensures that AI inferences are grounded in construct-relevant actions rather than incidental gameplay artifacts.

8.5.2 Evidence Modeling

Gameplay scenarios function as AI-readable task environments only when grounded in explicit evidence models. Drawing on ECD, competencies, evidentiary behaviors, and task conditions must be defined in advance so that AI systems can map raw interaction data to latent constructs in principled ways. Without explicit evidence models, AI analytics risk producing opaque or ambiguous inferences.

8.5.3 Engagement and Psychometric Control

AI-driven adaptation must balance learner motivation with psychometric rigor. While adaptive difficulty, feedback, and personalization can enhance engagement, they must be constrained to preserve comparability and interpretability of evidence across learners. Poorly regulated adaptation may introduce construct-irrelevant variance, whereas well-designed adaptive systems can improve evidence quality by sustaining effort and eliciting authentic problem-solving (Wouters et al., 2013).

8.5.4 Validation Cycles and Team Structures

AI-enabled assessment requires iterative cycles of modeling, training, validation, and revision. Validation extends beyond model accuracy to include scrutiny of feature selection, bias, and stability across contexts and populations. These processes depend on interdisciplinary collaboration among psychometricians, AI researchers, game designers, and learning scientists, each contributing domain-specific expertise to ensure that systems are adaptive, engaging, and psychometrically defensible.

8.6 Case Examples of AI-Enabled Game-Based Assessment

Concrete applications of AI-enabled GBA illustrate how the measurement principles and design frameworks discussed in earlier sections can be operationalized across diverse learning domains. These examples demonstrate how gameplay process data, interpreted through theory-driven inference models, can support assessment of complex competencies that are difficult to capture using traditional item-based formats.

8.6.1 Problem-Solving and Strategic Reasoning

GBAs of problem-solving increasingly rely on AI-driven models to infer learners' strategic planning, executive function, and adaptive reasoning by analyzing gameplay processes rather than final outcomes. In such systems, evidence is drawn from sequences of actions, timing patterns, strategy shifts, and responses to feedback, providing insight into how learners approach ill-structured problems over time. This process-oriented approach aligns with large-scale initiatives such as the OECD's Programme for International Student Assessment innovative assessment tasks, which emphasize complex problem-solving in dynamic environments (OECD, 2017).

By modeling problem-solving behavior as a trajectory rather than a single performance event, AI-enabled games can distinguish between learners who arrive at similar outcomes through qualitatively different strategies. From a measurement perspective, this distinction is critical: strategic efficiency, adaptability, and persistence are substantively meaningful dimensions of competence that are often invisible in traditional assessments. However, these inferences depend on explicit construct models and careful control of construct-irrelevant influences such as exploratory play styles or interface familiarity.

8.6.2 Language and Literacy Learning

Narrative- and dialogue-rich games provide a promising context for assessing language and literacy skills in authentic, context-sensitive ways. Supported by natural language processing techniques, such games can analyze learners' spoken or written language to infer discourse practices, reading comprehension, narrative reasoning, and pragmatic language use. Rather than eliciting isolated responses to decontextualized prompts, game-based language assessments situate language use within meaningful interactions, aligning assessment with communicative practice (Gee, 2007).

AI-based inference models in this domain can incorporate features such as lexical diversity, syntactic complexity, coherence, and responsiveness to conversational cues. When embedded within ECD frameworks, these features serve as evidence for well-defined linguistic constructs rather than as ad hoc indicators. At the same time, language-based game assessments raise particular validity and fairness concerns, including sensitivity to dialectal variation, multilingualism, and cultural norms of communication. Addressing these issues requires explicit modeling of response processes and careful validation across diverse learner populations.

8.6.3 Early Learning and Developmentally Sensitive Assessment

In early childhood contexts, AI-enabled GBAs offer opportunities to support developmentally appropriate measurement while accommodating constraints related to attention, communication, and variability in developmental trajectories. Games designed for young learners can infer learning progress from interaction patterns such as object manipulation, response latency, exploration sequences, and error correction, rather than relying on verbal explanations or written responses (Clark et al., 2016).

AI-driven adaptation allows tasks to adjust dynamically to a child's emerging abilities, supporting both engagement and measurement sensitivity. From a psychometric standpoint, however, such systems must carefully distinguish developmental change from measurement error and account for high within-child variability. Validity arguments in early learning contexts therefore place particular emphasis on response process evidence and consequences of use, given the formative and potentially high-impact nature of assessment outcomes.

8.6.4 Socio-Emotional and Collaborative Skills

AI-enabled GBAs are increasingly used to infer socio-emotional competencies such as persistence, self-regulation, collaboration, and empathy. In both individual and multiplayer game environments, machine learning models analyze behavioral patterns, including persistence in the face of challenge, help-seeking behavior, turn-taking, coordination, and responsiveness to peers.

These constructs are inherently contextual and socially situated, making them difficult to assess through traditional methods. Games provide structured yet flexible environments in which socio-emotional behaviors can be observed repeatedly and under varying conditions. However, the interpretive challenges are substantial. Observable behaviors may reflect situational strategies or cultural norms rather than stable dispositions. Consequently, assessment of socio-emotional skills requires especially careful construct definition, longitudinal evidence, and cautious interpretation, particularly when used for evaluative or high-stakes purposes.

8.7 Future Directions in Game-Based Assessment

As GBA transitions from experimental innovation to an increasingly institutionalized component of educational assessment systems, research attention has shifted from questions of feasibility and engagement toward issues of quality, scalability, integration, and governance. Recent scholarship reflects a maturing field in which methodological rigor, AI, system interoperability, and ethical accountability are central determinants of credibility and adoption.

8.7.1 Research Quality and Methodological Rigor

A defining future direction for GBA research is the continued elevation of methodological and psychometric rigor. Early work in the field focused on proof-of-concept demonstrations and motivational affordances, which were essential for establishing viability but insufficient for sustained assessment use. More recent research increasingly emphasizes theory-driven design, explicit construct modeling, and comprehensive validity arguments (Wouters et al., 2013).

Contemporary studies more frequently align game mechanics with formal evidence models and established assessment frameworks such as ECD. Advanced measurement approaches, including Bayesian modeling, latent variable techniques, and longitudinal analysis, are increasingly applied to gameplay data to support inference about competence, uncertainty, and learning trajectories. Despite these advances, research quality remains uneven, with small samples, limited replication, and inconsistent reporting practices constraining generalizability. Strengthening cumulative evidence through replication, shared datasets, and transparent reporting standards is therefore a central research priority.

8.7.2 Advanced AI and Data-Driven Inference

AI and machine learning will continue to expand the analytic power and scalability of GBA. Educational data mining and learning analytics support the modeling of high-frequency behavioral data, enabling assessment to move beyond static outcomes toward dynamic, process-based inference (Baker & Siemens, 2014). Advances in deep learning, sequence modeling, and multimodal data fusion increasingly enable real-time adaptation and learner profiling across large populations.

At the same time, reliance on advanced AI intensifies concerns about interpretability and validity. Many high-performing models function as opaque systems, complicating the articulation of evidence chains linking observed behaviors to inferred constructs. This tension between predictive accuracy and explainability represents a critical inflection point for the field, particularly as GBAs are considered for higher stakes or institutional decision-making. Future research is therefore likely to emphasize hybrid approaches that integrate theory-driven models with data-driven techniques, as well as explainable AI methods tailored to assessment contexts.

8.7.3 System Integration and Interoperability

Another key direction concerns the integration of GBAs within broader educational technology ecosystems. Increasingly, GBA systems are embedded within learning management systems, analytics platforms, and institutional data infrastructures rather than operating as standalone tools. Interoperability supports longitudinal evidence accumulation, cross-context inference, and coordinated instructional decision-making (Siemens, 2013).

The adoption of shared data standards and protocols enables gameplay-generated evidence to be combined with traditional assessments, instructional records, and demographic information, supporting more holistic learner profiles. At the same time, system integration introduces new challenges related to data quality, contextual validity, governance, and interpretation across platforms. Addressing these challenges requires not only technical solutions but also organizational capacity building and policy alignment.

8.7.4 Ethics, Fairness, and Governance

Ethical considerations are emerging as a defining concern in the next phase of GBA. These systems often collect detailed, continuous behavioral data, sometimes without learners' explicit awareness, raising questions about informed consent, transparency, data ownership, and appropriate use. Such concerns are amplified in AI-supported systems, where inference processes may be difficult to explain or contest.

Research highlights the risk of algorithmic bias, particularly when models are trained on data reflecting historical inequities or when game mechanics advantage learners with specific cultural or experiential backgrounds (Mittelstadt et al., 2016). Differences in prior gaming experience, accessibility needs, or familiarity with game conventions may introduce construct-irrelevant variance that undermines fairness. Future work increasingly emphasizes fairness-aware modeling, accessibility-informed design, and governance frameworks that clarify accountability and oversight. Treating ethics as a foundational design constraint, rather than a retrospective consideration, is essential for responsible scaling.

8.7.5 Research Priorities and Transformative Potential

Taken together, these trends point toward a set of research priorities that will shape the field's trajectory. Longitudinal validation across contexts, cross-game and cross-platform inference, and transparent reporting of models and assumptions are critical for building cumulative knowledge. Equally important is the distinction between incremental AI-driven enhancements to existing assessment practices and more transformative reconfigurations of how evidence about learning is generated, interpreted, and used.

Future research must therefore examine not only technical advances but also how GBA reshapes assessment ecosystems as a whole. The extent to which AI-enabled GBA can support valid, fair, and actionable decision-making at scale will ultimately determine its role in the future of educational measurement.

8.8 Conclusion

AI has the potential to transform educational games into scalable, adaptive assessment environments, but this potential can only be realized when assessment is firmly grounded in sound measurement theory. Defensible GBA requires clearly articulated constructs, transparent inference models, robust validation evidence, and rigorous ethical safeguards. Educational games are uniquely positioned to embed assessment within meaningful, engaging activities, enabling continuous feedback and personalized learning, but this integration must not compromise validity, fairness, or interpretability.

Looking ahead, the future of assessment is likely to be defined by AI-supported ecosystems in which learning, play, and measurement are seamlessly intertwined. Achieving this vision will require sustained interdisciplinary collaboration to refine modeling techniques, establish standards for validation and reporting, and ensure that ethical, legal, and social considerations are addressed proactively. By attending to these priorities, AI-driven GBA can evolve from a promising innovation into a reliable, equitable, and scientifically grounded component of contemporary educational measurement.

References

American Educational Research Association, American Psychological Association, & National Council on Measurement in Education. (2014). *Standards for educational and psychological testing*. Washington, DC: AERA.

Baker, R. S., & Inventado, P. S. (2014). Educational data mining and learning analytics. In J. Larusson & B. White (Eds.), *Learning analytics: From research to practice* (pp. 61–75). Springer. https://doi.org/10.1007/978-1-4614-3305-7_4

Baker, R., & Siemens, G. (2014). Educational Data Mining and Learning Analytics. In R. K. Sawyer (Ed.), *The Cambridge Handbook of the Learning Sciences* (2nd ed., pp. 253–272). Cambridge University Press. https://doi.org/10.1017/cbo9781139519526.016

Clark, D. B., Tanner-Smith, E. E., & Killingsworth, S. S. (2016). Digital games, design, and learning: A systematic review and meta-analysis. *Review of Educational Research, 86*(1), 79–122. https://doi.org/10.3102/0034654315582065

Dorans, N. J., & Cook, L. L. (2016). *Fairness in educational assessment and measurement*. Routledge.

DiCerbo, K. E., & Behrens, J. T. (2012). Implications of the digital ocean on current and future assessments. In R. Lissitz and H. Jiao (Eds.), *Computers and their impact on state assessment: Recent history and predictions for the future* (pp. 273–306). Charlotte, NC: Information Age Publishing. https://doi.org/10.1108/978-1-61735-727-520251015

Earl, L. M. (2013). *Assessment as learning: Using classroom assessment to maximize student learning* (2nd ed.). Corwin.

Embretson, S. E. (1998). A cognitive design system approach to generating valid tests: Application to abstract reasoning. *Psychological Methods, 3*(3), 380–396. https://doi.org/10.1037/1082-989X.3.3.380

Eseryel, D., Ge, X., Ifenthaler, D., & Law, V. (2011). Dynamic modeling as a cognitive regulation scaffold for complex problem-solving skills in an educational massively multiplayer online game environment. *Journal of Educational Computing Research, 45*(3), 265–286. https://doi.org/10.2190/ec.45.3.a

Eseryel, D., Guo, Y., & Law, V. (2012). Interactivity[3] design and assessment framework for educational games to promote motivation and complex problem solving skills. In D. Ifenthaler, D. Eseryel, & X. Ge (Eds.), *Assessment in game-based learning: Foundations, innovations, and perspectives* (pp. 257–285). New York: Springer.

Eseryel, D., Ifenthaler, D., & Ge, X. (2011). Alternative assessment strategies for game-based learning environments. In D. Ifenthaler, Kinshuk, P. Isaias, D. G. Sampson, & J. M. Spector (Eds.), *Multiple perspectives on problem solving and learning in the digital age* (pp. 159–178). New York: Springer.

Eseryel, D., Ifenthaler, D., & Ge, X. (2013). Validation study of a method for assessing complex ill-structured problem solving by using causal representations. *Educational Technology Research & Development, 61*(3), 443–463. https://doi.org/10.1007/s11423-013-9297-2

Eseryel, D., & Law, V. (2012). Effect of cognitive regulation in understanding complex science systems during simulation-based inquiry learning. *Technology, Instruction, Cognition, & Learning, 9*(1–2), 111–132.

Eseryel, D., Law, V., Ifenthaler, D., Ge, X., & Miller, R. B. (2014). An investigation of the interrelationships between motivation, engagement, and complex problem solving in game-based learning. *Educational Technology & Society, 17*(1), 42–53.

Gee, J. P. (2007). *What video games have to teach us about learning and literacy* (2nd ed.). Palgrave Macmillan.

Greeno, J. G. (1998). The situativity of knowing, learning, and research. *American Psychologist, 53*(1), 5–26. https://doi.org/10.1037/0003-066X.53.1.5

Ifenthaler, D., Eseryel, D., & Ge, X. (2012). Assessment in game-based learning. In D. Ifenthaler, D. Eseryel, & X. Ge (Eds.), *Assessment in game-based learning: Foundations, innovations, and perspectives* (pp. 3–10). New York: Springer.

Ifenthaler, D., & Yau, J. Y.-K. (2020). Utilising learning analytics to support study success in higher education: A systematic review. *Educational Technology Research and Development, 68*(4), 1961–1990. https://doi.org/10.1007/s11423-020-09788-z

Kane, M. T. (2006). Validation. In R. L. Brennan (Ed.), *Educational measurement* (4th ed., pp. 17–64). Westport, CT: Praeger.

Kane, M. T. (2013). Validating the interpretations and uses of test scores. *Journal of Educational Measurement, 50*(1), 1–73.

Kolen, M. J., & Brennan, R. L. (2014). *Test equating, scaling, and linking* (3rd ed.). New York: Springer. https://doi.org/10.1007/978-1-4939-0317-7

Mislevy, R. J., Almond, R. G., & Lukas, J. F. (2003). A brief introduction to evidence-centered design. *ETS Research Report Series, 2003*(1), i–29. https://scholar.google.com/citations?view_op=view_citation&hl=en&user=J6_-wesAAAAJ&citation_for_view=J6_-wesAAAAJ:M3ejUd6NZC8C

Mislevy, R. J., Almond, R. G., Lukas, J. F., & Steinberg, L. S. (2002). Design and analysis in task-based language assessment. *Language Testing, 19*(4), 477–496.

Mislevy, R. J., Behrens, J. T., Dicerbo, K. E., & Levy, R. (2012). Design and discovery in educational assessment: Evidence-centered design, psychometrics, and educational data mining. *Journal of Educational Data Mining, 4*(1), 11–48.

Mislevy, R. J., Steinberg, L. S., & Almond, R. G. (2003). On the roles of task model variables in assessment design. In S. Irvine & P. Kyllonen (Eds.), *Generalizing items for cognitive test: Theory and practice* (pp. 131–180). Springer.

Mittelstadt, B. D., Allo, P., Taddeo, M., Wachter, S., & Floridi, L. (2016). The ethics of algorithms: Mapping the debate. *Big Data & Society, 3*(2), 1–21. https://doi.org/10.1177/2053951716679679

National Research Council. (2007). *Taking science to school: Learning and teaching science in grades K-8*. National Academies Press.

OECD. (2017). *PISA 2015 Result (Volume V) collaborative problem-solving*. OECD Publishing. https://doi.org/10.1787/9789264285521-en

Pellegrino, J. W., Chudowsky, N., & Glaser, R. (2001). *Knowing what students know: The science and design of educational assessment*. National Academy Press.

Ryan, R. M., & Deci, E. L. (2000). Intrinsic and extrinsic motivations: Classic definitions and new directions. *Contemporary Educational Psychology, 25*(1), 54–67. https://doi.org/10.1006/ceps.1999.1020

Shaffer, D. W., Halverson, R., Squire, K. R., & Gee, J. P. (2005). Video games and the future of learning. *Phi Delta Kappan, 87*(2), 105–111. https://doi.org/10.1177/003172170508700205

Shute, V. J. (2011). Stealth assessment in computer-based games to support learning. In S. Tobias & J. D. Fletcher (Eds.), *Computer games and instruction* (pp. 503–524). Information Age.

Shute, V. J., & Ventura, M. (2013). *Stealth assessment: Measuring and supporting learning in video games*. MIT Press.

Siemens, G. (2013). Learning analytics: The emergence of a discipline. *American Behavioral Scientist, 57*(10), 1380–1400.

Siemens, G., & Baker, R. (2012). Learning analytics and educational data mining: Towards communication and collaboration. In *Proceedings of the 2nd international conference on learning analytics and knowledge* (pp. 252–254). ACM. https://doi.org/10.1145/2330601.2330661

Williamson, D. M., Bejar, I. I., & Mislevy, R. J. (2006). Automated scoring of complex tasks in computer-based testing: An introduction. In D. M. Williamson, R. J. Mislevey, & I. I. Bejar (Eds.), *Automated scoring of complex tasks in computer-based testing* (pp. 1–13). Lawrence Erlbaum Associates Publishers.

Wise, A. F., & Shaffer, D. W. (2015). Why theory matters more than ever in the age of big data. *Journal of Learning Analytics, 2*(2), 5–13.

Wouters, P., van Nimwegen, C., van Oostendorp, H., & van der Spek, E. D. (2013). A meta-analysis of the cognitive and motivational effects of serious games. *Journal of Educational Psychology, 105*(2), 249–265. https://doi.org/10.1037/a0031311

9

LARGE LANGUAGE MODELS IN ASSESSMENT

Christopher Ormerod, Alexander Kwako, Kai North, and Sue Lottridge

9.1 Introduction

Large language models (LLMs) have emerged as one of the most transformative technologies in artificial intelligence (AI), fundamentally changing how we interact with machines and process information. In this chapter, we provide a broad overview of LLMs in educational assessment: we discuss (1) validity in the context of educational applications of LLMs; (2) the technical underpinnings of LLMs; (3) how LLMs are applied to three common problems in educational assessment, i.e., automated scoring (AS), personalized feedback, and automatic item generation (AIG); and (4) how we can ensure that LLMs contribute to high-quality assessments.

9.1.1 Validity Theory and LLMs in Assessment

The integration of LLMs necessitates grounding in traditional validity theory, specifically Messick's (1987) unified framework and Kane's (2013) argument-based approach. Utilizing LLMs shifts the focus toward how these models represent underlying educational constructs. While we will see that LLMs have shown remarkable abilities in logic and problem-solving, when applying an LLM to an academic task such as the interpretation and application of a rubric, a central concern is construct representation: ensuring the LLM captures the intended skills rather than surface-level linguistic patterns. Furthermore, interpretive arguments must clearly define which claims can be made based on AI-generated outputs and identify where construct-irrelevant variance, such as algorithmic bias or model hallucinations, might undermine the integrity of test scores.

DOI: 10.4324/9781003621522-9

9.2 Technical Foundations for LLMs

This section provides a technical overview of LLMs, including foundations, capabilities, and practical considerations. We begin by exploring the underlying transformer architecture that enables these models. An LM is a function that approximates the probability of a word sequence, enabling content generation by iteratively predicting the next word. The term LLM typically refers to deep neural networks based on the transformer architecture (Vaswani et al., 2017). Depending on their components, these models come in three main variants: encoder-only, decoder-only, or encoder-decoder. The input into each type of model is defined by an input embedding, encoding semantic information, and a positional embedding, encoding relative positional information, as presented in Figure 9.1.

The core mechanism of the transformer is the layer-wise application of attention (Graves et al., 2006). Unlike prior neural network models that process text sequentially and then apply attention (Dong et al., 2017), attention layering allows the model to simultaneously weigh the relative importance of every word in the input context. This parallel processing is far more effective at capturing long-range dependencies in text. However, it also imposes a fundamental limitation: the entire input sequence must be processed at once. All transformer-based LLMs have a fixed maximum input size, known as the context length.

Modern generative LLMs are trained in the following three stages:

1 **Pretraining**: The model weights are optimized to predict the next word in a large corpus of unlabeled text.

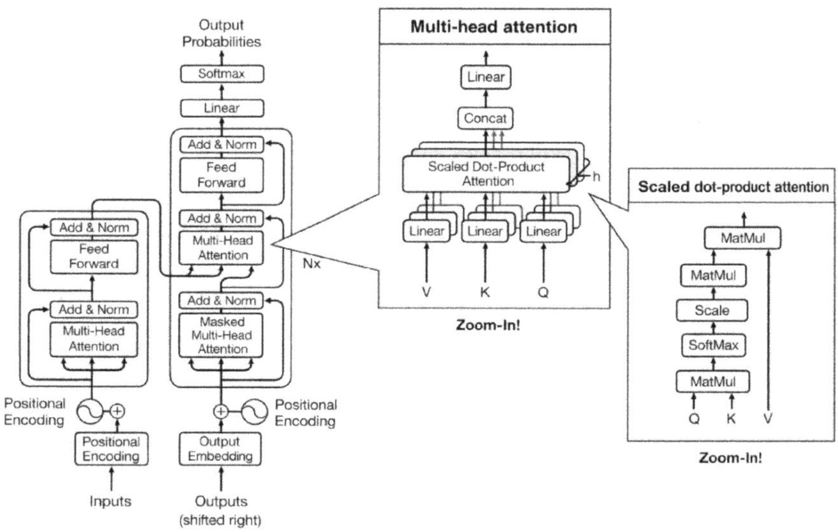

FIGURE 9.1 The transformer architecture.

TABLE 9.1 Example Chat Template

User	What is the capital of France?
Assistant	The capital of France is Paris.
User	What is the population?
Assistant	The city of Paris has a population of approximately 2.1 million people. However, the larger metropolitan area, often referred to as Grand Paris or the Île-de-France region, has a population of over 12 million.

2 **Instruction Tuning**: The model weights are then fine-tuned to complete a corpus of instructions.
3 **Refinement**: The model weights are then further fine-tuned to prefer labeled outputs.

The first two stages rely on variants of stochastic gradient descent, such as Adam (Kingma & Ba, 2017). We often refer to the first stage as semi-supervised (Chapelle et al., 2006), since next word prediction is a supervised task on unlabeled data; unlabeled data is not required to conform to any particular format and often is composed of academic, web-based, prose, dialogue, and code/mathematics (Gao et al., 2020). The second stage, instruction tuning, uses an instruction set that typically takes the form of a dialogue between a user and an assistant, where the user poses a task with relevant input, and the assistant provides task completion, with possible follow-up tasks and completions, as shown in Table 9.1.

The final stage, being the refinement process, uses reinforcement learning techniques such as direct preference optimization (DPO) (Ziegler et al., 2020). These techniques can be used to modify weights so that the outputs are more helpful and less harmful. The input for these methods is preferential pairs: the user specifies a task, and versions of the task completion are presented, with one preferred. This preference is encoded as a reward function, and the weights are updated to increase the likelihood of the preferred output.

9.2.1 Abilities of Generative LLMs

First, the LLM naturally possesses a set of abilities prescribed by the instruction-tuning stage of training; hence, it can generally complete tasks in the categories present in the corpus used in this stage. This corpus typically consists of tasks in the following categories:

1 **Natural Language Understanding**: Examples include classification tasks such as sentiment analysis or toxicity detection, and question-answering tasks such as multiple-choice questions (MCQs) and knowledge-based short-answer items.
2 **Natural Language Generation**: This includes summarization and content-generation tasks, such as generating stories, poems, and essays.

3 **Information Retrieval**: Identifying specific information, such as names, dates, and places, from a text.
4 **Logic and Coding**: The generation of step-by-step reasoning in addition to problem-solving in several different languages.
5 **Other**: This includes style transfer, translation, and data integration.

One key discovery about LLMs is that scaling their size generally improves their ability to complete unseen tasks. This characteristic gives rise to the notion of an emergent ability, which is any ability not present in smaller models but is present in larger models trained in the same way (Wei et al., 2022). The most prominent examples of emergent abilities are known as zero-shot, one-shot, and few-shot learning (Brown et al., 2020). These abilities refer to completing tasks with no examples, one example, or a few examples, respectively. We may see remarkable improvements in text classification with very few examples, which we consider emergent, as no such improvements are observed with much smaller models.

Researchers have sought to evaluate the abilities and limitations of LLMs using a collection of benchmarks, defined by a dataset and an evaluation metric. Some of the most common benchmarks include the Massive Multitask Language Understanding, Graduate-Level Google-Proof Q&A Benchmark (GPQA), HumanEval, MATH, and Multilingual Grade School Math (MGSM) (Alzahrani et al., 2024). Some of these benchmarks for popular models are presented in Table 9.2, with performance measured as accuracy, expressed as the percentage of tasks correctly completed.

A review of these patterns suggests that while models like GPT-4.5 and Gemini 2.5 Pro show high proficiency in reasoning-heavy benchmarks like MATH, performance varies significantly across domains such as coding (HumanEval) and graduate-level knowledge (GPQA). These differences highlight that no single model is superior across all assessment tasks, underscoring the need for domain-specific model selection. Lastly, we note that many models are trained to integrate information from external sources, a technique known as retrieval-augmented generation (RAG) (Saad-Falcon et al., 2024). RAG is a method of extending an LLM's ability to use up-to-date information not necessarily available during training.

TABLE 9.2 LLM Benchmark List

	MMLU	*GPQA*	*MATH*	*HumanEval*	*MGSM*
Claude 3.5 Sonnet	88.3	59.4	71.1	92.0	91.6
GPT-4.5	90.8	69.5	87.1	88.0	86.9
Gemini 2.5 Pro	84.1	80.3	95.2	82.0	92.2
Grok 3	81.4	84.0	94.2	86.5	91.3

9.2.2 *Limitations and Pitfalls of Using Generative LLMs*

The first limitation we mentioned was that the architecture imposes a limit on input length. For initial transformer-based LLMs such as the bidirectional encoder representations from transformers (BERT) (Devlin et al., 2018), the maximum sequence length was 512, limiting their applicability. Modern generative LLMs circumvent this limitation by using rotational positional embeddings (Su et al., 2024), which facilitates extended training on long contexts (Fu et al., 2024). While the resulting context length is still finite, in practice, it is sufficiently long for most applications. The relative effective context length (RECL), introduced by Dai et al. (2019), is a more practical measure, primarily because it captures a model's ability to extract information across long contexts. One of the more popular benchmarks for RECL has been the needle in a haystack test, which assesses an LLM's ability to retrieve key information from long distractor texts (Hsieh et al., 2024).

The use of RAG is also crucial in two other limitations of LLMs: the knowledge cutoff during pretraining and hallucinations. The knowledge cutoff refers to the fact that LLMs are static; hence, their weights do not change with prompting. LLMs are only aware of events learned through pretraining and will not naturally know about current events unless used in conjunction with RAG. The second pitfall, partly addressed by RAG, is that LLMs have a chance of presenting inaccurate content as truth, known as factual hallucinations, as well as flawed logic in multi-step tasks, referred to as reasoning hallucinations. Some famous examples of factual hallucinations include the model producing fictitious legal cases as precedent or citing nonexistent journal articles as proof of a particular concept or fact. Examples of reasoning hallucinations include inaccurate explanations of why a student's essay achieved a specific score or invalid reasoning for why a particular answer is correct. Some researchers have sought to quantify hallucination rates (Chelli et al., 2024), while others have sought to detect them (Farquhar et al., 2024).

9.2.3 *Prompt Tuning and Fine-Tuning*

Since the quality of their instructions influences LLMs' performance, prompt engineering is the practice of crafting effective prompts to maximize task performance. This enhancement often involves creating reusable prompt templates that contain instructions, conditions, and placeholders for dynamic content. To automate this process, frameworks like the open-source DSPy use optimizers to improve prompts based on performance metrics systematically (Opsahl-Ong et al., 2024), while closed-source platforms like OpenAI and Anthropic offer similar proprietary tools. However, closed-source LLMs are often updated behind the scenes, leading to model shift. As such, prompts may change in effectiveness when entered into an updated closed-source model, resulting in inconsistent output and poor reproducibility.

When prompt engineering fails to meet validation and reproducibility standards, the next step is fine-tuning an open-source model. Open-source LLMs can be saved locally with their weights being frozen, making them more reliable and consistent. However, full fine-tuning is computationally expensive, with a 1-billion-parameter model requiring over 16GB of GPU memory using standard optimizers, exceeding the capacity of most consumer-grade hardware. To address this challenge, researchers have developed parameter-efficient fine-tuning (PEFT) methods (Xu et al., 2023). The most popular technique, low-rank adaptation (LoRA) (Hu et al., 2021), works by freezing the model's original weights and training only a small set of new, "adapter" layers. This practice drastically reduces memory and computational requirements. When LoRA is combined with quantization, which is a technique for storing model weights at lower precision, the method is known as QLoRA (Dettmers et al., 2023). QLoRA enables fine-tuning large models on consumer hardware.

9.3 Generative Approaches to Automated Scoring

AS is an inexpensive alternative to scoring essays and short-constructed responses by hand. Prompt engineering, fine-tuning strategies, and data augmentation techniques have subsequently gained significant interest within the assessment community. This section provides an overview that compares previous scoring methods with approaches using generative LLMs.

9.3.1 Comparison with Previous Scoring Approaches

The earliest approaches to AS utilize hand-selected features to determine the quality of a student's answer (Page, 2003). These features ranged from length, syntactic complexity, vocabulary, readability, style, argumentation, relevance to the prompt, and more (Misgna et al., 2024). Traditional machine learning models used hand-crafted features to predict student scores. However, creating these features was costly and time-consuming, requiring extensive experimentation to optimize performance. The features were also highly context-dependent—those used for math problems differed significantly from those needed for essay assessment.

Word and document embeddings are used as an alternative to hand-crafted features. These are vector representations of words or documents that can capture semantics based on the statistical context of words (Le & Mikolov, 2014). Models trained on sequences of word embeddings of a large corpus of student responses provide vector representations to capture semantic relationships, which are then used as score predictors. Methods of computing word and document embeddings include Word2Vec (Le & Mikolov, 2014), GloVe (Pennington et al., 2014), and FastText (Bojanowski et al., 2017). Convolutional and recurrent neural network models trained using these packages were shown in several studies to outperform early feature-engineered approaches (Dong et al., 2017).

The BERT model captures long-distance dependencies and semantic representations using attention. This model was pre-trained on 3.3 billion tokens as a masked language modeling and next-sentence prediction model, learning bidirectional context to make predictions. For AS, an additional classification layer is appended to BERT and fine-tuned for scoring (Rodriguez et al., 2019). Variants of this approach have achieved state-of-the-art performance with better generalizability across item types than feature-engineered approaches (Xie et al., 2022). However, fine-tuning still requires large, expensive datasets to achieve optimal performance.

9.3.2 Approaches to Zero- and Few-Shot Scoring

Generative LLMs can match BERT-based approaches without fine-tuning and, after fine-tuning, potentially exceed them (Hou et al., 2025). This improved performance stems from vastly larger pretraining datasets—Llama 3 used 15 trillion tokens compared to BERT's 3.30 billion—providing a broader knowledge base, and from vastly larger model size—Llama 3 has 70 billion parameters compared to BERT's 330 million. Unlike BERT's masked language modeling, generative LLMs utilize additional information in the prompting, enabling zero-shot and few-shot prediction. This pretraining provides AS forms that do not require fine-tuning.

Mizumoto and Eguchi (2023) found promising results using GPT-3.5 for second-language essay scoring. Hou et al. (2025) showed that zero-shot prompts that provide the model with additional linguistic features (lemmas, nouns, sentence counts) consistently outperformed those without, matching BERT baseline performance when tested on GPT-4 and Mistral 7 and B. Yoshida (2024) found that GPT-3.5 performed best with few-shot prompts, while GPT-4.0 showed minimal improvement across prompt types. Stahl et al. (2024) tested various personas (teaching assistant, educational researcher, creative writing member) with Mistral 7B. They found that the academic researcher and teaching assistant personas achieved optimal performance, with further improvement from additional examples. Wang and Ormerod (2024) and Saad-Falcon et al. (2024) demonstrated excellent performance using few-shot prompting in combination with a RAG pipeline.

9.3.3 Fine-Tuning for Automated Scoring

Fine-tuning generative LLMs for AS is a less-explored approach compared to single-shot or few-shot prediction, which do not require further training. This limitation is primarily due to the time and cost needed to fine-tune recent LLMs, given their size. However, studies on AS that perform some form of fine-tuning provide excellent baselines, surpassing those of zero- and few-shot approaches. Ormerod and Kwako (2024) and Katuka, Gain, and Yu (2024) offered several cases in which PEFT methods, such as QLoRA, applied to open-source models, such as Llama (Meta, 2024), outperformed much larger single-shot models as well as BERT baselines (Rodriguez et al., 2019). While fine-tuning is predominantly applied to open-source models, Latif and Zhai (2023) fine-tuned GPT-3.5 to score science questions of varying types automatically. They trained GPT-3.5 over several epochs on approximately 7k student responses, each with a pre-assigned grade level.

9.3.4 *Data Augmentation for Scoring*

Data augmentation is the process of adding repurposed or synthetic data to a pre-existing dataset used for model fine-tuning to improve model performance. Synthetic data may be data created by artificial means, such as another model's predictions or AI-generated content. In sufficient quantities, synthetic data can boost model performance and be manipulated to reduce model bias or other unwanted characteristics.

Grammatical error correction (GEC) was one of the first applications of data augmentation in training generative models. By applying round-trip translation (RTT), Stahlberg and Kumar (2021) created a large corpus to train T5 models for GEC. Bayer et al. (2023) demonstrated that, when carefully applied, RTT can also provide value in text classification problems when the classification scheme does not change with paraphrasing; however, applications to assessment so far have not been as successful.

North and Ormerod (2025) used synthetic data to improve AS performance for the PERSUADE corpus (Crossley et al., 2022). They demonstrated that it was possible to train traditional LLMs, such as ELECTRA (Clark et al., 2020), with far less data. By fine-tuning Llama-3 on only 10% of the original PERSUADE corpus and then applying Llama-3 to predict student grades on the remaining 90% of the training corpus, the ELECTRA model performed significantly better than when trained on the original 10% alone. This result effectively shows that using generative models in a model distillation pipeline requires only a small amount of scored data to achieve AS performance comparable to that of traditional scoring models.

9.3.5 *Challenges to Implementation in Large-Scale Assessment*

Generative LLMs are a compelling alternative for AS because their performance can match that of previous methods without the costly fine-tuning required on specialized datasets. Furthermore, when fine-tuned, they can set a new state-of-the-art, particularly for complex tasks such as essay scoring (Ormerod & Kwako, 2024). Despite these advantages, deploying LLMs in large-scale assessment introduces significant challenges related to bias, data privacy, and the high computational resources required for their operation.

A primary fairness challenge arises from the observation by North and Ormerod (2025) that LLM-generated scores often have distributions that differ from those assigned by human experts. This systemic deviation can introduce novel biases not present in human scoring, raising significant concerns about equity. To mitigate this, researchers are exploring advanced fine-tuning techniques such as DPO, which aims to align a model's outputs more closely with human judgments and preferences.

Privacy and security present another major hurdle, especially with closed-source models. Because these models are trained on undisclosed data, sending them confidential student information or proprietary grading rubrics poses an unacceptable risk of data leakage in high-stakes testing. Open-source models offer a direct solution to this problem, as they can be hosted and trained securely in-house. This control, however, comes at the cost of high computational demands. While techniques such as LoRA and QLoRA can reduce the required GPU resources, their practical implementation demands specialized technical expertise.

9.4 Generating Personalized Feedback

Feedback consists of verification (e.g., a score) and elaboration (e.g., personalized guidance to help a learner improve) (Kulhavy & Stock, 1989). While this guidance can come from many sources, LLMs can automate their generation, providing the detailed and timely input that is crucial for effective learning (Shute, 2008). However, because simply presenting feedback is rarely sufficient for learning (Hattie & Timperley, 2007), automated feedback is most effective when integrated into broader educational tools, such as formative assessments or intelligent tutoring systems (ITSs). This section will provide an overview of effective feedback, review how LLMs generate it, and discuss its integration into tools designed to facilitate learning.

9.4.1 What Makes Feedback Effective?

Research shows that effective feedback is not one-size-fits-all; its impact depends on a complex interplay between the learner, the context, and the task. When designing automated feedback systems, it is crucial to consider not just what feedback to provide but also for whom and under what conditions. With this disclaimer in mind, we highlight several findings that are highly relevant to automated personalized feedback:

- **Feedback is most effective when it is timely** (Pridemore & Klein, 1995), yet not so immediate that it interrupts a learner's thought process. Ideally, the learner should be receptive to feedback or actively seek it (Corno & Snow, 1986; Hattie & Timperley, 2007).
- **Specificity matters** (Ranalli, 2018), but the type depends on the learner. While specific feedback is always more helpful than general advice, the best approach varies. Directive feedback (providing the correct answer) is often best for novices, whereas facilitative feedback (guiding without answering) is more beneficial for advanced learners (Black & Wiliam, 1998).

- **Engagement is essential.** For feedback to be effective, students must have the opportunity to engage actively with it (Fredricks et al., 2004; Zhang & Hyland, 2018; Wilson & MacArthur, 2024) and apply it to their learning goals (Black & Wiliam, 1998). Feedback that consists of simple reminders is often ignored and unlikely to lead to improvement (Link et al., 2022).
- **Feedback has emotional stakes.** Even when intended to be formative, feedback can be discouraging and negatively impact a student's motivation and performance if it is not delivered with care (Kluger & DeNisi, 1996).

9.4.2 Generating Feedback with LLMs

Automated feedback can be derived from LLMs through two primary methods: directly prompting a generative model or fine-tuning a model for a specific feedback-related task. Both approaches can enhance existing feedback systems and enable entirely new forms of educational guidance.

As previously mentioned, prompting is where an LLM is given instructions and a student's work to generate feedback. Advanced strategies like chain-of-thought prompting, assigning an expert persona, or using a second LLM to evaluate the feedback (an "LLM-as-judge" approach) can improve the quality of the output (e.g., Stahl et al., 2024; Phung et al., 2024).

Alternatively, an LLM can be fine-tuned to identify discourse elements like "claims" and "evidence" in student essays. The model's predictions can then be used to generate highly targeted feedback, such as suggesting a student add more evidence to support a claim or rewrite a sentence to establish a stronger argument (Baffour & Crossley, 2024; Lottridge et al., 2024).

Each method presents a clear trade-off. Prompting is easier to implement initially but can yield unreliable or unexpected output (Ji et al., 2023; Ye et al., 2023). Furthermore, due to an LLM's open-ended nature, quality is difficult to validate automatically (Ormerod & Kwako, 2024) and may be even more difficult to integrate into educational tools. In contrast, fine-tuning requires significant upfront effort, such as dataset creation and technical expertise, but yields more consistent, reliable, and targeted feedback that is easier to evaluate and align with specific educational goals.

9.4.3 Applications of Automated Personalized Feedback

While early ITSs provided sophisticated automated feedback, they lacked the flexibility offered by LLMs (Shute & Psotka, 1994; Shermis & Wilson, 2024). *Write On with Cambi!*, a formative assessment tool, exemplifies how fine-tuned LLMs can help students improve their argumentative writing (Lottridge et al., 2024).

In the tool, students submit an essay and are guided through a structured, multi-phase revision process. A series of fine-tuned models first evaluates high-level components, checking for key elements like a central claim, supporting evidence, and a conclusion. Only after these structural issues are addressed does the tool offer suggestions for surface-level edits, such as spelling and grammar. The process is interactive, waiting for the student's cue before moving to the next stage.

Write On with Cambi, being an interactive educational platform provided by Cambium Assessment, incorporates several principles of effective feedback. Its design is student-centered: feedback is timely but not interruptive, allowing students to control the pace. The suggestions are specific and actionable, often highlighting exact text or locations for revision. By following a pedagogically sound sequence, the tool encourages deep engagement and helps students improve their writing process in a structured way.

Example 9.1 Depicts Examples of Student-Centered Feedback Provided by Write On with Cambi

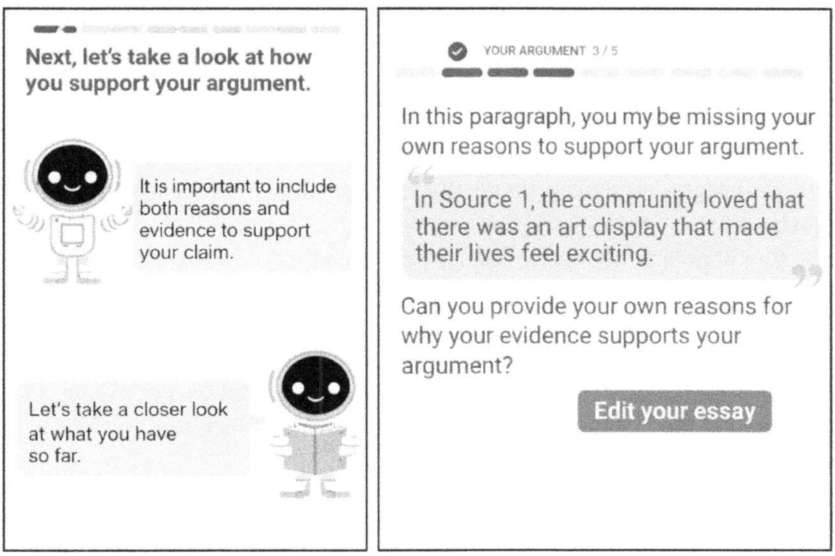

9.5 Generating Items and Content

AIG has a long history (Gierl & Haladyna, 2012). Most current research around AIG focuses on generating text-based MCQs. Yet there is also research on broader test content, such as diagram generation for math items (Lee et al., 2024) and the generation of informational passages for reading items (Bezirhan & von Davier, 2023). In high-stakes assessments, AIG is primarily used to populate item pools, which are field tested before use (LaFlair et al., 2023). LLMs are not used exclusively for generating items. They are also heavily employed in post-generation processing to find adequate distractors or filter items that fail to meet specific criteria, and LLMs are sometimes used for pre-generation processing or data mining (Tan et al., 2025).

9.5.1 Comparison with Template-Based Approaches

AIG traditionally relies on template-based approaches, which use highly structured item models with modular components (e.g., 5 + 3 = _ for single-digit addition). Templates produce predictable and controlled output. In contrast, many modern approaches use probability-based approaches (e.g., LLMs) to generate content. With LLMs, this is typically accomplished by prompting large, closed-source models.

The two methods present a clear trade-off in workflow and quality control. The template approach requires a significant upfront investment in designing item models but requires less post-generation validation. Conversely, prompting LLMs makes generating a high volume of varied content easy but requires extensive verification effort. LLMs can produce imbalanced domain coverage due to their inherent biases, generate factual inaccuracies or unexpected outputs (Ji et al., 2023; Ye et al., 2023), and struggle to create effective distractors (Attali et al., 2022). These weaknesses necessitate an iterative process of analyzing output and refining prompts.

Neither approach, however, has solved the challenge of accurately predicting item difficulty. Even simple template-based items can yield unexpected results, underscoring the need for field testing to calibrate items before use (LaFlair et al., 2023). Consequently, the primary role of AIG in high-stakes testing is to populate item banks for future calibration, not for dynamic, on-the-fly generation. While IRT parameter prediction models can reduce the scale of field testing, they are not yet precise enough to replace it.

9.5.2 Successfully Applying LLMs for AIG

Successful applications of prompting LLMs for AIG rely on several common strategies that circumvent the limitations of prompting described above. Note that strategies 1 and 2 are iterative processes that may involve many small-scale experiments.

1 Constrain the input (i.e., the prompt): It is helpful to start with a prompt that yields output as close to the ideal as possible. If further constraints are required, breaking the generation phase into multiple, smaller phases can help. Subject Matter Experts (SMEs) should be involved to ensure the output aligns with the domain and relevant standards.

2 Overgenerate and filter. Over-generating helps ensure that at least some items meet all criteria. Filtering involves applying foundational Natural Language Processing (NLP) techniques (e.g., cosine similarity) to remove output that is redundant or unlikely to meet the desired properties.
3 Evaluate or edit prospective items: Employ SMEs to evaluate or simply edit generated items. Manual evaluation can be time-consuming, so effective prompts and filters must be established in advance.

9.5.3 *Prompting for Content Creation*

A standard prompt for AIG typically includes instructions, a persona (e.g., "you are an expert test developer"), output format specifications, and a few examples to guide the model. This few-shot learning approach often outperforms zero-shot prompting (e.g., Bezirhan & von Davier, 2023), though the optimal number of examples should be empirically determined for each use case (Ripoll Y Schmitz & Sonnleitner, 2025).

To achieve greater control, complex generation tasks can be decomposed into a sequence of smaller, highly constrained prompts. For instance, instead of asking for a full passage at once, one can prompt for each sentence individually, specifying its unique topic, style, and complexity (Sayin & Gierl, 2024).

To generate multiple-choice distractors, one method is to repurpose keys from related items, using semantic similarity to select options that are plausible but not too obvious. Another approach is to prompt the LLM to generate distractors directly, for example, by instructing it to create an answer based on a specific misconception or a contradicting context (Attali et al., 2022).

When an LLM produces insufficient variation, modular elements can be added to the prompt to increase it. To generate content across a broader range of topics, for example, a variable can be added and populated from a curated list for each prompt call (e.g., Runge et al., 2024). Hierarchical templates can further structure this modularity for more complex generation tasks (Gierl & Lai, 2015).

9.5.4 *Post-Generation Processing*

A key strategy in AIG is to overgenerate and filter: produce a high volume of content, then systematically reduce it to a small, higher-quality set for SMEs to review. Recent work by Firoozi et al. (2025) provides a structured approach for this quality control process, specifically for multiple-choice test items. For example, Runge et al. (2024) generated 125,000 passages, which were filtered down to 900 before SME review.

The filtering process uses several techniques. The most common is post-generation filtering, where items are removed if they fail to meet specific constraints, such as word count, readability, structural rules (e.g., word count or Lexile score), or semantic similarity of distractors (Attali et al., 2022). Filtering can also be embedded within the prompt itself using an LLM-as-judge approach, where the model generates multiple options and then evaluates its own output to select the best one (Sayin & Gierl, 2024).

Furthermore, post-generation analysis is crucial for correcting unexpected biases in the generated content. For example, when an LLM overproduced items on a single subject, researchers refined their prompts to request rewrites using a curated list of subjects (Runge et al., 2024). This consequence highlights a critical principle: LLMs have non-intuitive behaviors and preferences, making iterative analysis and prompt refinement essential to achieve the desired results.

9.6 Ensuring Assessment Quality

Integrating LLMs into assessment programs requires upholding the core measurement principles of validity, reliability, and fairness. Validity is especially critical, as it concerns the degree to which evidence supports the interpretation of test scores for their proposed uses (AERA, APA, and NCME, 2014). Because LLMs fundamentally alter assessment processes, their use must be justified by a clear rationale demonstrating how this change supports, or even enhances, the intended score interpretations.

Therefore, validating an LLM-integrated assessment focuses on collecting evidence to prove it maintains or improves the integrity of score interpretations. This procedure requires a multifaceted approach, guided by the five sources of evidence outlined in the *Standards for Educational and Psychological Testing*: evidence based on test content, response processes, internal structure, relations to other variables, and the consequences of testing (AERA et al., 2014).

A foundational part of this validation is clearly defining the construct, which is the specific knowledge, skills, or traits the test is intended to measure. This definition must clarify how the construct differs from others and how it should relate to other variables. This process is shaped by the intended use of the scores and by the test design's mitigation of issues such as construct underrepresentation (insufficient measurement of the intended construct) and construct-irrelevant variance (measures unrelated to the construct).

9.6.1 Validation Methodologies

This section details validation methods for LLMs in assessment, as outlined in Tables 9.3 and 9.4. These validation methods follow critical steps in the LLM development pipeline. These are not to be interpreted as discrete steps but as a series of mutually reinforcing decisions that contribute toward an overarching validity argument (Kane, 2013). Ours is a practical framework, complementary to other frameworks that examine the validity of using LLMs in educational assessment (e.g., Casabianca et al., 2024).

TABLE 9.3 Validation Methods for Automated Scoring and Feedback

Validation Method	*Automated Scoring*	*Automated Feedback*
Rationale for use	Reduced cost and scoring time; consistency in scoring across time and testing occasions	More detailed information on characteristics of student responses, typically unscored
Human/AI interaction, with rationale	Fully AI, complementary AI/human, combined AI/human (Williamson et al., 2012)	Fully AI, AI with human edits
Rubric definition	The rubric used to assign scores is well defined, aligned with the item's design and intent, and reflects the range of performance expected for the item	Structured/Specific: Rubric used to evaluate feedback is well defined, aligned with item design and intent, and reflects the range of performances expected for the item Unstructured/General: Feedback aligns with rubric scores; evaluation of feedback addressed key aspects of the rubric; a feedback rubric is used to evaluate the quality of the feedback relative to humans
Human benchmark data	Evidence suggests that humans can be trained to apply a rubric accurately and fairly to all examinees	Structured/Specific: Evidence suggests that humans can be trained to apply feedback accurately and fairly to all examinees Unstructured/General: Human feedback exists that is of similar form and content as provided by AI (e.g., anchor paper descriptions of why scores were assigned)
LLM engine design	Choice of model, fine-tuning or prompting mechanism, score reproducibility, and data security/privacy are appropriate for use	Choice of model, fine-tuning or prompting mechanism, score reproducibility, and data security/privacy are appropriate for use
Training/Validation data	Responses representative of the range of examinee performances and scores, and of appropriate size to robustly examine performance	Responses representative of the range of examinee performances and feedback, and of appropriate size to robustly examine performance. Note that for unstructured feedback, this space may be quite large

(*Continued*)

TABLE 9.3 (Continued)

Validation Method	*Automated Scoring*	*Automated Feedback*
Statistical metrics for evaluation	Metrics examining the degree of agreement on the rubric	Metrics examining the degree of agreement on feedback assignment
Performance criteria	Thresholds for determining adequate agreement	Thresholds for determining adequate agreement
Relationship to other variables	Correlation with overall test score	Degree of alignment with the item scoring rubric
Downstream assessment quality impacts	IRT item parameter estimates Overall test reliability Overall test scores	Not applicable
Potential negative consequences	Attempts to game the LLM to obtain a higher score; lack of engagement; distrust of AI; potential for bias in scores	Feedback adopted without questioning; feedback is wrong and distracts the examinee; potential for bias in feedback; feedback creates gaming behavior
Monitoring plan with mitigations	Monitoring with human scoring is part of the deployment against performance criteria	Monitoring with human scoring is part of the deployment against performance criteria

The validation strategy is directly informed by the primary rationale for using an LLM. Common goals include reducing costs, increasing production speed, or improving the quality of scores, feedback, or test content. The chosen priority shapes the validation focus; for instance, a goal of cost reduction may only require showing that the LLM matches human performance, whereas a goal of program improvement would demand evidence of superior quality.

A core part of validation is defining the model of human-LLM interaction. The definition can range from fully automated LLM use to various hybrid approaches, such as an LLM drafting content for human review, an LLM refining human-created drafts, or humans and LLMs co-designing content interactively. The selected approach must be clearly justified based on the assessment's purpose and supported by evidence from the validation process.

The primary goal of using an LLM in assessment is to replicate the work of a well-trained human, whether for scoring, providing feedback, or developing test content. Adequate validation before deployment, therefore, requires several key components: a well-defined human judgment to serve as the ground truth, clear evaluation rubrics, and representative data for training and evaluation. These analyses must extend to test-taker subgroups to ensure fairness and can also include examining downstream impacts, such as the effect of automation on overall test scores.

Once deployed, validation must continue through ongoing monitoring to ensure both the LLM and human components of the system maintain quality. The supervision is necessary because human raters can drift, student responses can evolve

TABLE 9.4 Validation Methods for Automated Test Content Generation

Validation Method	*Automated Test Content Generation*
Rationale for use	Reduced development time; potentially higher-quality items
Human/AI interaction	Fully AI process with AI review; Interactive AI/human development; human development with AI review
Rubric definition	The rubric used to evaluate generated test content is well defined and represents the range of concerns for test development
Human benchmark data	Evidence suggests that humans can be trained to apply a rubric accurately and fairly to generated items
LLM engine design	Choice of model, fine-tuning or prompting mechanism, score reproducibility, and data security/privacy are appropriate for use
Training/validation data	Domain of test content and content development specifications are well defined; Items meeting requirements are available; Reviews of items are available using a well-defined rubric
Statistical metrics for evaluation	Human raters agree at adequate levels to be able to interpret rubric results; results are generally interpreted relative to the rubric scale for item review (e.g., content is usable with minimal modification)
Performance criteria	Criteria define when a generated item is acceptable for use or for human review and editing
Downstream assessment quality impacts	Psychometric quality of AI-generated items is computed, typically from field testing
Potential consequences	Negative: Examinees exhibit low engagement with LLM-generated content; LLM content does not span the breadth and depth of the topic; item development staff over-rely on AI-generated content at the expense of quality; generated items cannot be copyrighted or violate copyright/plagiarism
Monitoring plan with mitigations	Ongoing human review

with language and instruction, societal norms and values can change in ways that affect education, and test specifications can change over time. Consequently, most assessment programs deploy LLMs with continuous human oversight to monitor performance and refine the models as needed.

9.6.2 Human Oversight and Hybrid Approaches

Human oversight is fundamental to the responsible use of LLMs in assessment. In all cases, human-generated materials—whether scores, feedback evaluations, or test items—serve as the essential benchmark for training and evaluating these models.

For AS, human oversight is critical in two phases. First, human scores are used to evaluate and approve an LLM's performance before it can be used operationally. Second, once deployed, a hybrid approach is used, especially for high-stakes tests. This process often involves a portion of responses (typically 20%–35%) receiving a human score to monitor the LLM's performance, similar to a random audit. If the engine performs poorly on this sample, it can be retrained, and all responses rescored. Alternatively, this process can be used to route unusual or outlier responses to humans for accurate scoring. In low-stakes contexts, humans often can override automated scores they disagree with.

As with scoring, automated feedback systems require human oversight during the training and validation phases. Once deployed, monitoring varies by context. Since most automated feedback is for low-stakes purposes (e.g., formative), users are typically free to use, ignore, or modify the suggestions. However, it is crucial to collect evidence on how students and teachers use and alter this feedback to ensure it remains effective and aligned with scoring rubrics.

For test content, nearly all uses will involve significant human review, as LLMs cannot yet operate sufficiently well without it, and items must meet specific quality standards. This human-in-the-loop process generally takes one of three forms: (1) The LLM generates content that humans review and approve, often with minor edits. (2) Humans write initial drafts, and LLMs assist in the revision process. (3) Humans and LLMs co-generate content collaboratively.

The specific hybrid approach chosen will depend on organizational needs, the LLM's capabilities, and ongoing research to refine these models.

9.6.3 Quality Control Mechanisms

Quality control mechanisms require human oversight but also depend on the specific implementation and use case. Three key areas to consider are performance metrics, model robustness, and data hygiene.

First, precise performance metrics are a foundational QC measure, enabling interpretation and communication of results. While well defined for AS (e.g., agreement with human scores, distributional characteristics), these criteria are less developed for automated feedback and content generation (Williamson et al., 2012).

Second, model robustness is essential for handling data shifts and unusual inputs. For scoring, a model that gives high marks to gibberish erodes trust; this is often mitigated by using secondary models to flag such outliers. For content generation, robustness means handling ill-formed user prompts while ensuring the output is accurate, fair, and does not plagiarize existing text.

Third, good data hygiene supports QC. Using standard train/validation/test splits, a common practice in data science, ensures that model performance is generalizable and reproducible when moved from training to deployment. Quality control is critical, as technical reporting must accurately reflect the model's operational functioning.

9.6.4 Standards and Best Practices

Standards and best practices are well defined for AS, given its relatively long history in assessment; however, these are only emerging for automated feedback and for test content generation. In our view, the validation methods section provides an excellent approach to developing standards for these uses; however, the implementation details are yet to be defined. We expect these to emerge in the coming years.

Regardless, AS does provide excellent examples of standards that can likely be adapted for automated feedback and test generation. Excellent examples include the scoring section of the *ITC and ATP Guidelines for Technology-Based Assessment* (2023) and ETS's *Best Practices for Constructed-Response Scoring* (*2022*). Both examples closely align with the validation methods outlined above and provide substantial detail for each of their elements.

9.6.5 Implications for Educational Policy

Educational policy refers to a set of guidelines for decision-making; these can be law-driven and non-negotiable. The integration of LLMs into assessment for scoring, feedback, and test development can influence policy and impact policy. We describe a few in this section.

First, LLM integration must adhere to existing AI policies, which typically address data privacy and security, student safety through guardrails, and intellectual property concerns such as copyright and plagiarism, particularly in test generation. Second, procedural policies governing aspects like scoring timelines or item development requirements can both drive the rationale for LLM use (e.g., for speed) and provide a basis for impact analysis. These policies may mandate human participation, such as involving local educators in scoring, thereby shaping hybrid LLM approaches. Third, communication is a critical policy component. Test developers must create materials explaining AI use, rationale, benefits, and limitations in clear, non-technical language for a broad audience. The timing of this communication is crucial for stakeholder buy-in, as policy can shift based on public perception of LLM successes or failures.

Finally, Technical Advisory Committees, comprising measurement experts, review the validity and quality of LLM applications and provide recommendations on quality. Robust technical reporting remains critical to provide the evidence needed to justify the use of LLMs in assessment programs.

9.7 Ethical Considerations

The integration of LLMs into real-world applications, especially in critical domains like education, extends far beyond technical performance. Deploying these models responsibly requires a thorough examination of their societal and ethical implications. This section addresses these critical considerations, beginning with an analysis of model bias and fairness. It then explores the practical trade-offs between open-source and closed-source models, followed by a discussion of significant privacy and security risks. Finally, it examines how the technology impacts equity and the digital divide, highlighting disparities in adoption and access.

9.7.1 *Bias and Fairness Considerations*

When evaluating AS and feedback, it is essential to distinguish between two types of bias. Intrinsic bias originates from the training data itself, while extrinsic bias arises from the model's generation process and is measured against human-assigned scores, which serve as the ground truth (Guo et al., 2024).

Unlike other AS methods, LLMs can inherit biases from their vast pretraining data, which may persist after fine-tuning (Wang & Russakovsky, 2023). Two standard methods for detecting this bias in scoring are:

1. calculating the standardized mean difference in scores between demographic subgroups (Williamson et al., 2012) and between AI and human scores across subgroups, and
2. using matched sampling, which compares a subgroup to a sample from the general population that has been matched on ability level to control for pre-existing differences (Ormerod et al., 2022).

Studies using these methods find that fine-tuned LLMs often exhibit a slight positive bias for females over males and a negative bias for English language learners (Ormerod et al., 2022). Potential explanations include the model's reliance on response length, which can correlate with gender, and linguistic complexity, which can differ between native and non-native speakers (Liang et al., 2023). Although often small, these biases require continuous monitoring and mitigation.

9.7.2 *Open-Source vs Closed-Source Models*

User-friendly interfaces like ChatGPT have led to the widespread adoption of generative AI, with closed-source models dominating the market (81% share) and educational applications (Bilski, 2024). However, their lack of transparency and potential privacy risks create a strong need for open-source alternatives. While a performance gap has historically favored closed-source models, recent high-quality open-source releases from developers like DeepSeek, Qwen, and Meta are rapidly closing it. Figure 9.2, which shows the market share of LLM usage between 2023 and 2024, indicates the apparent dominance of closed-source models over their open-source counterparts.

The true power of open-source models lies not in matching general benchmarks but in their customizability. The debate is less about "open vs. closed" and more about "customized vs. large-scale." A smaller, open-source model fine-tuned for

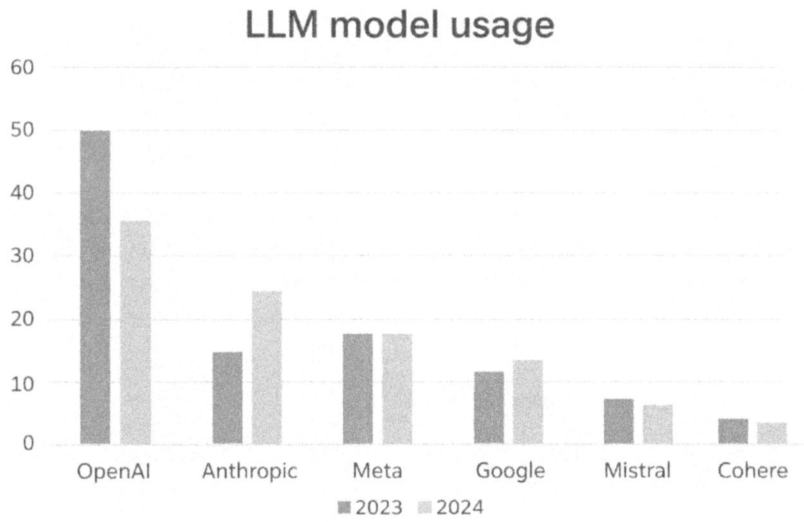

FIGURE 9.2 Market share of LLMs, 2023–2024.

a specific task, such as AS, can outperform a much larger, general-purpose model (Ormerod & Kwako, 2024). This outcome shows that highly specialized models can deliver superior performance on narrow tasks.

Furthermore, replicability, being a critical factor in assessment, is a significant challenge with closed-source models. Research findings can become impossible to replicate if a provider changes a model or its system prompts, as performance can degrade or change unpredictably over time (Chen et al., 2023). Open-source models, which can be self-hosted and version-controlled, offer a more stable and reliable foundation for scientific research.

9.7.3 Privacy and Security Considerations

The impact of AI on privacy and security is multifaceted. Using closed-source LLMs for large-scale assessment is complicated by privacy laws like the Family Educational Rights and Privacy Act (FERPA). Since student responses may contain personally identifiable information (PII), sending them to a third-party API for scoring constitutes a disclosure. FERPA imposes strict contractual limits, prohibiting the AI provider from using student data for future model training and requiring auditable security measures, such as encryption and access controls. These hurdles make implementing assessment using external APIs difficult.

Conversely, AI also offers tools to enhance security and privacy. PII, as defined by varying regulatory frameworks, includes not only direct identifiers like names but also indirect information from which an identity can be reasonably inferred. The process of removing this information is called anonymization. Traditional anonymization using named entity recognition is often limited to masking direct

PII (Singh & Narayanan, 2025). However, LLMs excel at inferring personal characteristics from indirect information (Staab et al., 2024), leading to more advanced techniques. One such method is adversarial anonymization, in which one LLM attempts to strip PII while a second LLM attempts to re-identify individuals in the data (Staab et al., 2025). This approach aligns better with stricter regulatory frameworks.

Finally, AI can address item security, which is crucial for test validity. When test items are exposed, test-takers with prior knowledge gain an unfair advantage. AI-driven item generation can mitigate this risk by creating vast item banks or generating dynamic content on demand, eliminating the need for prior knowledge.

9.7.4 Equity and the Digital Divide

The concept of the digital divide, traditionally focused on access to technology and infrastructure, has evolved. With the rise of AI, the divide now encompasses AI literacy and usage, creating new fault lines that often mirror and risk exacerbating existing societal inequalities (Khowaja et al., 2024). These disparities are particularly pronounced across socioeconomic status, race and ethnicity, and generational cohorts.

Socioeconomic status is a primary determinant in the AI divide. Individuals from higher income households and those with higher educational attainment are more likely to have access to AI tools and the training necessary to leverage them effectively. For instance, a Pew Research Center study (2023) found that 42% of adults in high-income households have used a tool like ChatGPT, versus only 14% in low-income households. This gap is critical, as a report from *Revelio Labs* (2025) claims that a worker adopting AI earns 10% more than one who does not, suggesting the AI divide could significantly widen economic inequality.

The divides are also clearly defined by generation. According to a Randstad report (2024), millennials are utilizing AI in their jobs at a greater rate than other generations, followed by Gen Z, Gen X, and Boomers. This trend is partly driven by attitudes toward AI, as both millennials and Gen Z seem more optimistic about the positive effects AI will have in the workplace. The same pattern appears along gender lines, with AI adoption rates among men twice those among women (*Revelio Labs*, 2025), threatening to worsen the gender pay gap as AI proficiency becomes more valuable (Table 9.5).

Significant disparities in AI adoption are also evident across racial and ethnic groups. A report from *Revelio Labs* (2025) highlights a notable trend: even after controlling for job roles and exposure, Asian professionals are adopting AI at approximately twice the rate of their White, Black, and Hispanic counterparts. Broader population data shows a similar pattern, with a Pew Research Center survey (2023) finding that 39% of Asian adults have used ChatGPT, compared to 23% of White adults, 21% of Hispanic adults, and 16% of Black adults. This differential

TABLE 9.5 Attitudes to AI (Revelio Labs, 2025)

	Millennials (%)	*Gen Z (%)*	*Gen X (%)*	*Boomers (%)*
Current generative AI usage at work	50	45	34	19
AI will make my work more interesting	53	52	41	35
AI will impact equity negatively	45	46	40	28
Who gets more opportunities to excel in AI	44	34	28	17
Companies are lagging in AI adoption	47	43	35	72

adoption creates a risk of certain minority groups being left behind in an increasingly AI-driven economy. Furthermore, it raises concerns about the development and deployment of AI, as a lack of diversity among creators and early adopters can perpetuate and amplify algorithmic bias against underrepresented groups.

9.8 Conclusions and Future Directions

In this section, we highlight some of the possibilities that are arising from the introduction of LLMs. In particular, we discuss emerging technologies and their potential to impact educational assessment.

9.8.1 Emerging Technologies and Improvements

From mid-2025 onward, the field of LLMs in educational assessment is moving rapidly beyond initial applications of prompting and basic fine-tuning. Several emerging technologies are beginning to shape the next generation of assessment tools, focusing on greater authenticity, reliability, and efficiency.

The next evolution of LLMs is the development of autonomous agents that can perform complex, multi-step tasks without continuous human intervention. These agents can use tools, access databases, and execute entire workflows. An "AI Assessment Designer" agent could be tasked with a high-level goal, such as "Create a 45-minute formative assessment for a 10th-grade biology unit on genetics, aligned with NGSS standards." The agent could then autonomously browse the curriculum, generate varied item types (multiple-choice, short-answer, diagram analysis), check them for bias using an external tool, and assemble them into a ready-to-deploy quiz within the school's learning management system, flagging only the most nuanced items for final human review. This technology automates the entire assessment *creation pipeline*, dramatically reducing teacher workload and ensuring alignment with standards.

9.8.2 A Multimodal Future

LLMs are rapidly evolving beyond text-only interfaces, increasingly adopting multimodal capabilities that allow them to process and generate information across various formats, including images, audio, and data visualizations. Models like OpenAI's GPT-4o and Google's Gemini can now "see" a student's work, "hear" a spoken response, and interpret complex diagrams. This fundamental shift from a purely linguistic to a multi-sensory understanding of information is poised to open new frontiers for educational research.

This transition enables researchers to move beyond analyzing written text and begin exploring a wider, more authentic range of student competencies. The potential outcomes for educational research are profound:

- **Assessing Complex, Non-Textual Skills**: Researchers can now design and automate the scoring of tasks that were previously impossible to evaluate at scale. This capability includes a student's ability to interpret a scientific diagram, explain a mathematical process verbally and draw on a digital whiteboard, or demonstrate procedural knowledge in a simulated environment. For example, an LLM could analyze both the final answer and the visual steps a student took to solve a geometry problem.
- **Analyzing Oral and Presentation-Based Assessments**: Multimodal models can transcribe and analyze the content, fluency, and structure of a student's spoken response or oral presentation. The transcription allows researchers to study the features of effective argumentation in a verbal context and develop new methods for providing feedback on public speaking and communication skills.
- **Enhancing Accessibility and Construct Validity**: Multimodality offers new avenues for accessible assessment, provided a clear distinction is maintained between accommodations and learning preferences. Researchers must investigate whether allowing alternative response modes (e.g., spoken vs. written) removes irrelevant barriers for students with disabilities—thereby preserving construct relevance—or if it fundamentally alters what is being measured. While student preferences can drive engagement, valid cross-modal scoring rubrics are essential to ensure scores remain comparable across modalities.

9.8.3 Potential Impact on Education

Based on our discussion, the integration of advanced, multimodal LLMs stands to impact the very foundation of education. The potential changes are not merely incremental; they represent a paradigm shift in how we assess knowledge, deliver instruction, and conceptualize the roles of students and teachers. The most significant impact will be on *what* we measure and *how* we measure it.

Education systems can shift focus from rote memorization to evaluating the complex skills needed for the modern world: critical thinking, oral communication, collaboration, and creative problem-solving. An assessment could be a student's recorded presentation, a video of them conducting a science experiment, or their interactive dialogue with an AI designed to probe their reasoning. The increase in modalities provides a much richer and more valid picture of a student's true capabilities, moving assessment from a single, high-stakes event to a continuous process embedded within learning itself.

Rather than replacing educators, this technology will fundamentally change and elevate their role in the classroom. AI will become a powerful "co-pilot" that handles routine, time-consuming tasks, freeing up teachers to focus on the deeply human aspects of education.

The ultimate impact of this technology is not predetermined. It will depend entirely on the choices made by educators, policymakers, researchers, and developers. If guided by rigorous research and a steadfast commitment to pedagogical principles and equity, these advancements have the potential to make education more personalized, authentic, and empowering than ever before. If not, they risk automating existing inequities and creating new ones. The central task for the field is to steer this transformation toward a more effective and just educational future.

Bibliography

AERA, APA, & NCME. (2014). *Standards for Educational and Psychological Testing.* Washington DC: American Educational Research Association.

Alzahrani, N., Alyahya, H. A., Alnumay, Y., Alrashed, S., Alsubaie, S., Almushaykeh, Y., Mirza, F., Alotaibi, N., Altwairesh, N., Alowisheq, A., Bari, M. S., & Khan, H. (2024). *When Benchmarks are Targets: Revealing the Sensitivity of Large Language Model Leaderboards* (arXiv:2402.01781). arXiv. https://doi.org/10.48550/arXiv.2402.01781

Attali, Y., Runge, A., LaFlair, G. T., Yancey, K., Goodwin, S., Park, Y., & von Davier, A. A. (2022). The interactive reading task: Transformer-based automatic item generation. *Frontiers in Artificial Intelligence*, *5*, 903077. https://doi.org/10.3389/frai.2022.903077

Baffour, P., & Crossley, S. (2024). Advances in automating feedback for argumentative writing: Feedback prize as a case study. In M. D. Shermis & J. Wilson (Eds.) *The Routledge International Handbook of Automated Essay Evaluation* (pp. 303–328). Routledge.

Bayer, M., Kaufhold, M.-A., & Reuter, C. (2023). A survey on data augmentation for text classification. *ACM Computing Surveys*, *55*(7), 1–39. https://doi.org/10.1145/3544558

Best Practices for Constructed-Response Scoring—McCaffrey—2022—ETS Research Report Series—Wiley Online Library. (n.d.). Retrieved May 22, 2024, from https://onlinelibrary.wiley.com/doi/full/10.1002/ets2.12358

Bezirhan, U., & von Davier, M. (2023). Automated reading passage generation with OpenAI's large language model. *Computers and Education: Artificial Intelligence*, *5*, 100161. https://doi.org/10.1016/j.caeai.2023.100161

Bilski, D. (2024, November 20). 2024: The state of generative AI in the enterprise. *Menlo Ventures*. https://menlovc.com/2024-the-state-of-generative-ai-in-the-enterprise/

Black, P., & Wiliam, D. (1998). Assessment and classroom learning. *Assessment in Education: Principles, Policy & Practice*, *5*(1), 7–74. https://doi.org/10.1080/0969595980050102

Bojanowski, P., Grave, E., Joulin, A., & Mikolov, T. (2017). Enriching word vectors with subword information. *Transactions of the Association for Computational Linguistics*, *5*, 135–146. https://doi.org/10.1162/tacl_a_00051

Brown, T., Mann, B., Ryder, N., Subbiah, M., Kaplan, J. D., Dhariwal, P., Neelakantan, A., Shyam, P., Sastry, G., & Askell, A. (2020). Language models are few-shot learners. *Advances in Neural Information Processing Systems*, *33*, 1877–1901.

Casabianca, J. M., McCaffrey, D. F., Johnson, M. S., Alper, N., & Zubenko, V. (2024). *Validity Arguments for Constructed Response Scoring Using Generative Artificial Intelligence Applications* (arXiv:2501.02334). arXiv.

Chapelle, O., Schölkopf, B., & Zien, A. (2006). *Semi-supervised Learning*. MIT Press.

Chelli, M., Descamps, J., Lavoué, V., Trojani, C., Azar, M., Deckert, M., Raynier, J.-L., Clowez, G., Boileau, P., & Ruetsch-Chelli, C. (2024). Hallucination rates and reference accuracy of ChatGPT and bard for systematic reviews: Comparative analysis. *Journal of Medical Internet Research, 26*, e53164. https://doi.org/10.2196/53164

Chen, L., Zaharia, M., & Zou, J. (2023). *How Is ChatGPT's Behavior Changing over Time?* (arXiv:2307.09009). arXiv. https://doi.org/10.48550/arXiv.2307.09009

Clark, K., Luong, M. T., Le, Q. V., & Manning, C. D. (2020). *Electra: Pre-training Text Encoders as Discriminators rather than Generators*. arXiv preprint arXiv:2003.10555.

Corno, L., & Snow, R. E. (1986). Adapting teaching to individual differences among learners. In M. C. Wittrock (Ed.), *Handbook of Research on Teaching* (3rd ed., pp. 605–629). Macmillan.

Crossley, S. A., Baffour, P., Tian, Y., Picou, A., Benner, M., & Boser, U. (2022). The persuasive essays for rating, selecting, and understanding argumentative and discourse elements (PERSUADE) corpus 1.0. *Assessing Writing, 54*, 100667. https://doi.org/10.1016/j.asw.2022.100667

Dai, Z., Yang, Z., Yang, Y., Carbonell, J., Le, Q. V., & Salakhutdinov, R. (2019). *Transformer-XL: Attentive Language Models Beyond a Fixed-Length Context* (arXiv:1901.02860). arXiv. https://doi.org/10.48550/arXiv.1901.02860

Dettmers, T., Pagnoni, A., Holtzman, A., & Zettlemoyer, L. (2023). QLoRA: Efficient finetuning of quantized LLMs. *Advances in Neural Information Processing Systems, 36*, 10088–10115.

Devlin, J., Chang, M.-W., Lee, K., & Toutanova, K. (2018). *BERT: Pre-training of Deep Bidirectional Transformers for Language Understanding* (arXiv:1810.04805). arXiv. https://doi.org/10.48550/arXiv.1810.04805

Dong, F., Zhang, Y., & Yang, J. (2017). Attention-based recurrent convolutional neural network for automatic essay scoring. *Proceedings of the 21st Conference on Computational Natural Language Learning (CoNLL 2017)*, 153–162. https://aclanthology.org/K17-1017/

Farquhar, S., Kossen, J., Kuhn, L., & Gal, Y. (2024). Detecting hallucinations in large language models using semantic entropy. *Nature, 630*(8017), 625–630. https://doi.org/10.1038/s41586-024-07421-0

Focus on Formative Feedback—Valerie J. Shute, 2008. (n.d.). Retrieved July 31, 2025, from https://journals.sagepub.com/doi/abs/10.3102/0034654307313795

Firoozi, T., Daniels, L., Daniels, V., & Gierl, M. (2025). An augmented intelligence system for automated quality control and feedback generation of multiple choice test items. In *International Conference on Artificial Intelligence in Education* (pp. 86–93). Springer Nature Switzerland.

Fredricks, J. A., Blumenfeld, P. C., & Paris, A. H. (2004). School engagement: Potential of the concept, state of the evidence. *Review of Educational Research*, 74(1), 59–109. https://doi.org/10.3102/00346543074001059

Fu, Y., Panda, R., Niu, X., Yue, X., Hajishirzi, H., Kim, Y., & Peng, H. (2024). *Data Engineering for Scaling Language Models to 128K Context* (arXiv:2402.10171). arXiv. https://doi.org/10.48550/arXiv.2402.10171

Gao, L., Biderman, S., Black, S., Golding, L., Hoppe, T., Foster, C., Phang, J., He, H., Thite, A., Nabeshima, N., Presser, S., & Leahy, C. (2020). *The Pile: An 800GB Dataset of Diverse Text for Language Modeling* (arXiv:2101.00027). arXiv. https://doi.org/10.48550/arXiv.2101.00027

Gierl, M. J., & Haladyna, T. M. (2012). Automatic item generation: An introduction. In M. J. Gierl, & T. M. Haladyna (Eds.) *Automatic Item Generation* (pp. 3–12) Routledge.

Gierl, M. J., & Lai, H. (2015). Automatic item generation. In S. Lane, M. R. Raymond, & T. M. Haladyna (Eds.) *Handbook of Test Development* (2nd ed., pp. 410–429). Routledge.

Graves, A., Fernández, S., Gomez, F., & Schmidhuber, J. (2006). Connectionist temporal classification: Labelling unsegmented sequence data with recurrent neural networks. *Proceedings of the 23rd International Conference on Machine Learning*, 369–376. https://doi.org/10.1145/1143844.1143891

Guo, Y., Guo, M., Su, J., Yang, Z., Zhu, M., Li, H., Qiu, M., & Liu, S. S. (2024). *Bias in Large Language Models: Origin, Evaluation, and Mitigation* (arXiv:2411.10915; Version 1). arXiv. https://doi.org/10.48550/arXiv.2411.10915

Hattie, J., & Timperley, H. (2007). The power of feedback. *Review of Educational Research*, *77*(1), 81–112. https://doi.org/10.3102/003465430298487

Hou, Z. J., Ciuba, A., & Li, X. L. (2025). *Improve LLM-based Automatic Essay Scoring with Linguistic Features* (arXiv:2502.09497). arXiv. https://doi.org/10.48550/arXiv.2502.09497

Hsieh, C.-P., Sun, S., Kriman, S., Acharya, S., Rekesh, D., Jia, F., Zhang, Y., & Ginsburg, B. (2024). *RULER: What's the Real Context Size of Your Long-Context Language Models?* (arXiv:2404.06654). arXiv. https://doi.org/10.48550/arXiv.2404.06654

Hu, E. J., Shen, Y., Wallis, P., Allen-Zhu, Z., Li, Y., Wang, S., Wang, L., & Chen, W. (2021). *LoRA: Low-Rank Adaptation of Large Language Models* (arXiv:2106.09685). arXiv. https://doi.org/10.48550/arXiv.2106.09685

ITC and ATP Guidelines for Technology-Based Assessment. (2023). https://www.intestcom.org/page/16

Ji, Z., Lee, N., Frieske, R., Yu, T., Su, D., Xu, Y., Ishii, E., Bang, Y. J., Madotto, A., & Fung, P. (2023). Survey of hallucination in natural language generation. *ACM Computing Surveys*, *55*(12), Article 248. https://doi.org/10.1145/3571730

Kane, M. T. (2013). Validating the interpretations and uses of test scores. *Journal of Educational Measurement*, *50*(1), 1–73.

Katuka, G. A., Gain, A., & Yu, Y.-Y. (2024). *Investigating Automatic Scoring and Feedback Using Large Language Models* (arXiv:2405.00602). arXiv. https://doi.org/10.48550/arXiv.2405.00602

Kennedy, B., Tyson, A., & Saks, E. (2023). *Public Awareness of Artificial Intelligence in Everyday Activities*. https://policycommons.net/artifacts/3450412/public-awareness-of-artificial-intelligence-in-everyday-activities/4250673/

Khowaja, S. A., Khuwaja, P., Dev, K., Wang, W., & Nkenyereye, L. (2024). ChatGPT needs spade (sustainability, privacy, digital divide, and ethics) evaluation: A review. *Cognitive Computation 16*(5), 1–23. https://doi.org/10.1007/s12559-024-10285-1

Kingma, D. P., & Ba, J. (2017). *Adam: A Method for Stochastic Optimization* (arXiv:1412.6980). arXiv. https://doi.org/10.48550/arXiv.1412.6980

Kluger, A. N., & DeNisi, A. (1996). The effects of feedback interventions on performance: A historical review, a meta-analysis, and a preliminary feedback intervention theory. *Psychological Bulletin*, *119*(2), 254–284. https://doi.org/10.1037/0033-2909.119.2.254

Kulhavy, R. W., & Stock, W. A. (1989). Feedback in written instruction: The place of response certitude. *Educational Psychology Review*, *1*(4), 279–308. https://doi.org/10.1007/BF01320096

LaFlair, G., Yancey, K., Settles, B., & Davier, A. A. v. (2023). Computational psychometrics for digital-first assessments: A blend of ML and psychometrics for item generation and scoring. In V. Yaneva & M. von Davier (Eds.) *Advancing Natural Language Processing in Educational Assessment* (pp. 107–123). Routledge.

Latif, E., & Zhai, X. (2023). *Automatic Scoring of Students' Science Writing Using Hybrid Neural Network* (arXiv:2312.03752). arXiv. https://doi.org/10.48550/arXiv.2312.03752

Le, Q., & Mikolov, T. (2014). Distributed representations of sentences and documents. *Proceedings of the 31st International Conference on Machine Learning*, 1188–1196. https://proceedings.mlr.press/v32/le14.html

Lee, G.-G., Latif, E., Wu, X., Liu, N., & Zhai, X. (2024). Applying large language models and chain-of-thought for automatic scoring. *Computers and Education: Artificial Intelligence*, *6*, 100213. https://doi.org/10.1016/j.caeai.2024.100213

Liang, W., Yuksekgonul, M., Mao, Y., Wu, E., & Zou, J. (2023). *GPT Detectors Are Biased against Non-native English Writers* (arXiv:2304.02819). arXiv. https://doi.org/10.48550/arXiv.2304.02819

Link, S., Mehrzad, M., & Rahimi, M. (2022). Impact of automated writing evaluation on teacher feedback, student revision, and writing improvement. Computer Assisted Language Learning, *35*(4), 605–634.

Lottridge, S., Burkhardt, A., Ormerod, C., Woolf, S., Young, M., Patel, M., Wang, H., Frost, J., McBeth, K., Benson, J., Flynn, M., Dwyer, K., Fitz, S., Berkheiser, R., Floyd, H., Davis, D., Godek, B., & Wilson, Q. (2024). *Write On with Cambi: The Development of an Argumentative Writing Feedback Tool*. Cambium Assessment. https://files.portal.cambiumast.com/corporate-site/documents/CAI_CSSC_NCME_Write_on_with_Cambi_White_Paper.pdf

Messick, S. (1987). Validity. *ETS Research Report Series*, *1987*(2), i–208.

Meta, A. (2024). Introducing meta llama 3: The most capable openly available LLM to date. *Meta AI*.

Misgna, H., On, B.-W., Lee, I., & Choi, G. S. (2024). A survey on deep learning-based automated essay scoring and feedback generation. *Artificial Intelligence Review*, *58*(2), 36. https://doi.org/10.1007/s10462-024-11017-5

Mizumoto, A., & Eguchi, M. (2023). Exploring the potential of using an AI language model for automated essay scoring. *Research Methods in Applied Linguistics*, *2*(2), 100050. https://doi.org/10.1016/j.rmal.2023.100050

North, K., & Ormerod, C. (2025). *Cyborg Data: Merging Human with AI Generated Training Data* (arXiv:2503.22736). arXiv. https://doi.org/10.48550/arXiv.2503.22736

Opsahl-Ong, K., Ryan, M. J., Purtell, J., Broman, D., Potts, C., Zaharia, M., & Khattab, O. (2024). *Optimizing Instructions and Demonstrations for Multi-Stage Language Model Programs* (arXiv:2406.11695). arXiv. https://doi.org/10.48550/arXiv.2406.11695

Ormerod, C., Lottridge, S., Harris, A. E., Patel, M., van Wamelen, P., Kodeswaran, B., Woolf, S., & Young, M. (2022). Automated short answer scoring using an ensemble of neural networks and latent semantic analysis classifiers. *International Journal of Artificial Intelligence in Education*. *33*(3), 467–496. https://doi.org/10.1007/s40593-022-00294-2

Ormerod, C. M., & Kwako, A. (2024). *Automated Text Scoring in the Age of Generative AI for the GPU-poor* (arXiv:2407.01873). arXiv. https://doi.org/10.48550/arXiv.2407.01873

Page, E. B. (2003). Project essay grade: PEG. In M. Shermis & J. Burstein (Eds.) *Automated Essay Scoring: A Cross-disciplinary Perspective* (pp. 43–54). Lawrence Erlbaum Associates Publishers.

Pennington, J., Socher, R., & Manning, C. (2014). GloVe: Global vectors for word representation. *Proceedings of the 2014 Conference on Empirical Methods in Natural Language Processing (EMNLP)*, 1532–1543. https://doi.org/10.3115/v1/D14-1162

Phung, T., Pădurean, V._A., Singh, A., Brooks, C., Cambronero, J., Gulwani, S., Singla, A., & Soares, G. (2024). Automating human tutor_style programming feedback: Leveraging GPT_4 tutor model for hint generation and GPT_3.5 student model for hint validation. In Proceedings of the 14th Learning Analytics and Knowledge

Conference (LAK '24) (pp. 12–23). Association for Computing Machinery. https://doi.org/10.1145/3636555.3636846

Pridemore, D. R., & Klein, J. D. (1995). Control of practice and level of feedback in computer-based instruction. *Contemporary Educational Psychology*, *20*(4), 444–450. https://doi.org/10.1006/ceps.1995.1030

Ranalli, J. (2018). Automated written corrective feedback: How well can students make use of it? *Computer Assisted Language Learning,* 31(7), 653–674. https://doi.org/10.1080/09588221.2018.1428994

Ripoll Y Schmitz, L. M., & Sonnleitner, P. (2025). Evaluating AI-generated vs. human-written reading comprehension passages: An expert SWOT analysis and comparative study for an educational large-scale assessment. *Large-scale Assessments in Education, 13,* Article 20. https://doi.org/10.1186/s40536-025-00255-w

Rodriguez, P. U., Jafari, A., & Ormerod, C. M. (2019). *Language Models and Automated Essay Scoring* (arXiv:1909.09482). arXiv. https://doi.org/10.48550/arXiv.1909.09482

Runge, A., Attali, Y., LaFlair, G. T., Park, Y., & Church, J. (2024). A generative AI-driven interactive listening assessment task. *Frontiers in Artificial Intelligence*, *7*. 1–21. https://doi.org/10.3389/frai.2024.1474019

Saad-Falcon, J., Khattab, O., Potts, C., & Zaharia, M. (2024). *ARES: An Automated Evaluation Framework for Retrieval-Augmented Generation Systems* (arXiv:2311.09476). arXiv. https://doi.org/10.18653/v1/2024.naacl-long.20

Sayin, A., & Gierl, M. (2024, March 1). Using OpenAI GPT to generate reading comprehension items. *EBSCOhost*. https://doi.org/10.1111/emip.12590

Shermis, M. D., & Wilson, J. (2024). Introduction to automated evaluation. In M. D. Shermis & J. Wilson (Eds.), The Routledge International Handbook of Automated Essay Evaluation (pp. 1 -[end]). Routledge.

Shute, V. J., & Psotka, J. (1994). Intelligent tutoring systems: Past, present, and future. In D. H. Jonassen (Ed.), *Handbook of Research for Educational Communications and Technology* (pp. 570–600). Macmillan.

Singh, D., & Narayanan, S. (2025). *Unmasking the Reality of PII Masking Models: Performance Gaps and the Call for Accountability* (arXiv:2504.12308). arXiv. https://doi.org/10.48550/arXiv.2504.12308

Staab, R., Vero, M., Balunović, M., & Vechev, M. (2024). *Beyond Memorization: Violating Privacy via Inference with Large Language Models* (arXiv:2310.07298). arXiv. https://doi.org/10.48550/arXiv.2310.07298

Staab, R., Vero, M., Balunović, M., & Vechev, M. (2025). *Large Language Models are Advanced Anonymizers* (arXiv:2402.13846). arXiv. https://doi.org/10.48550/arXiv.2402.13846

Stahl, M., Biermann, L., Nehring, A., & Wachsmuth, H. (2024). *Exploring LLM Prompting Strategies for Joint Essay Scoring and Feedback Generation* (arXiv:2404.15845). arXiv. https://arxiv.org/abs/2404.15845

Stahlberg, F., & Kumar, S. (2021). *Synthetic Data Generation for Grammatical Error Correction with Tagged Corruption Models* (arXiv:2105.13318). arXiv. https://doi.org/10.48550/arXiv.2105.13318

Su, J., Ahmed, M., Lu, Y., Pan, S., Bo, W., & Liu, Y. (2024). RoFormer: Enhanced transformer with rotary position embedding. *Neurocomputing*, *568*, 127063. https://doi.org/10.1016/j.neucom.2023.127063

Tan, B., Armoush, N., Mazzullo, E., Bulut, O., & Gierl, M. (2025). A review of automatic item generation techniques leveraging large language models. *International Journal of Assessment Tools in Education*, *12*(2), Article 2. https://doi.org/10.21449/ijate.1602294

The Generational Divide in AI Adoption | Randstad USA. (n.d.). Retrieved July 30, 2025, from https://www.randstadusa.com/business/business-insights/workplace-trends/generational-divide-ai-adoption/

This Gender Lags Behind in AI Adoption | Revelio Labs. (n.d.). Retrieved July 30, 2025, from https://www.reveliolabs.com/news/tech/this-gender-lags-behind-in-ai-adoption/

Vaswani, A., Shazeer, N., Parmar, N., Uszkoreit, J., Jones, L., Gomez, A. N., Kaiser, Ł., & Polosukhin, I. (2017). Attention is all you need. *Advances in Neural Information Processing Systems, 30,* 1–11. https://proceedings.neurips.cc/paper/2017/hash/3f5ee243547dee91fbd053c1c4a845aa-Abstract.html

Wang, A., & Russakovsky, O. (2023). *Overwriting Pretrained Bias with Finetuning Data*, 3957–3968. https://openaccess.thecvf.com/content/ICCV2023/html/Wang_Overwriting_Pretrained_Bias_with_Finetuning_Data_ICCV_2023_paper.html

Wang, Z., & Ormerod, C. (2024). *Generative Language Models with Retrieval Augmented Generation for Automated Short Answer Scoring* (arXiv:2408.03811). arXiv. https://doi.org/10.48550/arXiv.2408.03811

Wei, J., Tay, Y., Bommasani, R., Raffel, C., Zoph, B., Borgeaud, S., Yogatama, D., Bosma, M., Zhou, D., Metzler, D., Chi, E. H., Hashimoto, T., Vinyals, O., Liang, P., Dean, J., & Fedus, W. (2022). *Emergent Abilities of Large Language Models* (arXiv:2206.07682). arXiv. https://doi.org/10.48550/arXiv.2206.07682

Williamson, D. M., Xi, X., & Breyer, F. J. (2012). A framework for evaluation and use of automated scoring. *Educational Measurement: Issues and Practice*, *31*(1), 2–13. https://doi.org/10.1111/j.1745-3992.2011.00223.x

Wilson, J., & MacArthur, C. (2024). Exploring the role of automated writing evaluation as a formative assessment tool supporting self-regulated learning in writing. In M. D. Shermis & J. Wilson (Eds.), *The Routledge International Handbook of Automated Essay Evaluation* (pp. 197–220). Routledge.

Xie, J., Cai, K., Kong, L., Zhou, J., & Qu, W. (2022). Automated essay scoring via pairwise contrastive regression. In N. Calzolari, C.-R. Huang, H. Kim, J. Pustejovsky, L. Wanner, K.-S. Choi, P.-M. Ryu, H.-H. Chen, L. Donatelli, H. Ji, S. Kurohashi, P. Paggio, N. Xue, S. Kim, Y. Hahm, Z. He, T. K. Lee, E. Santus, F. Bond, & S.-H. Na (Eds.), *Proceedings of the 29th International Conference on Computational Linguistics* (pp. 2724–2733). International Committee on Computational Linguistics. https://aclanthology.org/2022.coling-1.240

Xu, L., Xie, H., Qin, S.-Z. J., Tao, X., & Wang, F. L. (2023). *Parameter-Efficient Fine-Tuning Methods for Pretrained Language Models: A Critical Review and Assessment* (arXiv:2312.12148). arXiv. https://doi.org/10.48550/arXiv.2312.12148

Zheng, L., Chiang, W.-L., Sheng, Y., Zhuang, S., Wu, Z., Zhuang, Y., Lin, Z., Li, Z., Li, D., Xing, E. P., Zhang, H., Gonzalez, J. E., & Stoica, I. (2023). *Judging LLM-as-a-Judge with MT-Bench and Chatbot Arena* (arXiv:2306.05685). arXiv. https://doi.org/10.48550/arXiv.2306.05685

Ye, H., Liu, T., Zhang, A., Hua, W., & Jia, W. (2023). *Cognitive Mirage: A Review ofHallucinations in Large Language Models*. arXiv. https://doi.org/10.48550/arXiv.2309.06794

Yoshida, L. (2024). The impact of example selection in few-shot prompting on automated essay scoring using GPT models. In A. M. Olney, I.-A. Chounta, Z. Liu, O. C. Santos, & I. I. Bittencourt (Eds.), *Artificial Intelligence in Education: 25th International Conference, AIED 2024* (pp. 61–73). Springer. https://doi.org/10.1007/978-3-031-64315-6_5

Zhang, Z. V., & Hyland, K. (2018). Student engagement with teacher and automated feedback on L2 writing. *Assessing Writing*, *36*, 90–102. https://doi.org/10.1016/j.asw.2018.02.004

Ziegler, D. M., Stiennon, N., Wu, J., Brown, T. B., Radford, A., Amodei, D., Christiano, P., & Irving, G. (2020). *Fine-Tuning Language Models from Human Preferences* (arXiv:1909.08593). arXiv. https://doi.org/10.48550/arXiv.1909.08593

10

MACHINE LEARNING–BASED METHODS FOR CHEATING DETECTION IN LARGE-SCALE ASSESSMENTS

Hong Jiao, Jiawei Xiong, and Chandramani Lnu

10.1 Introduction

Test fairness is an important consideration in the validity of inferences made based on test scores in high-stakes large-scale assessments. It assures that the inferences drawn from those scores, whether for licensure, college admissions, or educational accountability, are rendered justifiable (Cizek & Wollack, 2017). In recent years, the rapid integration of artificial intelligence (AI) has fundamentally reshaped this landscape, creating a dynamic race between security innovations and increasingly sophisticated cheating methodologies (Dawson, 2020). On the prevention and administration front, AI has become a critical ally. It is now widely employed in automated item generation to produce vast numbers of unique items, thereby mitigating the risk of item harvesting and identifying enemy items or mutually exclusive questions (Gierl & Haladyna, 2013). Furthermore, the increasing usage of remote testing during the pandemic has promoted AI-driven remote proctoring solutions with multiple functions such as monitoring biometric data, tracking gaze patterns, and flagging suspicious behaviors in real time (Hylton et al., 2016).

Along with the breakthroughs brought by AI, these technological advancements have also introduced unprecedented threats to test security. The assessment community now faces challenges ranging from the detection of AI-generated text and deep fakes to the use of smart wearable technology (e.g., smart glasses) and hardware-embedded AI capable of masking cheating behaviors (Hao & Fauss, 2022). While this broader AI landscape encompasses prevention, monitoring, and physical security, the foundation of forensic analysis remains the detection of anomalies within the assessment data itself. Therefore, while acknowledging the breadth of AI's influence on test security, this chapter specifically focuses on

DOI: 10.4324/9781003621522-10

the assessment data-driven detection of cheating behaviors. It demonstrates how machine learning and data augmentation techniques can be leveraged to identify the most challenging cases of likely cheaters in large-scale assessment.

10.1.1 Importance of Cheating Detection

Cheating is a threat to test fairness in large-scale assessments. In general, the intent of cheating is to spuriously increase the test scores unconditional on a test-taker's true latent ability. When certain test-takers use unauthorized external assistance to artificially boost their scores, it creates an unfair disadvantage for most of the test-takers who complete the test without such external assistance. Such behaviors raise concerns about test security and can compromise the validity of score interpretations. Thus, cheating detection is essential for ensuring test fairness, maintaining the integrity of assessment results, and preserving technical quality in the testing process. By identifying and addressing cheating behaviors, it protects test-takers from unfair disadvantages, safeguards the validity of score interpretations, and upholds the credibility of the testing results.

10.1.2 Types of Cheating Behaviors

Cheating in large-scale assessments can take multiple forms (Bernardi et al., 2008), occurring before, during, or after the administration of a test (Zhou & Jiao, 2023). Prior to test administration, some test-takers may gain unauthorized access to test items, allowing them to preview items in advance. This item pre-knowledge (Bernardi et al., 2008) could be gained due to planned stealing of test items for profit gains. While historical instances often involved individual coaching schools sending instructors to sit on live tests to memorize the items on operational forms and then share them with test-takers taking the test preparation courses, modern item harvesting has evolved into organized, high-end criminal activity. This includes the use of hidden cameras and sophisticated capturing devices to harvest content, which is then rapidly disseminated via social media, private chat rooms, and encrypted community forums. This commercialized aspect of pre-knowledge harvesting poses a significantly severe threat. Another type of cheating is related to instances where smart instructors created practice items that were like or almost the same as the operational items. With the advances in the generative AI (genAI) technology, the latter type of item pre-knowledge could become a more severe concern when items could be generated by prompting genAI tools such as ChatGPT, Gemini, Claude, and Grok using released practice items or compromised operational items from unauthorized channels.

During test administration, potential cheating behaviors include copying from other test-takers (McCabe, 2016), either by directly viewing nearby individual test-takers' answers or by exchanging signals, gestures, or coded messages. This is especially possible for linear tests when test items are listed in the same sequential order. Further, test-takers may get answers from a proctor due to group-level cheating. Another is the use of prohibited materials such as notes or electronic devices which may store answers or provide internet access. Seeking real-time assistance from others can also occur through texting or using concealed earpieces or eyeglasses to receive guidance from someone outside the testing room. Online searching is increasingly possible in computer-based or remote assessments if test-takers are not properly monitored, allowing them to search for answers online in real time. In some cases, proxy test-taking is arranged, where another person, often more knowledgeable, takes the test on behalf of the registered test-taker. Additionally, with remote or at-home testing, new variations have emerged, such as running multiple devices simultaneously, sharing screens with collaborators, or using AI-based tools to assist with problem-solving or use genAI to compose answers for constructed-response items or essay writing.

After test administration, cheating may involve altering responses, either by the test-taker or by others. In some cases, proctors such as classroom teachers may change students' answers to improve their scores. This group collusion may be driven by pressures to meet performance targets, enhance school rankings, or secure incentives tied to student achievement, but it fundamentally undermines the fairness and integrity of the assessment process and results.

In addition, it is worth highlighting genAI-related cheating, which could be fundamentally different from traditional non-AI-facilitated plagiarism or collusion. Traditional cheating can often be detected by comparing a test-taker's work to other test-takers' work or published material, when collusion typically leaves a trail of similarity between test-takers' responses, especially in constructed responses including essays. In contrast, genAI technology can essentially produce entirely original yet plausible content that doesn't directly copy existing sources given its strong summarization (Hua et al., 2025) and reasoning capabilities. These genAI or large language models (LLMs), such as generative pre-trained transformer (GPT), Gemini, Claude, Grok, or DeepSeek, can create essays, short answers, or even answer multiple-choice items in ways that appear authentic, coherent, and tailored to the prompt, making detection far more challenging. The spectrum of AI-driven cheating includes essay and free-response generation, code writing, reasoning or problem-solving steps for math or science questions, and potentially automated selection or reasoning for multiple-choice questions. Each type poses unique detection challenges; while essays might be flagged via AI-detection tools or stylistic analysis, AI-assisted multiple-choice answers could bypass plagiarism checks entirely, blending seamlessly with the test-taker's natural performance.

In summary, all these cheating behaviors engaged in different stages of test administration or reliance on genAI technology not only give an unfair advantage to those engaging in them but also compromise the reliability, validity, and fair use of the assessment results. To address the negative consequences of potential cheating, various methods and technologies have been developed to analyze test-taker responding behaviors and detect potential cheating.

10.2 Methods for Cheating Detection

Cheating detection has long been a critical concern in high-stakes, large-scale assessments. Different methods and techniques have been explored to address this concern (Cizek & Wollack, 2017; Kingston & Clark, 2014; Wollack & Fremer, 2013). These techniques and methods could be classified into device-based, human monitoring, or data-driven approaches. Some technology devices or tools are often used for monitoring and preventing cheating. These include surveillance cameras in testing rooms, AI-powered remote proctoring software, screen-locking browsers, detectors for electronic devices, earpieces, wearable-signal eyeglasses, or communication devices. In addition, human proctors are often trained to directly observe and report suspicious test-taking behaviors. In-person proctor monitoring is often implemented for test administration of large-scale assessments. Classroom teacher observations and peer reporting systems are often set in place for post-test investigation. An additional layer of protection relies on data-driven approaches to detect aberrant responding patterns or test-taking behaviors. These include statistical modeling of answer-change behaviors, psychometric analysis based on person-fit measures, response time analysis, IP address and location tracking for online tests, and plagiarism detection in written responses based on similarity measures, and more recently, the detection of genAI created answers to assessment tasks.

While a comprehensive array of forensic psychometric methods exists, including similarity analysis and score differencing (Cizek & Wollack, 2017), this chapter focuses on the latest advances in cheating detection using machine learning methods. For demonstration, we concentrate exclusively on AI-based methods for detecting likely cheaters who were flagged in an operational testing program, which do not necessarily require a *priori* assumptions regarding specific types of cheating behaviors. Though some studies used person-fit measures to flag potential cheaters, this chapter demonstrates how these specific psychometric indices are uniquely positioned to serve as engineered features for data augmentation within the machine learning framework discussed in the subsequent empirical example sections. Consequently, the following section highlights the specific psychometric and machine learning methods that are most feasible to this hybrid, data-augmented approach.

10.2.1 Psychometric Methods for Cheating Detection

One traditional method for detecting cheating in the era of paper-and-pencil tests (PPTs) was erasure analysis (Bishop & Egan, 2016; McClintock, 2015; Primoli et al., 2011; Qualls, 2001) based on aberrant answer-change patterns (Belov, 2015; Sinharay, Duong, & Wood, 2017; Sinharay & Johnson, 2017). Erasure analysis is a forensic method for detecting abnormal answer changes related to potential cheating in PPTs, especially when scoring is done from scanned bubble answer sheets. Erasure analysis focuses on unusually high rates of wrong-to-right answer changes. These patterns are typically investigated to determine if test-takers' answers were altered after the fact by a third party (e.g., a teacher, administrator, or proctor tampering with answer sheets) or if the test-taker engaged in strategic answer changes that deviate from the standard test-taker population. Unlike similarity analysis, erasure analysis is not a primary tool for detecting answer copying between test-takers but rather for identifying anomalous changes that suggest tampering answer records or data inconsistency. In computer-based testing, erasure or answer-change data can be captured with greater precision, allowing the exact sequence of selected options/answers to be tracked (Tiemann & Kingston, 2014).

10.2.1.1 Person-Fit Measures

Another widely used category of psychometric cheating detection methods involves analyzing item response data to assess person fit (Meijer & Sijtsma, 2001; Ranger, Schmidt, & Wolgast, 2020). Ranger et al. (2020) investigated 18 indicators for detecting cheating in e-exams in higher education. Their study included person-fit indices based on item responses, such as U1 (van der Flier, 1977), U3 (van der Flier, 1982), CS (Sato, 1975), and the H^T statistic (Sijtsma, 1986). It also examined response time–based indicators (Sinharay, 2018), including the KL statistic (Man et al., 2018), Z^2 statistic, and KT statistic, as well as response revision indicators (Bishop & Egan, 2016; Qualls, 2001), such as the number of revisions (N1, N2), wrong-to-right revisions (NC1, NC2), and revision time (T1, T2, T3). Additionally, the study considered an indicator assessing the relationship between responses and response time (Toton & Maynes, 2018), along with two other indicators based on the similarity of response patterns (Maynes, 2016; Zopluoglu, 2016). The study results indicated that the number of answer revisions was the most important predictor of cheating detection. In the meantime, indicators based on response time were able to flag potential cheaters. However, a word of caution is necessary regarding the effectiveness of person-fit indices. Research indicates that these statistics can be underpowered relative to specific forensic models and often yield high false-positive rates (Reise & Flannery, 1996). Therefore, when it detects cheating, considerable investigative work is required to ensure that the misfit is attributable to cheating and not to some other source of construct-irrelevant variance. For example, aberrant responding does not strictly imply cheating, but it may stem from construct-irrelevant variance, such as anxiety, fatigue, or distinct cognitive processing styles (Chen, 2004). Therefore, while person-fit indices serve as a reasonable strategy to initiate an investigation, they typically require considerable corroborative evidence to support a definitive inference of cheating or score cancellation.

10.2.1.2 Latent-Variable Model-Based Approaches

While traditional psychometric methods utilize item responses, more recent advances integrated process data in cheating detection. As reviewed in Ranger et al. (2020), item response time data can be easily collected and have been explored to detect compromised items and/or test-takers (Boughton, Smith, & Ren, 2016; Li, Wall, & Tang, 2018; Pan et al., 2022; Toton & Maynes, 2018). Various latent-variable models utilizing item responses and/or response times have been investigated for cheating detection (e.g., Chen et al., 2020; Marianti et al., 2014; Shu et al., 2013; Skorupski et al., 2016; Toton & Maynes, 2018; van der Linden & Guo, 2008; Wang et al., 2018; Wollack, 1997 ; Zhu et al., 2023) including mixture modeling, Bayesian change point analysis, gated item response modeling, and nominal response modeling. More recently, Man and Harring (2020) evaluated item pre-knowledge by applying a multiple-group joint model that incorporated item responses, response times, and visual fixation counts. Such joint modeling of multiple related data sources is expected to improve the accuracy of cheating detection. However, when process data becomes more complex in structure, parametric statistical models, especially latent variable-based modeling approaches, may not be sufficiently feasible to account for the complexity of data from multiple sources when the model assumptions are not satisfied.

In general, the effectiveness of existing psychometric methods depends on the satisfaction of strong assumptions. In addition to how well a measurement model fits the data, these methods often assume that the type of cheating is known. For example, detecting pre-knowledge using psychometric techniques may require knowing exactly which items were compromised, whether the answer key was leaked along with those items, or how much more quickly test-takers with pre-knowledge respond than honest test-takers. If any of these assumptions are untenable, researchers may choose inappropriate indices or end up with detectors that lack sufficient power to identify the breach. By contrast, machine learning approaches can often flag unusual response patterns without relying on such strong assumptions and rigid prior specifications. Further, when genAI tools such as ChatGPT are utilized for producing text-based responses to assessment items, traditional psychometric methods may not suffice for analyzing text data for cheating detection.

10.2.2 Machine Learning Methods for Cheating Detection

With the increasing prevalence of digital assessments, both product and process data can now be collected with ease. Leveraging advances in machine learning and deep learning (Jiao et al., 2023a), researchers have investigated a range of approaches for cheating detection, including supervised algorithms (e.g., Zhou & Jiao, 2022, 2023; Zopluoglu, 2019) and unsupervised algorithms (e.g., Gorgun & Bulut, 2022; Kim et al., 2016; Liao et al., 2021). More recently, deep learning methods (e.g., Ranger et al., 2022; Tang, et al., 2023) have been investigated for aberrant responding behavior detection and cheating detection.

The primary advantages of applying machine learning and deep learning algorithms to cheating detection lie in their ability to handle complex, non-linear, multi-dimensional, multimodal data in ways that traditional psychometric models and methods cannot. First, these approaches can capture intricate, non-linear relationships among diverse data sources in large-scale assessments including item responses, response times, and answer-change counts and patterns without being constrained by the strong assumptions underlying latent-variable psychometric models and methods. In addition, machine learning methods are highly flexible and scalable, making it possible to incorporate multimodal data, including biometric data like eye fixation, and other forms of sequential process data based on keystroke dynamics and mouse movements as they become available. They also support automated feature selection, enabling the identification of subtle patterns or combinations of indicators that may be overlooked by one single model or indicator based on traditional psychometric methods. Furthermore, ensemble and deep learning techniques can improve predictive accuracy by combining multiple weak learners or by learning hierarchical representations of complex data. Finally, machine learning models can be continuously updated and retrained as new assessment data accumulate, allowing cheating detection systems to adapt quickly to evolving cheating strategies while the traditional psychometric models and methods may only detect fixed types of cheating strategies.

10.2.2.1 Supervised Machine Learning Algorithms

Supervised machine learning methods can be employed to train cheating detectors when labeled data are available, such as cases where potential cheaters have been flagged. Cavalcanti et al. (2012) reviewed text mining methods for cheating detection and introduced two classification models based on Decision Tree algorithms. To address plagiarism involving paraphrasing and summarization, Chitra and Rajkumar (2015) developed a paraphrase recognition system using a support vector machine (SVM) approach. Sahu (2016) applied the K-nearest neighbor (K-NN) algorithm for pattern recognition to identify copied texts by comparing them against existing files. Zopluoglu (2019) employed eXtreme Gradient Boosting (XGBoost) to detect item pre-knowledge in a large-scale testing program. Similarly, Man et al. (2019) investigated both supervised algorithms (K-NN, random forest, and SVM) and unsupervised algorithms (K-means clustering and self-organizing maps) for fraud detection. Building on this line of work, Zhou and Jiao (2022, 2023) applied a stacking ensemble machine learning approach to integrate test-takers' item responses, response times, and augmented data for cheating detection. They further compared the performance of the stacking models with two other ensemble techniques (random forest and gradient boosting) as well as six individual non-ensemble machine learning models, including Decision Tree, Naïve Bayes, neural network, discriminant analysis, logistic regression, and SVM. These studies explored different machine learning models for different datasets. There is no unanimously identified best-performing model. As cheating detection is more an empirical question, it is recommended that different methods should be empirically compared to identify the model with the highest detection accuracy.

10.2.2.2 Unsupervised Machine Learning Algorithms

Whereas supervised machine learning algorithms adopt a confirmatory approach, unsupervised algorithms offer a more exploratory perspective for detecting potential cheaters. It is worth noting that when unsupervised machine learning methods are applied to cheating detection, most research focused on the identification of aberrant responding behaviors. This is because clustering or outlier anomalies do not necessarily indicate cheating. Nonetheless, the detection of such anomalies provides a valuable starting point for further investigation of potential cases of cheating. Clustering and anomaly detection are the two most commonly used unsupervised approaches in cheating detection. Liao et al. (2021) examined item harvesters who tried to memorize items and share items with future test-takers. Their study utilized the process data and the K-means clustering algorithm to learn the archetypes of test-taking processes, and those that deviated from the archetypes of responding patterns were flagged for further investigation. Man et al. (2019) explored unsupervised algorithms (K-means clustering and self-organizing maps) for fraud detection. Pan and Wollack (2023) used an ensemble-unsupervised-learning-based approach for detecting person and item pre-knowledge simultaneously.

Gorgun and Bulut (2022) explored six unsupervised anomaly detection methods (Gaussian mixture model, Bayesian Gaussian mixture model, Isolation Forest, Mahalanobis distance, local outlier factor, and Elliptic Envelope) for identifying aberrant responses in intelligent tutoring systems with the extremely sparse response data. Their findings showed that most methods flagged similar aberrant responses, though the local outlier factor produced notably different results. Mahalanobis distance proved to be a conservative detector, whereas Isolation Forest and Gaussian mixture models were more liberal. Overall, the study demonstrated that unsupervised anomaly detection methods are promising for identifying aberrant responses and recommended using multiple methods to improve accuracy.

10.2.2.3 Deep Learning Algorithms

In addition, recent research explored different deep learning methods for cheating detection. Tang et al. (2023) explored click-streaming data to detect atypical test-taking behaviors using a long short-term memory (LSTM) network. Clickstream records the details of user actions. Such unstructured data cannot be well modeled using traditional psychometric models due to its complexity and dynamic nature. This study introduces the model agreement index (MAI), quantifying how typical or atypical a test-taker's clickstream is relative to an expected behavior model trained with. Empirical findings show that test-takers with low MAI scores often struggled with repeatedly opening and closing tool widgets, resulting in wasted time. The study details the training of the LSTM, compares it to a "most common next action" baseline, and examines correlations between MAI and other behavioral indicators, such as answer changes, using data from a statewide testing program.

As Ranger et al. (2022) highlighted, supervised learning algorithms can achieve high accuracy for cheating detection; however, they require labeled datasets with known instances of potential cheaters, which are typically not available in the early stages of an assessment cycle. Their study explores the use of transfer learning by adapting a detector trained on one labeled dataset to a new, unlabeled dataset from a different test. Empirical results show that transferring a pre-trained detector improves accuracy over unsupervised approaches: a naive transfer, which simply reuses the detector, substantially increases accuracy, while transfer via the self-labeling algorithm yields a modest additional gain. These findings suggest that transfer learning offers a practical option of enhancing cheating detection early in the assessment process by capitalizing on existing trained detectors.

10.2.2.4 Language Models

Language models are the recent advances in natural language processing (NLP). Bidirectional Encoder Representations from Transformers (BERT; Devlin et al., 2018) stands out for leveraging the encoder of the Transformer architecture (Vaswani et al., 2017) to capture deep bidirectional context. Unidirectional models restrict learning to the immediate previous context by processing text sequentially (e.g., left-to-right), whereas bidirectional models consider the full context by accessing information from both preceding and succeeding words simultaneously. Unlike traditional unidirectional language models, BERT uses a masked language modeling objective. In this process, tokens (i.e., the basic units of text, such as words or sub-words) are randomly masked, and the model attempts to predict them based on the context provided by surrounding tokens. This allows the model to capture deep bidirectional relationships. These pretraining objectives allow BERT to learn rich, context-aware semantic and syntactic representations, achieving strong performance across a wide range of downstream tasks. Its encoder-only architecture enables robust language representations that can be fine-tuned for various applications, establishing BERT as a foundational model in modern NLP research.

BERT's success has inspired a range of adaptations aimed at improving model performance and efficiency. RoBERTa (Liu et al., 2019) refines BERT's pretraining by removing the next sentence prediction task, employing dynamic masking, and using larger datasets with longer training, achieving better generalization and linguistic pattern capture. DeBERTa (He et al., 2021) introduces disentangled attention that separates content and positional information, enhancing the modeling of word dependencies. ELECTRA (Clark et al., 2020) replaces masked language modeling with a replaced token detection objective, enabling sample-efficient learning and comparable or superior performance to BERT with fewer resources. ConvBERT (Jiang et al., 2020) integrates convolutional mechanisms into self-attention layers to capture both local and long-range dependencies efficiently, while DistilBERT (Sanh et al., 2020) uses knowledge distillation to produce a smaller, faster model that retains much of BERT's accuracy. Collectively, these innovations demonstrate how modifications to architecture, pretraining, and attention mechanisms can yield more effective and resource-efficient language models.

Language models for detecting AI-generated text responses can be trained or fine-tuned to analyze text to identify patterns indicative of machine generation. These models leverage linguistic cues, stylistic consistency, and statistical irregularities that often differ from human writing, such as repetitive phrasing, unusual syntax, or improbable word combinations. Detection models can be classifier-based, trained on examples of AI-generated versus human-written essays, or probabilistic, estimating the likelihood that text was produced by a language model. Yan et al. (2023) fine-tuned a RoBERTa model to classify AI- vs. human-generated essays. They further compared this language model's performance with an SVM model using features extracted by e-rater, an in-house proprietary automated scoring engine, with the former yielding higher detection accuracy. Jiao et al. (2023c) explored detection of essays generated by ChatGPT 3.5 and compared feature-based approaches to language model-based approaches. Supervised machine learning models were used for the feature-based approaches, including logistic regression, SVM, Naïve Bayes, gradient boosting, random forest, and Decision Tree, while the explored language models include BERT, ELECTRA, and ConvBERT. In general, language models performed better than the feature-based supervised machine learning models, with ELECTRA yielding the highest detection accuracy. However, Hua and Yao's (2024) study examined both supervised machine learning models (SVM, logistic regression, and XGBoost) and language models (BERT, ELECTRA, and RoBERTa) in detecting essays generated by multiple LLMs including GPT 3.5, GPT 4, GPT40, Gemini, Gemini Advanced, and Claude 3.5. Their study found feature-based SVM performed the best among all the studied models including language models. In the realm of high-stakes testing, organizations such as Duolingo have pioneered the application of these advanced NLP techniques and AI-generated text detection to secure remote assessments (Belzak et al., 2025).

Research findings on the top-performing models for detecting AI-generated text exhibit considerable variability, reflecting the differences in generating the data using genAI, evaluation criteria, and model training. While these detection methods demonstrate partial success in identifying synthetic text, their effectiveness is increasingly challenged by the rapid advancements in genAI technology as genAI is progressively capable of producing text that is not only more natural but also contextually sophisticated, incorporating nuanced linguistic patterns that closely mimic human-authored content. This evolution has precipitated a dynamic and ongoing competition between generative language models, which aim to produce undetectable outputs, and detection models, which are tasked with distinguishing artificial text from human-generated text. The continuous refinement of generative models, leveraging larger datasets, improved architectures, and advanced training techniques such as reinforcement learning or transfer learning, exacerbates the challenge for detection of AI-generated text responses in large-scale assessments in an ever-evolving technological landscape.

10.3 Data Augmentation in Cheating Detection

10.3.1 Class Imbalance in Cheating Detection

In cheating detection, class imbalance presents a critical challenge for supervised machine learning models, as the scarcity of positive cases can bias training, limit predictive performance, and skew the performance evaluation. For instance, in the publicly available dataset reported by Cizek and Wollack (2017), only 46 of 1,636 test-takers were flagged as likely cheaters, comprising just 2.81% of the sample. This extreme imbalance not only highlights the rarity of observed cheating in large-scale assessments but also underscores the methodological difficulty of developing models that can reliably identify such infrequent behaviors. This class imbalance between the likely cheaters (the minority class) and the large number of non-cheating test-takers (the majority class) may lead to under-representation of the minority class in model training. Without sufficient positive examples, supervised machine learning models may overfit the majority class (non-cheaters) and fail to detect subtle or emerging cheating behaviors. In this case, data augmentation is especially critical for developing machine learning models for cheating detection because labeled cases of potential cheaters are often rare, limited, and contain an extremely small portion of the total test-takers.

10.3.2 Data Augmentation

Data augmentation is a technique used in machine learning to increase the size, representation, and diversity of a dataset by generating modified or synthetic versions of existing data points. Its primary purpose is to improve the performance, robustness, and generalizability of machine learning models by exposing the trained models to a wider range of variations and scenarios. This approach is particularly valuable when training data is limited, unbalanced, or lacks sufficient diversity, as it helps ensure that models become more robust, generalizable, and adaptable to different conditions. In general, data augmentation can address issues related to class imbalance, limited data, data sparsity, overfitting, data privacy concerns and improve transfer learning.

Augmentation techniques such as generating synthetic response patterns, simulating unusual clickstream behaviors, or creating perturbed versions of known cheating cases may help artificially expand the dataset and introduce greater diversity and representation of cheating behaviors. This improves model robustness, enhances its ability to generalize the trained model to new or unseen cheating behaviors, and reduces the risk of bias toward the majority non-cheating class. Ultimately, data augmentation makes cheating detection systems more reliable, adaptable, and effective in real testing environments where genuine cheating data is scarce and evolving. Although much of the existing research on data augmentation originates from computer vision for image data and from speech processing, this chapter focuses on augmenting tabular and textual data for cheating detection in large-scale assessments, given item product and process data are often represented in tabular or text format such as essay writing and constructed responses.

According to Bayer et al. (2022), data augmentation methods can be generally classified into two categories: feature space and data space. Feature space augmentation seeks to increase the number of variables associated with each sample in a dataset. The rationale is similar to incorporating covariates in regression analysis, where auxiliary information is added to enrich the representation of each case and provide a more comprehensive basis for analysis. On the other hand, data space augmentation aims to increase both the sample size and the representativeness of a dataset, often using resampling techniques. When features are arranged in columns and cases in rows, feature space augmentation refers to increasing the number of columns (i.e., variables), whereas data space augmentation refers to increasing the number of rows (i.e., sample size or the number of cases). In cheating detection, features are usually behavioral indicators, such as response time patterns, navigation behaviors, and answer-change sequences that capture potential misconduct. However, the features used as data augmentation for cheating detection need to be examined carefully for validity considerations.

10.3.2.1 Methods for Tabular Data

Tabular data augmentation is especially relevant in cheating detection since item response data, process data collected from clickstreams, or log files are often structured as rows (test-takers) and columns (features). Feature space augmentation is about creating new variables (columns) that enrich the representation of each sample. The easiest feature space augmentation is to include test-takers' prior performance, or test-taking history as a repeater or not, as well as contextual data including testing conditions like time of day, device used, or test duration. Further, new features can be created based on existing ones, informed by domain-specific theory or knowledge. For example, the ratio of response time to item difficulty, the number of clicks per minute, can be derived using existing item-level information and item response time for each test-taker. Some other variables which can capture the interaction relationships among variables can be created. For example, a new feature can be derived based on the interaction of test-takers' latent ability in response accuracy and latent speed. In addition, summary statistics aggregated across items can be included to augment data such as minimum, maximum, mean, and variances of item response time (Zhou & Jiao, 2023) and maximum pause length. Furthermore, some mathematical transformations can be implemented, including polynomial transformation to capture non-linear relationships among the raw features, taking logarithmic, exponential transformations to convert the skewed distribution to be normally distributed, or categorizing continuous variables/features into categorical levels to better reveal patterns. For click-streaming or action sequence data, sequence embeddings using LSTM/Transformer hidden states can be added to augment feature space. In general, the augmented features are selected based on theory or empirical studies showing the new features are valid in improving the detection of potential cheating behaviors.

The representation of feature vectors plays a critical role in the performance of machine learning models (Heaton, 2020). In fact, insufficient feature representation can sometimes degrade prediction accuracy more severely than a limited number of training samples. Heaton (2020) emphasized that creating new features derived from existing ones can enrich the input representation and improve model performance. This feature space augmentation enhances the diversity and informativeness of the dataset. Several studies illustrate this approach. Micenková et al. (2015) applied outlier scoring functions to generate transformed features, thereby enriching the feature representation for learning. Devries and Taylor (2017) transformed existing data vectors within a learned feature space by encoding sequences, extracting context vectors, and applying transformations such as noise injection. Zopluoglu (2019) converted item responses into nominal response patterns to expand the feature space, while Zhou and Jiao (2023) augmented data at the base-model level in a stacking ensemble framework by incorporating features such as test-taking attempts and summary statistics. Zhou and Jiao (2022) also include the anomaly detection results to augment the feature space at the meta-model level for stacking modeling to increase the accuracy in cheating detection. Jiao et al. (2023b) incorporated person-fit measures to augment feature space for cheating detection. In general, these strategies help augment the feature space to improve the robustness and generalization of machine learning models for cheating detection.

Data space augmentation, on the other hand, aims to increase both the sample size and the representativeness of a dataset, thereby improving model training and generalization, by creating synthetic data points. This is often achieved through resampling techniques such as oversampling the minority class or generating synthetic samples. By enriching the dataset with additional or rebalanced examples, data space augmentation helps address issues such as class imbalance and insufficient diversity in the training data. One common technique is the synthetic minority oversampling technique (SMOTE; Chawla et al., 2002), which generates new samples for minority classes via interpolation between existing minority samples. Adaptive synthetic sampling approach for imbalanced learning (ADASYN; He et al., 2008), as an adaptive extension of SMOTE focuses on generating synthetic samples for harder-to-learn minority cases which are closer to the majority class or in overlapping regions to increase the representation of the difficult-to-classify cases. Different studies have explored these resampling methods for cheating detection. For example, Zhou and Jiao (2023) applied oversampling, undersampling, and SMOTE, based on the KNN algorithm, to produce synthetic cheater data and address class imbalance in cheating detection. Similarly, Tiong and Lee (2021) augmented their dataset by adding 60 synthetic samples representing aberrant behaviors in online exam settings. Across these studies, augmentation enriched the datasets by adding new samples, thereby improving model robustness.

10.3.2.2 Methods for Textual Data

Data augmentation for textual data is also classified into two categories (Bayer et al., 2022): feature space and data space. For feature space, Bayer et al. (2022) highlight the techniques of interpolation and noise injection. Wang and Yang (2015) used embeddings, which are dense numerical vector representations that capture the semantic meaning of text, to augment feature space. For data space, data augmentation can be implemented at character level (e.g., swapping letters to simulate typos), word level (e.g., synonym replacement), phrase level (e.g., paraphrasing specific clauses or idioms), and document level (e.g., translating and back-translating entire essays). The following highlights the methods that are more commonly used in data augmentation for text data. For a full review of data augmentation methods, readers may refer to Feng et al. (2021), Li et al. (2021), and Bayer et al. (2022).

Incorporating word or sentence embedding into the feature space is a common data augmentation method. When traditional machine learning or deep learning methods rely on engineered features, both static and contextual embeddings can be incorporated to augment feature space. Static embeddings are fixed vector representations of words that remain the same regardless of context. Models such as Word2Vec, GloVe, and FastText generate these embeddings by training on large text corpora, assigning each word in the vocabulary a single vector that captures general semantic and syntactic information. While static embeddings are computationally efficient and useful for many NLP tasks, they cannot capture polysemy or subtle context-dependent variations in meaning. This limitation has motivated the development of contextual embeddings.

Contextual embeddings are vector representations of words or tokens that dynamically capture their meaning based on the surrounding context within a sentence or document, unlike traditional static embeddings, which assign a single fixed vector per word. By taking into account the neighboring words and overall linguistic structure, contextual embeddings can distinguish between different senses of the same word and encode richer semantic and syntactic information. These embeddings are typically generated by deep neural network models, such as transformers, which process entire sequences and model dependencies between words, resulting in representations that adapt to varying contexts and significantly improve performance in natural language understanding tasks. Models used for generating contextual embeddings include embeddings from language models, BERT, RoBERTa, DeBERTa, GPT series, and T5 (Text-to-Text Transfer Transformer), to list a few. A full list of best-performing embedding models can be found at the Embedding Leaderboard from https://huggingface.co/spaces/mteb/leaderboard.

For data space, word-level data augmentation includes synonym replacement (Jungiewicz & Smywiński-Pohl, 2019; Zhang, Zhao, & LeCun, 2015), random swap which randomly swaps questions, random deletion, and random insertion as noise induction (Wei & Zou, 2019). For phrase and document-level data augmentation, backtranslation (Sennrich et al., 2016; Yu et al., 2018) as round-trip translation is often used to add more samples. Backtranslation is particularly valuable in cheating detection as it generates high-quality paraphrases that mimic the spinning tools or manual rewriting strategies often used by test-takers to mask plagiarism (Zhang et al., 2015). By training on these synthetic variations, machine learning models are powerful to detect paraphrased content that deviates from the original source material. For the most recent advances, genAI (Anaby-Tavor et al., 2020; Dai et al., 2023; Kobayashi, 2018; Qiu et al., 2020; Wu et al., 2019) can be used to create more sample answers for data augmentation using different prompting and fine-tuning strategies.

While data augmentation is standard in general NLP tasks, its application is particularly critical in the domain of test security for detecting AI-generated essays and obfuscated plagiarism. In operational settings, obtaining a large, labeled corpus of verified cheating responses is often difficult, resulting in severe class imbalance. Furthermore, sophisticated test-takers may employ adversarial strategies, such as paraphrasing or translating content back and forth, to evade simple similarity checks. Consequently, data augmentation techniques for text are not merely about increasing sample size. Instead, they serve to simulate these adversarial evasion behaviors, thereby enabling the training of robust detection models capable of identifying subtle variations of academic misconduct.

10.4 Empirical Examples

To illustrate the applications of the methods for data augmentation discussed in this chapter, this section presents empirical examples based on Zhou and Jiao (2022, 2023) and Jiao et al. (2023b) to demonstrate the increasing accuracy of cheating detection when data is augmented in terms of quantities and categories.

10.4.1 Data

The dataset used for this demonstration is publicly available from a large-scale licensure examination in which potential cases of cheating had been flagged (Cizek & Wollack, 2017). However, no information was provided about the type of cheating behaviors the flagged test-takers have engaged in. The test form included 170 dichotomous items administered to 1,636 test-takers, of whom 46 were identified as likely cheaters. The dataset contained item responses and response times for each of the 170 items, total response time per test-taker, and the number of test-taking attempts. In total, the original dataset comprised 342 variables.

Because only a small proportion of test-takers, 2.81% of the 1,636 test-takers were flagged as likely cheaters, the dataset exhibited significant class imbalance. To address this issue, resampling techniques were applied to the training set, each of the three studies experimented with different data augmentation methods.

10.4.2 Evaluation Criteria

Due to the class imbalance issue in cheating detection, overall accuracy defined as the proportion of correctly classified cases is not an appropriate metric for evaluating detection performance. For the imbalanced classification problem, model performance was primarily evaluated using the F1 score, which is the harmonic mean of recall and precision (Forman & Scholz, 2010). In addition, recall, precision, and the false-positive rate (FPR) were also reported. Recall (or sensitivity) measures the proportion of true positives (cheaters correctly identified) out of all actual cheaters. Precision measures the proportion of true positives among all test-takers predicted as cheaters. The FPR reflects the proportion of non-cheaters who were incorrectly classified as cheaters. Each of the evaluation criteria is defined as follows:

$$\text{Recall} = \frac{\text{TP}}{\text{TP} + \text{FN}}$$

$$\text{Precision} = \frac{\text{TP}}{\text{TP} + \text{FP}}$$

$$\text{F1 Score} = \frac{2 \times \text{Precision} \times \text{Recall}}{\text{Precision} + \text{Recall}} = \frac{2\text{TP}}{2\text{TP} + \text{FP} + \text{FN}}$$

$$\text{False Positive Rate } \left(\text{FPR}\right) = \frac{\text{FP}}{\text{FP} + \text{TN}}$$

where TP = true positives, FP = false positives, FN = false negatives, and TN = true negatives.

10.4.3 Data Augmentation

Study 1 based on Zhou and Jiao (2023) investigated the use of a stacking ensemble machine learning algorithm to detect cheating behaviors by analyzing item responses and response times from 170 items as well as augmented test-taker data. This study explored data augmentation at the feature space and data space. In the feature space, augmented features included the number of test-taking attempts and several summary statistics (the total test score and the total response time across all 170 items), along with the mean, median, maximum, and minimum item response times, with a total of 7 augmented features. Incorporating these augmented features represents a form of data augmentation, intended to provide higher-level information beyond what is captured by individual item responses. In total, 347 variables were included in the dataset.

To augment the data space, this study examined several resampling strategies to address class imbalance, including oversampling, undersampling, and a combination of both (referred to as dual resampling). Specifically, the SMOTE function was used for oversampling and the RandomUnderSampler function for undersampling in Python. To compare the effect of data augmentation on model performance, different class ratios of non-cheaters to cheaters were tested including 1:1, 2:1, 5:1, and 10:1 via different resampling strategies. All data augmentation strategies were applied at the base-model levels in the stacking ensemble model. The meta-model (a higher-level model ensembled over the base models) was developed only using the outputs from the base models using the augmented features (refer to Zhou and Jiao (2023) for details).

Study 2 based on Zhou and Jiao (2022) investigated data augmentation in the feature space within a blending ensemble framework at the meta-model level. Specifically, four anomaly detection techniques were used to generate outlier scores, which were incorporated alongside the most informative features selected from the original dataset by four feature selection methods. Four commonly used anomaly detection algorithms include Isolation Forest, Elliptic Envelope, One-Class SVM, and DBSCAN to capture different types of outliers (Jose, 2019). In addition, most effective features (a total of 33 features) identified for the base-model training were selected to augment data in the feature space for the meta-model development. When base models were trained, resampling via both oversampling (SMOTE) with a ratio of 0.4 and undersampling (RandomUnderSampling) with a ratio of 0.5 was utilized to augment data in the cheater groups and balance the sample sizes between the two classes.

Study 3 augmented the feature space by including both anomaly measures and person-fit measures. The four anomaly detection methods including Isolation Forest, Elliptic Envelope, Local Outlier Factor, and One-Class SVM produced outlier scores for each test-taker. In addition, 29 person-fit measures expanded those investigated by Ranger et al. (2020) to augment the feature space. These measures include Guttman-based indices: G statistics (Guttman, 1944), Norm Conformity Index (NCI, Tatsuoka, 1984); agreement-based indices: Agreement Index (A), Disagreement Index (D), Dependability Index (EI) (Kane & Brennan, 1980); correlation/covariance-based indices: point-biserial correlation (Donlan & Fischer, 1968), the Caution Index or C.Sato (Sato, 1975), C* (Harnisch & Linn, 1981), Gnormed (van der Flier, 1977), U3 (van der Flier, 1982) and standardized U3-ZU3 (van der Flier, 1982), H^T (Sijtsma, 1986), six indices proposed by Tatsuoka (1984) including ECI1, ECI2, ECI3, ECI4, ECI5, ECI6. Further, likelihood-based indices were also used for data augmentation, including L_0 (Levine & Rubin, 1979), L_z (Drasgow et al., 1985), L_z* (Snijders, 2001). Person outfit and infit mean squares and Z statistics (Wright & Stone, 1979) were included as augmented features after fitting the item response data to the Rasch model. Three response time-based indices further augmented the feature space including KT statistics by Ranger et al. (2020), Man et al. (2018), and Z-square (Fekken & Holden, 1992). As each person-fit index addresses different types of aberrant responding behaviors, the inclusion of these 29 person-fit indices was expected to augment the feature space and lead to more accurate cheating detection. Following the resampling ratios used in Zhou and Jiao (2023), this study adopted the same resampling ratios of 0.4 for the SMOTE oversampling and 0.5 for the random undersampling.

10.4.4 Results

Study 1 examined six machine learning models including Decision Tree, SVM, logistic regression, Naïve Bayes, discriminant analysis, and neural network alongside two ensemble models, random forest and gradient boosting as the base model. The predictions from these eight base models were then used to construct a meta-model. For the meta-model development, input data were sequentially tested, ranging from outputs of all base models to only the top two best-performing base models.

Figure 10.1, as adapted from Figure 8 in Zhou and Jiao (2023), summarizes the best-performing model, the meta-model stacked on two best-performing base models in comparison with the base models. This best-performing meta-model utilized the feature set combining item responses and summary statistics, with an undersampling ratio of 10:1 using discriminant analysis for stacking in the meta-model. The meta-model, stacked on the top two base models, outperformed all individual base classifiers, achieving an F1 score of 0.586, a recall of 0.638, a balanced precision of 0.551, and a low FPR of 0.014. Overall, among all models evaluated,

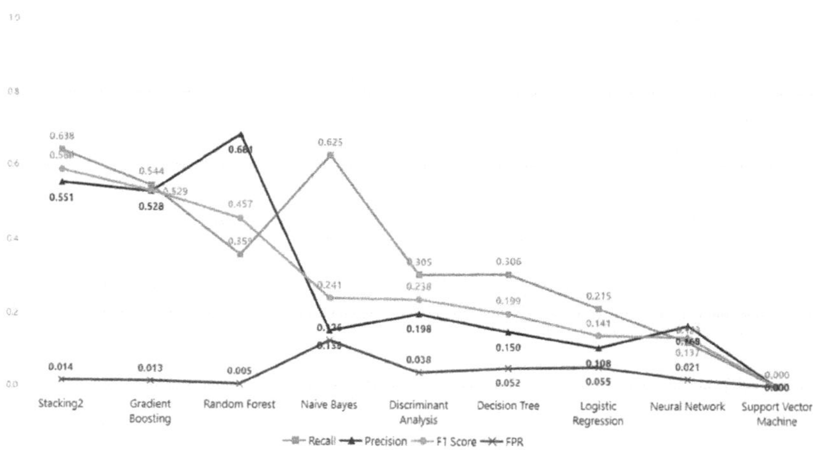

FIGURE 10.1 Comparison between the base models and the meta-model using discriminant analysis based on item responses and summary statistics. Adapted from Figure 8 of Zhou and Jiao (2023).

the discriminant analysis-based stacking meta-model with item responses and augmented summary statistics at a 10:1 undersampling ratio achieved the highest F1 score and balanced performance, with all key metrics: F1, recall, and precision exceeding 0.5, indicating effectiveness in detecting cheaters.

Study 2 trained the same eight base models as trained in Study 1, with a SMOTE rate of 0.4 and a RandomUndersampling rate of 0.5 to deal with class imbalance. Further, it trained a meta-model in blending, a special case of stacking. Ten most effective features were selected and used as features to train the meta-model for data augmentation. Further, four outlier scores from Isolation Forest, Elliptic Envelope, One-Class SVM, and DBSCAN were used as augmented data for the meta-model training. In addition to the augmented data, the meta-model was trained with input data ranging sequentially from the outputs of all base models to only the top two best-performing base models.

Figure 10.2, adapted from Figure 5 in Zhou and Jiao (2022), illustrates the performance of the best blended meta-model incorporating two types of augmented data, alongside the eight base models. The figure also includes the performance of the base models and the meta-models with different input data. Overall, the blended meta-model based on the six top-performing base models with both types of augmented data achieved the highest F1 score of 0.7857, balanced recall and precision (both above 0.5), and a relatively low FPR of 0.0064. Meta-models using only one type of augmented data, either outlier measures or the top selected effective features, still

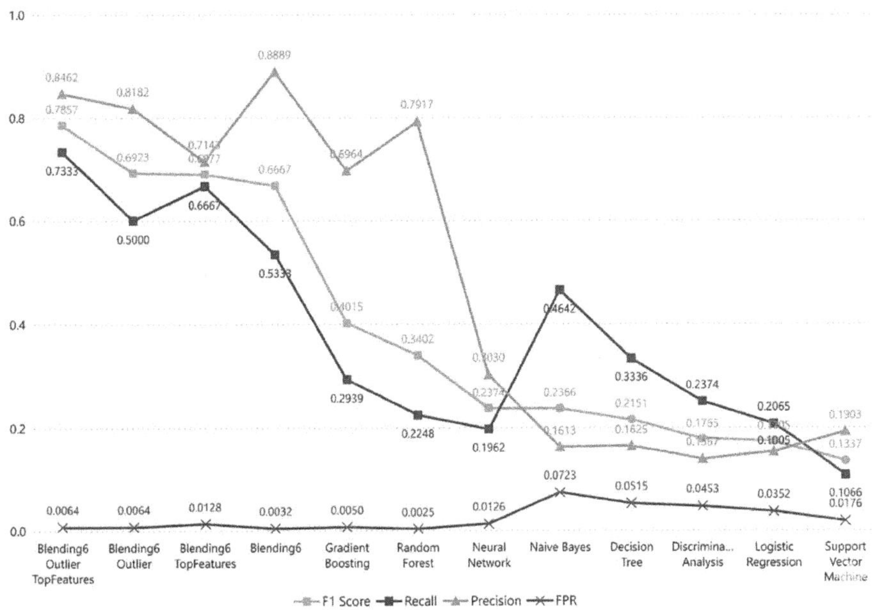

FIGURE 10.2 Model comparison among the base models and the meta-models with and without data augmentation. Adapted from Figure 5 of Zhou and Jiao (2022).

outperformed the blending approach without data augmentation. In comparison with the base models, including the ensemble models: gradient boosting and random forest, all blending-based meta-models demonstrated substantially superior performance.

Study 3 trained the same eight base models for meta-model development. In training the base model, in addition to the 347 features used in both Studies 1 and 2, this study augmented the feature space for the base-model training by adding 29 fit measures and 4 anomaly scores. Eight feature selection methods were applied to identify the top 10 most effective features from each method. After removing duplicates, 55 unique features remained. Combining the base models' outputs with the augmented features and a total of 63 features were used to train the meta-model. The meta-model achieved an F1 score of 0.85, a recall of 0.78, a precision of 0.99, and an FPR below 0.001 across all three meta-models: random forest, gradient boosting, and discriminant analysis. Compared with previous studies using the same dataset, the meta-models developed in this study demonstrated superior performance.

10.5 Summary and Discussion

The latest advances in machine learning and genAI have brought new perspectives as well as new challenges in cheating detection. This chapter introduces cheating detection methods using machine learning methods, deep learning models, and language models. Further, data augmentation integrating both psychometric methods and machine learning algorithms is demonstrated to increase detection accuracy via a series of empirical studies. Lastly, this chapter briefly introduces the methods for detecting essays produced by genAI.

While both supervised and unsupervised machine learning methods can be used for cheating detection, an important issue of class imbalance needs to be addressed when the cheater class, often the minority class, consists of an extremely small portion of the total sample. Further, traditional psychometric analysis of person-fit measures can be used for cheating detection. Such measures can be incorporated as augmented data in cheating detection using machine learning methods in addition to anomaly detection measures from machine learning. This chapter demonstrates the effectiveness of data augmentation for tabular data based on summary statistics, anomaly detection methods, and person-fit measures from traditional psychometric analysis. However, other data augmentation methods can be explored further such as the transformation of raw data, adding interaction terms to account for non-linear relationships among raw data, and adding noise to increase the diversity or variability of existing data.

In addition, genAI introduces a new type of cheating, as these tools can produce item responses including essays and extended constructed responses mimicking authentic responses generated by test-takers. Unlike traditional forms of cheating, AI-generated responses can be entirely original yet highly plausible, making them difficult to detect using conventional methods. Language models can play a significant role in detecting AI-generated responses in large-scale assessments. Studies (e.g.,

Jiao et al., 2023c; Yan et al., 2023) reported that in general language models such as RoBERTa and ELECTRA performed better than feature-based supervised machine learning models in detecting AI-generated essays. This chapter focuses primarily on cheating detection of AI-generated essays and text responses to constructed-response items. However, it is important to acknowledge that genAI can also be used to manipulate other item formats, such as multiple-choice or short-answer questions, by suggesting likely correct responses or patterns, further complicating detection efforts.

It is worthy of note that recent advances in cheating detection have increasingly emphasized hybrid models that combine unsupervised and supervised techniques, as well as ensemble learning approaches. The empirical examples illustrated the better performance of stacking ensemble models compared with individual base models. The models that integrate the strengths of different methods: unsupervised learning can uncover broad, previously unknown patterns of irregular behavior without requiring labeled data, while supervised learning can capture fine-grained anomalies based on prior knowledge and labeled examples of cheating. Ensemble methods, which aggregate multiple classifiers or detectors, further enhance robustness by reducing the risk of overfitting to specific behaviors and improving generalizability across contexts. These hybrid and ensemble approaches are becoming more common in cheating detection, as they offer a comprehensive framework for identifying both subtle individual and group irregularities.

It is worth noting that cheating detection is a challenging task in psychometric analysis. Cheating behaviors may take on different forms. In practice, it is difficult to distinguish cheating behaviors from other aberrant responding behaviors such as smart guessing or other factors which may lead to model fit issues. The analysis of item responses may not reveal sufficient information to detect cheating behaviors. We strongly advocate the use of process data and the integration of data from multiple sources and multiple modalities to conduct cheating detection to increase its power and accuracy. When the data becomes bigger and more complex, the latest advances of machine learning and AI technology will surely be a more viable analysis paradigm for cheating detection when the parametric psychometric methods and models may fall short.

This chapter focuses on detecting potential cheaters, rather than identifying compromised items, although effectively detecting compromised items is crucial for maintaining the quality of the item bank. Readers interested in detecting compromised items or simultaneous detection of pre-knowledge in both items and test-takers can refer to studies conducted by other researchers (e.g., Pan, 2022; Pan et al., 2022; Pan & Wollack, 2021; Pan & Wollack, 2023).

References

Anaby-Tavor, A. A., Carmeli, B., Goldbraich, E., Kantor, A., Kour, G., Shlomov, S., Tepper, N., & Zwerdling, N. (2020). Do not have enough data? Deep learning to the rescue! In *Proceedings of the AAAI Conference on Artificial Intelligence (AAAI-20)* (Vol. 34, pp. 7383–7390). AAAI Press. https://doi.org/10.1609/aaai.v34i05.6233

Bayer, M., Kaufhold, M.-A., & Reuter, C. (2022). A survey on data augmentation for text classification. *ACM Computing Surveys*, 55(7), 1–44. https://doi.org/10.1145/3544558

Belov, D. I. (2015). Robust detection of examinees with aberrant answer changes. *Journal of Educational Measurement*, 52, 437–456.

Belzak, W., Baig, B., Cardwell, R., Hastings, R., Horie, A., LaFlair, G., … & Shih, Y. S. (2025). *Duolingo English test: Security and score integrity*. Duolingo Research Report DRR-25-04, Duolingo English Test.

Bernardi, R., Baca, A., Landers, K., & Witek, M. (2008). Methods of cheating and deterrents to classroom cheating: an international study. *Ethics & Behaviors*, 18, 373–391. https://doi.org/10.1080/10508420701713030

Bishop, S., & Egan, K. (2016). Detecting erasures and unusual gain scores: Understanding the status quo. In G. Cizek & J. Wollack (Eds.), *Handbook of quantitative methods for detecting cheating on tests* (pp. 193–213). Routledge.

Boughton, K., Smith, J., & Ren, H. (2016). Using response time data to detect compromised items and/or people. In G. Cizek & J. Wollack (Eds.), *Handbook of quantitative methods for detecting cheating on tests* (pp. 177–190). Routledge. https://doi.org/10.4324/9781315743097

Cavalcanti, E. R., Pires, C. E., Cavalcanti, E. P., & Pires, V. F. (2012). Detection and evaluation of cheating on college exams using supervised classification. *Informatics in Education*, 11(2), 169–190.

Chawla, N. V., Bowyer, K. W., Hall, L. O., & Kegelmeyer, W. P. (2002). SMOTE: Synthetic minority over-sampling technique. *JAIR Journal of Artificial Intelligence Research*, 16, 321–357.

Chen, J. (2004). *Effects of test anxiety, time pressure, ability and gender on response aberrance*. The Ohio State University.

Chen, Y., Lu, Y., & Moustaki, I. (2020). *Detection of two-way outliers in multivariate data and application to cheating detection in educational tests*. arXiv:1911.09408. https://arxiv.org/ abs/1911.09408v2

Chitra, A., & Rajkumar, A. (2015). Plagiarism detection using machine learning-based paraphrase recognizer. *Journal of Intelligent Systems*, 25(3), 351–359. https://doi.org/10.1515/jisys-2014-0146

Cizek, G., & Wollack, J. (Eds.). (2017). *Handbook of quantitative methods for detecting cheating on tests*. Routledge.

Clark, K., Luong, M.-T., Le, Q. V., & Manning, C. D. (2020). Electra: Pre-training text encoders as discriminators rather than generators. In *International Conference on Learning Representations*. https://openreview.net/forum?id=r1xMH1BtvB

Dai, H., Liu, Z., Liao, W., Huang, X., Cao, Y., Wu, Z., … & Li, X. (2023). AugGPT: Leveraging ChatGPT for text data augmentation. *arXiv*. https://doi.org/10.48550/arXiv.2302.13007

Dawson, P. (2020). *Defending assessment security in a digital world: Preventing e-cheating and supporting academic integrity in higher education*. Routledge.

Devlin, J., Chang, M.-W., Lee, K., & Toutanova, K. (2018). BERT: Pre-training of deep bidirectional transformers for language understanding. *arXiv* preprint arXiv:1810.04805.

Devries, T., & Taylor, G.W. (2017). Dataset augmentation in feature space. *arXiv*, abs/1702.05538.

Donlon, T. F., & Fischer, F. E. (1968). An index of an individual's agreement with group determined item difficulties. *Educational and Psychological Measurement*, 28, 105–113.

Drasgow, F., Levine, M. V., & Williams, E. A. (1985). Appropriateness measurement with polychotomous item response models and standardized indices. *British Journal of Mathematical and Statistical Psychology*, 38, 67–86.

Feng, S. Y., Gangal, V., Wei, J., Chandar, S., Vosoughi, S., Mitamura, T., & Hovy, E. (2021). A survey of data augmentation approaches for NLP. In C. Zong, F. Xia, W. Li, & R. Navigli (Eds.), *Findings of the Association for Computational Linguistics: ACL-IJCNLP 2021* (pp. 968–988). Association for Computational Linguistics. https://doi.org/10.18653/v1/2021.findings-acl.84

Fekken, G. C., & Holden, R. R. (1992). Response latency evidence for viewing personality dimensions as schema indicators. *Journal of Research in Personality*, *26*(2), 103–120.

Forman, G., & Scholz, M. (2010). Apples-to-apples in cross-validation studies: Pitfalls in classifier performance measurement. *SIGKDD Explorations*, 12, 49–57.

Gierl, M. J., & Haladyna, T. M. (Eds.). (2013). *Automatic item generation: Theory and practice*. Routledge.

Gorgun, G., & Bulut, O. (2022). Identifying aberrant responses in intelligent tutoring systems: An application of anomaly detection methods. *Psychological Test and Assessment Modeling*, 64(4), 359–384.

Guttman, L. (1944). A basis for scaling qualitative data. *American Sociological Review*, 9, 139–150.

Hao, J. & Fauss, M. (2022, November). *Test security in remote testing age: Perspectives from process data analytics and AI.* Presentation at the 2022 annual Maryland Assessment Research Center virtual conference.

Harnisch, D. L., & Linn, R. L. (1981). Analysis of item response patterns: Questionable test data and dissimilar curriculum practices. *Journal of Educational Measurement*, 18, 133–146.

He, H., Bai, Y., Garcia, E. A., & Li, S. (2008, June). ADASYN: Adaptive synthetic sampling approach for imbalanced learning. In *2008 IEEE International Joint Conference on Neural Networks (IEEE World Congress on Computational Intelligence)* (pp. 1322–1328). IEEE. https://doi.org/10.1109/IJCNN.2008.4633969

He, P., Liu, X., Gao, J., & Chen, W. (2021). Deberta: Decoding-enhanced BERT with disentangled attention. https://arxiv.org/abs/2006.03654

Heaton, J. (2020). An empirical analysis of feature engineering for predictive modeling. *arXiv*. https://arxiv.org/abs/1701.07852

Hua, H., Jiao, H., & Wang, X. (2025, November). *Exploration of summarization by generative language models for automated scoring of long essays*. arXiv. https://doi.org/10.48550/arXiv.2510.22830

Hua, H., & Yao, C.-J. (2024). Investigating generative AI models and detection techniques: Impacts of tokenization and dataset size on identification of AI-generated text. *Frontiers in Artificial Intelligence*, 7, Article 1469197. https://doi.org/10.3389/frai.2024.1469197

Hylton, K., Levy, Y., & Dringus, L. P. (2016). Utilizing webcam-based proctoring to deter misconduct in online exams. *Computers & Education*, 92, 53–63.

Jiang, Z.-H., Yu, W., Zhou, D., Chen, Y., Feng, J., & Yan, S. (2020). ConvBERT: Improving BERT with span-based dynamic convolution. *Advances in Neural Information Processing Systems*, 33, 12837–12848.

Jiao, H., He, Q., & Yao, L. (2023a). Machine learning and deep learning in assessment. *Psychological Testing and Assessment Modeling*, 64(1), 178–189.

Jiao, H., Yadav, C., & Li, G. (2023b). Integrating psychometric analysis and machine learning to augment data for cheating detection in large-scale assessment. *PsyArXiv*. https://doi.org/10.31234/osf.io/fjz2c

Jiao, H., Yadav, C., Wan, L., Hendrickson, A., & Hua, W. (2023c, July). *Detecting essays produced by generative AI.* Paper presented at the Annual Meeting of the International Meeting of Psychometric Society (IMPS), College Park, MD.

Jose, C. (2019). Anomaly detection techniques in Python. *Medium.* https://medium.com/learningdatascience/anomaly-detection-techniques-in-python-50f650c75aaf

Jungiewicz, M., & Smywiński-Pohl, A. (2019). Towards textual data augmentation for neural networks: Synonyms and maximum loss. *Computer Science*, 20(1), 57–84. https://doi.org/10.7494/csci.2019.20.1.3023

Kane, M. T., & Brennan, R. L. (1980). Agreement coefficients as indices of dependability for domain referenced tests. *Applied Psychological Measurement*, 4, 105–126.

Kim, D., Woo, A., & Dickison, P. (2016). Identifying and investigating aberrant responses using psychometrics-based and machine learning-based approaches. In G. J. Cizek & J. A. Wollack (Eds.), *Handbook of quantitative methods for detecting cheating on tests* (pp. 70–97). Routledge.

Kingston, N., & Clark, A. (Eds.). (2014). *Test fraud: Statistical detection and methodology.* Routledge.

Kobayashi, S. (2018). Contextual augmentation: Data augmentation by words with paradigmatic relations. In *Proceedings of the 2018 Conference of the North American Chapter of the Association for Computational Linguistics: Human Language Technologies (NAACL-HLT 2018)* (Vol. 2, pp. 452–457). Association for Computational Linguistics. https://doi.org/10.18653/v1/n18-2072

Levine, M. V., & Rubin, D. B. (1979). Measuring the appropriateness of multiple-choice test scores. Journal of Educational Statistics, 4(4), 269–290.

Li, B., Hou, Y., & Che, W. (2021). Data augmentation approaches in natural language processing: A survey. *Journal of LaTeX Templates.* Advance online publication. https://github.com/BohanLi0110/NLP-DA-Papers/blob/main/DA_in_NLP.pdf

Li, Z., Wall, N., & Tang, H. (2018). A new statistic for detecting aberrant response time patterns in large-scale assessments. In *Paper presented at the annual meeting of the National Council on Measurement in Education (NCME),* New York. Retrieved from https://www.emetric.net/Content/pdf/Manuscript-Response%20Aberrance.pdf

Liao, M., Patton, J., Yan, R., & Jiao, H. (2021). Mining process data to detect aberrant test takers. *Measurement: Interdisciplinary Research and Perspectives*, 19(2), 93–105. https://doi.org/10.1080/15366367.2020.1827203

Liu, Y., Ott, M., Goyal, N., Du, J., Joshi, M., Chen, D., … & Stoyanov, V. (2019). RoBERTa: A robustly optimized BERT pretraining approach. *arXiv.* https://arxiv.org/abs/1907.11692

Man, K., & Harring, J. R. (2020). Assessing preknowledge cheating via innovative measures: A multiple-group analysis of jointly modeling item responses, response times, and visual fixation counts. *Educational and Psychological Measurement*, 81(3), 441–465.

Man, K., Harring, J., Ouyang, Y., & Thomas, S. (2018). Response time based nonparametric Kullback-Leibler divergence measure for detecting aberrant test-taking behavior. *International Journal of Testing*, 18, 155–177. https://doi.org/10.1080/15305058.2018.1429446

Man, K., Harring, J., & Sinharay, S. (2019). Use of data mining methods to detect test fraud. *Journal of Educational Measurement*, 56, 251–279. https://doi.org/10.1111/jedm.12208

Marianti, S., Fox, J.-P., Avetisyan, M., Veldkamp, B. P., & Tijmstra, J. (2014). Testing for aberrant behavior in response time modeling. *Journal of Educational and Behavioral Statistics*, 39(6), 426–451. https://doi.org/10.3102/1076998614559412

Maynes, D. (2016). Detecting potential collusion among individual examinees using similarity analysis. In G. J. Cizek & J. A. Wollack (Eds.), *Handbook of quantitative methods for detecting cheating on tests* (pp. 47–69). https://doi.org/10.4324/9781315743097-3

McClintock, J. C. (2015). Erasure analyses: Reducing the number of false positives. *Applied Measurement in Education*, 28, 14–32.

McCabe, D. (2016). Cheating and honor: Lessons from a long-term research project. In T. Bretag (Ed.), *Handbook of academic integrity* (pp. 187–198). Springer. https://doi.org/10.1007/978-981-287-098-8_35

Meijer, R. R., & Sijtsma, K. (2001). Methodology review: Evaluating person fit. *Applied Psychological Measurement*, 25(2), 107–135.

Micenková, B., Mcwilliams, B., & Assent, I. (2015). Learning representations for outlier de-tection on a budget. *arXiv:1507.08104*.

Pan, Y. (2022). *Detecting item preknowledge using machine learning techniques* [Unpublished doctoral dissertation]. University of Wisconsin-Madison.

Pan, Y., & Wollack, J. A. (2021). An unsupervised-learning-based approach to compromised items detection. *Journal of Educational Measurement*, 58(3), 413–433.

Pan, Y., Sinharay, S., Livne, O., & Wollack, J. A. (2022). A machine learning approach for detecting item compromise and preknowledge in computerized adaptive testing. *Psychological Test and Assessment Modeling*, 64(4), 385–424.

Pan, Y., & Wollack, J. A. (2023). A machine learning approach for the simultaneous detection of preknowledge in examinees and items when both are unknown. *Educational Measurement: Issues and Practice*, 42(1), 76–98.

Primoli, V., Liassou, D., Bishop, N. S., & Nhouyvanisvong, A. (2011, April). *Erasure descriptive statistics and covariates*. Paper presented at the Annual Meeting of the National Council of Measurement in Education, New Orleans, LA.

Qiu, S., Xu, B., Zhang, J., Wang, Y., Shen, X., De Melo, G., Long, C., & Li, X. (2020). EasyAug: An automatic textual data augmentation platform for classification tasks. In *Companion Proceedings of the Web Conference 2020 (WWW '20)* (pp. 249–252). Association for Computing Machinery. https://doi.org/10.1145/3366424.3383552

Qualls, A. (2001). Can knowledge of erasure behavior be used as an indicator of possible cheating? *Educational Measurement: Issues and Practice*, 20, 9–16.

Ranger, J., Schmidt, N., & Wolgast, A. (2020). The detection of cheating on e-exams in higher education—The performance of several old and some new indicators. *Frontiers in Psychology*, 11, Article 2390. https://doi.org/10.3389/fpsyg.2020.568825

Ranger, J., Schmidt, N., & Wolgast, A. (2022). Detecting cheating in large-scale assessment: The transfer of detectors to new tests. *Educational and Psychological Measurement*. Online First. https://doi.org/10.1177/00131644221132723

Reise, S. P., & Flannery, P. (1996). Assessing person-fit on measures of typical performance. *Applied Measurement in Education*, 9(1), 9–26.

Sahu, M. (2016). Plagiarism detection using artificial intelligence technique in multiple files. *International Journal of Scientific & Technology Research*, 5(04), 111–114.

Sanh, V., Debut, L., Chaumond, J., & Wolf, T. (2020). Distilbert, a distilled version of BERT: Smaller, faster, cheaper and lighter. https://arxiv.org/abs/1910.01108

Sato, T. (1975). *The construction and interpretation of S-P tables*. Meiji Tosho.

Sennrich, R., Haddow, B., & Birch, A. (2016). Improving neural machine translation models with monolingual data. In *Proceedings of the 54th Annual Meeting of the Association for Computational Linguistics (Volume 1: Long Papers)* (pp. 86–96). Association for Computational Linguistics. https://aclanthology.org/P16-1009/

Shu, Z., Henson, R., & Luecht, R. (2013). Using deterministic, gated item response theory model to detect test cheating due to item compromise. *Psychometrika*, 78, 1–17. https://doi. org/10.1007/s11336-012

Sijtsma, K. (1986). A coefficient of deviance of response patterns. *Kwant Method*, 7, 131–145.

Sinharay, S. (2018). A new person-fit statistic for the lognormal model for response times. *Journal of Educational Measurement*, 55, 457–476. Doi: 10.1111/jedm.12188

Sinharay, S., Duong, M. Q., & Wood, S. W. (2017). A new statistic for detection of aberrant answer changes. *Journal of Educational Measurement*, 54, 200–217.

Sinharay, S., & Johnson, M. S. (2017). Three new methods for analysis of answer changes. *Educational and Psychological Measurement*, 77, 54–81.

Skorupski, W., Fitzpatrick, J., & Egan, K. (2016). A Bayesian hierarchical model for detecting aberrant growth at the group level. In G. J. Cizek & J. A. Wollack (Eds.), *Handbook of quantitative methods for detecting cheating on tests* (pp. 232–244). Routledge

Snijders, T. A. B. (2001). Asymptotic null distribution of person fit statistics with estimated person parameter. *Psychometrika*, 66(3), 331–342. https://doi.org/10.1007/BF02294437

Tang, S., Samuel, S., & Li. Z. (2023). Detecting atypical test-taking behaviors with behavior prediction using LSTM. *Psychological Test and Assessment Modeling*, 65(2), 76–124.

Tatsuoka, K. K. (1984). Caution indices based on item response theory. *Psychometrika*, 49, 95–110.

Tiemann, G. C., & Kingston, N. M. (2014). An exploration of answer changing behavior on a computer-based high-stakes achievement test. In N. M. Kingston & A. K. Clark (Eds.), *Test fraud: Statistical detection and methodology* (pp. 158–174). Routledge.

Tiong, L., & Lee, H. (2021). E-cheating prevention measures: Detection of cheating at online examinations using deep learning approach – A case study. *arXiv:2101.09841v1.*

Toton, S., & Maynes, D. (2018). The use of data mining techniques to detect cheating. In H. Jiao, R. Lissitz, & A. Van Wie (Eds.), *Data analytics and psychometrics: Informing assessment practices* (pp. 77–108). Information Age Publishing.

van der Flier, H. (1977). Environmental factors and deviant response patterns. In Y. Poortinga (Ed.), *Basic problems in cross-cultural psychology* (pp. 30–35). Swets and Zeitlinger.

van der Flier, H. (1982). Deviant response patterns and comparability of test scores. *Journal of Cross-Cultural Psychology*, 13(3), 267–298. https://doi.org/10.1177/0022002182013003001

van der Linden, J. W., & Guo, F. (2008). Bayesian procedures for identifying aberrant response-time patterns in adaptive testing. *Psychometrika*, 73(3), 365–384. Retrieved from https://doi.org/10.1007/s11336-007-9046-8

Vaswani, A., Shazeer, N., Parmar, N., Uszkoreit, J., Jones, L., Gomez, A. N., Kaiser, q., & Polosukhin, I. (2017). Attention is all you need. *Advances in Neural Information Processing Systems*, 30, 6000–6010.

Wang, C., Xu, G., Shang, Z., & Kuncel, N. (2018). Detecting aberrant behavior and item preknowledge: A comparison of mixture modeling method and residual method. *Journal of Educational and Behavioral Statistics*, 43, 469–501.

Wang, W. Y., & Yang, D. (2015). That's so annoying!!!: A lexical and frame-semantic embedding based data augmentation approach to automatic categorization of annoying behaviors using #petpeeve tweets. In *Proceedings of the 2015 Conference on Empirical Methods in Natural Language Processing (EMNLP 2015)* (pp. 2557–2563). Association for Computational Linguistics. https://aclanthology.org/D15-1306/

Wei, J., & Zou, K. (2019). EDA: Easy data augmentation techniques for boosting performance on text classification tasks. In *Proceedings of the 2019 Conference on Empirical Methods in Natural Language Processing and the 9th International Joint Conference on Natural Language Processing (EMNLP-IJCNLP)* (pp. 6382–6388). Association for Computational Linguistics. https://aclanthology.org/D19-1670/

Wollack, J. A. (1997). A nominal response model approach for detecting answer copying. *Applied Psychological Measurement*, 21, 307–320.

Wollack, J., & Fremer, J. (eds.). (2013). *Handbook of test security*. Routledge.

Wright, B. D., & Stone, M. H. (1979). *Best test design. Rasch measurement*. Chicago, IL: Mesa Press.

Wu, X., Lv, S., Zang, L., Han, J., Hu, S. (2019). Conditional BERT contextual augmentation. In Rodrigues, J., et al. (Eds.), *Computational Science – ICCS 2019. ICCS 2019. Lecture Notes in Computer Science*, vol. 11539. Springer. https://doi.org/10.1007/978-3-030-22747-0_7

Yan, D., Fauss, M., Hao, J., & Cui, W. (2023). Detection of AI-generated essays in writing assessment. *Psychological Testing and Assessment Modeling*, 65(2), 125–144.

Yu, A. W., Dohan, D., Luong, M. T., Zhao, R., Chen, K., Norouzi, M., & Le, Q. V. (2018). QaNet: Combining local convolution with global self-attention for reading comprehension. In *6th International Conference on Learning Representations* (ICLR 2018 Conference Track Proceedings).

Zhang, X., Zhao, J., & LeCun, Y. (2015). Character-level convolutional networks for text classification. In *Advances in Neural Information Processing Systems (NeurIPS 2015)* (pp. 649–657). Neural Information Processing Systems Foundation.

Zhou, T., & Jiao, H. (2023). Exploration of the stacking ensemble machine learning algorithm for cheating detection in large-scale assessment. Educational and Psychological Measurement, 83(4), 831–854. https://doi.org/10.1177/00131644221117193

Zhou, T., & Jiao, H. (2022). Data augmentation in machine learning for cheating detection in large-scale assessment: An illustration with the blending ensemble learning algorithm. *Psychological Test and Assessment Modeling*, 64(4), 425–444.

Zhu, H., Jiao, H., Gao, W., & Meng, X (2023). Bayesian change point analysis approach to detecting aberrant test-taking behavior using response times. *Journal of Educational and Behavioral Statistics*. 48, 490-520. https://doi.org/10.3102/10769986231151961

Zopluoglu, C. (2016). Similarity, answer copying, and aberrance: understanding the status quo. In G. J. Cizek & J. A. Wollack (Eds.), *Handbook of quantitative methods for detecting cheating on tests* (pp. 25–45). Routledge. https://doi.org/10.4324/9781315743097-2.

Zopluoglu, C. (2019). Detecting examinees with item preknowledge in large-scale testing using extreme gradient boosting (XGBoost). *Educational and Psychological Measurement*, 79, 931–961. https://doi.org/10.1177/0013164419839439

11

INTERNATIONAL WORK IN AI FOR EDUCATIONAL ASSESSMENT

Hongyun Liu, Yongmei Zhang, and Fang Luo

11.1 Introduction

11.1.1 Global Educational Transformation and the Rising Assessment Challenge

Globalization has fundamentally transformed education systems worldwide, reshaping policies, curricula, and access to learning opportunities. This shift has fostered an interconnected knowledge economy where learners and institutions exchange resources across borders, promoting global collaboration and competitiveness. However, while globalization has supported greater educational equity, it has coincided with a rapid digital transformation in education, which generates massive volumes of learning data, opening new opportunities but also intensifying challenges for assessment systems.

One central challenge lies in the scale and heterogeneity of contemporary educational data. The growth of massive open online courses (MOOCs), virtual classrooms, and cross-border programs generates continuous streams of text, interaction logs, and multimedia content that traditional assessment systems cannot process efficiently. As a result, manual and paper-based approaches struggle to deliver timely, consistent, and personalized feedback. At the same time, international curricula and large-scale assessments such as International Baccalaureate (IB) and Programme for International Student Assessment (PISA) intensify demands for standardized yet context-sensitive evaluation, exposing the limited adaptability of existing systems in linguistically and culturally diverse settings (Makuvaza, 2025).

DOI: 10.4324/9781003621522-11

11.1.2 *AI as a Catalyst for Assessment Innovation and Global Learning Reform*

To address these challenges and unlock the full potential of globalized education, artificial intelligence (AI) has emerged as a transformative force capable of reshaping not only assessment practices but also the very architecture of international learning systems. By harnessing advanced computational techniques, AI introduces new possibilities for achieving scalability, precision, and adaptability that traditional assessment methods cannot deliver (Makuvaza, 2025). AI-enabled systems leverage technologies such as natural language processing (NLP), machine learning (ML), deep learning (DL), and neural networks (Ouyang et al., 2023), enabling them to process massive and diverse datasets efficiently. Crucially, AI's role extends beyond assessment application; it is fundamentally concerned with transforming learning. These systems can analyze unstructured data (e.g., open-ended responses, behavioral interaction logs), offer personalized feedback, and dynamically adjust to individual learner needs, thereby closing the feedback loop and making assessment an integral, formative part of the learning process itself. These capabilities position AI as a cornerstone of future assessment practices, enhancing both effectiveness and inclusivity on a global scale.

The practical impact of AI in educational assessment is increasingly evident across a range of applications, including automated scoring, learning analytics and diagnostic tools, predictive modeling for early intervention, and adaptive assessment systems. Together, these approaches enable scalable evaluation, personalized feedback, and timely instructional support across diverse learning contexts (Adnan et al., 2021; Banihashem et al., 2022; Ramesh & Sanampudi, 2022; Raza, 2023). Emerging applications, such as virtual reality (VR)–based and augmented reality (AR)–based assessments, which create simulated or digitally augmented environments, further extend evaluation to complex, authentic skill domains (Tang et al., 2022).

11.1.3 *Catalyzing Global Transformation: From System Implications to Chapter Contribution*

Beyond technical innovation, AI in assessment has far-reaching societal implications by reshaping more equitable, competency-based, and interconnected global learning ecosystems. Traditional assessment systems often privilege well-resourced institutions and regions, whereas scalable and low-cost AI-enabled tools, such as automated scoring and adaptive platforms, expand access to sophisticated evaluation and personalized feedback for learners in marginalized contexts. Importantly, AI-enabled diagnostics and predictive analytics extend beyond identifying learning gaps to supporting adaptive, learner-responsive systems that evolve over time, enabling educators to design individualized learning pathways and shifting support from remediation toward continuous capacity development. At a systemic level, AI facilitates the emergence of transnational learning networks by harmonizing assessment metrics and integrating multilingual, culturally responsive analytics, thereby transforming international collaboration from policy alignment to shared pedagogical innovation and joint knowledge creation.

More fundamentally, AI enables a shift from assessing learning to designing learning through assessment. Evaluation moves from a discrete, summative event to an embedded and adaptive process that dynamically adjusts instructional content, difficulty, and feedback to individual learners (Mousavinasab et al., 2021). Through multimodal and immersive assessment environments, AI-enabled analytics support the measurement of complex competencies such as problem-solving and collaboration, while reducing geographical barriers and enabling cross-border learning interactions (Mouw et al., 2025). Collectively, these developments mark a transition from rigid, standardized testing toward flexible, interoperable, and learner-centered assessment infrastructures.

This chapter aims to provide a global analysis of the transforming landscape of AI in educational assessment. Its objectives are threefold: (1) to present an overview of the current state of AI-enabled assessment, including key technological advancements and real-world applications; (2) to examine how AI is being implemented across different regions, countries, and educational contexts; and (3) to identify emerging practices, key challenges, and future trends. This chapter's distinct contribution lies in its synthesis of diverse international applications of AI in assessment, the distillation of practical lessons from global case studies, and the articulation of forward-looking recommendations. Together, these recommendations offer both implementation considerations and governance guidance to support education systems in harnessing AI ethically and effectively to transform assessment and learning at a global scale.

11.2 Current State and Applications of AI in Educational Assessment

11.2.1 Automated Scoring Systems in Large-Scale Assessments

11.2.1.1 Key Technologies and Methodological Approaches for Automated Scoring Systems

Automated scoring systems have evolved from rule-based similarity measures to advanced AI-enabled frameworks capable of handling complex and multimodal responses. Early methods, such as Levenshtein Distance and Cosine Similarity, focused on textual overlap, while subsequent NLP techniques incorporating word embeddings, part-of-speech tagging, and syntactic parsing enabled more precise semantic evaluation. Recent advances rely heavily on DL, particularly transformer-based models such as bidirectional encoder representations from transformers (BERT), alongside architectures including long short-term memory and capsule networks, to improve scoring accuracy for free-text responses. Beyond text, contemporary systems increasingly support visual and multimodal inputs (such as handwritten text, diagrams, and images) using optical character recognition (OCR), computer-vision metrics, graph-based models, and convolutional neural network-based symbol recognition (Wang et al., 2021). Large language models (LLMs) further extend automated scoring by evaluating coherence, argumentation, and domain-specific language rather than surface features alone, while lightweight transformer variants balance accuracy and computational efficiency in large-scale deployments (Fagbohun et al., 2024; Ormerod et al., 2021). Collectively, these developments enable automated scoring systems to operate reliably at scale, positioning them not merely as technical solutions for grading efficiency but as essential components of large-scale and cross-national assessment infrastructures.

11.2.1.2 Global Applications of Automated Scoring Systems: A Feature-Based Perspective

Across diverse countries and deployment contexts, a feature-based perspective offers a more systematic understanding of automated scoring systems than isolated case descriptions. Key comparative dimensions include multimodal processing and subject adaptability, which determine whether systems can assess text, diagrams, and visual content across domains such as language arts and STEM (Wang et al., 2021); scoring granularity and feedback richness, reflecting a shift from numeric scores toward rubric-based and diagnostic feedback aligned with instructional goals (Fagbohun et al., 2024); and explainability coupled with human-in-the-loop governance, which enhances transparency, trust, and fairness through hybrid scoring workflows (Ormerod et al., 2021). Effective large-scale implementation further depends on balancing scalability with local adaptation, requiring trade-offs among accuracy, cost, and usability while aligning models with local curricula, languages, and pedagogical practices. Taken together, these comparative dimensions reflect not only technical design choices but also differing institutional priorities related to validity, governance, and fairness in large-scale assessment contexts.

11.2.1.3 National Case Studies

The following case studies illustrate how automated scoring systems operationalize within distinct educational and cultural contexts. A comparative summary of the cases is provided in Table 11.1. In the United States, E-rater®, developed by the Educational Testing Service for exams like the GRE® and TOEFL®, represents a benchmark system for balancing governance requirements with scalability in high-stakes assessment (Attali & Burstein, 2006). To perform at a massive scale while adapting to different contexts, E-rater® takes advantage of

TABLE 11.1 Comparative Analysis of Global Automated Scoring System Case Studies

Dimensions	*Case Study 1: E-rater® (United States)*	*Case Study 2: EICTS (China)*
Context and purpose	**High-stakes assessment**: Used for exams like GRE® and TOEFL®; prioritizes governance, scalability, and validity in large-scale settings.	**Intelligent tutoring system**: Designed for Chinese composition instruction; prioritizes instructional feedback and diagnostic granularity.
Key technologies	Utilizes hundreds of NLP-based linguistic features rather than end-to-end DL to ensure operational scalability while maintaining construct explainability.	Integrates custom-trained OCR for handwriting processing and BERT for semantic analysis.
Psychometric strengths and focus	**Validity and human-in-the-loop governance:** 1 Ensures score validity through a hybrid human-machine verification model. 2 Provides actionable feedback on grammar and style (via Criterion®).	**Multimodality and diagnostic granularity:** 1 Processes handwritten inputs (multimodal). 2 Adopts a four-layer assessment framework (language, expression, anomaly, discourse) to generate detailed diagnostic reports.
Limitations and challenges	1 Potential construct under-representation: may disproportionately weigh organizational features compared to human raters. 2 Performance is highly dependent on training data quality.	1 Validity constraint: Effective for basic skills but less reliable for higher order thematic analysis. 2 Trade-off between scalability and local instructional adaptation.

hundreds of linguistic features based on NLP techniques rather than end-to-end DL. While human-AI agreement is consistently high across scoring engines, performance is often modulated by the nature of the training data and specific linguistic features. To maintain validity, the system prioritizes explainability and human-in-the-loop design: both E-rater® and a human rater score every essay. To provide actionable feedback, the system (and the related Criterion® tool) looks at dimensions like grammar and style, offering step-by-step guidance throughout the learning process.

In the Chinese educational context, the Elion Intelligent Composition Tutoring System, developed by East China Normal University and Microsoft Research Asia, illustrates how multimodality and scoring granularity can be prioritized in classroom-oriented writing assessment. To process handwritten submissions from children, the system employs a custom-trained OCR model, while BERT-based methods are used to analyze linguistic features in student writing. The system's strength lies in scoring granularity: it adopts a four-layer assessment framework (language application, expression, anomaly detection, discourse quality) to provide detailed diagnostic reports rather than a single grade (Zheng et al., 2023).

11.2.1.4 Implications and Future Directions

Viewed from a system-level perspective, automated scoring has become integral to the operation and governance of contemporary large-scale assessments, rather than a standalone grading technology. Automated scoring systems have evolved from rule-based methods to multimodal, AI-enabled frameworks that support large-scale assessment and instructional feedback. Recent advances increasingly balance accuracy, scalability, explainability, and feedback granularity, positioning automated scoring as not only an efficiency tool but also a potential support for formative assessment when aligned with pedagogical goals. Nonetheless, challenges remain in assessing higher order reasoning, ensuring fairness, and adapting to local contexts, underscoring the need for continued human oversight, transparent model design, and evaluation beyond average accuracy. Future progress will depend on close collaboration among researchers, educators, and policymakers to develop systems that are both technically robust and pedagogically meaningful.

11.2.2 Learning Analytics and Diagnostic Systems

11.2.2.1 Conceptual Foundations and Technological Framework

Learning analytics and diagnostic systems are central to AI-enabled educational assessment, providing continuous insights into learner behavior, engagement, and performance. Learning analytics focuses on the systematic collection and analysis of learner data to understand and optimize learning processes and environments (Siemens & Long, 2011), while diagnostic systems identify misconceptions, learning gaps, and skill deficiencies to generate actionable feedback for both educators and students. Advances in AI have enhanced these systems' ability to analyze complex, longitudinal, and heterogeneous data, enabling more accurate and context-sensitive evaluation. By tracking learning trajectories, identifying patterns of engagement and risk, and integrating multiple sources of learner evidence, these systems support timely, personalized interventions. Collectively, learning analytics and diagnostic systems transform assessment from retrospective outcome measurement into a continuous, predictive, and learner-centered process that supports development.

11.2.2.2 Global Applications and Platform Implementations

Around the world, various nations and institutions are exploring how AI can enhance the learning analytics systems to enable ongoing, learning-oriented assessment. These AI-enabled tools provide an adaptive framework, deliver continuous feedback, and support data-informed instructional planning. Platforms such as Open Learning Analytics enable cross-platform data integration, allowing educators to track real-time learner progress (Muslim et al., 2020). In the United States, universities like Purdue and Arizona State have implemented platforms such as Course Signals and Civitas Learning to boost student retention and performance. In Australia, Open Universities Australia uses the Personalized Adaptive Study Success system to deliver individualized curriculum planning for struggling students. The Open University in the United Kingdom has demonstrated how pedagogical strategies influence long-term engagement through comparative studies of over 40 learning designs (Hernández-de-Menéndez et al., 2022). These global efforts show how AI can support not only instructional efficiency but also educational equity by identifying learners who may otherwise be overlooked.

11.2.2.3 National Case Studies

A compelling example of a national learning analytics initiative can be found in Estonia, a country widely recognized as a global leader in digital education reform. Supported by strong governmental support and a commitment to equity, Estonia has leveraged its commitment to equitable learning and digital innovation to build one of the world's most advanced education systems. Central to this effort is a nationwide learning analytics platform that integrates data from schools and learning management systems. The platform aggregates information on attendance, assessments, and behavioral indicators to generate real-time insights at national, school, and classroom levels. This AI-enabled analysis facilitates both timely individual interventions and evidence-based systemic policymaking, exemplifying how integrated analytics can enhance personalized learning and governance. Estonia's model exemplifies how integrated analytics infrastructure can enhance both personalized learning and evidence-based policymaking.

11.2.2.4 Implications and Future Directions

In summary, learning analytics and diagnostic systems are transforming educational assessment through real-time, personalized feedback. They advance formative assessment while supporting educational equity and personalization. As seen in countries like Estonia, AI integration in diagnostics is becoming a global reality.

Its effective deployment, however, demands attention to ethics, data privacy, and infrastructure gaps. Moving forward, collaboration among policymakers, educators, and technologists is essential to create scalable, transparent, and culturally responsive systems that serve diverse learners worldwide.

11.2.3 Predictive Modeling for Early Intervention

11.2.3.1 Data, Modeling Approaches, and Rationale for Early Risk Prediction

To support timely intervention and improve academic outcomes, predictive modeling has become a central approach for identifying students at academic risk in digitally mediated learning environments. Contemporary educational systems generate large-scale data that broadly include student profile information (e.g., demographic characteristics and prior academic performance) and behavioral engagement data reflecting learners' interactions with educational platforms (Hung et al., 2017). By analyzing patterns within these data, AI-enabled predictive models can detect early signals of disengagement or learning difficulty and inform targeted, personalized support strategies. A range of ML and DL approaches, complemented by NLP for unstructured textual data, has been applied to early risk prediction (Robinson et al., 2016). The effectiveness of these models depends largely on the characteristics, availability, and granularity of the underlying data, highlighting the importance of aligning modeling choices with specific educational contexts.

11.2.3.2 Global Applications of Predictive Analytics and Early Intervention Systems

Predictive analytics has been widely deployed in education worldwide, enhancing student retention and performance. In Europe, German universities have demonstrated success, with Berens et al. (2019) achieving prediction accuracies of 79%–85% in the first semester and 90%–95% by the fourth semester using ML methods. In North America, Matz et al. (2023) combined socio-demographic data and app engagement metrics to predict attrition more accurately. In Asia, Chung and Lee (2019) developed a dropout early warning system for Korean high school students. In Africa, Masabo et al. (2023) successfully implemented ML techniques for early detection of at-risk students in Rwanda's higher education system. South America has seen success in Uruguay, where Queiroga et al. (2022) launched a nationwide K–12 learning analytics initiative.

11.2.3.3 National Case Studies

Building on the global trend of using predictive analytics to support at-risk students, India has emerged as a notable example of large-scale implementation of

AI-enabled dropout prediction systems. Student dropout rates remain particularly acute in developing countries, with India facing significant challenges across educational levels. The average annual dropout rate for secondary schools in India was over 12% in 2022, while primary education showed lower but still concerning dropout patterns (Mehta, 2023). The state of Andhra Pradesh emerged as a pioneering example. In December 2015, the Andhra Pradesh Government partnered with Microsoft to develop an AI-powered dropout prediction system using the Azure Machine Learning platform. By leveraging the power of ML and analytics, a Microsoft app is able to predict the chances of a student dropping out, based on patterns identified from complex datasets. In 2018–2019, the platform identified 19,500 probable dropouts in the Vishakhapatnam district alone, with key factors including insufficient furniture and inadequate toilet infrastructure.

11.2.3.4 Implications and Future Directions

Predictive modeling has become a key component of early intervention in contemporary education, enabling the identification of at-risk students and the provision of timely, personalized support at scale. By integrating student profiles, fine-grained behavioral data, and advanced ML techniques, these systems show strong potential to improve retention, academic success, and educational equity. However, challenges related to data quality, model interpretability, and potential bias persist, and predictive accuracy alone is insufficient without adequate institutional capacity, teacher engagement, and ethical governance. Future efforts should therefore prioritize transparent, context-sensitive, and ethically grounded predictive systems developed through close collaboration among educators, policymakers, and technologists.

11.2.4 Adaptive and Personalized Assessment Technologies

11.2.4.1 Conceptual Foundations and Key Technologies for Adaptive and Personalized Assessment

AI-enabled adaptive and personalized assessment represents a shift from static testing toward more flexible and learner-centered evaluation, aiming to improve both measurement precision and assessment efficiency. These developments are grounded in advances in psychometric theory, particularly item response theory (IRT), whose parameter invariance enables dynamic item selection across test forms and time points (Chang, 2015). Building on IRT, computerized adaptive testing personalizes item selection based on test-taker responses, improving accuracy, reducing test length, and enhancing engagement, with demonstrated benefits in inclusive and special education. Extensions such as time-sensitive IRT models further refine ability estimation by incorporating response-time information (Ince & Özbay, 2025).

Beyond unidimensional ability estimation, multidimensional IRT and diagnostic classification models support finer grained assessment of complex skills and provide diagnostic feedback on mastery and misconceptions (Templin & Bradshaw, 2014). Multistage adaptive testing (multistage tailored testing, MST) balances adaptability with test control and security and has been adopted in large-scale assessments such as the Duolingo English Test (Duolingo, 2025). More broadly, Computational Psychometrics integrates psychometric modeling with AI and data science to analyze process data (e.g., keystrokes and response patterns) and support functions such as remote proctoring (von Davier & Halpin, 2022; Martínez-Comesaña et al., 2023). Complementing this approach, Learning Analytics and Automated Item Generation further extend adaptive assessment by enabling behavior prediction, personalized learning support, and scalable item bank development.

11.2.4.2 Overview of AI Tools for Adaptive and Personalized Learning Experiences

Advances in learning analytics, NLP, and automated assessment have enabled the translation of AI techniques into practical tools that support adaptive and personalized learning. Among these, intelligent tutoring systems (ITSs) are one of the most established approaches, designed to emulate core tutoring functions by analyzing learner data to deliver individualized instruction and feedback. Typically structured around domain, student, and tutoring models, ITSs adapt learning at both task-selection and step-by-step levels. Recent progress in conversational AI and NLP has further enhanced their responsiveness, with growing evidence that ITS can also support the development of metacognitive skills such as self-explanation. Beyond tutoring, adaptive learning platforms extend personalization across broader instructional contexts by using ML to analyze learner profiles, behaviors, and performance data to recommend tailored content, pathways, and feedback. Automated assessment and feedback systems play a complementary role by enabling timely, data-driven formative assessment, supporting instructional decision-making during learning (Khlaif et al., 2025).

11.2.4.3 National Case Studies

One illustrative example is Singapore's Student Learning Space (SLS), an AI-enabled national online learning platform developed by the Ministry of Education to promote personalized and inclusive learning experiences. Supported by AI tools, the SLS platform increases student engagement with content, ensures inclusivity and accessibility, improves assessment analytics, and boosts productivity. Widely adopted by schools across Singapore, the platform has significantly transformed traditional classroom practices. A key component is the adaptive learning system (ALS), which customizes learning paths and provides instant feedback based on student readiness. Since 2023, the ministry has introduced five AI-enabled tools, including three "learning feedback assistants" for math, English, and short-answer responses; the ALS; and an "Authoring Copilot" that supports teachers to plan lessons (Ministry of Education Singapore, 2025). Together, these tools offer students personalized feedback and corrections, while also enabling teachers to plan lessons more effectively and efficiently.

Another complementary example can be found in Australia's implementation of adaptive testing within National Assessment Program – Literacy and Numeracy (NAPLAN), a nationwide assessment administered annually to students in Years 3, 5, 7, and 9 that occurs annually. To improve accuracy, NAPLAN moved from a paper-based test to an online MST testing design. This system adjusts question difficulty based on each student's performance. A student's final score is determined by both the number and the difficulty of the questions that were answered correctly. This adaptive approach enhances measurement precision without lengthening the test and also helps students to stay engaged. Some key challenges have been matching results from the new adaptive tests with historical data and ensuring accessibility for students with disabilities. To address these issues, NAPLAN updated its measurement scales and proficiency standards in 2023. A comparative summary of the two cases is provided in Table 11.2.

11.2.4.4 Implications and Future Directions

In summary, adaptive and personalized assessment technologies are transforming learning measurement through dynamic, responsive evaluations. Advances in psychometrics, AI analytics, and national implementations are shifting assessment from static testing to continuous instructional support. By combining adaptive testing, automated feedback, and learning analytics, these systems enhance precision, engagement, and instructional relevance. Key challenges include ensuring fairness, transparency, and accessibility across diverse learners, and balancing personalization with standardization in high-stakes settings. Future work should prioritize interpretable models, ethical governance, and teacher-AI collaboration to ensure these systems are pedagogically meaningful and socially responsible.

11.2.5 Immersive and Experiential Assessment Using VR/AR

11.2.5.1 VR and AR Technologies as Foundations for Immersive Educational Assessment

To transform education through immersive learning experiences, VR and AR are emerging technologies that go beyond traditional methods. VR creates fully digital environments that immerse users through headsets or specialized devices, replacing the physical world with a virtual one (Verner et al., 2022). In contrast, AR enhances the real world by overlaying digital information onto users' views using

TABLE 11.2 Comparative Analysis of Adaptive Assessment Case Studies

Dimensions	*Case Study 1: Student Learning Space (Singapore)*	*Case Study 2: NAPLAN (Australia)*
Context and purpose	**National personalized learning platform**: Used for daily instruction and formative assessment; prioritizes student engagement and teacher support.	**High-stakes national assessment**: Used for annual literacy and numeracy testing (Years 3, 5, 7, 9); prioritizes measurement precision and accuracy at scale.
Key technologies	**Utilizes adaptive learning system (ALS)** and AI-enabled "feedback assistants" (for math, English, and short answers) to customize learning paths.	**Utilizes multistage tailored testing (MST)** to adjust question difficulty based on student performance.
Psychometric strengths and focus	**Feedback and customization:** 1. Provides instant, targeted hints to students (formative). 2. Supports teachers with AI "Copilot" for lesson creation. 3. Enhances inclusivity and accessibility.	**Precision and engagement:** 1. Enhances measurement precision without increasing test length. 2. Maintains student engagement by matching difficulty to ability. 3. Scoring considers item difficulty.
Challenges addressed	**Productivity and efficiency**: Boosts teacher productivity in lesson planning and provides scalable feedback across subjects.	**Continuity and standards**: Updated measurement scales in 2023 to address challenges in linking historical data and ensuring accessibility.

glasses, lenses, or mobile apps. Both VR and AR enable interactive learning with complex materials, fostering enriched experiences. These technologies depend on advanced hardware like head-mounted displays (HMDs), motion sensors, and spatial computing platforms, to create engaging simulations. Additionally, VR and AR are also enhancing educational assessments by improving accuracy, engagement, and interactivity, allowing educators to design personalized, dynamic assessments that cater to individual learning styles, which is difficult to achieve with traditional methods. In a broader context, the integration of VR/AR as educational tools holds immense potential, especially with the recent availability of functional generative AI, which further enhances their capabilities.

11.2.5.2 Measurement Advantages of VR/AR-Based Immersive Assessment

VR/AR-based assessments have emerged as transformative instruments for evaluating practical competencies across multidisciplinary domains, offering significant advantages over traditional assessment methods. These immersive technologies offer distinctive advantages for assessment applications. VR enhances measurement precision through accurate recording of behavioral metrics such as response times and movement patterns. At the same time, AR augments traditional assessment contexts by overlaying digital information onto real-world environments, enabling more naturalistic skill evaluation while maintaining environmental authenticity. Both technologies demonstrate enhanced participant engagement and reduced test anxiety through immersive, interactive experiences that mitigate the artificial constraints inherent in paper-based or laboratory assessments. Furthermore, VR's capacity to replicate high-fidelity, standardized scenarios and AR's ability to contextualize assessments within authentic settings collectively enhance ecological validity, thereby improving the generalizability and predictive validity of assessment outcomes across diverse real-world applications.

11.2.5.3 Applied Case Studies of VR/AR Assessment Systems

As VR and AR technologies mature, they are increasingly applied across teaching, skills training, and assessment. For example, Wang et al. (2024) developed a VR-based assessment framework for medical skills using simulated appendectomy procedures. Guided by the Substitution-Augmentation-Modification-Redefinition model, the system integrated competency evaluation, assessment tasks, performance data, and feedback within an immersive virtual operating room. Students performed surgical procedures using HMDs, while the system automatically captured behavioral indicators such as operation time, spatial accuracy, and prompt usage to provide both formative and summative feedback. The results indicated high assessment fidelity, comprehensive coverage of learning outcomes, and strong student acceptance of VR-based evaluation.

Similarly, Dinc et al. (2021) proposed an AR-driven assessment framework for chemistry education through the ARChem virtual laboratory. The platform combined AR experiments with embedded quiz-based assessments to evaluate students' theoretical understanding and practical skills. Automatic scoring, immediate feedback, and gamified modes enabled multi-level proficiency assessment while enhancing engagement. This AR-based approach supported dynamic, interactive, and personalized assessment across different levels of learner competence.

11.2.5.4 Implications and Future Directions

Overall, VR- and AR-based immersive assessments signal a shift toward more authentic and skill-oriented educational measurement by enabling context-rich tasks, fine-grained behavioral capture, and closer alignment between learning objectives and evaluation. Empirical evidence suggests that these environments can improve ecological validity and learner engagement, particularly for assessing complex, real-world competencies. Nevertheless, large-scale adoption remains constrained by infrastructure demands, cost, accessibility, and the need for robust validation across diverse contexts. Future progress will depend on integrating immersive technologies with AI-enabled analytics and adaptive feedback, alongside the development of rigorous validity frameworks and ethical, inclusive implementation strategies to support their sustainable use in mainstream educational systems.

11.3 Emerging Trends and Future Directions

11.3.1 Integration of Multimodal AI for Holistic Evaluation

11.3.1.1 From Traditional Classroom Evaluation to Multimodal AI-Enabled Assessment

Traditional classroom evaluation has relied primarily on teachers' observations of students' behaviors, emotions, and task completion, which limits assessment to observable outcomes and a single evaluative perspective. Such approaches often overlook learning processes, introduce subjective bias, and suffer from weak coherence among evaluative criteria, thereby constraining validity and reliability. In response, advances in AI and educational technology have driven a shift toward smart classroom environments and multimodal, AI-enabled assessment. By integrating multimodal data with pedagogical frameworks, these approaches overcome the unidimensional nature of traditional evaluation, enabling a more holistic and process-oriented understanding of learning dynamics and supporting more targeted instructional decision-making.

11.3.1.2 Multimodal Learning Analytics: Frameworks and Data Sources

Multimodal learning analytics enhances the understanding of learning processes by integrating heterogeneous data streams that are difficult to interpret in isolation. At its core, this approach relies on multimodal data fusion, defined as the computational integration of multiple sensory inputs, such as linguistic, visual, behavioral, and physiological signals, to construct a high-fidelity representation of learners' cognitive, affective, and behavioral states. By capturing the interactions among these dimensions, multimodal fusion frameworks achieve stronger predictive validity than unimodal analyses. In classroom-based learning evaluation, multimodal data typically include four categories: (1) behavioral data, such as gestures and body movements extracted through computer-vision techniques like skeletal keypoint recognition using OpenPose (Zhao & Liang, 2023); (2) affective data derived from facial expressions (Yang et al., 2011) and speech features, including speech rate and intonation (Grawemeyer et al., 2017); (3) cognitive and physiological data, such as eye-tracking indicators of attention distribution (Hutt et al., 2019), heart rate variability (Giannakos et al., 2019), and electrodermal activity (Pijeira-Díaz et al., 2018); and (4) interaction data, including response accuracy and participation patterns in classroom activities (Zhao & Liang, 2023). Together, these multimodal data sources, when integrated through appropriate fusion techniques, enable a more holistic and process-oriented evaluation of learning than traditional outcome-based approaches.

11.3.1.3 Challenges, Ethical Considerations, and Future Directions

While multimodal assessment offers significant potential, its implementation is tempered by several critical challenges. Data privacy remains a primary concern, as collecting sensitive information such as facial and physiological data must comply with ethical norms. Furthermore, the interpretability of algorithms is essential, as the decision logic of complex fusion models needs transparency to facilitate teachers' understanding of evaluation results (Lee et al., 2025). Finally, achieving technical adaptability requires a balance between the feasibility of technological applications and the effectiveness of multimodal tasks in learning assessment. Future efforts should focus on optimizing lightweight models to promote the widespread adoption of multimodal assessment across educational scenarios, truly realizing a closed loop of "assessment as learning".

11.3.2 Blockchain Integration for Secure Data Management

11.3.2.1 Rationale and Technological Foundations

As digital transformation accelerates in the educational assessment, the need for secure, tamper-proof, and verifiable management of assessment data and credentials has become critical. Traditional data systems often fall short in addressing issues such as credential fraud, data interoperability, and student privacy. To address these issues, blockchain technology has emerged as a promising solution, offering a decentralized, transparent, and immutable ledger system that can enhance the integrity and reliability of educational data management.

One of the core strengths of blockchain lies in its decentralized architecture, which eliminates the need for a central authority to manage and verify data. This structure distributes identical copies of a ledger across a network of nodes, ensuring that no single party can unilaterally alter information without consensus. Such decentralization significantly reduces the risk of data tampering, unauthorized access, or single points of failure that plague centralized systems (Nakamoto, 2009). In addition, blockchain uses cryptographic hash functions to secure data blocks. Each block contains a hash of the previous block, creating an immutable and traceable chain of information. Even a small change in data will alter the hash, immediately signaling tampering attempts. Smart contracts, which are self-executing code stored on blockchain, add another layer of security and automation. These contracts can enforce access controls, automate credential issuance, and ensure that data transactions follow predefined rules, without human intervention or bias. Collectively, these technical features make blockchain particularly well-suited for storing and verifying assessment records, academic achievements, and digital credentials.

11.3.2.2 Core Applications and Value Proposition

Blockchain offers a robust foundation for rethinking how educational assessment data is verified, shared, and protected. One of its key strengths lies in enabling automatic and trustworthy verification of credentials and transcripts, which is particularly beneficial for international students and cross-border academic recognition (Ocheja et al., 2022). By design, blockchain ensures data immutability, making it highly effective in preventing diploma fraud and reinforcing trust across educational institutions. This reliability also supports the long-term tracking of individualized learning trajectories, providing a secure historical record that can inform personalized educational planning (Bhaskar et al., 2020). At the same time, blockchain's support for self-sovereign identity frameworks allows learners to share their data across platforms while maintaining privacy and ownership. For educators and policymakers, blockchain offers increased confidence in the authenticity and portability of assessment outcomes (El Koshiry et al., 2023), which is especially relevant in the context of globalized education systems and online learning environments. Together, these capabilities make blockchain a promising enabler of transparent, secure, and learner-centered assessment ecosystems in the digital age.

11.3.2.3 Implications and Future Directions

In summary, the integration of blockchain technology in educational assessment marks a significant step toward secure, transparent, and globally interoperable data management. While persistent challenges exist in technical scalability, institutional adoption, and regulatory alignment, the increasing number of pilot programs and government-supported initiatives indicates a promising development trajectory. As trust, privacy, and verifiability become paramount in digital education, blockchain stands as a key enabler of secure and learner-centric innovation.

11.3.3 Personalization and Lifelong Learning Assessment

11.3.3.1 AI-Enabled Personalization across the Lifelong Learning Continuum

Building on the applications discussed in Section 11.2.4, emerging trends point toward even greater personalization in lifelong learning. AI plays a central role by analyzing large amounts of data to tailor content and learning pace for continuous skill development (Bayly-Castañeda et al., 2024). A defining trend in lifelong learning assessment is the increasing use of AI to support highly personalized learning pathways, in which content delivery, learning pace, and assessment are dynamically adapted to individual learner profiles. To deliver increasingly sophisticated educational experiences, future AI-enabled systems will analyze learner profiles to recommend highly relevant content. In addition to adaptive learning, AI will provide real-time feedback, automated assessment, and personalized career guidance. Generative AI tools, such as chatbots, will offer tailored guidance based on individual progress. Personalization will be further enhanced through emerging technologies, including VR and AR, affective computing, AI-enabled content curation, and intelligent "learning agents". Taken together, these developments indicate a shift in assessment from stage-bound evaluations tied to formal schooling toward continuous, personalized mechanisms that accompany learners across the lifelong learning continuum.

11.3.3.2 Credentialing, Workforce Alignment, and Data Governance

As AI-enabled personalization expands across lifelong learning, assessment systems are increasingly shaped by data governance, credential recognition, and workforce alignment, extending beyond instructional design alone. A core requirement for scalable lifelong learning assessment is learner-centric data governance, which emphasizes individual control, transparency, and secure data portability across educational and employment contexts. Finland's MyData initiative exemplifies this approach by enabling individual data control and seamless data flows to support personalized services. In parallel, assessment practices are shifting toward granular competency recognition through microcredentials and digital badges, which allow continuous, verifiable documentation of skills across learning and career trajectories. Such mechanisms support dynamic skill profiles that can be updated and recognized across institutions and labor markets, as illustrated by initiatives such as digital open badges and AI Skills Passport programs. In this context, assessment functions not merely as an instructional mechanism but as a connective interface linking education systems, labor markets, and governance frameworks through shared data, credentials, and competency representations.

Beyond formal education, AI-enabled assessment increasingly supports workforce upskilling and reskilling by aligning individual competencies with evolving labor market demands. Governments and organizations employ AI-based skills tracking and training initiatives to address labor shortages and cultivate future-ready talent (Calonge et al., 2026), with national strategies such as the UAE's National AI Strategy 2031 demonstrating systemic integration of assessment, credentialing, and workforce development. As AI becomes more prevalent in education and assessment, ethical governance has become central, with growing emphasis on transparency, accountability, and ensuring that AI augments rather than replaces human judgment. Developing AI literacy, combining technical competence with ethical awareness and social responsibility, has been highlighted as a priority by

UNESCO (2025) and the World Economic Forum (2025). At the regulatory level, policies such as the EU AI Act (European Parliament and Council of the European Union, 2024) and national guidelines increasingly prioritize data protection, safety, and misuse prevention. In light of generative AI-related academic integrity concerns, assessments are shifting toward open-ended, process-oriented formats that prioritize critical thinking and reasoning (Khlaif et al., 2025).

11.3.3.3 Challenges and Future Directions

Despite the potential of AI-enabled personalization in lifelong learning assessment, its widespread implementation presents significant ethical and practical issues. Key challenges involve algorithmic bias, fairness, and transparency in automated decisions, especially when outcomes influence educational or career pathways. Extensive data collection further heightens privacy and accountability risks, necessitating strong governance frameworks and meaningful learner agency. Enhancing AI literacy is also vital for critical interpretation of feedback and preserving human oversight. Future efforts should prioritize process-oriented, authentic assessments that foster critical thinking, while fostering collaboration across stakeholders to develop transparent, inclusive, and trustworthy systems. Addressing these concerns is central to building equitable, human-centered assessment frameworks that effectively support lifelong learning at scale.

11.3.4 Cross-national Standards and Global Challenges

11.3.4.1 International Large-Scale Assessments and AI-Related Standard Development

To reflect the growing significance of AI in education, international organizations such as United Nations Educational, Scientific and Cultural Organization (UNESCO) and the Organisation for Economic Co-operation and Development (OECD) have begun integrating AI into their educational assessment agendas. For the OECD, PISA 2029 will introduce a new assessment area, "Media and Artificial Intelligence Literacy". This test will simulate environments where students interact with AI through platforms like the Internet, social media, and generative AI tools, assessing their digital and AI literacy (OECD, n.d.). Developed jointly by the European Union and the OECD, with support from Code.org and experts, this framework underscores AI's growing importance in large-scale educational evaluations. As a result, corresponding standards are evolving over time to keep pace with technological advancements and changing educational needs.

Additionally, the International Association for the Evaluation of Educational Achievement (IEA), a major international assessment organization, has released the new technical standards for 2025 (IEA, 2025). This is a comprehensive revision since 1999, highlighting significant changes in the field of international assessment. Key updates include computer-based assessments with elements like process data collection, AI scoring integration, and adaptive designs. In particular, detailed standards have been established for AI-based automated scoring. Only by fully establishing operational standards for the program can the reliability and high efficiency of AI be guaranteed, enabling it to better assist manual scoring.

11.3.4.2 Fragmented Global Landscape and the Move toward Cross-National Alignment

Although there is no global AI-enabled education assessment standard like PISA, which is led by a single organization, multiple international organizations and standardization institutions are actively exploring and formulating relevant guidelines. We can see that from policy guidance and cross-border multilateral cooperation to technical guidelines, all are laying the foundation for AI-enabled educational assessment. In the future, as pilot experience and high-quality cases continue to accumulate and international consensus deepens, we are expected to see more systematic and universal cross-national assessment standards and practical plans.

11.3.4.3 Cognitive Risks of AI Use in Assessment and Capability-Oriented Responses

The impact of AI on educational assessment is inherently mixed, requiring vigilance toward its cognitive risks, particularly false content and algorithmic bias. LLMs are prone to hallucinations, generating outputs that deviate from established knowledge or fabricate facts, which may mislead users in the absence of effective evaluation mechanisms (Maleki et al., 2024). In addition, AI systems can reproduce or amplify human-like biases related to race and gender, potentially exacerbating inequality. Evidence suggests that interaction with biased algorithms may even intensify human biases in perception, emotion, and social judgment, effects not observed in human-to-human interactions (Glickman & Sharot, 2025). Moreover, recent findings indicate that LLMs may exhibit "self-preference", favoring AI-generated product descriptions and thereby demonstrating a form of anti-human bias (Laurito et al., 2025). If left unregulated, these cognitive deficiencies may lead to broader cultural and ethical harms.

11.3.4.4 Summary and Future Directions

Overall, AI is gradually being incorporated into international educational assessment through large-scale initiatives, evolving technical standards, and emerging policy guidance. While organizations such as the OECD and IEA are actively advancing AI-related assessment frameworks, global practices remain uneven and fragmented, reflecting differences in regulatory environments, technical capacity, and educational priorities. At the same time, concerns related to algorithmic bias, hallucination, and cognitive influence underscore the importance of treating AI not only as a technical tool but also as a socio-educational actor. Moving forward, continued efforts toward cross-national coordination, clearer operational standards, and capability-oriented AI education will be essential to support the responsible and effective integration of AI into global assessment systems.

11.4 Conclusion and Recommendations

As discussed in this chapter, AI-enabled educational assessment is reshaping how learning is evaluated and supported in response to pressing global challenges such as equity, skills development, and cross-national comparability. In an increasingly globalized educational environment, the capacity to assess learning outcomes across diverse contexts is no longer optional; it is a prerequisite for informed policy and effective practice. Building on the cases and analyses presented, collaboration, customization, and controversy emerge as central to understanding the international trajectory of this transformation.

Collaboration underpins the scalable use of AI assessment, as illustrated by international MOOCs and cross-border platforms that integrate large, diverse learner datasets for benchmarking, research, and capacity building. Customization reflects AI's capacity to support learner-centered and context-sensitive assessment, enabling alignment with local curricula, languages, and individual learner profiles through adaptive and diagnostic systems. At the same time, controversy remains integral to this transformation, as unresolved issues related to data privacy, security, ethical governance, and uneven infrastructure continue to constrain large-scale and interoperable deployment. While technologies such as blockchain offer promising support for secure credentialing, global standards and shared ethical frameworks remain uneven and slow to emerge.

Looking forward, the convergence of multimodal AI, blockchain-secured credentialing, and internationally recognized evaluation protocols offers a pathway toward greater interoperability, transparency, and trust. Realizing this potential will require sustained collaboration, sensitivity to local contexts, and a balanced approach to innovation and ethics, ensuring that AI-enabled assessment advances both excellence and equity worldwide. As AI becomes deeply integrated into educational assessment, actionable recommendations are proposed for key stakeholders:

For Educators and Teacher Trainers:

Develop Critical AI Assessment Literacy: Critically evaluate the design, limitations, and potential biases of AI-enabled assessment tools, and integrate algorithmic fairness into digital pedagogy.

Champion the Human-in-the-Loop Model: Use AI-generated diagnostics and feedback to inform, rather than replace, professional judgment and personalized student support.

For Educational Administrators and Institutional Leaders:

Implement Tiered Piloting and Ethical Audits: Adopt phased AI deployment with systematic impact, bias audits, and clear institutional policies for data governance and accountability.

Invest in Infrastructure and Capacity Building: Support equitable AI integration through sustained investment in digital infrastructure and staff development focused on ethical data use.

For Psychometricians and Assessment Experts:

Pioneer Validity Frameworks for AI: Develop and validate psychometric standards for AI-enabled assessments that address fairness, explainability, and cross-context generalizability.

Foster Open Science and Benchmarking: Promote open, privacy-preserving benchmarks to enable transparent and cross-cultural evaluation of AI assessment systems.

For Policymakers and International Organizations:

Establish Agile, Principle-Based Governance: Advance flexible international guidelines for ethical AI assessment that safeguard data sovereignty, equity, and cross-border recognition.

Catalyze Equitable Innovation Ecosystems: Fund open, modular, and low-cost AI assessment infrastructures to support under-resourced systems and reduce global assessment disparities.

Through such coordinated, role-specific actions grounded in ethical commitment and collaborative spirit, the global education community can steer the development of AI-enabled assessment. The ultimate goal is to harness this transformative power not merely for measurement efficiency, but to foster a more authentic, equitable, and human-centric future for learning worldwide.

Acronym Glossary

AI	artificial intelligence
ALS	adaptive learning system
AR	augmented reality
BERT	bidirectional encoder representations from transformers
DL	deep learning
EICTS	Elion Intelligent Composition Tutoring System
HMDs	head-mounted displays
IEA	International Association for the Evaluation of Educational Achievement
IRT	item response theory
ITS	intelligent tutoring systems
LLMs	large language models
ML	machine learning
MOOCs	massive open online courses
MST	multistage tailored

NAPLAN	National Assessment Program – Literacy and Numeracy
NLP	natural language processing
OCR	optical character recognition
OECD	Organisation for Economic Co-operation and Development
PISA	Programme for International Student Assessment
SLS	Student Learning Space
VR	virtual reality

References

Adnan, M., Habib, A., Ashraf, J., Mussadiq, S., Raza, A.A., Abid, M., Bashir, M., & Khan, S.U. (2021). Predicting at-risk students at different percentages of course length for early intervention using machine learning models. *IEEE Access, 9,* 7519–7539. https://doi.org/10.1109/ACCESS.2021.3049446

Attali, Y., & Burstein, J. (2006). Automated essay scoring with e-rater® V.2. *Journal of Technology, Learning, and Assessment, 4*(3), 1–32.

Banihashem, S. K., Noroozi, O., van Ginkel, S., Macfadyen, L. P., & Biemans, H. J. A. (2022). A systematic review of the role of learning analytics in enhancing feedback practices in higher education. *Educational Research Review, 37*, 100489. https://doi.org/10.1016/j.edurev.2022.100489

Bayly-Castañeda, K., Ramírez-Montoya, M.-S., & Morita-Alexander, A. (2024). Crafting personalized learning paths with AI for lifelong learning: A systematic literature review. *Frontiers in Education, 9*, 1424386. https://doi.org/10.3389/feduc.2024.1424386

Berens, J., Schneider, K., Gortz, S., Oster, S., & Burghoff, J. (2019). Early detection of students at risk–predicting student dropouts using administrative student data from german universities and machine learning methods. *Journal of Educational Data Mining, 11*(3), 1–41.

Bhaskar, P., Chandan, K., & Joshi, A. (2020). Blockchain in education management: Present and future applications. *Interactive Technology and Smart Education, 18*(1), 1–17. https://doi.org/10.1108/ITSE-07-2020-0102

Calonge, D. S., Kamalov, F., Aguerrebere, P. M., Hassock, L., Smail, L., Yousef, D., Thadani, D. R., Kwong, T., & Abdulla, N. (2026). Upskilling and reskilling in the United Arab Emirates: Future-proofing careers with AI skills. *Journal of Adult and Continuing Education, 32*(1), 98–126. https://doi.org/10.1177/14779714251315288

Chang, H.-H. (2015). Psychometrics behind computerized adaptive testing. *Psychometrika, 80*(1), 1–20. https://doi.org/10.1007/s11336-014-9401-5

Chung, J. Y., & Lee, S. (2019). Dropout early warning systems for high school students using machine learning. *Children and Youth Services Review, 96*, 346–353.

Dinc, F., De, A., Goins, A., Halic, T., Massey, M., & Yarberry, F. (2021). ARChem: Augmented reality based chemistry LAB simulation for teaching and assessment. In *2021 19th International Conference on Information Technology Based Higher Education and Training (ITHET)* (pp. 1–7). https://doi.org/10.1109/ITHET50392.2021.9759587

Duolingo. (2025). *Duolingo English Test: Technical Manual. Duolingo Research Report.* Duolingo. https://englishtest.duolingo.com/research

El Koshiry, A., Eliwa, E., Abd El-Hafeez, T., & Shams, M. Y. (2023). Unlocking the power of blockchain in education: An overview of innovations and outcomes. *Blockchain: Research and Applications, 4*(4), 100165. https://doi.org/10.1016/j.bcra.2023.100165

European Parliament and Council of the European Union. (2024). *Regulation (EU) 2024/1689 of the European Parliament and of the Council of 13 June 2024 Laying Down Harmonised Rules on Artificial Intelligence (Artificial Intelligence Act) and Amending Certain Union Legislative Acts. Official Journal of the European Union*, L, 2024/1689. https://data.europa.eu/eli/reg/2024/1689/oj

Fagbohun, O., Iduwe, N. P., Abdullahi, M., Ifaturoti, A., & Nwanna, O. M. (2024). Beyond traditional assessment: Exploring the impact of large language models on grading practices. *Journal of Artificial Intelligence, Machine Learning and Data Science, 2*(1), 1–8.

Giannakos, M. N., Sharma, K., Pappas, I. O., Kostakos, V., & Velloso, E. (2019). Multimodal data as a means to understand the learning experience. *International Journal of Information Management, 48*, 108–119.

Glickman, M., & Sharot, T. (2025). How human–AI feedback loops alter human perceptual, emotional and social judgements. *Nature Human Behaviour, 9*(2), 345–359. https://doi.org/10.1038/s41562-024-02077-2

Grawemeyer, B., Mavrikis, M., Holmes, W., Gutiérrez-Santos, S., Wiedmann, M., & Rummel, N. (2017). Affective learning: Improving engagement and enhancing learning with affect-aware feedback. *User Modeling and User-Adapted Interaction, 27*(1), 119–158.

Hernández-de-Menéndez, M., Morales-Menendez, R., Escobar, C. A., & Ramírez Mendoza, R. A. (2022). Learning analytics: State of the art. *International Journal on Interactive Design and Manufacturing, 16*(3), 1209–1230. https://doi.org/10.1007/s12008-022-00930-0

Hung, J.-L., Wang, M. C., Wang, S., Abdelrasoul, M., Li, Y., & He, W. (2017). Identifying at-risk students for early interventions—A time-series clustering approach. *IEEE Transactions on Emerging Topics in Computing, 5*(1), 45–55. https://doi.org/10.1109/TETC.2015.2504239

Hutt, S., Krasich, K., Mills, C., Bosch, N., White, S., Brockmole, J. R., & D'Mello, S. K. (2019). Automated gaze-based mind wandering detection during computerized learning in classrooms. *User Modeling and User-Adapted Interaction, 29*(4), 821–867. https://doi.org/10.1007/s11257-019-09228-5

IEA. (2025). *IEA's technical standards for international large-scale assessment.* International Association for the Evaluation of Educational Achievement.

Ince, N. Ç., & Özbay, E. (2025). Enhancing ability estimation with time-sensitive IRT models in computerized adaptive testing. *Applied Sciences, 15*(13), 6999. https://doi.org/10.3390/app15136999

Khlaif, Z. N., Alkouk, W. A., Salama, N., & Abu Eideh, B. (2025). Redesigning assessments for AI-enhanced learning: A framework for educators in the generative AI era. *Education Sciences, 15*(2), 174.

Laurito, W., Davis, B., Grietzer, P., Gavenčiak, T., Böhm, A., & Kulveit, J. (2025). AI–AI bias: Large language models favor communications generated by large language models. *Proceedings of the National Academy of Sciences, 122*(31), Article e2415697122. https://doi.org/10.1073/pnas.2415697122

Lee, G., Shi, L., Latif, E., Gao, Y., Bewersdorff, A., Nyaaba, M., … & Zhai, X. (2025). Multimodality of ai for education: Towards artificial general intelligence. *IEEE Transactions on Learning Technologies, 18*, 666–683. https://doi.org/10.1109/TLT.2025.3574466

Makuvaza, S. (2025). The implications of ignoring the cultural and linguistic needs of children with disabilities during psychological assessment: A critical analysis. *International Journal of Educational Development in Africa, 9*, 1–15. https://doi.org/10.25159/2312-3540/15710

Maleki, N., Padmanabhan, B., & Dutta, K. (2024). AI hallucinations: a misnomer worth clarifying. In *2024 IEEE Conference on Artificial Intelligence (CAI)* (pp. 133–138). IEEE. https://doi.org/10.1109/CAI59869.2024.00033

Martínez-Comesaña, M., Rigueira-Díaz, X., Larrañaga-Janeiro, A., Martínez-Torres, J., Ocarranza-Prado, I., & Kreibel, D. (2023). Impact of artificial intelligence on assessment methods in primary and secondary education: Systematic literature review. *Revista de Psicodidáctica, 28*, 93–103.

Masabo, E., Nzabanita, J., Ngaruye, I., Ruranga, C., Nizeyimana, J. P., Uwonkunda, J., & Ndanguza, D. (2023). Early detection of students at risk of poor performance in Rwanda higher education using machine learning techniques. *International Journal of Information Technology, 15*(6), 3201–3210.

Matz, S. C., Bukow, C. S., Peters, H., Deacons, C., Dinu, A., & Stachl, C. (2023). Using machine learning to predict student retention from socio-demographic characteristics and app-based engagement metrics. *Scientific Reports, 13*(1), 5705.

Mehta, A. (2023). A study of the status & public financing of elementary education in India: With special reference to Jharkhand state. *Vinoba Bhave Journal of Economics, 9*(1), 129–137.

Ministry of Education Singapore. (2025). *Artificial intelligence in education: EdTech Masterplan 2030*. Ministry of Education Singapore. https://www.moe.gov.sg/education-in-sg/educational-technology-journey/edtech-masterplan/artificial-intelligence-in-education

Mousavinasab, E., Zarifsanaiey, N., Niakan Kalhori, S. R., Rakhshan, M., Keikha, L., & Ghazi Saeedi, M. (2021). Intelligent tutoring systems: A systematic review of characteristics, applications, and evaluation methods. *Interactive Learning Environments, 29*(1), 142–163. https://doi.org/10.1080/10494820.2018.1558257

Mouw, J. M., Fokkens-Bruinsma, M., & Snippe, A. (2025). Assessing complex skills in a virtual reality context: Capturing the development of pre-service teachers' classroom management strategies. *Education Sciences, 15*(1), 2–21. https://doi.org/10.3390/educsci15010002

Muslim, A., Chatti, M. A., & Guesmi, M. (2020). Open learning analytics: A systematic literature review and future perspectives. In N. Pinkwart & S. Liu (Eds.), *Artificial intelligence supported educational technologies* (pp. 3–29). Springer. https://doi.org/10.1007/978-3-030-41099-5_1

Nakamoto, S. (2009). *Bitcoin: A peer-to-peer electronic cash system*. https://bitcoin.org/bitcoin.pdf

Ocheja, P., Agbo, F. J., Oyelere, S. S., Flanagan, B., & Ogata, H. (2022). Blockchain in education: A systematic review and practical case studies. *IEEE Access, 10*, 99525–99540. https://doi.org/10.1109/ACCESS.2022.3206791

OECD. (n.d.). *PISA 2029: Media and artificial intelligence literacy*. Organisation for Economic Co-operation and Development. Retrieved August 6, 2025, from https://www.oecd.org/en/about/projects/pisa-2029-media-and-artificial-intelligence-literacy.html

Ormerod, C. M., Malhotra, A., & Jafari, A. (2021). *Automated essay scoring using efficient transformer-based language models*. ArXiv. https://arxiv.org/abs/2102.13136

Ouyang, F., Dinh, T. A., & Xu, W. (2023). A systematic review of AI-enabled educational assessment in STEM education. *Journal for STEM Education Research, 6*(3), 408–426. Education Database; Education Research Index. https://doi.org/10.1007/s41979-023-00112-x

Pijeira-Díaz, H. J., Drachsler, H., Kirschner, P. A., & Järvelä, S. (2018). Profiling sympathetic arousal in a physics course: How active are students? *Journal of Computer Assisted Learning, 34*(4), 397–408.

Queiroga, E. M., Batista Machado, M. F., Paragarino, V. R., Primo, T. T., & Cechinel, C. (2022). Early prediction of at-risk students in secondary education: A countrywide K-12 learning analytics initiative in Uruguay. *Information, 13*(9), 401.

Ramesh, D., & Sanampudi, S. K. (2022). An automated essay scoring systems: A systematic literature review. *Artificial Intelligence Review, 55*(3), 2495–2527. https://doi.org/10.1007/s10462-021-10068-2

Raza, F. (2023). AI in education: Personalized learning and adaptive assessment. *Cosmic Bulletin of Business Management, 2*(1), 280–297. https://doi.org/10.13140/RG.2.2.24796.77446

Robinson, C., Yeomans, M., Reich, J., Hulleman, C., & Gehlbach, H. (2016). Forecasting student achievement in MOOCs with natural language processing. In *Proceedings of the Sixth International Conference on Learning Analytics & Knowledge* (pp. 383–387). https://doi.org/10.1145/2883851.2883932

Siemens, G., & Long, P. (2011). Penetrating the fog: Analytics in learning and education. *EDUCAUSE Review, 5*, 30–32. https://doi.org/10.17471/2499-4324/195

Tang, Y. M., Chau, K. Y., Kwok, A. P. K., Zhu, T., & Ma, X. (2022). A systematic review of immersive technology applications for medical practice and education, trends, application areas, recipients, teaching contents, evaluation methods, and performance. *Educational Research Review, 35*, 100429. https://doi.org/10.1016/j.edurev.2021.100429

Templin, J., & Bradshaw, L. (2014). Hierarchical diagnostic classification models. *Psychometrika, 79*(2), 210–230. https://doi.org/10.1007/s11336-013-9362-0

UNESCO. (2025). *What's worth measuring? The future of assessment in the AI age*. UNESCO.

Verner, I., Cuperman, D., Perez-Villalobos, H., Polishuk, A., & Gamer, S. (2022). Augmented and virtual reality experiences for learning robotics and training integrative thinking skills. *Robotics, 11*(5), Article 5. https://doi.org/10.3390/robotics11050090

von Davier, A. A., & Halpin, P. F. (Eds.). (2022). *Computational psychometrics: New methodologies for a new generation of digital learning and assessment.* Springer.

Wang, S., Li, Y., & Li, Y. (2021). Instance-level graph grammars for layout analysis of scientific diagrams. In *Proceedings of the IEEE/CVF International Conference on Computer Vision (ICCV)* (pp. 2223–2232).

Wang, Y., Li, Y., Chen, C., Zhang, W., Wang, Y., Sha, K., & Wang, S. (2024). Research on virtual reality-based assessment framework and application path in medical education. *PLOS ONE, 19*(11), e0310782. https://doi.org/10.1371/journal.pone.0310782

World Economic Forum. (2025). *Why AI literacy is now a core competency in education.* World Economic Forum.

Yang, M. T., Cheng, Y. J., & Shih, Y. C. (2011). Facial expression recognition for learning status analysis. In *International Conference on Human-Computer Interaction* (pp. 131–138). Springer Berlin Heidelberg.

Zhao, Q., & Liang, Z. (2023). Research on multimodal based learning evaluation method in smart classroom. *Learning and Motivation, 84*, 101943.

Zheng, C., Guo, S., Xia, W., & Mao, S. (2023). 小花狮:基于大语言模型的中文作文智能辅导系统 [Xiao Hua Shi: A large language model-based intelligent tutoring system for Chinese composition]. *Chinese/English Journal of Educational Measurement and Evaluation, 4*(3), Article 4. https://doi.org/10.59863/WNPU9372.

12

KEY CONSIDERATIONS FOR ASSESSING AND SUPPORTING COLLABORATION WITH AI

Peter W. Foltz

12.1 Introduction

Collaboration is a foundational skill in both education and the evolving workforce. Its importance stems from how collaborative work drives higher-level thinking, improves outcomes, and prepares individuals for complex, interconnected job environments (Graesser et al., 2018; Lai et al., 2017; National Research Council, 2015). Collaboration is defined as a "coordinated, synchronous activity that is the result of a continued attempt to construct and maintain a shared conception of a problem" (Roschelle and Teasley, 1995, p. 70). In essence, it is more than just working together; it is about creating a "joint problem space" (Dillenbourg, 1999) to reach a shared solution (e.g., OECD, 2017).

The rise of automation, cross-functional teams, and project-based work in the global economy has heightened the need for strong collaborative abilities. Employers increasingly report that "soft skills" such as collaboration, problem-solving, and adaptability are as critical as technical expertise for advancement, career resilience, and innovation (e.g., Autor, Levy, and Murnane, 2003; Hosseinioun et al., 2025; Letsky et al., 2008). By 2030, up to 39% of essential workforce skills are expected to shift, with collaboration, creative thinking, and social influence remaining core priorities (World Economic Forum, 2025). In education, collaborative learning exposes students to diverse perspectives, teaches them to solve problems collectively, and nurtures social skills. Meta-analyses of studies on collaborative problem-solving (CPS) in the classroom show that it helps students develop critical thinking, communication, and leadership skills, while also boosting confidence and engagement (Springer et al., 1999; Xu et al., 2023). Thus, collaboration not only underpins effective learning; it also future-proofs students and workers, equipping them for the demands of a rapidly shifting work landscape and ensuring their ability to thrive in diverse, technology-rich environments.

DOI: 10.4324/9781003621522-12

To place greater emphasis on collaboration, however, requires agreed-upon definitions of what constitutes collaboration skills, as well as robust approaches for assessing, providing feedback on, and teaching these skills. Educational institutions and countries have responded to this need for better standards, training, and assessments by integrating these skills into curricula, developing new assessment frameworks, and adapting educational policies (e.g., Care et al., 2012; Fiore et al., 2018; Graesser et al., 2018; National Research Council, 2015; OECD, 2017). These frameworks and policies have influenced educational practice and led to the adoption of standardized assessment approaches, such as the OECD's Programme for International Student Assessment (PISA) 2015 CPS assessment.

Despite universal agreement about the importance of collaborative skills, assessment and feedback on collaboration is still an emerging field. The paucity of development is due to several factors.

- Collaboration is a *complex, multifaceted construct.* It blends cognitive (problem-solving, reasoning), social (turn-taking, influencing, conflict resolution), and emotional (empathy, trust-building) components. Different disciplines operationalize collaboration definitions and construct differently, making it hard to align measures. Domain-specific norms that are considered adequate in one learning or professional context might not translate to another.
- Collaboration behaviors are highly *context-dependent.* In an online asynchronous undergraduate planning group, members may focus more on maintaining engagement and interpreting intent. In contrast, a face-to-face group of middle school STEM students may need to focus more on building shared understanding of the problem space. Task-specific demands may further elicit different collaborative patterns. Short-term activities may focus on rapid progress to a solution, while long-term activities may cause greater emphasis on building relationships and connections among group members.
- Collaboration is *dynamic, unfolding over time.* Thus, a single snapshot or a post hoc assessment may miss essential patterns. These patterns may also indicate the progress of teams in a nonlinear way. Teams may have phases of conflict, silence, or divergence that are necessary for eventual success. However, these phases may look like poor performance when observed in isolation.
- Collaboration is inherently *multimodal and multiparty* (e.g., Blikstein and Worsley, 2016). Evidence for collaboration may come through speaking, writing, facial expressions, gestures, or entries into a digital workspace. Subtle patterns in multimodal features may indicate important factors, such as how an individual influences a group, which can affect the group's solution outcome.

Overall, these factors indicate that to assess collaboration successfully, there must be a shift from simple, one-dimensional measures to dynamic models that account for the nuances of interpersonal interactions, verbal and non-verbal communication, and evolving team norms. Automating measurement using AI-based methods holds promise for addressing these complexities. By pairing well-designed collaboration frameworks with robust AI-based assessment techniques, it is possible to obtain compelling characterizations of collaborative performance and to develop novel approaches to supporting students and teachers. Beyond applying sound frameworks and accurate AI, a range of other critical factors is implicated in the design of realistic and sustainable educational applications for collaboration. Deploying such assessment technology in real-world applications can be cumbersome for data collection, which directly affects the kinds of tasks and interactions that can be used. It can further require complex assessment models that enable reliable, valid inferences about individuals and group performance. We therefore advocate a balanced, human-centered integration of AI to develop collaborative assessment approaches. This chapter presents a taxonomy of factors to consider for successfully implementing AI-based solutions to support collaboration. It then provides a real-world example of an implementation and how it aligns to these factors.

12.2 Characterizing Collaboration Skills

To assess collaboration, we first need to identify the targeted skills. Skills frameworks provide clear, objective, and standardized criteria for evaluating individual and team competencies, ensuring that skill assessments are fair, reliable, and aligned with the goals of the educational or workplace experience (e.g., Zajac et al., 2021). Several frameworks have been developed for measuring CPS, each emphasizing different aspects and contexts. These frameworks aim to capture the cognitive and social skills essential for individuals and teams to work together to solve complex problems effectively. However, some frameworks primarily focus on assessment of groups in education, while others focus on team performance in the workforce. Here, we focus on a few key frameworks.

12.2.1 Collaboration Frameworks

The Assessment and Teaching of 21st Century Skills (ATC21S) project developed a concept for assessing and teaching CPS skills, focusing on teachable skills (Griffin et al., 2012). Its theoretical framework included:

- *Participation*: Encompasses the general level of involvement, interaction with others, and responsiveness to others, as well as the motivational aspects needed for task completion.
- *Perspective taking*: Involves understanding and responding to others, contextualizing utterances, integrating contributions, and tailoring one's communication (audience design).
- *Social regulation*: Addresses how groups productively work with member diversity. This involvement includes metamemory (knowledge about oneself), transactive memory (knowledge about collaborators' strengths and weaknesses),

negotiation skills (for resolving conflicts), and initiative skills (responsibility for group progress).

The ATC21S framework focused on human-to-human interactions in authentic, less scripted problem-solving and interaction situations. For example, students working in small-group class exercises. While this approach provided greater ecological validity, the scoring of group performance was not highly amenable to automation, as it relied on skill descriptors that were not easily quantifiable (e.g., "The student uses highly organized, evidence-based communication to keep the team focused on the goal"). This complication meant that the framework required more laborious human annotation of student skills.

The OECD's PISA framework was designed to assess CPS skills, surveying 15-year-old students across 52 countries and economies (OECD, 2017). It defined CPS competency as

> the capacity of an individual to effectively engage in a process whereby two or more agents attempt to solve a problem by sharing the understanding and effort required to come to a solution, and pooling their knowledge, skills, and efforts to reach that solution.
>
> *(OECD, 2017)*

The framework was structured around two main dimensions.

The Cognitive Dimension (Task Work) focused on individual problem-solving competencies adapted from PISA 2012, including:

- *Exploring and understanding*: Interpreting initial and newly uncovered information about a problem.
- *Representing and formulating*: Identifying approaches, strategies, and relevant artifacts to solve the problem.
- *Planning and executing*: Constructing and enacting plans and actions (physical, social, or verbal).
- *Monitoring and reflecting*: Tracking progress toward goals and reflecting on the quality of progress or solutions.

The Collaborative Dimension (Teamwork) focused on the social processes involved in collaboration:

- *Establishing and maintaining shared understanding*: Tracking team members' knowledge, perspectives, and a shared vision of problem states and activities.
- *Taking appropriate actions to solve the problem*: Performing physical and communicative actions that advance the solution.
- *Establishing and maintaining group organization*: Helping organize or reorganize the group based on members' knowledge, skills, abilities, and resources, including role assignment and handling obstacles.

These two dimensions intersect to form a 12-skill matrix for CPS assessment. The PISA assessment was designed to be automatically scored with individual students interacting with two or more computer-based agents in constrained situations, where the students could choose from fixed discourse responses in a scripted conversation. These limitations in the assessment approach were due to the need to deliver equivalent assessments across counties, to ensure that student performance was not dependent on other students, and to ensure that all students encountered the same situations to assess the full range of skills from the framework.

The CPS framework introduced by Sun et al. (2020) extends the PISA framework, with a greater focus on tasks such as joint analysis, negotiation, and knowledge construction. A key component of this framework was identifying discourse components that occur during interactions and serve as indicators of the skills. These indicators focused on specific, measurable utterances (what is said) and actions (what is done) in digital environments (e.g., *Agreeing on how the team will communicate or take turns before starting the task*). By focusing on the assessment of human-human interaction through language indicators, the framework supports open and natural language conversations in unconstrained digital environments. This strategy allows analysis of a much broader range of discourse moves and interaction patterns, enabling a more comprehensive measurement of CPS skills that were constrained in PISA's limited communication settings.

Other frameworks have focused more on teamwork, emphasizing their applicability to measuring workforce performance. The O'Neil et al. (2003) framework draws on the teamwork literature to identify features necessary for optimizing team performance outcomes. Key skills include the following:

- *Adaptability*: Monitoring the team and task, and responding to emerging problems.
- *Coordination*: Synchronizing and integrating group activities to ensure timely task completion.
- *Interpersonal skills*: Cooperating and accommodating other group members.
- *Leadership*: Providing direction for the group.
- *Communication skills*: Exchanging information clearly and accurately.

These skills are combined with *problem-solving strategies* (traditional cognitive strategies) and *metacognition* (self-regulatory components like planning and monitoring). O'Neil et al. (2003) further identify approaches to automated analyses of these skills, including applying Bayesian networks to detect causal influences of team performance.

Salas et al. (2005) similarly define a "Big Five" of teamwork skills. They identify five core components, *team leadership*, *mutual performance monitoring*, *backup behavior*, *adaptability*, and *team orientation*, as essential for teamwork. These five skills are supported by three fundamental coordinating mechanisms: shared mental models, closed-loop communications, and mutual trust. This model has been influential in the design of workforce assessments and training, for example, in healthcare (e.g., Ashour et al., 2025) and policing (e.g., Espevik et al., 2022).

Despite the variety of frameworks, there are strong commonalities to assessing collaboration. For example, successful collaboration requires task work (problem-solving strategies, planning, monitoring) and teamwork (communication, coordination, relationship management). Most frameworks integrate aspects of interpersonal and metacognitive processing alongside problem-solving behaviors. Whether called "monitoring and reflecting" (PISA), "social regulation" (ATC21S), or "mutual performance monitoring" (Big Five), there is agreement that awareness of progress and the ability to adjust strategies are critical skills. All frameworks are rooted in real-world collaborative contexts (e.g., education, workforce, or both), even if the assessment delivery method (e.g., scripted versus open dialogue) varies for practical reasons. Finally, they all operationalize collaboration through behavioral indicators—e.g., turn-taking, perspective taking, adaptability, leadership actions—making skills assessable through observation or automated analysis. However, some frameworks are more amenable to automated assessment. For example, the Sun et al. (2020) framework can be readily applied using natural language processing of collaborative discourse moves. This application results from the framework's linkage to computationally instantiable skill indicators. In contrast, the Big Five dimensions are defined very broadly, which typically requires analysis based on human observation.

12.3 Linking Frameworks to Assessment Development

While a framework provides an accounting of the skills, there needs to be a straightforward, principled approach to mapping those skills to evidence. Evidence-centered design (ECD) (Mislevy et al., 2006) provides a comprehensive framework for designing and deploying multimodal, multiparty AI-based assessments by outlining what is measured (student model), where it is measured (task model), and how it is calculated (evidence model). ECD is highly applicable to developing ways to assess complex skills like collaboration, which often involve vast amounts of high-granularity log or verbal data from digital environments that need to be converted into measures. Applied to CPS frameworks, ECD helps conceptualize complex CPS skills and extract evidence from detailed records of individuals' actions and discourse.

ECD helps clarify the link between what is being measured and the specific claims about those features. It starts with a student model (the claims you want to make about knowledge, skills, or abilities), then works backward to define the evidence you need and the tasks that can elicit that evidence. For AI assessments, this prevents the common problem of measuring what is easy to capture (e.g., word counts, click rates) instead of what is actually important for the construct (e.g., verbal indicators of negotiation, specific transfer of knowledge from one person to another). Thus, ECD keeps the analysis focused on the *construct-relevant* features rather than spurious correlations. Because collaborative data may be inherently multimodal (e.g., speech, text, gesture, and action logs), defining the constructs ahead of time specifies which modalities are relevant in different situations, which features to extract, and how those features support inferences about the constructs.

ECD further helps make AI-based assessments more transparent and defensible. Enforcing explicit reasoning about *why* a given behavior, response, or pattern of interaction provides evidence for a construct removes some of the "black boxiness" of the AI's assessment system. As AI detects individual markers of behavior, these markers can be explicitly mapped back to specific pieces of evidence for the constructs, providing a more transparent accounting of the analysis process. This transparency can be essential for stakeholder trust (learners, educators, policymakers) to help clarify how AI is applied to complex multimodal data. Thus, applying ECD in the design of assessments provides a purposeful, evidence-driven, and defensible approach to developing valid, fair, and meaningful measures of collaborative performance.

As an example of explicitly incorporating ECD into a CPS framework, the in-task assessment framework (I-TAF) (Kerr et al., 2016) was specifically designed to support the assessment of complex skills, such as CPS, within digital environments that generate large amounts of data, such as mouse-click and chat-message logs. A key feature of I-TAF is its use of a CPS ontology (e.g., student model), which provides a theory-driven, hierarchical representation of the CPS constructs and related skills. This ontology allows the framework to define the construct space at multiple levels of granularity, from high-level skills down to low-level observable behaviors. It then connects this behavioral evidence based on a specific task environment (task model). For example, behavioral evidence may be based on log data of student actions or on particular types of communication in an electronic simulation. The systematic rules that link behavioral evidence to high-level skills (the evidence model) provide a means to extract evidence of CPS skills from fine-grained data. This systematic approach enables automated analyses of team interactions and communication, providing a theory-motivated, in-depth assessment that can handle large datasets and deliver timely feedback, which is crucial for moving beyond time-intensive human annotation of collaborative data. An excellent example of the implementation of incorporating ECD within a collaborative platform is in the EPCAL platform (Educational Testing Service Platform for Collaborative Assessment and Learning) (Hao et al., 2017b). EPCAL was built to enable the control and manipulation of group variables, allowing the study of collaboration at scale while ensuring that the rich process data aligns with the evidence model. Thus, incorporating collaboration frameworks with explicit mapping of behavioral evidence to the skills provides a pathway to automating assessment.

12.4 Dimensions of Collaborative Assessment

Identifying collaboration skills and mapping them to behavioral evidence is a critical component for developing computer-based collaborative assessment and support systems. However, building AI technology for the assessment and support of collaboration skills cannot be examined in isolation from the contexts to which it is being applied. Overall, technology has assessed collaboration skills more tractable for broader, more realistic situations. Thus, it is essential to look broadly at the many roles that technology plays across all aspects of supporting collaboration. For example, it can (1) be used to present and control the task situation, (2) provide virtual teammates that respond to users based on an analysis of the situation (e.g. Fiore and Wiltshire, 2016), (3) collect the evidence such as speech, eye gaze, pointing, work products, logs of actions, (4) apply models to analyze the evidence automatically, (5) provide feedback to group teammates, and (6) generate reports or dashboards to external observers or teachers.

Furthermore, we need to consider the many potential dimensions of the collaborative situation, including the types of collaboration constructs being assessed, the testing environment, the types and number of teammates (both AI or humans), the types of data being collected, indicators of collaboration (verbal, eye gaze, etc.), the types of AI models being applied, the ethics of collecting the data, and how and when the results of the assessments are used to provide feedback about participant performance. These dimensions introduce trade-offs in fidelity of measurement, mapping to real-world examples, ease of administration, how the results can be used, and scalability for large-scale classroom or high-stakes assessment use. In Table 12.1, the key dimensions to be considered for automating assessment and supporting collaboration are enumerated. A commentary is then provided on these dimensions. These dimensions are divided into five key domains of consideration. In addition, the table provides a mapping of these dimensions to layers of ECD, along with whether they are critical considerations for the technical implementation. It is important to note, though, that much of what is considered "implementation" is also strongly related to the "task model" layer in ECD.

12.4.1 Context and Setup

The context and setup domain address the foundational conditions under which AI-based collaborative assessments are designed and conducted. The context begins by clarifying the purpose of assessment: formative (to guide learning in progress), summative (to evaluate learning at the end), or diagnostic (to identify strengths and needs before instruction). Each purpose carries implications for how the assessment is structured, the stakes involved, and the types of feedback provided. For example, developing a formative application requires mapping the identified skills to specific, pedagogically effective feedback. The interaction environment—whether simulated, live, or hybrid—shapes both the realism and the controllability of the collaboration scenario. For example, live interactions can capture authentic dynamics but introduce much greater variability. Classrooms can have sources of unanticipated interruptions, additional background noise, and fewer restrictions on off-task behavior. Simulated settings offer tighter control but may limit natural behaviors and ease of deployment. Likewise,

TABLE 12.1 Key Dimensions for Consideration of the Implementation of Automated Collaborative Assessment and Support

Development Domain	*Collaborative Assessment Dimension*	*Categories (Not Comprehensive)*	*Alignment to ECD Layers/ Implementation Factors*
Context and setup	Purpose of assessment	Formative, summative, diagnostic	Implementation
	Interaction environment	Simulated, live, hybrid	Task model
	Data types/ease of collection	Spoken audio, video, log files, student responses	Implementation
	Task structure and control	Firmly directed by tasks (multiple choice, SJT), semi-structured, open-ended (e.g., open conversations)	Task model
	Teammate embodiment (nature of teammate)	Virtual teammate, human, human-in-the-loop	Task model
Modeling and evidence	Targeted competencies	CPS, social-emotional, pedagogical moves, domain knowledge	Student model
	Granularity of analysis	Individual, dyad, whole team	Student model
	Collaboration evidence sources	Group work product, verbal expressions, turn-taking, influenced eye gaze, pointing, situation judgment, action logs, survey instruments, observer notes, or scores	Evidence model
	Analytic model(s)	Simple counts, statistical, Bayesian, semantic features, LLM models	Evidence model
	Data integration method	Single modality, multimodal, separate, multimodal-integrated	Evidence model
	Data access and privacy constraints	Full access, restricted, anonymized	Implementation
Timing	Timeliness of data collection and analysis	Real-time, near-real-time, post hoc analysis	Implementation
	Timing of AI feedback	Real-time concurrent with group task, near real time, post hoc	Task model

(Continued)

TABLE 12.1 (Continued)

Development Domain	*Collaborative Assessment Dimension*	*Categories (Not Comprehensive)*	*Alignment to ECD Layers/ Implementation Factors*
Feedback and use	Nature of AI feedback	Collaborative moves, team processes, domain scaffolding, reports, critical incidents, scoring	Task model
	Target of feedback	Individual, team, teachers, evaluators	Task model
Scope and scale	Scalability of assessment	Pilot, small-scale, large-scale	Implementation
	Context sensitivity	Domain-general, domain-specific, context-adapted, culturally appropriate	Implementation

task structure and control can range from tightly scripted tasks to open-ended problem-solving, each influencing the degree of spontaneity and the types of competencies that can be observed.

Data collection choices (e.g., spoken audio, video, log files, final products) depend on feasibility and the richness of desired evidence. Spoken audio, video, and log files provide rich, unobtrusive data collection. However, they require precise mapping of the constructs to these evidence sources. Final products can provide effective indicators of the group outcomes but may miss the processes that allowed the group to get there. The data types also introduce privacy considerations. Collecting video and audio data in real-world situations, such as classrooms, can require higher levels of consent, particularly with minors. Finally, teammate embodiment—whether AI is interacting as a virtual teammate, humans are interacting with each other, a human-in-the-loop mode is acting as an AI-based agent, or just feedback is provided graphically—can affect the participant's engagement, trust, and interaction patterns (e.g., Forsyth et al., 2019; Franklin and Graesser, 1996). Thus, the design of AI-based virtual teammates requires careful consideration of how feedback/responses will be generated, such as through natural language generation or canned rule-based responses.

12.4.2 Modeling and Evidence

The modeling and evidence domain focuses on what is measured and how evidence is captured, processed, and interpreted. As described in the sections on skills frameworks and ECD, this domain involves identifying targeted competencies, which may include CPS skills, socio-emotional skills, pedagogical moves, or domain-specific knowledge, such as STEM. These skills may be defined by the granularity of analysis (e.g., whether skill measures are at the individual or group level), since this influences both data needs and analytic methods. The domain further identifies the evidence sources, which might include verbal and non-verbal data (e.g., turn-taking, gaze, pointing), artifacts of work (e.g., group products), or observer ratings. The choice of these sources depends on what can be measured in the collaborative situation and their successful mapping to skills.

Analytic models encompass the full range of computational and statistical approaches used to extract evidence from the collaborative data. At the simplest level, these may include frequency counts or basic descriptive statistics to capture participation rates, turn-taking, or contribution patterns (e.g., Gonzales et al., 2009). However, AI-based models have become increasingly sophisticated at recognizing speech, analyzing and annotating language, measuring collaborative performance from log files, recognizing gestures, processing eye gaze and emotion from facial features, and fusing multiparty, multimodal data. Reviewing all the approaches is beyond the scope of this chapter. Von Davier et al. (2017) provide a comprehensive overview of computational methods for assessing collaboration across contexts and the application of psychometric methods for validation while examining their applicability in both workforce and educational settings. Ouyang and Zhang (2024) and Tan et al. (2022) provide reviews of AI-based analytics for computer-supported cooperative learning. Giannakos et al. (2022) and Ochoa et al. (2022) provide an overview of multimodal learning analytics (MMLA) and fusion approaches.

Communication among team members is one of the richest sources of evidence on team processes and cognition (e.g., Cooke et al., 2017; Foltz et al., 2007). Discourse moves that correspond to aspects of collaboration, such as negotiation, acknowledging, building shared knowledge, and establishing common ground, can be mapped to indications of collaborative skills. Analyzing the semantic, structural, and sequential features of the discourse enables the interpretation of the meaning being expressed. This approach has been widely used with a variety of natural language processing methods, such as latent semantic analysis (Foltz & Martin, 2008; Martin and Foltz, 2004), Naïve Bayes classifiers of n-grams (Flor et al., 2016), conditional random fields of label sequences (Hao et al., 2017a), word embedding models such as BERT and Word2Vec (Pugh et al., 2021; Sun et al., 2020), and, most recently, using large language models (LLMs) (Lee et al., 2025; Spain et al., 2025). These approaches have demonstrated accuracies consistent with human annotation of discourse categories, thereby considerably speeding and automating the characterization of states of collaboration through language. Nevertheless, spoken discourse must first be processed by an automatic speech recognition (ASR) system. While ASR can have accuracies of word error rates (WERs) of less than 5% in quiet controlled conditions, performance in real-world noisy environments and with young participants shows WERs of 20%–80%, meaning much of the discourse may be lost or generated incorrectly (e.g., Foltz et al., 2003; Southwell et al., 2022).

Collaboration is less about the outcomes and more about how the group arrived at them. Process data logs provide rich information about how individuals and groups take actions, coordinate tasks, share knowledge, and transition between problem-solving and coordination states. Features for process data can include (1) temporal information such as response latencies and idle time, indicating engagement or level of coordination; (2) sequences such as n-grams of actions and transitions between states, indicating patterns of collaborative workflows; (3) participation such as turn frequencies and dominance ratios, indicating balance in the group and effective turn-taking; and (4) discourse-based markers, indicating transitions from one kind of discourse move to another and changes in sentiment.

A variety of modeling approaches have been used to characterize such process data. For example, He (2023) and He et al. (2017) analyzed the processes underlying students' actions in the PISA 2015 CPS assessment, providing a direct mapping to the targeted CPS skills. Social network analysis has been used to represent collaboration as a network of relations among participants and actions. This approach allows measurement of aspects of centrality, density, and cohesion as indicators of equitable participation, influence, and coordination (e.g., Martinez et al., 2003; Puntambekar, 2013). Hidden Markov models enable the detection of latent collaboration states and the timing of state transitions (e.g., Xiao et al., 2021).

As the field becomes better able to collect diverse data streams, such as video, audio, and logs of actions, there is a greater need for MMLA to integrate the data and provide a more holistic and nuanced understanding of group dynamics (e.g., Cohn et al., 2024; Worsley and Blikstein, 2018; Yuan et al., 2025). MMLA approaches fuse information from various modalities, such as verbal and written communication, facial expressions, gestures, eye gaze for joint visual attention, physiological sensors, and action log files, enabling a deeper accounting of behaviors, affective states, and cognitive processes during collaborative tasks. For instance, combining prosodic and transcribed speech can provide a more comprehensive language representation, while integrating features from natural language, video, and audio can significantly improve predictive performance in collaborative settings. Studies have shown that multimodal systems are consistently more accurate than their best unimodal counterparts, with an average improvement of nearly 10% (e.g., Cohn et al., 2024; D'Mello and Kory, 2015; Ma et al., 2022). As such, these MMLA approaches provide a means to move from analyzing individual evidence streams in isolation to unified models that yield richer interpretations but require more sophisticated pipelines.

12.4.3 Timing and Feedback

The nature of AI feedback can vary widely, from identifying collaborative moves and diagnosing team processes to providing domain-specific scaffolding, generating incident reports, or scoring performance. These outputs can support formative learning, summative evaluation, or even predictive analytics for intervention planning. Critical, though, is to ensure that the feedback is tied back to the CPS constructs and also provided in ways interpretable by the end-user. Generative AI offers a means to interpret CPS analyses and convert them into feedback. However, LLM models need to be carefully trained and assessed to ensure the accuracy of the feedback. For example, Wang and Demszky (2023) found that feedback to teachers on their coaching methods, while relevant to improving instruction, was often not novel or insightful.

The target of feedback, whether an individual, a team, or educators/observers, shapes its tone, granularity, and actionable quality. Feedback to individuals may highlight specific contributions and areas for growth, while team-level feedback may focus on coordination, negotiation, and collective decision-making. When directed at teachers or evaluators, AI feedback can inform instructional planning, targeted support, and resource allocation. Designing for the intended user requires balancing interpretability, specificity, and alignment with broader learning goals.

Timing considerations are crucial for both data collection and use in AI-enabled assessments. Data collection and analysis can range from real-time streaming to near-real-time or post hoc analysis. However, each choice affects the immediacy of feedback, the scalability, and the computational requirements. High-stakes settings may require batch analysis for accuracy, while learning-support contexts may prioritize rapid feedback, even at the cost of model reliability.

Feedback delivered concurrently with a group task can shape ongoing collaboration but must be designed to avoid disrupting natural interaction or creating cognitive overload. Post hoc feedback may allow for deeper analysis and reflection, but it loses the opportunity to shape behavior in the moment. Thus, in formative contexts, it is critical not just to measure the fidelity of the model's characterization of CPS skills, but also to assess how well the feedback derived from that measurement drives effective changes in collaboration. A lower-fidelity model that can be run in real time may be as effective as, or more effective than, a high-fidelity model that requires greater computational costs or post hoc processing. Balancing these trade-offs requires aligning timing with the assessment's purpose, stakes, and the learners' needs.

12.4.4 Scope and Scale

Scope and scale address broader implementation considerations, ensuring that the assessment can operate effectively in its intended environments and that the evaluation is both valid and practical. Scalability of assessment involves planning for pilot phases, small-scale trials, and eventual large-scale deployment, each with distinct infrastructure, training, and quality assurance needs. Successful scaling requires not only robust technical systems but also organizational buy-in, stakeholder trust, and adaptability to different contexts. Key considerations for implementing CPS-based systems include how to collect data in a non-intrusive, ethical manner. Collecting audio and video in the classroom or workplace can be logistically complicated to implement, particularly if instructors or students need to set up and run the system. For example, if facial features or gestures are used, how will the system ensure that cameras are placed to capture users appropriately? If microphones are used, does each student need a separate microphone, or can a single microphone be placed in the center of a group? How much background noise is acceptable for the effective performance of the system?

The implementation scope must also consider how the CPS assessment and training align with the organization's goals. For instance, what kind of professional development around the CPS constructs and how they tie into the organization's curriculum will be provided? How will the results of assessments or feedback from the CPS system be incorporated into teachers' assessment workflow or learning plans? Additionally, educational organizations will want CPS systems that align with their curriculum and specific standards that may vary by state and district. AI-based collaborative assessments can be designed as domain-general (applicable across many subjects), domain-specific (tailored to a particular discipline), or context-adapted (customized to local needs, culture, and constraints). When deploying a system, how much work will be needed to assess transferability, comparability of results, and localization across different contexts?

More specifically, for defining the scope of the assessment, it is essential to recognize that effective collaboration looks fundamentally different across cultural contexts. What constitutes productive participation, appropriate communication styles, or effective leadership varies substantially between individualistic and collectivistic cultures, high-context and low-context communication environments, and societies with different power distance norms (e.g., Gelfan and Realo, 1999). For instance, in some East Asian educational contexts, silence and careful observation may signal deep engagement and respect rather than disengagement. At the same time, direct disagreement might be seen as face-threatening rather than as productive debate (Broeder, 2021). Similarly, turn-taking patterns, the role of hierarchy in decision-making, and expectations around consensus-building versus individual accountability all carry cultural meanings that can be misread by AI systems trained primarily on Western, educated, industrialized, rich, and democratic populations. An AI system that privileges verbal contribution frequency or direct challenge as markers of collaboration quality may systematically disadvantage students from cultures where these behaviors are considered inappropriate or disrespectful.

Practically implementing culturally responsive collaboration assessment requires both technical and participatory approaches. ECD can help by building culturally responsive assessment frameworks by making explicit the claims, evidence, and warrants that connect observable behaviors to underlying collaborative competencies for specific cultures. AI models can be further developed using diverse training data that represent multiple cultural contexts. These models can incorporate techniques such as domain adaptation or transfer learning to account for population differences and include uncertainty quantification to detect when the assessment model is operating outside its validated contexts. However, technical solutions alone are insufficient. Meaningful accommodation of socio-cultural variation demands ongoing collaboration with educators, students, and cultural experts from target communities throughout the design process, from initial competency modeling through validation studies. This participatory approach helps ensure that frameworks do not simply impose dominant cultural norms but genuinely recognize diverse forms of collaborative excellence, while also acknowledging that some collaborative competencies (such as coordinating toward shared goals or building on others' ideas) may have cross-cultural validity, even as their behavioral manifestations vary.

12.5 Supporting Small-Group Collaboration in Classrooms with the Community Builder

To illustrate the dimensions outlined in Table 12.1 in a concrete implementation of a collaborative system, we describe the development of the Community Builder (CoBi) and provide links to key design considerations in that table. CoBi is a multiparty AI partner primarily to help middle school students develop better small-group collaborative learning skills (Breideband et al., 2023). It is designed to enhance students' collaborative learning skills, particularly focusing on the relationship dimension of collaboration. It aims to empower teachers and students by providing valuable insights that facilitate more meaningful and engaging collaborative learning experiences. It specifically targets the relationship dimension of collaboration, fostering positive team dynamics and treating collaboration as an intrinsic goal. During collaborative sessions, CoBi automatically identifies and visualizes expressions of "socially uplifting discourse" in student group speech related to specific Community Agreements (CAs), derived from the OpenSciEd K-12 science materials aligned to national standards (OpenSciEd, n.d.). These CAs are mutually agreed-upon norms of behavior co-negotiated by students and their teachers to guide classroom collaboration. It currently focuses on supporting three CAs: community building (or being committed to our community), moving and thinking forward, and being respectful. A key aspect of CoBi is the extraction and presentation of "noticings"—specific examples of positive instances of the CAs from student speech. This qualitative feedback is designed to promote reflection and transparency, helping students understand how their talk contributes to community building in collaborative settings.

Classroom implementation of CoBi's design is rooted in extensive co-design workshops with youth, who expressed a desire for AI to help them build strong communities in class (Chang et al., 2022). It operates through four distinct phases in the classroom:

1 *Co-negotiation of Agreements*. With teacher guidance, students work in small groups to articulate and input their own examples of the CAs into the CoBi

interface. This initial step ensures that the norms are mutually agreed upon and relevant to the students' context.

2 *Real-Time Discourse Analysis and Visualization*. Students then engage in collaborative learning tasks. As they perform the tasks, CoBi actively analyzes their spoken discourse for instances of these agreements, referred to as "noticings". Audio is captured via tabletop omnidirectional microphones (Yeti Blue) placed with each group. These microphones were specifically chosen for their affordability and ease of use in capturing conversations from two to four students. The audio is streamed in 10-second chunks, processed with Whisper for Automatic Speech Recognition (ASR), and then analyzed by fine-tuned RoBERTa language models. To protect student privacy, the results are aggregated across student groups and visualized at the classroom level. Teachers can monitor these visualizations in real time, which might include a radar chart for a quantitative summary or a growing tree animation in which flowers bloom, indicating different agreements (see Figure 12.1).

3 *Collaborative Reflection*. After a collaborative learning task, teachers use CoBi's visualizations to guide students in reflecting on how well their group discourse aligned with their co-negotiated CAs. This process is designed to foster deeper insights into collaboration dynamics and enhance the overall learning experience.

4 *Fostering AI Literacy*. Teachers have the option to reveal the top-ranked "noticings" (specific examples of positive instances of CAs) that CoBi identified during the session. This transparency is crucial, as it invites deeper reflection and discussion about the strengths and limitations of AI systems. For example, students might discuss potential miscategorizations due to noisy audio or missed contextual cues, thereby also developing critical 21st-century AI literacy skills.

In the context of the dimensions in Table 12.1, CoBi serves as a formative assessment, running in real time in live classroom environments where there is a lack of

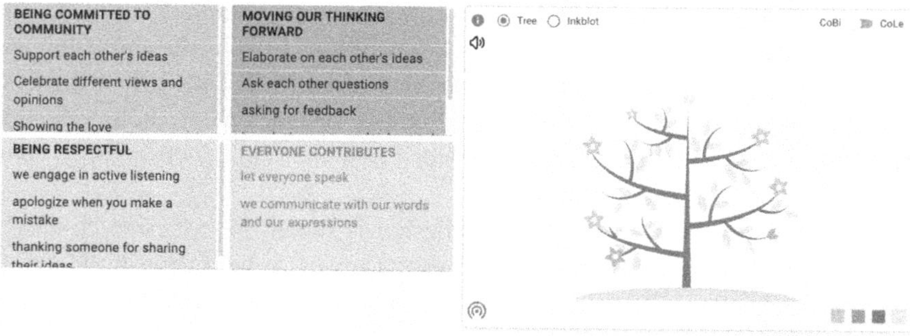

FIGURE 12.1 CoBi student agreements and tree representation of adherence to agreements.

strong task structure or controls. CoBi can be applied across a range of collaborative tasks and can process students' open-ended communication. The AI partner is embodied as a set of visualizations of adherence to CAs and examples of noticings. Presenting aggregated visualizations to students and teachers was a deliberate design decision, as it reduces student distractions, allowing them to be more focused on their collaborative tasks than on the results of the collaboration. CoBi is displayed on a large screen in the classroom, allowing students and the teacher to view the results of their collaborative efforts in real time during the tasks. Teachers can use the visualizations for discussion after completing collaborative tasks to engage students in thinking more deeply about how well the collaboration went during the tasks.

12.5.1 Modeling and Evidence in CoBi

To assess the collaborative discourse, the streamed audio chunks are processed using Whisper, a state-of-the-art open-access ASR model fine-tuned on children's speech (see Southwell et al., 2022) to transcribe individual utterances. A significant challenge in this step is the noisy classroom environment, which includes overlapping student chatter, background noise, and the inherent variability and less clear speech patterns of children compared to adults. These environments lead to high WERs of 60%–70% across various middle school datasets. However, when the ASR output was used in downstream NLP-based classification tasks for CPS utterances, the effects of WER could be significantly ameliorated (see Ezema et al., 2025; Southwell et al., 2022). For example, using only utterances with high ASR confidence reduces classification errors, ensuring that the agent characterizes only student utterances that it is sure about. It should be noted that racial bias in ASR systems is also a concern. Studies have shown lower accuracy for Black speakers compared to white speakers due to differences in acoustic patterns. These errors can cascade and negatively affect downstream discourse classification if left unmitigated (e.g., Ezema et al., 2025).

CoBi primarily uses fine-tuned RoBERTa models to classify student utterances. The models were individually fine-tuned on human-annotated datasets with binary labels for each CA (Chandler et al., 2024). The CA labels and annotation approach was adopted to align with the constructs from the CPS framework from Sun et al. (2020). The models were further fine-tuned and tested on annotated data from entirely different collaborative tasks and contexts to develop more generalized models (e.g., Chandler et al., 2025). To enhance robustness to ASR errors and improve generalizability, CoBi incorporates ASR-augmentation during fine-tuning (Chandler et al., 2024). This technique involves training models on both human-transcribed and ASR-transcribed utterances, effectively doubling the training data and exposing the model to the types of errors encountered in real-world settings. The method has shown notable improvements in accuracy and has reduced the performance gap between human and ASR transcripts. The models output a probability between 0 and 1 for each utterance, indicating the likelihood that it exemplifies a particular CA, with probabilities greater than 0.5 signaling a positive match. CoBi also generates "noticings", which are specific, positive exemplars of the CAs identified from student speech.

It should be noted that other models are being explored, including LLMs such as Mistral 7B (Jiang et al., 2023). The LLM models are used in configurations such as few-shot prompting or combined with support vector machine classifiers for their embeddings to enhance generalizability across diverse contexts and curricula.

From the perspective of modeling, evidence, and feedback in Table 12.1, the computational models are directly aligned with the CA constructs by being fine-tuned on human-annotated data in which utterances are labeled for the presence or absence of these specific CAs. The "noticings" extracted and presented as feedback are concrete instances of these collaborative behaviors, directly illustrating how students' talk embodies the CAs. The feedback visualizations further guide students and teachers in reflecting on how well their collaborative discourse aligns with these co-negotiated agreements, thereby supporting the development of critical collaboration skills and AI literacy. This focus aligns with the concept of criterion validity, ensuring that the models align with constructs meaningful to stakeholders and educational outcomes, such as whether students are advancing their thinking or being respectful.

12.5.2 Scope and Scale of CoBi

As of now, CoBi has been used by 100s of student groups from multiple school districts. From a scale perspective, CoBi is built on a scalable, modular architecture hosted in the Amazon Web Services, ensuring secure data access and storage. Data collection in the classroom requires only a Chromebook and a Yeti Microphone for each group, since all AI processing occurs on the backend. CoBi is integrated into a larger multimodal intelligent analyzer suite of AI and multimodal analysis tools for broader research into classroom interactions. While CoBi initially relied primarily on language, ongoing work includes integrating non-verbal cues (e.g., gestures, posture, eye gaze) to create a more comprehensive and robust model of collaboration, thereby acknowledging diverse communication styles (D'Mello et al., 2024).

Overall, CoBi aims to cultivate crucial social and AI literacy skills through multiparty and multimodal data analysis in authentic educational contexts. It goes beyond traditional approaches to assessing and teaching collaboration by providing aggregated feedback that helps students and teachers reflect on and understand how their communication relates to the collaborative processes that are part of the CAs. As such, the approach is to change the narrative so that instead of AI policing collaborative behavior, it supports students in adhering to mutually agreed CAs. The approach is therefore designed to fundamentally shift the role of AI in collaborative settings by empowering students to develop better collaborative relationships and social skills rather than merely extending traditional models of one-on-one tutoring or systems that provide intrusive interventions into collaboration.

12.6 Conclusions

Measuring and supporting collaborative skills is hard (e.g., Liu et al., 2016; Stecher and Hamilton, 2014). Over the past 20 years, there have been significant advancements in the development of frameworks and agreement on what constitutes collaboration skills. With greater incorporation of digital technologies in the classroom, there are more opportunities to capture rich contextual information about student collaboration. AI technology has advanced at an exponential rate, with LLMs able to process complex multimodal data in real time. However, while there are collaborative skills, frameworks, and a variety of AI techniques that are being widely researched in the assessment and computer-supported cooperative learning literature, very few have been applied in real-world, large-scale use for performance measurement or learning (e.g., Lane et al., 2023). The PISA 2015 CPS assessment (OECD, 2017) was an exception in that it was administered across countries to a sample of over 100,000 15-year-olds. However, it was only run once on a select population. Further, critiques of the PISA approach have questioned the fidelity of the computer-based measurement approach to the target constructs and the extent to which individual students' judgments on the task would map to collaboration in real-world settings (Shaw and Child, 2017). Thus, at this time, there are no large-scale collaborative assessments in use, nor is there any widely adopted educational software explicitly designed to support or assess collaboration.

One reason for the lack of widespread classroom adoption is that multimodal data collection presents substantial privacy and consent challenges that must be carefully navigated. The collection of speech, video, facial expressions, eye gaze patterns, and other biometric data from students raises particularly sensitive concerns that may reveal intimate information about students' emotional states, attention patterns, and even health conditions beyond what is pedagogically relevant (e.g., Prinsloo et al., 2023). Thus, for such data collection to be realized, the field first needs to demonstrate to students, parents, teachers, and administrators that providing their data creates that educational value through the collaboration tools. This improvement can be achieved by showing how AI can partner with students and teachers to support learning in transparent, critiquable ways, such as CoBi's noticings. Second, we need to transform informed consent from a simple binary opt-in/opt-out decision to a continuous, measurable process that maintains transparency and accountability throughout data collection (e.g., Jin et al., 2024). Regulatory complexities compound this privacy challenge, as different laws govern different aspects of student data: FERPA restricts disclosure of education records, COPPA requires parental consent for collecting information from children under 13, and PPRA governs surveys touching on sensitive topics, creating a patchwork of requirements that educators and researchers must navigate while ensuring students' rights and dignity are protected.

If we examine where collaboration is being measured at scale, we must look to the workplace, where consent is less stringent. For example, in the medical field, surveys, observations, and structured questionnaires are regularly used to assess perceptions, attitudes, communication, leadership, and interactions (Kash et al., 2018; Peltonen et al., 2020). A meta-analysis of studies of teamwork examined 51 research articles on 72 unique interventions and 8,439 participants. It showed that they primarily used performance outcome measures, human observations, and survey results rather than automated skill measures (McEwan et al., 2017). Although workplaces are now highly digitized, with email, messaging, communication logs, and performance measurement, there is still no broad adoption of automated analyses of teamwork (e.g., Lane et al., 2023).

Thus, the field is at a point where we need to consider what will be required to advance collaboration beyond lab experiments, demos, small classroom implementations, and human observations. Frameworks and AI models that can accurately assess collaboration are only a small part of what is needed to successfully implement, validate, and deploy collaboration at scale. What is required is a rethinking of how collaboration is assessed and taught. While there are standards for teaching and assessing these skills, collaboration is not a curriculum in its own right. Collaboration skills need to be embedded into many contexts (e.g., Science, Math, Design) where negotiation, coordination, and knowledge sharing are critical to performing and learning tasks. To achieve this, collaborative technologies should be generalizable across multiple contexts. This will ease the development and integration into various curricula, as well as make learning tools and assessments more acceptable to schools and existing teaching practices.

The continuous evolution of AI will further enable more sophisticated analysis of collaborative interaction data. LLMs are quickly changing the nature of the learning data that can be analyzed, showing that the assessment of higher order thinking skills, as well as focused feedback, is more tractable (e.g., Foltz, Sawaya, and Chandler, in press; Hao, 2025; Lodzikowski et al., 2024). For example, the office of Education Technology's Future of Teaching and Learning (2023) states, "Going forward, we must build on AI capabilities that connect with principles of collaborative and social learning and which respect the student not just for their cognition but also for the whole human skill set" (p. 54). The field is rapidly embracing research on approaches to integrating non-verbal communication (gestures, posture, eye gaze) for improved accuracy and a more holistic understanding of collaboration. However, there is also a crucial need for transparent, ethical, and equitable frameworks for AI integration in both classrooms and high-stakes assessments. Thus, there will need to be an increased promotion of responsible innovation in the development and deployment of these technologies. The benefits of learning will need to be balanced with the challenges of privacy loss and concerns about measurement accuracy. To achieve this vision, the field will need to draw insights from educators, measurement specialists, cognitive scientists, AI innovators, ethicists, and human-computer interaction specialists to build a balanced human-centered approach to integrating AI to support collaboration.

Acknowledgments

This research was supported by the NSF National AI Institute for Student-AI Teaming (iSAT) under grants DRL 2019805 and DRL 2454151. The opinions expressed are those of the author and do not represent views of the NSF.

References

Ashour, H. M. A. A. A., Abou Hashish, E. A. O., & Awad, N. H. A. (2025). From awareness to action: Investigating the impact of big-five teamwork model awareness on rationing of nursing care and patient-centered care. *BMC Nursing, 24*(1), 133.

Autor, D. H., Levy, F., & Murnane, R. J. (2003). The skill content of recent technological change: An empirical exploration. *The Quarterly Journal of Economics, 118*(4), 1279–1333.

Blikstein, P., & Worsley, M. (2016). Multimodal Learning Analytics: A methodological framework for research in constructivist learning. *Journal of Learning Analytics, 3*(2), 220–238.

Breideband, T., Bush, J., Chandler, C., Chang, M., Dickler, R., Foltz, P., ... & D'Mello, S. (2023, October). The Community Builder (CoBi): Helping students to develop better small group collaborative learning skills. In *Companion publication of the 2023 conference on computer supported cooperative work and social computing* (pp. 376–380).

Broeder, P. (2021). Informed communication in high context and low context cultures. *Journal of Education, Innovation, and Communication, 3*(1), 13–24.

Care, E., Griffin, P., & McGaw, B. (2012). *Assessment and teaching of 21st century skills.* Dordrecht: Springer.

Chang, M. A., Philip, T. M., Cortez, A., McKoy, A., Sumner, T., & Penuel, W. R. (2022). Engaging youth in envisioning artificial intelligence in classrooms: Lessons lèarned. Digital promise and the International Society of the Learning Sciences Rapid Community reports. https://par.nsf.gov/biblio/10499515.

Chandler, C., Breideband, T., Reitman, J. G., Chitwood, M., Bush, J. B., Howard, A., ... & D'Mello, S. K. (2024). Computational modeling of collaborative discourse to enable feedback and reflection in middle school classrooms. In *Proceedings of the 14th learning analytics & knowledge conference (LAK 2024).* New York: ACM.

Chandler, C., Raju, R., Reitman, J. G., Penuel, W. R., Ko, M., Bush, J. B., ... & D'Mello, S. K. (2025). Improving the generalizability of models of collaborative discourse. In *Proceedings of the 18th international conference on educational data mining* (pp. 215–227).

Cohn, C., Davalos, E., Vatral, C., Fonteles, J. H., Wang, H. D., Ma, M., & Biswas, G. (2024). Multimodal methods for analyzing learning and training environments: A systematic literature review. *arXiv preprint arXiv:2408.14491.*

Cooke, N. J., Gorman, J. C., & Kiekel, P. A. (2017). Communication as team-level cognitive processing. In M. Letsky & N. W. Warner (Eds.), *Macrocognition in teams* (pp. 51–64). Boca Raton, FL: CRC Press.

Dillenbourg, P. (1999). What do you mean by collaborative learning? In P. Dillenbourg (Ed.), *Collaborative-learning: Cognitive and computational approaches* (pp. 1–19). Oxford: Elsevier.

D'Mello, S. K., Biddy, Q., Breideband, T., Bush, J., Chang, M., Cortez, A., ... & Whitehill, J. (2024). From learning optimization to learner flourishing: Reimagining AI in education at the Institute for Student-AI Teaming (iSAT). *AI Magazine, 45*(1), 61–68.

D'Mello, S. K., & Kory, J. (2015). A review and meta-analysis of multimodal affect detection systems. *ACM Computing Surveys (CSUR), 47*(3), 1–36.

Espevik, R., Johnsen, B. H., & Hystad, S. W. (2022). Police dyads within an operational simulation: An empirical test of the research propositions made in the "big five" teamwork approach. *Journal of Police and Criminal Psychology, 37*(4), 844–855.

Ezema, K., Chandler, C., Southwell, R., Cholendiran, N., & D'Mello, S. (2025, April). "It feels like we're not meeting the criteria": Examining and mitigating the cascading effects of bias in automatic speech recognition in spoken language interfaces. In *Proceedings of the 2025 CHI conference on human factors in computing systems* (pp. 1–13).

Fiore, S. M., Graesser, A., & Greiff, S. (2018). Collaborative problem-solving education for the twenty-first-century workforce. *Nature Human Behaviour, 2*(6), 367–369.

Fiore, S. M., & Wiltshire, T. J. (2016). Technology as teammate: Examining the role of external cognition in support of team cognitive processes. *Frontiers in Psychology, 7*, 1531.

Flor, M., Yoon, S. Y., Hao, J., Liu, L., & von Davier, A. (2016, June). Automated classification of collaborative problem-solving interactions in simulated science tasks. In *Proceedings of the 11th workshop on innovative use of NLP for building educational applications* (pp. 31–41).

Foltz, P. W., Laham, D., & Derr, M. (2003, October). Automated speech recognition for modeling team performance. In *Proceedings of the human factors and ergonomics society annual meeting* (Vol. 47, No. 4, pp. 673–677). Los Angeles, CA: SAGE Publications.

Foltz, P. W., Lavoie, N., Oberbreckling, R., & Rosenstein, M. (2007). Tools for automated analysis of networked verbal communication. *Network Science Report, 1*, 1.

Foltz, P. W., & Martin, M. J. (2008). Automated communication analysis of teams. In E. Salas, C. F. Goodwin, & C. S. Burke (Eds.), *Team effectiveness in complex organizations: Cross-disciplinary perspectives and approaches* (pp. 445–466). Milton Park: Routledge.

Foltz, P. W., Sawaya, S., & Chandler, C (in press). From theory to practice: Using large language models to measure and support collaborative skills. In M. C. Mayrath, D. Robinson, & J. Behrens (Eds.), *The handbook of generative AI in education.* New York: Springer.

Forsyth, C. M., Luce, C., Zapata-Rivera, D., Jackson, T. G., Evanini, K., & So, Y. (2019). Evaluating English language learners' conversations: Man vs. machine. *Computer Assisted Language Learning*, 32(4), 398–417.

Franklin, S., & Graesser, A. (1996). Is it an agent, or just a program?: A taxonomy for autonomous agents. In *International workshop on agent theories, architectures, and languages* (pp. 21–35). Berlin, Heidelberg: Springer.

Gelfand, M. J., & Realo, A. (1999). Individualism-collectivism and accountability in intergroup negotiations. *Journal of Applied Psychology, 84*(5), 721–736.

Giannakos, M., Spikol, D., Di Mitri, D., Sharma, K., Ochoa, X., & Hammad, R. (Eds.). (2022). *The multimodal learning analytics handbook.* Berlin: Springer.

Graesser, A. C., Fiore, S. M., Greiff, S., Andrews-Todd, J., Foltz, P. W., & Hesse, F. W. (2018). Advancing the science of collaborative problem solving. *Psychological Science in the Public Interest, 19*(2), 59–92. https://doi.org/10.1177/1529100618808244.

Griffin, P., McGaw, B., & Care, E. (2012). *Assessment and teaching of 21st century skills.* Dordrecht: Springer.

Gonzales, A. L., Hancock, J. T., & Pennebaker, J. W. (2009). Language style matching as a predictor of social dynamics in small groups. *Communication Research, 37*(1), 3–19. https://doi.org/10.1177/0093650209351468.

Hao, J. (2025, August 8). AI for educational assessment: Opportunities and challenges through the lens of evidence-centered design and measurement values. https://doi.org/10.35542/osf.io/dacxj_v2.

Hao, J., Chen, L., Flor, M., Liu, L., & von Davier, A. A. (2017a). CPS-Rater: Automated sequential annotation for conversations in collaborative problem-solving activities. *ETS Research Report Series, 2017*(1), 1–9.

Hao, J., Liu, L., von Davier, A. A., Lederer, N., Zapata-Rivera, D., Jakl, P., & Bakkenson, M. (2017b). EPCAL: ETS platform for collaborative assessment and learning. *ETS Research Report Series, 2017*(1), 1–14.

He, Q. (2023). Collaborative problem-solving design in large-scale assessments: Shedding lights in sequential conversation-based measurement. *International Journal of Assessment Tools in Education, 10*(Special Issue), 194–207.

He, Q., von Davier, M., Greiff, S., Steinhauer, E. W., & Borysewicz, P. B. (2017). Collaborative problem solving measures in the Programme for International Student Assessment (PISA). In A. A. von Davier, M. Zhu, & P. C. Kyllonen (Eds.), *Innovative assessment of collaboration* (pp. 95–111). Berlin: Springer International Publishing/Springer Nature. https://doi.org/10.1007/978-3-319-33261-1_7.

Hosseinioun, M., Neffke, F., Zhang, L., & Youn, H. (2025). Skill dependencies uncover nested human capital. *Nature Human Behaviour, 9*(4), 1–15.

Jiang, A. Q., Sablayrolles, A., Mensch, A., Bamford, C., Chaplot, D. S., de las Casas, D., …, & El Sayed, W. (2023). *Mistral 7B*. arXiv. https://arxiv.org/abs/2310.06825.

Jin, Y., Echeverria, V., Yan, L., Zhao, L., Alfredo, R., Tsai, Y. S., … & Martinez-Maldonado, R. (2024). FATE in MMLA: A student-centred exploration of fairness, accountability, transparency, and ethics in multimodal learning analytics. *arXiv preprint arXiv:2402.19071.*

Kerr, D., Andrews, J. J., & Mislevy, R. J. (2016). The in-task assessment framework for behavioral data. In A. A. Rupp & J. P. Leighton (Eds.), *The Wiley handbook of cognition and assessment: Frameworks, methodologies, and applications* (pp. 472–507). New York: John Wiley & Sons.

Lai, E. R., DiCerbo, K. E., & Foltz, P. (2017). *Skills for today: What we know about teaching and assessing collaboration.* London: Pearson. https://www.pearson.com/content/dam/one-dot-com/one-dot-com/global/Files/efficacy-and-research/skills-for-today/Collaboration-FullReport.pdf.

Lane, J. N., Leonardi, P. M., Contractor, N. S., & DeChurch, L. A. (2023). Teams in the digital workplace technology's role for communication, collaboration, and performance. *Small Group Research, 55*(1), 139–183. https://doi.org/10.1177/10464964231200015 (original work published 2024).

Lee, Y., Kwon, C., Seoh, S., Gweon, G., Stamper, J., & Rosé, C. P. (2025). Capturing collaborative competency with GPT-4o and ENA. In *Proceedings of the 18th international conference on computer-supported collaborative learning-CSCL 2025* (pp. 72–80). International Society of the Learning Sciences.

Letsky, M. P., Warner, N. W., Fiore, S., & Smith, C. A. P. (2008). *Macrocognition in teams: Theories and methodologies*. London: Ashgate.

Liu, L., Hao, J., von Davier, A. A., Kyllonen, P., & Zapata-Rivera, J. D. (2016). A tough nut to crack: Measuring collaborative problem solving. In *Handbook of research on technology tools for real-world skill development* (pp. 344–359). New York: IGI Global Scientific Publishing.

Lodzikowski, K., Foltz, P. W., & Behrens, J. T. (2024). Generative AI and its educational implications. In T. Kourkoulou, D. O. Tzirides, B. Cope, & M. Kalantzis (Eds.), *Trust and inclusion in AI-mediated education: Where human learning meets learning machines* (pp. 35–57). Cham: Springer Nature.

Kash, B. A., Cheon, O., Halzack, N. M., & Miller T. R. (2018). Measuring team effectiveness in the health care setting: An inventory of survey tools. *Health Services Insights*, 24(11), 1178632918796230. https://doi.org/10.1177/1178632918796230. PMID: 30158825; PMCID: PMC6109848.

Ma, Y., Celepkolu, M., & Boyer, K. E. (2022). Detecting impasse during collaborative problem solving with multimodal learning analytics. In *LAK22: 12th international*

learning analytics and knowledge conference. ACM, Online USA (pp. 45–55). https://doi.org/10.1145/3506860.3506865.
Martin, M. J., & Foltz, P. W. (2004). Automated team discourse annotation and performance prediction using LSA. In *Proceedings of the human language technology conference / North American chapter of the Association for Computational Linguistics annual meeting HLT/NAACL* (pp. 97–100).
Martınez, A., Dimitriadis, Y., Rubia, B., Gómez, E., & De la Fuente, P. (2003). Combining qualitative evaluation and social network analysis for the study of classroom social interactions. *Computers & Education*, *41*(4), 353–368.
McEwan, D., Ruissen, G. R., Eys, M. A., Zumbo, B. D., & Beauchamp, M. R. (2017). The effectiveness of teamwork training on teamwork behaviors and team performance: A systematic review and meta-analysis of controlled interventions. *PloS one*, *12*(1), e0169604.
Mislevy, R. J., Steinberg, L. S., Almond, R. G., & Lukas, J. F. (2006). Concepts, terminology, and basic models of evidence-centered design. In D. M. Williamson, R. J. Mislevy, & I. I. Bejar (Eds.), *Automated scoring of complex tasks in computer-based testing* (pp. 15–47). Mahwah, NJ: Routledge.
National Research Council. (2015). *Enhancing the effectiveness of team science*. Washington, DC: The National Academies Press.
Ochoa, X., Lang, C., Siemens, G., Wise, A., Gasevic, D., & Merceron, A. (2022). Multimodal learning analytics-rationale, process, examples, and direction. In C. Lang, G. Siemens, A. F. Wise, D. Gasevic, & A. Merceron (Eds.), *The handbook of learning analytics* (pp. 54–65). Vancouver, BC: SoLAR.
OECD. (2017). PISA 2015 results: Collaborative problem solving.
Office of Educational Technology, US Department of Education. (2023). Artificial intelligence and the future of teaching and learning: Insights and recommendations. https://files.eric.ed.gov/fulltext/ED631097.pdf.
O'Neil, H. F., Chuang, S., & Chung, G. K. W. K. (2003). Issues in the computer-based assessment of collaborative problem solving. *Assessment in Education: Principles, Policy & Practice*, *10*, 361–373. https://doi.org/10.1080/0969594032000148190.
OpenSciEd (n.d.). OpenSciEd: Creating classrooms with inspired educators & motivated learners. https://www.openscied.org. Retrieved: 8-10-2025.
Ouyang, F., & Zhang, L. (2024). AI-driven learning analytics applications and tools in computer-supported collaborative learning: A systematic review. *Educational Research Review*, *44*, 100616.
Peltonen, J., Leino-Kilpi, H., Heikkilä, H., Rautava, P., Tuomela, K., Siekkinen, M., … & Stolt, M. (2020). Instruments measuring interprofessional collaboration in healthcare - A scoping review. *Journal of Interprofessional Care*, *34*(2), 147–161. https://doi.org/10.1080/13561820.2019.1637336. Epub 2019 Jul 23. PMID: 31331216.
Prinsloo, P., Slade, S., & Khalil, M. (2023). Multimodal learning analytics—In-between student privacy and encroachment: A systematic review. *British Journal of Educational Technology*, *54*(6), 1566–1586.
Pugh, S., Subburaj, S. K., Rao, A. R., Stewart, A. E., Andrews-Todd, J., & D'Mello, S. K. (2021, November). Say what? Automatic modeling of collaborative problem solving skills from student speech in the wild. In *Proceedings of the 14th international conference on educational data mining* (pp. 208–218). Educational Data Mining.
Puntambekar, S. (2013). Mixed methods for analyzing collaborative learning. In A. M. O'Donnell & C. E. Hmelo-Silver (Eds.), *The international handbook of collaborative learning* (pp. 220–230). New York: Routledge.

Roschelle, J., & Teasley, S. D. (1995, August). The construction of shared knowledge in collaborative problem solving. In *Computer supported collaborative learning* (pp. 69–97). Berlin, Heidelberg: Springer.

Salas, E., Sims, D. E., & Burke, C. S. (2005). Is there a "big five" in teamwork?. *Small Group Research, 36*(5), 555–599.

Shaw, S., & Child, S. (2017). Utilising technology in the assessment of collaboration: A critique of PISA's collaborative problem-solving tasks. https://www.repository.cam.ac.uk/bitstreams/93e115d5-0c71-4286-a3c4-b28fdf1b2413/download.

Southwell, R., Pugh, S., Perkoff, M., Clevenger, C., Bush, J. B., Lieber, R., … & D'Mello, S. K. (2022). Challenges and feasibility of automatic speech recognition for modeling student collaborative discourse in classrooms. In *Proceedings of the 15th international educational data mining conference (EDM 22)* (pp. 302–315).

Spain, R., Min, W., Kumaran, V., Pande, J., Saville, J., & Lester, J. (2025). Applying large language models to enhance dialogue and communication analysis for adaptive team training. *International Journal of Artificial Intelligence in Education, 34*(4), 1–35.

Springer, L., Stanne, M. E., & Donovan, S. S. (1999). Effects of small group learning on undergraduates in science, mathematics, engineering, and technology: A meta-analysis. *Review of educational research, 69*(1), 21–51.

Stecher, B. M., & Hamilton, L. S. (2014). *Measuring hard-to-measure student competencies: A research and development plan. Research report.* Santa Monica, CA: RAND Corporation.

Sun, C., Shute, V., Stewart, A., Yonehiro, J., Duran, N., & D'Mello, S. K. (2020). Toward a generalized competency model of collaborative problem solving. *Computers & Education, 143*, 103672.

Tan, S. C., Lee, A. V. Y., & Lee, M. (2022). A systematic review of artificial intelligence techniques for collaborative learning over the past two decades. *Computers and Education: Artificial Intelligence, 3*, 100097.

von Davier, A. A., Zhu, M., & Kyllonen, P. C. (2017). *Innovative assessment of collaboration.* Cham: Springer.

Wang, R. E., & Demszky, D. (2023). Is chatgpt a good teacher coach? Measuring zero-shot performance for scoring and providing actionable insights on classroom instruction. *arXiv preprint arXiv:2306.03090.*

World Economic Forum. (2025). The future of jobs report 2025. Retrieved from: https://www.weforum.org/publications/the-future-of-jobs-report-2025/in-full/3-skills-outlook/.

Worsley, M., & Blikstein, P. (2018). A multimodal analysis of making. *International Journal of Artificial Intelligence in Education, 28*(3), 385–419. https://doi.org/10.1007/s40593-017-0160-1.

Xiao, Y., He, Q., Veldkamp, B. P., & Liu, H. (2021). Exploring latent states of problem-solving competence using hidden Markov modeling on process data. *Journal of Computer-Assisted Learning, 37*(5), 1232–1247.

Xu, E., Wang, W., & Wang, Q. (2023). The effectiveness of collaborative problem solving in promoting students' critical thinking: A meta-analysis based on empirical literature. *Humanities and Social Sciences Communications, 10*(1), 1–11.

Yuan, Y., Li, Z., & Zhao, B. (2025). A survey of multimodal learning: Methods, applications, and future. ACM *Computing Surveys, 57*(7), 1–34.

Zajac, S., Woods, A., Tannenbaum, S., Salas, E., & Holladay, C. L. (2021). Overcoming challenges to teamwork in healthcare: A team effectiveness framework and evidence-based guidance. *Frontiers in Communication, 6*, 606445.

13

THE IMPACT OF ARTIFICIAL INTELLIGENCE ON VALIDITY AND TEST VALIDATION

Stephen G. Sireci, Sergio Araneda, and Javier Suárez-Álvarez

13.1 The Impact of Artificial Intelligence on Validity and Test Validation

Validity has been described as one of the most important concepts in educational and psychological testing (American Educational Research Association [AERA] et al., 2014, p. 11). This importance stems from the fact that, with respect to educational and psychological tests, validity refers to the soundness of the theoretical, logical, and empirical basis for supporting the claims of a testing program. That is, validity refers to the degree to which evidence and theory support the use of a test for a particular purpose.

Before drilling in on the impact of artificial intelligence (AI) on validity, we need to unpack the many layers within this seemingly simple definition. Terms like "evidence," "theory, "use," and "purpose" require explanation of what they mean in the context of testing, particularly when AI is used in various aspects of test development, administration, scoring, score reporting, and score interpretation. In this chapter, we first present an overview of these conceptions. Then, we describe how they are being affected by the use of AI. At the time of this writing (January 2026), AI is transforming all aspects of educational and psychological testing from determining what is possible to be measured to generating test content, scoring responses, and reporting scores. In this chapter we explore how these changes affect the degree to which evidence and theory support the use of a test. As will become evident, the most fundamental aspects of validity and validation endure in this era of AI; however, how we approach them and validate a testing program require new perspectives.

DOI: 10.4324/9781003621522-13

13.1.1 Understanding Validity

Given that validity refers to the degree to which evidence and theory support the use of a test for a particular purpose, testing agencies must document their rationale for why the test is needed (i.e., the theory supporting test use) and the evidence they acquire to support test use. In this regard, we understand validity not as a fixed property of a test enabling users to make any interpretation or justify any use, but rather as contingent on a specific context of use. That is, a test does not "possess" or "not possess" validity, because validity refers to the justification of interpretations, decisions, and actions that are made on the basis of test scores. In this age of AI, such justification is even more important because what a test is measuring, how it is being measured, and what the scores mean can be less transparent relative to traditional tests.

The first two steps in responsible test development are articulating the purposes of a testing program and describing what the tests measure. For tests to fulfill their intended purposes, which includes proper interpretation of test results, these two steps are non-negotiable. Their non-negotiability becomes even more obvious when it is realized that they set the stage for test validation. We describe the importance of each step next.

13.1.2 Articulating Test Purposes and Uses

Tests are developed with specific purposes in mind. This is both an observation coming from the decades of practice in test development and an acknowledgment that tests are technologies, and as in any technology, there is an explicit intention for creating the test. It is incumbent upon the creator of a test (or testing agency) to not only clearly define those purposes but to also define the intended uses (Kane, 2013; Sireci & Benitez, 2023). The intended purposes and uses of a testing program set the targets for test design, development, and test validation. Because validity refers to the degree to which evidence and theory support the use of a test for a particular purpose, those particular (intended) purposes define the inferences and actions to be validated.

It is important to note that tests may be used for purposes other than for which they were originally designed. In such cases, it is incumbent upon the test *user* to justify that particular use through theory and evidence. Thus, for every test use, validity evidence must be presented to justify that use. Such evidence signals to test-takers, users, and society in general that the claims made about what test results mean have value, and that the actions made on the basis of test scores are justified by evidence.

AI is likely to enhance the different types of purposes educational and psychological tests can fulfill. For example, if a purpose of a test is to provide diagnostic information for individual students, or for a classroom of students, AI can help accomplish that goal by better summarizing test-takers' performance, either for individual test-takers or for groups of test-takers. Recent work in this area includes the use of AI for making narrative descriptions to summarize the results across a large group of students or across multiple assessments for an individual student. Similarly, AI is being used to enhance the feedback provided to students after they take a test. These improved "selling points" of a testing program need to be validated to see if they truly provide valuable information. Thus, the need to validate each purpose of a testing program is not new, but the new purposes and claims AI makes possible are new and will continue to expand in the future. These AI-enhanced purposes are likely to expand what needs to be validated in contemporary testing programs.

13.1.3 Describing What a Test Measures

Theories motivating and describing what a test measures come from different sources depending on the testing context. In many educational contexts, theories of learning and curriculum standards will define the knowledge and skills targeted by a test and how students' responses to test items are reflective of those knowledge and skills. In licensure and certification testing, such as when candidates are tested for a license in hair styling, accounting, nursing, and so forth, analyses of the knowledge, skills, and abilities needed for safe and successful practice are typically used to describe what is measured by the test. In psychological contexts, such as identifying a psychiatric disorder, measuring anxiety, personality, and other psychological phenomena, theories of behavior, personality, attitudes, neuropsychology, and pathology are also used to define what is measured.

There are so many different attributes measured by educational and psychological tests that the term *construct* was introduced to explain what is being measured by a test. In introducing the concept, Cronbach and Meehl (1955) defined a construct as

> some postulated attribute of people, assumed to be reflected in test performance...We expect a person at any time to possess or not possess a qualitative attribute...or to possess some degree of a quantitative attribute...
>
> *(p. 283)*

Psychometricians (those who develop and evaluate tests) have found the notion of a construct helpful in several ways, including defining what is measured on a test, and providing a framework for validation research. For example, the term *construct representation* has been used to describe the degree to which a test represents the domain of knowledge, skill, attitude, personality, and so forth that it attempts to measure. If tests are measuring other attributes or behaviors not included in the construct definition, those "nuisance" factors are referred to as *construct irrelevant*. Thus, validity in testing is supported by providing evidence of (a) construct representation, and (b) a lack of construct irrelevance. Focusing on invalidity, Messick (1989) wrote, "Tests are imperfect measures of constructs because they either leave out something that should be included ... or else include something that should be left out, or both" (Messick, 1989, p. 34). Thus, the notions of construct representation and construct irrelevance are important in evaluating the degree to which a test is fulfilling its intended purposes (Sireci, 2020, 2021).

We believe defining what a test is measuring will become more important in the age of AI-enhanced testing because it is often elusive to understand how AI generates its output and to defend the process in construct-relevant terms (Dorsey & Michaels, 2022a). For example, if test developers and researchers cannot defend the use of AI in generating test content from a theoretical perspective, the resulting content that is generated must be defended based on experts' notions of the degree to which the content is relevant to and representative of the targeted construct (Sireci, 1998a, b; Sireci & Faulkner-Bond, 2014). When assessments are based on analysis of existing data on a person, or supplemented by such data, a strong theory should be provided regarding how those data support the intended construct interpretations. In non-psychometric terms, those who develop and use tests must provide evidence the assessments measure what they intend them to measure, and such claims begin with adequate definition of what a test is intended to measure and the appropriate use of test results.

In summary, test developers are responsible for describing what it is an assessment is measuring as well as the intended uses of test results. This "construct definition" and associated "intended use statement" establish a shared understanding of what is measured between the testing agency and all "interest holders" (test-takers, test users, policy makers, etc.). In addition, it allows for a shared understanding of the value intended to be gained from using the test results.

13.1.4 Test Validation and Validity Evidence

In the previous section, we briefly defined the concept of test validity and some terms important for understanding it. In this section, we describe *test validation*, which is the process of evaluating a test based on (a) how it was developed, and (b) investigations of its quality and utility. Both (a) and (b) involve analysis of evidence and underscore the importance of including quality control procedures and following best practices when developing tests, but also conducting additional studies to ensure the test is fulfilling its specific purposes. The process of test validation is essentially evaluation, with an implied summary judgment that the use of the test for a particular purpose is justified based on the evidence evaluated. Thus, tests are "validated" for a specific purpose when the accumulated evidence supports such a conclusion.

As we describe in subsequent sections of this chapter, the use of AI in assessment likely requires additional studies than those heretofore seen in the validity literature. However, AI can also be used to enhance validity studies by providing new ways to gather validity evidence (Dorsey & Michaels, 2022b).

The AERA et al. (2014) *Standards* describe five sources of validity evidence "that might be used in evaluating the validity of a proposed interpretation of test scores for a particular use" (p. 13). These sources are validity evidence based on (a) test content, (b) response processes, (c) internal structure, (d) relations to other variables, and (e) consequences of testing. At the time of this writing, these *Standards* are being revised, and it is expected a sixth source of validity evidence, based on interpretations of test scores, will be added. These different sources of evidence illustrate the types of studies that can be done to investigate specific aspects of validity and to answer important validity questions, such as "Does the test measure what it claims to measure?", "Does the test produce comparable scores across different testing formats?", and "Is the test biased against certain types of test-takers?". In this section, we briefly describe these five sources of validity evidence and how they can be used to develop a *validity argument*, which is a synthesis of the evidence and theory that supports the use of a test for a particular purpose.

Validity evidence based on test content refers to information that reflects the degree to which the content of a test is consistent with the intended testing purposes (Sireci & Benitez, 2023). Such information is typically based on independent analysis of test content by external subject-matter experts (SMEs) that review and rate test items and scoring rubrics with respect to the degree to which they adequately represent the constructs stipulated by the test developers. Content validity studies structure the item review task in different ways and often involve critiquing the *alignment* of the objectives measured by test items to their intended objectives (Martone & Sireci, 2009; Sireci & Faulkner-Bond, 2014). Recently, AI has been used to provide alignment data by performing similar item-objective congruence ratings to those provided by human experts or by aligning objectives across different types of curricula or job tasks (Butterfuss & Doran, 2024; Mena Serrano et al., 2023).

Validity evidence based on response processes refers to data provided by investigations into whether the cognitive processes and behaviors used by test-takers to solve problems on an assessment are those that are intended to be measured. Traditional forms of validity evidence based on response processes come from many sources, including think-aloud studies where test-takers explain their reasoning while responding to items and tasks on an assessment, or to cognitive interviews where hypothesis-driven questions are asked of test-takers after they have taken an assessment. Mathematical modeling of task features that affect item difficulty (e.g., Embretson, 1983) is another form of validity evidence based on response processes. More recently, the "log data" provided by digitally-based assessments have been used to provide validity evidence based on response processes (e.g., Araneda et al., 2022, He et al., 2023a, 2023b; Zumbo & Hubley, 2017), and it is in this regard that AI techniques are proving particularly helpful. For example, AI can be used to search through the huge amounts of log data to identify patterns of responses that reveal test-takers' strategies or thought processes while responding to items.

Validity evidence based on internal structure refers to analysis of test-takers' responses to test items to understand the structure of these data and to evaluate whether the observed structure is consistent with the structure described in the construct definition (i.e., whether the observed structure of the data conforms to the intended structure). This type of evidence is statistical and uses dimensionality detection or confirmation techniques such as exploratory or confirmatory factor analysis (Rios & Wells, 2014), or model residual analysis such as the degree to which observed test data fits an item response theory model (e.g., Hambleton & Rovinelli, 1986). Validity evidence based on test structure can also be used to evaluate whether the structure of a test is consistent across different subgroups of test-takers or across different modes of taking an assessment (e.g., tablet vs. cell phone). Wells (2021) provided a comprehensive overview of how to conduct such "measurement invariance" analyses. A fascinating emerging application of AI in the area of validity evidence based on internal structure is the use of large language models to derive the dimensional structure of the text comprising a test based on item features such as semantic meaning, linguistic complexity, and other attributes (Sese, 2025; see also Golino & Epskamp, 2017; Guenole et al., 2025; Martínez-García et al., 2025). Like other validity applications, it is likely AI will greatly expand the repertoire of tools psychometricians have at their disposal for gathering and analyzing validity evidence based on internal structure.

Validity evidence based on relations to other variables comes from research studies that include test scores as one variable in the analysis and data from other sources as additional variables in the analysis. These studies probe and document the relationship between test scores and both construct-relevant and irrelevant factors. A common example of a construct-relevant study is the relationship between admissions test scores and subsequent performance in high school or college based on grade point average. Correlations between students' prior test scores and subsequent GPAs would be expected to be large and positive, given the predictive purpose of such assessments. Regression models where GPA is predicted by students' test scores and other admissions criteria (e.g., high school grades) are also typically conducted in the context of admissions testing and can be used to evaluate the strength of prediction across different groups of test-takers (e.g., Sireci & Talento-Miller, 2006). An example of a construct-irrelevant validity analysis would be investigating the relationship between digital proficiency and scores on a reading assessment, or between linguistic complexity and scores on a mathematics assessment. In both cases, high correlations would signify the presence of construct-irrelevant factors on test performance and undermine a validity argument. We expect AI may make it easier to collect data on external variables to gather validity evidence (e.g., Schoenegger et al., 2025).

Validity evidence based on testing consequences refers to results from investigations of the impact use of a test has on individuals, communities, organizations, and society in general. Traditional studies have focused on the impact of test results on "property rights" such as earning a credential or being hired by an employer. If tests are used as a primary criterion for such rewards, the degree to which attainment is reached by test-takers from different subgroups should be evaluated for potential bias against subgroups. For example, the United States Equal Employment Opportunity Council uses a "four-fifths" rule for evaluating adverse impact of selection procedures against minority groups. Specifically, if the passing rate for a minority group is less than 80% of that of the majority group, the minority group can bring a legal challenge against the testing program (U.S. Equal Employment Opportunity Commission, 2010). Validity evidence based on testing consequences includes more comprehensive analyses tied to the intended consequences of a testing program. For example, for tests that are designed to improve instruction, studies could be done to evaluate changes in teaching practices related to implementation of the testing program (Lane, 2014). Validity investigations should include both evidence that the intended purposes of a testing program are being realized, while unintended, negative effects are not occurring. AI may be useful in providing such evidence in the form of simulation studies that model the scenarios of different potential testing outcomes, but of course such evidence would need to be carefully interrogated.

Validity evidence based on appropriate interpretations of test scores is a source of validity evidence proposed by O'Leary et al. (2017) that results from systematic study of the degree to which the intended interpretations and actions of test results are appropriately being made by test users. For example, if classroom teachers are expected to act on test results to target instruction to their students, they must be able to understand the information contained in test score reports in the ways the test developers intended. Similarly, if feedback on assessments is intended to help students understand and correct their errors, they must understand the feedback for that intended effect to be realized. Studies on how well users interpret test scores are rare, but needed. It will be interesting to see if AI can be helpful to test developers and researchers in this area.

13.1.5 Summarizing and Documenting Validity Evidence: The Validity Argument

In the previous section, we described different sources of validity evidence and highlighted where applications of AI may be particularly helpful. In this section, we stress the importance of summarizing validity evidence and theory so that potential test users can make an informed decision regarding the utility of a test for their purposes, and whether all stakeholders can trust the information provided by test scores. The summary and documentation of all validity evidence can be thought of as producing a "validity argument" (Kane, 1992, 2006, 2013) that contends the accumulated evidence supports use of the test for the intended interpretations and uses. Although the validity argument is a summary document that allows for informed decisions regarding test use, it is also comprehensive, and a result of extensive prior planning of the types of evidence that should be gathered and interrogated to evaluate the degree to which a test is fulfilling its intended purposes and not resulting in unintended consequences. Given the power AI has shown promise in summarizing large amounts of data, we expect AI will be used to summarize the results of individual studies (particularly qualitative studies that involve large amounts of interview or focus group data), as well as assisting in aggregating the various results into a coherent validity argument.

13.2 AI-Enhanced Assessments and Their Impact on Validity

In the previous sections, we described traditional notions of test validity and validation, and how AI may relate to research and practice in educational and psychological testing. In this section, we first describe the emergent types of AI-based assessments and how their features impact many of the topics already covered.

AI-based assessment refers to the use of AI technologies, including machine learning (ML), deep learning (DL), and their intersection with natural language processing (NLP), to design, deliver, score, interpret, and enhance educational and psychological assessments (Bulut et al., 2024; Dorsey & Michaels, 2022a; Hao et al., 2024; Suárez-Álvarez et al., 2026). These systems can automate item generation, adapt test content to learners in real time, provide immediate and personalized feedback, and support educators with data-driven insights for instruction and intervention (Yaneva & von Davier, 2023). While we acknowledge the growing influence of AI-enabled educational tools, such as learning analytics dashboards (Susnjak et al., 2022), or intelligent tutoring systems (Graesser et al., 2016), these tools are not a primary focus of this chapter. Our focus is instead on AI-based assessments explicitly designed to measure or certify skills or used to monitor educational systems, ensure accountability, and guide instruction (Borgonovi & Suárez-Álvarez, 2025).

AI-based assessments extend beyond traditional testing by enabling dynamic, scalable, and more personalized evaluation of people's skills, while also introducing new challenges related to validity and fairness (Suárez-Álvarez et al., 2026). Table 13.1 summarizes how various AI-based applications in educational assessment contribute to and potentially threaten validity. The table highlights the dual role of AI as both a catalyst for innovation and a source of new psychometric risks. In the following sections, we revisit validity frameworks to help maximize the benefits of AI-based assessments while minimizing associated risks. But first, we provide a summary of the benefits and risks to validity posed by various AI-based applications in educational assessment.

13.2.1 Construct Identification and Development

AI technologies enable the identification and refinement of emerging constructs that are increasingly relevant in digitally mediated learning environments. Constructs

TABLE 13.1 Validity Benefits and Threats Associated with AI-Based Assessment Applications

AI-Based Applications	*Validity Benefits*	*Validity Threats*	*References*
Construct identification and development	Supports definition of technology-driven constructs (e.g., AI literacy, prompt engineering)	Construct underrepresentation	Dorsey and Michaels (2022a), Hao et al. (2024), Swiecki et al. (2022) and Yan et al. (2024)
Automated item generation	Enhances content coverage, cost-efficient item development	Risk of generating low-quality or biased items	LaFlair et al. (2023), Suárez-Álvarez et al., (2026), von Davier (2018) and von Davier et al. (2024)
Innovative item types	Increases authenticity and learner engagement	May introduce construct-irrelevant variance and accessibility barriers	Foster and Piacentini (2023) and Swiecki et al. (2022)
Item parameter calibration	Reduces the need for extensive pilot testing	Risk of inaccurate parameter estimation	Guenole et al. (2024), Suárez-Álvarez et al. (2026), and Tran et al. (2025)
Content alignment	Reduces workload for SMEs via AI-assisted mapping	Potential misalignment b/w items and standards	Butterfuss and Doran (2024)
Automated scoring	Improves scoring efficiency and reduces human bias	Limited transparency and interpretability of scoring algorithms	Bejar (2017), LaFlair et al. (2023), Lane (2023) and Shermis (2022)
Personalization	Allows adaptation to individual learner needs	Challenges for strict standardization and comparability, stereotypical outcomes	Arslan et al. (2024), Sireci et al. (2024) and Yan, von Davier, and Weiss (2024)
Test security	Enhances test fraud detection and proctoring	May be difficult to establish item equivalency and comparability	Foster (2020)

such as AI literacy, computational thinking, and prompt engineering are beginning to shape the measurement landscape. AI-driven pattern recognition in large-scale data, such as log files, learner interactions, and open-ended responses, can help conceptualize and operationalize these constructs in novel ways (Araneda et al., 2022; Hao et al., 2024; He et al., 2023a, 2023b; Swiecki et al., 2022).

However, the reliance on AI introduces the risk of construct underrepresentation. AI systems may favor features that are easily extracted or modeled, such as lexical patterns or surface behaviors, potentially neglecting the deeper cognitive or socio-emotional dimensions intended by the assessment (Dorsey & Michaels, 2022a; Hao et al., 2024). This bias toward quantifiable features can distort construct validity if not addressed through robust theoretical grounding and human oversight.

13.2.2 Automated Item Generation

Automated item generation (AIG) leverages AI to produce large volumes of test items from templates, facilitating broad content coverage and reducing development costs (LaFlair et al., 2023; Luecht, 2025; von Davier, 2018). By systematically generating item variants, AIG enhances generalizability and construct representation while supporting adaptive delivery. However, AIG can also amplify threats to validity if the generation process lacks adequate human quality control. Poorly specified item models or biased training data can result in items that are linguistically or culturally inappropriate, inaccurate in terms of difficulty, or misaligned with the intended construct (Huggins-Manley et al., 2022; Suárez-Álvarez et al., 2026; von Davier et al., 2024; Varrasi et al., 2026). These risks underscore the need for iterative human-in-the-loop validation, especially in high-stakes, multicultural and multilingual contexts.

13.2.3 Innovative Item Types

The use of AI enables the development of innovative item formats such as interactive simulations, scenario-based assessments, and chat-based dialogues. These item types offer richer representations of applied skills and decision-making processes, enhancing ecological and consequential validity (Foster & Piacentini, 2023; Swiecki et al., 2022). Such designs are particularly valuable in domains requiring dynamic reasoning or interpersonal competencies. However, innovative formats may inadvertently introduce construct-irrelevant variance if test-takers differ in their familiarity with digital interfaces or if the simulation environment is not equitably accessible. Differences in digital literacy, connectivity, or assistive technology compatibility can undermine the fairness and comparability of results (Huff & Sireci, 2001; Swiecki et al., 2022).

13.2.4 Item Parameter Calibration

AI can assist in estimating pseudo-item parameters by leveraging methods such as Bayesian networks or ML regression to infer item parameters based on item features or prior information (Tran et al., 2025). These approaches reduce the logistical burden of traditional pilot testing while accelerating the development of calibrated item banks (Guenole et al., 2024; Suárez-Álvarez et al., 2026). This innovation offers improvements over traditional statistical models used to estimate item complexity (Embretson, 1983; Sheehan & Mislevy, 1990). That said, the use of pseudo-item parameters requires empirical verification to ensure that item parameter estimates are not unstable or biased (Guenole et al., 2024; Suárez-Álvarez et al., 2026). The degree to which these new approaches to item calibration support valid and fair score interpretations still requires additional research (Varrasi et al., 2026). However, some testing programs are already reporting promising results using these AI-based approaches (AlKhuzaey et al., 2023; Runge et al., 2024; Yancey et al., 2024).

13.2.5 Content Alignment

As mentioned earlier, AI algorithms can be used to map assessment items to learning standards or curriculum frameworks, thereby assisting with instructional alignment and reducing the burden on SMEs. When properly trained, these tools can improve the transparency and efficiency of alignment processes (Butterfuss & Doran, 2024). However, one caution in this area is automated alignment systems remain vulnerable to misclassification errors and lack the nuanced judgment human experts bring to interpreting curriculum intent. Misalignments can lead to misleading conclusions about instructional effectiveness or learner progress (Butterfuss & Doran, 2024), threatening both the content and consequential aspects of validity.

13.2.6 Automated Scoring

Automated scoring systems, powered by NLP and DL, provide rapid and consistent evaluation of open-ended responses, such as essays, short answers, and even spoken interactions. These systems reduce scoring costs, minimize rater bias, and offer scalable feedback mechanisms (Bejar, 2017; LaFlair et al., 2023; Lane, 2023; Shermis, 2022). However, algorithmic scoring models often operate as "black boxes," making it difficult to ensure that scores reflect the intended construct. This opacity poses a threat to interpretive validity and challenges test developers' ability to audit scoring processes, especially in high-stakes, multicultural and multilingual environments (Dorsey & Michaels, 2022a; Hao et al., 2024).

13.2.7 Personalization

AI supports adaptive testing and personalized learning paths that respond to individual learner characteristics. By tailoring assessment content to ability levels and preferences, these systems can increase engagement, reduce anxiety, and improve measurement precision, especially for historically underserved learners (Arslan et al., 2024; Sireci et al., 2024; Suárez-Álvarez et al., 2024; Yan et al., 2024). Yet, personalization also presents comparability challenges (Bennett, 2023). When different learners receive distinct items, it becomes difficult to ensure their scores are equated or interpretable on a common scale. These concerns are particularly salient in contexts involving certification, placement, or accountability but are less likely to be consequential for assessments designed to support learning (Sireci, 2021; Sireci et al., 2024).

13.2.8 Test Security

AI-enabled proctoring and fraud detection tools enhance test security by monitoring for anomalous behaviors, including eye movement patterns, browser activity, and audio cues. These tools can deter misconduct and protect the integrity of high-stakes assessments (Foster, 2020). However, maintaining test security through frequent form rotations or reactive item removal may affect test form equivalency over time, reducing score stability and longitudinal comparability (Foster, 2020). Moreover, excessive reliance on surveillance may raise ethical concerns about student privacy and autonomy.

13.3 Validation Research for AI-Based Assessments

Because AI has the potential to change the very notion of what constitutes a "test," it will likely impact validation practices by extending them to ensure construct definition is well understood and any non-transparent (i.e., "black box") uses of AI promote rather than diminish validity. The breadth and sophistication of AI-driven computational methods are expanding rapidly, making previously inconceivable forms of assessment increasingly feasible (Dorsey & Michaels, 2022a). For instance, conversational assessment agents (Karatay & Xu, 2025) are being used to assess communication skills as are simulations enhanced with AI for learning and assessment (Hicke et al., 2025).

AI is poised to alter core validity practices—not by discarding them, but by forcing a re-examination of long-held assumptions. If we compare the practices of AI validation (i.e., how AI tools are evaluated outside of educational testing) with test validation, new emergent practices can be noticed. For example, capacity studies are often undertaken for applications of AI to understand what other things an AI technology can do beyond its immediate purpose (Carro et al., 2025; Xia et al., 2024). Also, as mentioned earlier, when assessments are enhanced using AI, if opaque models are used, they will need to be quantified and interpreted (Huggins-Manley et al., 2022; Molnar, 2025).

Nevertheless, even when AI is used throughout the entire assessment process—to score, interpret, or inform decisions—the underlying requirement for validity remains—evaluating the degree to which a test is fulfilling its intended purposes and not resulting in unintended consequences. Notably, many of the evidentiary sources proposed by Cronbach and Meehl (1955), Messick (1989), and others as part of validation are still applicable: group differences, correlation/regression analyses, factor analyses, studies of change over occasions, studies of response process, etc. Even when a model is opaque, as long as it yields a quantifiable outcome, those validation procedures can be applied.

However, a significant shift emerges when AI systems do not require the generation of a single, unified score to support decision-making. Unlike traditional assessments, which rely on one-dimensional scoring models, AI systems can leverage complex, multi-dimensional outputs. In neural networks, for instance, decision-making may rest on a high-dimensional vector produced in the final layers—effectively functioning as a score, though not in the conventional sense. This evolution challenges the conventional notion of what we mean by a "score" in testing. As such, validity frameworks may require updating to accommodate systems in which numerical representations are more complex than a single summary metric; even when applied to a single instrument, we might still label a "test."

Another way in which AI challenges validity theory is by prompting a reconsideration of the very concept of a "test." If we adopt the broad definition of measurement as the assignment of numbers or categories to individuals, then many AI models—particularly those used for classification or prediction—fall within the scope of measurement. However, this equivalence obscures an important distinction. The opaqueness and non-interpretable nature of many AI models introduce a qualitative difference when compared to traditional tests. A test is not merely a technological system that assigns outputs to individuals; it is a structured experience designed to elicit behavior or responses from a person to support specific inferences. Tests are intentionally designed to provoke cognitive or emotional responses, making the test-taking experience central to the validity of the inferences drawn. Implicit in this design is an assumption of explainability and generalizability—that the functioning of the test can be understood, and that its results can be meaningfully extended beyond the specific instance of administration. In contrast, many AI applications operate without such transparency or theoretical grounding, which suggests validation would need to include transparent explanation of the construct relevance of what is presented to test-takers and how they respond to test content.

Dorsey and Michaels (2022a) described this complexity of using AI to assist in test development and scoring, while ensuring construct representation and valid score interpretation. As they put it,

> We may use Natural Language Processing (NLP) methods to score interviews, essays, or other forms of text-based assessments, while overlooking the fact that language/text exists at multiple levels of abstraction: syntactic, lexical, semantic, and pragmatic, involving a host of construct-based inferences—ones that involve complex interactions between culture and language. Thus, based on modern validity frameworks, a more rigorous standard might be to provide evidence that NLP-based algorithms accurately understand the words/text being

produced, recognize the supporting reason(s) provided by a test-taker, and evaluate the relevance and appropriateness of the reasoning provided.

(p. 268)

As AI continues to permeate various domains, emerging technologies may increasingly fulfill roles traditional tests have occupied within societal systems—guiding decisions, allocating opportunities, and certifying competencies—without resembling conventional assessments in form or function. As the boundaries of testing and AI permeation blur, the frameworks we use to judge the appropriateness of test inferences and uses must adapt accordingly. Thus, we encourage readers to use AI to augment, not replace, traditional validation methods. That said, we note regulatory efforts aimed at governing AI will likely have ripple effects beyond AI itself, influencing a wide array of hybrid systems where AI is an auxiliary or foundational component. These broader shifts suggest that the future of validity theory will be shaped not only by psychometric advances but also by evolving societal expectations, technological architectures, and legal frameworks.

13.3.1 How Does AI Affect Construct Representation and Interpretation?

It is difficult to fully anticipate how AI will evolve, given its rapid development, the substantial investments it attracts, and the wide array of hopes and interests it embodies. AI remains a dynamic and experimental domain—a "boiling pot" of innovation. However, even amid this uncertainty, some likely impacts on construct representation in assessment can already be discerned. In its most immediate applications, AI has begun to alter how constructs are operationalized, detected, and inferred. Whether through NLP, behavioral tracking, or multimodal data integration, AI introduces new ways of capturing evidence about learners that may diverge from traditional construct definitions. This shift challenges validity theorists to reconsider how well the data captured by AI systems align with the intended constructs, and whether these systems are measuring what they claim to measure—or, alternatively, introducing new constructs altogether without explicit theoretical grounding.

For example, the use of AI in item generation is pushing the boundaries of how we define the "content domain" in assessment. Traditionally, a content domain was articulated through blueprints, frameworks, or a set of behaviors and competencies that the test was intended to represent. However, AI-driven item generation often relies on explicit input—such as text corpora, curricular documents, or other source materials—to guide the creation of items. As a result, the materials themselves increasingly function as de facto definitions of the content domain. This shift foregrounds the role of content sources not merely as references, but as active components in construct representation. Furthermore, to preserve test integrity and avoid item predictability from commonly available preparation materials, test developers may now require a "golden" or restricted content source—a curated, confidential body of knowledge that guides item generation while remaining inaccessible to test-takers. This introduces a novel layer of complexity to construct representation, where the boundaries between construct, content, and security protocols begin to blur.

In this regard, AI is amplifying a long-standing yet often underexamined issue in assessment: the divergence between the stated content domain and the actual content domain used to construct a test. While this discrepancy has always existed to some degree, the use of AI in item generation makes it more visible and potentially more consequential. In practice, we can think of three overlapping sets: (a) the intended or theoretical content domain, as defined by standards or blueprints; (b) the source material used—especially in AI-driven processes—to generate test items; and (c) the actual content presented to test-takers. Misalignments among these sets give rise to different forms of construct misrepresentation. For instance, if the source materials used by an AI model introduce biases or omit critical content areas, the resulting items may distort the construct being assessed—even if the test appears to follow the original blueprint. These tensions underscore the need to revisit how construct representation is defined, operationalized, and audited in an era where AI plays a growing role in test development.

This tension in construct representation becomes even more pronounced when generative AI is tasked with producing entire tests. What a test developer assumes the content domain to be and what the AI model actually draws upon to generate items may diverge in subtle, but significant ways. Even when a large language model (LLM) provides explanations about how it interprets prompts or follows guidelines, its internal processes remain largely opaque. As such, relying solely on its assurances is insufficient. To ensure fidelity to the intended construct, it becomes essential to conduct post hoc analyses—examining the generated items and mapping them back onto a formal blueprint or content specification. This process of alignment verification may emerge as a critical best practice in the use of generative AI for AIG, helping to safeguard construct representation and maintain the validity of resulting score interpretations.

Any time AI is used to impersonate an SME, human rater, or another role traditionally held by humans within the assessment process, the risk of construct misrepresentation emerges. Importantly, this risk is not necessarily greater than that posed by human involvement—after all, human judgment is itself a source of opacity and variability in testing (Dorsey & Michaels, 2022a). However, the substitution of AI for human roles brings renewed scrutiny to issues of transparency, bias, and fidelity to construct representation. Just as explainability is increasingly demanded of AI systems, similar standards might reasonably be applied to human raters, whose cognitive processes are no less opaque. Nevertheless, existing research indicates LLMs do not impersonate human roles with uniform accuracy. Their performance can vary significantly depending on context and is shaped by training data that are often proprietary and heavily influenced by Western, particularly American, cultural and linguistic norms. This raises concerns about construct distortion when

LLMs are deployed in diverse educational or psychological contexts, as their interpretations and outputs may not reflect the intended construct in a culturally responsive or contextually appropriate manner (Huggins-Manley et al., 2022).

A particular caution arises when LLMs are used to impersonate test-takers. Emerging research has explored the use of synthetic respondents—AI-generated proxies for real test-takers—as a method for attributing item characteristics or simulating response patterns (Liu et al., 2025). This approach often involves detailed profiling of learners, followed by logical modeling of responses based on assumed knowledge structures (e.g., if a student knows X and Y, they are predicted to answer in a specific way). While promising for purposes such as item calibration or test form evaluation, this procedure demands its own rigorous validation framework.

One of the most substantive ways to validate synthetic response generation is by comparing AI-generated "clones" with real test-takers who share similar profiles. Crucially, such validation should not be limited to matching answers alone, but should also involve response process evidence—for example, comparing think-aloud protocols or reasoning paths. If this technique becomes widely used, but is implemented without adequate safeguards, it poses significant risks for construct misrepresentation, potentially undermining the interpretive validity of test scores derived from such data.

When AI is used for scoring, several critical risks must be carefully considered. One of the most pressing concerns is the potential for algorithmic bias (International Test Commission [ITC] & Association of Test Publishers [ATP], 2022). Depending on how the AI system is trained, the underlying data may contain biases—whether historical, cultural, or demographic—that become embedded in the model and subsequently influence the scoring outcomes. These biases can manifest globally, affecting all examinees, or locally, disproportionately impacting specific subgroups or geographic regions. This issue, widely recognized as algorithmic bias, has been extensively documented in the AI ethics and fairness literature (Baker & Hawn, 2022; Bulut et al., 2024; Dorsey & Michaels, 2022a). The challenge is particularly acute with opaque, or "black-box," AI models, where the internal decision-making processes are not easily interpretable. In response, a growing body of statistical and computational methods have been developed to detect, quantify, and mitigate such biases, including fairness metrics, bias audits, and post hoc adjustment techniques (Thompson et al., 2021; Chen et al., 2023). Nonetheless, the use of these tools requires deliberate integration into the validation process to ensure automated scoring systems do not compromise the fairness and validity of test score interpretations.

In addition, recent advances in AI have placed unprecedented stress on test security. While AI offers promising tools for personalizing assessments and enhancing test design (Sireci et al., 2024), it simultaneously enables new and increasingly sophisticated forms of cheating. In the past two years alone, numerous cases have emerged involving AI-assisted misconduct, including browser extensions that generate real-time responses, wearable devices like smart glasses connected to LLMs, and even the use of deepfakes for identity fraud (e.g., Goodier, 2025). From a validity perspective, such breaches are not merely procedural violations—they represent direct threats to the interpretability and defensibility of test scores. Furthermore, when some individuals have access to AI-enhanced cheating tools while others do not, the issue transcends validity and becomes one of fairness. The dual impact on both the accuracy of inferences and the equity of testing conditions underscores the urgent need to integrate test security considerations into contemporary validity frameworks. Thus, the degree to which cheating and other security threats are present remains an important validation consideration in this age of AI.

13.4 Methods for Evaluating AI Assessments: User and Test-Taker Experience

In traditional assessment contexts, test design has often prioritized psychometric rigor over the experience of the test-taker. Recent work in educational measurement (Araneda, 2023) has argued for a reimagining of test validity through an experiential lens—one that considers the lived experience of the test-taker as integral to the success and fairness of the assessment. This shift aligns with broader trends in human-centered design and reflects growing recognition that interface design, feedback structures, and perceptions of fairness influence both engagement and performance.

Under this experiential view, validity is framed not only as a technical property of score interpretation, but also as a socio-technical accomplishment, dependent on the successful implementation of a design that is experienced as meaningful, accessible, and appropriate. Within this framework, user experience (UX) research becomes validity-relevant: understanding and optimizing test-taker experience supports the legitimacy of the inferences drawn from assessment results. Techniques such as think-aloud protocols, usability testing, and emotion tracking are therefore essential tools for gathering experiential evidence in support of test validity, and co-design (involving test-takers and other stakeholders in assessment design and revision) will be particularly valuable (Sireci et al., 2025).

The integration of AI into assessment systems—via automated scoring, adaptive testing, or generative item design—has introduced new dynamics to the test-taker experience. These AI-driven systems not only present content, but also adapt in real time based on user interaction, influencing both the content and structure of the assessment. This evolution requires extending UX considerations into the domain of algorithmic experience (AX), which refers to the subjective and behavioral experience of interacting with algorithmic systems (Shin et al., 2020). In AI-enhanced assessments, AX includes

- the perception of how adaptive engines select and present items
- the interpretability and perceived fairness of automated scoring
- the responsiveness and credibility of AI tutors or conversational agents
- the overall predictability and transparency of system behavior

Negative AX—such as feelings of being unfairly judged by an opaque algorithm or confusion due to unpredictable item selection—can compromise trust in the system and, by extension, the legitimacy of the assessment outcomes.

The field of human-AI interaction has begun to formalize frameworks for evaluating algorithmic systems from a user-centered perspective. For instance, studies by Wang et al. (2019) proposed conceptual frameworks for assessing trust, perceived agency, and explainability in AI interactions. Such frameworks are directly applicable to AI-driven testing environments, where perceptions of fairness, clarity, and control can shape both user engagement and response processes (Huggins-Manley et al., 2022).

To ensure validity in AI-enhanced assessments, AX research should be integrated into test design and validation processes. Mixed-method approaches—combining behavioral logs, qualitative interviews, and affective data—can reveal critical insights into how test-takers experience algorithmic assessments and how systems might be improved to support equitable and trustworthy measurement.

13.4.1 Synthetic Data Simulating Test-Takers and SME

Recent advances in LLMs have opened new opportunities for simulating test-taker responses and SME feedback using synthetic data. This method offers scalable, cost-effective alternatives for early-stage item evaluation and test development. Two lines of research demonstrate the feasibility and challenges of this approach.

Liu et al. (2025) examined whether LLMs can simulate student responses to college algebra items with psychometric fidelity. They prompted six different models—including GPT-3.5, GPT-4, and LLaMA 3—to generate responses, comparing them to actual responses from undergraduate students. Results showed that some LLMs outperformed humans in mean proficiency but lacked the distributional variability found in real populations. While no single model could fully emulate human proficiency distributions, assembling multiple LLMs yielded a synthetic respondent pool with improved alignment to human data. Their study also introduced augmentation strategies, mixing real and synthetic responses, showing that hybrid samples (e.g., 50% human, 50% LLM) yielded improved parameter recovery under item response theory. Thus, LLMs can function as "virtual examinees" to reduce the burden of data collection while preserving psychometric rigor.

In parallel, Lu and Wang (2024) proposed the concept of generative students—LLM-simulated learners with predefined profiles of strengths and weaknesses. These generative agents were used to evaluate and flag problematic items during the item development process. By controlling the skill mastery patterns, they were able to simulate nuanced test-taking behaviors and validate whether items aligned with intended constructs. This approach reflects a shift from generic response simulation to intentional, profile-based modeling of cognition and performance, bringing test development closer to theory-driven validation practices. Furthermore, by simulating SME behavior alongside students, their framework enables parallel validation of both response plausibility and rationale coherence—key dimensions in modern assessment design.

The potential of LLM-based data simulation for assessment development and validation is promising. Many forms of validity evidence—especially those grounded in empirical item analysis, test piloting, or response process evaluation—require extensive data collection from human participants, which is costly, time-consuming, and logistically complex. The strategic use of large language models to simulate or augment human responses offers a scalable alternative to gather validity evidence based on response processes or internal structure that can reduce research burden while preserving analytical rigor. If robust validation frameworks can be established to support the full use of synthetic data, this approach could offer not only a complement but, in some contexts, a viable substitute for early-stage empirical testing. In this sense, LLM-based simulation holds the potential to become a transformative tool for data augmentation, allowing developers to explore item functioning, refine test blueprints, and surface construct-irrelevant variance—all before real examinees ever engage with the test.

13.4.2 Evaluating Scoring Engines

In educational measurement, scoring functions—whether human or algorithmic—are central components of the interpretation argument. A test interpretation reflects a claim about an underlying psychological attribute based on a defined response process. The validity of such inference rests in part on whether the scoring mechanism properly captures the intended construct. In the case of AI-based scoring engines, this extends beyond the accuracy of output labels to include questions about construct representation, stability across contexts, and the transparency of decision-making.

Messick (1989) emphasized scoring as a design act—one that embodies assumptions about what constitutes evidence of knowledge or ability. The appropriateness of scoring models, particularly when they are automated, must be evaluated not only in terms of criterion performance (e.g., agreement with human raters) but also in relation to construct relevance and construct underrepresentation. For example, if an AI scoring engine favors verbosity or syntactic complexity over conceptual accuracy, it may systematically reward irrelevant features, thus compromising the fidelity of the score to the intended construct.

The AERA et al. (2014) *Standards* similarly stress that validation of automated scoring systems should include empirical studies of inter-rater agreement, error patterns, and generalizability across diverse subgroups and prompt types. It is also essential to interrogate the human-AI interaction dynamics in hybrid scoring systems, where human raters may be influenced by AI recommendations—an under-explored area with implications for both validity and fairness.

13.4.3 Evaluating Potential Biases in Scoring Engines

Bias in testing is traditionally conceptualized as construct-irrelevant variance—systematic errors that unfairly advantage or disadvantage particular groups, regardless of the intended construct being measured (Messick, 1989). In AI-augmented assessments, potential sources of bias expand considerably. Scoring engines and item generators trained on large-scale corpora may inherit societal biases encoded in those data, reproducing disparities that are difficult to detect without careful design and evaluation. Dorsey and Michaels (2022a) aptly point out that AI-based scoring algorithms can perpetuate human biases, while also adding unique biases rooted in the algorithm or the training data.

Cronbach and Meehl's (1955) emphasis on *nomological networks*—that is, the web of theoretical and empirical relationships among constructs—provides a foundation for detecting biased functioning. When observed patterns of scoring or prediction diverge from expected relationships across groups, it may suggest that the score is contaminated by irrelevant features. This is further formalized in modern practice through statistical tools such as differential item functioning and differential prediction analyses, both of which are recommended by the AERA et al. (2014) *Standards* as critical for evaluating fairness.

For AI-based systems, bias evaluation must extend beyond outputs to the design pipeline itself: the training data, prompt engineering, and feedback loops that shape model behavior. Methods such as counterfactual fairness testing (Kim & Kim, 2025) and intersectional audit studies (Morina et al., 2019; Ovalle et al., 2023) are gaining prominence as tools to evaluate whether scoring models systematically underperform for particular populations or misrepresent the intended constructs in ways that correlate with race, gender, language, or other demographic attributes.

Ultimately, the evaluation of both scoring engines and bias must be tied to a theory of validity as a social and ethical responsibility (Huggins-Manley et al., 2022; Messick, 1989). Validity is not only a matter of internal technical coherence, but also of the consequences of test use for individuals and groups. As algorithmic assessment becomes more widespread, these evaluative responsibilities grow—requiring psychometricians to engage deeply with both foundational theory and emerging computational methods.

13.5 Conclusions

In this chapter, we began with an explanation of the foundational concepts of validity such as defining testing purpose and the construct to be tested and gathering evidence to confirm a test is operating as intended and having the intended outcomes. We then described how AI applications in assessment require us to think more broadly about how to stay true to these foundational concepts when AI makes aspects of test development, administration, scoring, or score interpretation less transparent. Cautions that deserve more attention in validation include focusing on how content is created and represents the intended construct, how scores or other information is produced from the interactions of test-takers with the test, and investigation of potential biases based on ML algorithms and the data on which they are trained.

As we consider the impact of AI on assessments, one conclusion is clear—validation becomes more important and will require more effort relative to traditional assessments. Traditional tests have been criticized for their lack of transparency with respect to how they transform students' responses to a scale score. In this age of AI, the testing inputs and outputs will increasingly be based on algorithms and models that will not be well understood by most stakeholders in the testing process. Validating the construct relevance and fairness of these approaches and their results thus becomes an important addition to test validation.

References

AlKhuzaey, S., Grasso, F., Payne, T., & Tamma, V. (2023). Text-based question difficulty prediction: A systematic review of automatic approaches. *International Journal of Artificial Intelligence in Education, 34*, 862–914. https://doi.org/10.1007/s40593-023-00362-1.

American Educational Research Association, American Psychological Association, & National Council on Measurement in Education. (2014). *Standards for educational and psychological testing*. Washington, DC: American Educational Research Association.

Araneda, S. (2023). *An experiential approach to test design and validation* [Doctoral dissertation, University of Massachusetts Amherst]. ScholarWorks@UMass Amherst. https://doi.org/10.7275/33072110.

Araneda, S., Lee, D., Lewis, J., Sireci, S. G., Moon, J. A., Lehman, B., … & Keehner, M. (2022). Exploring relationships among test takers' behaviors and performance using response process data. *Education Sciences, 12*, 104. https://doi.org/10.3390/educsci12020104.

Arslan, B., Lehman, B., Tenison, C., Sparks, J. R., López, A., Gu, L., & Zapata-Rivera, D. (2024). Opportunities and challenges of using generative AI to personalize educational assessment. *Frontiers in Artificial Intelligence, 7*, 1–8. https://doi.org/10.3389/frai.2024.1460651.

Baker, R. S., & Hawn, A. (2022). Algorithmic bias in education. *International Journal of Artificial Intelligence in Education, 32*(4), 1052–1092.

Bejar, I. I. (2017). Threats to score meaning in automated scoring. In K. Ercikan & J. Pellegrino (Eds.), *Validation of score meaning for the next generation of assessments* (pp. 75–84). New York: Routledge. https://doi.org/10.4324/9781315708591.

Bennett, R. E. (2023). Toward a theory of socioculturally responsive assessment. *Educational Assessment, 28*(2), 83–104. https://doi.org/10.1080/10627197.2023.2202312.

Borgonovi, F., & Suárez-Álvarez, J. (2025). *How can adult skills best meet the demands of the 21st century?* OECD Social, Employment, and Migration Working Papers, No. 319, OECD Publishing, Paris. https://doi.org/10.1787/853db37b-en.

Bulut, O., Beiting-Parrish, M., Casabianca, J. M., Slater, S. C., Jiao, H., Song, D., … & Morilova, P. (2024). The rise of artificial intelligence in educational measurement: Opportunities and ethical challenges. *arXiv preprint arXiv:2406.18900.*

Butterfuss, R., & Doran. H. (2024, February). *An application of text embeddings to support alignment of educational content standards*. Paper presented at the Generative Artificial Intelligence for Measurement and Education meeting. Available at https://hdoran.github.io/Blog/ContentMapping.pdf.

Carro, R., Liao, B., Hase, P., Chaudhary, S., & Bansal, M. (2025). A conceptual framework for AI capability evaluations. *arXiv*. https://arxiv.org/abs/2406.06562.

Chen, R. J., Wang, J. J., Williamson, D. F., Chen, T. Y., Lipkova, J., Lu, M. Y., … & Mahmood, F. (2023). Algorithmic fairness in artificial intelligence for medicine and healthcare. *Nature Biomedical Engineering, 7*(6), 719–742.

Cronbach, L. J., & Meehl, P. E. (1955). Construct validity in psychological tests. *Psychological Bulletin, 52*(4), 281.

Dorsey, D. W., & Michaels, H. R. (2022a). Validity arguments meet artificial intelligence in innovative educational assessment. *Journal of Educational Measurement, 59*, 267–271.

Dorsey, D. W., & Michaels, H. R. (2022b). Validity arguments meet artificial intelligence in innovative educational assessment: A discussion and look forward. *Journal of Educational Measurement, 59*, 389–394.

Embretson (Whitley), S. (1983). Construct validity: construct representation versus nomothetic span. *Psychological Bulletin, 93*, 179–197.

Foster, D. (2020). *SmartItems: Stop fraud, improve fairness, and upgrade the way you test.* Midvale, UT: Caveon.

Foster, N., & Piacentini, M. (Eds.) (2023). *Innovating assessments to measure and support complex skills*. Paris: OECD Publishing. https://doi.org/10.1787/e5f3e341-en.

Golino, H. F., & Epskamp, S. (2017). Exploratory graph analysis: A new approach for estimating the number of dimensions in psychological research. *PLOS ONE, 12*(6), e0174035. https://doi.org/10.1371/journal.pone.0174035.

Goodier, M. (2025, June 15). Revealed: Thousands of UK university students caught cheating using AI. *The Guardian*. Retrieved from https://www.theguardian.com/education/2025/jun/15/thousands-of-uk-university-students-caught-cheating-using-ai-artificial-intelligence-survey.

Graesser, A., Hu, X., Nye, B., & Sottilare, R. (2016). Intelligent tutoring systems, serious games, and the Generalized Intelligent Framework for Tutoring (GIFT). In H. F. O'Neil, E. L. Baker, & R. S. Perez (Eds.), *Using games and simulations for teaching and assessment: Key issues* (pp. 58–79). Routledge. https://doi.org/10.4324/9781315817767.

Guenole, N., D'Urso, E., Samo, A., & Sun, T. (2024, April 14). *Pseudo Factor Analysis of Language Embedding Similarity Matrices: New Ways to Model Latent Constructs*. [Preprint]. PsyArXiv. https://doi.org/10.31234/osf.io/vf3se_v2.

Guenole, N., D'Urso, E. D., Samo, A., Sun, T., & Haslbeck, J. (2025, March 12). Enhancing scale development: Pseudo factor analysis of language embedding similarity matrices. OSF. https://osf.io/.

Hambleton, R. K., & Rovinelli, R. J. (1986). Assessing the dimensionality of a set of test items. *Applied Psychological Measurement, 10*(3), 287–302.

Hao, J., von Davier, A. A., Yaneva, V., Lottridge, S., von Davier, M., & Harris, D. J. (2024). Transforming assessment: The impacts and implications of large language models and generative AI. *Educational Measurement: Issues and Practice, 43*, 16–29. https://doi.org/10.1111/emip.12602.

He, Q., Borgonovi, F., & Suárez-Álvarez, J. (2023a). Clustering sequential navigation patterns in multiple-source reading tasks with dynamic time warping method. *Journal of Computer Assisted Learning, 39*(3), 719–736. https://doi.org/10.1111/jcal.12748.

He, Q., Shi, Q., & Tighe, E. (2023b). Predicting problem-solving proficiency with hierarchical supervised models on response process. *Psychological Test and Assessment Modeling, 65*(1), 255–281.

Hicke, Y., Geathers, J., Rajashekar, N., Chan, C., Jack, A. G., Sewell, J., … & Kizilcec, R. (2025). MedSimAI: Simulation and formative feedback generation to enhance deliberate practice in medical education. *arXiv preprint arXiv:2503.05793.*

Huff, K. L., & Sireci, S. G. (2001). Validity issues in computer-based testing. *Educational Measurement: Issues and Practice, 20*(3), 16–25.

Huggins-Manley, A. C., Booth, B. M., & D'Mello, S. K. (2022). Toward argument-based fairness with an application to AI-enhanced educational assessments. *Journal of Educational Measurement, 59*, 362–388.

International Test Commission and Association of Test Publishers. (2022). *Guidelines for technology-based assessments* (J. Weiner & S. Sireci, Eds.). Available at https://www.intestcom.org/page/28.

Kane, M. (2006). Validation. In R. L. Brennan (Ed.), *Educational measurement* (4th ed., pp. 17–64). Washington, DC: American Council on Education/Praeger.
Kane, M. (2013). Validating the interpretations and uses of test scores. *Journal of Educational Measurement, 50*, 1–73.
Kane, M. T. (1992). An argument-based approach to validity. *Psychological Bulletin, 112*, 527–535.
Karatay, Y., & Xu, J. (2025). Exploring the potential of conversational AI for assessing second language oral proficiency. *TEOSL Quarterly*. https://doi.org/10.1002/tesq.70003.
Kim, W., & Kim, H. (2025). Counterfactual fairness evaluation of machine learning models on educational datasets. *arXiv preprint arXiv:2504.11504.*
LaFlair, G., Yancey, K., Settles, B., & von Davier, A. A. (2023). Computational psychometrics for digital-first Assessments: A blend of ML and psychometrics for item generation and scoring. In V. Yaneva & M. von Davier (Eds.), *Advancing natural language processing in educational assessment* (pp. 107–123). New York: Routledge. https://doi.org/10.4324/9781003278658.
Lane, S. (2023). Validity, fairness, and technology-based assessment. In V. Yaneva & M. von Davier (Eds.), *Advancing natural language processing in educational assessment* (1st ed.). Routledge. https://doi.org/10.4324/9781003278658-11
Lane, S. (2014). Validity evidence based on testing consequences. *Psicothema*. https://doi.org/10.7334/psicothema2013.258.
Liu, Y., Bhandari, S., & Pardos, Z. A. (2025). Leveraging LLM respondents for item evaluation: A psychometric analysis. *British Journal of Educational Technology, 56*(3), 1028–1052.
Lu, X., & Wang, X. (2024, July). Generative students: Using llm-simulated student profiles to support question item evaluation. In *Proceedings of the Eleventh ACM Conference on Learning@ Scale* (pp. 16–27).
Luecht, R. M. (2025). *Assessment engineering in test design: Methods and practices*. New York: Routledge. https://doi.org/10.4324/9781003451051.
Martínez-García, J., Montaño, J. J., Jiménez, R., Gervilla, E., Cajal, B., Núñez, A., … & Sesé, A. (2025). Decoding artificial intelligence: A tutorial on neural networks in behavioral research. *Psicothema, 36*(2), 77–95.
Martone, A., & Sireci, S. G. (2009). Evaluating alignment between curriculum, assessments, and instruction. *Review of Educational Research, 4*, 1332–1361.
Mena Serrano, F., Smith, N., & Suárez-Álvarez, J. (2023, October). *Evaluating existing standard alignment studies using NLP*. Paper presented at the annual meeting of the Northeastern Educational Research Association, Trumbull, CT.
Messick, S. (1989). Validity. In R. L. Linn (Ed.), *Educational measurement* (3rd ed., pp. 13–103). American Council on Education & Macmillan.
Molnar, C. (2025). *Interpretable machine learning: A guide for making black box models explainiable* (3rd ed.). Available at https://christophm.github.io/interpretable-ml-book/.
Morina, G., Oliinyk, V., Waton, J., Marusic, I., & Georgatzis, K. (2019). Auditing and achieving intersectional fairness in classification problems. *arXiv preprint arXiv:1911.01468.*
O'Leary, T. M., Hattie, J. A. C., & Griffin, P. (2017). Actual interpretations and use of scores as aspects of validity. *Educational Measurement: Issues and Practice, 36*(2), 16–23.
Ovalle, A., Subramonian, A., Gautam, V., Gee, G., & Chang, K. W. (2023, August). Factoring the matrix of domination: A critical review and reimagination of intersectionality in ai fairness. In *Proceedings of the 2023 AAAI/ACM Conference on AI, Ethics, and Society* (pp. 496–511).
Rios, J., & Wells, C. S. (2014). Validity evidence based on internal structure. *Psicothema, 26*(1), 108–116.

Runge, A., Attali, Y., LaFlair, G. T., Park, Y., & Church, J. (2024). A generative AI-driven interactive listening assessment task. *Frontiers in Artificial Intelligence, 7*, 1–21, 1474019. https://doi.org/10.3389/frai.2024.1474019.

Schoenegger, P., Greenberg, S., Grishin, A., Lewis, J., & Caviola, L. (2025). AI can outperform humans in predicting correlations between personality items. *Communications Psychology, 3*, Article 23. https://doi.org/10.1038/s44271-025-00205-w

Sese, A. (2025, July). *Mapping construct representations: Integrative approaches to content validity and latent structures*. Paper presented at the XI onference of the European Methodology Association, Tenerife, Spain.

Shermis, M. D. (2022). Anchoring validity evidence for automated scoring. *Journal of Educational Measurement, 59*, 314–337.

Sheehan, K., & Mislevy, R. J. (1990). Integrating cognitive and psychometric models to measure document literacy. *Journal of Educational Measurement, 27*, 255–272.

Shin, D., Zhong, B., & Biocca, F. A. (2020). Beyond user experience: What constitutes algorithmic experiences? *International Journal of Information Management*, *52*, 102061.

Sireci, S. G. (1998a). Gathering and analyzing content validity data. *Educational Assessment, 5*, 299–321.

Sireci, S. G. (1998b). The construct of content validity. *Social Indicators Research, 45*, 83–117.

Sireci, S. G. (2020). De-"constructing" test validation. *Chinese/English Journal of Educational Measurement and Evaluation, 1,* 1–13. 教育测量与评估双语季刊. Available at: https://www.ce-jeme.org/journal/vol1/iss1/3 [https://doi.org/10.59863/CKHH8837].

Sireci, S. G. (2021). Valuing educational measurement. *Educational Measurement: Issues and Practice, 40*(1), 7–16. https://doi.org/10.1111/emip.12415.

Sireci, S. G., & Benitez, I. (2023). Evidence for test validation: A guide for practitioners. *Psicothema, 35*(3), 217–226.

Sireci, S. G., Crespo Cruz, E., Suárez-Álvarez, J., & Rodriguez, G. (2025). Understanding UNDERSTANDardization research. In R. Bennett, L. Darling-Hammond, & A. Badrinarayan (Eds.), *Socioculturally responsive assessment: Implications for theory, measurement, and systems-level policy* (pp. 415–433). New York: Routledge.

Sireci, S. G., & Faulkner-Bond, M. (2014). Validity evidence based on test content. *Psicothema, 26*, 100–107. https://doi.org/10.7334/psicothema2013.256.

Sireci, S. G., Suárez-Alvárez, J., Zenisky, A. L., & Oliveri, M. E. (2024). Evolving educational testing to meet students' needs: Design-in-real-time assessment. *Educational Measurement: Issues and Practice, 43*(4), 112–118.

Sireci, S. G., & Talento-Miller, E. (2006). Evaluating the predictive validity of Graduate Management Admissions Test Scores. *Educational and Psychological Measurement, 66*, 305–317.

Suárez-Ávarez, J., Oliveri, M. E., Zenisky, A., & Sireci, S. G (2024). Five key actions for redesigning adult skills assessments from learners, employees, and educators. *Journal for Research on Adult Education, 47*, 321–343. https://doi.org/10.1007/s40955-024-00288-8

Suárez-Álvarez, J., He, Q., Guenole, N., & D´Urso, D. (2026). Using artificial intelligence in test construction: A practical guide. *Psicothema, 38*(1), 1–12. https://doi.org/10.70478/psicothema.2026.38.01

Susnjak, T., Ramaswami, G. S., & Mathrani, A. (2022). Learning analytics dashboard: A tool for providing actionable insights to learners. *International Journal of Educational Technology in Higher Education, 19(12)*, 1–23. https://doi.org/10.1186/s41239-021-00313-7.

Swiecki, Z., Khosravi, H., Chen, G., Martinez-Maldonado, R., Lodge, J. M., Milligan, S., … & Gaševi´c, D. (2022). Assessment in the age of artificial intelligence. *Computers and Education: Artificial Intelligence, 3*, 100075. https://doi.org/10.1016/j.caeai.2022.100075.

Thompson, H. M., Sharma, B., Bhalla, S., Boley, R., McCluskey, C., Dligach, D., … & Afshar, M. (2021). Bias and fairness assessment of a natural language processing opioid misuse classifier: Detection and mitigation of electronic health record data disadvantages across racial subgroups. *Journal of the American Medical Informatics Association, 28*(11), 2393–2403.

Tran, P., Feng, W., Sireci, S. G., McNichols, H., & Lan, A. (2025). Using item features to calibrate educational test items: Comparing artificial intelligence and classical approaches. *American Journal of Education and Learning, 10*(2), 178–189. https://doi.org/10.55284/ajel.v10i2.1543.

U.S. Equal Employment Opportunity Commission. (2010). *Fact sheet on employment tests and selection procedures*. Washington, DC: U.S. Equal Employment Opportunity Commission. Available at https://www.eeoc.gov/policy/docs/factemployment_procedures.html.

Varrasi, S., Platania, G. A., Castellano, S., Ferraioli, F., Massimino, S., Vicario, C. M., Di Nuovo, S., & D'Urso, E. D. (2026). Expanding psychometrics with pretrained language models: Evaluating pseudo-factor analysis in applied and multilingual contexts. *Methods in Psychology*, 14, Article 100244. https://doi.org/10.1016/j.metip.2026.100244

von Davier, A. A., Runge, A., Park, Y., Attali, Y., Church, J., & LaFlair, G. (2024). The item factory: Intelligent automation in support of test development at scale. In H. Jaio & R. Lissitz (Eds.), *Machine learning, natural language processing, and psychometrics* (pp. 1–25). Charlotte, NC: Information Age Publishing.

von Davier, M. (2018). Automated item generation with recurrent neural networks. *Psychometrika, 83*(4), 847–857. https://doi.org/10.1007/s11336-018-9608-y.

Wang, D., Yang, Q., Abdul, A., & Lim, B. Y. (2019, May). Designing theory-driven user-centric explainable AI. In *Proceedings of the 2019 CHI Conference on Human Factors in Computing Systems* (pp. 1–15).

Wells, C. S. (2021). *Assessing measurement invariance for applied research*. Cambridge: Cambridge University Press.

Xia, B., Lu, Q., Zhu, L., & Xing, Z. (2024, July). An AI system evaluation framework for advancing AI safety: Terminology, taxonomy, lifecycle mapping. In *Proceedings of the 1st ACM International Conference on AI-Powered Software* (pp. 74–78).

Yan, D., von Davier, A. A., & Weiss, D. (Eds.) (2024). *Research for practical issues and solutions in multistage-adaptive testing*. Oxfordshire: Taylor and Francis.

Yancey, K. P., Runge, A., LaFlair, G., & Mulcaire, P. (2024). BERT-IRT: Accelerating item piloting with BERT embeddings and explainable IRT models. In *Proceedings of the 19th Workshop on Innovative Use of NLP for Building Educational Applications* (pp. 428–438). Available at https://aclanthology.org/2024.bea-1.35.pdf.

Yaneva, V., & von Davier, M. (Eds.) (2023). *Advancing natural language processing in educational assessment*. New York: Routledge. https://doi.org/10.4324/9781003278658.

Zumbo, B. D., & Hubley, A. M. (Eds.) (2017). *Understanding and investigating response processes in validation research*. Cham: Springer Press.

14

THE TRANSFORMATIVE POTENTIAL OF AI IN LARGE-SCALE ASSESSMENTS

Ummugul Bezirhan and Matthias von Davier

14.1 Introduction

Artificial intelligence (AI) is rapidly transforming the landscape of educational assessment. Once dependent solely on human expertise, assessment systems are now increasingly supported or even driven by intelligent algorithms capable of scoring, generating, classifying, and assembling test content. These advancements find their way into large-scale assessments, including international large-scale assessment (ILSA) programs such as Trends in International Mathematics and Science Study (TIMSS), Progress in International Reading Literacy Study (PIRLS), and Programme for International Student Assessment (PISA), as well as national assessments such as the National Assessment of Educational Progress (NAEP). Given the essential role these programs play in monitoring educational progress, guiding policy, and informing system-level decisions, the increasingly central role of AI within them carries both significant promise and profound responsibility.

Over the past decade, AI technologies have evolved from experimental tools into essential components of assessment systems. Innovations in machine learning (ML) and natural language processing (NLP) now enable the automatic scoring of open-ended responses (e.g., Tyack et al., 2024; Jung et al., 2025; Mizumoto & Eguchi, 2023), the generation of items aligned with curriculum frameworks (e.g., Bezirhan & von Davier, 2023; Gorgun & Bulut, 2025), and the assembly of adaptive tests tailored to students' abilities. In ILSAs, where cross-linguistic and cross-cultural fairness is paramount, large language models (LLMs) enable new possibilities for automated scoring across languages, generation of culturally appropriate content, and alignment with curricular and international frameworks. These innovations support the development and implementation of assessments that are not only psychometrically robust but also operationally sustainable on a global scale.

DOI: 10.4324/9781003621522-14

Despite these advancements, the use of AI in assessment is not without risk. Key concerns include privacy, algorithmic bias, lack of transparency, cultural and linguistic fairness, and the potential erosion of validity arguments when black box models are adopted without sufficient documentation or interpretability. As researchers have emphasized, AI can perpetuate historical inequities if its design and deployment are not carefully checked through ongoing bias monitoring, scale drift analysis, and validation studies (e.g., Bulut et al., 2024; Chang, 2024; Ho, 2024).

Because AI systems operate differently from traditional psychometric models, their adoption may alter several elements of a comprehensive validity argument (Ercikan, 2025). Automated scoring may introduce learned decision rules that may not align with the intended construct, raising questions on internal structure and generalizability. AI-driven item generation may potentially change how the construct domain is covered, with implications for content validity and construct representation. Similarly, embedding-based alignment tools rely on semantic similarity and require careful evaluation to determine when these approaches meaningfully reflect the underlying construct. Throughout this chapter, we highlight these interactions and identify where existing methodologies provide adequate guidance and where AI-specific extensions to current practices may be needed.

To ensure responsible implementation, leading organizations advocate for aligning AI-enhanced assessment systems with existing measurement standards such as the Standards for Educational and Psychological Testing (American Educational Research Association, American Psychological Association, and National Council on Measurement in Education [AERA, APA, and NCME], 2014) while also developing new guidance specific to AI's unique capabilities and risks (Ho, 2024). A recurring recommendation in the literature is the adoption of a human-in-the-loop approach (Burstein, 2023), in which psychometricians, educators, and domain experts collaborate with AI to ensure quality, fairness, and contextual relevance. In addition, privacy concerns must be addressed when using cloud-based services, such as scoring written student responses that may potentially contain identifiable information.

This chapter is intended for psychometricians, assessment developers, policymakers, and researchers who are considering or implementing AI-based processes in large-scale assessment programs. We focus on four use cases that are most consequential for ILSAs: automated scoring, item generation, test assembly, and item alignment, drawing on recent research, pilot implementations, and ethical frameworks. Our aim is not to provide an exhaustive catalog of AI applications in education but rather to examine those that directly reshape large-scale assessment ecosystems and to identify both the opportunities they offer for innovation and the boundaries that must be respected. Ultimately, this chapter advocates an approach that leverages AI to extend human capability while preserving human decision-making at key points and upholding the principles of equity and interpretability that are fundamental to responsible assessment.

14.2 Important Use Cases of AI in Large-Scale Assessments

The integration of AI into large-scale assessment programs is most apparent in four key domains: automated scoring, item generation, item verification and alignment, and test assembly. These use cases represent the core functions where AI technologies are currently being researched, piloted, and implemented. Each application seeks to address longstanding challenges in assessment, such as scalability, consistency, timeliness, and resource intensiveness, while introducing new capabilities.

14.2.1 Automated Scoring

Automated scoring has been used in educational measurement for decades, employing NLP and computational linguistics methods, as well as statistical models, to evaluate examinee responses to open-ended questions. It represents one of the most mature applications of ML and AI in educational measurement across contexts, including K–12 assessments, licensure, and certification programs, particularly for evaluating proficiency in writing, reading, and mathematics (Foltz et al., 2020). Its application is especially critical in large-scale assessments, where scoring open-ended responses at scale presents persistent logistical, financial, and psychometric challenges. Human scoring of constructed-response (CR) items is not only expensive and labor-intensive but also prone to inconsistency due to rater variability, fatigue, or cross-cultural misinterpretation (e.g., Bejar, 2017; Jung et al., 2025). These challenges are amplified in multilingual assessments, where responses in many countries, often with 100 or more language versions, must be scored reliably and fairly.

Automated scoring systems have evolved significantly over the past two decades. Early systems, including Project Essay Grader (Page, 1966), *e-rater* (Enright & Quinlan, 2010; Burstein et al., 2013), and Intelligent Essay Assessor (Foltz et al., 1999), relied on expert-engineered features such as grammar, syntax, vocabulary, and coherence. These systems were primarily developed for scoring essays in monolingual, high-stakes assessments. More recent developments have incorporated ML and NLP (Flor & Hao, 2022) to move beyond fixed feature sets, enabling models to learn scoring patterns from large corpora of human-scored responses. With the rise of deep learning techniques and transformer-based language models, the capacity of AI to understand and evaluate diverse and complex student responses has improved dramatically (Ormerod et al., 2021).

While these technical advances are substantial, they also introduce important validity considerations. Traditional automated scoring systems based on hand-crafted features offered transparency in how scoring decisions were made - human reviewers could trace specific linguistic features to understand the score assignment. Modern neural network approaches, particularly deep learning-based models, operate as "black boxes," making it more challenging to establish construct representation evidence to ensure that models are scoring the intended construct rather than surface features or other confounding variables. This shift necessitates more rigorous validation protocols, including careful attention to differential performance across demographic groups and examination of what linguistic and semantic features drive scoring decisions.

In the context of ILSAs, Jung et al. (2022) conducted a foundational study demonstrating that artificial neural networks (ANNs) could effectively score short CR items in TIMSS math and science using U.S. data. Their approach focused on four dichotomously scored items, showing that ANNs trained on human-labeled data achieved high average agreement with human raters across the four items ($r = 0.91$). Furthermore, they introduced a method to improve scoring quality by weighting training data based on item response theory (IRT)-estimated scores, thereby filtering noisy labels and reducing model variance. This approach showed promise not only in maintaining scoring accuracy but also in enhancing psychometric reliability.

Building on these results, Jung et al. (2024) addressed a central challenge in ILSAs: scoring multilingual responses. Rather than developing separate models for each language, a costly and often impractical practice considering the operational scale of ILSAs, the authors proposed a pipeline that combined machine translation (MT) with ANN-based scoring. Using responses in six languages across eight countries, including both Latin and non-Latin scripts, the responses were translated into English using both Google Translate and ChatGPT and then scored using a bag-of-words (Harris, 1954) model combined with a fully connected feed-forward neural network.

Extending this line of research, Jung et al. (2025) used data from three science items, including all participating countries (52 countries and 42 languages) in TIMSS 2023, and compared multiple automated scoring methods, including both supervised and unsupervised (LLM) models. The multiple MT approach combined with ANNs (MMT_ANNs) achieved the highest performance across countries and items, with average exact agreement ranging from 92.5% to 95% and Cohen's kappa from 0.83 to 0.87. The MMT_ANNs method strategically selects either Google Translate or ChatGPT for different languages and individual responses, demonstrating effectiveness for low-resource languages. Notably, the approach successfully translated more than 99% of responses, with only 0.81% remaining untranslated on average, and achieved standardized mean differences of 0, indicating that scores obtained from human and automated systems were nearly identical.

Analyses of scoring discrepancies revealed that disagreements primarily stemmed from three sources: human scoring inconsistencies across and within countries, translation difficulties with responses that were heavily misspelled, and challenges posed by low-resource languages. The study documented important patterns: in one country, human raters applied scoring criteria more strictly than in other countries, marking responses with older terminology or indirect keyword explanations as incorrect, while the automated system consistently classified these as correct based on the proper content alignment with the rubric. Similarly, identical misspelled responses in a language used in multiple countries were scored differently across these countries. While scorers in one country marked them incorrect, those in others accepted the misspelled responses, whereas the automated system scored them consistently in every case. These findings highlight a fundamental challenge for the field: when human scoring shows cross-country variability, establishing appropriate validity benchmarks becomes complex.

Importantly, these results suggest that automated scoring can serve as an effective and cost-efficient quality control (QC) measure in ILSAs, potentially reducing reliance on additional human raters while maintaining scoring consistency across diverse linguistic contexts.

For image-based CR items, von Davier et al. (2023) and Tyack et al. (2024) demonstrated the strong potential of convolutional neural networks (CNNs) for scoring TIMSS graphical items. The authors showed that CNNs substantially outperformed feed-forward neural networks on a TIMSS 2019 graphical item requiring students to draw figures on a digital grid, achieving classification accuracy of up to 97.53% and, in some cases, correctly identifying responses that human raters had misclassified. Extending this work to eight graphical response items, Tyack et al. (2024) reported accuracies exceeding 98% across diverse mathematical tasks and complexity levels. Importantly, model-guided error analyses revealed that up to 2% of responses were incorrectly or inconsistently scored by humans, illustrating both the limitations of human scoring as a reference standard and the value of the AS systems for QC.

Together, these studies paved the way for the implementation of automated QC procedures during the scoring of TIMSS 2023 CR items (Bookbinder et al., 2023) to improve scoring consistency, transparency, and reliability on a global scale. In parallel, current efforts are extending these innovations to even more complex response types beyond short-answer CR and graphical items. A fully unsupervised scoring pipeline has been developed to rescore the PIRLS 2021 CR items without any human-labeled training data (Jung, Bezirhan et al., 2025). This approach leverages LLMs, MT, prompt engineering techniques, and semantic similarity metrics to assign and validate scores. These developments mark a significant shift toward scalable, multilingual, and unsupervised AI-driven scoring solutions in ILSAs, further challenging traditional human-centered scoring paradigms and expanding the scope of AS to more nuanced student responses.

These technical advances also require careful consideration of the validity of inferences drawn from AI-generated scores. Although agreement with human ratings is often treated as the primary indicator of model performance, human and automated scoring processes differ fundamentally (Ercikan & McCaffrey, 2022). We assume that properly trained human raters expend their best effort to understand content and make informed judgments, while AI systems identify systematic patterns correlated with construct indicators. When assessment tasks are designed for human scoring, these differences could create inferential gaps if the features captured by AI are not aligned with construct-relevant evidence. An ECD perspective helps mitigate this risk by ensuring coherence among the construct model, task model, and evidence model, thereby ensuring that automated scoring targets theoretically meaningful features (Ercikan & McCaffrey, 2022). Traditional validity frameworks (Messick, 1989; Kane, 2006) require reconsideration across five sources of evidence: content, response processes, internal structure, generalization, and consequential validity. In addition to these approaches, argument-based validation frameworks (Kane, 2013; Chapelle et al., 2011) have gained traction in automated scoring research (Xi, 2010; Enright & Quinlan, 2010; Huawei & Aryadoust, 2023), providing operationalized criteria that link AS systems to construct definitions and guide evaluation standards, including association with human scores, fairness, relationships with external variables, reliability across tasks and forms, and impact of use (Ramineni & Williamson, 2013). These multiple frameworks emphasize the need for comprehensive validity evidence rather than relying solely on human-machine agreement statistics.

To address these validity requirements, we propose an operational implementation of LLM-based scoring for ILSAs that follows a QC-integrated pipeline. Pre-processing serves as the first layer of protection, ensuring ethical compliance through multilingual personally identifiable information detection and masking before responses enter cloud-based systems. At the same time, language validation checks confirm data quality and address consequential validity concerns about student privacy and appropriate data handling. The scoring prompt construction step directly operationalizes ECD principles: prompts incorporate item stems, complete scoring guides, example responses at different score levels, and explicit scoring instructions, making the AI scoring process conceptually analogous to how human raters are trained to apply scoring criteria. During scoring, complete audit trails document all API interactions and model output, addressing transparency requirements essential for content-related validity evidence. Post-processing quality checks address fairness and internal structure concerns by examining translation quality to detect hallucinations that could introduce construct-irrelevant variance. In addition, consistency checks ensure lexically similar responses receive identical scores, reducing arbitrary scoring variation. Finally, cross-country and cross-language reliability analyses provide evidence for generalization, with systematic flagging of responses that show inconsistencies across countries or languages, prompting expert review when automated scoring may be capturing unintended features. This multi-stage process creates the documentation and QCs necessary to support defensible validity arguments for AI-based scoring in ILSAs.

These innovations offer substantial benefits to large-scale assessment programs. First, they reduce the operational burden of human scoring, which often involves recruiting and training hundreds of raters across participating countries. Scoring training accounts for approximately 25% of the international meeting expenditures required to conduct international assessments, in addition to substantial expenditures to hire human scorers in each participating country. Second, they enable faster turnaround times compared to a fully human scoring framework. Third, they help ensure comparability of scoring, an essential condition for valid cross-national inference in ILSAs.

In summary, automated scoring in ILSAs is no longer a distant goal but a practical and increasingly validated solution. By integrating MT, ANNs, LLMs, and domain-aligned QC frameworks, ILSAs can move toward more scalable, equitable, and data-rich systems while maintaining the core measurement principles.

14.2.2 Automated Item Generation

Item development is among the most expensive, time-consuming, and labor-intensive aspects of assessment development because it relies heavily on subject-matter experts (SMEs). SMEs draft each item, followed by iterative rounds of review and revision to ensure alignment with established quality standards (Haladyna & Rodriguez, 2013). However, this manual approach introduces inconsistencies stemming from differences in SME expertise and interpretations, and it lacks scalability and operational efficiency, limiting responsiveness to evolving assessment needs. To address these limitations, automated item generation (AIG) emerged as a promising alternative. Initially defined as the use of cognitive and psychometric theories supported by computer technology to systematically produce test items (e.g., Hornke & Habon, 1986; Embretson & Yang, 2007; Gierl & Haladyna, 2012; Gierl & Lai, 2013), AIG offers a scalable solution that reduces human burden while maintaining construct alignment.

Early implementations of AIG primarily relied on item templates, i.e., structured item formats predefined by SMEs for generating questions. While effective for producing large numbers of items, this approach was limited to narrowly defined item types and lacked the flexibility to support diverse item formats. Furthermore, the initial setup of these templates still required significant input from SMEs, which ultimately constrained the scalability of the approach in operational settings. Alternative strategies leveraged traditional NLP techniques (Shin, 2021), such as part-of-speech tagging, topic modeling, and noun phrase extraction, to automatically generate items (e.g., Flor & Riordan, 2018; Mazidi, 2017; Shin, 2021). These innovations removed some constraints of template-based AIG, but their rule-based structure often failed to produce items with semantic richness or sufficient alignment with cognitive targets. A more significant breakthrough came with neural network models, particularly LSTM-based recurrent neural networks, which allowed systems to learn directly from text corpora and simulate human-like item construction (von Davier, 2018).

The introduction of transformer-based language models marked a dramatic leap forward in AIG capabilities. Models such as the Bidirectional Encoder Representations from Transformers (BERT; Devlin et al., 2018), the Text-to-Text Transformer (T5, Raffel et al., 2020), and the Generative Pretrained Transformer (GPT; Radford et al., 2019) often approach human-level performance in diverse language tasks (Hansen & Hebart, 2022). GPT-2, for instance, was utilized for generating medical licensing tasks (von Davier, 2019), personality question generation (Hommel et al., 2022; Götz et al., 2023), and distractor generation (Offerijns et al., 2020), though it required extensive pre-training and fine-tuning on large, domain-specific datasets to adapt effectively to the demands of AIG (von Davier, 2019).

With the development of GPT-3, AIG research entered a new phase. GPT-3 introduced few-shot and zero-shot learning capabilities, enabling users to generate coherent, contextually appropriate outputs with minimal input via prompt engineering (Brown et al., 2020). This advancement enabled a shift away from reliance on large, labeled training datasets toward flexible, scalable item generation using natural language instructions. Early studies used GPT-3 to generate reading comprehension passages for both expository and narrative texts as well as accompanying comprehension items and distractors for MC questions for the Duolingo English Test (Attali et al., 2022; Park et al., 2022), adopting "human-in-the-loop AI" in their pipelines to evaluate the fairness and possible bias in the automatically generated test passages and items (Burstein et al., 2021).

Bezirhan and von Davier (2023) conducted one of the first empirical studies to systematically evaluate the use of LLMs for generating reading assessment content. They introduced a structured prompt engineering framework that guided GPT-3 to generate Lexile-controlled passages suitable for Grade 4 reading assessments modeled on existing PIRLS passages. They also incorporated a human-in-the-loop approach into their story-generation framework to enable light post-editing and mitigate potential bias and factual inaccuracies. Following these checks, a panel of recruited judges rated each AI passage alongside a matched PIRLS original on a four-point Likert scale. Across all comparisons, 92%–97% of judges rated the AI passages as adequate for fourth-grade readers. These findings provide encouraging evidence for face and content plausibility; however, adequacy ratings alone do not demonstrate full construct validity. This must be complemented through field testing with students and psychometric validation beyond expert adequacy ratings, similar to the validation process for human-written content. Moreover, engagement ratings for the AI passages were on par with, or in some cases exceeded, those of the original texts, while coherence scores remained comparable. Notably, judges did not perceive the AI passages as containing more distracting material than the human-authored passages, and in one literary comparison, they found the AI passages to contain less distracting content. These findings suggest that, when combined with effective prompt design and targeted human oversight, LLMs can produce full-length, psycholinguistically appropriate reading passages that rival the quality of human-authored materials, offering a scalable and valid alternative for content development in educational assessments.

Subsequent studies extended this paradigm to other domains using GPT-3.5 and GPT-4. For example, LLMs were employed to generate content in reading comprehension (e.g., Sayin & Gierl, 2024; Schmitz & Marie, 2025), medical sciences (e.g., Kıyak et al., 2024; Laohawetwanit et al., 2024), undergraduate programming (Doughty et al., 2024), and mathematics (e.g., Hwang & Utami, 2024; Kuusemets et al., 2024), with psychometric analyses revealing that 40%–70% of AI-generated items met conventional difficulty levels and discrimination thresholds. Understanding why the remaining 30%–60% of items failed to meet thresholds, whether due to systematic issues in prompt engineering frameworks, inherent model limitations, or the need for more refined filtering mechanisms, represents an essential direction for improving AIG quality and efficiency.

These developments reflect a broader shift from template-based approaches toward flexible, prompt-driven pipelines. Prompt engineering has emerged as a critical component in the design of effective and responsible AIG frameworks. While it is now technically possible to prompt a chatbot (such as ChatGPT) to generate items, doing so without scaffolding often yields content comparable to what a novice item writer might produce, which would be low in quality, misaligned with cognitive targets, and inconsistent with established assessment frameworks. Therefore, developing workflows that ensure construct and framework alignment in AIG is crucial. In educational settings, assessment items must adhere to strict blueprints that specify grade level, content domain, and cognitive processes. For instance, in the PIRLS reading assessment, questions must be text-dependent, non-overlapping in inference, independent across items, and mapped to comprehension-process constraints that cannot be satisfied by generic prompts alone. Thus, prompt engineering must translate these complex design specifications into precise natural language instructions. Researchers have explored various strategies to improve prompt fidelity, such as embedding structured learning objectives (e.g., Bloom's taxonomy), defining output formats, and employing few-shot examples to guide response generation (Doughty et al., 2024). Additionally, role-based prompting, where the model is instructed to act as an SME or item writer, has been shown to improve both relevance and quality (Lin & Chen, 2024).

A recent study by Bezirhan et al. (2025) introduced a structured framework for generating reading comprehension items aligned with the PIRLS assessment using LLMs. This work extended prior prompt engineering research by embedding PIRLS item-writing guidelines directly into prompts and operationalizing the assessment blueprint as natural language input for GPT-based item generation. The process followed a multi-stage AIG pipeline, beginning with the input of stimulus passages, a reference passage, and item examples. Prompt templates were designed to reflect core PIRLS principles, such as process-specific comprehension targets and item independence, and were used to generate initial candidate items via GPT-4. These were then passed through a filtering stage utilizing a suite of semantic and lexical similarity metrics (BLEU, ROUGE-L, METEOR, and cosine similarity via BERT embeddings) to identify items most representative of the passage content and intended comprehension process. The remaining subset was subjected to human expert review, during which items were edited or discarded based on alignment with PIRLS constructs, cognitive process, and linguistic appropriateness. Finally, the remaining items were psychometrically evaluated with fourth-grade students and compared with human-authored counterparts, demonstrating comparable performance across difficulty and discrimination indices.

Building on our previous work (Bezirhan et al., 2025), we propose a generalized AIG pipeline (see Figure 14.1) that integrates key components of item development: alignment with an assessment framework, prompt engineering, automated content generation, and quality assurance through automated and human review. The pipeline begins with the specification of a target assessment framework, including grade

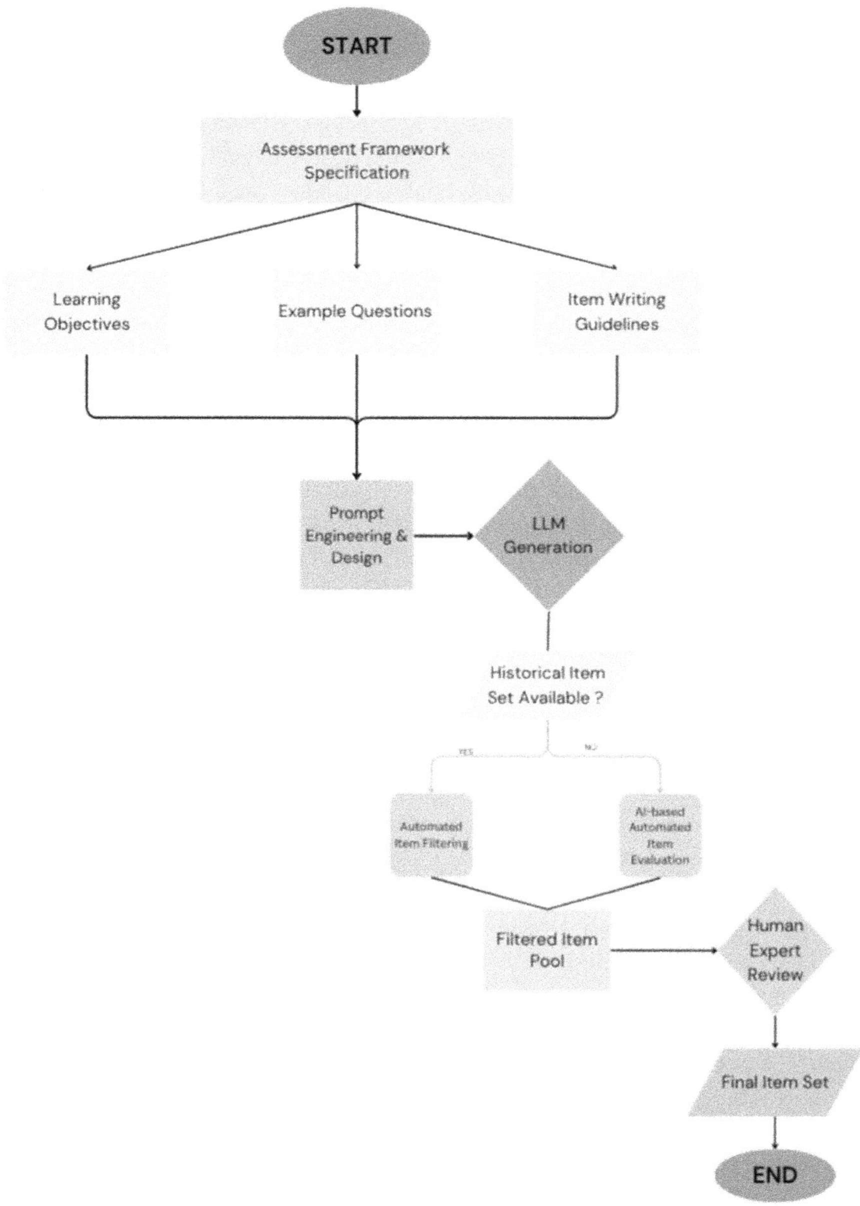

FIGURE 14.1 General AIG pipeline

level, content domain, cognitive processes, and item-format constraints, which serves as the foundation for prompt design. Prompts are carefully constructed to reflect these blueprint elements and can include exemplar items, stimulus texts, or targeted learning objectives. Once finalized, the prompts are passed to an LLM which generates a pool of candidate items aligned with the framework. In contexts where historical items are available, the generated items can be filtered using lexical and semantic similarity metrics to identify those that best match the style, complexity, and content of previously validated items. This automated filtering step helps narrow the item pool to high-quality candidates before human review. However, in settings without access to legacy items, researchers can adopt alternative automated evaluation strategies drawn from recent literature. These include using LLM-based reviewer models (e.g., instruction-tuned GPT variants) to rate item quality along dimensions such as clarity, alignment, and cognitive demand (e.g., Gorgun & Bulut, 2025; Säuberli & Clematide, 2024), or prompting the model to self-assess and revise its outputs (Tan et al., 2024). While these automated techniques are not yet a substitute for human validation, they offer a scalable means of eliminating low-quality outputs and reducing the reviewer burden. The remaining items proceed to a human-in-the-loop review, where SMEs assess fidelity to the construct, factual accuracy, linguistic appropriateness, and fairness. Once curated, items can be field-tested and psychometrically calibrated.

This generalized AIG pipeline can also be accompanied by concrete monitoring indicators that support operational use in large-scale assessments. Useful metrics include the proportion of AI-generated items retained after SME review; the extent to which accepted items satisfy blueprint constraints on content, cognitive processes, and formats; the percentage of piloted items that achieve acceptable item-fit statistics; and comparative differential item functioning (DIF) analyses for AI-generated versus human-authored items. Reporting these indicators would provide clearer baselines for evaluating AIG pipelines, helping understand not only whether AI can generate items but also under what conditions those items are psychometrically and substantively comparable to established item pools.

By incorporating the assessment blueprint into the generative process, this pipeline ensures that LLM outputs are pedagogically sound and psychometrically defensible. Its modular structure enables adaptability across domains and model types, while its combined use of automated and human validation ensures scalability and QC. As such, this pipeline represents a forward-compatible approach to AIG that can evolve alongside advances in the domains of language processing and psychometrics.

14.2.3 Item Verification and Alignment

Item verification, alignment, and content mapping have long served as foundational components of assessment validation frameworks. Historically, alignment procedures required SMEs to manually evaluate the compatibility between test items, instructional materials, and learning standards (AERA, APA, & NCME, 2014). Alignment was often conducted through multi-day workshops or panel reviews, using curriculum mapping techniques and qualitative judgments to ensure content validity (Porter et al., 2008). While effective, these approaches were inherently labor-intensive and limited in scalability.

Recent advances in NLP and LLMs have introduced more systematic and scalable approaches to content alignment (e.g., Butterfuss & Doran, 2025; Camilli, 2024; Camilli & Suter, 2024). Zhou and Ostrow (2022) trained transformer-based models to align test items with educational standards, achieving modest predictive performance due to reliance on averaged word-level embeddings and lack of contextual nuance. In contrast, Khan et al. (2021) introduced a Catalog system, which utilized transformer-based sentence embeddings to match science–related reading passages to Next-Generation Science Standards.

Building on this, others advocated for NLP-assisted (rather than NLP-based) frameworks that integrate sentence embeddings and semantic similarity to support SME decision-making. Butterfuss and Doran (2025) proposed a method using cosine similarity of transformer-generated text embeddings to pre-rank potential standard-to-standard matches, significantly reducing the cognitive workload on SMEs. Their framework emphasized that ML should organize and prioritize candidate alignments, but final decisions must remain in the hands of expert reviewers. Similarly, Camilli (2024) extended the role of embeddings by applying regression techniques to investigate the alignment between Common Core State Standards and NAEP item specifications. Later, Camilli and Suter (2024) applied clustering techniques, including k-means, to group standards and items based on their semantic similarity. Their findings reinforced the utility of embedding-based frameworks not just for alignment tasks but also for construct validity and coherence analysis across hierarchical contents. While embedding-based semantic similarity provides valuable preliminary evidence of construct alignment, it is only one component of a broader validation framework that must be complemented by empirical psychometric evidence.

While alignment has historically focused on standards and curricular frameworks, ensuring that AI-generated items meet psychometric expectations introduces a new set of challenges. In recent years, significant research efforts have shifted toward the a priori prediction of item properties as a proxy for psychometric alignment (AlKhuzaey et al., 2023). Early work in this area used surface features like word frequency, readability, and sentence length to predict difficulty (e.g., Freedle & Kostin, 1993; Perkins et al., 1995). With the evolution of NLP, researchers began using context-aware embeddings to extract semantic features, enabling more accurate, text-based difficulty predictions (e.g., Mikolov et al., 2013; Yaneva et al., 2019).

Transformer-based models have further advanced this line of research. Yeung et al. (2019), for instance, used BERT to generate distractors of controlled difficulty by computing semantic similarity within multiple-choice contexts. More recent applications have applied these models, both fine-tuned and zero-shot, to predict item difficulty and response time with a somewhat higher accuracy than traditional methods (e.g., Yaneva et al., 2020; Benedetto et al., 2023; Demirkaya et al., 2025). Tran et al. (2025) extend this trajectory by showing that manual features, chain-of-thought reasoning, and fine-tuned LLMs together explain approximately 60% of the variance in IRT difficulty parameters across mathematics items. Their findings highlight the potential of AI-based feature extraction for identifying items whose empirical difficulty is likely to fall outside target ranges. These approaches are particularly relevant in AI-assisted item generation, where psychometric quality must be anticipated and monitored during item generation, not just after empirical validation. This need arises in part from the scale and speed at which AI-based AIG can produce items. This high-volume output increases the risk of producing items that are misaligned with the intended content domain, cognitive demand, and difficulty distribution. Without early-stage psychometric checks, there is a greater likelihood of producing unusable items that would be costly to identify and filter post hoc. Therefore, integrating psychometric monitoring into the generation pipeline becomes a practical necessity. While human-written items are also subject to review and validation, their manageable volume and slower production pace typically allow these processes to be conducted post hoc without overusing resources.

Despite significant progress in national- and state-level assessments (e.g., Webb, 1997; Forte, 2017), alignment research within ILSAs remains comparatively underexplored. TIMSS systematically maintains content alignment through rigorous item development processes and expert reviews. Building on these advances and the principles of evidence-centered design (Mislevy et al., 2003), Bezirhan and von Davier (2025) proposed an LLM-based classification model to ensure alignment of items with the TIMSS assessment framework. Their study evaluated GPT-4o's ability to classify TIMSS mathematics items into content and cognitive domains and to assign difficulty levels. Using a structured prompt engineering approach grounded in the TIMSS framework, the model demonstrated high accuracy for content classification (~95%) and moderate performance for cognitive domains and difficulty. These results suggest that LLMs, when guided by structured frameworks and dynamic prompting, can serve as reliable co-reviewers in assessment development pipelines, reducing SME workload while preserving construct validity.

The trajectory of item verification and alignment research has evolved from expert-only judgment models to hybrid frameworks that combine the scalability of NLP with the nuance of human expertise. Text embeddings and transformer-based models now serve as powerful tools to reduce SME burden and support alignment across items, standards, and specifications. The emerging consensus is that hybrid pipelines that use LLMs or embedding models for rapid filtering, followed by targeted SME or psychometric review, offer the best balance of efficiency and validity for large-scale item verification and alignment.

14.2.4 Automated Test Assembly

Conventional test construction is still dominated by human content experts who handpick items, iterate through multiple review cycles, and manually balance content coverage and statistical targets. This has involved time-intensive review processes in which human experts iteratively select and revise items to meet test blueprint or framework specifications. However, such methods are increasingly impractical given the scale and complexity of modern assessments. Manual form assembly is not only expensive and inefficient but also prone to inconsistencies and construct underrepresentation (van der Linden, 2005), particularly when attempting to meet the fine-grained content and cognitive distribution targets mandated by international frameworks such as TIMSS or PIRLS.

Blueprint adherence is particularly critical in large-scale assessments because it underpins the validity of score interpretations and the cross-national or longitudinal comparability of scores. Frameworks typically specify detailed proportions of items across content domains, cognitive processes, and item types. For example, the TIMSS 2023 mathematics framework requires that 65% of eighth-grade items be aligned with either the applying or the reasoning cognitive domain. When tests deviate from these specifications, either by overrepresenting certain content or cognitive areas or underrepresenting others, inferences about construct coverage from test scores may be compromised. Blueprint violations have been shown to lead to infeasible test assembly models, particularly when item banks lack sufficient coverage of targeted domains (Spaccapanico Proietti et al., 2020). Moreover, failure to meet blueprint constraints has downstream implications for psychometric analyses, reporting, and policy interpretation, especially in trend assessments that rely on consistent content representation across cycles.

To address these challenges, automated test assembly (ATA) approaches have emerged as viable solutions. van der Linden's (2005) linear-models framework formalized ATA as a mixed-integer linear programming (MILP) problem, in which the algorithm uses modern solvers such as *lp_solve* (Berkelaar et al., 2004) to reliably generate near-optimal forms subject to multiple psychometric and blueprint constraints. However, when item banks are large and complex, blueprints often yield infeasible or suboptimal solutions with standard MILP formulations. The integration of metaheuristic algorithms such as genetic algorithms and cuckoo search has enhanced ATA capabilities by providing robust solutions to multi-criteria optimization problems that require careful balancing of test information targets, item overlap specifications, and exposure control parameters (Jin & Pan, 2025).

In parallel, AI-based approaches are transforming the test assembly process by leveraging ML, reinforcement learning, and NLP to enhance both form construction and adaptive delivery. Neural computerized adaptive testing, for instance, frames item selection as a reinforcement learning problem and directly learns a selection algorithm from the data (Zhuang et al., 2022). Other approaches, such as Bandit CAT, employ contextual bandits and Thompson sampling to incorporate uncertainty and adaptively control item exposure during form delivery, as in the Duolingo English Test (Sharpnack et al., 2024). These systems have been shown to reduce test length without sacrificing measurement precision, offering considerable gains in efficiency.

AI-enhanced assembly methods also enable more adaptive and group-targeted assessments that better reflect individual learner competencies. Recent advances in explainable AI (XAI) further enhanced these systems by introducing interpretability layers into adaptive testing and test assembly, enabling LLMs to generate human-readable rationales for item selection (Cheng et al., 2024). These approaches hold promise for educational assessment, potentially leading to systems that are not only efficient and psychometrically sound but also transparent, diagnostic, and learner-centered.

14.3 Impact of AI on Assessment Practices

AI has fundamentally transformed the landscape of educational assessment by reducing the manual effort required in scoring and assessment development. Tasks that previously required extensive human labor can now be augmented or partially automated using LLMs and NLP techniques. Automated scoring systems, for example, have demonstrated high levels of agreement with human raters, significantly reducing turnaround times while maintaining reliability (e.g., Jung et al., 2025; Tyack et al., 2024). Similarly, AI-based AIG systems have the potential to accelerate the creation of items aligned with assessment frameworks, thereby populating item banks more quickly and with greater coverage across domains (Bezirhan et al., 2025).

In addition to efficiency gains, these algorithms offer scalable solutions. This increased scalability is particularly valuable for ILSAs, which must deliver consistent, valid assessments across diverse linguistic, cultural, and educational contexts. AI-enhanced test assembly and scoring systems enable these assessments to scale without compromising psychometric quality. Additionally, as AI models mature, which happens at a pace that can only be described as “blink and you will miss it”, they offer greater transparency and auditability, features that are indispensable in international comparative studies where reliability, fairness, and defensibility are paramount.

The growing prevalence of computer-based assessments has enabled the collection of rich process data, such as response times, frequency of item revisits, keystrokes, clickstreams, and navigation patterns, that capture how examinees interact with tasks. These temporally structured data offer valuable insights into aberrant behaviors (e.g., Demirkaya et al., 2023; van der Linden & Belov, 2023), test-taking strategies (e.g., Bezirhan et al., 2021; Leng et al., 2024), and engagement (e.g., Ulitzsch et al., 2020, 2022). However, their complexity requires sophisticated methods to extract meaning. Recent advances in ML and AI have enabled researchers to analyze sequential process data through techniques such as autoencoders, contextual embeddings, RNNs, and Markov models. These approaches allow for anomaly detection, identification of latent cognitive strategies, and group comparisons in problem-solving processes (e.g., Bulut, Gorgun et al., 2024; Pokropek et al., 2024; Zhang et al., 2024). This line of work aligns with the field of computational psychometrics, which integrates ML and AI models with psychometric theory to handle large-scale and multimodal data from digital learning and assessment (von Davier et al., 2021). The incorporation of such multimodal data opens new avenues for interpreting student learning processes, particularly using open-ended and technology-enhanced items (Hao et al., 2024).

At a broader level, the insights derived from AI-enabled assessment systems can inform instructional decisions and education policy. By aggregating and analyzing assessment data across schools, regions, or populations, AI can help identify systemic gaps in achievement, monitor curriculum effectiveness, and support more personalized and equitable learning pathways. ML models have been increasingly applied to ILSA data to predict student performance and uncover factors contributing to academic success. For example, explainable deep learning (Elouafi et al., 2025) and gradient-boosting models (Nadaf et al., 2022), trained on TIMSS data, have shown that variables such as metacognitive strategy use, instructional time, and school-climate indicators are among the strongest drivers of mathematics achievement. At the same time, applications of neural network and ensemble models to PISA science data (Huang et al., 2021) and curriculum-sensitive classifiers to TIMSS science data (Song & Cutumisu, 2025) demonstrate that ML can accurately forecast performance. When combined with XAI methods, these models can produce interpretable insights such as feature importance rankings that aid policymakers and educators in understanding why certain student groups may be falling behind. Such capabilities provide stakeholders, educators, administrators, and policymakers with actionable insights into improving educational outcomes.

14.4 Ethical Concerns

The integration of AI into educational assessment comes with ethical challenges. As AI systems increasingly influence how assessments are developed, scored, and interpreted, the field must confront issues related to algorithmic bias, transparency, data privacy, automation bias, and the erosion of human oversight.

A foundational gap in the field is the absence of formal guidelines for the use of AI in educational measurement. The Standards for Educational and Psychological Testing (AERA, APA, and NCME, 2014), the central reference for validity, reliability, and fairness in assessment, currently offers no guidance specific to AI.

To address this gap, Burstein (2023) and colleagues introduced the Responsible AI Standards (RAIS), the first institutional framework outlining the ethical and technical responsibilities for deploying AI in educational assessments. The RAIS document highlights core principles such as transparency, inclusivity, and continuous monitoring and serves as an important foundation for future revisions of the Standards. Another vital contribution to the discourse on AI ethics in educational assessment is the report by Johnson et al. (2025), outlining five core principles for responsible AI in measurement and learning: fairness and bias mitigation, privacy and security, transparency and accountability, educational impact and integrity, and continuous improvement. The NCME's Special Interest Group on AI in Measurement and Education released a white paper that provides a comprehensive, field-wide perspective on these issues. This collaborative effort brings together multiple researchers to explore the ethical implications of AI-powered tools, address challenges such as automation bias and environmental sustainability, and propose actionable frameworks for responsible AI integration in educational measurement (Bulut et al., 2024).

Transparency is one of the most frequently mentioned concerns of AI-based assessment systems. Transformer-based models often operate as black boxes, making it difficult to trace the rationale behind specific outputs. Without interpretable decision-making processes, it becomes challenging to validate AI outputs within established psychometric standards (Hao et al., 2024; Dorsey & Michaels, 2022). This lack of interpretability can undermine the defensibility of test results and limit stakeholders' ability to challenge or verify scoring decisions.

To mitigate this, researchers advocate the use of XAI methods and hybrid systems, in which AI-generated outputs are reviewed or supplemented by human experts. While transparency and bias are widely acknowledged concerns, operationalizing safeguards requires concrete methodologies. Several established psychometric tools can be adapted to AI-based workflows. DIF analyses, for example, can be applied to compare human- and AI-based scores across demographic subgroups to detect systematic disparities in model behavior. Bias dashboards, which continuously monitor model outputs across subgroups, item types, and languages, provide a scalable mechanism for detecting patterns of drift or construct-irrelevant variance. Item- and response-level anomaly detection, along with a human-in-the-loop design, can provide oversight for edge cases, novel responses, or flagged inconsistencies.

Algorithmic bias remains a critical concern in AI systems. Because LLMs are trained on historical data that reflect societal structures and disparities, they may inadvertently reproduce entrenched biases such as gendered language, colonial curricular framing, or digital access gaps in their outputs. For instance, LLMs may encode stereotypical associations or fail to recognize dialectal and culturally specific expressions, thereby disadvantaging students from underrepresented linguistic or cultural groups (Bulut et al., 2024; Gallegos et al., 2024). Bias in AI models can emerge from multiple sources: skewed training data, unequal representation of subpopulations, or unintended correlations learned during training. In educational assessment, such biases can result in systematic disadvantages for underrepresented linguistic or cultural groups, threatening the equity of test score interpretations (Ho, 2024; Bulut et al., 2024). To mitigate these risks, robust fairness evaluations are essential.

Equally concerning is the phenomenon of automation illusion, a cognitive bias in which stakeholders overrely on machine-generated outputs because of their speed, precision, and perceived objectivity, even in the presence of uncertainty or error. As emphasized throughout this chapter, AI systems are most effective when designed to augment rather than replace human expertise, at least at this stage. Uncritical reliance on automated scoring or item classification models, particularly in the absence of human oversight, increases the risk that flawed outputs will be accepted without adequate scrutiny (Chang, 2024; Owan et al., 2023). This underscores the importance of maintaining human-in-the-loop frameworks to ensure interpretability, contextual sensitivity, and alignment with intended constructs.

Data privacy and security concerns are equally critical in the deployment of AI within educational assessment. AI systems, especially those hosted on cloud-based platforms, may inadvertently expose sensitive student information. To mitigate privacy risks, institutions should prioritize the use of locally deployed models when feasible, minimizing external data transmission. Additionally, adopting privacy-preserving API protocols, such as encrypted communication channels, tokenized access, and strict usage logging, can help ensure that student data remains protected throughout the assessment pipeline. Embedding these safeguards into system design is essential for maintaining trust and complying with legal and ethical standards for educational data use.

The environmental impact of generative AI has been widely debated, particularly in relation to the energy demands of training and deploying LLMs. However, it is important to contextualize these concerns within the scope of educational assessment. In practice, most AI applications in this domain rely on inference rather than training, and their power consumption is comparatively modest. For example, scoring an open-ended response using a locally hosted generative model consumes approximately 2 watt-hours per response, equivalent to less than $0.001 in energy cost. When scaled to a full assessment administration (e.g., 135 items, 800 responses per item, across 60 countries), which translates to a carbon footprint equivalent to 0.0147 transatlantic flights. In contrast, traditional human scoring requires extensive training in ILSAs; these training sessions involve logistics such as approximately 280 international flights, 700 hotel nights, and 1,500 scoring days across national centers, which represent a substantial environmental burden. While sustainability must remain a consideration in AI adoption, the evidence suggests that many educational use cases, particularly those replacing high-emission workflows, can be part of the solution rather than the problem.

14.5 Future Directions

As the field advances, several key areas warrant research and development. One important area is the emerging field of large multimodal models that integrate text, audio, video, and image inputs. So far, only a handful of applications of AI in education research focus on multimodal models. These models promise richer representations of learner competencies, particularly in domains such as scientific experimentation, oral language proficiency, and creative problem-solving. However, such advances will require new validity arguments, multimodal annotation protocols, and psychometric models capable of handling complex data (Hao et al., 2024).

As educational needs evolve, assessments will increasingly aim to measure new competencies such as collaboration, creativity, digital literacy, and AI literacy. These are constructs that are difficult to capture using traditional test formats. AI may potentially play a vital role in operationalizing and evaluating these competencies, especially through dynamic simulations and real-time performance analysis (Hao et al., 2024). However, this demands close attention to construct representation, cultural appropriateness, and language equity in AI-enabled designs, especially in multilingual settings such as ILSAs. It is important to note that ILSAs require AI systems designed from the ground up for multilingual and cross-cultural contexts. This includes developing culturally responsive models, advancing multilingual educational LLMs, and creating international frameworks for equitable AI performance across diverse linguistic and cultural groups.

Finally, a vital future direction involves the development of formalized, domain-specific AI guidelines for educational measurement. While efforts such as the Duolingo Responsible AI Standards and NCME's Special Interest Group on AI in Measurement and Education are promising (Burstein, 2023; Bulut et al., 2024), there is a need for a community-wide conversation about AI-specific extensions to validity and reliability standards. Hao et al. (2024) advocate for a temporal stance that recognizes scale drift and mandates periodic revalidation of AI systems, particularly as data distributions, models, and societal contexts evolve.

To support these efforts, interdisciplinary collaboration across psychometrics, computer science, data science, education, and ethics will be essential. Future research should prioritize XAI, longitudinal impact studies, and infrastructure for sharing benchmarks and evaluation protocols across programs and contexts.

14.6 Conclusion

AI has brought transformative capabilities to large-scale educational assessment, enabling unprecedented levels of scalability, efficiency, and personalization. Through applications in automated scoring, item generation, test assembly, and item verification, AI is expanding possibilities in psychometric practice. However, these advances must be approached with measured caution. The risks of over-adaptation, including uncritical reliance on automated outputs, insufficient validation of AI systems, and removal of human expertise, are as significant as the opportunities. These advances necessitate renewed commitments to fairness, transparency, and construct validity.

As this chapter has illustrated, responsible implementation of AI requires more than technical sophistication; it demands a principled and measured approach grounded in psychometric theory. AI applications in education are not intended to replace human expertise but rather to amplify and support it, creating systems in which human judgment and machine intelligence co-evolve to uphold the foundational values of educational measurement.

Moving forward, the field must embrace the dual challenge of innovation and governance. By investing in validation, ethical safeguards, and community standards, we can ensure that AI-driven assessments are not only efficient and scalable but also fair, inclusive, and educationally meaningful.

References

AlKhuzaey, S., Grasso, F., Payne, T. R., & Tamma, V. (2023). Text-based question difficulty prediction: A systematic review of automatic approaches. *International Journal of Artificial Intelligence in Education*, 34(3), 862–914.

American Educational Research Association, American Psychological Association, & National Council on Measurement in Education. (2014). *Standards for Educational and Psychological Testing*. Washington, DC: American Educational Research Association.

Attali, Y., Runge, A., LaFlair, G. T., Yancey, K., Goodwin, S., Park, Y., & Von Davier, A. A. (2022). The interactive reading task: Transformer-based automatic item generation. *Frontiers in Artificial Intelligence*, 5, 903077.

Bejar, I. I. (2017). A historical survey of research regarding constructed-response formats. In R. Bennett & M. von Davier (Eds.), *Advancing Human Assessment. Methodology of Educational Measurement and Assessment* (pp. 556–633). Cham: Springer. https://doi.org/10.1007/978-3-319-58689-2_18

Benedetto, L., Cremonesi, P., Caines, A., Buttery, P., Cappelli, A., Giussani, A., & Turrin, R. (2023). A survey on recent approaches to question difficulty estimation from text. *ACM Computing Surveys*, 55(9), 1–37.

Berkelaar, M., Eikland, K., & Notebaert, P. (2004). *lp_solve (Version 5.1.0.0) [Computer software]*. https://lpsolve.sourceforge.net/

Bezirhan, U., & von Davier, M. (2023). Automated reading passage generation with OpenAI's large language model. *Computers and Education: Artificial Intelligence*, 5, 100161.

Bezirhan, U., & von Davier, M. (2025, October). AI-Based Classification of TIMSS Items for Framework Alignment. In *Proceedings of the Artificial Intelligence in Measurement and Education Conference (AIME-Con): Full Papers* (pp. 134–141). Pittsburgh, PA: National Council on Measurement in Education. https://aclanthology.org/2025.aimecon-main.15/

Bezirhan, U., von Davier, M., & Grabovsky, I. (2021). Modeling item revisit behavior: The hierarchical speed–accuracy–revisits model. *Educational and Psychological Measurement*, 81(2), 363–387.

Bezirhan, U., Wry, E., Goren, S., & von Davier, M. (2025, July). AI-driven item generation for PIRLS. *Presentation at the International Meeting of the Psychometric Society (IMPS)*, Minneapolis, MN.

Bookbinder, A., Tyack, L., Aldrich, C. E., Khorramdel, L., & Mao, T. (2023). Automated and human scoring in TIMSS. *TIMSS*, 7–1.

Brown, T. B., Mann, B., Ryder, N., Subbiah, M., Kaplan, J., Dhariwal, P., … Amodei, D. (2020). Language models are few-shot learners. In H. Larochelle, M. Ranzato, R. Hadsell, M. F. Balcan, & H. Lin (Eds.), *Advances in Neural Information Processing Systems* (Vol. 33, pp. 1877–1901). Vancouver: Curran Associates, Inc.

Bulut, O., Beiting-Parrish, M., Casabianca, J. M., Slater, S. C., Jiao, H., Song, D., … & Morilova, P. (2024). The rise of artificial intelligence in educational measurement: Opportunities and ethical challenges. arXiv preprint arXiv:2406.18900.

Bulut, O., Gorgun, G., & He, S. (2024). Unsupervised anomaly detection in sequential process data: Insights from PIAAC-Problem-solving tasks. *Zeitschrift für Psychologie*, 232(2), 74–94. https://doi.org/10.1027/2151-2604/a000558

Burstein, J. (2023). Responsible AI standards. Retrieved from https://duolingo papers. s3.amazonaws.com/other/DET±Responsible±AI±033123.pdf

Burstein, J., LaFlair, G. T., Kunnan, A. J., & von Davier, A. A. (2021). A theoretical assessment ecosystem for a digital-first assessment—The Duolingo English Test. DRR-21-04.

Burstein, J., Tetreault, J., & Madnani, N. (2013). The e-rater ®automated essay scoring system. In M. D. Shermis & J. Burstein (Eds.), *Handbook of Automated Essay Scoring: Current Applications and Future Directions* (pp. 55–67). New York: Routledge.

Butterfuss, R., & Doran, H. (2025). An application of text embeddings to support alignment of educational content standards. *Educational Measurement: Issues and Practice*, 44(1), 73–83.

Camilli, G. (2024). An NLP crosswalk between the common core state standards and NAEP item specifications. arXiv preprint arXiv:2405.17284.

Camilli, G., & Suter, L. (2024). NLP cluster analysis of common core state standards and NAEP item specifications. arXiv preprint arXiv:2412.04482.

Chang, H. H. (2024). Harnessing AI for educational measurement: Standards and emerging frontiers. *Journal of Educational and Behavioral Statistics*, 49(5), 702–708.

Chapelle, C. A., Enright, M. K., & Jamieson, J. M. (Eds.) (2011). *Building a Validity Argument for the Test of English as a Foreign LanguageTM*. New York: Routledge.

Cheng, C., Zhao, G., Huang, Z., Zhuang, Y., Pan, Z., Liu, Q., ... & Chen, E. (2024, November). Towards explainable computerized adaptive testing with large language model. In Y. Al-Onaizan, M. Bansal, & Y.-N. Chen (Eds.), *Findings of the Association for Computational Linguistics: EMNLP 2024* (pp. 2655–2672). Miami, FL: Association for Computational Linguistics. https://doi.org/10.18653/v1/2024.findings-emnlp.149

Demirkaya, O., Bezirhan, U., & Zhang, J. (2023). Detecting item preknowledge using revisits with speed and accuracy. *Journal of Educational and Behavioral Statistics*, 48(4), 521–542.

Demirkaya, O., Wei, H. R., & Johnson, E. (2025, October). Simulating rating scale responses with LLMs for early-stage item evaluation. In *Proceedings of the Artificial Intelligence in Measurement and Education Conference (AIME-Con): Full Papers* (pp. 385–392). Pittsburgh, PA: National Council on Measurement in Education.

Devlin, J., Chang, M. W., Lee, K., & Toutanova, K. (2018). Bert: Pre-training of deep bidirectional transformers for language understanding. arXiv preprint arXiv:1810.04805.

Dorsey, D. W., & Michaels, H. R. (2022). Validity arguments meet artificial intelligence in innovative educational assessment. *Journal of Educational Measurement*, 59(3), 267–271.

Doughty, J., Wan, Z., Bompelli, A., Qayum, J., Wang, T., Zhang, J., ... & Sakr, M. (2024, January). A comparative study of AI-generated (GPT-4) and human-crafted MCQs in programming education. In *Proceedings of the 26th Australasian Computing Education Conference* (pp. 114–123). New York: Association for Computing Machinery.

Elouafi, A., Tammouch, I., Eddarouich, S., & Touahni, R. (2025). Uncovering key factors of student performance in math: An explainable deep learning approach using TIMSS 2019 data. *Information*, 16(6), 480.

Embretson, S. E., & Yang, X. (2007). Automatic item generation and cognitive psychology. In C. R. Rao, & S. Sinharay (Eds.), *Handbook of Statistics. Psychometrics* (Vol. 26, pp. 747–768). North Holland: Elsevier.

Enright, M. K., & Quinlan, T. (2010). Complementing human judgment of essays written by English language learners with e-rater® scoring. *Language Testing*, 27(3), 317–334.
Ercikan, K. (2025). Efficacy, validity and fairness considerations in AI-Driven assessments. In E. M. Tucker, E. Armour-Thomas, & E. W. Gordon (Eds.), *Handbook for Assessment in the Service of Learning* (Vol. 1). Amherst, MA: University of Massachusetts Amherst Libraries
Ercikan, K., & McCaffrey, D. F. (2022). Optimizing implementation of artificial-intelligence-based automated scoring: An evidence centered design approach for designing assessments for AI-based scoring. *Journal of Educational Measurement*, 59(3), 272–287.
Flor, M., & Hao, J. (2022). Text mining and automated scoring. In A. A. von Davier, R. J. Mislevy, & J. Hao (Eds.), *Computational Psychometrics: New Methodologies for a New Generation of Digital Learning and Assessment: With Examples in R and Python* (pp. 245–262). Cham: Springer International Publishing.
Flor, M., & Riordan, B. (2018, June). A semantic role-based approach to open-domain automatic question generation. In *Proceedings of the Thirteenth Workshop on Innovative use of NLP for Building Educational Applications* (pp. 254–263).
Foltz, P. W., Laham, D., & Landauer, T. K. (1999). The intelligent essay assessor: Applications to educational technology. *Interactive Multimedia Electronic Journal of Computer-Enhanced Learning*, 1(2), 939–944.
Foltz, P. W., Yan, D., & Rupp, A. A. (2020). The past, present, and future of automated scoring. In D. Yan, A. Rupp, & P. W. Foltz (Eds.), *Handbook of Automated Scoring: Theory into Practice* (pp. 1–9). New York: CRC Press.
Forte, E. (2017). *Evaluating Alignment in Large-Scale Standards-Based Assessment Systems*. Washington, DC: Council of Chief State School Officers.
Freedle, R., & Kostin, I. (1993). The prediction of TOEFL reading comprehension item difficulty for expository prose passages for three item types: Main idea, inference, and supporting idea items. *ETS Research Report Series*, 1993(1), i–48.
Gallegos, I. O., Rossi, R. A., Barrow, J., Tanjim, M. M., Kim, S., Dernoncourt, F., … & Ahmed, N. K. (2024). Bias and fairness in large language models: A survey. *Computational Linguistics*, 50(3), 1097–1179.
Gierl, M. J., & Haladyna, T. M. (2012). *Automatic Item Generation: Theory and Practice*. New York: Routledge. https://doi.org/10.4324/9780203803912
Gierl, M. J., & Lai, H. (2013). Using automated processes to generate test items. *Educational Measurement: Issues and Practice*, 32, 3650.
Gorgun, G., & Bulut, O. (2025). Instruction-tuned large-language models for quality control in automatic item generation: A feasibility study. *Educational Measurement: Issues and Practice*, 44(1), 96–107.
Götz, F. M., Maertens, R., Loomba, S., & van der Linden, S. (2023). Let the algorithm speak: How to use neural networks for automatic item generation in psychological scale development. *Psychological Methods*, 29(3), 494.
Haladyna, T. M., & Rodriguez, M. C. (2013). Developing and validating test items. New York: Routledge.
Hansen, H., & Hebart, M. N. (2022). Semantic features of object concepts generated with GPT 3. arXiv preprint arXiv:2202.03753.
Hao, J., von Davier, A. A., Yaneva, V., Lottridge, S., von Davier, M., & Harris, D. J. (2024). Transforming assessment: The impacts and implications of large language models and generative AI. *Educational Measurement: Issues and Practice*, 43(2), 16–29.
Harris, Z. S. (1954). Distributional structure. *Word*, 10(2–3), 146–162.

Ho, A. D. (2024). Artificial intelligence and educational measurement: Opportunities and threats. *Journal of Educational and Behavioral Statistics*, 49(5), 715–722.

Hommel, B. E., Wollang, F. J. M., Kotova, V., Zacher, H., & Schmukle, S. C. (2022). Transformer-based deep neural language modeling for construct-specific automatic item generation. *Psychometrika*, 87(2), 749–772.

Hornke, L. F., & Habon, M. W. (1986). Rule-based item bank construction and evaluation within the linear logistic framework. *Applied Psychological Measurement*, 10, 369–380.

Huang, S., Jiang, Y., Yin, H., & Jong, M. S. Y. (2021). Does ICT use matter? The relationships between students' ICT use, motivation, and science achievement in East Asia. *Learning and Individual Differences*, 86, 101957.

Huawei, S., & Aryadoust, V. (2023). A systematic review of automated writing evaluation systems. *Education and Information Technologies*, *28*(1), 771–795.

Hwang, W. Y., & Utami, I. Q. (2024). Using GPT and authentic contextual recognition to generate math word problems with difficulty levels. *Education and Information Technologies*, 29(13), 1–29.

Jin, C., & Pan, W. (2025). A hybrid model based on learning automata and cuckoo search for optimizing test item selection in computerized adaptive testing. *Scientific Reports*, 15(1), 18218.

Johnson, M. S. (2025). *Responsible AI for Measurement and Learning: Principles and Practices. Research Report. RR-25-03*. ETS Research Report Series.

Jung, J. Y., Bezirhan, U., & von Davier, M. (2025, October). Input optimization for automated scoring in reading assessment. In *Proceedings of the Artificial Intelligence in Measurement and Education Conference (AIME-con): Full Papers* (pp. 1–8). Pittsburgh, PA: National Council on Measurement in Education.

Jung, J. Y., Tyack, L., & von Davier, M. (2022). Automated scoring of constructed-response items using artificial neural networks in international large-scale assessment. *Psychological Test and Assessment Modeling*, 64(4), 471–494.

Jung, J. Y., Tyack, L., & von Davier, M. (2024). Combining machine translation and automated scoring in international large-scale assessments. *Large-scale Assessments in Education*, 12(1), 10.

Jung, J. Y., Tyack, L., & von Davier, M. (2025). Towards the implementation of automated scoring in international large-scale assessments: Scalability and quality control. *Computers and Education: Artificial Intelligence*, 8, 100375.

Khan, S., Rosaler, J., Hamer, J., & Almeida, T. (2021). Catalog: An educational content tagging system. In *Proceedings of the 14th International Conference on Educational Data Mining (EDM 2021),* Virtual from Paris. International Educational Data Mining Society. Lin, Z., & Chen, H. (2024). Investigating the capability of ChatGPT for generating multiple-choice Reading comprehension items. *System*, 123, 103344. https://doi.org/10.1016/j.system.2024.103344

Kane, M. (2006). Content-related validity evidence in test development. In T. M. Haladyna & S. M. Downing (Eds.), *Handbook of Test Development* (Vol. 1, pp. 131–153). New York: Routledge.

Kane, M. T. (2013). Validating the interpretations and uses of test scores. *Journal of Educational Measurement*, 50(1), 1–73.

Kıyak, Y. S., Coşkun, Ö., Budakoğlu, I. İ., & Uluoğlu, C. (2024). ChatGPT for generating multiple-choice questions: Evidence on the use of artificial intelligence in automatic item generation for a rational pharmacotherapy exam. *European Journal of Clinical Pharmacology*, 80(5), 729–735.

Kuusemets, L., Parve, K., Ain, K., & Kraav, T. (2024). Assessing AI-generated (GPT-4) versus human created MCQs in mathematics education: A comparative inquiry into vector topics. *International Journal of Education in Mathematics, Science and Technology*, 12(6), 1538–1558.

Laohawetwanit, T., Apornvirat, S., & Kantasiripitak, C. (2024). ChatGPT as a teaching tool: Preparing pathology residents for board examination with AI-generated digestive system pathology tests. *American Journal of Clinical Pathology*, 162(5), 471–479.

Leng, D., Bezirhan, U., Khorramdel, L., Fishbein, B., & Davier, M. V. (2024). Examining gender differences in TIMSS 2019 using a multiple-group hierarchical speed-accuracy-revisits model. *Educational Measurement: Issues and Practice*, 43(3), 64–75.

Mazidi, K. (2017, April). Automatic question generation from passages. In *International Conference on Computational Linguistics and Intelligent Text Processing* (pp. 655–665). Cham: Springer.

Messick, S. (1989). Meaning and values in test validation: The science and ethics of assessment. *Educational Researcher*, 18(2), 5–11.

Mikolov, T., Chen, K., Corrado, G., & Dean, J. (2013). Efficient estimation of word representations in vector space. arXiv preprint arXiv:1301.3781.

Mislevy, R. J., Almond, R. G., & Lukas, J. F. (2003). A brief introduction to evidence-centered design. *ETS Research Report Series*, 2003(1), i–29.

Mizumoto, A., & Eguchi, M. (2023). Exploring the potential of using an AI language model for automated essay scoring. *Research Methods in Applied Linguistics*, 2(2), 100050.

Nadaf, A., Monroe, S., Chandran, S., & Miao, X. (2022, July). Learning factors for TIMSS math performance evidenced through machine learning in the UAE. In *International Conference on Artificial Intelligence in Education Technology* (pp. 47–66). Singapore: Springer Nature Singapore.

Offerijns, J., Verberne, S., & Verhoef, T. (2020). Better distractions: Transformer-based distractor generation and multiple choice question filtering. arXiv preprint arXiv:2010.09598.

Ormerod, C. M., Malhotra, A., & Jafari, A. (2021). Automated essay scoring using efficient transformer-based language models. arXiv preprint. https://doi.org/10.48550/arXiv.2102.13136

Owan, V. J., Abang, K. B., Idika, D. O., Etta, E. O., & Bassey, B. A. (2023). Exploring the potential of artificial intelligence tools in educational measurement and assessment. *Eurasia Journal of Mathematics, Science and Technology Education*, 19(8), em2307.

Page, E. B. (1966). The imminence of… grading essays by computer. *The Phi Delta Kappan*, 47(5), 238–243. https://www.jstor.org/stable/20371545

Park, Y., LaFlair, G. T., Attali, Y., Runge, A., & Goodwin, S. (2022). *Interactive reading—the duolingo english test*. Duolingo Res., Pittsburgh, PA, USA, White Paper DDR-22-02.

Perkins, K., Gupta, L., & Tammana, R. (1995). Predicting item difficulty in a reading comprehension test with an artificial neural network. *Language Testing*, 12(1), 34–53.

Pokropek, A., Żółtak, T., & Muszyński, M. (2024). Identifying careless responding in web-based surveys: Exploiting sequence data from cursor trajectories and approximate areas of interest. *Zeitschrift für Psychologie*, 232(2), 95–108. https://doi.org/10.1027/2151-2604/a000555

Porter, A. C., Polikoff, M. S., Zeidner, T., & Smithson, J. (2008). The quality of content analyses of state student achievement tests and content standards. *Educational Measurement: Issues and Practice*, 27(4), 2–14.

Radford, A., Wu, J., Child, R., Luan, D., Amodei, D., & Sutskever, I. (2019). Language models are unsupervised multitask learners. *OpenAI Blog*, 1(8), 9.

Raffel, C., Shazeer, N., Roberts, A., Lee, K., Narang, S., Matena, M., … & Liu, P. J. (2020). Exploring the limits of transfer learning with a unified text-to-text transformer. *Journal of Machine Learning Research*, 21(140), 1–67.

Ramineni, C., & Williamson, D. M. (2013). Automated essay scoring: Psychometric guidelines and practices. *Assessing Writing*, 18(1), 25–39.

Säuberli, A., & Clematide, S. (2024). Automatic generation and evaluation of Reading comprehension test items with large language models. In R. Wilkens, R. Cardon, A. Todirascu, & N. Gala (Eds.), *Proceedings of the 3rd Workshop on Tools and Resources for People with Reading Difficulties (READI) @ LREC-COLING 2024* (pp. 22–37). Torino: ELRA and ICCL. https://aclanthology.org/2024.readi-1.3

Sayin, A., & Gierl, M. (2024). Using OpenAI GPT to generate reading comprehension items. *Educational Measurement: Issues and Practice*, 43(1), 5–18. https://doi.org/10.1111/emip.12590

Schmitz, R. Y., & Marie, L. (2025). Evaluating AI-generated vs. human-written reading comprehension passages: an expert SWOT analysis and comparative study for an educational large-scale assessment. *Large-scale Assessments in Education*, 13(1), 1–29.

Sharpnack, J., Hao, K., Mulcaire, P., Bicknell, K., LaFlair, G., Yancey, K., & von Davier, A. A. (2024). Banditcat and autoirt: Machine learning approaches to computerized adaptive testing and item calibration. arXiv preprint arXiv:2410.21033.

Shin, E. (2021). Automated item generation by combining the non-template and template based approaches to generate reading inference test items. (Doctoral dissertation, University of Alberta). https://ualberta.scholaris.ca/server/api/core/bitstreams/dd99144e-6919-49b5-8304-f1332a207cfe/content

Song, Y., & Cutumisu, M. (2025). Using machine learning to predict student science achievement based on science curriculum type in TIMSS 2019. *International Journal of Science Education*, 47(9), 1105–1149.

Spaccapanico Proietti, G., Matteucci, M., & Mignani, S. (2020). Automated test assembly for large-scale standardized assessments: Practical issues and possible solutions. *Psych*, 2(4), 24.

Tan, B., Armoush, N., Mazzullo, E., Bulut, O., & Gierl, M. (2024). A review of automatic item generation techniques leveraging large language models. EdArXiv Preprints. https://doi.org/10.35542/osf.io/6d8tj

Tran, P., Feng, W., Sireci, S. G., McNichols, H., & Lan, A. (2025). Using item features to calibrate educational test items: Comparing artificial intelligence and classical approaches. *American Journal of Education and Learning*, 10(2), 178–189.

Tyack, L., Khorramdel, L., & von Davier, M. (2024). Using convolutional neural networks to automatically score eight TIMSS 2019 graphical response items. *Computers and Education: Artificial Intelligence*, 6, 100249.

Ulitzsch, E., He, Q., & Pohl, S. (2022). Using sequence mining techniques for understanding incorrect behavioral patterns on interactive tasks. *Journal of Educational and Behavioral Statistics*, 47(1), 3–35.

Ulitzsch, E., von Davier, M., & Pohl, S. (2020). A hierarchical latent response model for inferences about examinee engagement in terms of guessing and item-level non-response. *British Journal of Mathematical and Statistical Psychology*, 73(1), 83–112. https://doi.org/10.1111/bmsp.12188

Webb, N. L. (1997). Criteria for alignment of expectations and assessments in mathematics and science education. Research Monograph No. 6.

Xi, X. (2010). Automated scoring and feedback systems: Where are we and where are we heading? *Language Testing*, 27(3), 291–300.

van der Linden, W. J. (2005). *Linear Models for Optimal Test Design*. New York: Springer New York.

van der Linden, W. J., & Belov, D. I. (2023). A statistical test for the detection of item compromise combining responses and response times. *Journal of Educational Measurement*, 60(2), 235–254. 10.1111/jedm.12346

von Davier, M. (2018). Automated item generation with recurrent neural networks. *Psychometrika*, 83(4), 847–857.

von Davier, M. (2019). Training Optimus prime, MD: Generating medical certification items by fine-tuning OpenAI's gpt2 transformer model. arXiv preprint arXiv:1908.08594.

von Davier, A. A., Mislevy, R. J., & Hao, J. (Eds.) (2021). *Computational Psychometrics: New Methodologies for a New Generation of Digital Learning and Assessment*. New York: Springer. https://www.springer.com/gp/book/9783030743932

von Davier, M., Tyack, L., & Khorramdel, L. (2023). Scoring graphical responses in TIMSS 2019 using artificial neural networks. *Educational and Psychological Measurement*, 83(3), 556–585.

Yaneva, V., Baldwin, P., & Mee, J. (2019, August). Predicting the difficulty of multiple choice questions in a high-stakes medical exam. In *Proceedings of the Fourteenth Workshop on Innovative use of NLP for Building Educational Applications* (pp. 11–20). Florence: Association for Computational Linguistics.

Yaneva, V., Baldwin, P., & Mee, J. (2020, May). Predicting item survival for multiple choice questions in a high-stakes medical exam. In *Proceedings of the Twelfth Language Resources and Evaluation Conference* (pp. 6812–6818). Marseille: European Language Resources Association.

Yeung, C. Y., Lee, J. S., & Tsou, B. K. (2019). Difficulty-aware distractor generation for gap-fill items. In *Proceedings of the 17th Annual Workshop of the Australasian Language Technology Association* (pp. 159–164). Sydney: ALTA.

Zhang, S., Tang, X., He, Q., Liu, J., & Ying, Z. (2024). External correlates of adult digital problem-solving process: An empirical analysis of PIAAC PSTRE action sequences. *Zeitschrift für Psychologie*, 232(2), 120–136. https://doi.org/10.1027/2151-2604/a000554

Zhou, Z., & Ostrow, K. S. (2022, June). Transformer-based automated content-standards alignment: A pilot study. In *International Conference on Human-Computer Interaction* (pp. 525–542). Cham: Springer Nature Switzerland.

Zhuang, Y., Liu, Q., Huang, Z., Li, Z., Shen, S., & Ma, H. (2022, June). Fully adaptive framework: Neural computerized adaptive testing for online education. In *Proceedings of the AAAI Conference on Artificial Intelligence* (Vol. 36, No. 4, pp. 4734–4742). Palo Alto, CA: AAAI Press.

INDEX

Note: *Italic* and **Bold** page numbers refer to figures and **tables**. Page numbers followed by 'n' refer to notes.

For Product Safety Concerns and Information please contact our EU representative GPSR@taylorandfrancis.com
Taylor & Francis Verlag GmbH, Kaufingerstraße 24, 80331 München, Germany

www.ingramcontent.com/pod-product-compliance
Ingram Content Group UK Ltd.
Pitfield, Milton Keynes, MK11 3LW, UK
UKHW020155200926
475702UK00016B/2725
9781041028031